W9-DHR-870

English Writing and Language Skills

Complete Course

Critical Readers and Contributors

The authors and the publisher wish to thank the following people, who helped to evaluate and to prepare materials for this series:

Charles L. Allen, Baltimore Public Schools, Baltimore, Maryland
Kiyoko B. Bernard, Huntington Beach High School, Huntington Beach, California
Sally Borengasser, Rogers, Arkansas
Deborah Bull, New York City, New York
Joan Colby, Chicago, Illinois
Phyllis Goldenberg, North Miami Beach, Florida
Beverly Graves, Worthington High School, Worthington, Ohio
Pamela Hannon, Kirk Middle School, Cleveland, Ohio
Carol Kuykendall, Houston Public Schools, Houston, Texas
Wayne Larkin, Roosevelt Junior High School, Blaine, Minnesota
Nancy MacKnight, University of Maine, Orono, Maine
Catherine McCough, Huntington Beach Union School District, California
Lawrence Milne, Ocean View High School, Long Beach, California
Al Muller, East Carolina University, Greenville, North Carolina
Dorothy Muller, East Carolina University, Greenville, North Carolina
John Nixon, Santa Ana Junior College, Santa Ana, California
Jesse Perry, San Diego City Schools, California
Christine Rice, Huntington Beach Union School District, Huntington Beach, California
Jo Ann Seiple, University of North Carolina at Wilmington, Wilmington, North Carolina
Joan Yesner, Brookline, Massachusetts
Seymour Yesner, Brookline Education Center, Massachusetts

Classroom Testing

The authors and the publisher also wish to thank the following teachers, who participated in the classroom testing of materials from this series:

David Foote, Evanston High School East, Evanston, Illinois
Theresa Hall, Nokomis Junior High School, Minneapolis, Minnesota
Carrie E. Hampton, Sumter High School, Sumter, South Carolina
Pamela Hannon, Proviso High School East, Maywood, Illinois
Wayne Larkin, Roosevelt Junior High School, Blaine, Minnesota
Grady Locklear, Sumter High School, Sumter, South Carolina
William Montgomery, Hillcrest High School, Jamaica, New York
Josephine H. Price, Sumter High School, Sumter, South Carolina
Barbara Stilp, North High School, Minneapolis, Minnesota
Joseph Thomas, Weymouth North High School, East Weymouth, Massachusetts
Travis Weldon, Sumter High School, Sumter, South Carolina

Teachers of the Huntington Beach Union High School Writing Program

Cassandra C. Allsop
Eric V. Emery
Michael Frym
Barbara Goldfein
Joanne Haukland
Don Hohl
Sandra Johnson
Carol Kasser
Patricia Kelly
Stephanie Martone
Lawrence Milne
Richard H. Morley
John S. Nixon
Catherine G. McCough
Kathleen C. Redman
Christine Rice
Michael D. Sloan
S. Oliver Smith
Glenda Watson
Dorothy Augustine, District Consultant in Writing

English Writing and Language Skills

Complete Course

W. Ross Winterowd

Patricia Y. Murray

HARCOURT BRACE JOVANOVICH, PUBLISHERS
Orlando New York Chicago Atlanta Dallas

HBJ

The Series:

English Writing and Language Skills, First Course
English Writing and Language Skills, Second Course
English Writing and Language Skills, Third Course
English Writing and Language Skills, Fourth Course
English Writing and Language Skills, Fifth Course
English Writing and Language Skills, Complete Course

A test booklet and teacher's manual are available for each title.

W. ROSS WINTEROWD is the Bruce R. McElderry Professor of English at the University of Southern California. Since 1975, Dr. Winterowd has traveled widely as a writing consultant for numerous schools in North America.

PATRICIA Y. MURRAY is director of the writing program and the writing laboratory at the University of Michigan—Flint. Dr. Murray taught junior and senior high school English in the Los Angeles city schools. She is also a consultant in curriculum development and teacher training.

Design: Michael Rogondino

Photo Credits 7, Harry Wilks, Stock, Boston; 7, © Peter Menzel, Stock, Boston; 40, © Ken Graves, Jeroboam, Inc.; 40, Lionel J-M Delevingne, Stock, Boston; 43, Lee Youngblood; 43, Robert Bull; 46, Lee Youngblood; 47, © Frank Siteman, Stock, Boston; 47, © Laurence Cameron, Jeroboam, Inc.; 78, Louis & Virginia Kay, DPI; 79, © Peter Menzel, Stock, Boston; 307, W. Eugene Smith; 379, M. C. Escher: *Portrait of the Artist's Father, G. A. Escher.* © BEELD-RECHT, Amsterdam/VAGA, New York. Collection Haags Gemeentemuseum, The Hague, 1981. 402, Laurence Cameron, Jeroboam, Inc.; 446, © Frank Siteman, Jeroboam, Inc.; 448, California Historical Society, Title Insurance & Trust Co. (L.A.) Collection of Historical Photographs; 475, United Press International; 476, © Frank Siteman, Jeroboam, Inc.

Printed in the United States of America

ISBN 0-15-311555-6

Contents

3 Reading

4 Sentence Combining

6 Using Grammar

9 Testing

PART

1 Writing

1 Personal Writing

Writing About Yourself

Personal writing—writing about yourself—includes many different types, or *genres.* You may choose to record thoughts and observations about your experiences in a letter, in a diary or journal, in an informal essay, or in an autobiography. These forms of writing share one important element; they emphasize the personal life of the writer.

The purpose of personal writing is to re-create experiences, ideas, and impressions that are valuable to you.

Whatever form you choose, personal writing is a storehouse of events from your life: people, places, and emotions that might otherwise be forgotten. This storing of observations and thoughts allows writers to use their personal writing as a source of ideas for other genres such as formal essays, novels, poems, or plays.

One important characteristic of personal writing is its natural style.

The basic style of personal writing is casual and conversational, whether for an audience of one in a private diary, an audience of friends in a letter or public journal, or the general audience addressed by the personal essay or autobiography. Personal writing is not stiff and formal; instead, it uses the language of daily speech. Good personal writing is filled with specific details and vivid descriptions that re-create experiences for readers. In general, personal writing is lively and colorful.

In this chapter you will read about two types of personal writing: the journal and the personal essay. You will learn how to use the skills of personal writing to improve your powers of observation, descriptive abilities, and natural writing style.

Following this selection is a For Discussion activity.

Reading Personal Writing

The following passages by the Welsh poet Dylan Thomas come from an essay titled "Reminiscences of Childhood." As you read, listen to the writer's natural, conversational language and notice the specific details.[1]

Chips are french fries.

A *pence* is the British plural of *penny*.

> Never was there such a town as ours, I thought, as we fought on the sandhills with rough boys or dared each other to climb up the scaffolding of half-built houses soon to be called Laburnum Beaches. Never was there such a town, I thought, for the smell of fish and chips on Saturday evenings; for the Saturday afternoon cinema matinees where we shouted and hissed our threepences away; for the crowds in the streets with leeks in their hats on international nights; for the park, the inexhaustible and mysterious, bushy red-Indian hiding park where the hunchback sat alone and the groves were blue with sailors. The memories of childhood have no order, and so I remember that never was there such a dame school as ours, so firm and kind and smelling of galoshes, with the sweet arid fumbled music of the piano lessons drifting down from upstairs to the lonely schoolroom, where only the sometimes tearful wicked sat over undone sums, or to repeat a little crime—the pulling of a girl's hair during geography, the sly shin kick under the table during English literature. Behind the school was a narrow lane where only the oldest and boldest threw pebbles at windows, scuffled and boasted, fibbed about their relations—
>
> "My father's got a chauffeur."
>
> "What's he want a chauffeur for? He hasn't got a car."
>
> "My father's the richest man in the town."
>
> "My father's the richest man in Wales."
>
> "My father owns the world."
>
> And swapped gob-stoppers for slings, old knives for marbles, kite strings for foreign stamps.

For Discussion

1. In the excerpt from "Reminiscences of Childhood," Dylan Thomas recounts specific childhood activities and the sights and sounds he associates with them. For example, he recalls the smell of fish and chips and the shouting and hissing in the movie theater on Saturday afternoon. What other specific activities does he recall? What sensory details—details of sight, sound, taste, smell, and texture—does he use?
2. Dylan Thomas combines natural language with poetic observations to make his descriptions interesting. For example, there is a casual tone in the opening sentence, "Never was there such a town as ours." What other examples show the use of natural, or conversational, language?

Writing Practice 1

In the passages from "Reminiscences of Childhood," Dylan Thomas concentrates on his memories of the town where he grew up and of the school he

---

[1] From "Reminiscences of Childhood" from *Quite Early One Morning* by Dylan Thomas. Copyright 1945 by New Directions Publishing Corporation. Published by J. M. Dent & Sons, England. Reprinted by permission of New Directions and David Higham Associates Limited.

Use the Preparing to Write section that follows to help you find ideas for this assignment.

attended. Select a place from your own childhood, such as your town or school; the park where you used to play; the beach, woods or fields; or the streets of your city. Write your memories of this place, including specific activities and the sensory impressions that go with them. Try to remember how things looked; what sounds you associate with each experience; what smells, tastes, and textures you remember. Tell the reader about these memories, using natural, conversational language.

Preparing to Write

Dylan Thomas writes that "The memories of childhood have no order, . . ." When you begin thinking about a specific place from your childhood, you will note that bits of remembered scenes and experiences come to you at random. One way to retain all of these experiences is to record them on a list before you write.

Find a place where you can sit quietly and then let your mind wander over your experiences. If, for example, you have chosen to write about a street of the city where you grew up, visualize yourself doing what you used to do with your friends: playing catch, skipping rope, or just sitting on the steps and talking with your best friend. At the top of your list, write the specific activity as it comes to you.

SITTING ON THE STEPS

Next, ask yourself what *specific* details you associate with that activity. Where were the steps? What were you looking at? Add such details to your list.

SITTING ON THE STEPS

Cracks in the concrete, grass growing through
Looking at the store windows across the street
  green and white awnings
  paint chipping off the lettering: Estelle's Beauty Salon
Watching older kids play stickball in the street
Talking to Mrs. Ellis, who lived upstairs and cried a lot

Then ask what sounds you associate with those steps, perhaps conversations with friends or just the sounds of the city:

Car horns, sometimes yelling drivers, "Get out of the streets, kids"
All the kids laughing and yelling back
Slap, slap, slap of the jumping rope game down the block
Kids' mothers calling them, "Judy! Paul! Dinner!"
"I heard Lisa has a crush on you." "Does not." "You wanna bet?"

Then try to recall the various smells, both pleasant and unpleasant, that you associate with the place you write about:

Smells of dinners cooking, coming out of the windows and down to the street
The steamy, spicy smell when the sausage vendor came by with his cart
The smell of rain on cement
The smell of the garbage trucks going by

The senses of taste and smell are closely related. Write the tastes you recall from this childhood experience:

> After playing all afternoon, ice water so cold it hurt my teeth
> Walking home past the fruit stand, buying a warm, yellow banana
> Sitting on the steps, eating roasted pumpkinseeds at Halloween

Finally, the sense of touch and texture is important. Try to recall how things felt to you as a child and add those details to your list:

> Playing jacks, sweeping the jacks up off the rough cement
> The spongy, hard feel of a softball and the tingle as it hits my hands
> Stair railings made of metal, ice-cold in the winter
> Edges of library books poking me in the stomach as I walk home

As you think of specific sensory details, other memories will come to you. Include on your list all the associations you can recall, and then write about the ones that most completely describe the experience. Describe the memories in simple words, as if talking with a friend, using *I*, *my*, and *we*.

Keeping a Journal

A *personal journal* is a record of the writer's experiences, thoughts, and observations.

The words *journal* and *diary* both derive from words meaning "daily," since their original purpose was to provide a daily account of events. Journals are now used for many different purposes. Many writers, for example, keep journals as a source of ideas for future writing, using them as a storehouse of personal reactions and impressions of people, places, new experiences, and ideas. Another important purpose of journal writing is to provide a way of reexperiencing important times in your life. In this way journal writing can often give you a new perspective on your life, both as you live through events and experiences, and as you look back on them.

Some personal journals are intended to be private, like diaries, but many writers keep journals that they plan to make public one day. The journal you will keep in this chapter is a public journal, to be shared with your classmates and teacher. (If you wish to write about private thoughts and feelings, do so in a private journal you keep at home.) Your teacher will tell you how to keep your public journal, perhaps in a loose-leaf or spiral notebook or in a special section of your English notebook.

Learning to Observe

Observation is essential to good writing. It is an especially important skill in journal writing and in other personal writing, where the purpose is to record your observations of the world around you and to describe your reactions, thoughts, and emotions.

The following excerpt, "Cambridge Notes," from the college notebooks of the poet Sylvia Plath, combines observations of the writer's physical world and observations about herself. (Cambridge is a university in England.) As you read, notice the specific details the writer uses to describe her surroundings, as well as the observations she makes about her feelings.[1]

The *bronze boy* is a statue of a boy holding a dolphin.

> So, now I shall talk every night. To myself. To the moon. I shall walk, as I did tonight, jealous of my loneliness, in the blue-silver of the cold moon, shining brilliantly on the drifts of fresh-fallen snow, with the myriad sparkles. I talk to myself and look at the dark trees, blessedly neutral. So much easier than facing people, than having to look happy, invulnerable, clever. With masks down, I walk, talking to the moon, to the neutral impersonal force that does not hear, but merely accepts my being. And does not smite me down. I went to the bronze boy whom I love, partly because no one really cares for him, and brushed a clot of snow from his delicate smiling face. He stood there in the moonlight, dark, with snow etching his limbs in white, in the semicircle of the privet hedge, bearing his undulant dolphin, smiling still, balancing on one dimpled foot.

For Discussion

1. In "Cambridge Notes" Sylvia Plath describes a private experience: a walk she took to be by herself and think. In her notebook she records what she saw and how she felt during this walk. She describes the "blue-silver" moon shining and sparkling on the new snow. What other concrete details does she use to describe her observations during the walk?
2. Part of the description in "Cambridge Notes" tells of the writer's loneliness. She says that talking to herself is easier than being with people and trying to appear happy. What feelings does she have about walking alone in the moonlight? Why does she look for the statue of the boy holding the dolphin? What feelings does she associate with the statue?

Writing Practice 2

You may wish to read the Using Specific Details section that follows before you write this entry.

In "Cambridge Notes" Sylvia Plath describes walking through a place that was familiar to her. For a journal entry describe a walk you have taken through a familiar place. Use specific sensory details to describe what you observed, and include how you reacted to your observations and also how you felt during the walk.

Writing Practice 3

The photographs on page 7 show unusual, or exotic, settings. Select one of the photographs and examine it closely; then write a journal entry about it. Imagine that you have just returned from a walk through the scene or from an exploration of the scene. Describe what you saw and how you reacted to being there, using sensory details to make your descriptions more interesting.

---

[1]Excerpt from "Cambridge Notes" in *Johnny Panic and the Bible of Dreams* by Sylvia Plath.

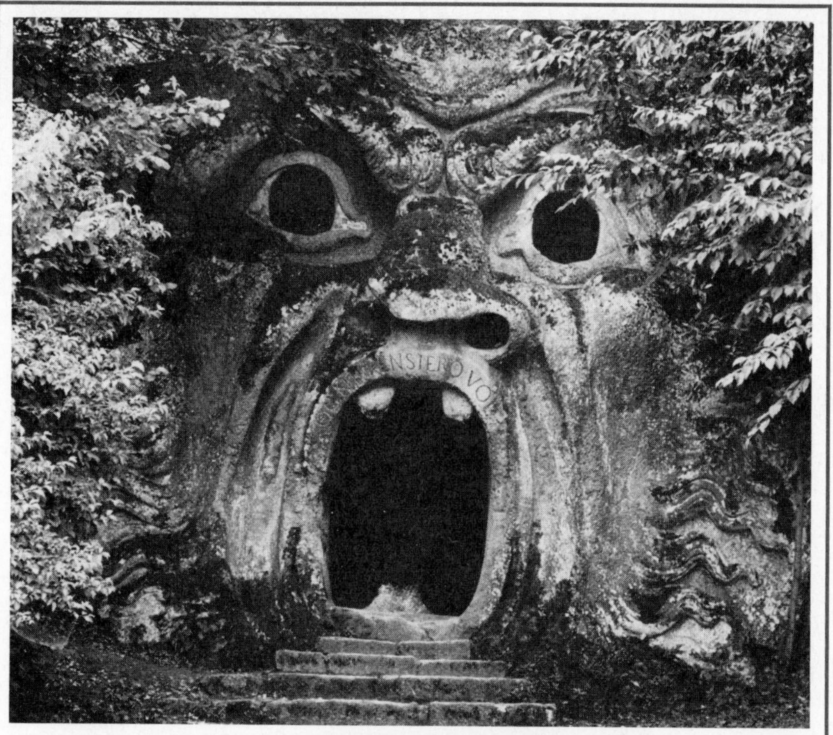

Using Specific Details

As you develop your skills as an observer, you also need to develop your ability to "translate" your observations into precise language. Using specific details is one important way to give the reader an accurate, vivid description of your observations.

Specific details re-create sights, sounds, tastes, smells, and textures for the reader.

In the following excerpt from "The Gastronomical Me," M. F. K. Fisher describes her memory of women working in the heat of the summer to complete the task of canning. The year she recalls is 1912. As you read, pay attention to the visual and other sensory details that Fisher uses to describe the scene.[1]

> The first thing I remember tasting and then wanting to taste again is the grayish-pink fuzz my grandmother skimmed from a spitting kettle of strawberry jam. I suppose I was about four.
>
> Women in those days made much more of a ritual of their household duties than they do now. Sometimes it was indistinguishable from a dogged if unconscious martyrdom. There were times for This, and other equally definite times for That. There was one set week a year for "the sewing woman." Of course, there was Spring Cleaning. And there were other periods, almost like festivals in that they disrupted normal life, which were observed no matter what the weather, finances, or health of the family.
>
> Many of them seem odd or even foolish to me now, but probably the whole staid rhythm lent a kind of rich excitement to the house-bound flight of time.
>
> With us, for the first years of my life, there was a series, every summer, of short but violently active cannings. Crates and baskets and lug-boxes of fruits bought in their prime and at their cheapest would lie waiting with opulent fragrance on the screened porch, and a whole battery of enameled pots and ladles and wide-mouthed funnels would appear from some dark cupboard.
>
> All I knew then about the actual procedure was that we had delightful picnic meals while Grandmother and Mother and the cook worked with a kind of drugged concentration in our big dark kitchen, and were tired and cross and at the same time oddly triumphant in their race against summer heat and the processes of rot.
>
> Now I know that strawberries came first, mostly for jam. Sour red cherries for pies and darker ones for preserves were a little later, and then came the apricots. They were for jam if they were very ripe, and the solid ones were simply "put up." That, in my grandmother's language, meant cooking with little sugar, to eat for breakfast or dessert in the winter which she still thought of in terms of northern Iowa.
>
> She was a grim woman, as if she had decided long ago that she could thus most safely get to Heaven. I have a feeling that my Father might have liked to help with the cannings, just as I longed to. But Grandmother, with that almost joyfully stern bowing to duty typical of religious women, made it clear that helping in the kitchen was a bitter heavy business forbidden certainly to men, and generally to children. Sometimes she let me pull stems off the cherries, and

---

[1] From "The Gastronomical Me" in *The Art of Eating* by M. F. K. Fisher.

one year when I was almost nine I stirred the pots a little now and then, silent and making myself as small as possible.

But there was no nonsense anyway, no foolish chitchat. Mother was still young and often gay, and the cook too . . . and with Grandmother directing operations they all worked in a harried muteness . . . stir, sweat, hurry. It was a pity. Such a beautifully smelly task should be fun, I thought.

Asceticism is a belief in self-denial and self-discipline.

In spite of any Late Victorian asceticism, though, the hot kitchen sent out tantalizing clouds, and the fruit on the porch lay rotting in its crates, or readied for the pots and the wooden spoons, in fair glowing piles upon the juice-stained tables. Grandmother, saving always, stood like a sacrificial priestess in the steam, "skimming" into a thick white saucer, and I, sometimes permitted and more often not, put my finger into the cooling froth and licked it. Warm and sweet and odorous. I loved it, then.

The specific sensory details that M. F. K. Fisher uses in the preceding passage help to make the scene, over half a century old, come to life. She describes the "grayish-pink fuzz" from the "spitting kettle of strawberry jam" and the "opulent fragrance" of fruit waiting in "crates and baskets and lug-boxes . . . on the screened porch." What other specific details does Fisher use to describe the kitchen, the women in it, and the work of canning? Which of the senses does Fisher emphasize most in the passage?

Writing Practice 4

In a journal entry describe either the experience of eating a food that you enjoy very much or that of having to eat a food that you do not like. You may write about an early memory, as M. F. K. Fisher does, or about a recent experience. Use specific sensory details to make your description come alive for the reader. Include a brief description of the situation, as Fisher does when she describes the canning activity surrounding her memory of tasting the jam.

Reading Journal Writing

In 1973 John Coleman took a leave of absence from his job as president of Haverford College to work as a manual laborer because he was disturbed by the lack of understanding between the academic community and the other working communities in America. The following entries are from a journal that he kept about that experience, published under the title *Blue-Collar Journal.* As you read, notice how John Coleman uses specific, descriptive details to make vivid observations about what he sees, thinks, and feels.[1]

Following this selection is a For Discussion activity.

Saturday, April 7

Saturday meant that most adults were at home on the route. So were school-age children. I thought this might mean more talk back and forth as I made the rounds today. There were many people outdoors, tending to their spring yard chores. Most of them looked friendly enough. While I wouldn't have time to talk at length, there was time to exchange the greetings that go with civilized ways.

---

[1] Excerpts from *Blue-Collar Journal: A College President's Sabbatical* by John R. Coleman. Copyright © 1974 by John R. Coleman (J. B. Lippincott Co.). Reprinted by permission of Harper & Row, Publishers, Inc. and Collier Associates.

That is where I got my shock.

I said hello in quite a few yards before the message sank in that this wasn't the thing to do. Occasionally, I got a straight man-to-man or woman-to-man reply from someone who looked me in the eye, smiled, and asked either "How are you?" or "Isn't this a nice day?" I felt human then. But most often the response was either nothing at all, a look of surprise that I had spoken and used a familiar tongue, or an overly sweet hello.

Both men and women gave me the silent or staring treatment. A woman in housecoat and curlers putting her last tidbit of slops into the pail was startled as I came around the corner of her house. At the sound of my greeting, she gathered her housecoat tightly about her and moved quickly indoors. I heard the lock click. In a way I was flattered by that, even though I had nothing more than picking up her trash on my mind. Another woman had a strange, large animal, more like a vicuña than anything else, in her yard. I asked her what kind of dog it was. She gaped at me. I thought she was hard of hearing and asked my question louder. There was a touch of a shudder before she turned coldly away. A man playing ball with his two young sons looked over in response to my voice, stared without a change of face, and then calmly threw the next ball to one of the boys. And so it went in almost every yard.

The sweet treatment came from women alone. From the way they replied and asked after my health, I knew that at the day's end when they listed the nice things they had done, there would be a place on the list for "I spoke to the trashman today."

Monday, April 9

A dump is not a pretty place. To a novice there is a fascinating rhythm about it as the steady streams of trucks flow in and out and the two heavy tractors dart back and forth leveling out the new loads of trash. But to find beauty it is necessary to look up at the blue sky above and the flocks of seagulls gliding back and forth in effortless flight over their food.

At this time of year, a garbage man's job doesn't smell nearly as much as I had expected. A few backyard cans made me turn up my nose, but most smells were more varied than strong. The dump is different. The noxious odors hang heavy in the air, rich and full. Nor is it possible to turn one's head away, as I could with the more objectionable cans. There was nowhere to find lighter air once we got into those vast acres of waste. The only escape was in dropping the load and getting out of there fast.

That relief is impossible for the attendant who patrols the dump and shows each of the many trucks where to deposit its load. His red plastic cape both identifies him as the traffic man and keeps the seagull droppings off his clothes. If I saw this forty-five-year-old white man on the street, with his clean-cut face and well-greased hair, I would never connect him with this job. I wonder how he got there and what pride he is allowed from his work. Someone has tried to elevate the task by giving it a fancy name: he is called a landfill inspector. That's about like calling those of us on the truck environmental control agents.

The dump is so new a world to me that today I just stood gaping while our load dropped to the ground. The volume and variety of what is thrown away are enough to leave me both frightened and sad. My picture of affluence in America is no longer going to be one of all those young people eating in the Oyster House or even of those elegant homes on the Main Line where I live. It will be a livelier, uglier scene: an unending line of refuse trucks spilling their loads of half-used goods on the ground and rushing back to get more before dark.

I lived and worked in India as a consultant for one year. In Calcutta I saw men, women, and children comb through wretched piles of garbage in the streets to extract anything that could possibly be used again. On any one day on this one single dump in America, there are riches enough to lift a thousand Indians' lives toward the stars.

Today I brought back a single souvenir from the mountains of refuse on the dump. I spotted a pile of bold blue-and-white cards with words so fitting for the job I am doing—and the one I'll go back to soon—that I had to take one along. It says: "IF WE DID SOMETHING WRONG, TELL US. IF WE DID SOMETHING RIGHT, TELL US."

I wonder who tells the landfill inspector when he does something right. . . .

For Discussion

1. John Coleman's journal combines observations about the people he encounters, the work he does, and the dump site. He notices how people treat him in his role as trash collector. For example, he relates that many people give him the "silent treatment," and he gives a specific example of a woman "in housecoat and curlers" who quickly goes indoors and locks her door when he speaks to her. What other specific observations does Coleman make about the appearance and behavior of the people he encounters?
2. What specific, descriptive details does the writer use to convey his impressions of the garbage dump? For example, he talks about the rhythms of the trucks that "flow in and out." What visual details does he use? What details of smell?
3. John Coleman's journal contains many comments on how people treat garbage collectors and also on the garbage dump itself. Why do his observations there leave him "frightened and sad"? What other direct observations does he make?

Writing Practice 5

Write a journal entry about an experience you have had while working with other people. Perhaps, like John Coleman, you might write about an experience at work and how you were treated as a worker. Perhaps you will write about working at a task with a friend or relative. Explain how you felt about what you were doing. Describe where you were and the people you encountered, by using specific sensory details. Write in a natural tone of voice, as if you were relating your experience to a friend.

Revising Journal Entries

An important part of every type of writing, including personal writing, is the rereading and reworking stage. After you have completed a journal entry and have laid it aside for a day or so, you are ready to revise it.

Revision is the process of making changes to improve a piece of writing.

When writers submit private journals for publication, they frequently revise their work by deleting entries not suitable for a general audience, by adding more extensive descriptions or specific sensory details, and by making other changes to improve the writing style. While it is possible to revise your work immediately after you finish writing, it is advisable to allow at least a day to pass between the writing and revising stages. This short break allows you to come back to your writing refreshed and helps you to read what you have written with a more critical eye.

Writing Practice 6

Use the following guidelines to revise one of the journal entries you have written in this chapter.

1. The entry has a natural, conversational style.
2. The entry is interesting to the general reader.
3. People, places, and events that might be unfamiliar to the general reader are explained.
4. The writer makes exact observations about the people, places, and experiences he or she describes.
5. The entry uses specific sensory details in its descriptions.

When you have completed a satisfactory revision, you are ready for the final stage, which is proofreading.

Proofreading Journal Entries

Proofreading is an American word derived from publishing terminology, meaning "to read and correct proofs (typeset material) before the final production of a book."

The term *proofreading* generally means "the correcting of a manuscript before submitting it to another reader."

The process of proofreading is simple, but it requires concentration. When you proofread a composition, you examine each line carefully for errors in grammar, spelling, punctuation, and style. Many proofreaders recommend using a ruler to scan a work from the bottom to the top of the page and from right to left. This backward manner of reading forces you to examine each word separately, making it easier to catch mistakes.

To avoid writing corrections by hand each time, proofreaders use a set of symbols to make corrections. The list on page 13 shows commonly used proofreading symbols and their meanings. You can learn to use them in your own work to save time during the proofreading process.

Edited Standard English is discussed on pages 359–360.

Since proofreading is the final stage in the writing process, it is your last chance to make improvements in your manuscript. The following Checklist for Proofreading, which reviews features of Edited Standard English (ESE), will help you make full use of the proofreading process. Copy it into your notebook and each time you complete a writing assignment that should

Symbols for Proofreading

Symbol	Meaning	Example
cap ≡	Capitalize	cap everglades
lc /	Lowercase letters	lc a National Park
¶	New Paragraph	¶ The Everglades, a low-lying marshy area in South Florida, covers an area of about 5,000 square miles.
no ¶	No new paragraph	no¶ Once the home of the Seminole Indians, the Everglades today is a haven for such endangered species as the crocodile, egret, and the bald eagle.
∧	Insert letter, word, or phrase; called a *caret;* also used to indicate where a change is to be made	The survival of the Everglads depends on a constant supply of fresh water. The large amount of construction in the Miami area may have endanger this supply.
stet	Leave as is (from the Latin phrase meaning "let it stand"); used to indicate that a marked change is not to be made.	Ramps built over the marshy areas enable visitors to come close to the wildlife and unusual vegetation which that fill the area. stet
∿	Transpose	As it blows across the swa grass, the wind makes a low sound moaning.
⁀‿	Delete space	Signs through out the park remind visitors that the park belongs to the wildlife, and that it is the humans who are the visitors.
#	Insert space	A delicate ecological balance mustbe preserved if the wildlife is to survive.

conform to ESE, check your writing carefully against each item on the checklist. Make corrections on your final copy or draft only if you can do so neatly; if the corrections are messy or make your paper difficult to follow, copy your paper over, including your corrections.

The section For Extra Help that follows the Checklist for Proofreading tells you where features of Edited Standard English are explained in this textbook.

Checklist for Proofreading

1. The paper is carefully written or typed and is not marred by inkblots, messy smudges, or crossed-out words.
2. Sentence structure is accurate. There are no fragments or run-on sentences. Punctuation is used correctly to link compound sentences.
3. Singular verbs are used with singular subjects, and plural verbs with plural subjects.
4. All pronouns have clear antecedents. Plural pronouns are used to refer to plural nouns, and singular pronouns are used with singular nouns.
5. Pronouns are the correct subject or object form.
6. Singular pronouns such as *either, each, anybody, everybody,* or *nobody* are used with singular verbs.
7. The writer uses verb tense consistently and accurately.
8. The writer avoids unnecessary shifts in pronouns, such as *I* to *you,* or *they* to *you.*
9. Confusing verbs such as *lie/lay, sit/set, leave/let* are used correctly.
10. The endings *-s, -'s, -ing,* or *-ed* are used correctly with nouns and verbs.
11. Participial phrases, prepositional phrases, and dependent clauses are clearly attached to the words they modify, to avoid misunderstanding.
12. Capitalization is used correctly at the beginning of sentences and with proper nouns and adjectives.
13. Each word is spelled correctly.
14. Punctuation is used correctly throughout the writing.
15. Contractions such as *they're, it's,* or *you're* are not confused with possessive pronouns.
16. Confusing words such as *farther/further, fewer/less* or sound-alikes such as *desert/dessert, since/sense* are used and spelled correctly.
17. Dialogue is punctuated and capitalized correctly.
18. Slang and other words or phrases not a part of Edited Standard English are used only when they are appropriate.

For Extra Help

Sentence Structure	Pages 487–517
Subject-Verb Agreement	Pages 421–429
Pronoun Reference	Pages 398–399
Pronoun Form	Pages 392–397
Indefinite Pronoun Agreement	Pages 423–425
Pronoun-Antecedent Agreement	Pages 398–400
Irregular Verbs	Pages 409–411
Confusing Verbs	Pages 430–432
Noun Plurals and Possessives	Pages 368–375
Misplaced and Dangling Modifiers	Pages 531–532
Capitalization	Pages 582–595
Spelling	Pages 596–615
Punctuation	Pages 550–581
Contractions	Page 573
Words That Sound the Same	Pages 597–608
Punctuating Dialogue	Pages 577–581
Using Edited Standard English	Pages 359–361

Writing Practice 7

Use the Checklist for Proofreading to proofread a journal entry that you have already revised. (Your teacher may want to check your revision before you begin the proofreading process.) Using the proofreading symbols in this section, make any necessary corrections on your manuscript. If necessary, rewrite your entry, incorporating the changes you have marked.

Further Uses for Journal Writing

Each of the remaining chapters of this textbook contains suggestions for further journal entries. In addition, you may want to use your journal as a kind of practice field for other types of writing. Many writers who keep journals use them to jot down ideas for compositions, quick impressions of people or places they will write about in greater detail later, beginning lines or images of poems, opinions about current events, and so on. The writing practice assignments that follow can also be used as suggestions for further journal writing.

Writing Practice 8

You can use your journal as a place to increase your ability to write about specifics, as opposed to generalities. The general words in the following list can be related to specific, concrete thoughts and experiences. Select one of them and write a journal entry relating that word to a specific experience or to a specific time and place to remember. Use sensory images and details in your description.

Example

a. General Word: Boredom

a. Journal Entry: *Late Saturday morning, mid-August. I am sitting at the kitchen table, feeling lazy, trying to wake myself up with thoughts of a day all to myself. But the heat takes away all my good resolutions—I look at the dishes I promised to do, think about finishing that letter to David, and idly glance through the paper to see what is playing at the movies. The clock keeps ticking away. Boredom usually makes me hungry. I ate breakfast only an hour ago, but I decide that some food will bring me around, so I hunt around for an orange in the refrigerator. Mother comes in as I stand peeling the bright, fragrant skin; she looks at me, then at the undone dishes, and walks out again. I sigh. The orange tastes cold and sweet on my tongue. If I were a puppy, I could give myself a good shake and be ready for action. As it is, I feel like one big yawn.*

GENERAL WORDS

1. Aggressive
2. Alienation
3. Depressing
4. Desolate
5. Excellent
6. Exciting
7. Experience
8. Fun
9. Handsome
10. Humorous
11. Lonely
12. Love
13. Proud
14. Responsible
15. Tedious

Writing Practice 9

Use your journal to keep a daily account of a subject or activity over a period of time—a week, a month, a school term, and so on. Use one of the following suggestions for journal writing or write on a subject or activity of your own choice.

1. Dreams: a record of the dreams you remember each morning
2. Books: your impressions of and reactions to the books you read
3. Mastery of something: for example, a record of your progress as you learn to play a musical instrument
4. Sports: your thoughts and feelings about a specific team that you follow
5. Seasons: descriptions of the landscape where you live as it changes during a season or a month or through several seasons

Writing the Personal Essay

The *personal essay* is the most structured type of personal writing. It sets forth comments on one theme or on a theme as it relates to a series of connected events in the life of the writer.

Like a journal entry, the personal essay records experiences, thoughts, and impressions in a natural writing style. Unlike a journal entry, the personal essay always concentrates on and develops one specific theme and is, for this reason, more highly structured than a journal entry. Many of the same skills you learned in journal writing, however, also apply to writing a personal essay. You will need to observe accurately and to convey your observations using specific details. Your journal can be an excellent source of ideas to develop in personal essays.

Structuring the Personal Essay

The term *personal essay* applies to a wide range of personal writing: essays that grow out of ideas, essays that are inspired by specific experiences or specific incidents, essays that are written in response to public events or private emotions. In spite of this variety, you will find that most personal essays are structured around five elements: the *central theme;* the *narrative element* of the action or actions illustrating the theme; the *narrator and characters;* the *descriptive details* of setting, action, characters, and ideas; and the *commentary.*

Central Theme

The *central theme* is the main idea that the writer develops in the personal essay.

The theme that the writer chooses to focus on in a personal essay always relates personally to the writer's life. For example, imagine that you were assigned to write a personal essay on the subject of books. Your central theme could relate to your own reading habits, to the role that books played in your childhood or play in your present life, or to some other direct personal experience with books. It would not be appropriate to write about the reading habits of Americans in general or about how books get on the best seller list, even though you may have information about these subjects. The theme of the personal essay relates to you, the writer, and to your own direct experiences.

The following excerpt is the first paragraph of a personal essay written in 1926 by British novelist E. M. Forster. Its title, "My Wood," gives you a general idea that the essay will deal with a piece of property that the writer owns. E. M. Forster uses the introductory paragraph to set forth the specific theme of the essay.

A book refers to the writer's famous novel, *A Passage to India.*
Cheque is the English spelling of *check.*
Forster speaks of *shame* here in a tongue-in-cheek fashion, but private ownership of property was a highly disputed issue when this essay was written.

> A few years ago I wrote a book which dealt in part with the difficulties of the English in India. Feeling that they would have had no difficulties in India themselves, the Americans read the book freely. The more they read it the better it made them feel, and a cheque to the author was the result. I bought a wood with the cheque. It is not a large wood—it contains scarcely any trees, and it is intersected, blast it, by a public footpath. Still, it is the first property that I have owned, so it is right that other people should participate in my shame, and should ask themselves, in accents that will vary in horror, this very important question: What is the effect of property upon the character? Don't let's touch economics; the effect of private ownership upon the community as a whole is another question—a more important question, perhaps, but another one. Let's keep to psychology. If you own things, what's their effect on you? What's the effect on me of my wood?[1]

As in the preceding paragraph, most writers introduce the theme of the essay in the introduction so that the reader knows from the outset what to expect. In E. M. Forster's essay the theme is stated in one sentence: "What's the effect on me of my wood?" You may formulate the theme of a personal essay as a question or as a statement, but in general you should include it as one clear sentence somewhere in the first paragraph.

Notice that Forster himself avoids the general application of the theme of his essay when he writes, "Don't let's touch economics; the effect of private ownership upon the community as a whole is another question. . . ." He is focusing his essay specifically on his own reactions to ownership. He uses contractions—"Let's keep to psychology"—and he uses simple, conversational language.

Writing Practice 10

On a separate sheet of paper, write two sentences that introduce the themes of two personal essays you would like to write. You may formulate each theme as a question, or you may formulate it as a direct statement. The topic for each sentence should be different and should relate to you personally. Do not write general themes about opinions on current events. Write about something that is part of your personal experience.

You may use the following suggestions to help find essay themes, or you may use your journal entries as a source of ideas.

1. The effect that having (or not having) something has had on you
2. How a particular habit you have affects your life
3. The impact a particular person has made on your life
4. An interest you have that sets you apart from others in some way (for example, an unusual hobby, an interest in another culture, etc.)
5. Your feelings about a particular place and its effect on you

---

[1]Excerpted from "My Wood" in *Abinger Harvest;* copyright 1936, 1964 by E. M. Forster. Reprinted by permission of Harcourt Brace Jovanovich, Inc. and Edward Arnold Ltd.

The Narrative Element

Personal essays often contain *narrative passages*, passages that relate incidents or experiences in chronological order.

Chronological order means "order in time."

You will often find narrative passages mixed in with descriptive passages or commentary in a personal essay. For example, in the following paragraph from "My Wood," E. M. Forster explains the effect his wood has on him by relating an incident. As you read, notice how he combines the narrative (storytelling) element with commentary about it. (In the preceding paragraph Forster explained that, in the first place, his wood made him feel heavy.)[1]

> In the second place, it makes me feel it ought to be larger.
>
> The other day I heard a twig snap in it. I was annoyed at first, for I thought that someone was blackberrying, and depreciating the value of the undergrowth. On coming nearer, I saw it was not a man who had trodden on the twig and snapped it, but a bird, and I felt pleased. My bird. The bird was not equally pleased. Ignoring the relation between us, it took fright as soon as it saw the shape of my face, and flew straight over the boundary hedge into a field, the property of Mrs. Henessy, where it sat down with a loud squawk. It had become Mrs. Henessy's bird. Something seemed grossly amiss here, something that would not have occurred had the wood been larger. I could not afford to buy Mrs. Henessy out, I dared not murder her, and limitations of this sort beset me on every side. Ahab did not want that vineyard—he only needed it to round off his property, preparatory to plotting a new curve—and all the land around my wood has become necessary to me in order to round off the wood. A boundary protects. But—poor little thing—the boundary ought in its turn to be protected. Noises on the edge of it. Children throw stones. A little more, and then a little more, until we reach the sea. Happy Canute! Happier Alexander! And after all, why should even the world be the limit of possession? A rocket containing a Union Jack, will, it is hoped, be shortly fired at the moon. Mars. Sirius. Beyond which . . . But these immensities ended by saddening me. I could not suppose that my wood was the destined nucleus of universal dominion—it is so very small and contains no mineral wealth beyond the blackberries. Nor was I comforted when Mrs. Henessy's bird took alarm for the second time and flew clean away from us all, under the belief that it belonged to itself.

Canute: an ancient king of the Britons who believed he could rule the sea. *Alexander:* Alexander the Great, who conquered all of the known world by the age of thirty.

In the preceding paragraph Forster narrates the incident involving the bird to explain what he means about feeling that the wood should be larger. How does this incident help you understand his point? What specifically is he saying about his property and the bird?

The story about the bird is woven into Forster's commentary about the age-old desire to conquer. How does Forster use the incident of the bird to tie his thoughts together at the end of the paragraph? What is he implying in the final sentence?

---

[1]Excerpted from "My Wood" in *Abinger Harvest;* copyright 1936, 1964 by E. M. Forster. Reprinted by permission of Harcourt Brace Jovanovich, Inc. and Edward Arnold Ltd.

Writing Practice 11

Imagine that you are going to write a personal essay that you will illustrate with a narrative passage: an incident or experience that you will tell in chronological order. You may use one of the theme statements you wrote for Writing Practice 10 or invent a new theme to write about. If, for example, you wrote about a person who had an important influence on your life, you might relate an incident illustrating this person's importance to you. Write a paragraph including the narrative account of the incident or experience you choose. Remember to use chronological order to make your narration clear to the reader.

The Narrator and Characters

The *narrator* is one who tells, or narrates, the events or presents the ideas in an essay.

In many personal essays the narrator is the central or the only character. In fiction the narrator can be the writer or one or more of the characters within the story; in personal essays the narrator is always assumed to be the writer.

The writer describes other characters in a personal essay only when they figure importantly in the essay as a whole. Unlike journal writing, which is less structured and may follow the writer's inclination for describing people or places that come to mind, the personal essay must stay focused on its main theme and may introduce characters only when they relate directly to it.

There are many different methods for presenting and describing characters. One method is to tell about the characters chiefly through physical details, a method used by Virginia Woolf's niece Angelica to describe her famous aunt in the following passage.[1]

> She was the most enchanting aunt that anyone is ever likely to have. . . To start with there was her beauty, her rare and special physical beauty which reminded one of the most aristocratic and nervous of racehorses or greyhounds and which fascinated me and possessed me even as a child. Her face with its vulnerable narrow temples and deeply hooded grey-green eyes shutting at an unexpected moment like the eyes of a bird and then opening to pierce me with a glance of amused intelligence. Above all her sensitive and sardonic mouth with a very pronounced downward curve, expressive often of the most intense amusement. Then her gestures which were somewhat jerky, her long hands waving a still longer cigarette-holder. She would puff the smoke out of the corner of her mouth and chuckle at some secret and intimate joke that we shared between us.

The preceding passage presents a kind of portrait of Virginia Woolf. The descriptive details, such as her "deeply hooded grey-green eyes shutting at an unexpected moment like the eyes of a bird," give the reader a clear visual impression. What other descriptive details does Angelica Bell use to portray Virginia Woolf? The description of Virginia Woolf piercing her niece with "a glance of amused intelligence" shows a woman who is quick-witted and

---

[1]From David Garnett, *Great Friends*. Copyright © 1979 by David Garnett. (New York: Atheneum, 1980). Reprinted with the permission of Atheneum Publishers and Angelica Garnett.

observant. What other impressions of Virginia Woolf's character does this physical portrait convey?

The following description, also of Virginia Woolf, uses a different method of presenting a character. Here the writer David Garnett is talking directly about Woolf's character rather than her physical description.[1]

> There was a strange contradiction in Virginia. She was so beautiful, so tall, so aristocratic and in many ways so fastidious. But she had a sense of humour that would stick at nothing, like Shakespeare's, or Chaucer's. And she had an appetite and a relish for life that one finds most often in market women.
>
> Nothing made her wish to avert her eyes and cross to the other side of the street. Like Rembrandt she could have found the subject for a work of art in a side of beef.
>
> Because of this there were no doors closed to her: she could pluck the secret from the heart of an old dried-up lawyer, a charwoman or a young actor enjoying his first triumph. Whenever Virginia appeared she brought a new treasure trove with her, something that she had heard in the street, been told over the counter, found in an old letter. After she had been to a party she would come round and regale her sister with an account of it, and what she said might have been written by Thackeray if he had been a poet with a completely uninhibited sense of humour. She was vain and sensitive to criticism, but she liked making herself into a ridiculous figure and laughing at herself.
>
> Almost all her stories had one point, one object: to catch the unique living self that makes one human being different from another.
>
> When she went into the street, she saw the same crowds that we all do, hurrying and scurrying along like disordered sheep. But for her the spectacle was, I think, an illusion. She never forgot that each figure was not a unit in a mass, but an individual with a secret. So that even in Oxford Street there was no crowd, and on the Downs the sheep were not a flock: the shepherd or his dog could tell each one apart.

Market women are women who sell goods and produce in open-air markets.

Thackeray was a British novelist famous for writing about people and society.

In the preceding passage are many specific, descriptive details, but they have primarily to do with Virginia Woolf's character—her personality and attitudes about people and herself—rather than her physical presence. Notice that although Garnett writes about her personality in general, he illustrates his main points about Virginia Woolf with specific examples and details. How does he illustrate what he calls the "strange contradiction" in her personality? How does he illustrate her "relish for life"?

Both types of character descriptions, the physical description related to personality and the direct personality description, appear in personal essays. In your own personal essay writing, select the method that best fits the character you are portraying, but remember to describe in depth only those characters who relate to the main theme.

Writing Practice 12

Imagine that you are writing a personal essay that focuses on a theme concerning one central character and yourself, the narrator. Write one paragraph

---

[1] From David Garnett, *Great Friends*. Copyright © 1979 by David Garnett. (New York: Atheneum, 1980). Reprinted with the permission of Atheneum Publishers and A. P. Watt Ltd.

about the central character as if the paragraph were from your essay. You may describe the character through a physical portrait that tells something about your character's personality, or you may talk about the personality directly. Remember in either case to use specific details and examples to aid description.

Descriptive Details

The use of descriptive details is also discussed on pages 8–9.

Descriptive details help to make the subject of a personal essay seem real and vivid. Specific observations about people, places, ideas, emotions, and states are all made more precise for the reader through descriptive details.

Using descriptive details in the personal essay is similar to using them in journal writing and in other types of personal writing. As with character description, however, you must remember to describe in detail only when the description is integral to the central theme. Your descriptions should never be simply ornamental in the personal essay.

The following paragraph by Roger Kahn describes one of the special pitches mastered by Preacher Roe, a famous pitcher with the Brooklyn Dodgers. Notice the descriptive details that Kahn uses to help the reader visualize the process of throwing the spitball.[1]

> Roe chewed Beech-Nut gum, which he says gave him a slicker saliva than any other brand. To throw a spitter, you use a fast-ball motion, but squeeze as you release the ball. The effect you want, Roe says, is like letting a watermelon seed shoot out from between your fingers. The fingertips have to be both damp and clean. Before throwing the spitball, Roe cleaned his fingers by rubbing them on the visor of his cap. Between innings he dusted the visor with a towel. To "load one," Roe wiped his large left hand across his brow and surreptitiously spat on the meaty part of the thumb. The broad base of the hand was his shield. Then pretending to hitch his belt, he transferred moisture to his index and middle fingers. Finally, he gripped the ball on a smooth spot—away from seams—and threw. The spitter consistently broke down.

Broke down means "curved abruptly downward toward the plate."

While much descriptive writing focuses on an object or a person, the descriptive details that Kahn observes in the preceding paragraph show the reader the process of throwing a spitball. The pitcher says the effect "is like letting a watermelon seed shoot out from between your fingers." Kahn states that before throwing the spitter, the pitcher cleans his fingers "by rubbing them on the visor of his cap." What other specific details about the process do you learn from the paragraph?

Descriptive details can also be used in personal essays to illustrate the ideas of the writer. Instead of simply stating ideas, the writer uses specific details to make those clear to the reader. In the following passage from "My Wood," notice how E. M. Forster uses details to describe the effect that owning property has on him.

---

[1]Excerpt from p. 306 in *The Boys of Summer* by Roger Kahn. Copyright © 1971, 1972 by Roger Kahn. Reprinted by permission of Harper & Row, Publishers, Inc. and William Morris Agency, Inc. on behalf of the author.

The New Testament states that it is easier for a camel to pass through the eye of a needle than for a rich man to enter Heaven.

> In the first place, it makes me feel heavy. Property does have this effect. Property produces men of weight, and it was a man of weight who failed to get into the Kingdom of Heaven. He was not wicked, that unfortunate millionaire in the parable, he was only stout; he stuck out in front, not to mention behind, and as he wedged himself this way and that in the crystalline entrance and bruised his well-fed flanks, he saw beneath him a comparatively slim camel passing through the eye of a needle and being woven into the robe of God. The Gospels all through couple stoutness and slowness. They point out what is perfectly obvious, yet seldom realized: that if you have a lot of things you cannot move about a lot, that furniture requires dusting, dusters require servants, servants require insurance stamps, and the whole tangle of them makes you think twice before you accept an invitation to dinner or go for a bathe in the Jordan.[1]

E. M. Forster uses a humorous description of the "unfortunate millionaire" getting stuck because of his enormous size as he tries to enter the Kingdom of Heaven. What specific, descriptive words portray this scene? (For example, look at the word *crystalline* and contrast it with the words describing the rich man.) What other details does Forster use to illustrate his idea that property makes him feel heavy?

To understand the full effect that descriptive detail has on writing, try to imagine either of the preceding examples without the illustrations. If you take away the descriptive detail, the passages become flat and colorless statements of observations instead of lively presentations of scenes and ideas.

Writing Practice 13

Write one paragraph of a personal essay, illustrating observations of a scene, person, event, or idea, by using descriptive details. You may use one of the theme statements you wrote for Writing Practice 10 or you may write on another theme of your choice. (Look through your journal entries for suggestions on subjects.)

Commentary

The *commentary* a writer makes in a personal essay includes direct comments, as well as reflections and observations about the central theme.

The purpose of commentary is to communicate directly with the reader about the theme of the essay. The commentary has a single focus, just as the essay has a single, central theme. In most personal essays, commentary is interspersed throughout the essay, as in the paragraphs by E. M. Forster.

The following paragraph is the concluding paragraph of an essay on working in a hospital by Richard Wright. His commentary about working in the hospital as a black man overseen by whites is also woven into the rest of the piece. The commentary here relates to an incident he has just described in which a fight broke out between two hospital workers, and all the exper-

---

[1] Excerpted from "My Wood" in *Abinger Harvest;* copyright 1936, 1964 by E. M. Forster. Reprinted by permission of Harcourt Brace Jovanovich, Inc. and Edward Arnold Ltd.

imental animals were thrown from or escaped from their cages. The workers sorted them out as best they could, but no one reported what had happened. Wright worries about the experiments but decides not to tell anyone.[1]

> I brooded, of course, upon whether I should have gone to the director's office and told him what had happened, but each time I thought of it I remembered that the director had been the man who had ordered the boy to stand over me while I was working and time my movements with a stop watch. He did not regard me as a human being. I did not share his world. I earned thirteen dollars a week and I had to support four people with it, and should I risk that thirteen dollars by acting idealistically? Brand and Cooke would have hated me and would have eventually driven me from the job had I "told" on them. The hospital kept us four Negroes, as though we were close kin to the animals we tended, huddled together down in the underworld corridors of the hospital, separated by a vast psychological distance from the significant processes of the rest of the hospital—just as America had kept us locked in the dark underworld of American life for three hundred years—and we had made our own code of ethics, values, loyalty.

The preceding passage clearly shows Richard Wright's conflict of feelings about what happened: his sense of responsibility toward his work and his resentment at being treated as a menial. What is Wright's attitude about the director of the hospital? How does he describe his thought process and final decision not to go to the director and report what happened?

Writing Practice 14

Select one of the sentences you wrote as a theme sentence in Writing Practice 10 or use a new theme topic. Remember that your theme should relate to a personal experience of your own. Write at least one paragraph of a personal essay on this theme, paying special attention to the commentary. Your comments should convey your thoughts, feelings, and reactions to the theme of the essay. (As you write, remember to follow chronological order if narrating an incident, to describe important characters, and to use descriptive details.)

Reading the Personal Essay

Following this selection is a For Discussion activity.

The following personal essay, "The Death of the Moth," was written by Virginia Woolf, British novelist, essayist, and critic. (Descriptions of her appear earlier in this chapter.) As the title indicates, the essay deals with the death of a moth: a death that the writer observes. As you read, notice how Woolf combines narration, description, and commentary.[2]

> Moths that fly by day are not properly to be called moths; they do not excite that pleasant sense of dark autumn nights and ivy-blossom which the com-

---

[1]Excerpt from pp. 58–59 in *American Hunger* by Richard Wright. Copyright 1944 by Richard Wright. Copyright © 1977 by Ellen Wright. Reprinted by permission of Harper & Row, Publishers, Inc.

[2]From "The Death of the Moth" in *The Death of the Moth and Other Essays* by Virginia Woolf, copyright 1942 by Harcourt Brace Jovanovich, Inc.; copyright 1970 by Marjorie T. Parsons, Executrix. Reprinted by permission of Harcourt Brace Jovanovich, Inc., the Literary Estate of Virginia Woolf, and the Hogarth Press Ltd.

monest yellow-underwing asleep in the shadow of the curtain never fails to rouse in us. They are hybrid creatures, neither gay like butterflies nor sombre like their own species. Nevertheless the present specimen, with his narrow hay-coloured wings, fringed with a tassel of the same colour, seemed to be content with life. It was a pleasant morning, mid-September, mild, benignant, yet with a keener breath than that of the summer months. The plough was already scoring the field opposite the window, and where the share had been, the earth was pressed flat and gleamed with moisture. Such vigour came rolling in from the fields and down beyond that it was difficult to keep the eyes strictly turned upon the book. The rooks too were keeping one of their annual festivities; soaring round the tree tops until it looked as if a vast net with thousands of black knots in it had been cast up into the air; which, after a few moments, sank slowly down upon the trees until every twig seemed to have a knot at the end of it. Then, suddenly, the net would be thrown into the air again in a wider circle this time, with the utmost clamour and vociferation, as though to be thrown into the air and settle slowly down upon the tree tops were a tremendously exciting experience.

Benignant means "kind and gracious."

Vociferation means "loud, insistent shouting."

The same energy which inspired the rooks, the ploughmen, the horses, and even, it seemed, the lean bare-backed downs, sent the moth fluttering from side to side of his square of the window-pane. One could not help watching him. One was, indeed, conscious of a queer feeling of pity for him. The possibilities of pleasure seemed that morning so enormous and so various that to have only a moth's part in life, and a day moth's at that, appeared a hard fate, and his zest in enjoying his meagre opportunities to the full, pathetic. He flew vigorously to one corner of his compartment, and, after waiting there a second, flew across to the other. What remained for him but to fly to a third corner and then to a fourth? That was all he could do, in spite of the size of the downs, the width of the sky, the far-off smoke of houses, and the romantic voice, now and then, of a steamer out at sea. What he could do he did. Watching him, it seemed as if a fibre, very thin but pure, of the enormous energy of the world had been thrust into his frail and diminutive body. As often as he crossed the pane, I could fancy that a thread of vital light became visible. He was little or nothing but life.

The *downs* are low hills.

Yet, because he was so small, and so simple a form of the energy that was rolling in at the open window and driving its way through so many narrow and intricate corridors in my own brain and in those of other human beings, there was something marvellous as well as pathetic about him. It was as if someone had taken a tiny bead of pure life and decking it as lightly as possible with down and feathers, had set it dancing and zigzagging to show us the true nature of life. Thus displayed one could not get over the strangeness of it. One is apt to forget all about life, seeing it humped and bossed and garnished and cumbered so that it has to move with the greatest circumspection and dignity. Again, the thought of all that life might have been had he been born in any other shape caused one to view his simple activities with a kind of pity.

After a time, tired by his dancing apparently, he settled on the window ledge in the sun, and, the queer spectacle being at an end, I forgot about him. Then, looking up, my eye was caught by him. He was trying to resume his dancing, but seemed either so stiff or so awkward that he could only flutter to the bottom of the window-pane; and when he tried to fly across it he failed. Being intent on other matters I watched these futile attempts for a time without thinking, unconsciously waiting for him to resume his flight, as one waits for a machine, that has stopped momentarily, to start again without considering the reason of its failure. After perhaps a seventh attempt he slipped from the wooden ledge and fell, fluttering his wings, on to his back on the window sill. The helplessness of his attitude roused me. It flashed upon me that he was in difficulties; he could no longer raise himself; his legs struggled vainly. But, as I stretched out a pencil, meaning to help him to right himself, it came over me that the failure and awkwardness were the approach of death. I laid the pencil down again.

The legs agitated themselves once more. I looked as if for the enemy against which he struggled. I looked out of doors. What had happened there? Presumably it was midday, and work in the fields had stopped. Stillness and quiet had replaced the previous animation. The birds had taken themselves off to feed in the brooks. The horses stood still. Yet the power was there all the same, massed outside indifferent, impersonal, not attending to anything in particular. Somehow it was opposed to the little hay-coloured moth. It was useless to try to do anything. One could only watch the extraordinary efforts made by those tiny legs against an oncoming doom which could, had it chosen, have submerged an entire city, not merely a city, but masses of human beings; nothing, I knew had any chance against death. Nevertheless after a pause of exhaustion the legs fluttered again. It was superb this last protest, and so frantic that he succeeded at last in righting himself. One's sympathies, of course, were all on the side of life. Also, when there was nobody to care or to know, this gigantic effort on the part of an insignificant little moth, against a power of such magnitude, to retain what no one else valued or desired to keep, moved one strangely. Again, somehow, one saw life, a pure bead. I lifted the pencil again, useless though I knew it to be. But even as I did so, the unmistakable tokens of death showed themselves. The body relaxed, and instantly grew stiff. The struggle was over. The insignificant little creature now knew death. As I looked at the dead moth, this minute wayside triumph of so great a force over so mean an antagonist filled me with wonder. Just as life had been strange a few minutes before, so death was now as strange. The moth having righted himself now lay most decently and uncomplainingly composed. O yes, he seemed to say, death is stronger than I am.

For Discussion

1. In "The Death of the Moth" Virginia Woolf tells of a personal experience that had meaning for her. In your own words, explain the theme of the essay. (Think, for example, about how this incident causes the writer to reflect on life and death.) Be prepared to discuss specific observations that Woolf makes about the moth's life and death.
2. The narrative element in "The Death of the Moth" is skillfully woven in with the description of the setting and of the moth, and with Woolf's commentary about what is happening. How does Woolf lead into the narrative in the first paragraph? How does she relate the description of the setting in the beginning back to the moth? Go carefully through the essay and observe how Woolf moves from description to narration to commentary, and find examples of these transitions.
3. Woolf begins to use chronological order in the second paragraph to portray the movement of the moth, describing it "fluttering side to side" at

the window-pane. Where else does she use chronological order to make the sequence of action easy to follow?

4. The two characters in "The Death of the Moth" are Virginia Woolf (the narrator) and the moth. The narrator uses a great deal of descriptive detail to portray the moth for the reader. At first she describes it as a "specimen," with "narrow hay-coloured wings, fringed with a tassel of the same colour" that seems "content with life." Find other specific details that Woolf uses to describe the moth and its movements. What does she feel for the moth? How does she describe her feelings?
5. Woolf uses descriptive details throughout the essay to convey her impressions of setting, the time of day and year, and the sights and sounds of other life around her. Find examples of these details and be prepared to discuss their significance to the theme of the essay.

Writing Practice 15

Use the Gathering Ideas for Writing section that follows to help you with ideas for this assignment.

Write a complete personal essay either based on a theme that you have already used or on a new theme. You may look at suggestions for theme sentences given in Writing Practice 10, consult your journal for ideas, or use the Gathering Ideas for Writing section that follows. It will be helpful to review the five elements of the personal essay before you begin writing.

Gathering Ideas for Writing

Virginia Woolf's essay "The Death of the Moth" works by taking a seemingly insignificant event and using it to describe and comment on the process of death, and to reflect on life by way of contrast.

You may also want to write about an event or experience that happens every day, but that has a larger importance for you. What this event or experience is depends on you—your habits, thoughts, observations, your way of life. For example, if you enjoy experiencing nature, perhaps you will observe the first day the wind smells of autumn, the first bird flying south for the winter, or the first clump of violets in the spring—any event or process of nature that you observe firsthand and that causes an emotional or intellectual response in you. If you live in a town or city, you might observe the crowds of people and your own feelings of pleasure or displeasure about being one in the midst of so many. Another possibility is to observe the many different kinds of people that inhabit a city or the personalities that different blocks or areas of a city seem to take on.

Your interests or hobbies can also provide starting places for personal essays. If you enjoy sports, for example, you may want to write an essay describing how Little League playing taught you something important about working with others, or how learning to swim taught you something about self-sufficiency.

The key to writing a strong personal essay is to select a theme that you have experienced personally and directly. Perhaps you reacted by feeling curiosity and intellectual stimulation, as E. M. Forster did when he was moved to write "My Wood." Perhaps you felt intense empathy with another life, as Virginia Woolf did in "The Death of the Moth." Remember that you do not have to write on an unusual subject to have a good essay. Both Forster and Woolf write about fairly commonplace subjects—owning property and watching an insect die—but they relate these experiences to their own ideas and feelings and then draw conclusions about the experiences.

Revising the Personal Essay

The process of revision is discussed on pages 61–62.

Use the following checklist to revise your personal essay. (Your teacher may wish to see the first draft of your essay before you begin the revision.)

Checklist for Revising the Personal Essay

1. The writing style is natural and informal.
2. The essay focuses on one central theme.
3. The narrative, or storytelling, element of the essay is presented in chronological order.
4. Characters important to the essay are described so that their behavior or their significance is made clear.
5. Descriptive details about characters, setting, ideas, and feelings are used to help convey the writer's experience.
6. The writer's commentary on the central theme is an essential part of the essay.

Writing Practice 16

Revise your personal essay, using the preceding checklist. After you have made a complete revision, proofread the essay for errors in usage and mechanics by using the Checklist for Proofreading on page 14.

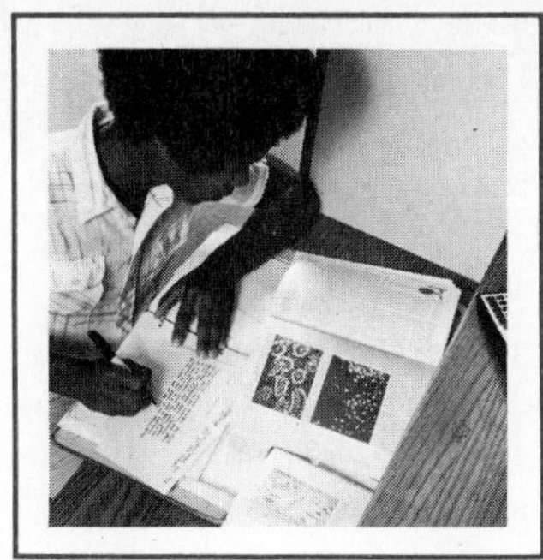

2 Discovering Ideas for Writing

Generating Ideas for Writing

Almost every writer has had the experience of facing a blank sheet of paper with no idea of how to go about filling it. Even though the writer may be an "expert" on the subject, ideas about it seem in short supply. In this situation certain methods for generating ideas can be especially useful. This chapter presents several methods to help you generate and develop ideas of your own for writing. You will learn how to discover what you already know about a subject and how to build on that knowledge. You will also read about different methods for organizing and analyzing the information that you find.

Brainstorming: Starting with What You Know

Brainstorming is the process of stimulating creative thinking by letting your mind wander freely over a subject.

Brainstorming is primarily a group activity in which everyone shares ideas as quickly and freely as possible, making no judgments about which ones are good or bad, sensible or silly. The initial purpose of brainstorming is to come up with as many ideas as possible, not to judge them as serious or trivial. Legend has it that Albert Einstein asked himself a seemingly trivial question: "What would the universe be like if I perceived it from a streetcar going at the speed of light?" From this question resulted the theory of relativity, not to mention the atom bomb and nuclear power. Creative thinkers must allow themselves to think about the trivial and the impossible—and the purpose of brainstorming is to bring about this kind of freethinking.

For group brainstorming, the procedure is to decide on a general subject to explore and then to focus attention on it, contributing ideas, associations, and suggestions quickly and freely. To brainstorm alone sit quietly with a sheet of paper in front of you and concentrate on the subject that you have chosen. Letting your mind roam freely, jot down the ideas, impressions, and associations that come to you.

Writing Practice 1

Decide on a subject for brainstorming. (You may select one from the list of subjects included with this writing practice or create one from your own imagination.) If you brainstorm alone, sit quietly by yourself and let your thoughts wander over your subject. On a sheet of paper, jot down ideas and impressions as they come to you. Do not discard ideas if they seem silly at the time. Remember that your purpose is to accumulate ideas. If you brainstorm as a group, use the following directions.

1. Form into groups of four or five.
2. Choose one member of the group to be the recorder. He or she will write all of the ideas on the board or on a sheet of paper.
3. Let one member of the group start the session by stating one idea concerning the subject. Remember that no one is to judge this idea.
4. After the session has begun, members should state ideas or call up associations as quickly as possible. Have the recorder keep a list of these thoughts.
5. As more and more ideas are brought out, group members should find it easier to suggest new thoughts. Continue to record all ideas until time is up.

SUBJECTS FOR BRAINSTORMING

How to improve the school cafeteria

Alternate energy sources

Plot for a soap opera

Advantages and disadvantages of a college education

Freedom of speech

Popular music

Computers

Combating inflation

How to be happy

Farming the oceans

Clustering

Clustering is an interesting and unusual version of brainstorming.

While brainstorming works best as a group activity, clustering is a technique that you can use either with a group or by yourself. For example, assume that you are part of a group that is exploring what the word *education* means to the members. The first step is to put that word in the center of a sheet of paper or on the blackboard.

Now begin to brainstorm. As you think of ideas, write them around the first word. Show how the ideas relate to each other by circling them and drawing lines. After a few minutes you might have a diagram that looks like the following one.

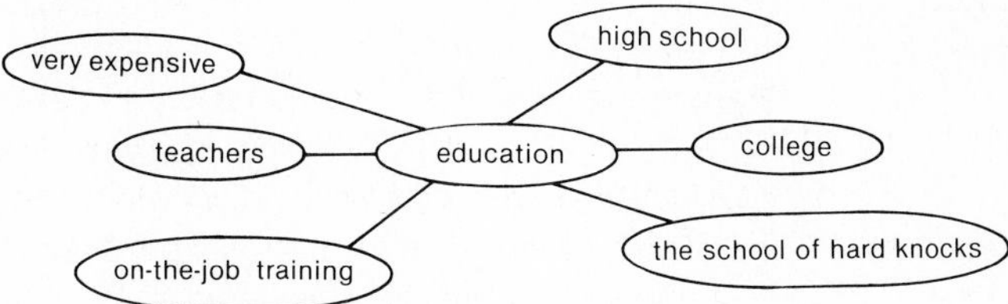

As with brainstorming, one idea will suggest another, so after fifteen minutes or half an hour, you might have developed something like the following diagram.

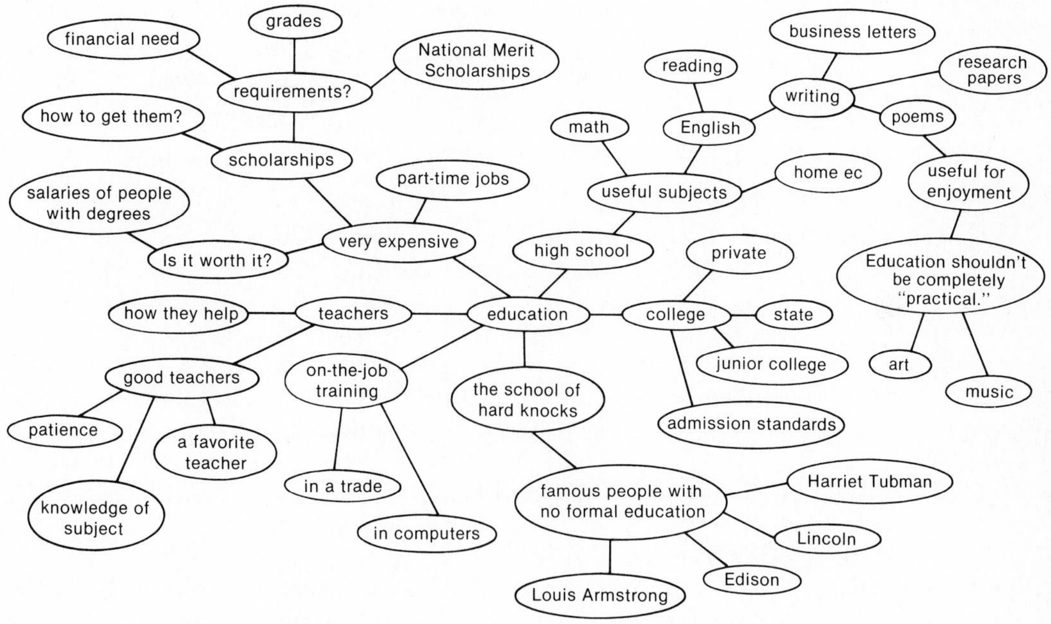

The only limits to clustering are time and space!

The clusters around *education* would probably give you many ideas about the subject—more than enough to get you started on an essay, which might have six sections: high school education, college education, learning through experience, on-the-job training, teachers, costs, and so on. Or it might be that you would choose to write a whole essay on one of those subjects. If you chose to write on the costs of a college education ("very expensive"), you would need to do research in the library to find what costs are at various colleges and universities, what scholarships are available and what the requirements are, how to get financial aid, and so on. If you chose to write on useful subjects, you could draw on your own experience. You might even want to make "useful subjects" the center of your cluster and add more ideas.

Writing Practice 2

No one in the world knows more about how you write a theme for your English class than you do. You probably have never thought about what you do, however—how you get ready to write, your favorite place for writing, or how you organize your writing. For you, writing essays is probably something like riding a bicycle: you can do it, but you have never tried to explain how. Use the following diagram as a starter for a clustering exercise on the subject "Writing themes." Put down as many ideas as you possibly can. Save your cluster for later use.

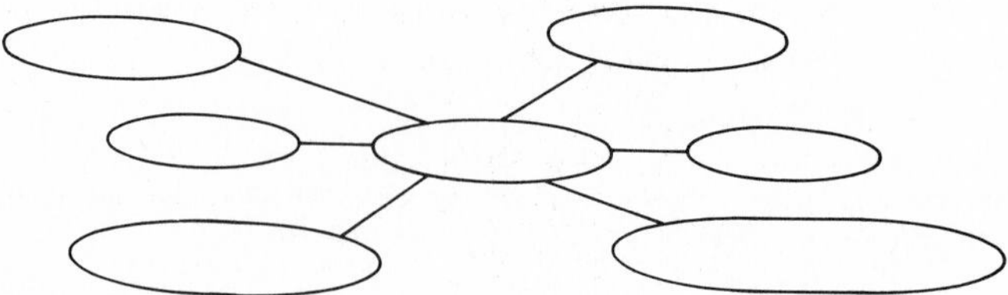

Writing Practice 3

Some words have many shades of meaning for different people: *winter*, *spring*, *vacation*, *work*, *north*, *south*, *Asia*, *Europe*, and *America*, for instance. Either by yourself or with a group, use clustering to find the meanings that one of those words (or a similar one of your choice) has for you or for you and members of your group. Once you have finished the clustering, discuss this question: Have you developed enough ideas for an essay on the meanings of the word? What might some of the major sections of the essay be?

Making Changes

Often, changes will improve a thing, an idea, or a piece of writing. For example, you might want to think about changing a common bathtub to make it more practical, comfortable, and useful. Or suppose that you have an idea about how to organize a backpacking club at your school, but before you present that idea to your friends and classmates, you want to make it as perfect as possible. Of course, as a writer you always want to change your essays, stories, and poems to bring them to their best possible form. When you change anything, there are only four possible actions you can perform:

1. You can *add* something.

    You might add a padded headrest to the bathtub to make it more comfortable.

Your proposal for a backpacking club contains five reasons for establishing it, and you can add a sixth. Your essay does not have a clearcut ending, so you add one.

2. You can *delete* something (take it away).

   You remove the shower curtain from around your bathtub because you never use the shower and the curtain gets in the way.

   One of your proposals concerning the backpacking club is impractical, so you delete it.

   A paragraph in your theme is irrelevant, and you cross it out.

3. You can *substitute* one thing for another.

   You substitute a rubber plug in your bathtub for the mechanical one that did not work very well.

   For the impractical suggestion that the backpacking club climb Mount Everest in Tibet, you substitute the proposal that the group climb Mount Whitney in California.

   For the irrelevant paragraph in your essay, you substitute one that relates directly to your topic.

4. You can *rearrange* parts.

   You put the water controls of your bathtub on the side, where you can reach them when you are lying down.

   You rearrange the paragraphs in your essay so that your discussion is more logical.

As with brainstorming, you should record every change you can think of. When you are discovering ideas, do not try to judge whether they are good or bad—just get as many as possible; you can discard the trivial or impractical ones when you plan what you will write.

Writing Practice 4

By yourself or with a small group, suggest ways in which one of the following common items could be improved: a toothbrush, an electric stove, the room in which your English class meets, a newspaper, the can that contains frozen orange juice, a lawn mower, or a similar object of your choice. Record your ideas on a sheet of paper or on the board under the headings *Add, Delete, Substitute,* and *Rearrange.*

Writing Practice 5

Think about your own writing process. How might you improve your ability to write by making additions, deletions, substitutions, and rearrangements? You can apply these questions to *places, equipment, feelings, planning, getting started, revising, purposes,* and *"props."* Jot your ideas down on a sheet of paper under the headings *Add, Delete, Substitute,* and *Rearrange* and save them for later use.

The *5WHow?* Questions

When a reporter writes about an event in the news, he or she tries to answer a standard set of questions for you: *Who* was involved? *What* happened? *When* did it happen? *Where* did it happen? *Why* did it happen? and *How* did it happen? When you are writing about events, these questions (called the *5WHow?* questions) can help you gather the ideas that you need to report what happened.

When using the *5WHow?* system, remember that these are not short-answer questions. Instead, use them to explore the event thoroughly, thinking of as many details as possible about the event. For example, the following report is not a very good one, even though it answers all of the *5WHow?* questions.

> Because he detests chores, Anthony Walters avoided doing the dishes after dinner at his home last night by claiming that he had three hours of studies to complete.
>
> *Who?* Anthony Walters
> *What?* Avoided doing the dishes
> *When?* Last night
> *Where?* At his home
> *Why?* Detests chores
> *How?* By claiming that he was overloaded with homework

If that is all there is to be said about the event, then it is not worth writing about. However, the answers to the *5WHow?* questions can be more detailed, creating a piece of writing that might interest readers, such as the following one.

> My younger brother, Anthony John Walters, has always detested household chores, and he is always at work on new techniques for avoiding them. He appears to be a completely normal twelve-year-old who tries to set records for length of time gone without bathing and whose idea of cleaning up his room is to throw all his old school papers, comic books, dirty T-shirts, and unwanted records into the closet. My parents tend to overlook these qualities, though, because Anthony truly likes schoolwork as much as he detests chores. Mom and Dad are happy that he is a good student and encourage him whenever they can.
>
> Since we were young, our parents have taught Anthony and me responsibility by giving us alternating chores. One week I take out the garbage, the next week I set the table, and every other Saturday one of us helps with general housecleaning or special "projects" Mom or Dad dreams up for us. We're also supposed to take turns doing the dishes. For some reason Anthony hates doing the dishes more than all other chores combined, and he is a master of inventing excuses to avoid doing his duty. The excuse I liked best was his scheme for a friend to telephone him with a desperate request for help in preparing for a test. It worked fine the first three times, but after that even my trusting mother became suspicious and called the parents of my brother's accomplice. I liked that one best because my brother had to do the dishes by himself for two weeks as punishment.
>
> Last night, however, I found that my brother had used all that time scrubbing away to dream up a new routine. As we were eating, he knitted his brow

and talked about schoolwork, complaining that his teachers had all given him huge assignments due the next morning—a theme for English, a chapter of American history to be studied for a quiz, and a dozen tough math problems. He shook his head sadly and sighed, "I wish all the teachers would get together so they didn't all give so much work at the same time."

I glared at him from across the table, but he looked back with an expression of perfect innocence.

Supper ended, and Anthony jumped up from the table to clear the dishes. "I'd better do the dishes now so I can begin studying," he said earnestly.

Mom and Dad looked at one another, and I had a sinking feeling in my stomach. Dad looked at Anthony and declared, "Since you have so much to do tonight, I'm sure your brother will do the dishes for you this time. You can do the same for him when he needs extra study time." Dad smiled at me. My study habits were a sore point between us. I opened my mouth to argue, but I knew that it was no use. Fate had caught up with me—Fate and the scheming mind of my little brother.

The preceding essay, written from the viewpoint of Anthony's brother, gives full answers to the questions of *Who? What? When? Where? Why?* and *How?* Even a simple event such as the one in the preceding example can be interesting if the writer supplies enough details, and the *5WHow?* questions can help you gather such details.

Writing Practice 6

At the top of each of six sheets of scratch paper, write one of the *5WHow?* questions. Now think of an event that recently happened at your home or school. Then list as many details as you can about the *who, what, when, where, why,* and *how* of the event under the appropriate headings.

Writing Practice 7

From your literature anthology or from some other source, select a short story or poem. Read the selection over and then ask yourself the *5WHow?* questions about it. Answer the questions on a sheet of paper, and then jot down ideas for writing about the selection or discussing it.

A New Set of Questions

One important decision that you must make when gathering information for writing is which discovery technique to use. Brainstorming and clustering are most useful, for example, when you are just beginning to explore a subject and have no specific ideas about how to investigate it. The *5WHow?* system is helpful when you want a formula for gathering basic, specific information about an event.

A new set of questions, called the *Pentad,* can help you to investigate a subject in greater depth.[1]

---

[1]This section is based on ideas in *Rhetoric: Discovery and Change* by Richard E. Young, Alton L. Becker, and Kenneth E. Pike (New York: Harcourt Brace Jovanovich, 1971).

The Pentad questions can be posed about any subject in the following manner.

1. *What is the action?* What is happening, has happened, or will happen?

2. *Who are the actors?* Who are the people responsible for or involved in the action? What are these people like?

3. *What is the scene?* Where and when does the action happen?

4. *What is the method or agency?* By what means or with what instrument is the action performed?

5. *What is the purpose?* Why does the action happen?

An *action* is any physical or mental thing that has happened or is happening. An event, such as walking to school, is an action. (An event of nature, such as a tornado or an earthquake, is not considered an action; instead, it is an occurrence. An *action* is committed with a purpose in mind.) All creative works (such as poems, stories, plays, paintings, and pottery) are actions because they have happened as the result of someone's mental and physical actions. Concepts and ideas are actions because they have happened in someone's mind.

Those who perform actions are called *agents.* When you ask the question *Who?* you are really inquiring about the agent or agents.

The time and place of an action might be called the *scene.* Therefore, when you ask *Where?* and *When?* you are asking about scene.

Most actions are performed by means of some thing or things. For example, in a murder mystery the detective always looks for the murder weapon—the means with which the crime was committed. When you talk with a friend or write anything, you use language as your means to do so. When you drive a nail, you use a hammer. When you ask your teacher to excuse you from turning in a paper, you probably use "psychology." All of these "things" through which actions are accomplished are *agencies.* An *agency* is something that is used to make an action possible. When you ask *How?* you are really asking about agency.

Finally actions are performed for some reason—for a *purpose.* When you ask *Why?* you are asking questions about purpose.

The following list of terms gives a summary of the Pentad questions and their meanings.

Action:	Any physical or mental thing that has happened or is happening (not a natural occurrence, such as a tornado)
Actor:	The person who performs the action or who is involved in it
Scene:	The time and place of the action
Method:	The means through which the action is performed
Purpose:	The reason for the action (the motive)

Applying the Pentad Questions

The following letter is from the "Dear Abby" advice column. As you read it, imagine what letter you would have written in reply, had you been in Abby's place.[1]

> Dear Abby,
>
> Please don't laugh, for this is a serious problem. I am a girl, nearly 17, who wants more than anything else in the world to become a bullfighter. When I tell people that this is my ambition, they think I am kidding, but I'm not.
>
> I know it is an unusual profession for a woman, but I can't see any reason why a woman shouldn't be as good as a man when it comes to bullfighting, do you?
>
> I have never been to see a bullfight, but those I've seen in the movies and on TV look like the most exciting sport in the world. It takes grace and lots of guts, and I've got both.
>
> Can you tell me how to get into this line of work? I know I can't get any training in this country, but I am willing to go to Mexico or even to Spain if necessary.
>
> [signed] Future Bullfighter

Suppose that you were Abigail Van Buren and had to compose a reply to the letter. What would you tell the young woman? Your answers to the following questions might help you give a complete answer.

1. Concerning the *action:* What do you know about bullfighting? What happens in a bullfight? How do you feel about what happens? Other questions about action?
2. Concerning *actors:* What sort of people do you suppose bullfighters are? What sort of person do you suppose the writer of the letter is? What can you learn about "Future Bullfighter" from the letter? Other questions about actors?
3. Concerning *scene:* What influence should time and place have on your answer (for example, the United States of America in the 1980s)? Other questions about scene?
4. Concerning *method:* What would the girl need in order to become a bullfighter? Money? Training? Physical ability? Courage? Cruelty? Other questions about method?
5. Concerning *purpose:* Why do you think the girl wants to become a bullfighter? Why do you think anyone wants to become a bullfighter? Other questions about purpose?

In the following answer notice how Abby concentrates on *action, scene,* and *purpose.*

> Dear Bullfighter,
>
> Since bullfighting is outlawed in the United States, you would have to get your training in a country that permits it [*Scene*]. But before you do anything,

[1]"Dear Abby" column from *The Los Angeles Times* February 10, 1980.

may I make a suggestion? Ask yourself why you want "more than anything else in the world" [*Purpose*] to excel in the brutal and bloody business of torturing and killing animals for sport and entertainment [*Action*].

Writing Practice 8

From a newspaper at home or in your school library, select a letter to an advice columnist and then ask yourself the Pentad questions on page 36 about it. Jot down your answers on a sheet of paper, noting the ones that seem most relevant to the response you would give to the writer. Then write the letter as if you were the advice columnist.

Using the Pentad for Research

The Pentad questions can guide you in researching and writing about topics that are outside your general knowledge. For example, assume that you are writing a paper on Stonehenge, the prehistoric arrangement of stones on the Salisbury Plain in England, as a research project. To help narrow your subject to a specific topic, you gather as much information as possible by reading, by talking with teachers who know something about the subject, and, if possible, by consulting with someone who has visited Stonehenge.

To guide you in your research, you might ask yourself the Pentad questions, taking notes as you answer them. The following example shows how one writer did this. As you follow the example, notice that each of the Pentad questions has been broken down into more specific questions.

Questions About the Action

1. What is it?

   Stonehenge is a circular formation of huge, upright stone slabs and cross-piece stones located on the Salisbury Plain in Wiltshire, England. It is the most famous prehistoric monument in a system of similar ruins extending from southern Sweden through the British Isles, France, Spain, and Portugal.

2. What happened?

   Stonehenge was constructed over a period of 200 years during the second millennium (somewhere between 1900–1700 B.C.) as a place of worship or as a sophisticated astronomical observatory.

3. What is happening?

   Research is still being conducted by scientists in order to learn more about the origin and purpose of Stonehenge. In addition, Stonehenge is a world-famous tourist site.

4. What will happen?

   Investigations of Stonehenge, including future excavations, will continue. The mystery and beauty of Stonehenge will continue to attract visitors.

5. What could happen?

> Archaeological evidence could be uncovered to throw more light on the builders of Stonehenge, on the connection between Stonehenge and the more than 50,000 prehistoric stone monuments across Europe, or on the reason for the apparently abrupt stop to the building of the megalithic structures.

Notice that the first preceding action question is, *What is it?* Although this might seem a simple question to ask, it can help you discover important information about your subject that you might otherwise have not included. The remaining four action questions cover actions that are happening now, those that have happened in the past, and those that will or could happen in the future. Not all of these questions are relevant to every topic, and often you will generate overlapping information. When you apply the action questions to your own topic, use the ones that are relevant.

Writing Practice 9

Select one of the following actions or substitute a similar one of your choice. Then apply the relevant action questions on pages 38–39 to your subject. Write the appropriate questions and your answers on a separate sheet of paper.

1. The American space program
2. The cosmetics industry in the United States
3. A key battle in American history
4. Current research on dolphin communication
5. Shopping centers
6. Inflation in the United States
7. A specific rule governing student behavior at your school
8. The role of computers in the United States during the late 1900s
9. A form of music, such as jazz or rock
10. The saying, "Beauty is in the eye of the beholder."

Writing Practice 10

Select one of the photographs on page 40 and write a journal entry describing what you see. To discover ideas for your entry, apply the action questions to the photograph.

Questions About the Actors

The actors of the Pentad are the people responsible for and involved in the action. In some situations, such as science fiction, the actors might be nonhumans (such as robots or a form of extraterrestrial life). The following questions relate to the actors.

1. Who or what is responsible for the action?
2. What are the actors like?

The following notes show how one writer applied the actor questions to the subject of Stonehenge.

1. Who or what is responsible for the action?

Three separate groups of people were involved in the construction at Stonehenge. The first construction was started by people known to archaeologists as the Windmill Hill People, native hunters and farmers who dug a large circular ditch at the site and piled earth into steep banks on either side. Scientists date this first construction somewhere around 1900 B.C.

The second wave of construction, by a group known as the Beaker People, began around 1750 B.C. These were the people who brought the enormous stones—megaliths weighing up to five tons each—and organized them in two concentric (arranged around the same center) circles.

The third wave of construction, by a group called the Wessex People, began in approximately 1700 B.C. and finished the construction, called Stonehenge III, with more complex alignments of stones, perhaps for observing the skies.

As Stonehenge is not the oldest of the megalithic constructions, another theory states that there was a priestly class or a class of architects who traveled throughout Europe exchanging information on assembling the monuments. This theory explains the network of monuments and their strong resemblance to one another.

2. What are the actors like?

The Windmill Hill People are believed to have been peaceful and productive, with a strong religion. They left pottery and tools such as adzes, arrowheads, axes, scrapers for leatherwork, and millstones for grinding. These people practiced collective burial in large stone tombs, interring food, tools, and pottery with their dead. Graves were aligned east and west, in the direction of the rising and setting sun.

The Bronze Age wave of builders, the Beaker People, are known for their custom of burying beakers (pottery drinking cups) with their dead. They are thought to have been powerful and energetic people, better organized and less peaceful than the Windmill Hill People. They buried their dead in pairs or individually, as contrasted with the group burials of the earlier inhabitants, in small graves marked by mounds. The dead were buried in a sitting position, knee-to-chin, fully clothed and with their valuables, such as vessels and ornaments of gold, jet, and amber.

The Wessex People, also during the Bronze Age, appeared around 1700 B.C. Although their graves contained daggers and bows, their weapons seem more ceremonial in nature than the battle-axes of the Beaker People. The Wessex People seem to have preserved only their chieftains; no graves of ordinary citizens have been discovered. Because Baltic amber, Egyptian bead, Scottish jet, and Normandy-styled bowls were found in their graves, these rulers are thought to have been international traders, bartering for luxuries from the Baltic to the Mediterranean.

The writer has collected detailed information about the actors involved in the building of Stonehenge. When the writer actually prepares the report, he or she might decide that some of the information is not relevant to the restricted topic and so discard it.

Writing Practice 11

Apply the actor questions to a topic from the list on page 39 or to a similar topic of your choice. (You may want to use the topic you chose for Writing Practice 8.) Write the appropriate questions and your answers to them on a sheet of paper. Remember to collect as much detailed information as possible.

Writing Practice 12

Imagine that you know the people involved in the action of one of the photographs on page 43. You can imagine that they are related to you, that they are friends or acquaintances, or that you have some other association with them. Then write a journal entry or a descriptive paragraph describing the people in the photograph that you chose. To gather information for your entry or paragraph, apply the actor questions from the Pentad.

Questions About the Scene

Scene questions relate to the time and place of the action. The following questions illustrate how to ask about details of scene.

1. Where is the action happening?
2. Where did the action happen? (for past action)
3. Where will the action happen? (for future action)
4. What is the place like?
5. When did the action happen? (for past action)
6. When will the action happen? (for future action)
7. What is the historical background of the action?

Using scene questions that are appropriate to investigating the subject of Stonehenge produces the following information.

1. Where is the action happening?

    Stonehenge is located in Wiltshire, England, on the Salisbury Plain.

2. When did the action happen?

    Stonehenge has been a feature of the Salisbury Plain landscape for over 3600 years.

3. What is the place like?

    The great megaliths of Stonehenge are enclosed within a circular ditch and are approached by a wide roadway called the Avenue. There are four series of stones within the trench: (1) a circle of sandstones with connecting lintels, (2) a circle of bluestone megaliths, (3) within that, a horseshoe-shaped arrangement surrounding an oval-shaped group of stones, and (4) the Altar Stone at

the center. The Avenue points northeast to the Heel Stone, a megalith that marks the midsummer sunrise.

It is possible to mark solstices, equinoxes, and other more sophisticated astronomical observations by the stones even today.

4. When did the action begin?

The first construction at Stonehenge is thought to have begun around 1900 B.C. and continued, through two new groups of builders, over the following 200 years.

5. What is the historical background of the action?

The building of Stonehenge did not follow a direct evolution, with one construct building up from the previous one. The first stage included a large circle of holes surrounding an arrangement of circular ditches and elevated mounds; the circle opened up on a pathway to a special area marked with a large standing stone called the Heel Stone, which told the exact point of the midsummer sunrise.

During the second stage the circular enclosure was surrounded by megaliths arranged in two concentric circles; this structure also left an opening directed toward the Heel Stone.

The third builders of Stonehenge removed the double circle of megaliths (no one has discovered where they were taken) and replaced them with eighty-one boulders of the same stone as the Heel Stone. The builders also added four boulders within the circle to mark sunrise and sunset, moonrise and moonset.

One leading theory about Stonehenge is that it was always used for astronomical purposes but that as more was learned about observing the heavens, the different builders rebuilt and improved its structure for more exact observations and calculations.

Not all of the preceding scene questions will be appropriate to every topic, and some questions will produce similar information. However, asking yourself about the past, present, and future scene will help you to understand your subject more fully. As you write, you can eliminate irrelevant or repetitious information.

Writing Practice 13

Apply the Pentad scene questions to a topic from the list on page 39 or to a topic of your choice. (You may wish to continue using the topic from Writing Practice 11.) Write the appropriate questions and their answers on a separate sheet of paper.

Writing Practice 14

Assume that you have just returned from a place in one of the photographs on page 43 and then write a journal entry describing the place or a letter to a friend in which you describe the scene. To discover ideas for your entry or letter, apply the Pentad scene questions to the scene that you have chosen.

Questions About Method

In examining method the Pentad asks, *What means are used to bring about the action?* The following notes show how one writer used the Pentad method questions to gather information about the means by which Stonehenge was constructed.

1. What methods were used to build Stonehenge?

   There is still much scientific speculation about how the enormous boulders of Stonehenge were transported there. Most experts believe that (as in the building of the pyramids of Egypt) humans were used to drag the boulders from their source, which was a great distance from the Stonehenge site. They had no wheels to ease their task and no horses to help pull the boulders.

2. What methods were used to predict the movements of celestial bodies at Stonehenge?

   Evidence that Stonehenge was primarily an astronomical observatory (or a sun-moon temple, as some call it) comes from the alignment of the stones with significant stages in the progression of the sun and the moon across the skies. The intricate series of stones in Stonehenge III can be used in a number of different ways, sighting the heavens from one particular viewpoint or another, to observe or predict the movement of heavenly bodies.

Writing Practice 15

Think of two or more questions that you could ask about your topic that have to do with the method in which the action was performed. Apply these method questions to a topic from the list on page 39 or to a similar one of your choice. Write the appropriate questions and their answers on a separate sheet of paper. (You may wish to continue using your topic from previous Writing Practice assignments.)

Questions About Purpose

The final Pentad question deals with the purpose of the action: *For what purpose, or reason, does the action occur?* (Remember that an event such as a hurricane or a tornado is not considered an action.) The following information was gathered by applying the Pentad purpose question to the subject of Stonehenge.

1. What was the purpose of Stonehenge?

   The main purpose of Stonehenge seems to have been the prediction of sun and moon movements at crucial alignments.

   Stonehenge was an astronomical observatory capable of yielding precise calculations, most probably used as a calendar for determining when to plant crops. Moreover, it was probably also a temple; religious leaders may have used knowledge of the movements of the skies to maintain their power. They could call worshipers together to observe the midsummer sunrise over the Heel Stone, knowing exactly the day on which it would come. They could also assemble people for eclipses and for the midwinter sunrise through another configuration at Stonehenge. Furthermore, since the progression of structures at Stonehenge reveals an increasingly sophisticated knowledge of astronomical observation, Stonehenge's builders probably enjoyed the mental exercise of watching and predicting the movement of the stars and planets, just as people do today.

Writing Practice 16

Using the same topic you have used with previous Pentad exercises or a new one you select for this assignment, apply the Pentad purpose question. Write the question and your answer on a sheet of paper. Remember to make your answer as detailed as possible.

For Your Journal

It is interesting to imagine what archaeologists 2,000 years from now would make of some of the structures and objects in contemporary American civilization. Select one of the photographs on these pages and write a journal entry about it as though you were a scientist from the year 4000. Imagine that you have just discovered the structure or object in the photograph and are writing suggestions about its use or purpose for one of your colleagues.

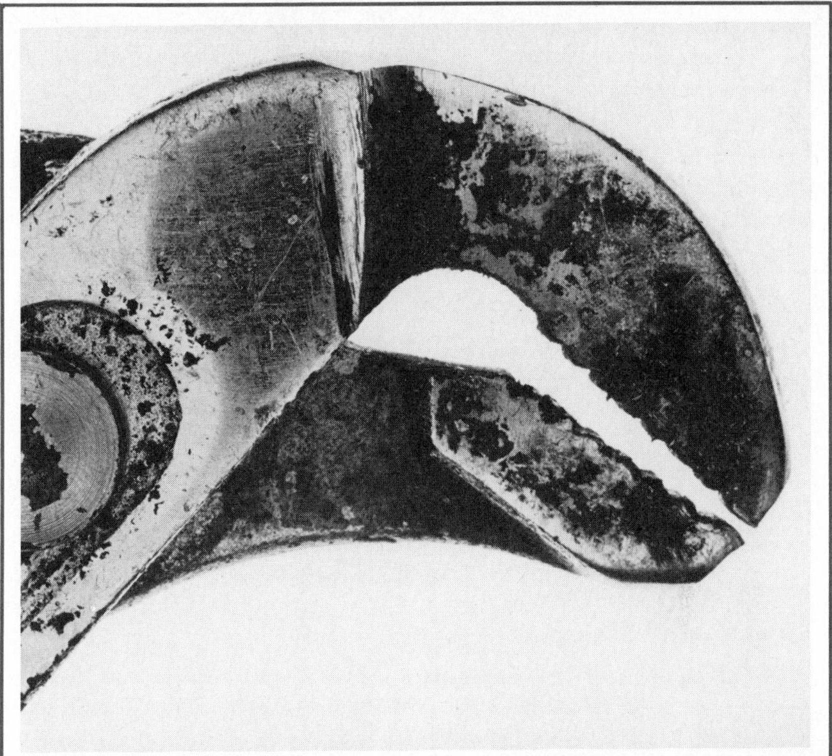

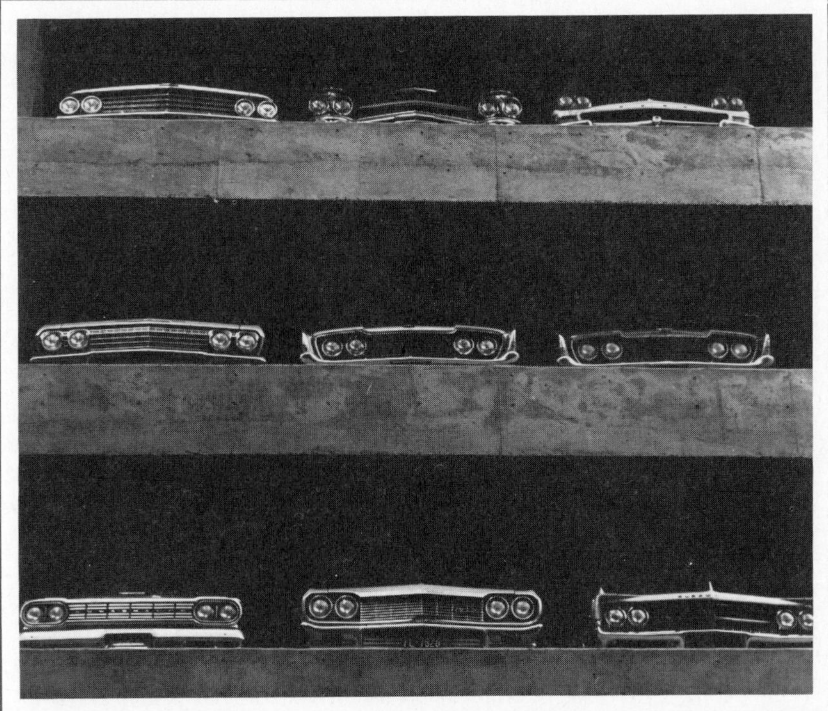

Changing Viewpoints

A helpful method for discovering ideas for writing is to change your viewpoint, or way of looking at a subject. In the following sections you will learn to look at a subject from three viewpoints: (1) as it appears frozen in time and space, (2) as it changes or varies over time and space, and (3) as it is made up of working parts that together fit into a much larger background. These three viewpoints can be expressed by means of the following questions.

1. What is it?
2. How does it change or vary?
3. What are its relationships? (How do its parts work together? How is it related to a larger background?)

What Is it?

When you ask *What is it?* about a subject, you are asking about its identity. Look first at its features or characteristics. The features of a subject—whether it is a concrete one (such as a pencil or a television set) or an abstract one (such as education or sports)—are its characteristics. These characteristics are what distinguish an object or idea from other objects or ideas like it. For example, what features make a chair different from a stool, a snack from a meal, or a grade school from a high school? When you study the features of a subject, you "freeze" it in time and space, just as you would if you photographed it, to study it minutely.

If your subject is a person or an organization, the *What is it?* question focuses on the person's physical characteristics or on a description of the organization. Assume, for example, that your subject is *Trade unions*. From this viewpoint you would define the subject *Trade unions*, asking yourself who composes them, what they do, and what their purpose is.

Using comparison and contrast is a good way to gather information about a subject's identity. For example, how do present-day trade unions compare with the craft guilds of medieval Europe? Was their basic purpose the same? Did they represent similar types of workers? By exploring these similarities and differences, you can broaden your understanding of the nature of the trade union.

Ideas and concepts can also be examined by using the *What is it?* question, since the first step in describing a concept is to make a definition. Assume, for example, that your subject is *Tragedy*. Most dictionaries define *tragedy* as "a drama with a serious theme that is brought to an unhappy conclusion." You can broaden this definition by examining a particular kind of tragedy, such as Elizabethan tragedy, or you can describe your concept further by relating tragedy to one particular drama, such as *Hamlet*.

Comparing and contrasting your idea or concept with other similar subjects will help to increase your understanding of it. For example, you could compare Greek tragedy with tragedy in twentieth-century drama. Within this framework you could concentrate specifically on comparing and contrasting one figure from Greek tragedy, such as Oedipus, with a figure from twentieth-century drama, perhaps Willy Loman in *Death of a Salesman.* This comparison and contrast would focus primarily on two different views of the nature of tragedy, rather than on similarities in the definition.

Writing Practice 17

Think of a person (such as a figure from history or someone in the news) or an organization of people (such as a club, a political party, or a religious group) as the general subject for this assignment. Then use the following *What is it?* questions to gather information about the subject, jotting down your answers on a separate sheet of paper. When you have finished, use the ideas you discovered to write a paragraph describing the person or organization you have chosen.

1. What are the physical characteristics or important defining characteristics of your subject?
2. What are the most striking or essential features of your subject?
3. What does your subject do, or what is the purpose of your subject?
4. In what way is your subject important? (Give specific information or examples.)
5. How does your subject compare and contrast with other similar subjects? (Compare and contrast your subject with a *specific* person or group.)

Writing Practice 18

Select one of the following IDEAS OR CONCEPTS as your subject for this assignment or use a similar one of your choice. Then select one of the QUESTIONS TO ASK YOURSELF that follow the list of subjects, jotting down your answers on a sheet of paper. Finally use the information that you gather to write a detailed description of your idea or concept.

IDEAS AND CONCEPTS

1. Middle class
2. Honesty
3. Empire
4. Courtesy
5. Individualism
6. Art
7. Evil
8. Progress
9. Comedy
10. Freedom of speech

QUESTIONS TO ASK YOURSELF

1. What is the definition of the subject? (First write out your own definition and then check the dictionary definition.)
2. What are the similarities between the subject you have chosen and other similar subjects?
3. What are the differences between this subject and other similar subjects?

How Does it Change or Vary?

Asking yourself how your subject has changed over time or how it can change (or vary) without losing its identity is another way to discover ideas. For instance, since the first television sets were mass produced in the United States, they have undergone many changes. They are much smaller and slimmer, receive much better pictures, and cost much less. In addition, the sets are available in many variations. They come with screens as small as a watch crystal or as large as a movie screen. They can be installed in walls or automobiles, or they come in large consoles with radios and record players. However, regardless of the changes television sets have undergone over the years and regardless of the variations available, the television set has remained a television set. There is a limit to which an item can be changed and still retain its identity. For example, if a television set were to be changed by removing its capacity for receiving images, it would no longer be a television set; instead, it would be the equivalent of a radio.

To view the subject *Trade unions* from the second viewpoint, you would ask yourself how the nature and purpose of trade unions have changed over time. For example, you might want to study the Knights of Labor in the early nineteenth century through the real growth of the unions around the turn of the century, or you might want to study the changes in unions from the turn of the century to the present or any other time framework that makes sense to you. You would also ask yourself how the unions can vary without becoming something other than trade unions. For instance, if unions began opening and running factories themselves rather than representing people who worked for those factories, would they still be trade unions?

You can also examine how an idea or a concept changes over time. In studying tragedy, for example, you would learn that in the Middle Ages *tragedy* referred not to drama but to narratives about how people of high rank fell to low estate and that not until the sixteenth century was tragedy associated with the theater in England. You can also ask how ideas and concepts change without losing their basic identity. For example, some scholars believe that real tragedy deals only with heroic figures and that twentieth-century drama about ordinary people should not be defined as tragedy. Other scholars believe that tragedy is a reflection of the beliefs and values of various societies and that definitions of tragedy must change as societies change. (There will often be disagreement about the extent to which a subject can vary without losing its identity.)

Writing Practice 19

Select one of the following SUBJECTS or use one of your own choice (perhaps the subject you used for Writing Practice 18). Gather information about your chosen subject by asking yourself the question *How does it change or vary?* Use this information to write a paragraph describing how your subject has changed or is in the process of changing. If appropriate, include information about how it can vary without losing its identity. The specific QUESTIONS TO ASK YOURSELF that follow the list of SUBJECTS will help you to explore your subject.

SUBJECTS

1. Poetry
2. Your high school
3. Television
4. The Presidency of the United States
5. A particular fad that is popular around your school now
6. Conservation
7. Rock music
8. Public transportation
9. The space program of the United States

QUESTIONS TO ASK YOURSELF

1. How has the subject changed over time? (If appropriate, select a specific time period to address.)
2. Is the change caused by natural or internal forces?
3. Is the change caused by outside forces, such as the influence of other people or forces of nature?
4. What is the most significant factor in the change?
5. To what extent can the subject change without losing its identity?
6. How does the subject vary?
7. To what extent can the subject vary without losing its identity?

What Are Its Relationships?

The third viewpoint about a subject can be expressed by the question *What are its relationships?* This viewpoint concerns both the parts of the subject and how they work together and how the subject fits against a larger background. In other words, you are considering the subject as both a system in itself (parts that work together) and as part of a larger system.

Most subjects have definite parts: the American government is composed of legislative, judicial, and administrative branches—the Congress and Senate, the courts, and the Presidency; most essays are made up of an introduction, a body, and a conclusion; the main parts of an automobile are the body, engine, power train, and chassis. In addition, these parts work together a certain way to create the subject.

To understand trade unions you must know both their parts and how these parts work together to form a system. Trade unions are generally composed of members and leaders who form various committees through which most of the work is accomplished. Then you would ask yourself how these parts work together to accomplish the purpose of a trade union. For example, you would want to know how workers join, how leaders are elected, and how decisions are made. To understand the subject *Tragedy* you would first need to know that it has the following elements: a character who is the central figure, a struggle against opposing forces of some sort (often fate), and a disastrous end for the character. Then you would need to know how these parts work together to produce the tragedy.

In addition to having an internal system, subjects themselves can also be placed into larger systems. For instance, a high school has many parts that work together to accomplish the purpose of educating students of a certain age. In addition, a high school is only part of a larger educational system that includes elementary schools, middle schools, colleges, universities, and trade or technical schools. One larger system of which trade unions are a part is the economy in general. How do trade unions affect other parts of the economy? What role do they play in the economy? Another system might be the political system. What influence do trade unions have as a political force?

The larger system of which tragedy is a part might be drama, or it might be entertainment in general. To put the subject of tragedy into a larger context, you could examine the role of tragic plays in Greek, Elizabethan, or contemporary drama, or you could look at tragic drama as it relates to other forms of entertainment.

Writing Practice 20

Select one of the following SUBJECTS or use one of your own choice. (You may want to continue with a subject from a previous Writing Practice.) Then use the QUESTIONS TO ASK YOURSELF that follow the list of subjects and write your answers on a sheet of paper. Finally, write two paragraphs about your subject, one describing how the parts of the subject work together and another explaining how your subject relates to a larger background.

SUBJECTS

1. Protein
2. Money
3. Language
4. The Great Lakes
5. Magic
6. Fashion
7. Trains
8. The Supreme Court
9. Basketball
10. Jazz

QUESTIONS TO ASK YOURSELF

1. What are the different parts of the subject?
2. What are the most significant parts of the subject?
3. How do the parts of the subject work together to accomplish its purpose?
4. How does the subject fit into a larger system or systems?
5. How do these other systems work with the subject?

Writing Practice 21

Use one of the following subjects as the basis for an essay that will explain the subject to someone who knows nothing about it. Use each of the three viewpoints discussed in the preceding sections to gather the ideas that you need for the explanation.

1. A team sport, such as baseball
2. A movie or book that you enjoyed
3. A process, such as refinishing a piece of furniture
4. A concept, such as honesty
5. An object, such as a lawn mower
6. An activity, such as acting in a school play
7. Something that you particularly like or dislike
8. Your reasons for liking or admiring some person
9. Your plans for the future
10. An important event in your life

Changing Viewpoints to Analyze Problems

The "viewpoints" technique is extremely useful when you must analyze a problem and recommend solutions.

Often you know that all is not right with some process or some thing but cannot state concisely and exactly what the problem is; therefore, you cannot recommend solutions. Consider, for example, the following situations:

> An employee at a fast-food restaurant knows that the operation is not as efficient as it might be and would like to suggest ways to increase efficiency.
>
> A group of students complains about the intramural sports program in their school. The principal challenges them to prepare a report analyzing the problem in detail and recommending solutions.
>
> A student is dissatisfied with one of her research papers and wants to find ways to improve it.
>
> Another student wants to "turn over a new leaf"—to understand what has been wrong with his study and work habits in the past and make improvements for the future.

For situations such as the preceding ones, the "viewpoints" technique can be of great help.

Writing Practice 22

For help with this assignment, use the Preparing to Write section on pages 54–55.

Choose something that you think needs improvement, do an analysis of the problem, and suggest ways of making changes. If you do not have a topic in mind, you can use one of the following problems.

1. Making your home or some part of it a more efficient place
2. Improving the attractiveness of some area of your city or community (for example, a park or business area)
3. Making improvements in something you have produced (for example, a piece of carpentry, a story, or a dress)
4. Solving problems of pollution control
5. Helping people with self-destructive tendencies (for example, smoking cigarettes) to overcome them

6. Improving the public transportation system in your city or area
7. Making the perfect mousetrap
8. Improving some dish, such as stew or quiche
9. Solving problems with the American system of Presidential elections
10. Maintaining civil rights while crime steadily increases

Preparing to Write

At the top of a blank sheet of paper, write the question that will help you to explore your subject from the first of the three viewpoints: *What is it?* Then record ideas about the identity and features of your subject. What is the definition of your subject? What does it mean to you and to others you know? What is the dictionary definition of your subject? For example, what are its physical characteristics, such as colors, dimensions, sounds, smells, tastes, textures, temperature, dampness, or dryness? How do these features differ from those of other similar subjects?

At the top of the second sheet of paper, write the question that will help you to discover ideas about your subject from the third viewpoint: *What are its relationships?* (For this assignment consider the second viewpoint—*How does it change or vary?*—last.)

What are the major parts of your subject? How do these parts work together? (Try drawing a diagram.) Are human actions involved? If so, what are they? Machines? Natural forces, such as winds or tides? Speeds: slow or fast? Nature of movement: jerky or smooth? Other questions about operation?

On the second sheet also record ideas about how your subject fits into or relates to a larger system. For example, the recreational program of a community is one system within the whole system of the community, which also includes systems such as police and fire departments, schools, and health care. The can opener in your kitchen is a system within the system of food preparation in your home. The Supreme Court of the United States is a system within the American system of justice.

Does your subject fit into its larger system well or badly? Why? How could the relationship be changed? Different chain of command? Better communication? Should the subject be removed from its present system and be placed within another? What are other questions regarding the larger system of your subject?

It may take you several days, or even weeks, to gain all of the ideas possible about your subject. You may want to do research, conduct interviews, or visit some place for a close inspection. However, before you proceed to the remaining viewpoint, complete your research.

When you have completed your research, consider the possible changes that will result in an improvement. At the top of a third sheet of paper, write the question that will help you to discover ideas for changes: *How does it change or vary?* On the basis of ideas and data that you have gathered, what changes would you recommend for improvement? The recommendations that you make must be possible to carry out and must not change the identity of your subject. For example, if you are suggesting improvements in your school's extracurricular programs, you should not make recommendations that would cost more money than is available. A report on the cafeteria at a summer camp should not recommend that food be served by waiters and waitresses in formal uniforms because then the cafeteria would become a restaurant.

Writing Practice 23

Using the principles of organization discussed in other chapters of the "Writing" part of this textbook, prepare a report or an essay on your topic. First present the details that will allow readers to understand the problem. Then make detailed recommendations for a solution or for improvement. If possible, present your report to some person or group that might use it as the basis for action.

Writing Practice 24

Using notes that you have made in this chapter, write an essay about your own writing process. You can organize your essay in any way that you choose, but if you can discover no other way, you might want to use the following informal outline.

Introduction: Your attitude toward writing essays

A description of what you do when you write
- Planning
- Writing
- Revising

The influence of your background and personality on your writing

The place or places where you write
- Description of them
- Their effect on your writing

Your best times for writing

Your favorite writing equipment

Props (such as snacks or music)

3 Writing Paragraphs

Paragraph Writing

In your reading you have probably encountered many different kinds of paragraphs. In dialogue, for example, paragraph indentions indicate when the speaker changes. In other kinds of prose, writers often use single-sentence paragraphs to mark a transition from one idea to the next or to emphasize an important idea. Still another type of paragraph is a related group of sentences that develop or explain a main idea.

In this chapter you will study the structure of the paragraph that develops and explains a main idea.This type of paragraph is often called an *expository paragraph.*

Methods of Paragraph Development

Expository paragraphs may be developed by several different methods or by a combination of methods. In the following sections, you will study the *Topic-Restriction-Illustration* (*TRI*) pattern and its variations. You will also study paragraphs developed by means of comparison, analogy, and cause and effect.

The TRI Pattern

One method of paragraph development that is useful particularly in expository writing is called the *Topic-Restriction-Illustration (TRI) pattern.*

In a TRI paragraph each part of the TRI represents a sentence or group of sentences. The *topic sentence* states the general topic of the paragraph. The *restriction sentence* limits, or restricts, the general topic to the specific topic that the paragraph will discuss. The *illustration sentences* develop the main idea of the paragraph by providing examples, reasons, data, descriptive details, or other information.

In the basic TRI pattern the topic sentence comes first, as in the following example by W. H. Auden from an essay "The Almighty Dollar."[1]

> Political and technological developments are rapidly obliterating all cultural differences and it is possible that, in a not remote future, it will be impossible to distinguish human beings living on one area of the earth's surface from those living on any other, but our different pasts have not yet been completely erased and cultural differences are still perceptible.

The preceding topic sentence states that the general topic of the paragraph is *Cultural differences among people arising from their different pasts.* The restriction sentence then follows:

> The most striking difference between an American and a European is the difference in their attitudes towards money.

The restriction sentence narrows the general subject of cultural differences to two specific cultures, America and Europe, and the specific issue of attitudes toward money in these cultures.

The illustration sentences elaborate on these differences:

1. Every European knows, as a matter of historical fact, that in Europe wealth could only be acquired at the expense of other human beings, either by conquering them or by exploiting their labor in factories.
2. Further, even after the Industrial Revolution began, the number of persons who could rise from poverty to wealth was small; the vast majority took it for granted that they would not be much richer nor poorer than their fathers.
3. In consequence, no European associates wealth with personal merit or poverty with personal failure.

The three illustration sentences of the paragraph discuss the European attitude toward money, its origins, and its consequences.

Written in an essay, the paragraph appears in the following form.

> Political and technological developments are rapidly obliterating all cultural differences and it is possible that, in a not remote future, it will be impossible to distinguish human beings living on one area of the earth's surface from those living on any other, but our different pasts have not yet been completely erased and cultural differences are still perceptible. The most striking difference between an American and a European is the difference in their attitudes towards money. Every European knows, as a matter of historical fact, that in Europe wealth could only be acquired at the expense of other human beings, either by conquering them or by exploiting their labor in factories. Further, even after the Industrial Revolution began, the number of persons who could rise from poverty to wealth was small;

---

[1]Excerpt from "Postscript: The Almighty Dollar" in *The Dyer's Hand and Other Essays* by W. H. Auden.

the vast majority took it for granted that they would not be much richer nor poorer than their fathers. In consequence, no European associates wealth with personal merit or poverty with personal failure.

The preceding paragraph begins by introducing the idea that *While in the future people may share a global culture, for the present there are still perceptible cultural differences among nations.* This statement is the general topic of the paragraph. The restriction sentence limits this general idea to a specific comparison of attitudes toward money in America and Europe. After restricting the topic, Auden then explains the European attitude toward money in three illustration sentences. Each one adds a new piece of information about the restricted, not the general, topic of the paragraph.

Although most statements of topic and restriction are expressed in one sentence each, there is no general rule about the number of illustrations to include. Use as many as you need to make your point clearly and thoroughly.

Writing Practice 1

The chapter "Discovering Ideas for Writing" on pages 29–55 gives several methods for finding ideas that you can use for this assignment.

Select two of the following topic sentences for an expository paragraph or, with your teacher's permission, substitute two similar sentences of your own. For each topic sentence write a restriction sentence followed by three or four illustration sentences. When you have finished, write each TRI in regular paragraph form.

1. Sports may be hazardous to your health.
2. The arts are important to society.
3. Over the years I have perfected the art of (studying/avoiding work/amusing myself/etc.).
4. Some people regard movies as an escape, but for me they are something more.
5. I believe in patriotism.
6. Learning a foreign language can help you understand another culture.
7. The United States should be (more/less) active in aiding needy or developing countries.
8. The wilderness is a precious resource.
9. Some television advertisements are amusing, but there is one I cannot stand to watch.
10. Keeping up with current events is an important part of becoming a good writer.

Varying the Basic TRI Pattern

Varying the structure of paragraphs is an important part of good writing. There are several methods of altering the basic TRI paragraph pattern.

One variation called the *Topic-Illustration* pattern combines the topic and restriction parts of the pattern into one sentence.

The TI pattern presents the general topic and restricts it in the same sentence. The writer then uses the rest of the paragraph for illustrations, as in the following example from an essay on food in Elizabethan England by M. F. K. Fisher titled "A Pigges Pettie Toes."[1]

> Even in the lusty days of Elizabeth's long reign, when England's blood ran, perhaps, at its fastest and finest, there were melancholy observers of what seemed signs of weakening in the nation's appetite. Who could tell where things would end, when already the most reputable of rich merchants were copying an effeminate Italian mannerism, and carrying their silver and gold forks about with them instead of eating with their fingers and knives as good Englishmen had been glad to do for centuries? And the ladies, lying in bed until six o'clock in the morning! When they arose, they breakfasted like babies, thinking they could start the day decently on a pot of ale and but one meager pound of bacon. The Queen, God be thanked, paid no attention to the new-style finicking, and made her first meal of the day light but sustaining: butter, bread (brown, to stay in the stomach longer and more wholesomely than white), a stew of mutton, a joint of beef, one of veal, some rabbits in a pie, chickens, and fruits, and beer and wine to wash all down in really hygienic fashion.

In the preceding paragraph the topic and restriction are combined in the first sentence. This sentence restricts the general topic, *Food in Elizabethan England*, to the more specific topic of what some contemporary observers saw as "signs of weakening" in English appetites. These tendencies are humorously illustrated by the remaining sentences. What specific examples does Fisher cite as evidence? What information does the final illustration provide?

Another way to vary the basic Topic-Restriction-Illustration pattern is to change the position of each part within the paragraph.

For example, you could write a paragraph with the topic-restriction sentence in the middle rather than at the beginning. You could also invert the order completely and write a Reverse TRI paragraph.

The *Reverse TRI* pattern begins with illustration sentences and works from that point to conclude with the topic or topic-restriction sentence.

The following paragraph from an essay by Nora Ephron, titled "Bernice Gera, First Lady Umpire," uses the Reverse TRI pattern. The topic-restriction sentence is underlined.[2]

> It took four years for Bernice Gera to walk onto that ball field, four years of legal battles for the right to stand in the shadow of an "Enjoy Silver Floss Sauerkraut" sign while the crowd cheered and young girls waved sheets reading "Right On, Bernice!" and the manager of the Geneva Phillies welcomed her to the game. "On behalf of professional baseball," he said, "we say good luck and God bless you in your chosen profession." And the band played and the spot-

---

[1]From "Serve It Forth" in *The Art of Eating* by M. F. K. Fisher. Copyright © 1937, 1943, 1954, 1971 by M. F. K. Fisher. Reprinted with permission of Macmillan Publishing Co., Inc. and Lescher & Lescher, Ltd.

[2]Excerpt from "Bernice Gera, First Lady Umpire" in *Crazy Salad: Some Things About Women* by Nora Ephron. Copyright © 1975 by Nora Ephron. Reprinted by permission of Alfred A. Knopf, Inc.

lights shone and all three networks recorded the event. Bernice Gera had become the first woman in the 133-year history of the sport to umpire a professional baseball game.

The illustration sentences in the preceding paragraph give information about the background and the setting for the main topic, or idea: *Bernice Gera became the first woman umpire in the history of baseball.*

Writing Practice 2

Each of the sentences that follow is a combination topic-restriction sentence. Select two of them or use similar sentences of your own choice. Then on a separate sheet of paper, write three or four illustration sentences for each topic-restriction sentence. Begin each paragraph with the topic-restriction sentence and write each paragraph in standard paragraph form.

1. Part of baseball's appeal is its emphasis on the individual player.
2. Learning how to drive a car was one of the (most important/exciting) experiences of my life.
3. Scarcity of natural resources is one of the most significant problems in this country today.
4. Working (in a store/as a baby-sitter/etc.) has taught me a lot.
5. When I think of my childhood, I see a movie screen filled with images I will never forget.

For Your Journal

After reading the paragraph from "A Pigges Pettie Toes" in the preceding section, perhaps you reflected on your own eating habits or on those of others. Are there foods or combinations of foods you enjoy eating that others find strange? Have your parents ever remarked on your eating habits? What food memories from your childhood stand out most? Do you recall the dull flavor of strained peas, the tartness of a fall apple, your first experience with a gloriously sticky pizza? Write a journal entry or entries about experiences from the present or the past involving food. Use specific details to help the reader share your experience.

Writing Practice 3

Select one of the following topic-restriction sentences or substitute one of your own. Then write a paragraph using the Reverse TRI pattern. Include at least three illustration sentences and end the paragraph with a topic-restriction sentence.

1. Animal communication is a fascinating field of study.
2. Revision is an essential part of the writing process.
3. Penalties for driving while intoxicated are not severe enough.

4. Active participation in student government is essential.
5. Then the mysterious sounds ceased, and the castle was plunged into silence.

Revising Paragraphs

Revision is also discussed on pages 11–12.

Revision is the process of making improvements in a piece of writing.

When you revise your writing, you read through it carefully, making corrections and improvements as needed. For some writers revision is a continuous process; as they write, they keep rereading the previous sentences, examining each one individually and as a part of the overall work. After they have finished, they reread to be certain of the total effect. Other writers like to get all their ideas down on paper before revising; they write an entire paragraph or essay and then go back and evaluate their work. Use whichever approach to revision best fits your writing habits, but remember that revision is essential to all good writing.

The following suggestions will guide you in revising your paragraphs.

1. The first stage in revising your paragraph is to examine each sentence individually.

Each of your sentences, by itself, should make a clear statement about the paragraph topic. However you have positioned the topic sentence within your paragraph, remember that only the topic sentence gives general information. The other sentences proceed from the topic sentence and give specific information about it.

2. The second stage in revising is to examine each sentence as it relates to the paragraph as a whole.

Each sentence in your paragraph should contribute a new piece of information. Rewrite or delete any sentences that repeat information or any illustration sentence that does not contribute specific information to the paragraph. If you find an illustration sentence that does not relate directly to the restriction sentence, rewrite or delete it.

3. The third stage is examining your paragraph as a whole.

Consider each paragraph as a separate unit of information that presents and develops a topic. When you reread your paragraph, make certain that you have stated your main idea clearly and that you have illustrated it with sufficient examples, details, data, or other information.

The following checklist for revising paragraphs covers all of the items on paragraph writing discussed in this chapter. For now, check your paragraphs against only those items you have studied; as you work through the chapter, refer to the checklist for help in revision, adding additional points as you study them. After revising each paragraph, proofread for features that are not a part of Edited Standard English by using the Checklist for Proofreading on page 14.

Checklist for Revising Paragraphs

1. The paragraph has a clear central idea. If appropriate, this idea is expressed in a topic sentence.
2. The central idea is sufficiently restricted to be developed in a paragraph. If appropriate, the restriction is expressed in a separate sentence or combined with a statement of the topic in a topic-restriction sentence.
3. The central idea is adequately developed with illustration sentences giving specific information about it.
4. A paragraph developed through comparison is organized either by a block or a point-by-point method; the points of comparison are similar.
5. A paragraph developed by analogy uses a simpler idea or process or other model to help explain a more complex one. The comparison by analogy is carried throughout the paragraph.
6. A paragraph developed by cause-and-effect reasoning discusses either immediate or underlying causes, and immediate or long-range effects.
7. The paragraph has unity. The main idea is apparent; every sentence in the paragraph supports or develops the main idea. If a "clincher" sentence is appropriate, it focuses the reader's attention back on the main idea or presents a final interesting piece of information.
8. The paragraph is coherent. Sentences are arranged in an orderly progression; transitions, connecting pronouns, paraphrase, repetition, or parallel structure are used to link ideas.

In addition to this checklist, you can use the following suggestions by George Orwell to help improve your writing.[1]

> Never use a metaphor, simile, or other figure of speech which you are used to seeing in print.
>
> Never use a long word where a short one will do.
>
> If it is possible to cut a word out, always cut it out.
>
> Never use the passive where you can use the active.
>
> Never use a foreign phrase, a scientific word, or a jargon word if you can think of an everyday English equivalent.
>
> Break any of these rules sooner than say anything outright barbarous.

Development by Comparison

The purpose of comparison is to identify ways in which items are similar and ways in which they differ.

When you use comparison to develop a paragraph, you liken and contrast ideas and concepts, people, places, experiences, points of view, and so on.

---

[1]Excerpted from "Politics and the English Language" in *Shooting an Elephant and Other Essays* by George Orwell. Copyright 1946 by Sonia Brownell Orwell, copyright 1974 by Sonia Orwell. Reprinted by permission of Harcourt Brace Jovanovich, Inc., A.M. Heath & Company Ltd. as agents for the estate of the late George Orwell, and Martin Secker & Warburg.

Comparison paragraphs help the reader to understand more about both items by showing them in relation to one another, and by discussing the significance of their similarities and differences.

When you make a comparison, the items being compared must share a common element. For example, you could compare the British Parliament with the U.S. Congress because each is a legislative body. The novels of J. R. R. Tolkien and C. S. Lewis can be compared because both authors write fantasies with religious overtones.

The individual points within any comparison that you make must be similar. Suppose, for example, that you are writing a comparison of British and American football. It would not be appropriate to discuss game strategies for one and the history of the other. Each major point that you make must be discussed for each item of the comparison: the history, players, and method of scoring of British football must be accompanied by a discussion of the history, players, and method of scoring of American football.

Some comparisons concentrate on the similarities between items, and some focus on the differences. The nature of your subject will tell you whether it is more appropriate to emphasize the likenesses or the differences. If, for example, you are writing a comparison of the painters Mary Cassatt and Edgar Degas, you might emphasize the similarity of their styles, as Degas was a great influence on Cassatt. On the other hand, in comparing Elizabeth I of England with Mary, Queen of Scots, you would probably emphasize the differences between them in terms of their power and personalities.

Two basic comparison methods are the *block method* and the *point-by-point method.*

With the *block method* of comparison, the items are compared separately; ideas about each item are grouped together. The block method is used most frequently to contrast, rather than to liken, two parts of a comparison. For example, in W. H. Auden's paragraph on page 57 from "The Almighty Dollar," Auden presents his discussion of the European attitude toward money in one section, or block. He contrasts this with the American attitude toward money, which he writes about in a separate paragraph.

In the following passage from *Zen and the Art of Motorcycle Maintenance*, Robert M. Pirsig compares a romantic view of the world with a classic viewpoint, using the block comparison method.[1]

A *mode* is a way of being or acting.

> The romantic mode is primarily inspirational, imaginative, creative, intuitive. Feelings rather than facts predominate. "Art" when it is opposed to "Science" is often romantic. It does not proceed by reason or by laws. It proceeds by feeling, intuition and esthetic conscience. In the northern European cultures the romantic mode is usually associated with femininity, but this is certainly not a necessary association. The classic mode, by contrast, proceeds by reason and by laws—which are themselves underlying forms of thought and behavior. In the European cultures it is primarily a masculine mode and the fields of

---

[1]Excerpt from *Zen and the Art of Motorcycle Maintenance* by Robert M. Pirsig.

science, law and medicine are unattractive to women largely for this reason. Although motorcycle riding is romantic, motorcycle maintenance is purely classic. The dirt, the grease, the mastery of underlying form required all give it such a negative romantic appeal that women never go near it.

Pirsig states in the preceding paragraph that the romantic way of looking at the world is based on feeling rather than fact. How does this contrast with the classic viewpoint? What other points of comparison does Pirsig make between the romantic and classic modes? For example, how does he use the terms *masculine* and *feminine* to describe the different viewpoints?

In the *point-by-point method*, the items being compared are not separated. Instead, both likenesses and differences are discussed for each item before the writer moves on to the next point. This method is useful when there are many specific points of comparison, when the differences between the two parts are subtle and need special explanation, or when you are emphasizing the similarities between the two parts of the comparison.

The following paragraph uses a point-by-point comparison to discuss the silent film comics Charlie Chaplin and Buster Keaton. As you read, notice each specific point in the comparison of the two stars.

Both Charlie Chaplin and Buster Keaton began as vaudeville comics and later moved on to successful careers in silent film comedy. Both were known to millions for film characters who projected a unique comic vision of the world. Chaplin's "Little Tramp," with his bowler, twirling cane and teetering walk, was an appealing figure of impoverished gentility and innocence whose only assets were his decency and his faith in an orderly universe. The film personality of Keaton, called the "Great Stoneface," was distinguished by the somber, stony expression of a man who has seen everything and is beyond ordinary surprise, joy, or sorrow. Chaplin and Keaton's humor grows from the incongruity between a situation and their comic character's response. In Chaplin's world, the Little Tramp is happily ignorant of danger, maintaining a daffy optimism and grace in the face of harsh reality. Starving during a bitter Alaskan winter, the Tramp cheerfully boils his shoe and serves it up with a gentlemanly flourish. In Keaton's world, the comic imbalance grows from his character's stone-faced stoicism confronting an absurd world. When his house collapses around him, he watches soberly, picks up the walls, and begins again. As the catastrophes mount, Keaton's deadpan response becomes more hilarious; he has transcended everything, even despair. When romance appears in Chaplin's films, the Little Tramp's heroine stays above the silly pratfalls and comic convolutions of his world. Significantly, his goodness and faith triumph and he usually wins her in the end. Keaton's world, however, immerses the delicate heroine in its catastrophes, and she is as likely as anyone else to be the victim of ignoble tumbles in the mud. In this world, fate provides no reward for good intentions and the hero often winds up having offended and lost the woman he hoped to win.

The preceding paragraph compares the comic characters of Chaplin and Keaton by examining their similarities and differences. The first point of the comparison looks at the personality of each character. What characterizes Chaplin's Little Tramp as opposed to Keaton's Great Stoneface? The second point of the comparison focuses on how Chaplin and Keaton create humor for their characters. How are their attitudes toward the world different? What is the final point of the comparison?

For help with this assignment, use one of the methods discussed in the chapter "Discovering Ideas for Writing" on pages 29–55.

To revise your paragraph, use the Checklist for Revising Paragraphs on page 62.

Writing Practice 4

Select one of the following suggestions for comparison/contrast paragraphs or write a similar comparison/contrast topic of your own. You may focus on the similarities or on the differences between the two parts of your comparison/contrast. Use whichever comparison/contrast method, block or point-by-point, is more appropriate to your topic.

1. Compare and contrast two Presidents (or other historical figures, such as rulers, inventors, philosophers, artists, writers).
2. Compare and contrast two types of relaxation or entertainment.
3. Compare yourself (getting up in the morning, going to school, or in another situation) on your best days as opposed to your worst days.
4. Compare and contrast the way your school or student government is run with an ideal school or student government.
5. Compare and contrast two sports teams or two orchestras.

Development by Analogy

An *analogy* is a type of comparison.

An analogy in expository writing is similar to a metaphor in imaginative writing. Both the analogy and the metaphor make comparisons of seemingly unlike items rather than making the standard comparison of like items. Consider, for example, the following analogy by Sylvia Plath.[1]

> If a poem is concentrated, a closed fist, then a novel is relaxed and expansive, an open hand: it has roads, detours, destinations; a heart line, a head line; morals and money come into it. Where the fist excludes and stuns, the open hand can touch and encompass a great deal in its travels.

It is not usual to compare a poem to a closed fist, or a novel to an open hand; but making this comparison helps the reader to understand their differences.

The purpose of analogy is to explain a difficult or unusual concept by comparing it with something simpler.

Like an extended metaphor in a poem or novel, an analogy will often be followed through an entire piece of writing. In the following excerpts from an essay titled "Feeding the Mind" by Lewis Carroll, the analogy carried throughout is the feeding of the body compared with the "feeding," or education, of the mind. As you read, notice the specific points of comparison that Carroll describes.

Lewis Carroll is the pseudonym for Charles L. Dodgson, a British mathematician famous for his *Alice in Wonderland*.

---

[1]Excerpt from "A Comparison" in *Johnny Panic and the Bible of Dreams* by Sylvia Plath. Copyright © 1956, 1962 by Sylvia Plath. Published by Faber & Faber of London, copyright © 1977 by Ted Hughes. Reprinted by permission of Harper & Row, Publishers, Inc., and Olwyn Hughes as agent for the author.

Considering the amount of painful experience many of us have had in feeding and dosing the body, it would, I think, be quite worth our while to try to translate some of the rules into corresponding ones for the mind. First, then, we should set ourselves to provide for our mind its *proper kind* of food; we very soon learn what will, and what will not, agree with the body, and find little difficulty in refusing a piece of the tempting pudding or pie which is associated in our memory with that terrible attack of indigestion, and whose very name irresistibly recalls rhubarb and magnesia; but it takes a great many lessons to convince us how indigestible some of our favorite lines of reading are, and again and again we make a meal of the unwholesome novel, sure to be followed by its usual train of low spirits, unwillingness to work, weariness of existence—in fact by mental nightmare. Then we should be careful to provide this wholesome food in *proper amount.* Mental gluttony, or overreading, is a dangerous propensity, tending to weakness of digestive power, and in some cases to loss of appetite; we know that bread is a good and wholesome food, but who would like to try the experiment of eating two or three loaves at a sitting? I wonder if there is such a thing in nature as a *fat mind?* I really think I have met with one or two minds which could not keep up with the slowest trot in conversation, could not jump over a logical fence to save their lives, always got stuck fast in a narrow argument, and, in short, were fit for nothing but to waddle helplessly through the world. . . .

Mr. Oliver Wendell Holmes, in his very amusing book *The Professor at the Breakfast-table,* gives the following rule for knowing whether a human being is young or old. "The crucial experiment is this. Offer a bulky bun to the suspected individual just ten minutes before dinner. If this is easily accepted and devoured, the fact of youth is established." He tells us that a human being, "if young, will eat anything at any hour of the day or night."

To ascertain the healthiness of the *mental* appetite of a human animal, place in its hands a short, well-written, but not exciting treatise on some popular subject—a mental *bun,* in fact. If it is read with eager interest and perfect attention, *and if the reader can answer questions on the subject afterwards*, the mind is in first-rate working order; if it be politely laid down again, or perhaps lounged over for a few minutes, and then, "I can't read this stupid book! Would you hand me the second volume of *The Mysterious Murder?*" you may be equally sure that there is something wrong in the mental digestion.

In the first paragraph Lewis Carroll states that people should provide the "proper kind of food" for their minds: Books are to the mind what food is to the stomach. How does he carry through with this analogy in the paragraph? What specific points of comparison does he make between physical eating and mental feeding?

The paragraph goes on to discuss feeding the mind with the "proper amount" of food. What specific comparisons does Carroll make between an overweight person and one with a "fat mind"?

How does Carroll extend the food analogy in the next paragraph? What further comparison does he introduce with the quotation from Oliver Wendell Holmes?

Writing Practice 5

Select one of the following suggestions for paragraphs developed by analogy or write a similar topic of your own. First list the specific points of comparison

For help with this assignment, use one of the methods discussed in the chapter "Discovering Ideas for Writing" on pages 29–55.

To revise your paragraph, use the Checklist for Revising Paragraphs on page 62.

your analogy will contain. Then write a paragraph developing the analogy on a separate sheet of paper.

1. Explain your reading habits by analogy.
2. Explain how a car engine (or other mechanical construct) works by analogy.
3. Explain how to make friends (or enemies) by analogy.
4. Explain how to act on a first date by analogy.
5. Explain how to play tennis (or basketball or how to ride a horse, etc.) by analogy.
6. Use a watch as an analogy for describing the body.
7. Use a factory as an analogy for describing school.
8. Use falling down a mountain as an analogy for falling asleep.
9. Use making a physical object (such as a table or a pot) as an analogy for making a story, a poem, or an essay.
10. Use the life process to describe the rise and fall of a nation, an empire, or a sports team.

Development by Cause and Effect

A good deal of expository writing explores the causes of an event, action, or situation and the resulting effects.

When you think in terms of *cause and effect*, you ask the questions, *Why did this occur?* and *What was the result?*

Because cause-and-effect paragraphs pose questions, you will often find them presented in a question-and-answer format. The paragraph will state the topic as a question about cause, such as, "How did the Beatles influence American culture?" and then discuss the effects the Beatles had, in the rest of the paragraph.

Analysis by cause and effect can be subdivided into smaller categories. First, you can examine the immediate (or precipitating) cause, or you can examine the underlying cause or causes. For example, the immediate cause of World War I was the assassination of Archduke Francis Ferdinand of Austria-Hungary in 1914. The underlying causes, however, included territorial and economic rivalry among the nations of Austria-Hungary, Russia, Germany, France, and Great Britain, going back almost half a century.

Second, you can examine the direct or immediate effects of an event, an action, or a situation, or you can look at its long-range effects. One immediate aftereffect of World War I, for example, was the move to create the League of Nations; another was the Treaty of Versailles that forced Germany alone to assume guilt for the war. In terms of long-range effects, some historians believe that the peace treaties signed after World War I were responsible for the economic misery in Europe. This misery led to a new spirit of nationalism in Germany and ultimately contributed to the causes of World War II. As this example shows, the study of cause and effect is seldom clear-cut. The effects of one action can in turn become the causes of another.

The following paragraph from George Orwell's famous essay "Politics and the English Language" uses a cause-and-effect approach to the language of politics. Orwell argues that politicians use vague or jargon-laden speech to distract their listeners from the real meaning of their words.[1]

A *euphemism* is a word or phrase that seems less offensive than the one it replaces.

> In our time, political speech and writing are largely the defense of the indefensible. Things like the continuance of British rule in India, the Russian purges and deportations, the dropping of the atom bombs on Japan, can indeed be defended, but only by arguments which are too brutal for most people to face, and which do not square with the professed aims of political parties. Thus political language has to consist largely of euphemism, question-begging and sheer cloudy vagueness. Defenseless villages are bombarded from the air, the inhabitants driven out into the countryside, the cattle machine-gunned, the huts set on fire with incendiary bullets: this is called *pacification*. Millions of peasants are robbed of their farms and sent trudging along the roads with no more than they can carry: this is called *transfer of population* or *rectification of frontiers*. People are imprisoned for years without trial, or shot in the back of the neck or sent to die of scurvy in Arctic lumber camps: this is called *elimination of unreliable elements*. Such phraseology is needed if one wants to name things without calling up mental pictures of them. Consider for instance some comfortable English professor defending Russian totalitarianism. He cannot say outright, "I believe in killing off your opponents when you can get good results by doing so." Probably, therefore, he will say something like this: "While freely conceding that the Soviet régime exhibits certain features which the humanitarian may be inclined to deplore, we must, I think, agree that a certain curtailment of the right to political opposition is an unavoidable concomitant of transitional periods, and that the rigors which the Russian people have been called upon to undergo have been amply justified in the sphere of concrete achievement."

In the preceding paragraph George Orwell begins by stating that political language "in our time" (this essay was published in 1945) is used chiefly to defend brutal actions by governments. This purpose, "the defense of the indefensible," is the *cause* of political language being euphemistic and vague. The *effect* is the language itself in that state.

Except with very simple cause-and-effect topics, it is generally better to focus on one step in the cause-and-effect process in a single paragraph. For example, you could first discuss the immediate cause-and-effect relationship of your topic and then discuss in a later paragraph the underlying causes and long-term effects.

Writing Practice 6

Select one of the following suggestions for cause-and-effect paragraphs or write one of your own. First, write out a clear statement of the cause in one sentence and list the effect or effects. Then write a cause-and-effect paragraph

---

[1]Excerpted from "Politics and the English Language" in *Shooting an Elephant and Other Essays* by George Orwell. Copyright 1946 by Sonia Brownell Orwell, copyright 1974 by Sonia Orwell. Reprinted by permission of Harcourt Brace Jovanovich, Inc., A.M. Heath & Company Ltd. as agents for the estate of the late George Orwell, and Martin Secker & Warburg.

For help with this assignment, use one of the methods discussed in the chapter "Discovering Ideas for Writing" on pages 29–55.

To revise your paragraph, use the Checklist for Revising Paragraphs on page 62.

on a separate sheet of paper. Decide before you write whether you will focus on the immediate or underlying cause and on the immediate or long-term effects.

1. What are the main causes and effects of a historical event (such as the Battle of Hastings, the attacks on Fort Sumter or Pearl Harbor, the signing of the Yalta Pact, Watergate)?
2. What, in your opinion, are the chief causes of dissatisfaction with public education?
3. What, in your opinion, are the chief causes of a "good life"?
4. Draw on your own observation or reading to describe the chief effects of prejudice.
5. Draw on your own observation or reading to describe the chief effects of television viewing on daily life.

Writing Unified Paragraphs

Unity, the quality of wholeness, is essential to good paragraph writing.

A unified paragraph presents one complete unit of information or sequence to the reader; the relationship of each sentence to the main idea is clear. An important way to ensure unity is to be certain that each sentence relates directly to the main idea of the paragraph. Any idea, no matter how interesting, that strays from the main idea should not be included: instead, it can be developed in a later paragraph.

Clincher Sentences

Another way to unify paragraphs is to use a *clincher sentence*.

A *clincher sentence* is one that provides a strong ending for a paragraph.

All paragraphs do not require clincher sentences; in fact, you will most often find them at the end of essays or at the end of a distinct section of an essay.

Clincher sentences can also be used to sum up the main idea or intent of the paragraph, as in the Nora Ephron paragraph on pages 59–60 about Bernice Gera that concludes: "Bernice Gera had become the first woman in the 133-year history of the sport to umpire a professional baseball game." If you were writing a concluding paragraph to an essay that covered several important points, a clincher sentence summing up your ideas would be a good way of reemphasizing them for the reader.

A clincher sentence can also be used to add a new piece of information to a paragraph. Often this type of clincher sentence is used as a transition from one section of an essay to another, as in the following example from an essay on publicity by John Berger. What is the clincher sentence?

> It is important here not to confuse publicity with the pleasure or benefits to be enjoyed from the things it advertises. Publicity is effective precisely because it feeds upon the real. Clothes, food, cars, cosmetics, baths, sunshine are real things to be enjoyed in themselves. Publicity begins by working on a natural appetite for pleasure. But it cannot offer the real object of pleasure and there is no convincing substitute for a pleasure in that pleasure's own terms. The more convincingly publicity conveys the pleasure of bathing in a warm, distant sea, the more the spectator-buyer will become aware that he is hundreds of miles away from that sea and the more remote the chance of bathing in it will seem to him. This is why publicity can never really afford to be about the product or opportunity it is proposing to the buyer who is not yet enjoying it. Publicity is never a celebration of a pleasure-in-itself. Publicity is always about the future buyer. It offers him an image of himself made glamorous by the product or opportunity it is trying to sell. The image then makes him envious of himself as he might be. Yet what makes this self-which-he-might-be enviable? The envy of others. Publicity is about social relations, not objects. Its promise is not of pleasure, but of happiness: happiness as judged from the outside by others. The happiness of being envied is glamour.[1]

The final statement, "The happiness of being envied is glamour," provides the essay with an interesting clincher sentence.

Writing Practice 7

Remember to use your journal to help you find ideas for writing.

Choose one of the following five suggestions for a paragraph topic or write a similar one of your own. On a separate sheet of paper, write a clear statement of your paragraph idea in one or two sentences (a topic-restriction sentence or both a topic and a restriction sentence). Then write a paragraph developing your main idea, supporting it with illustrations, or using comparison, analogy, or cause and effect. Be sure to include sufficient details to support your main idea. As you write, pay special attention to unity. End your paragraph with a clincher sentence.

1. Compare how you feel at your age now with the way you thought you would feel when you were younger.
2. Use the analogy of a menu to describe the many choices that you face in your life.
3. Use an analogy to describe the three branches of the United States government.
4. Discuss two important causes of the American Revolution.
5. What have been the effects of television on study habits of teenagers?

Writing Coherent Paragraphs

Sentences in a coherent paragraph follow an orderly arrangement so that the links between sentences are made clear to the reader. You can improve the

[1] From *Ways of Seeing* by John Berger (Pelican Books, 1972) p. 132. Copyright © 1972 by Penguin Books Ltd. Reprinted by permission.

coherence of your writing by deciding on a logical organization for each paragraph and by using any of several other methods you will study in the final sections of this chapter.

Sentence Organization

There are three general methods of sentence organization that you can use to make your paragraphs more coherent: chronological order, spatial arrangement, and order of importance.

Use *chronological order* for paragraphs that present events or sequences of ideas as they happen in time.

When you explain a process, the sequence of an event, or a series of ideas, chronological order helps you present this information clearly, step by step, to the reader. The chronology can cover a short or long time span. For example, you could use chronological organization in a paragraph describing the process of programming a computer, the sequence of events leading up to the signing of the Magna Carta, or a progression of ideas about the solar system from Copernicus to the present.

In the following paragraph from an essay titled "We've Never Asked a Woman Before," biographer Catherine Drinker Bowen uses chronological order to give the reader a historical perspective on the achievements of women. Words that indicate chronological organization are underlined.[1]

> Without a clear view of their capabilities, men and women cannot function. Convince a two-legged man that he has but one leg, and he will not be able to walk. A writer must know her horizon, how wide is the circle within which she, as artist, extends. The world still professes to wonder why there has been no female Shakespeare or Dante, no woman Plato or Isaiah. Yet people do what society looks for them to do. The Quaker Meeting House has existed for centuries, but it has produced no Bach and no B Minor Mass. Music was not desired by Quakers, it was frowned on. Poetry, fiction, playwriting have been expected from women only recently, as history counts time. Of the brilliant, erratic Margaret Cavendish, her husband, the Duke of Newcastle, remarked, circa 1660, "A very wise woman is a very foolish thing." As lately as 1922, Christina Rossetti's biographer wrote of her, that "like most poetesses, she was purely subjective, and in no sense creative." What a beautiful triple sneer, and how it encompasses the entire second sex!

In the preceding paragraph Bowen uses a chronological progression to discuss what society expects and has expected from women. The examples she gives to support her idea occur in a historical framework, or are ordered in time.

Use *spatial organization* to describe the location in space of people or objects.

In the following paragraph from an essay titled "An Englishman's Outrageous View of Texas Football," the writer J. B. Priestley describes his first

---

[1]From "We've Never Asked a Woman Before" by Catherine Drinker Bowen, from *The Atlantic Monthly*, March 1970. Copyright © 1970 by Catherine Drinker Bowen. Reprinted by permission of Harold Ober Associates Incorporated.

experience at an American football game. As you read, notice which sentences tell about the location of the people and things that Priestley observes. Which words and phrases indicate spatial organization?[1]

Deprecatory means "apologetic" or "belittling."

> The professor and I carried our cushions to the top of the stand and then found our places among a group of his colleagues, of both sexes, belonging to the departments of language and literature. Nodding and smiling a welcome, Middle English, Romance Languages, Modern Novel and Elizabethan Drama pleasantly acknowledged my presence, with that slight archness and hint of the deprecatory which scholars display when discovered attending some unscholarly college function. From this height, the whole stadium was spread below us, all open to our view. The scene had more color than we find in our football grounds. The crowd opposite, mostly students in colored shirts and blouses, looked almost like a vast heap of those tiny sweets known in my childhood as "hundreds and thousands." Two large students' military bands, one in orange uniforms, the other in purple, the colors of their respective teams, could just be distinguished, massed together, on the lower slopes, where the sousaphones gleamed and blared. In the space between the touchline and the stand, there were cheerleaders in white, men and girls, already beginning to signal to and encourage, with enormous rhythmical gestures, their obedient sections of students. One end of the ground, to my right, was dominated by an illuminated electric clock, ready to mark off every second of play. Above the crowd at the other end, lower than we were, I could see ranks of parked cars, extending apparently into far, open country, glittering, glimmering and then fading into the haze, like some plague of gray and green beetles unaccountably stricken with death. Down on the turf a host of players, enough to make a dozen teams, all uniformed, leather-armored, numbered, were throwing passes and punting the balls and loosening up. Other men, mostly in white, not cheerleaders but athletic directors, coaches, referees and linesmen, trainers and first-aid men, were gathering along the touchlines. From somewhere behind us, voices through loudspeakers, harsh and appallingly amplified, made announcements, called doctors to the telephone. The bowl, you might say, was busy.

From the "top of the stand" where Priestley sits, he has a panoramic view of the entire football field and stadium. The first observation he makes is of the "crowd opposite" him dressed in bright colors. Next, he describes the bands located "on the lower slopes." What other sentences in the paragraph gives details about people or things from Priestley's vantage point or as they are placed in relation to one another?

Use *order of importance* to indicate order by rank or significance.

A writer may use order of importance to list ideas, facts, reasons, or other illustrations. The most common sequence of order of importance is from least important to most important point. Order of importance is sometimes called *climactic order*, because the paragraph builds to a climax.

The following paragraph from an essay by E. B. White organizes its information by order of importance. Which words and phrases indicate the order of importance?

---

[1] From "An Englishman's Outrageous View of Texas Football" from *Journey Down a Rainbow* by J. B. Priestley and Jacquetta Hawkes. Reprinted by permission of A. D. Peters & Co. Ltd.

> There are roughly three New Yorks. There is, first, the New York of the man or woman who was born here, who takes the city for granted and accepts its size and its turbulence as natural and inevitable. Second, there is the New York of the commuter—the city that is devoured by locusts each day and spat out each night. Third, there is the New York of the person who was born somewhere else and came to New York in quest of something. Of these three trembling cities the greatest is the last—the city of final destination, the city that is a goal. It is this third city that accounts for New York's high-strung disposition, its poetical deportment, its dedication to the arts, and its incomparable achievements. Commuters give the city its tidal restlessness, natives give it solidity and continuity, but the settlers give it passion. And whether it is a farmer arriving from Italy to set up a small grocery store in a slum, or a young girl arriving from a small town in Mississippi to escape the indignity of being observed by her neighbors, or a boy arriving from the Corn Belt with a manuscript in his suitcase and a pain in his heart, it makes no difference: each embraces New York with the intense excitement of first love, each absorbs New York with the fresh eyes of an adventurer, each generates heat and light to dwarf the Consolidated Edison Company.[1]

E. B. White states that the last New York that he describes is the greatest. What reasons does he give for the feeling that this particular New York is the greatest?

Writing Practice 8

The following topics are suggestions for paragraphs to be organized by chronological order, spatial order, or order of importance. Select one or write a similar topic of your own. Then on a separate sheet of paper, write a paragraph based on your topic, paying special attention to the organization.

To find ideas for this assignment, use one of the methods discussed in the chapter "Discovering Ideas for Writing."

1. To get to school on time on Monday morning takes great organization.
2. The problem of pollution has increased over the last fifty years.
3. An aerial view of my (town/city/neighborhood/etc.) would show you why I think it is so (beautifully/badly/confusingly) laid out.
4. There are three essential elements to a really bad horror film.
5. My family has a strong sense of our heritage.
6. When you open the hood of an automobile, you need to know the location of certain basic parts.
7. There are a number of ways that the student government in this school could be improved.
8. Looking at different works by the same author can tell you a great deal about the author's basic attitudes and concerns.
9. From the top of a (building/mountain/bluff) the scene below me was beautiful.
10. Everyone has to live by certain rules; the rules at my house are simple.

---

[1]Excerpt from p. 121 in "Here Is New York" from *Essays of E.B. White.* Copyright 1949 by E. B. White. Reprinted by permission of Harper & Row, Publishers, Inc.

For Your Journal

J. B. Priestley's essay "An Englishman's Outrageous View of Texas Football" is interesting partly because it gives the view of an outsider about an experience that many people have had: attending a football game. Think about another common event or experience and take a moment to reflect on how you would view it if you were a visitor from another country or even from another planet. In your journal write a description of this event or experience from the point of view of an outsider. Be sure to include descriptions of the sights, sounds, and other sensory details that relate to your event or experience.

Using Transitions to Improve Coherence

Transitions are words or phrases that help link sentences together.

The purpose of using transitions is to improve coherence within a paragraph by indicating the connection or relationship between sentences. Transitions help the reader follow the writer's thoughts from one point to another.

There is a wide variety of transitions. Some show overall organization, such as chronological order, spatial order, or order of importance; some indicate logical connections; some introduce illustrations, comparisons, or conclusions.

Transitions are also referred to as *transitional devices*, *linking expressions*, or *connectives*.

The following paragraph from Catherine Drinker Bowen's essay, "We've Never Asked a Woman Before," uses three common transitions: *yet*, *therefore*, and *but*. As you read, notice how each transition helps you follow her train of thought.[1]

> For thirty years I have been writing about lawyers and the law. And for almost as many years I have been the recipient of invitations to stand on platforms and address large assemblies of legal experts. I enjoy receiving these invitations; it shows that people are reading my books. Yet I often hesitate; the program means serious preparation. A non-lawyer—and a non-man—cannot stand up and talk drivel for thirty minutes or fifty (as specified) to a hall bristling with five hundred or so hard-minded professional gentlemen. Therefore I hold off, saying into the telephone that I haven't the time; I am writing a new book and must stay home by myself, where writers belong. Perhaps the committee will send a letter, giving details? "Mrs. Bowen!" says an urgent voice from Houston or San Francisco. "This is our law society's big annual celebration. We've had Senator Fulbright as speaker, and Wechsler of Columbia, and the Lord Chief Justice of England [and God and Santa Claus]. But we've never asked a woman before."

In the preceding paragraph Bowen uses transitions to make her writing more coherent. The first transition, *yet*, introduces a contrasting statement: The writer enjoys receiving invitations to speak *yet* she often hesitates about

---

[1]From "We've Never Asked a Woman Before" by Catherine Drinker Bowen, from *The Atlantic Monthly*, March 1970. Copyright © 1970 by Catherine Drinker Bowen. Reprinted by permission of Harold Ober Associates Incorporated.

accepting. The second transition, *therefore,* sets up a conclusion to a train of thought: The writer thinks about how much work it is to prepare a speech and *therefore,* as a result, she holds off accepting the invitations. The final transition, *but,* introduces another contrasting statement: The various law societies have asked many important figures, *but* they have never invited a woman before. These transitions all serve to link and connect ideas within the paragraph, making its sequence of ideas clear and easy to follow.

Choose transitions according to their use.

The particular transition word or phrase that you use depends on its purpose within the sentence or paragraph. The following list of transitions is organized according to use; one group of transitions is appropriate to show chronological order, another to show spatial order, and still another to indicate order of importance. Other groups are appropriate to introduce ideas, to continue with a sequence of ideas, or to present contrasting ideas.

As you write your own paragraphs, use this list as a reference until you are familiar with all the transitions included and can use them easily in your own writing. As you read, be aware of the many other transitions that writers often use.

TRANSITIONS	USES
for example, for instance	to introduce illustrations
also, and, another, besides, furthermore, in addition, moreover, too	to add illustrations
although, but, despite, however, in the same way, in spite of, nevertheless, nonetheless, on the contrary, on the other hand, similarly, still, yet	to show contrasting statements or comparisons and contrasts
first, second, third, eventually, finally, later, meanwhile, next, now, presently, then, thereafter	to show chronological order
about, above, across, around, at the top, behind, below, beyond, far, far away, here, near, on the left, on the right	to show spatial order
least, least important, more importantly, most important	to show order of importance
as a result, because, finally, for this reason, in conclusion, therefore, thus, so	to make a conclusion, to indicate purpose or a result

Writing Practice 9

Revise your paragraph, using the Checklist for Revision on page 62.

For this assignment use the paragraph you wrote for Writing Practice 8 or select another topic that you can develop with chronological, spatial, or climactic order. Then write a paragraph based on that topic. As you revise your paragraph, pay particular attention to the transitions appropriate to its organizational method. Make use of at least three transitions from the list on this page.

Further Methods to Improve Coherence

You can also improve the coherence of your writing by using connecting pronouns, paraphrase, repetition, and parallel structure.

Connecting pronouns help coherence by referring to nouns in a previous sentence, thus emphasizing the connection in thought from one sentence to the next and avoiding unnecessary repetition.

You will find that substituting connecting pronouns for nouns is one of the most widely used methods of improving coherence. In the following paragraph, notice how the underlined pronouns help link the thoughts from one sentence to another.

> Agatha Christie was a British author known throughout the world for her intriguing mystery novels. When she died at the age of eighty-six, she had published more than ninety-four volumes. Many of them were translated into several different languages. Although the famous author rarely accepted requests for interviews, writer Gwen Robyns has pieced together some of Agatha Christie's personal ideas about writing in a biographical study called *The Mystery of Agatha Christie.* For example, in its earliest stages a new mystery was for Mrs. Christie a process of mental organization. Only after perceiving a plot clearly in her mind was she ready for the commitment of beginning to type her new work. As she wrote it, often in her long walks across the fields near her home, Mrs. Christie tested the effectiveness of characters' conversations by repeating their speeches aloud. When she was worried by difficulties and problems in her writing, she busied herself with humdrum household chores. She let her mind wander as she worked until solutions to them popped into her head.

The connecting pronoun *she* in the second sentence refers to Agatha Christie mentioned in the first sentence; the pronoun connects these two sentences and avoids unnecessary repetition. What nouns do the other underlined pronouns in the paragraph replace? What sentences do these pronouns link?

The purpose of *paraphrase* (rewording) is to remind the reader of a thought from one sentence by rephrasing it in a subsequent sentence.

In this way paraphrase connects ideas between sentences and helps avoid unnecessary repetition of words and phrases. In the following paragraph the paraphrasing is underlined and explained in brackets.

> Mrs. Christie often wrote the concluding chapter of a mystery first since this procedure [paraphrase of *writing the concluding chapter first*] permitted her to gather the clues together, to alter minor details, and to tie up any loose ends in the story [paraphrase of *mystery*]. Because her principal involvement with the mysterious entanglements of plot superseded her other concerns about each work [paraphrase of *mystery*], Christie described characters briefly in one or two sentences and trimmed description of setting to a few well-chosen sentences. The master mystery writer [paraphrase of *Mrs. Christie*] admitted that she wouldn't discuss a new novel until the who-dun-it [paraphrase of *mystery*] was completed. She believed that if she discussed her work-in-progress [paraphrase of *new novel*], she would grow dissatisfied with it. Initiating each new novel with enthusiasm, Mrs. Christie conceded that she often wanted to

> desert a project [paraphrase of *new novel*] halfway through it. In spite of her many achievements, the famous novelist [paraphrase of *Mrs. Christie*] once commented: "People think that writing must be easy for me. It isn't. It's murder. . . . I never have much faith in my writing—I am always scared that people will find out that I really can't write."

Paraphrasing in the preceding paragraph made the writer's train of thought easy to follow and also avoided the overuse of words such as *Mrs. Christie*, *mystery*, and *new novel*.

When you use paraphrasing in your own writing, remember never simply to substitute a more-impressive-sounding word for a simple word. Also, do not try to use paraphrase when repetition is acceptable. For example, if you write an essay about the effects of drinking coffee, you do not need to paraphrase the word *coffee* each time you use it. Substituting *steaming black liquid* or *caffeinated beverage* for *coffee* can sound pretentious or artificial.

Properly used *repetition* can be an aid to linking ideas within a paragraph.

It is not always necessary to use pronouns or paraphrase to avoid repeating the same word: in some cases selective repetition of a word or phrase can help emphasize an important point or help connect ideas in a paragraph. You should choose your repeating words and phrases carefully. If you are not careful, the repetition can become monotonous and detract from coherence. Always reread your work to make sure that the words you repeat help improve coherence.

The following paragraph by sportswriter Roger Angell uses repetition to emphasize the main idea of his paragraph, which is the dimension of time in baseball. In contrast to the Agatha Christie paragraph in which the writer uses paraphrase to avoid repeating the words *mystery* and *Mrs. Christie*, Angell repeats the word *time* throughout to give his paragraph coherence.[1]

> The last dimension is time. Within the ballpark, time moves differently, marked by no clock except the events of the game. This is the unique, unchangeable feature of baseball, and perhaps explains why this sport, for all the enormous changes it has undergone in the past decade or two, remains somehow rustic, unviolent, and introspective. Baseball's time is seamless and invisible, a bubble within which players move at exactly the same pace and rhythms as all their predecessors. This is the way the game was played in our youth and in our fathers' youth, and even back then—back in the country days—there must have been the same feeling that time could be stopped. Since baseball time is measured only in outs, all you have to do is succeed utterly; keep hitting, keep the rally alive, and you have defeated time. You remain forever young. Sitting in the stands, we sense this, if only dimly. The players below us—Mays, DiMaggio, Ruth, Snodgrass—swim and blur in memory, the ball floats over to Terry Turner, and the end of this game may never come.

The repetition of the word *time* is effective in the preceding paragraph because time is its theme. Moreover, there is no effective paraphrase for the

---

[1]From "The Interior Stadium" in *The Summer Game* by Roger Angell. Copyright © 1971 by Roger Angell. Originally appeared in *The New Yorker*.

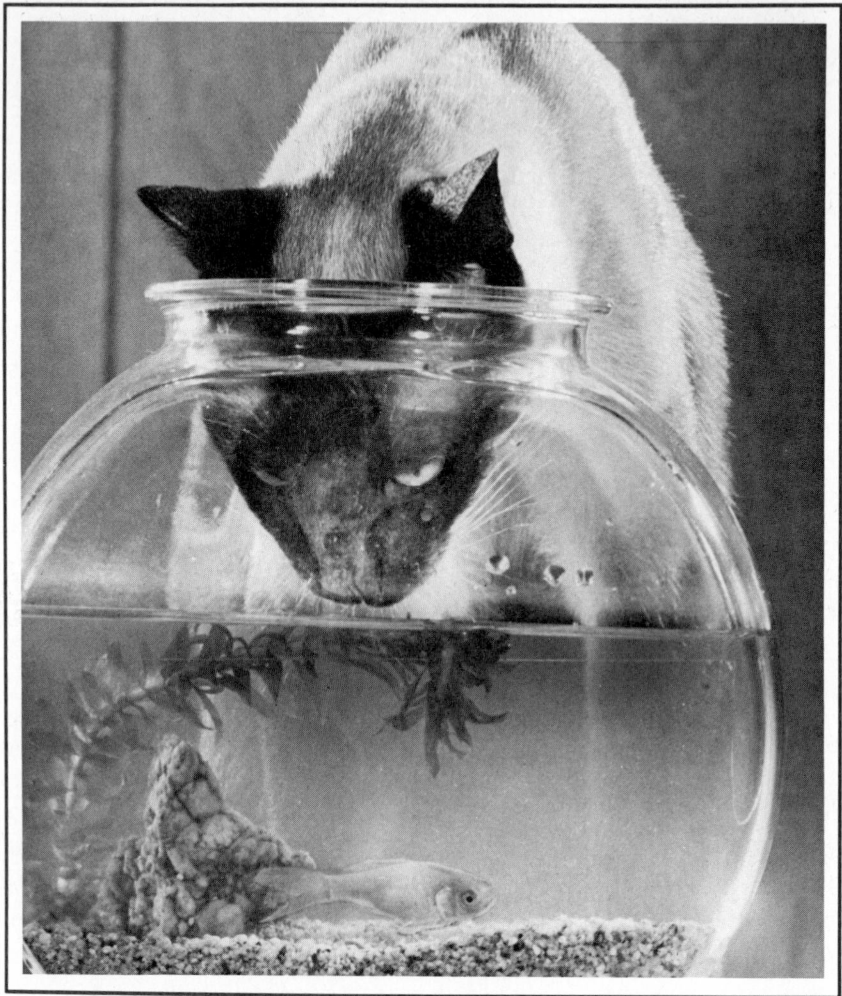

word *time* that would have been appropriate to the paragraph. Why is *time* as a repeating word more interesting than *copywriter* or *pet food* as repeating words?

A specific type of repetition that helps paragraph coherence is called *parallel structure.*

Parallel structure means "the similar wording or arrangement of words in a sentence or series of sentences." The famous statement by Julius Caesar, "I came, I saw, I conquered," is an example of parallel structure within one sentence.

Parallel structure draws the reader's attention to the thoughts being expressed with similar wording and reinforces their similarity. You can use parallel structure to emphasize an important point, as in the following paragraph from an essay by Sylvia Plath titled "A Comparison." Notice the parallel structure with the repetition of "farther than" in the final sentence.

> Surely the great use of poetry is its pleasure—not its influence as religious or political propaganda. Certain poems and lines of poetry seem as solid and miraculous to me as church altars or the coronation of queens must seem to people who revere quite different images. I am not worried that poems reach relatively few people. As it is, they go surprisingly far—among strangers, around the world, even. Farther than the words of a classroom teacher or the prescriptions of a doctor; if they are very lucky, farther than a lifetime.[1]

The parallelism in the final line emphasizes Plath's idea about the effect of poetry, and the repetition gives a sense of completion to the paragraph.

Parallel structure can also be used to emphasize the logical connection between thoughts. For example, in the paragraph you read by John Berger on

---

[1] Excerpt from "A Comparison" in *Johnny Panic and the Bible of Dreams* by Sylvia Plath. Copyright © 1956, 1962 by Sylvia Plath. Published by Faber & Faber of London, copyright © 1977 by Ted Hughes. Reprinted by permission of Harper & Row, Publishers, Inc., and Olwyn Hughes as agent for the author.

page 70, parallel structure was used extensively for emphasis: "*The more* convincingly publicity conveys the pleasure of bathing in a warm, distant sea, *the more* the spectator-buyer will become aware that he is hundreds of miles away from that sea and *the more* remote the chance of bathing in it will seem to him [*italics* added]." What other examples of parallel structure do you find in the paragraph? How do they help coherence?

Writing Practice 10

Choose one of the following suggestions as a topic for a paragraph or substitute a similar topic of your own. Decide which method of development you will use in the paragraph before you write. As you write, pay special attention to connecting pronouns, paraphrasing, and parallel structures, underlining them as you go along.

To find ideas for this paragraph, consider using the Pentad approach discussed on pages 35–46.

1. Compare your ideas about success with those of a close friend or family member.
2. Explain why conservation (or an issue of your choice) is important.
3. Explain how the Electoral College works.
4. Describe your school layout and give suggestions for improving it.
5. Relate an experience that changed your mind about something.

Writing Practice 11

Use the paragraph you wrote for Writing Practice 10 or any other paragraph you have written for this section and revise it, paying special attention to repetition and parallel structure. Use parallel structure within the paragraph *at least once* and repeat a key word or phrase *at least three times.* If you prefer, you may write a new paragraph, using parallel structure and repetition, for this writing practice.

Writing Practice 12

For help with revision, refer to the Checklist for Revision on page 62.

Select one of the photographs on pages 78–79 and write a paragraph describing it, using spatial organization and repetition. (You can imagine that you are looking at the scene in the photograph or that you are inside the scene.) Select one feature or detail to focus on for your repeating word or phrase. Remember to use sensory details to make your description come alive for the reader.

For Your Journal

After reading Roger Angell's paragraph on the sense of time (page 77), perhaps you recall an experience of time that seemed different from other kinds of time. It might have been an experience of feeling that time was passing swiftly or the experience of a few moments that felt like an eternity. As a journal entry, describe your experience and the thoughts and feelings you had about time.

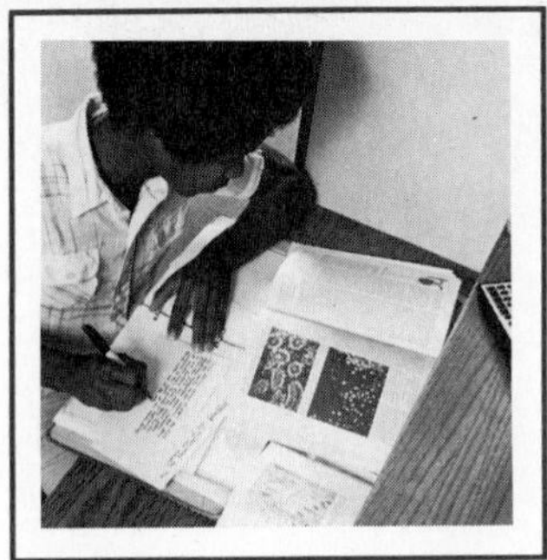

4 Writing Exposition

The Uses of Exposition

Expository writing is used for many purposes. Some of the most frequent uses are discussed in the following sections.

1. *To Give Directions*[1]

> Williamsburg is located on Interstate 64, about halfway between Richmond and Norfolk, and about 150 miles (240 km) south of Washington, D.C. There is direct daily service by Amtrak from New York, Philadelphia, Baltimore, and Washington. By bus Greyhound serves Williamsburg directly, and Trailways goes to Richmond and Norfolk. Air service to Patrick Henry International Airport near Newport News connects to Williamsburg by a twenty-minute ride in an airport limousine or rented car.
>
> —from *Travel/Holiday*, December, 1980

A good set of directions (1) gives all of the necessary information but no unnecessary details, (2) is clear, and (3) does not contain irrelevancies.

Writing Practice 1

Write a set of directions for getting from one place in your city or area to another. If relevant include information about the various means of transportation. When you finish, ask yourself whether your instructions follow the rules of quantity, quality, and relevance. If they are weak in any of those areas, revise them, making necessary changes.

2. *To Give Instructions*

---

[1]Excerpt from "Directions to Williamsburg" by Robert S. Milne from *Travel/Holiday*, December 1980. Reprinted with permission of Travel/Holiday, Travel Building, Floral Park, New York.

High-Temperature Roasting of Turkey

Season a stuffed turkey with salt and place it on its side in a roasting pan fitted with a rack. Place slices of fat salt pork over the breast and spread the bird generously with butter. Cook in a preheated hot oven (425° F.) fifteen minutes, then turn on the other side and cook fifteen minutes longer.

Reduce the heat to moderate (375° F.) and continue roasting, turning the bird from side to side and basting often with fat from the pan. If the fat tends to burn, add a few tablespoons of water.

Allow twenty minutes a pound for roasting.

Place the turkey on its back for the last fifteen minutes of cooking. Pierce the thigh for doneness; if the juice that runs out is clear with no tinge of pink, the bird is done.[1]

—from *The New York Times Cook Book*

In writing instructions, be certain that each step is explained in its proper sequence, as is the case in the instructions for roasting a turkey: first do this, then do that, and then do the next operation.

Writing Practice 2

Prepare a set of instructions for doing something. For example, you might present your favorite recipe or tell how to make something, such as how to develop a roll of film or change the oil in a car. When you finish writing, evaluate your instructions against the points in the following brief checklist. If necessary revise your instructions to eliminate weaknesses.

1. The instructions are clear.
2. All necessary information is included.
3. All of the information is relevant.

3. *To Present Facts*[2]

Tower of London, ancient fortress in London, England, just east of the City and on the north bank of the Thames, covering about 13 acres (5.3 hectares). Now used mainly as an arsenal, it was a royal residence in the Middle Ages. Later it was a jail for illustrious prisoners. The Tower is enclosed by a dry moat, within which are double castellated walls surrounding the central White Tower. Although Roman foundations were discovered as additions and changes were made, and tradition makes Julius Caesar the founder, the White Tower was built c. 1078 by Gundulf, bishop of Rochester; the exterior was restored by Sir Christopher Wren. Various towers subsequently built were used as prisons; one of them now houses a collection of medieval arms and armor, and another (the Wakefield Tower) contains the crown jewels. The Traitors' Gate (giving access by water from the Thames) and the Bloody Tower are associated with many historically noted persons, including Queen Elizabeth I (when still prin-

---

[1] "High Temperature Roasting of Turkey" from *The New York Times Cook Book* by Craig Claiborne.

[2] Entry for "Tower of London" from *The New Columbia Encyclopedia*.

> cess), Sir Thomas More, Anne Boleyn, Catherine Howard, Lady Jane Grey, the 2nd earl of Essex, Sir Walter Raleigh, and the duke of Monmouth. Many persons beheaded within the Tower precincts, or on the neighboring Tower Hill, were buried in the Chapel of St. Peter ad Vincula. The Yeomen of the Guard ("Beefeaters"), dressed in Tudor garb, still guard the Tower. Its north bastion was destroyed in air raids in 1940. See R. J. Minney, *The Tower of London* (1971).
>
> —from *The New Columbia Encyclopedia*

The facts in the preceding paragraph concern the location, history, and present-day use of the Tower of London.

Writing Practice 3

Choose a place that you know well but that is unknown to anyone else in your class—for example, your room at home, a relative's house or apartment, or some place that you go with your family. In a paragraph or two give the important facts about this place. When you finish, check your work for quantity, quality, and relevance. If it is weak in any one of these areas, revise it, making the necessary changes.

4. *To Explain Ideas and Opinions*

> Joan Bremer, Editor
> Bryant High Banner
>
> Dear Ms. Bremer:
>
> The calendar at Bryant High is not well planned and results in much wasted time.
>
> This year the first semester does not end until January 15, and winter vacation lasts through January 4. This means that there are only ten days of school between the end of winter vacation and the end of the semester. During this "lame duck" period no one does any serious work; the students just mark time, and the teachers spend their class periods in review and "enrichment" activities.
>
> It would be much more efficient to have the semester end at winter vacation. Then when students returned in January, they would be ready to start serious work on new classes. Furthermore, summer vacation could begin a week or two earlier, giving students a better chance to obtain summer jobs.
>
> Sincerely,
>
> Jean Safier

In this letter to the editor of her school newspaper, a student has explained her opinion concerning the academic calendar. Almost all newspapers have "opinion" pages, in which readers can express their ideas about subjects currently in the news. Letters to editors are part of the American heritage: in their first newspaper the Colonists began to express their opinions about politics, taxation, religion, commerce, education, and countless other subjects of concern. The freedom to express one's opinions has always been a cherished right of Americans, and the ability to express one's opinions in writing has been important to citizens.

Writing Practice 4

Think of a current issue relating to your school, city, or nation about which you have an opinion. Then write an opinion letter to the editor of your school or local newspaper, explaining how you feel about the issue. After writing, ask yourself whether your letter has the important qualities of exposition: quantity, quality, and relevance. Revise your writing if necessary. If you wish to mail your letter, check it carefully against the proofreading checklist on page 14 before doing so.

Qualities of Exposition

Two important qualities of expository writing are that it presents information and that it avoids truisms.

Information is "news"—something that you did not already know. The statement "There are twelve inches in a foot" is true, but it is probably not informative to you, for you already know that information. Of course, what is information for you might not be for another person. For example, your school's location is not news to you; you already know it. However, a statement of the exact location would be informative to someone who wanted to visit the school but did not know precisely where it was located.

To be informative a piece of writing must square with reality. If you believe that the earth is flat, then you might take the following statement as a piece of information: "Sailors who go beyond a certain point fall off the face of the earth." If you do not believe the flat-earth theory, then you will not take such statements as informative.

A *truism* is a statement with which most everyone would agree but that is too obvious to mention. For example, most people would agree that running twenty-five miles is hard work, that everyone should plan for the future, and that the course of true love never runs smoothly. The problem with these statements is that they are not news to anyone; they are not informative. Therefore, though everyone might admit their truth, they are unnecessary and boring.

For Discussion

On a sheet of paper, make a list of all of the expository writings that you have read in the last twenty-four hours. Remember that all instructions are exposition and that most labels contain expository writing. Textbooks, newspapers, magazines—all are largely or completely expository. When you have finished your list, see if the items can be categorized according to the purposes for which you read. Did you read anything—such as a textbook or newspaper article—merely to learn about a subject? Did you read any exposition for pleasure? How about sets of instructions for doing something (for example, assembling a toy or an appliance)? Did you read any directions for getting to some place? Be prepared to discuss in class the purposes for expository writing.

The Writer's Promises

When you write exposition, you make certain promises to your readers.

First, unless there is a good reason to think otherwise, readers assume that you are *sincere* in what you write.

Second, the writer promises to provide readers with all necessary information, but no more than is necessary.

This promise concerns *quantity*. A writing teacher is talking about this promise when she or he says to a student, "You haven't given me enough details" or "Your ideas need further development," or, on the other hand, "You're being redundant; you've already made this point."

Third, the writer promises readers to express ideas as clearly as possible.

Obscure or muddled expression of ideas annoys most readers, making them unwilling to accept the writer's message. This promise involves *quality*.

Finally, you promise your readers that everything you write will pertain to your subject; that is, everything will be *relevant*.

Whenever a reader says, "I wonder how this statement relates to the subject," the problem of relevance has appeared. For example, the last sentence in the following paragraph seems irrelevant.

> Mexican breads and pastries are rightly considered among the best in the world, and travelers returning from Mexico to the United States often bring large sacks of baked goods with them. *Tecate is just across the border from California.*

For Discussion

Find and bring to class a piece of exposition that has one or more of the following characteristics: insincerity, too little or too much information, muddled expression of ideas, or irrelevant ideas. With your teacher and classmates discuss why these characteristics make the expository writing ineffective. How should it be changed to make it an effective piece of communication? (You might begin your search by looking at advertisements.)

Violating the Rules

Sometimes, good writers purposely violate the rules of sincerity, quantity, quality, and relevance to achieve certain effects. Writers often create humor by violating one or more of the four rules. For example, Woody Allen gives the following tongue-in-cheek description of a college course.[1]

> *Fundamental Astronomy:* A detailed study of the universe and its care and cleaning. The sun, which is made of gas, can explode at any moment, sending our entire planetary system hurtling to destruction; students are advised what the average citizen can do in such a case. They are also taught to identify various

[1] "Fundamental Astronomy" from "Spring Bulletin," which appears in *Getting Even* by Woody Allen.

> constellations, such as the Big Dipper, Cygnus the Swan, Sagittarius the Archer, and the twelve stars that form Lumides the Pants Salesman.

Because no sane person could talk sincerely about the care and cleaning of the universe, the first sentence is a clue to readers that the course description will be humorous. Since everyone knows that the sun is made of gas, the second sentence violates the rule of *quantity*. The main device of humor in the description, though, is *irrelevancy;* none of the subject matter listed is relevant to a course in fundamental astronomy.

For Your Journal

In your journal write four humorous paragraphs, basing each one on the violation of one of the four rules.

Examples

Sincerity: *I propose a new extracurricular activity for our school: demolition derbies. Money that is now spent on sports, band, and orchestra could be used to buy old cars for the derbies, which could be held on the school athletic field. If these funds were not enough to supply each student with a car, teachers' salaries could be cut.*

Quantity: *Darlene is the most beautiful girl I have ever known; she is my ideal. In case you have never seen her, let me describe her to you. Her fingernails are immaculately clean and neatly trimmed.*

Using the Rules

The four rules discussed in the preceding section—sincerity, quantity, quality, and relevance—suggest some important guidelines for writers. When you begin to revise, consider the following items.

1. The writer is sincere about his or her statements, and readers believe that sincerity.
2. Readers are given all of the information they need, but no more than they need.
3. Ideas are expressed clearly.
4. All of the ideas are relevant to the subject at hand.

Facts and Opinions in Exposition

A *factual statement* relates to the physical world; it can be proved or disproved by measurements, counts, experiments, or research.

An *opinion* is a belief about a subject.

It is a fact, for example, that the Constitution of the United States was amended to give voting rights to eighteen-year-olds. Whether or not you think that was a good idea is a matter of *opinion.*

The following are examples of factual statements and the opinions that might be formed from them.

FACTUAL STATEMENTS	OPINIONS
Mount Whitney in California rises to an altitude of 14,494 feet (4,418 meters).	Mount Whitney, rearing above the other peaks in the Sierra Nevada chain, is majestic.
Locke High School now has an enrollment of 5,501 students and a teaching staff of 89, which yields a teacher-student ratio of one to 61.1.	The teacher-student ratio at Locke High School is far too high.
The Lincoln Memorial, a monument consisting of 164 acres (66 hectares) in Potomac Park, Washington, D.C., is dedicated to the memory of President Abraham Lincoln.	The Lincoln Memorial, one of the most moving tributes ever dedicated to the memory of a former President, represents all that is good in this country.

For Discussion

Like most exposition the following brief essay, "Comrade Lonelyhearts," published in *Time* magazine, contains a mixture of factual statements and opinions. Which of the statements in the essay are factual? Which are opinions?[1]

Male, 27, worker, loyal and sincere, father employed, younger brother and sister at university, 5 feet 1 inch tall, spine slightly crooked, seeks to marry employed woman comrade.

The idea was considered bourgeois decadence just a few years ago, but suddenly lovelorn Chinese are aggressively looking for Comrade Right. The Tianjin Daily, a newspaper that used to reject all advertising, now has classified columns filled with personals. Pamphlets give tips on dating. And, in Peking, the government has opened four official matchmaking centers. At one office in Ritan Park, 4,000 hopefuls have plunked down the $1.35 registration fee, handed over 2-inch-square photographs and scribbled descriptions of themselves and the mate of their dreams. "Some got a lot of help from the photographers," admits Song Baojie, a cheery matchmaker. But the Ritan office has matched up 600 couples over the past three months—and 200 fell in love.

Moral Codes: The Chinese seem to know less about romance than China's population (1 billion) might indicate. Since the revolution, love has taken a back seat to politics in China. Add rigid moral codes and no night life and it's clear why there are a lot of lonely Chinese. Now the government wants to change that—although its motives may not be entirely altruistic. "These young people are agonizing over their failure to wed," said one newspaper. "Their enthusiasm for work and study is dampened."

Altruistic means "motivated by unselfish concern for others."

A flood of manuals is helping Chinese make up for lost time. One, "The Art of Dating," advises young men to tote a badminton racquet and a book on the first date "to give the girl the impression you are studious and healthy." It also alerts young women to the body language of an undesirable Lothario. "The unscrupulous type," it says, "rounds corners at full speed on his bicycle."

---

[1] "Comrade Lonelyhearts" by John Brecher and Melinda Liu from *Newsweek*, December 29, 1980.

At the matchmaking centers, love can triumph even over party. Men are allowed to request non-Communist partners. "That way," explained one employee, "the woman will be sure to stay home and cook instead of going to meetings all the time." Even so, the go-between centers are hardly hangouts for swinging singles. The austere Chongwen office has a bare cement floor, a coal-burning stove and crude pencil marks on the wall to measure the height of incoming unmarrieds. A lanky, rosy-cheeked young woman with crimson gloves and royal blue socks—and sporting an upswept hair-do—strode in recently and whispered with an employee. The matchmaker pulled out the résumé of a potential mate and flashed the photograph. The woman dallied over the picture for several minutes, then shook her head and walked out. "Too short," explained the official. "She was 5 feet 7, the tallest girl to sign up here."

Tall and Handsome: The men are picky, too. One man strolled into the Ritan Park center not long ago, looking every inch a heartthrob. He was extremely tall, handsome and 29 years old. His parents were killed during the Cultural Revolution. The factory where he worked employed scores of eligible women. "None is ideal," he said. The matchmaker squinted at the suitor's résumé, leafed through some files and came up with a pleasant looking, if slightly homely, typist. After a moment's deliberation, the bachelor decided against an introduction. He left sadly, not knowing that a lonely, 5-foot-7 lady with red gloves and a beehive hair-do, perhaps the woman of his dreams, was waiting for him—no farther away than the dossier bank at the Chongwen office of love.

The Expository Composition

A type of exposition commonly found in English classrooms is the expository composition.

An *expository composition*, or *essay*, usually consists of several related paragraphs that give information.

Although you may never write an expository composition once you leave school, the process of doing so is a valuable experience. By developing an idea and by discovering and arranging the information that explains it, you learn much about clear thinking and about the effective presentation of ideas.

In the following sections you will study the process of developing a topic, formulating a thesis, gathering information, ordering the information, and writing an expository essay.

Subject and Topic

Very often an assignment for writing an expository essay begins with a general subject, one that covers much ground and that needs to be narrowed. Consider, for example, the subject *Poetry*. As a subject, poetry is vast, including its history from ancient times to the present, the various kinds of poetry (for example, lyric and epic, rhymed and free verse), various opinions about what makes a poem good or bad, poets, readers of poems, and countless other items. A complete discussion of poetry would require many thick volumes.

From the enormous territory named "poetry," the writer must choose a small plot that he or she can cover in detail. In a brief essay of, say, 500 words, it would be possible to discuss the meaning of one poem or the difference between an Elizabethan and an Italian sonnet.

The following are examples of general subjects and topics that might be derived from them.

SUBJECTS	WRITING TOPICS
Automobiles	Buying a subcompact car
Bandits	Jesse James' last robbery
Composition	Writing a good first paragraph
Democracy	The need for more democracy in my home
Environment	The problem of litter in Central Park
Final exam	How to prepare for a final exam in history
Grades	How to improve the grading system in my English class
History	The day the Mormons entered the Salt Lake Valley
Illness	My appendectomy
Knowledge	What I learned on my first job
Money	Planning a yearly budget in a time of inflation
Names	The meanings of some common American first names

The preceding topics would serve for relatively short papers. Some of them, of course, would demand research. (If you were to write about Jesse James' last robbery—in Northfield, Minnesota—you would probably need to spend some time in the library with books, magazines, and encyclopedias.) Other topics would result from your own experience and knowledge. (You are the world's greatest expert on what you learned on your first job.)

Writing Practice 5

On a sheet of paper, write down five general subjects that interest you—advertising, quackery in medicine, diets, shopping, and so on. Next to each subject write a topic that would be suitable for a short expository essay.

From Topic to Thesis

The *thesis* in a piece of writing is the point that the writer intends to make.

The thesis is a clear indication of what the writer will cover in the essay. For example, consider the following subject and topic.

Subject: Knowledge
Topic: What I learned on my first job

From the preceding topic it is difficult to tell exactly what direction the writer's paper will take; what the writer learned could be skills, such as operating machinery, or techniques of getting along with people. The following thesis statement, however, explains the writer's purpose in greater detail, giving a clearer indication of the essay's content: "A lesson that I learned on my first job changed my whole attitude toward work and a career."

The following are other examples of theses developed from topics.

SUBJECT	TOPIC	THESIS STATEMENT
Automobiles	Buying a subcompact car	In choosing a subcompact, you should (a) make certain that all members of your family can be comfortable riding in it, (b) be certain that service and parts are easily available, (c) compare the rates of depreciation of value among the cars that interest you.
Illness	My appendectomy	My appendectomy taught me that the care of nurses is as important as the medical knowledge of doctors when one is ill.
Pets	Spending money on pet supplies	Americans spend an enormous amount of money on food, medical care, and even clothing and toys for their household pets.

Writing Practice 6

For this activity use the writing topics you developed for Writing Practice 5 or create five new ones. Then write a thesis statement for each topic, using the ones in the preceding section as models.

Gathering Information

You are probably involved in the process of gathering information about your subject from the time you first begin thinking about it. In fact, your choice of subject is probably influenced by what you already know about it.

The chapter "Discovering Ideas for Writing" (pages 29–55) discusses several different systems for discovering ideas. Such systems can be helpful to you at several stages in your writing. For example, if you have a subject but cannot think of a narrowed topic, then you might brainstorm the subject to find ideas for a limited topic. Having developed a topic, you might use a system such as brainstorming, the Pentad, or changing perspectives to discover what you already know about your topic or what you need to find out through reading and through other kinds of research.

Writing Practice 7

Using one of the systems discussed in the chapter "Discovering Ideas for Writing," develop a list of details to use in your expository essay. If you find that you must do more reading or other research before proceeding with your essay, make a note of the areas in which you lack information.

Taking Notes From the time that you first begin thinking about an expository essay until you actually begin writing, you may find that you have forgotten many details. If you take notes from the beginning, however, you will have a record of ideas.

Notes can be in the form of words, phrases, sentences, or even whole paragraphs. A good system is to use a separate note card for each idea. You might also want to write a slug, or heading, that will help you to identify the content, at the top of the card. For example, the following note cards represent notes made on the topic *The superwoman myth*.

Personal Experience

my aunt

Advertisements

Advertisements frequently portray women who are not only successful in business, but who are also outstanding wives and mothers.

Women's Movement

In many respects the Women's Movement has had positive effects: women who were not content to remain at home feel more comfortable in the business world. In other ways, however, the effects of the Women's Movement have been negative. Although more and more women are working, no one has really helped them deal with the guilt they feel at leaving their children and homes. Consequently, they feel that they must become "superwomen," equally talented on all fronts.

Writing Practice 8

Prepare a set of note cards for a topic you develop for an expository essay. (You may wish to work with a topic you have already used in this chapter, or you may want to create a new one for this assignment.) Use either the standard-sized 4 × 6 index cards or slips of paper you cut to that size. In an upper corner of each card, write a slug that will help you to identify the content.

Ordering and Outlining Information

The formal outline is discussed on pages 137–138.

An *outline* is a listing of the main points of a book, a composition, or any other piece of writing. Outlines may be either *formal* or *informal.*

Formal outlines, usually composed after the piece of writing is completed, show exactly what points the writer covers. *Informal outlines* are constructed before the writing begins, and they often change as the writing progresses. They are like road maps in that they give direction; they are unlike road maps in that the writer can change them as he or she finds new ideas.

In making an informal outline as a guide, the writer lists main points and any thoughts that he or she might have about the subject. As the writing goes on, the outline can be changed: More ideas can be added, and any can be crossed out. The following notes are for an expository essay on the topic *The superwoman myth.* As you read them over, look for general headings under which they could be arranged.

Advertisement for perfume that shows a woman coming home from her job as an executive and changing into a glamorous dress for her husband

General emphasis on success in our culture

In one way "labor-saving" devices have actually contributed to the problem. Before vacuum cleaners were invented, for example, women were not expected to clean their houses daily.

Greek mythology—Hera, Aphrodite

The Women's Movement

Wonder Woman on television and in the comics—strong, capable, yet attractive

Superb executive

This problem came very close to home recently when my aunt resigned as an attorney for a large corporation. She felt that she could not be less than a perfect wife and mother, and her job did not leave her with the time or energy to accomplish this perfection.

Commercial in which a woman is shown beating her husband in a game of pool after they have both returned from work

Attitudes toward women have changed; Victorians did not expect women to succeed in business and industry.

Lack of role models for women

A *Waltons* episode showed how women did what was once considered "men's work" during World War II.

Betty Friedan

Guilt that women feel about leaving home and family

Women must realize that they cannot be perfect.

Although there are many ways to organize the information in the preceding notes, five general headings suggest themselves:

Definition of the myth
Evolution of the myth
Continuation of the myth
Personal experience with the myth
Combating the myth

Developing an informal outline by arranging specific details under these general headings might help the writer to decide on the following preliminary organization for the paper.

- Definition of the myth
    - Origins in the "Wonder Woman" story
    - The modern superwoman
        - Superb executive
        - Excellent wife and mother
        - Attractive appearance
        - Good athlete
- Evolution of the myth
    - Victorian attitude
    - Role of women during World War II
    - Effect of the Women's Movement
- Continuation of the myth
    - Advertisements
    - Lack of role models
    - Guilt of women
- Personal experience with the myth
- Combating the myth
    - Knowledge of the myth
    - Acceptance of imperfections

Notice that not all of the notes were included in the informal outline. Some, such as the note on Greek goddesses and the note about modern "labor-saving" devices, did not fit and were discarded. Later, when the paper is actually written, the writer might choose to alter the outline by adding or discarding more ideas.

An informal outline, unlike a formal one, does not have a numbering system; however, in the preceding sample outline, you can easily tell which are the main ideas and which are details that develop those ideas. The writer has left space between each main idea division, and supporting details are indented (moved a few spaces to the right) under the major headings.

Writing Practice 9

Using notes you already have for an expository essay or ones you write for this assignment, prepare an informal outline. Use the sample outline in the preceding section as a model.

Reading an Expository Essay

Aldous Huxley, the author of the following essay, "Time and the Machine," was born in England in 1894. In the 1930s he moved to California where he lived until his death in 1963. As you read the essay, decide whether Huxley's work meets the criteria of sincerity, quantity, quality, and relevance. Following the essay is a For Discussion activity.[1]

An *analogue* is something having a partial resemblance to something else; *aniline* is a derivative of benzene used in making dyes.

James Watt invented the condensing steam engine in 1765; George Stephenson invented the steam locomotive in 1814.

> Time, as we know it, is a very recent invention. The modern time-sense is hardly older than the United States. It is a by-product of industrialism—a sort of psychological analogue of synthetic perfumes and aniline dyes.
>
> Time is our tyrant. We are chronically aware of the moving minute hand, even of the moving second hand. We have to be. There are trains to be caught, clocks to be punched, tasks to be done in specified periods, records to be broken by fractions of a second, machines that set the pace and have to be kept up with. Our consciousness of the smallest units of time is now acute. To us, for example, the moment 8:17 A.M. means something—something very important, if it happens to be the starting time of our daily train. To our ancestors, such an odd eccentric instant was without significance—did not even exist. In inventing the locomotive, Watt and Stephenson were part inventors of time.
>
> Another time-emphasizing entity is the factory and its dependent, the office. Factories exist for the purpose of getting certain quantities of goods made in a certain time. The old artisan worked as it suited him, with the result that consumers generally had to wait for the goods they had ordered from him. The factory is a device for making workmen hurry. The machine revolves so often each minute; so many movements have to be made, so many pieces produced each hour. Result: the factory worker (and the same is true of the office worker) is compelled to know time in its smallest fractions. In the handwork age there was no such compulsion to be aware of minutes and seconds.
>
> Our awareness of time has reached such a pitch of intensity that we suffer acutely whenever our travels take us into some corner of the world where people

---

[1] "Time and the Machine" from *The Olive Tree* by Aldous Huxley. Copyright 1937 by Aldous Huxley; renewed © 1965 by Laura A. Huxley. Reprinted by permission of Mrs. Laura Huxley, Chatto & Windus Ltd., and Harper & Row, Publishers, Inc.

are not interested in minutes and seconds. The unpunctuality of the Orient, for example, is appalling to those who come freshly from a land of fixed mealtimes and regular train services. For a modern American or Englishman, waiting is a psychological torture. An Indian accepts the blank hours with resignation, even with satisfaction. He has not lost the fine art of doing nothing. Our notion of time as a collection of minutes, each of which must be filled with some business or amusement, is wholly alien to the Oriental just as it was wholly alien to the Greek. For the man who lives in a preindustrial world, time moves at a slow and easy pace; he does not care about each minute, for the good reason that he has not been made conscious of the existence of minutes.

This brings us to a seeming paradox. Acutely aware of the smallest constituent particles of time—of time, as measured by clockwork and train arrivals and the revolutions of machines—industrialized man has to a great extent lost the old awareness of time in its larger divisions. The time of which we have knowledge is artificial, machine-made time. Of natural, cosmic time, as it is measured out by sun and moon, we are for the most part almost wholly unconscious. Preindustrial people know time in its daily, monthly, and seasonal rhythms. They are aware of sunrise, noon, and sunset; of the full moon and the new; of equinox and solstice; of spring and summer, autumn and winter. All the old religions have insisted on this daily and seasonal rhythm. Preindustrial man was never allowed to forget the majestic movement of cosmic time.

Piccadilly is an important business street in London.

Industrialism and urbanism have changed all this. One can live and work in a town without being aware of the daily march of the sun across the sky; without ever seeing the moon and stars. Broadway and Piccadilly are our Milky Way; our constellations are outlined in neon tubes. Even changes of season affect the townsman very little. He is the inhabitant of an artificial universe that is, to a great extent, walled off from the world of nature. Outside the walls, time is cosmic and moves with the motion of sun and stars. Within, it is an affair of revolving wheels and is measured in seconds and minutes—at its longest, in eight-hour days and six-day weeks. We have a new consciousness; but it has been purchased at the expense of the old consciousness.

For Your Journal

In his essay "Time and the Machine," Aldous Huxley has some unusual thoughts on the concept of time, a subject people take mostly for granted. Think about other concepts that govern your life, but that you have never stopped to analyze, perhaps space, motion, distance, life, death, and so on. Have modern Americans changed in their approach to any of these concepts? For example, how have television and the telephone changed the concept of space and of distance? How have medical advances changed the concepts of life and death? Write in your journal about one or more of these concepts and how you think each has changed for humanity over the past fifty years or so.

For Discussion

1. In your opinion does Aldous Huxley sound sincere in "Time and the Machine"? Why do you think so?

2. Does Huxley fulfill the criterion of quantity? Does he develop his ideas with sufficient details? With what details does he support his belief that time is a tyrant in modern society?
3. Does Huxley fulfill the criterion of quality? In your own words state the main ideas of his essay.
4. Does Huxley fulfill the criterion of relevance? Do you find any ideas in the essay that do not seem to belong?
5. What is the subject of this essay? The topic? In your own words give a thesis statement for the essay.

Writing the First Draft

As you begin writing, pay particular attention to the order in which you present your ideas. Usually readers will pay most attention to the first and last parts of a piece of writing; therefore, you might want to put your most important ideas in those positions. Another possibility is to begin with the least important ideas, thus creating a kind of suspense for the reader as you build to the more important thoughts. Still another approach is to proceed from the least complex to the most complex ideas.

A useful way of arranging ideas in an expository essay is in a cause-effect pattern, as Aldous Huxley does in the sample essay on pages 94–95. After his initial statement that "Time is our tyrant," Huxley discusses causes for this situation: industrialism and urbanism. At the end of the essay Huxley describes the effect: while gaining a new sense of time, modern people have lost "the old consciousness."

The first paragraph of the essay should both introduce the main idea and capture the reader's interest.

Although professional writers may not make a direct statement of their main idea, including one in the first paragraph of your essay will give both you and your readers a sense of direction. A frequently used technique is to begin the introductory paragraph with some interesting information and to end it with a statement of the main idea as you have worded it in your thesis statement.

You can capture your reader's attention in your introduction in any of several ways. You might begin with a bold statement, with an interesting quotation or statistic, or with a straightforward statement of the main idea. The following introductions from the expository essays of professional writers illustrate these methods.

> Time, as we know it, is a very recent invention. The modern time-sense is hardly older than the United States. It is a by-product of industrialism—a sort of psychological analogue of synthetic perfumes and aniline dyes.
>
> —from "Time and the Machine" by Aldous Huxley

> The desire to hold a paid job has become so compelling that some 24 to 27 million people not now employed in full-time jobs—women, young people,

and old people in particular—are waiting to take jobs if they become available.
—from "The New Psychological Contracts at Work" by Daniel Yankelovich

> With the onset of the vacation season the real problem of the new leisure becomes obvious. Leisure pastime in this country has become so complicated that it is now hard work.
> —from "The Paradox of the New Leisure" by Russell Baker

The purpose of the concluding paragraph is to leave the reader with a sense of completeness.

If the essay is short, simply repeating the main points you have covered is not an effective way to end. You may, however, rephrase the main idea expressed in the opening paragraph. Russell Baker, author of "The Paradox of the New Leisure," ends his essay in the following way.

> With its genius for self-adjustment, the society has turned leisure into labor. We are not far from the time when a man after a hard weekend of leisure will go thankfully off to his job to unwind.

As you write your first draft, keep in mind the importance of adequate development, unity, and coherence.

In an adequately developed essay, the thesis statement is supported or explained with a sufficient number of specific details. (If you have prepared a preliminary outline, each major heading might become the topic sentence for a paragraph.) To be unified, details in the composition must be arranged in some kind of logical order, and each detail must clearly support or develop the thesis statement.

The use of transition words is discussed on pages 74–75.

Coherence in an essay may be achieved by using several devices: repetition of key words and phrases, consistency of point of view and tone, and transition words. Aldous Huxley uses two of these techniques in his essay "Time and the Machine" (pages 94–95). For example, the following sentences are the topic sentences for each of the first four paragraphs in the essay. Notice how the word *time* is repeated in each of the sentences. In addition, the *italicized* words are different ways of expressing the idea of the tyranny of time.

> Time, as we know it, is a very recent invention.
>
> Time is our *tyrant.*
>
> Another *time-emphasizing entity* is the factory and its dependent, the office.
>
> Our *awareness of time* has reached such a *pitch of intensity* that we *suffer acutely* whenever our travels take us into some corner of the world where people are not interested in minutes and seconds.

Aldous Huxley begins his essay in the first-person plural when he writes, "Time, as *we* know it, is a very recent invention [*italics* added]," and he maintains that point of view. Notice how often throughout the essay he uses the first-person plural pronouns *we, us,* and *our.* In this way Huxley includes his readers among those who are affected by this "modern time-sense." The tone that Huxley establishes at the beginning of the essay—that of the knowledgeable essayist—is maintained. Nowhere in the essay does Huxley use slang, colloquialisms, contractions, or usage features that are not a part of Edited Standard English. Notice, however, that much of his language is direct and simple: "Time is our tyrant," "The factory is a device for making workmen hurry," "This brings us to a seeming paradox," and so on.

Writing Practice 10

Using your informal outline as a guide, write the first draft of an expository essay. If you have not completed the following steps, do so before beginning to write.

1. Begin with a narrowed topic.
2. Develop a thesis statement from the topic.
3. Use one or more systems for gathering information.
4. Take notes.
5. Prepare an informal outline.

Defining Your Audience

The way you write is determined largely by the person or people for whom you are writing. For example, if an expert on language is writing for other experts, he or she can use words that nonexperts would not understand:

> Language has both a syntagmatic and a paradigmatic dimension.

To explain that same idea to a less expert audience, however, the language expert would need to write quite differently:

> The parts of a sentence relate to one another. The subject names the doer of the action, the verb names the action, and the object names the receiver of the action:

SUBJECT	VERB	OBJECT
Marvin	hit	Merlin.

> This relationship among sentence parts is the *syntagmatic dimension* of language. We can make substitutions for each major sentence part, so that *Marvin* can become *The bad-tempered man*, and *Merlin* can become *the innocent victim*.

SUBJECT	VERB	OBJECT
The bad-tempered man	hit	the innocent victim.

> This ability to make substitutions is the *paradigmatic dimension* of language.

When you *talk* to different groups of people, you make changes in what you say and the way you say it, depending on your audience. Speaking to small children, you avoid long words and complicated sentence structure. When you speak to someone in authority, such as your high school principal, you are more formal and polite than when you speak to close friends. If you are talking about baseball to a British friend who does not understand the game, you would define your terms, which would not be necessary for someone who understands the game. ("Casey struck out. That is, he made three swings at the ball without hitting it.")

When you write, you must also keep your audience in mind. An essay in which you explained the rules and procedures for playing baseball might be interesting and informative to your British friend if he or she wanted to learn about the game, but would probably not interest most of your friends since they already know about baseball. (On the other hand, you might have special knowledge that would interest even "experts.")

Writing Practice 11

For this activity use the first and second paragraphs of a rough draft for an expository essay. First, define the audience for which you are writing. (Your teacher may wish you to consider him or her and your classmates as your audience.) Then, select an audience from the following list that is different from the one for which you have written your rough draft. Finally, rewrite at least two paragraphs of your rough draft for your new audience. Think about changes in word choice, sentence structure, and language that you will need to make. Be certain that your essay is informative for that new audience.

1. Readers of *Seventeen* magazine (audience consists primarily of teenage girls)
2. Readers of *Reader's Digest* (audience consists mostly of adults; articles are general interest)
3. Readers of your school newspaper
4. Readers of your city or county newspaper
5. Readers of *Time* or *Newsweek* magazine (audience consists mostly of adults; articles are on topics of current national interest)

Establishing Tone

Tone is the attitude the writer assumes toward his or her readers.

The choices the writer makes about diction (words), sentence length and complexity, grammatical features, and point of view will determine how the writer sounds to readers. In most exposition the writer wishes to assume an informative and knowledgeable attitude and so avoids grammatical features that do not conform to Edited Standard English. In addition, however, the writer may decide to adopt a more or less formal tone.

The levels of usage are discussed on pages 356—357.

A formal tone of writing can be achieved by writing from a third-person point of view and by avoiding slang, colloquialisms, and contractions. Also, writers using a formal tone tend to use longer and more complex sentences. For a more informal tone writers might use the first-person point of view and use features of more informal English, such as colloquialisms and contractions.

Each of the following pieces of writing is from an expository essay. What is the tone of the first piece? Of the second? How can you tell?

> Smiling begins during the first few weeks of life, but to start with it is not directed at anything in particular. By about the fifth week it is being given as a definite reaction to certain stimuli. The baby's eyes can now fixate objects. At first it is most responsive to a pair of eyes staring at it. Even two black spots on a piece of card will do. As the weeks pass, a mouth also becomes necessary. Two black spots with a mouth-line below them are now more efficient at eliciting the response. Soon a widening of the mouth becomes vital, and then the eyes begin to lose their significance as key stimuli. At this stage, around three to four months, the response starts to become more specific. It is narrowed down from any old face to the particular face of the mother. Parental imprinting is taking place.[1]
>
> —from "A Baby Learns to Smile" by Desmond Morris

> Without being too pompous about it, I think I can say I speak for one of the largest unorganized groups in the world—the unpublished authors. We write as though our lives depended on it—yet we have long since adapted ourselves to the icy truth that we will never get into print. Why do we do it? Because it happens to please us. In my own case I enjoy it.[2]
>
> —from "Confessions of an Unpublished Writer" by Babette Blaushild

The excerpt from "A Baby Learns to Smile" is written in a formal tone. The writer has distanced himself by writing in third person. There are no slang, colloquialisms, or contractions, and although sentence length varies, the sentence structure is fairly complex. In the excerpt from "Confessions of an Unpublished Writer," however, the writer brings herself closer to readers by addressing them directly from the first-person point of view. Also, the vocabulary is not difficult, and the sentences are less complex than those of the Desmond Morris piece.

Writing Practice 12

Analyze the rough draft of the introduction to your expository essay for tone. First, be certain that you sound knowledgeable and informative. Then, classify your introduction as having either a formal or an informal tone. Finally, if the introduction has a formal tone, rewrite it so that it has an informal one. If it sounds informal, rewrite it to give it a formal tone. When you finish, compare the two versions. Which do you prefer and why?

Revising the Essay

If possible, put your first draft aside for several days before beginning the revision. This elapsed time will give you a more objective view of your own writing. Then read over the rough draft, evaluating it against the items in the following checklist. You may find that you need to add, delete, or rearrange ideas, but almost all writers make substantial changes at this stage. In

---

[1] From *The Naked Ape* by Desmond Morris. Copyright © 1967 by Desmond Morris. Reprinted by permission of McGraw-Hill Book Company.

[2] From "Confessions of an Unpublished Writer" by Babette Blaushild in *Saturday Review*, 1963. Copyright © 1963 by *Saturday Review*. All rights reserved. Reprinted by permission.

fact, most professional writers make major revisions several times before they are satisfied.

Checklist for Revising the Expository Composition

1. The writer presents information and avoids truisms.
2. The writer follows the four rules of sincerity, quantity, quality, and relevance.
3. Factual statements within the essay are accurate; opinions are presented as such and not as factual statements.
4. The topic is sufficiently limited for a short expository essay.
5. Ideas in the essay are arranged in some kind of logical organization.
6. The main idea is clearly stated early in the essay.
7. The introduction captures the reader's interest.
8. The conclusion leaves the reader with a sense of completeness.
9. The thesis statement is adequately developed.
10. The essay is unified.
11. The essay is coherent.
12. The topic and language of the essay are appropriate for the audience.
13. The writer establishes a tone and maintains it throughout the essay.
14. The writer adopts a point of view and maintains it throughout the essay.

Writing Practice 13

Using the checklist in the preceding section, revise the rough draft of your essay. (Your teacher may wish to see it first.) When you have finished, recopy the essay and check it for features that do not conform to Edited Standard English by using the Checklist for Proofreading on page 14.

Kinds of Expository Essays

Expository essays may be divided into several categories, depending on how the writer presents the information. Two common kinds of expository essays are definition and analysis. Your entire essay may fit into one of the categories, or part of it may be developed through one of these approaches.

Essay of Definition

One of the most important parts of communication is an understanding of the definition of words and terms. For example, unless agreement is reached, speakers are likely to disagree about the meaning of the word *success*. To one speaker *success* may mean having a lot of money and a job with status; to another the word might mean inner satisfaction and happiness.

In an *essay of definition,* a word or term is thoroughly defined.

One approach the writer might take is to give the dictionary definition of the term and then to extend that definition. An extended definition can include examples of the word or term, a discussion of its important characteristics and its history, and an explanation of variations in meaning.

The following sample essay, "Newspaperese" by Richard D. Altick, defines the term *newspaperese.*[1]

> The jargon peculiar to newspapers is a combination of the cliché, dead wood, and the weak passive or impersonal construction. The great objection to it, as to all jargon, is that it is machine-made. It is written according to formula, and material written to formula inevitably loses much of its color and interest. Here is a short sampling of newspaper clichés together with their simpler equivalents:

The death toll rose to ten today in the wake of the disastrous fire . . . (*or:* Death today claimed four more victims . . .)	Four more people died as a result of the fire . . .
The mercury soared to a record high for the year (*or* plummeted to a new low) . . .	Today was the hottest (*or* coldest) day of the year . . .
At an early hour this morning the identity of the victim had not yet been established . . .	Early this morning the body was still unidentified . . .
Traffic was snarled (*or* paralyzed, *or* at a standstill, *or* moved at a snail's pace, *or* crept bumper to bumper) as snow blanketed the metropolitan area . . .	The snowfall slowed traffic . . .
State Police, aided by local law enforcement officers, today were combing the area adjacent to Center City in search of clues that might lead to the solution of the mystery of the murder-kidnapping . . .	State and local police were looking for clues to the man who kidnaped and murdered . . .
Three persons suffered injuries when the automobile in which they were riding figured in a collision with a large truck . . .	Three persons were hurt when their car hit a big truck . . .
As he completed his investigation, the coroner said it was his opinion that death was instantaneous . . .	The coroner thought the man had been killed instantly . . .

Epithet means "an adjective, noun, or phrase used to describe someone or something."

> In addition, there are numerous single words, especially epithets and verbs, which are seemingly indispensable to newspaper reporting. Any better-than-

[1]From "Newspaperese" from *Preface to Critical Writing,* Fifth Edition by Richard D. Altick.

ordinary fire or auto accident is *spectacular;* an accident that is more peculiar than disastrous is *freak;* when public men approve of something they *hail* it, when they disapprove of it they *attack* it, and when they want something they *urge* it; when two factions have a disagreement they *clash;* when anything is announced it is made *public;* and when men accuse others of wrongdoing they *allege.* (*Assert,* another newspaper war horse, has a slightly less negative connotation.)

The weak passive is used in newspaper writing for essentially the same reason it is used in governmental correspondence: to achieve the impersonal note, and thus, in many instances, to disclaim direct responsibility for statements that are based on hearsay. When newspapers send a reporter for an eyewitness story of a disaster or a court trial, or when they quote a press release or statements made during an interview, they can state positively that this and that are true. But much news cannot be treated in so open and confident a fashion—news based on private information picked up by reporters or on rumors circulating in the city hall or the stock exchange. Although the papers wish to relay this news, they cannot do so on their own authority; the man who gave the reporter his information refuses to be quoted, and the public will be suspicious of anything plainly labeled "rumor." The solution, then, is to use weak passive or impersonal constructions which do not require an agent: "It was revealed (*or* learned *or* reported)" (*not:* the City Commissioner told our reporter but warned him not to use his name); "indications increased" or "a survey today showed" (*not:* our reporter asked several people, and their replies, when put together, suggested). Another device of passing on news without revealing its source (or, it may be, without revealing that it has no source outside the mind of an inventive reporter) is the use of those mysterious oracles, the *officials who asked that their names be withheld, spokesmen, informed quarters, observers,* and *sources usually considered reliable.* Judged from the viewpoint of clear, accurate communication, "newspaperese" has as little to recommend it as does any other kind of roundabout, machine-made language.

One particular brand of newspaper jargon, the language of the sports page, deserves special study. Sports writers, perhaps because they deal with lively, entertaining matters that seldom have dead-serious implications, have greater freedom, and indeed a greater necessity, than do other reporters to invent new ways of saying things. Sports pages are filled with metaphorical language. When first used, such terms add a welcome novelty to the narration of what are, after all, fairly routine events. (One baseball game differs from another only in details, not in general pattern: usually a game has nine innings, each inning is divided into halves, a side is always retired after the third out.) But, like all clichés, sports-page terms soon lose their vividness through overuse. Reporters keep on employing them just the same: *four-bagger* or *circuit clout* for *home run, coveted pasteboards* for *hard-to-get tickets, grid classic* for *big game, thinclads* for *track team, signal-caller* for *quarterback, tankmen* for *swimmers, century* for *100-yard dash, swivel-hipped pigskin toter* for *agile ball-carrier,* and so on.

In "Newspaperese" Richard Altick begins with a straightforward definition: "The jargon peculiar to newspapers is a combination of the cliché, dead wood, and the weak passive or impersonal construction." He then discusses the characteristics of newspaperese (the cliché, dead wood, and the weak passive), giving specific examples of each. Finally, he discusses in detail one particular variation of newspaperese: sports writing.

Writing Practice 14

Using one of the following subjects or one of your own choosing, write an extended essay of definition. Follow the steps outlined in this chapter for writing an expository essay. Your purpose is to define thoroughly the word or term that is your topic.

1. Feminism
2. Teenager
3. Soap opera
4. Propaganda
5. The American character
6. Cable television
7. Fads
8. A good job
9. Hero
10. "Come in from the cold" (expression used by intelligence agents)

Essay of Analysis

An essay of analysis may be either process analysis or item analysis.

In *process analysis* the writer's purpose is to explain how a process works.

In analyzing the process—creating special effects for a movie, perfecting a tennis backhand, building a log cabin, earning an *A* in English—the writer examines the individual parts of the process and how they work together. Usually this is done in the order of the steps of the process.

In *item analysis* the writer's purpose is to examine the reasons for a situation.

The situation may be inflation, a high crime rate, low school attendance, or a poor television production, but the writer looks for underlying reasons and causes that have resulted in that situation. For example, in the following essay Mollie Panter-Downes analyzes a political situation in England. During the elections for representatives to the European Parliament, few British people voted. (The European Parliament is the legislative body of an association of Western European countries called the European Economic Community.) After giving background information about the election, the writer categorizes and explains the reasons for the poor showing. As you read the essay, look for these reasons.[1]

The major political parties in Great Britain are the Conservative party and the Labour party.

An *M.P.* is a member of Parliament.

After last month's enormous political excitement here in Britain, the election of representatives to the European Parliament took place on June 7th in such a deep, inattentive calm that it might have been deciding something on another planet. The result, which sent Conservative winners romping off to Strasbourg in even greater preponderance than that of the Conservative M.P.s entrenched at Westminster, followed a campaign that was impersonally short of all the usual trimmings. London showed no sign of knowing that anything was afoot. In country towns to the south, which are prosperous Conservative strongholds and therefore, it is always said, contain more conscientious voters

---

[1] From "Letter From London" by Mollie Panter-Downes in *The New Yorker*, July 2, 1979, p. 68.

than Labour areas do, one noticed a slight blooming of party posters among the late lilacs in front gardens. There were apparently few local meetings and no door-to-door campaigning. It was predicted all along that the turnout would be low. Yet when the melancholy figures began to trickle in—on the night of the count both television channels took part in an elaborate election-results program that went on cheerily analyzing and hooking up with other voting capitals long after the majority of this section of Europe's new constituents had certainly yawned their way to bed—the undreamed-of-faintness of Britain's voice in the European concert was a shock that the press and the political commentators castigated as "appalling."

All sorts of reasons other than indifference or downright hostility were given to explain why things had turned out even worse than expected. The party organizations were tired and short of money after fighting the general election, and the public could not summon up much interest in another lot of political faces showing up so soon on their TVs, this time holding forth about Europe. The huge size of the Euro-constituencies into which Britain was carved up was daunting to many, since British election campaigns have traditionally preserved a personal, almost village character. Great slabs of the electorate were joined together willy-nilly with places beyond their normal constituency boundaries. For example, a sizable number of annoyed people who live in West Surrey found themselves pruned from the rest of the county and grafted on to part of Hampshire and all the Isle of Wight to form a new hybrid known as Wight and Hampshire East.

The lineup of candidates was unlikely to galvanize anybody. They included local-government figures, farmers, Eurocrats from Brussels, and professional men and women, with a sprinkling of past and present members of both Houses of Parliament and a few top executives who appear now and then in TV political discussions that do not attract popular audiences. Many citizens who were interested in the outcome and intended to use their vote had no idea what their candidate looked or sounded like. With one exception, the candidates were little-known players requesting to be sent out to bat for England in the unfamiliar Strasbourg field, and the lack of cheers for them—or, indeed, of any sound at all—was not surprising. It was possibly a nonpartisan relief to many to be able to pick out from their blurred mental snapshot of the chosen team the crisply trenchant silhouette of Mrs. Barbara Castle, a strong anti-Common Market left-winger and former minister, who stood down in the general election this May and won Greater Manchester North resoundingly for Labour as a Euro-candidate. She is now sixty-seven, and her looks—red-headed, attractive, neat as an extremely sharp pin—and her often vituperative North Country voice tirelessly drilling into Tory policies have been very well known indeed over the years.

Trenchant means "forceful" or "vigorous."

Vituperative means "scolding."

The threatening hint in Labour's European-election manifesto that Britain might withdraw from the European Economic Community if desired reforms did not come quickly has now been shelved for the next five years or so. Pro-Europe and anti-Europe voters are united for once, however, in approving the Thatcher Government's speedy announcement that although a new cordial era has come at last, this government will be every bit as tough as the last lot in pressing for a reduction in the disproportionately hefty contribution that Britain pays into the Community's budget. The message of the fainthearted June 7th vote was clearly that for most of the British people Europe is still "them," and has not become "us."

At the time of this election, Margaret Thatcher was Prime Minister of Great Britain.

To analyze the poor voter turnout, Mollie Panter-Downes looks at the reasons for the British voters' lack of interest. She explains, for example, that this election may have come too soon after the British national elections and that too few voters knew the candidates other than by name. What are other reasons she cites?

Writing Practice 15

Using one of the following subjects or another similar one that you select, write an essay of either process or item analysis. Follow the steps outlined in the previous section for writing an expository essay.

1. Tuning up a car
2. Reducing urban crime
3. Why the Social Security system doesn't work
4. A successful running program
5. How cable television affects the community
6. Maintaining an all-volunteer army successfully
7. The effects of caffeine on the body
8. A bad television program
9. Why society doesn't place more value on its senior citizens
10. How to save money on clothes

Subjects for Expository Compositions

The following list of general subjects is intended to give you help in finding ideas for your writing. Most of the subjects need further limiting before they are useful as topics for an expository composition.

AUTOMOBILES AND DRIVING

Teenage drivers
Buying a used car
Maintaining a car
Raising the driving age to eighteen
Reducing accidents
The car of tomorrow
Mandatory helmet laws for motorcycle riders
Mandatory seat belt laws
How the automobile changed America
Establishing national driving laws

EDUCATION

Alternatives to college
Dropouts
Standardized testing
The honor system
The ideal school
Women in service academies

Making schools safe
Abolishing attendance laws
Student government
The school of tomorrow

ENVIRONMENT
Noise pollution
Saving an endangered species
Mining coal
Smog in Los Angeles
Effects of pesticides
Dangers of cigarette smoke to nonsmokers
Disposing of toxic wastes
Acid rain
The effects of chemical fertilizers
Using resources wisely

FOOD
America's love for fast food
Health foods
Vegetarianism
The perfect hamburger
Saving money on groceries
Packaging for foods
Additives in foods
Artificial sweeteners
Tips for beginning cooks
Kitchen gadgets

HEALTH
Jogging for health
Importance of fiber in the diet
Important vitamins and minerals
Harmful diets
Dieting safely
Aerobic exercise
Yoga
The effects of cholesterol
Low-carbohydrate diets
The health food business

HUMAN BRAIN
Sleeping
Dreaming
Brain damage from smoking or drugs
How memory works
Theories of creativity
Mental retardation
How humans see
How humans taste
How humans smell
How humans hear

LIFE STYLES
Working parents
Male/female roles
Using credit cards wisely
Coping with inflation
Caring for a younger brother or sister
Living in a computer age
The teenager of today
Making a career decision
The definition of an adult
Dating

MEDICINE
The shortage of nurses
Lengthening the life span
Cloning
Future dental care
Nuclear medicine
Preventive health care
Careers in medicine in the year 2500
Conquering cancer
The common cold
Migraine headaches

MUSIC
Punk rock
Disco
Performing styles of popular performers
Effect of the Beatles on later music
Buddy Holly and rock-and-roll
The job of a disc jockey
How records are marketed
Buying a stereo system
What country music says
The origins of jazz

POLITICS
Definition of a Liberal
Definition of a Conservative
Amending the Constitution
An outstanding Justice of the Supreme Court
An outstanding President
Direct election of the President
Abolishing or strengthening the United Nations
The United States' involvement with Vietnam
A woman President
A six-year term for the President

SCIENCE
The space shuttle
Aviation safety
Problems of space travel

Weightlessness in space
The first astronauts
Computers for the home
The effects of sugar
The harmful effects of smoking
Communication satellites
Life in the year 3000

SPORTS

Professional boxing
Women in high school athletics
Physical education as a required course
The Olympics
Abolishing high school football
Improving a team's poor record
An outstanding coach
History of a sport
Sportsmanship
High salaries for professional athletes

TELEVISION AND MOVIES

A good television show or movie
A bad television show or movie
How television changed Americans
Screen stars of the 1980s
Clay animation in films
Soap operas
Television news programs
Editing movies for television
Harmful effects of television
Television commercials

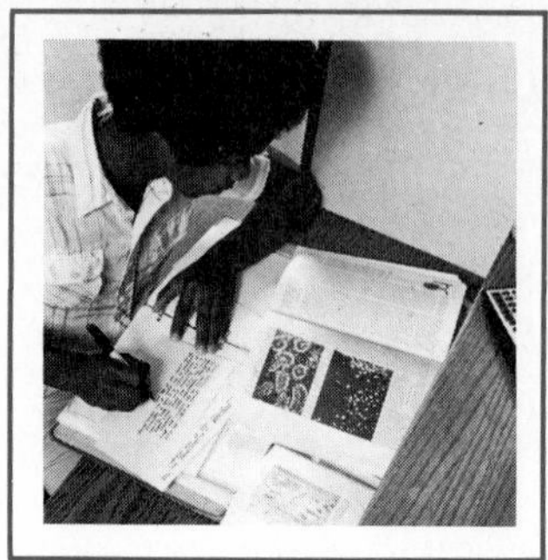

5 Critical Writing

Writing About Short Stories, Novels, and Plays

It is important to remember that writing critically about a subject—literature or film, for example—does not necessarily mean finding fault. It means reading and viewing carefully, with an understanding of how literature and films are structured. It also means that you analyze, evaluate, and then comment upon selected elements of the work.

Almost all short stories and novels share common elements. First, there are *characters*, humans or nonhumans, who think, feel, act, and respond in their fictional world much as you do in the real world. These characters perform actions based on *motives*, or reasons. These motivated actions, which make up the *plot* of the story, frequently arise from a *conflict*, or problem, and take place against a background of time and place, called a *setting*. Finally, the way the story is told, its *style*, helps readers to interpret its significance or meaning.

Writing About Characters

Most stories have two kinds of characters: major and minor. *Major characters* carry the burden of the plot and take part in most of the action. One of the major characters may be a *protagonist*, someone who has a problem to solve or a conflict to resolve before there can be a satisfactory ending. The protagonist's problems may be caused by an *antagonist*, someone against whom the protagonist struggles to resolve the conflict. Sometimes, the antagonist is not a person at all, but a force of nature, an animal, or circumstance.

Minor characters enrich a story or play by providing the major characters with further complications and by reflecting character traits that amuse, puzzle, entertain, and inform readers about the main ideas of the story.

Characters, whether major or minor ones, can be either *round* or *flat.* A *round character* is one that is dynamic, capable of growth and change. A *flat character* is a static one, frequently *stereotyped,* who does not grow or change during the story. If this character is a stereotype (such as the hanging judge of old Westerns or the street-wise, gum-chewing, joke-cracking newspaper reporter), you need to try to determine what the character contributes to the story.

Writers help readers visualize and understand characters in a number of ways. For example, in the following passage from "The Infant Prodigy" by Thomas Mann, the central character is introduced through direct description. As you read, notice the details of appearance and background that help you to see the infant prodigy.[1]

> The infant prodigy entered. The hall became quiet.
>
> It became quiet and then the audience began to clap, because somewhere at the side a leader of mobs, a born organizer, clapped first. The audience had heard nothing yet, but they applauded; for a mighty publicity organization had heralded the prodigy and people were already hypnotized, whether they knew it or not.
>
> The prodigy came from behind a splendid screen embroidered with Empire garlands and great conventionalized flowers, and climbed nimbly up the steps to the platform, diving into the applause as into a bath; a little chilly and shivering, but yet as though into a friendly element. He advanced to the edge of the platform and smiled as though he were about to be photographed; he made a shy, charming gesture of greeting, like a little girl.
>
> He was dressed entirely in white silk, which the audience found enchanting. The little white jacket was fancifully cut, with a sash underneath it, and even his shoes were made of white silk. But against the white socks his bare little legs stood out quite brown; for he was a Greek boy.

For Discussion

1. Notice the air of anticipation as the young performer enters the room. What details in the first two paragraphs describe the atmosphere in the concert hall?
2. What picture of the infant prodigy do you have as you read the third paragraph? How do "diving into the applause as into a bath" or "advanced to the edge of the platform and smiled as though he were about to be photographed" help you visualize the boy?

A writer may also introduce a character to you indirectly through what other characters say about him or her. In the opening scene of the play *Hedda Gabler* by Henrik Ibsen, two characters who have kept house for the previous occupants are talking about the arrival of the new ones. As you read their conversation, notice what bits of information and description you get about two major characters, Hedda and George Tesman.

---

[1]Excerpt from "The Infant Prodigy" in *Stories of Three Decades* by Thomas Mann, translated by H.T. Lowe-Porter. Copyright 1936 and renewed 1964 by Alfred A. Knopf, Inc. Reprinted by permission of Alfred A. Knopf, Inc.

BERTA. Well, but there's another thing, Miss. I'm so mortally afraid I shan't be able to suit the young mistress.

MISS TESMAN. Oh, well—just at first there may be one or two things—

BERTA. Most like she'll be terrible grand in her ways.

MISS TESMAN. Well, you can't wonder at that—General Gabler's daughter! Think of the sort of life she was accustomed to in her father's time. Don't you remember how we used to see her riding down the road along with the General? In that long black habit—and with feathers in her hat?

BERTA. Yes, indeed—I remember well enough! But good Lord, I should never have dreamt in those days that she and Master George would make a match of it.

MISS TESMAN. Nor I. But, by-the-bye, Berta—while I think of it: in future you mustn't say Master George. You must say Dr. Tesman.

BERTA. Yes, the young mistress spoke of that too—last night—the moment they set foot in the house. Is it true, then, Miss?

MISS TESMAN. Yes, indeed it is. Only think, Berta—some foreign university has made him a doctor—while he has been abroad, you understand. I hadn't heard a word about it, until he told me himself upon the pier.

BERTA. Well, well, he's clever enough for anything, he is. But I didn't think he'd have gone in for doctoring people too.

MISS TESMAN. No, no, it's not that sort of doctor he is. *(Nods significantly.)* But let me tell you, we may have to call him something grander before long.

BERTA. You don't say so! What can that be, Miss?

MISS TESMAN *(smiling).* Wouldn't you like to know! *(With emotion.)* Ah, dear, dear—if my poor brother could only look up from his grave now, and see what his little boy has grown into! *(Looks around.)* But bless me, Berta—why have you done this? Taken the chintz covers off all the furniture?

BERTA. The mistress told me to. She can't abide covers on the chairs, she says.

MISS TESMAN. Are they going to make this their everyday sitting room then?

BERTA. Yes, that's what I understand—from the mistress. Master George—the doctor—he said nothing.[1]

For Discussion

1. What do you learn about Hedda and George from the conversation?
2. Do the characters seem to be enthusiastic about the young couple's arrival? How can you tell?
3. Although Hedda has not yet entered the action of the play, what do you think she may be like from the few details you have in this short scene?

Writing Practice 1

For this assignment select a short story or play from your literature anthology or a library book. Then make a list of the major characters in the story or play and a list of the character traits each possesses. For instance, in the short story "Flight" by John Steinbeck, the young boy Pepe has character traits of trustworthiness, tenderness, determination, and fear of the unknown. Write

---

[1] Excerpt from "Hedda Gabler" from *Henrik Ibsen: The Complete Major Prose Plays,* translated by Rolf Fjelde. Copyright © 1965, 1970, 1978 by Rolf Fjelde. Reprinted by arrangement with The New American Library, Inc., New York, New York.

down on a sheet of paper as many character traits as you can for each of the major characters. Finally, decide whether the individual characters are rounded or flat types or whether they are stereotyped figures, and write several sentences explaining and supporting your answer.

Writing About Action

The plot of a story proceeds in a series of events: from beginning to middle to end. The plot is often started on its way through one or more complications or problems that affect the protagonist and other characters. As the plot becomes more complex and perhaps interwoven with other minor plots, a *climax*, or *turning point*, is reached. This turning point may be an unexpected discovery, a crucial decision, or a resolution of the conflict. The reader finishes the story with a sense of release from the tension created by the plot. In many stories, however, just as in real life, the conflict is not completely resolved. Instead, the resolution finds the protagonist changed as a result of the conflict, perhaps a little more mature, sadder but wiser.

Plots do not always proceed from Day 1 to Day 20 in orderly fashion. Writers may employ a technique called the *flashback* or the *flash forward* to give readers a glimpse of what happened before or what will happen in the future. Knowledge of earlier events helps the reader interpret and understand the motivations of characters. Seeing what lies ahead gives the reader a different perspective on present action and allows him or her to understand more fully how actions or circumstances contribute to the ending.

Writing Practice 2

For this assignment select a short story or play you have read recently or a film you have seen recently. Then on a sheet of paper, write down the major events, or actions, that happen in the story. Try to arrange them in the order in which they happen. Now think about the turning point in the plot. Which event, decision, or act eventually led to a resolution? Write a short paragraph explaining what the climax was and why you think it was the turning point in the story.

Writing About Motivation

Characters may be motivated by emotions—fear, pain, love, guilt—and by deliberate decisions that show them reacting to situations and other characters. Some stories may seem at first to be merely a sequence of events—one thing after another. Most well-written stories, however, are not simply a series of happenings; rather, the actions arise from characters. Things happen because people in a story respond to ideas, other people, and situations. As a reader you can take into account what characters say, what they do, what others say about them, and what others do in relation to them. You can also be aware of *foreshadowing*, the technique of hinting about events to come through description of setting, minor events, conversations between characters, and the tone of the story's narrator.

In the ancient Greek tragedy *Medea*, Jason, who sought the legendary Golden Fleece, has cast off his foreign wife, Medea, and married a Greek princess. In the following scene Medea is preparing to send wedding gifts to Jason's new wife. Actually, Medea seeks revenge and has poisoned the gifts. In the dialogue unnatural events in nature are discussed. These strange and unnatural things parallel the unnatural, evil revenge Medea is planning.[1]

MEDEA. These are the gifts I am sending to the young bride; this golden wreath
And this woven-gold veil. They are not not without value; there is nothing like them in the whole world, or at least
The Western world; the God of the Sun gave them to my father's father, and I have kept them
In the deep chest for some high occasion; which has now come.
I have great joy in giving these jewels to Creon's daughter, for the glory of life consists of being generous
To one's friends, and—merciless to one's enemies—you know what a friend she has been to me. All Corinth knows.
The slaves talk of it. The old stones in the walls
Have watched and laughed.
(MEDEA *looks at the gold cloth, and strokes it cautiously with her hand. It seems to scorch her fingers.* THIRD WOMAN *has come nearer to look; now starts backward.)*
MEDEA. See, it is almost alive. Gold is a living thing: such pure gold.
(NURSE *enters from up Right; crosses to foot of steps.)*
But when her body has warmed it, how it will shine!
(To the NURSE.*)*
Why doesn't he come? What keeps him?
NURSE *(evidently terrified).* Oh, my lady: presently.
I have but now returned from him. He was beyond the gate, watching the races—where a monstrous thing
Had happened: a young mare broke from the chariot
And tore with her teeth a stallion.
MEDEA *(stands up, shakes out the golden cloak, which again smoulders. She folds it cautiously, lays it in the leather case. The light has darkened again. She looks anxiously at the clouded sun).* He takes his time, eh? It is intolerable
To sit and wait.
(To the SERVING WOMEN.*)*
Take these into the house. Keep them at hand
For when I call.
(They take them in. MEDEA *moves restlessly, under extreme nervous tension; speaks to the* NURSE. NURSE *crosses below steps to stage Left, then up two steps.)*
You say that a mare attacked a stallion?
NURSE. She tore him cruelly.
I saw him being led away: a black racer: his blood ran down
From the throat to the fetlocks.

---

[1]Excerpt from *Cawdor and Medea* by Robinson Jeffers. Copyright 1928, 1956 by Robinson Jeffers. Reprinted by permission of New Directions Publishing Corporation.

MEDEA. You're sure he's coming. You're sure?
NURSE. He said he would.
MEDEA. Let him make haste, then!
SECOND WOMAN *(she crosses to Left below* NURSE*).* Frightening irrational things
Have happened lately; the face of nature is flawed with omens.
FIRST WOMAN *(crosses to Left, joining* SECOND WOMAN*).* Yesterday evening a slave
Came up to the harbor-gate, carrying a basket
Of new-caught fish: one of the fish took fire
And burned in the wet basket with a high flame: the thing was witnessed
By many persons.
THIRD WOMAN *(crosses Left of other* TWO WOMEN, *joining them).* And a black leopard was seen
Gliding through the marketplace—
MEDEA *(abruptly, approaching the* WOMEN*).* You haven't told me yet: do you not think that Creon's daughter
Will be glad of those gifts?
FIRST WOMAN. O Medea, too much wealth
Is sometimes dreadful.
MEDEA. She'll be glad, however. She'll take them and put them on, she'll wear them, she'll strut in them,
She'll peacock in them. I see him coming now—the
*(*THREE WOMEN *retire to up Left corner.* NURSE *sits below Left pillar.)*
whole palace will admire her. Stand away from me, women,
While I make my sick peace.

For Discussion

1. Unusual events, such as a mare attacking a stallion, are revealed in the preceding dialogue. What other strange things are discussed? What are omens?
2. One woman says, "O Medea, too much wealth/Is sometimes dreadful." How do you think this comment foreshadows Medea's revenge?
3. If you have read *Medea*, you know that the gold cloth burns the new wife's skin and causes her to die painfully. What lines in the dialogue foreshadow this event? To answer this question, look at how the gold cloth is described.

Writing Practice 3

Think about the conflict or problem in a story or film you have read or seen recently. What was the conflict or problem, and why did the protagonist react to it as he or she did? Also, think about what other characters did and what they said about the protagonist. When you can answer the question *Why did events happen as they did?* write a brief explanation of what happens and why the events happen.

Writing About Setting

The *setting* of a story or film may be as important to the meaning as the characters themselves. As you analyze a story, decide the time and place in which it takes place. You can do this easily if the story includes place names and dates, but you can also determine the setting by looking carefully at how characters speak, dress, and behave; and at the writer's description of places, such as homes, fields, forests, towns, and schools. However, a story may take place in an unspecified time and place, perhaps even inside a character's mind. You will need to look for clues in the context of the story itself to determine setting in these cases.

For example, in her novel *Jane Eyre*, Charlotte Brontë describes Jane's arrival at Ferndean, the home of her employer, Mr. Rochester. As you read the following description from that scene, notice how details of the physical setting suggests a foreboding, gloomy atmosphere.

> To this house I came, just ere dark, on an evening marked by the characteristics of sad sky, cold gale, and continued small, penetrating rain. The last mile I performed on foot, having dismissed the chaise and driver with the double remuneration I had promised. Even when within a very short distance of the manorhouse, you could see nothing of it; so thick and dark grew the timber of the gloomy wood about it. Iron gates between granite pillars showed me where to enter, and passing through them, I found myself at once in the twilight of close-ranked trees. There was a grass-grown track descending the forest aisle, between hoar and knotty shafts and under branched arches. I followed it, expecting soon to reach the dwelling; but it stretched on and on, it wound far and farther: no sign of habitation or grounds was visible.
>
> I thought I had taken a wrong direction and lost my way. The darkness of natural as well as of sylvan dusk gathered over me. I looked round in search of another road. There was none: all was interwoven stem, columnar trunk, dense, summer foliage—no opening anywhere.
>
> I proceeded: at last my way opened, the trees thinned a little; presently I beheld a railing, then the house—scarce, by this dim light, distinguishable from the trees; so dank and green were its decaying walls. Entering a portal, fastened only by a latch, I stood amidst a space of enclosed ground, from which the wood swept away in a semicircle. There were no flowers, no garden-beds; only a broad gravel-walk girdling a grass-plot, and this set in the heavy frame of the forest. The house presented two pointed gables in its front: the windows were latticed and narrow: the front-door was narrow too, one step led up to it. The whole looked, as the host of Rochester Arms had said, "quite a desolate spot." It was as still as a church on a week-day: the pattering rain on the forest leaves was the only sound audible in its vicinage.
>
> "Can there be life here?" I asked.

For Discussion

1. The road leading to Mr. Rochester's house is dark, isolated, and difficult to follow. What words or phases in the preceding passage suggest the isolation and apparent lack of life?
2. What words and phrases tell you how Jane feels about the place?

3. How effective is the question that Jane asks herself: "Can there be life here?" Have the descriptive details suggested something about life at the Rochester house?
4. What specific details help you to determine where and when this story takes place?

Writing Practice 4

Recall a story or film you have enjoyed and think about its setting. On a sheet of paper, identify the time and place in which the story takes place. If the scene changed from place to place or from time to time, note the background of the major part of the action. As you recall the background, jot down the clues you can remember that told you where and when the story took place. For example, in the film *Julia* the action takes place primarily in Europe, especially in Paris and Vienna. The time is shortly before and at the beginning of World War II. In the dialogue specific places, people, and events are named to tell viewers about time and place. The costumes worn by the actors, the models of cars and trains, and the interior decoration of homes and hotels are further clues to establish the story's background.

Writing About Style

When you look at a writer's *style*, you analyze imagery, symbols, irony, point of view, and other identifiable uses of language.

1. *Imagery*

Similes and metaphors are discussed on pages 229–230.

Imagery is the use of language to appeal to the senses and to make ideas, actions, and characters vivid. Images are frequently found in comparisons, especially in figures of speech such as *similes* and *metaphors*. In the passage from *Jane Eyre* on page 116, the narrator says that the manor house of Mr. Rochester "was as still as a church on a weekday." This simile directly compares the house to an empty church, thus emphasizing its isolation and emptiness.

2. *Symbolism*

A *symbol* is usually some concrete object or place that suggests complex ideas and associations. Symbols are not just stuck into stories for readers to find, however; they are a natural part of the story in which they appear. Some symbols are traditional ones that most readers recognize: a cross, which is associated with sacrifice; a rose, which represents beauty; or water, which may suggest birth, death, resurrection, or life. Other symbols may be private ones a writer employs to explain a point of view.

Writing Practice 5

For this assignment select a story or play in which a symbol or symbols play an important part. (For example, the valuable pearl found by the poor fisherman in John Steinbeck's novel *The Pearl* is at the same time a genuine pearl worth a great deal of money and a symbol of unmanageable wealth and bad fortune. Although it promises much, it brings nothing but disaster.) Write a brief explanation of the significance and meaning of the symbol you select. Show its importance in the story as well as its further meaning as you interpret the story.

3. *Point of View*

Stories are told from a *point of view*.

As you read literature, keep in mind that although authors *write* their stories, someone else *tells* them. That someone is a narrator, and the narrator may tell a story from any one of several points of view. A narrator may tell the story from *first-person point of view*. In first-person narration a character who refers to herself or himself as *I* narrates the story and plays a part in it at the same time. For example, in the following passage from Alice Walker's story "Everyday Use," a successful daughter, Dee, returns with her boyfriend to visit her mother and sister Maggie, who have remained on the farm where they grew up. As the story opens, the mother is thinking about Dee's visit and about Maggie's reaction to it. Notice how the narrator describes her own feelings. How is the narrator able to say how Maggie will react to her sister's visit?[1]

> I will wait for her in the yard that Maggie and I made so clean and wavy yesterday afternoon. A yard like this is more comfortable than most people know. It is not just a yard. It is like an extended living room. When the hard clay is swept clean as a floor and the fine sand around the edges lined with tiny, irregular grooves anyone can come and sit and look up into the elm tree and wait for the breezes that never come inside the house.
>
> Maggie will be nervous until after her sister goes: she will stand hopelessly in corners homely and ashamed of the burn scars down her arms and legs, eyeing her sister with a mixture of envy and awe. She thinks her sister has held life always in the palm of one hand, that "no" is a word the world never learned to say to her.

The mother is able to describe Maggie's reaction to the visit because she knows her daughter so well. A first-person narrator does not have magical powers. He or she cannot know the thoughts and feelings of other characters unless that knowledge is based on observation, as it was in the preceding example.

The *third-person point of view*, in which the narrator is not a character in the story, has several versions, depending upon how involved the narrator is with the characters in the story. At one extreme is the *omniscient* (all-knowing) *narrator* who knows everything that happens in the story and can describe what all characters think and feel. Since this narrator knows everything, he or she may pass judgment on what happens, may at times speak directly to the reader, and may interpret meanings.

Another third-person narrator, sometimes called a *selective omniscient narrator*, speaks through the thoughts of one of the characters but under-

---

[1]From "Everyday Use" from *In Love And Trouble* by Alice Walker. Copyright © 1973 by Alice Walker. Reprinted by permission of Julian Bach Literary Agency, Inc. and Harcourt Brace Jovanovich, Inc.

stands the thoughts of other characters from the outside only. In such stories the view of the world comes through the mind and senses of one character, usually a major one. The reader can only go where the narrator goes. In the following excerpt from a short story by John Galsworthy, for example, the narrator shows readers Mr. Nilson's limited world only through his words and feelings. What words and phrases in the selection identify the narrator as a selective omniscient narrator?[1]

> As Mr. Nilson, well known in the City, opened the window of his dressing room on Campden Hill, he experienced a peculiar sweetish sensation in the back of his throat, and a feeling of emptiness just under his fifth rib. Hooking the window back, he noticed that a little tree in the Square Gardens had come out in blossom, and that the thermometer stood at sixty. "Perfect morning," he thought; "spring at last!"
>
> Resuming some meditations on the price of Tintos, he took up an ivory-backed handglass and scrutinized his face. His firm, well-coloured cheeks, with their neat brown moustaches, and his round, well-opened, clear grey eyes, wore a reassuring appearance of good health. Putting on his black frock coat, he went downstairs.
>
> In the dining room his morning paper was laid out on the sideboard. Mr. Nilson had scarcely taken it in his hand when he again became aware of that queer feeling. Somewhat concerned, he went to the French window and descended the scrolled iron steps into the fresh air. A cuckoo clock struck eight.

The words, "he experienced a peculiar sweetish sensation in the back of his throat," identify the narrator as omniscient. Since nowhere in the story does the narrator reveal thoughts and feelings of other characters, he can be classified as a selective omniscient narrator. Unless he had access to the thoughts of Mr. Nilson, the narrator could not know that the character was experiencing a feeling of emptiness.

Another kind of third-person point of view presents a narrator who simply records what is said and what happens. This narrator functions something like a sound camera, picturing events and recording dialogue, but doing so *objectively*. Such a narrator does not comment or enter any character's mind. A narrator cannot be completely removed from the story, of course, for just as a camera selects and limits what viewers see and hear, so does the narrator select what readers learn about characters and events. This point of view generally has the most action. Since it does not interpret, the reader is allowed to do his or her own interpreting.

Writing Practice 6

For this assignment select a short story or novel you have read recently. Write a brief explanation of the point of view from which the story is told. Identify the narrator by name, if there is one, and define the kind of point of view as first or third person. If it is a third-person point of view, further identify it as *omniscient*, *selective omniscient*, or *objective*. Then give examples of the narrator's point of view by citing words and phrases.

---

[1]From *Caravan* by John Galsworthy. Reprinted by permission of The Society of Authors as the literary representative of the Estate of John Galsworthy.

Suggestions for Writing About Literature

When you write critically about literature or film, the suggestions in this section will help you organize and present your ideas.

1. Focus the subject of your paper.

When you write about a novel, play, or film, narrow the subject to a manageable topic for a single essay. In Margaret Mitchell's *Gone with the Wind*, for example, *The impact of the Civil War on the South* is a very large subject. Your essay might divide that subject into smaller topics such as the following:

Southern Attitudes Toward the War
Resourcefulness and Courage as Theme in *Gone with the Wind*

By narrowing or restricting the subject, *The impact of the Civil War on the South*, you are better able to relate the topic to specific incidents and characterizations in the novel. By relating directly and specifically to the novel itself, you are better able to develop your idea, strengthen your argument, and clarify your point of view.

To write an essay analyzing characterization in *Gone with the Wind*, you might limit your discussion to one or two major characters, to a group of characters that play an essential part in the story development, or to a feature of characterization, such as jealousy or patriotism. Some possible topics for a paper on characterization might be the following:

The Transformation of Scarlett O'Hara
Scarlett and Melanie: the Love-Hate Relationship
The People of Tara: a View of the Old South
Character and Caricature in *Gone with the Wind* [the film]

To write an essay analyzing plot, you can focus on a single incident or a sequence of incidents to show how they contribute to the conclusion. The following are examples of possible topics about plot:

TITLE	SUBJECT	TOPIC
a. "The Most Dangerous Game" [short story]	A manhunt	Rainsford's ironic situation as the hunted "game"
b. M*A*S*H [film]	Staying sane in wartime	Absurd comic behavior as an antidote for life in depressing times
c. *Riders to the Sea* [drama]	The conflict between humanity and nature	The role of fate in resolving the conflict between Maurya's family and the violent sea

2. Write a thesis statement.

A carefully written thesis statement establishes your topic, your point of view, and your reason for writing. Think of a thesis statement as a kind of summary statement of your interpretation. In the play *Pygmalion*, George Bernard Shaw explores the romantic possibilities of opposite characters' attracting each other. If you were to write about this topic, you might consider the following sentence as your thesis statement:

> In *Pygmalion* although Shaw explores the romantic possibilities of the characters, he is more interested in the social satire that the change in Eliza permits him to develop.

If you have seen *My Fair Lady*, the musical version of Shaw's play, you might note that *My Fair Lady* has a "happy ending" with Eliza and Professor Higgins as a romantic pair, but the original play does not end that way. In fact, Shaw writes in the Epilogue that Eliza marries Freddy instead. This difference could make the basis for a comparison between the two versions of the same story and produce a thesis statement like the following one.

> In contrast to the romantic ending of *My Fair Lady*, Shaw's *Pygmalion* is more true to the characters. By having Eliza marry Freddy rather than Higgins, he gives us a more realistic view of marriage and the relation between the sexes.

Writing Practice 7

For this assignment select a topic you have already used or select a new one. Then write a thesis statement for a critical essay about that topic.

3. Give detailed support from the story or film.

Once you have decided on your thesis, develop your essay by citing specific events, dialogue, or descriptive passages from the story or film itself. On page 116 of this textbook, a passage from *Jane Eyre* describes the approach to the manor house. In an essay whose thesis is that the author of *Jane Eyre* uses details of setting to suggest isolation and lifelessness, you would cite some of those details: "the iron gates between granite pillars," the path that stretched a long way through uninhabited land, the "decaying walls" of the house, and the narrowness of the windows and front door.

Using quoted material is discussed on page 135.

When you can best support your thesis by quoting directly from the story, remember to use quotation marks. These marks show your reader that the words they enclose are from the original work. A direct quotation is most useful when it summarizes a theme or point of view expressed by the narrator or a character, but short quoted phrases or lines are also useful when you want to demonstrate the author's use of language. Avoid using too many long quotations that could better be condensed by paraphrasing.

4. Paraphrase difficult or lengthy material.

A *paraphrase* is a restatement or rewording of the original material. In an essay you can paraphrase to cut down on the length of the material and to avoid giving too many long quotations. Once you begin paraphrasing, however, be careful to restate only those portions of the story that support and develop your thesis statement. Otherwise, you will simply be retelling the story and using many details that do not relate to your thesis.

5. Write in present tense.

Although a story or film was written in the past, you should write your essay in the present tense, because you are talking about the characters and actions as they appear to you today. The following example illustrates this:

> In "The Tale of Sir Launcelot of the Lake," Sir Thomas Malory *shows* readers a picture of life in King Arthur's time through descriptions of battles and tournaments between knights, conversations between ladies and courtly gentlemen, and tales of daring adventures.

6. Organize your essay.

One way to decide on a thesis statement for a critical paper about literature is to review the story, perhaps even reread it to refresh your memory. As you do, take notes on your reactions to characters and events. Note also the ideas you find developing as the plot unfolds. Jot down comments about the author's style of writing, point of view, use of symbols, imagery, or any other device that contributes to the effectiveness of the story. If you are writing about a film, try to see it a second time. Pay particular attention to the *way* the film tells the story: the use of musical background, the selection of objects and places photographed, the angle of camera shots, and sound effects. Write down your notes on the film as soon as possible after seeing it.

Once you have reviewed the story and made notes on it, look at them closely to see how they might be grouped according to topics. Perhaps you have noted several ideas about the author's use of imagery or minor characters who add comedy. Write your notations under the headings *Use of Imagery* and *Minor Characters Who Add Comedy*. Include not only specific details from the story itself but also your comments and responses to them. Use these notations as a worksheet from which to formulate a thesis statement and draw specific details for support.

The next step is to decide what kind of essay you want to write. Perhaps you want to *compare and contrast* two characters from a play or to *analyze and evaluate* the author's use of simile and metaphor. Another possibility would be to *explain* the theme by examining how it is presented through plot or characterization.

An essay about literature may be about any aspect of it: plot, character, setting, motivation, conflict, and style. When you have reviewed the story and arranged your notes on it, ask yourself what you liked most about the story, what affected you most strongly, and what you would like to explain to others about it. Then you will be better able to decide what the purpose of your essay will be: to explain, analyze, describe, or evaluate.

Suggestions for Topics

For papers that compare:

> The roles of two characters in the same story, such as Viola and Olivia in Shakespeare's *Twelfth Night*, or Brutus and Cassius in *Julius Caesar*

Two characters or groups of characters in different works by the same author, such as Jim in Joseph Conrad's *Lord Jim*, and the young captain in *The Secret Sharer*

Two works of literature that explore similar themes, such as *A Separate Peace* and *Catcher in the Rye*

Two versions of the same story, such as *Romeo and Juliet* and *West Side Story*

For papers that analyze and evaluate:

The role of setting in developing the theme in Emily Brontë's *Wuthering Heights*

The importance of light and dark imagery in *Oedipus the King* or *Romeo and Juliet*

Symbolism in *The Glass Menagerie*

The effectiveness of comic scenes in *Hamlet*

Coincidence in *The Return of the Native*

Significance of "the beast" in *Lord of the Flies*

For papers that explain and describe:

The meaning of the ending of *2001: A Space Odyssey*

The function of the chorus in Greek tragedy

Elements of the Chivalric Code in the Arthurian legends

Animal Farm as a parable and warning

Writing Practice 8

Select a title of a novel, short story, play, or film you have read or seen recently. If you prefer, choose a title you have written about before in this chapter or one you are now studying. Decide upon an interesting topic for an essay about that work of literature or film. Then prepare, organize, and write your essay on that topic.

Revising Your Essay

Just as you have for your other writing, check your essay to be certain that it communicates your main idea clearly. Use the following checklist to help you revise your work.

Checklist for the Critical Essay

1. The essay reflects your understanding of the story or film.
2. If necessary or appropriate to the subject of the essay, you found information in reference or other books to help support your thesis.
3. The essay is focused on one main topic.
4. The first paragraph states a thesis that sets forth your topic, your point of view, and how you will develop the topic.
5. You have used sufficient specific detail from the story or film itself to support and develop your topic.
6. If you have used direct quotations, they are enclosed in quotation marks or indented depending upon their length.

7. In order to shorten lengthy material or explain difficult passages, you have paraphrased.
8. The essay is in present tense.
9. The essay is organized with a beginning that contains your thesis, a body that develops and supports it, and a conclusion that summarizes or rephrases the thesis to emphasize it.

6 Writing the Research Paper

The Research Paper

The *research paper* is an extended, formal composition presenting information gathered from a number of sources.

Although a research paper is similar to a long expository essay, it includes more library resources and identifies those sources in footnotes and a bibliography. While some research papers are strictly informational, others draw a new conclusion from the facts they reveal. Typical of the informational kind would be a report on career opportunities in computer technology or a study of the Appalachian dialect. Papers that attempt to reach a conclusion often seek an answer to a question: How will computer technology affect education in the next two decades? What new food sources are available to feed an expanding world population?

Because a research paper requires independent and responsible work, it is important to understand each step in the process. You will find the paper easier to write, and you will produce a better final product if you schedule enough time to carefully complete each of the following steps.

1. Choose and limit a topic.
2. Survey resources.
3. Prepare a preliminary outline.
4. Gather information.
5. Reevaluate.
6. Organize a formal outline.
7. Write the rough draft.
8. Write the final draft with footnotes and bibliography.

Step One: Choosing and Limiting a Topic

Some teachers consider the choice of topic so important to the success of the final paper that they assign subjects they know students can manage. If you are free to make this decision yourself, choose a topic that will genuinely interest you, since you will be spending much time and effort learning about it. If your teacher indicates a certain length for the assignment, keep that guideline in mind.

Remember that your topic must be general enough so that you can locate sources providing pertinent information, yet limited enough so that ideas can be discussed in some depth.

A quick check of library resources will help you decide whether a topic is adequately limited or narrowed. Suppose you have always enjoyed reading about animals and decide to write about *Animals in zoos*. However, since your local and school libraries each contain five or six books on that topic, you realize you must limit your emphasis even more. Tentatively, you decide to explore some specific aspect of the zoo: the zoo veterinarian's work, the zoo's preservation of rare species, or recent changes in the nature of zoos. Since you can locate only one chapter on zoo design but no magazine articles, that topic seems too limited. After further investigation you decide on *Recent changes in zoos* as a limited topic because you can locate some sources, but the amount of information is not overwhelming.

Consider the scope of a topic before you make a decision. Topics that cover long time spans (*The history of the zoo* or *Veterinary medicine from its beginning to the present day*) are probably too general as are topics that cover many categories or groups (*Zoos throughout the world* or *Famous veterinarians*). On the other hand, beware of topics that are too limited in time or scope: *How lions are housed at the San Diego Zoo* or *The feeding of pandas at the National Zoo*.

Writing Practice 1

Divide a sheet of paper into two columns with the headings *Subjects* and *Limited Topics*. List five general subjects that appeal to you in the first column. In the second column write five limited topics for a short research paper developed from the subjects in the first column. You may use subjects from the following list.

1. Invention of the phonograph
2. History of surgery
3. Migrant workers in America
4. The development of alternative living spaces
5. Alternative schooling in America
6. Recent ocean exploration
7. History of a major business or industry in your area
8. Legends about ancient mythological heroes
9. History of photography

10. Famous Hispanic-American writers
11. Development of criminology
12. Problems of public transportation in the United States
13. Theories about the aging process
14. Patent medicines in early America
15. Famous women in science

Step Two: Surveying Resources

You will avoid problems later if you take time to get an overview of your topic, to develop a controlling purpose statement, and to locate the resources you will need.

Getting an Overview

For detailed information on library resources, see the chapter "Library Resources" on pages 234–257.

Students sometimes decide on a topic, check out several books, and hurriedly begin taking notes. Later, as they organize the final paper, they realize they have dozens of note cards covering unessential information but that they lack information on a key concept. An *overview*, or broad understanding of the topic gained from reading several general background sources, will eliminate such wasted or incomplete research.

For example, if you have decided to write about some aspect of animal life in the zoo, you might read the entry on *zoos* in the *World Book Encyclopedia*. Be sure to check the yearbooks for encyclopedias, too, because these annual volumes update all entries and feature special articles; for example, the *1980 Yearbook* for the *World Book Encyclopedia* features an article on zoo vets.

The *Readers' Guide* will also help you locate information, but remember that your goal now is to gain a general background. Choose articles addressed to the general public and articles under broad topic headings. If your topic is *Changes in zoos*, a general article about the new zoo in *Time* magazine will be more valuable than a *Scientific American* article about the breeding of the Père David deer in a specific zoo.

Also, spend some time examining the library shelf containing books on your topic. Quickly look at individual works, noting the chapter headings and major divisions. If a book contains a general introduction or preface about your topic, skim that section quickly. Although you might list unfamiliar words and names of people or places that seem important, try to avoid taking lengthy notes at this stage.

Developing a Controlling Purpose

At this point you are ready to give your paper a single focus, or *controlling purpose*. By limiting the topic to a specific attitude, a central idea, or a question, the writer establishes an important sense of direction early in the writing process. Because this controlling purpose aims research toward a specific goal, it helps the writer to recognize information that readers will need and to avoid unrelated information.

A student interested in the modern zoo might choose one of the following as a controlling-purpose statement; notice that each of these also suggests something about the paper's organization and development.

1. The new breeding programs in American zoos play an important role in preserving rare animal species. (This controlling purpose suggests an attitude toward the new zoo that the writer will support and prove in the paper.)
2. Zoos have changed dramatically in the last fifty years. (This purpose suggests that the student will explore several changes, perhaps contrasting zoos of the past with those of today.)
3. Zoos have changed for many reasons. (This purpose suggests that the student will focus on the reasons for change.)

As your research progresses and you become more knowledgeable about the topic, reevaluate your controlling purpose; revise it if the focus of your research changes.

Preparing a Working Bibliography

A *working bibliography* lists all the books, magazines, and newspaper articles, pamphlets, and other information sources that might be used, in alphabetical order by the author's last name. While the working bibliography lists all potential sources, the *final bibliography*, attached to the research paper, includes only those sources the writer actually used.

For detailed information on library resources, see the chapter "Library Resources" on pages 234–257.

Preparation of a working bibliography ensures that adequate sources have been located from a search of the card catalogue, *Readers' Guide*, vertical file, and specialized reference works. In your investigation of the card catalogue and *Readers' Guide*, remember to check broad general headings that may include a topic. For example, if your topic is *A modern zoo*, check "Zoology," "Conservation-Wildlife," and "Animals—Endangered Species" as well as "Zoos."

In a bibliography a standard form governs the order in which author, title, and publishing details are listed and separated by marks of punctuation. You will save time later by listing these items correctly in your working bibliography. Check with your teacher about the bibliography form you should use, as there are several acceptable ones. In this chapter the MLA form, developed by the Modern Language Association and explained in the *MLA Handbook*, is used.

A good approach is to record the necessary information about the author, title, publisher, and publication date of each source on a separate note card. Using this method for the working bibliography makes the preparation of a final bibliography easier.

The following source card shows the bibliography form for a book by one author; the slightly different forms for magazine and newspaper articles, pamphlets, and other sources appear in the list following the sample source card. Notice the circled numbers in the upper-right corner identifying this title as Source 1. Using this source number later on note cards prevents having to recopy bibliography details on each note card.

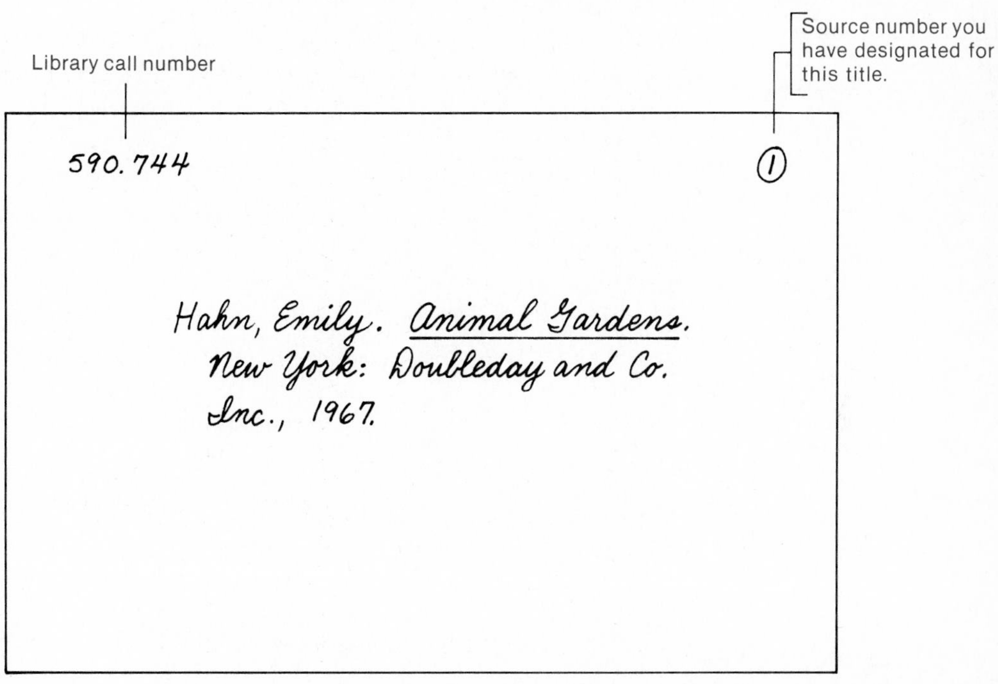

Library call number
Source number you have designated for this title.
590.744
①
Hahn, Emily. Animal Gardens.
New York: Doubleday and Co.
Inc., 1967.

The following list shows the MLA bibliography form for other kinds of sources. The punctuation marks in these examples have been emphasized so you will become familiar with their use in bibliographies.

BOOKS BY ONE AUTHOR

Pennycook, Andrew. *Codes and Ciphers: Amazing Ways to Scramble and Unscramble Secret Messages*. New York: David McKay Co., Inc., 1978. (Notice that the subtitle is included as part of the complete title.)

BOOK BY MORE THAN ONE AUTHOR

Crerar, Thomas and David King. *Choice of Words*. New York: Oxford University Press, 1969.

A WORK IN SEVERAL VOLUMES OR PARTS

Parrington, Vernon. *Main Currents in American Thought: The Romantic Revolution in America, 1800–1860*, Vol. II. New York: Harcourt, Brace and World, Inc., 1927.

WORK WITHIN A COLLECTION OF PIECES BY DIFFERENT AUTHORS

Welty, Eudora. "A Worn Path." In *By and About Women: An Anthology of Short Fiction*, ed. Beth Kline Schneiderman. New York: Harcourt Brace Jovanovich, Inc., 1973.

ARTICLE FROM A CRITICAL EDITION OR CASEBOOK

Widmer, Kingsley. "Black Existentialism: Richard Wright." *Modern Black Novelists: A Collection of Critical Essays*. Ed. M. G. Cooke. Englewood Cliffs, N.J.: Prentice-Hall, Inc., 1971.

EDITION OF A WORK OF LITERATURE

Wharton, Edith. *The House of Mirth*. Introd. Irving Howe. New York: Holt, Rinehart, and Winston, Inc., 1962.

ARTICLE IN AN ENCYCLOPEDIA OR OTHER REFERENCE WORK (NO AUTHOR GIVEN)

"Wright, Frank Lloyd." *Encyclopaedia Britannica: Macropaedia*. 1979 ed.

ARTICLE FROM AN ENCYCLOPEDIA OR OTHER REFERENCE BOOK

Marty, Martin E. "*Resurgent Fundamentalism*." *Encyclopaedia Britannica: 1980 Book of the Year*, pp. 606–7. (Articles in references arranged alphabetically need not be identified by volume and page.)

ARTICLE FROM A MONTHLY MAGAZINE

Hahn, Emily. "Eleventh Hour." *The New Yorker*, 1 Sept. 1980, pp. 37–69.

ARTICLE FROM A NEWSPAPER (NO AUTHOR GIVEN)

"Minimum Wage to Rise Again." *Decatur Herald*. 10 Oct. 1979, Sec. 1, p. 2, cols. 3–4.

ARTICLE FROM A NEWSPAPER

Stevens, Michelle. "Home or Hospital Birth? Center Offers Alternative." Chicago *Sun–Times*. 2 March 1981, p. 7, cols. 1–2.

REVIEW OF A FILM, BOOK, OR PLAY

Raynor, Vivien. "Picasso, of Course, Is Everywhere." Rev. of *The Shock of the New*, by Robert Hughes. *The New York Times Book Review*, 15 Feb. 1981, p. 3.

A SOURCE NOT IN PRINT FORMAT

McCluskey, Paul. Personal Interview. 28 Feb. 1981.

Frost, Robert. *Frost Reads His Poetry*. Caedmon, XC 783, 1952. (Use this format for records.)

PAMPHLET

The MLA Handbook. 2nd ed. New York: The Modern Language Association, 1970.

U.S. Bureau of Labor Statistics. *Productivity.* Washington, D.C.: GPO, 1958.

If an item of information is not available, record that fact by writing *no author, no date of publication, no place,* etc., on the bibliography card. Later, when you organize the final bibliography, you will know you did not forget to record this information.

Writing Practice 2

Use the card catalogue and the *Readers' Guide* to find at least three articles that provide general background information about your research topic or a topic you choose for this assignment. On a separate sheet of paper, list these sources. In a paragraph summarize what you learned from reading the articles to get an overview of the topic.

Writing Practice 3

Using materials in your library, prepare a working bibliography for your research paper by filling out a card for each source you plan to use. (If you are not writing a paper, select a topic for this assignment and prepare five bibliography cards.)

Writing Practice 4

On a sheet of paper, write four possible controlling-purpose statements for your research paper topic.

Step Three: Formulating Basic Questions

The process of taking notes will be easier if you formulate a list of basic questions to guide your research. The techniques described in the chapter "Discovering Ideas for Writing" (pages 29–55) can be used to develop a list of basic questions. For example, the five-question approach, called the *Pentad,* might lead to the following basic questions relating to the topic of the modern zoo.

1. What is the *action?* What is happening, has happened, or will happen?
   What is happening now in American zoos?
2. Who are the *actors?* Who are the people involved in the action?
   Who or what is responsible for the change in focus of the modern zoo?
3. What is the *agent?* By what means or with what instrument is the action performed?
   How have conservationists been involved in zoos' efforts to preserve species?
4. What is the *scene?* Where and when does the action happen?
   At what zoos are these changes being made?

5. What is the *purpose?* Why does the action happen?
   What is the purpose of the wild animal park?

When your list of basic questions is complete, arrange the questions as a preliminary outline. Although this outline will help you anticipate the important questions your paper will have to answer, it will probably require some revision as your research progresses. If you discover new points that need to be included, add them. If a point later seems unrelated to the scope of the final paper, remove it from the outline.

Writing Practice 5

Keeping in mind your controlling purpose and the information you gained from the overview of your topic, write a list of basic questions on your research paper topic. Use one of the information-gathering techniques in Chapter 2 as an aid.

Step Four: Taking Notes

Producing a good research paper that skillfully combines detailed facts from many sources requires excellent organization and careful note taking. The process will be easier if you use file cards, recording one item of information from a particular source on each card.

The examples on page 133 are note cards for a paper on *How zoos have changed*. The circled number in the upper-right corner indicates the source of this information; since the bibliography card with the same number lists all information about title, author, and publication, there is no need to repeat it on each note card. The *slug,* or topic heading, in the upper-left corner identifies the main idea of the note and allows the writer to organize the cards later without rereading each one.

Recording notes on cards in this manner has several advantages. A final paper on the modern zoo might contain a lengthy paragraph on innovations in animal exhibits; the supporting details for this paragraph might come from four different sources. Shuffling through pages of notes from a source to locate the necessary information is difficult and time consuming. With the information recorded on cards, the writer can simply pull out those carrying the slug *Animal exhibits* and arrange and rearrange them to produce the best order.

Evaluating Sources

You will probably use both *primary* and *secondary sources* in your paper.

Primary sources are firsthand documents.

For example, an entry in a zoologist's notebook, the memoir of a zookeeper, or an interview with a director of a zoo would be primary sources.

A *secondary source* is one written about some aspect of the primary source.

For example, the biography of Gerald Durrell, a famous zoo director and naturalist, or a magazine article written from interviews with zookeepers is a secondary source.

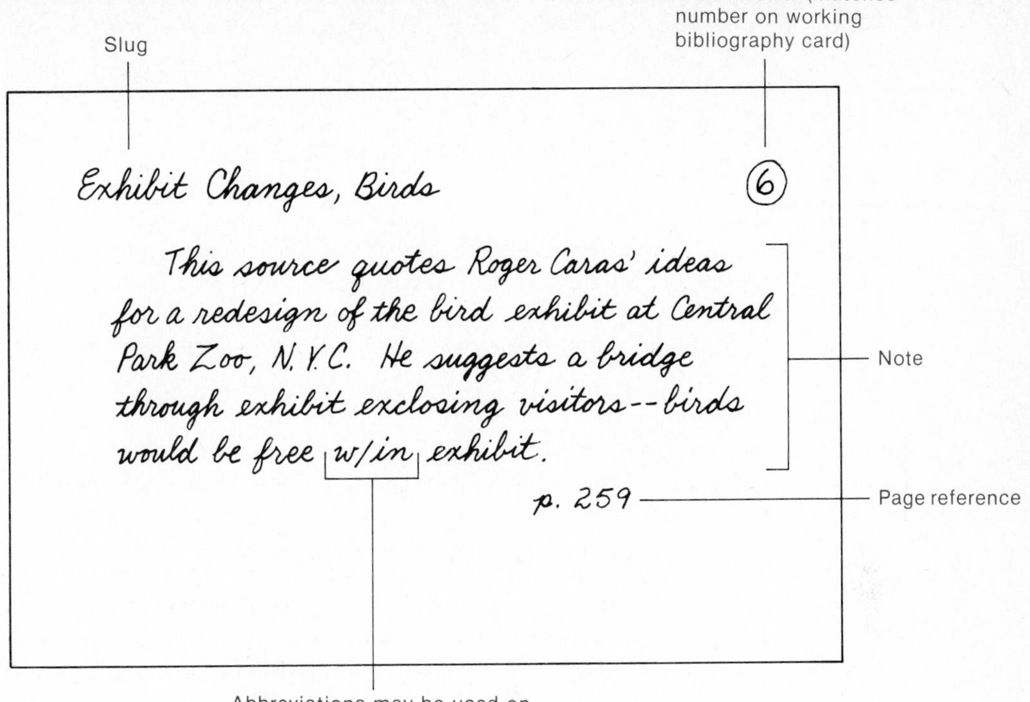
Slug
Source number (matches number on working bibliography card)
Exhibit Changes, Birds
6
This source quotes Roger Caras' ideas for a redesign of the bird exhibit at Central Park Zoo, N.Y.C. He suggests a bridge through exhibit enclosing visitors--birds would be free w/in exhibit.
p. 259
Note
Page reference
Abbreviations may be used on note cards.

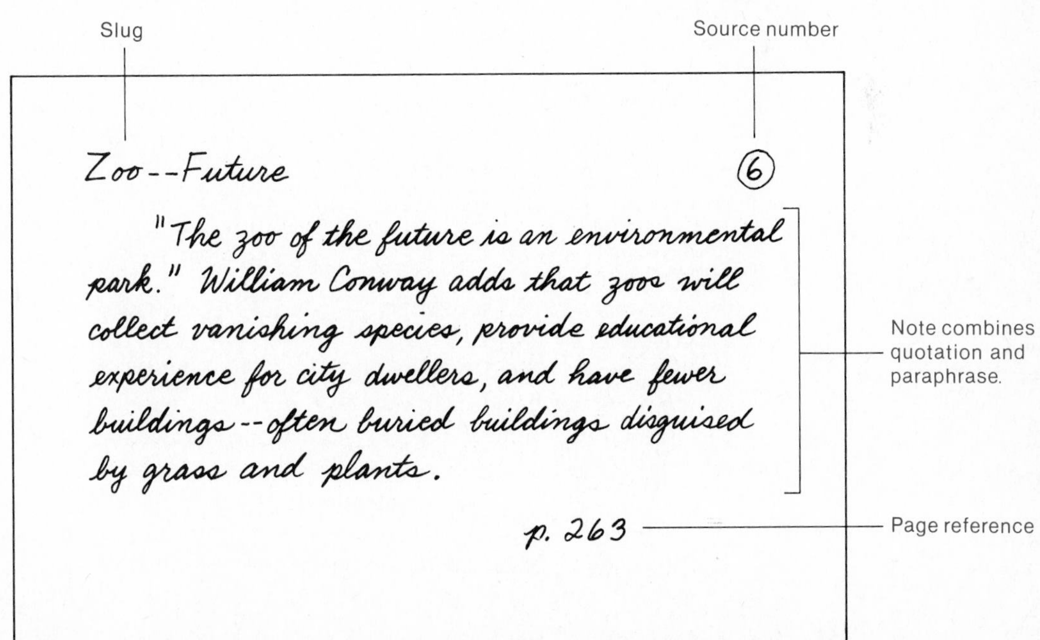
Slug
Source number
Zoo--Future
6
"The zoo of the future is an environmental park." William Conway adds that zoos will collect vanishing species, provide educational experience for city dwellers, and have fewer buildings--often buried buildings disguised by grass and plants.
p. 263
Note combines quotation and paraphrase.
Page reference

Not all sources are equally reliable or valuable. If your topic is *The modern zoo*, you might limit your sources to those written in the past ten years; for this reason Emily Hahn's *Animal Gardens*, published in 1967, is not a valuable resource. The author's reputation and expertise should also be considered. Sometimes, you can discover which authors are most respected by noting references to them in other sources. Also, the bibliographies at the end of books and articles often reveal which works are most respected or most important to understanding a topic. In addition, consider the audience for which a source was intended; articles in popular general magazines often do not have the authority of articles written for specialized journals. A quotation about zoos from *Audubon*, a publication of the Audubon Society, carries more weight than a travel feature about zoos appearing in a teen fashion magazine.

Reading Selectively

Survey a resource before you begin taking notes and use your preliminary outline to guide your reading. For a book read the chapter titles in the table of contents and the topics listed in the index at the back to locate those sections that provide specific information on your topic. Scan magazine articles and chapters of books for the main idea, noting headings, subheadings, and *italicized* words. Then read the material before you take notes rather than recording as you read; you may discover the author's first explanation of a term is not the best one or that an entire chapter is quickly summarized in the last few pages.

Adding Source Numbers

Before you write the note on a card, put the circled bibliography card number for that source in the card's upper-right corner. If *Lifeboats to Ararat* is source number 4, every note card with information from this source should have the circled number 4 in the upper-right corner. Under the source number place the page number(s) covered by that note. You may also want to put a topic heading in the upper-left corner of the card. (See the two sample note cards on page 133.)

Writing the Note

Usually a note card summarizes or paraphrases information found in a primary or secondary source.

To *paraphrase* information, read the source several times and then write a version that restates the ideas in your own words. Since your note cards are for your use, you may want to use phrases or abbreviations (*ex.*, rather than *example*) rather than complete sentences. However, the note must be complete enough so that you will understand it later.

The following selection is an original passage from the magazine article "Wildlife in Danger." As you read the selection, try to determine the paragraph's main ideas so that you can restate them in your own words.

> In the U.S., perhaps the most encouraging augury for preservation was the passage by Congress of the 1973 Endangered Species Act. Under the act, the Department of the Interior gives absolute protection to any species that it terms "endangered," and as much protection as its experts deem desirable to animals on a list of "threatened species." For each listed animal, the department's Office of Endangered Species must come up with a plan to guarantee its survival.[1]

The *summary* is a shortened version of a long work or passage.

The summary concentrates on main ideas but eliminates long description, excessive wordiness, unnecessary details, and some examples and illustrations. The following paraphrase is a summary of the preceding passage from "Wildlife in Danger."

> An encouraging sign for wildlife preservation, the Endangered Species Act of 1973 directed the Department of the Interior to provide protection for endangered or threatened species and to propose survival plans for such wildlife.

The process of paraphrasing or summarizing information is important; recording information in your own words will help you to understand the topic and to write a better paper. The final paper should be your work in your words, not a hodgepodge of borrowed passages. Submitting a paper with the words or the ideas of another presented as your own work is *plagiarism*, a dishonest practice you should conscientiously avoid.

Direct Quotations

Although quotations should be used sparingly, when an author states information especially clearly or forcefully, you may want to quote those words exactly. If you are writing about a work of literature, you can quote lines from the work to support your ideas. Also, if a writer is particularly associated with a phrase, even of one or two words, the phrase should be quoted. (Example: *Lincoln spoke of a government "for the people."*)

Always record an author's words exactly and place quotation marks around the words on the note card. If you abbreviate the quote by omitting a portion of the original, use an ellipsis (three spaced periods) to indicate the omission. Notice the ellipsis on the note card on page 136.

Brackets can be used to indicate that you have changed a word in the original quotation; however, this is done only rarely. The second quotation on page 136 originally began with the pronoun *they*. The student has inserted the word *primates* in brackets to avoid quoting the previous paragraph.

Writing Practice 6

Write note cards for your research paper from sources you have located, using your basic questions as a guide. Paraphrase or summarize information, using quotations only when they are especially appropriate.

---

[1]From "Wildlife in Danger" from *Newsweek*, January 6, 1975.

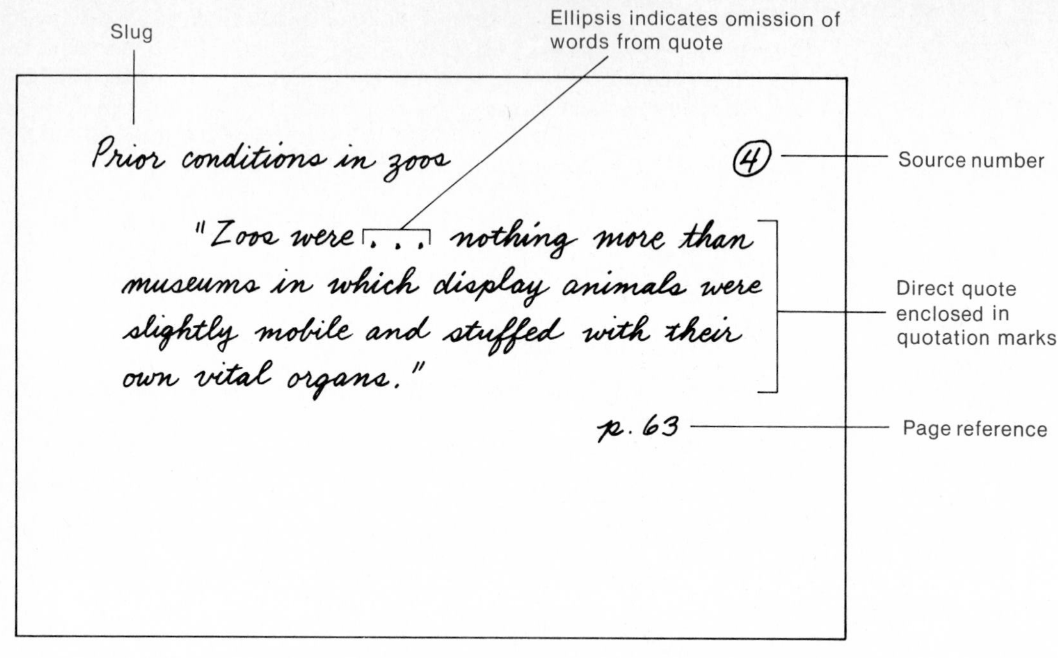

Slug
Ellipsis indicates omission of words from quote
Prior conditions in zoos
4
Source number
"Zoos were . . . nothing more than museums in which display animals were slightly mobile and stuffed with their own vital organs."
Direct quote enclosed in quotation marks
p. 63
Page reference

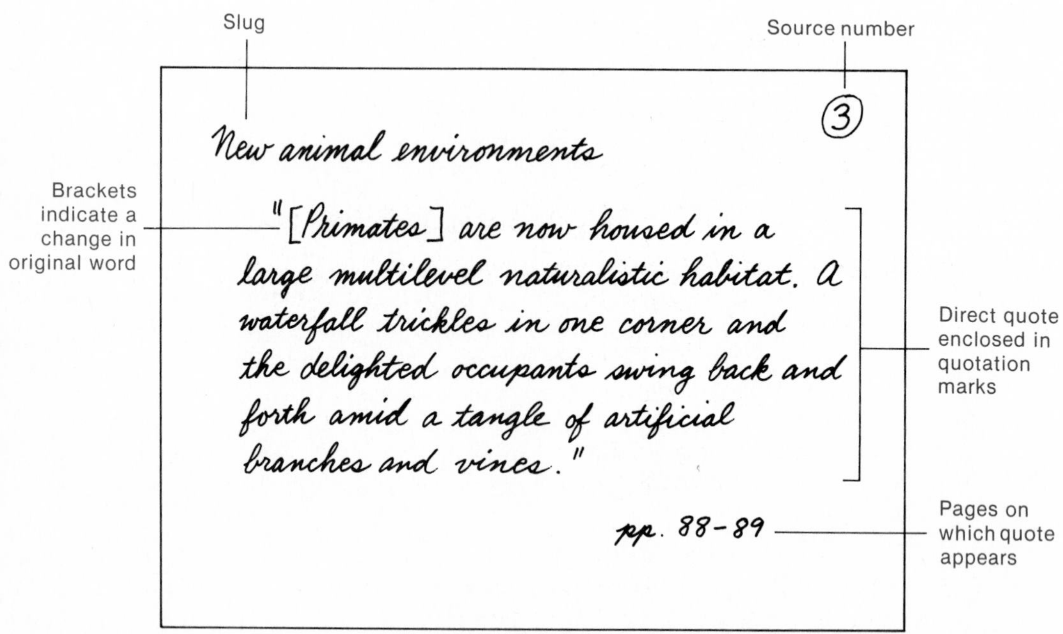

Slug
Source number
3
New animal environments
Brackets indicate a change in original word
"[Primates] are now housed in a large multilevel naturalistic habitat. A waterfall trickles in one corner and the delighted occupants swing back and forth amid a tangle of artificial branches and vines."
Direct quote enclosed in quotation marks
pp. 88-89
Pages on which quote appears

Step Five: Reevaluating Your Work Before you prepare a formal outline and begin writing your research paper, review the headings of your note cards and reevaluate both your controlling-purpose statement and preliminary outline. If you have discovered important new materials or if the purpose of your paper has changed, make revisions now. To help you reevaluate your work, consider the following questions.

1. Have you discovered new information that changes the emphasis of your paper? Should you modify your controlling purpose to reflect this new focus or add another heading to your preliminary outline?
2. Is there a topic in your outline that is not adequately treated by your note cards? Should you eliminate the topic or locate more information to develop it adequately?
3. Have you recorded information unrelated to your topic? If so, set these note cards aside; perhaps you can use this material to develop an interesting introduction or conclusion. Avoid using it where it does not fit.

Step Six: Organizing the Formal Outline

For more information on writing a thesis statement, see pages 89–90.

If you use the slugs, or topic headings, on your note cards to group related cards in stacks, writing the formal outline should not be difficult. Rearrange the cards, eliminating any that do not fit, until you have the best possible sequence for developing the controlling purpose.

Some instructors ask students to include a thesis statement at the beginning of the outline. Even if your teacher prefers an outline without a thesis statement, now is a good time to state your controlling purpose as a single declarative statement that presents the central idea of your research paper.

The *formal outline* uses Roman numerals (I, II, III), capital letters (A, B, C), and Arabic numbers (1, 2, 3) to show the relationship of major and minor ideas in the paper.

All the headings in a formal outline share a similar grammatical structure. In a *sentence outline* each point, major or minor, is stated as a complete sentence; in a *topic outline* all the headings are written as words and phrases. These two forms should not be mixed in the same outline.

The sample research paper on pages 146–150 was written from the following topic outline.

Thesis Statement: Improvements in zoo design, educational programs, and conservation efforts are characteristic of the modern zoo.

I. Zoo design
   A. Hagenbeck's influence
   B. The wild animal park
   C. Naturalistic exhibits
      1. World of birds
      2. Tropics exhibit

II. Educational programs
   A. Children's zoos
   B. Behavioral shows
   C. Other innovations

III. Conservation of endangered species
    A. The disinterest of older zoos
    B. The program of modern zoos
        1. Breeding loans
        2. Golden marmoset
        3. ISIS
    C. Problems of conservation with the Siberian tiger

The following example shows how the second division of the previous outline would look in a sentence outline.

II. The modern zoo has expanded its educational programs.
    A. Children's zoos are now commonplace.
    B. Zoos often provide behavioral shows.
    C. A variety of innovations gives visitors more information about exhibits.

Notice that there are always two or more divisions under a heading or none at all; an *A* requires at least a *B*, a *1* requires at least a *2*.

Divisions (or subheadings) are used when a broad topic is broken down into smaller topics. When the major topic cannot be subdivided into two or more parts, there is no reason for a subheading.

Writing Practice 7

Using information from your note cards, write either a formal sentence or a topic outline for your research paper. Ask your teacher if the thesis statement should be included.

Step Seven: Writing the Rough Draft

Writing the first, or rough, draft will be easier if your note cards are organized to correspond with your outline. If you discover that some notes do not fit the final organization of the paper or that you need more details to develop your topic, take time to delete or add more information.

Qualities of good exposition are discussed in the chapter "Writing Exposition."

The research paper possesses all the characteristics of a well-developed expository essay. The introduction should catch the reader's attention and introduce the central idea, or thesis statement. Each paragraph in the body of the paper should be restricted to one idea. This central idea should be adequately and clearly developed with examples, facts and statistics, the steps in a process, or some other method of paragraph development. Transition devices should be used between sentences and paragraphs to help the reader move from idea to idea and to show the relationships between these ideas. The conclusion should restate the paper's central idea in an interesting way and reveal the significance of the research.

Research papers sometimes vary in formality. A paper about local history that includes personal interviews with local residents might be written in the first person. A more formal paper based completely on library research would probably be written without reference to yourself.

Two special aspects of writing a rough draft for a research paper are incorporating quoted material and adding footnotes.

Using Quotations

Over the years researchers have developed standard methods for adding quotations to the research paper.

Long quotations, usually more than three lines of poetry or five lines of prose, are set off from the body of the paper and introduced with a short statement followed by a colon. Any of the following methods could be used to introduce a long quotation.

> In *The New Yorker* magazine the director of the Bronx Zoo commented:
>
> In *Living Trophies* Peter Batten wrote:
>
> Commenting on the development of natural habitats in zoos, Perry makes this observation:
>
> A noted critic of zoo management has stated:

Each line of a long quotation is also indented five spaces from the left-hand margin, the beginning of each paragraph being indented a total of ten spaces. If you write your paper in longhand, emphasize that you are quoting directly by making the indentation obvious and by introducing the quotation. Because this special format identifies the quotation, the quotation marks at the beginning and end of the passage are omitted.

Because *short quotations* of fewer than three lines are not indented, quotation marks are used at the beginning and end of the passage to indicate that the words are a quotation. A short quotation should not upset the smooth flow of the sentence or paragraph in which it appears. Instead, the writer should create a smooth transition between the quoted material and the rest of the sentence. Notice how this transition is achieved in the following examples of short quotations.

> Thomas Lovejoy, chairman of the Wildlife Trust International, addressed zoo directors as the Noahs of the future who must realize that "a place in tomorrow's biota, or in the ark that zoos can provide, will be by invitation only."[1]
>
> He added that it is now "necessary to decide which species zoos should undertake to breed and save and which will have to be allowed to totter or fly into the sunset of oblivion."[2]
>
> Current statistics support the accuracy of one zoo director's prediction that zoos would gradually become "producers instead of consumers of wildlife."[3]

Adding Footnotes

Footnotes tell readers the sources for important information or direct quotations used in the paper. Because these notes originally appeared at the foot of each page, they were labeled *footnotes*. Today they often appear on a separate page at the end of the paper as *endnotes*. No matter where they are located, footnotes have several important functions: (1) they give authors credit for unique facts, original theories, and words quoted exactly; (2) they provide specific details about references that allow the reader to locate the footnoted material quickly in the original source; and (3) they reassure readers that the material is not speculation or hearsay, but the result of the writer's sound research.

You may be unsure about what material to footnote. Direct quotations must always be footnoted even if the quotation is only two or three words. Information that is unique to a particular author is also footnoted even if you do not quote that information word for word. However, if a fact or idea appears so frequently that giving credit to a particular source seems impossible, a footnote is not necessary. For example, since most naturalists generally acknowledge that environments imitating natural habitats are more beneficial to wildlife breeding, that information would not be footnoted. A writer also would not footnote the date of the Endangered Species Act since that information is undisputed fact.

Although the absence of a necessary footnote can be considered plagiarism, a research paper can also include excessive footnotes. If several sentences or all the information in a paragraph is drawn from a single source, one footnote can be used at the end of the paragraph. To gain a better understanding of when footnotes are required, pay attention to their use in the books and magazines you read.

Some writers include footnotes in the rough draft, placing the information in parentheses immediately after the material to which it refers; others prefer to record footnotes on note cards or a sheet of paper. Later, these footnotes are moved to the bottom of the page or assembled at the end of the paper.

Keep the following points in mind as you write footnotes.

1. Footnoted material in the text of the paper is numbered consecutively (1, 2, 3, etc.).
2. A footnote matching the number in the text of the paper appears at the bottom of the page or at the end of the paper.
3. The *superscripts* (the slightly raised numbers after footnoted material in the text and before the footnotes) tell the reader which footnote to consult for the source of that information.
4. When footnotes appear at the bottom of the page, four lines of space separate the last line of text and the first footnote.
5. The first line of the footnote is indented five spaces.
6. Footnote numbers (superscripts) are raised by half a line.
7. One space separates the raised footnote number and the beginning of the footnote itself.
8. Information within the footnote is single spaced; the footnotes are separated from one another by a double space.
9. An abbreviated form is used for the second and all later footnotes referring to a source already footnoted.

Notice that the order and punctuation used in footnotes differ from that used in a bibliography. The following sample footnotes illustrate the MLA form for various sources of information. Your teacher may ask you to use this form or another one. The punctuation marks in these examples have been emphasized so you will become familiar with their use in footnotes. (See also the footnotes for the sample research paper on page 150.)

BOOK BY ONE AUTHOR

[1] Andrew Pennycook, *Codes and Ciphers: Amazing Ways to Scramble and Unscramble Secret Messages* (New York: David McKay Co., Inc., 1978), p. 20.

BOOK BY MORE THAN ONE AUTHOR

[2] Thomas Crerar and David King, *Choice of Words* (New York: Oxford University Press, 1969), pp. 88–91.

A WORK IN SEVERAL VOLUMES OR PARTS

[3] Vernon Parrington, *Main Currents in American Thought: The Romantic Revolution in America*, 1800–1860, Vol. II (New York: Harcourt, Brace and World, Inc., 1927), p. 41.

WORK WITHIN A COLLECTION OF PIECES BY DIFFERENT AUTHORS

[4] Eudora Welty, "A Worn Path," in *By and About Women: An Anthology of Short Fiction*, ed. Beth Kline Schneiderman (New York: Harcourt Brace Jovanovich, Inc., 1973), p. 319.

ARTICLE FROM A CRITICAL EDITION OR CASEBOOK

[5] Kingsley Widmer, "Black Existentialism: Richard Wright," in *Modern Black Novelists: A Collection of Critical Essays*, ed. M. G. Cooke (Englewood Cliffs, N.J.: Prentice-Hall, Inc., 1971), pp. 84–86.

EDITION OF A WORK OF LITERATURE

[6] Edith Wharton, *The House of Mirth*, introd. Irving Howe (New York: Holt, Rinehart, and Winston, Inc., 1962), p. 201.

ARTICLE IN ENCYCLOPEDIA OR OTHER REFERENCE WORK (NO AUTHOR GIVEN)

[7] "Wright, Frank Lloyd," *Encyclopaedia Britannica: Macropaedia*, 1979 ed. (Articles in references arranged alphabetically need not be identified by volume and page.)

ARTICLE IN ENCYCLOPEDIA OR OTHER REFERENCE WORK

[8] Martin E. Marty. "Resurgent Fundamentalism," *Encyclopaedia Britannica: 1980 Book of the Year*, pp. 606–7.

ARTICLE FROM A MONTHLY MAGAZINE

[9] Emily Hahn, "Eleventh Hour," *The New Yorker*, 1 Sept. 1980, p. 38.

ARTICLE FROM A NEWSPAPER (NO AUTHOR GIVEN)

[10] "Minimum Wage to Rise Again," *Decatur Herald*, 10 Oct. 1979, Sec. 1, p. 2, cols. 3–4.

ARTICLE FROM A NEWSPAPER

[11] "Michelle Stevens, "Home or Hospital Birth? Center Offers Alternative," Chicago *Sun–Times*, 2 March 1981, p. 7, cols. 1–2.

REVIEW OF FILM, BOOK, OR PLAY

[12] Vivien Raynor, "Picasso, of Course, Is Everywhere," *The Shock of the New*, by Robert Hughes, *The New York Times Book Review*, 15 Feb. 1981, p. 3.

A SOURCE NOT IN PRINT FORMAT

[13] Personal interview with Thomas J. Brennan, 28 Feb. 1981.

[14] Robert Frost, "Stopping by Woods on a Snowy Evening," *Robert Frost Reads His Poetry*, Caedmon, XC 783, 1952. (Recording)

A PAMPHLET

[15] Modern Language Association of America, *MLA Handbook*, 2nd ed. (New York): MLA, 1970, p. 13.

[16] U.S. Bureau of Labor Statistics, *Productivity* (Washington, D.C.: GPO 1958), p. 10.

There is no need to repeat the complete information about a source in later footnotes referring to it. Instead, provide complete information in the first reference and use an abbreviated form (the author's last name and the page number) in all other footnotes referring to that work. If your footnotes include two or more books written by the same author, add an abbreviated form of the title after the author's last name. The following example shows how this abbreviated form looks.

[1]Emily Hahn, *Animal Gardens* (New York: Doubleday and Co., Inc., 1967), p. 40.

[2]Bernard Livingston, *Zoo: Animal, People, Places* (New York: Arbor House Publishing Co., 1974), p. 235.

[3]Livingston, p. 235.

[4]Emily Hahn, "Eleventh Hour," *The New Yorker*, 1 Sept. 1980, p. 38.

[5]Hahn, "Eleventh," p. 39.

Writing Practice 8

The following list contains all the information needed to number and write the footnotes for a short research paper. On a separate sheet of paper, write the footnotes in the following order. Use the MLA form found on pages 141–143 or the form recommended by your teacher.

1. Reference to page 117 of *The Americans: The National Experience*, published in New York in 1965 by Vintage Books. Daniel Boorstin is the author.
2. A reference to page 401 of *Illinois: A History of the Prairie State* by Robert P. Howard. Published by William C. Eerdsmans Publishing Co., of Grand Rapids, Michigan in 1972.
3. A reference to Paul M. Angle's *Bloody Williamson: A Chapter in American Lawlessness*, a 1952 publication of Alfred Knopf, Inc., of New York. The reference is to page 81.
4. A second reference to Howard's book. Reference is to page 400.
5. A reference to *Prairie State: Impressions of Illinois, 1673–1967, by Travelers and Other Observers*, published by the University of Chicago Press, located in Chicago, in 1968. The reference is to page 333. The book's editor is Paul Angle.
6. A second reference to *Prairie State: Impressions of Illinois, 1673–1967, by Travelers and Other Observers*. The reference is to pages 370–71.
7. A reference to page 14 of an anonymous article appearing in the January 16, 1975, issue of the magazine *Senior Scholastic*. The article's title is "How Good Were the Good Old Days? Chicago in 1874."
8. A reference to page 75 of the article "Prairie Cattle Kings of Yesterday" by George Ade in the July 4, 1931, *Saturday Evening Post*.
9. A reference to Richard Sennett's book *Families Against the City: Middle Class Homes of Industrial Chicago, 1872–1900*, published in 1970 in New York by Vintage Books. The reference is to page 141.
10. A second reference to Sennett's book. Reference is to page 140.

Writing Practice 9

With the aid of your note cards and formal outline, write the rough draft of your research paper. Remember to add footnotes where they are needed and to insert quotations correctly.

Step Eight: Writing the Final Bibliography

The *final bibliography* includes only those sources you used in gathering information for your research paper.

After checking the information on your bibliography cards for accuracy, arrange them alphabetically by the author's last name. If no author is listed for a source, alphabetize it by the first major word in the title. In very lengthy bibliographies, sources are also subdivided by types: books, articles, films, pamphlets, each alphabetized under a separate heading.

Write the bibliography on a separate sheet of paper under the heading *Bibliography*. If an entry requires more than one line, indent the second and all other lines five spaces. If two sources were written by the same author, the author's name is not repeated in the second listing; a long dash is used instead for all other sources by that author. The following example shows how two works by Emily Hahn would be listed in a bibliography.

Hahn, Emily. *Animal Gardens*. New York: Doubleday and Co., Inc., 1967.

———. "Eleventh Hour." *The New Yorker*, 1 Sept. 1980, pp. 37–69.

Look closely at the sample bibliography on page 150. Notice that the listings for magazine and newspaper articles include the page numbers on which the article can be found, but that no page numbers are listed for books. This bibliography conforms to the MLA style, although your teacher may prefer that you use another accepted style.

Step Nine: Writing the Final Draft

Carefully revise your rough draft before you begin the final draft, reading through it several times to determine the effectiveness of your organization and wording. Are you satisfied with each paragraph's organization and development? If you find details in a paragraph that do not relate to the central idea or paragraphs that do not relate to the thesis of the paper, remove or change them. Since research papers often involve technical words and concepts, be sure that unfamiliar words or ideas are clearly explained. Finally, consider elements of style: Is there any unnecessary repetition? Are there spots where wording could be more precise?

Use the revision checklist on page 146 as a guide in revising your research paper.

Notice the improvement that results with the revisions in the following paragraph from a research paper on the modern zoo.

The change in wording creates a better transition between text and quotation.

Current statistics support the accuracy of one zoo director's prediction ~~when he said "I believe zoos are gradually becoming~~ that zoos would gradually become producers instead of consumers of wildlife." In 1979 the National Zoo alone had over 450 specimens involved in breeding loans. In 1969, ~~there were~~ when only 250 golden marmosets ~~existing~~ existed in Brazil, ~~which is~~ their native habitat/, ~~In 1969~~ the National Zoo began a breeding

This information is unrelated to the paragraph's main idea.

Combining these sentences eliminates a series of short, choppy sentences.

Word choice is improved.

program with four of these animals. ~~Marmosets are delicate creatures and acquire colds, measles, and other viruses easily. As a result, the zoo keeps marmosets isolated from visitors. The zoo also had trouble deciding on an appropriate diet for these animals; when protein was added to their diet, reproduction increased.~~ By 1978 the zoo had recorded the births of one hundred new marmosets. Some species, most notably the Père David's deer, Prezewolski's horse, and the wisent, are extinct in their native habitat. They exist only in zoos, where ~~Zoos'~~ careful conservation programs have saved them. Breeding programs are now so extensive ~~big~~ that American zoos have created a computerized inventory cataloging system called ISIS (International Species Inventory). This program, almost a computerized dating system for animals, provides detailed information about specific animals and helps zoo directors avoid the problem of inbreeding that can occur when a species dwindles to a small number.

Writing Practice 10

On a separate sheet of paper, organize and write the following sources as a final bibliography. Refer to the information on pages 128–131 for extra help.

1. A book by Paul Angle entitled *Bloody Williamson: A Chapter in American Lawlessness.* This work was published in New York by Alfred A. Knopf, Inc., in 1952.
2. A work published by William C. Eerdsmans of Grand Rapids, Michigan in 1952. The book is *Illinois: A History of the Prairie State* by Robert P. Howard.
3. A work called *Prairie State: Impressions of Illinois, 1673–1967, by Travelers and Other Observers.* Paul M. Angle edited the book, which was published by the University of Chicago Press in Chicago in 1968.
4. An anonymous article in *Senior Scholastic* titled "How Good Were the Good Old Days? Chicago in 1874." The article appeared on pages 14–15 in the January 16, 1975, edition of the magazine.
5. An article called "Where Gangsters Fell—Then and Now" on pages 42–46 of the *Chicago Tribune,* Sec. 9, Col. 1, for February 11, 1979. The article was written by W. K. Murray.

Writing Practice 11

Using the Checklist for Revising the Research Report that follows and any suggestions your teacher may add, revise your rough draft and write a final version of your research report. Remember that revision is not a patchwork process. When they read the final draft, readers should not be aware of your changes. As a final step, proofread your paper, using the proofreading checklist on page 14.

As a further aid, use the checklist for revising expository compositions on page 101.

Checklist for Revising the Research Report

1. The subject is limited to a topic that can be developed in a research paper.
2. The topic is adequately developed with factual information from outside sources.
3. Each item of information in the final paper explains or develops the topic in some way.
4. Important theories, unusual or specific facts, and quotations are footnoted.
5. Information in footnotes is ordered correctly, and footnotes follow a standard form, such as MLA.
6. Information in the bibliography is ordered correctly according to a standard form.
7. If quotations are used, they are placed correctly in the paper.

Reading a Research Report

The New Zoo

The gray cement floor of the small cage is littered with straw. Except for a metal door at the rear and a drain in the center of the floor, the enclosure is an unbroken expanse of tiled walls and metal bars. At one end flies buzz around a heap of wilted lettuce while a small African sand cat hunches listlessly beside a pool of stagnant water. Attached to the black bars at the front of the cage, a small sign announces that in the wild this predator roams a large range—from topical rain forests to cold, mountainous regions.

Incorporate short quotations smoothly in text.

Such living spaces, termed "scruffy, little animal slums"[1] by at least one zoo director, are being replaced with more spacious, aesthetic environments at many zoos. At one American zoo the African sand cat has found a new home with similar predators from Africa and Asia in a naturalistic environment. In a simulated desert cave, dim overhead lights cast a red glow that allows visitors to observe the predators' nighttime behavior. In the first exhibit two African sand cats move back and forth across the desert vegetation, rocks, and sand. No bars, metal doors, or cement floors mar the impression that these cats are part of a natural scene. In fact, the cats find their new quarters so realistic that they have produced four litters since the exhibit opened two years ago.

Indent the first word of each paragraph five spaces.

This award-winning Predator Ecology Exhibit, housed at the Brookfield Zoo near Chicago, is only one example of the sweeping changes in design, educational programs, and animal conservation that characterize the modern zoo.

Introduce long quotations.

Much of the improvement in zoo design grew from the thinking of one man, Carl Hagenbeck. Hagenbeck defined his goal as follows:

> I desired, above all things to give the animals the maximum of liberty. I wished to exhibit them not as captives, confined to narrow spaces, and looked at between bars, but as free to wander from place to place within as large limits as possible, and with no bars to obstruct the view and serve as a reminder of captivity. . . . I wished my new park to be a great and enduring example of the benefits that can be wrought by giving the animals as much freedom and placing them in as natural an environment as possible.[2]

Ellipsis indicates that material has been omitted from the quotation.

Although Hagenbeck introduced the zoological park concept at the Stellingen Zoo outside Hamburg in 1907, the trend toward naturalistic exhibits developed slowly, accelerating only in the past two decades as zoo directors noted the popularity of commercial safari or wildlife parks.

As they renovate and update their buildings, older zoos with limited space are employing Hagenbeck's philosophy to create more naturalistic living areas within the zoo's existing structure. The World of Birds at the hundred-year-old Bronx Zoo is an outstanding example of such an approach. The forty-story structure, built in curves and spirals, displays exotic bird species in lush, open-fronted environments that skillfully simulate natural habitats as diverse as African jungle, swamplands, arid desert, and rain forest. In such a setting visitors learn not only what the birds look like but also how they behave. Because the birds prefer the higher light level and vegetation of the exhibit area to the deliberately dark, barren visitors' corridors, few barriers are needed throughout the building.[3]

In 1981 Brookfield Zoo, another older institution, located outside Chicago, opened one of the world's largest indoor naturalistic exhibits. The Tropics Exhibit, housed in a huge structure resembling several sports stadiums placed end to end, contains three separate zoogeographic environments: Asian, African, and South American. Visitors can observe gorillas, pygmy hippos, small chimps, brightly colored birds, reptiles, and amphibians mingling in tropical settings complete with waterfalls, rocky cliffs, and natural plantings. During a tour of the exhibit, Tom Brennan, a zoo official, explained the careful detail and planning that enhances the realism. A bridge through the center of the African section allows visitors a better view of the hippos in the pond below. Barriers of rock separate gorillas from other species they might harm, but a special path under a waterfall allows the more adventurous visitor a closer look at these creatures. Since chimps are unfailingly attracted to spices, small caches of these treats are located high in the tops of trees to ensure that the animals will spend time at that level—just across from the visitors' ramp.[4]

Raise footnote number by half a line.

Exhibits at smaller zoos have taken another direction—toward specialization. In the past small zoos often had what some zoo experts call "postage stamp collections"[5]—isolated and unrelated specimens of animal species from around the world. Today many small zoos are, instead, developing exceptional displays of animals of one kind or animals from a particular region. The Wildfowl Trust in England, for example, displays 125 of the world's 147 varieties of waterfowl, but that is all it displays.[6] One of the most imaginative zoos with a specialized collection, the Arizona-Sonora Desert Museum, exhibits only those animals native to the regions of New Mexico, Arizona, and California that make up the Sonora Desert.

Innovations in zoo educational programs already provide a richer experience for zoo visitors. Noting that crowds always gather when keepers work with the animals, zoos have incorporated these interactions as part of their regular program.

Children's zoos, where young visitors can pet small animals or learn about diet and behavior as keepers feed baby animals, are now commonplace. Keepers often must train large aquatic animals, such as dolphins, porpoises, or sea lions, to obey commands so that they can receive medical attention or pools can be cleaned. Some zoos now present these training sessions as daily public shows, adding activities that allow visitors to observe the animals' natural behavior, such as the sea lion's ability to locate an object by underwater vibrations.[7]

Although printed signs still exist throughout the zoo, today they are more interesting and instructive. A large graphic information board, for example, might explain what messages baboons communicate through raised eyebrows, hand slapping, or facial grimaces. Other innovations include talking labels or audio tours on portable recorders, multiple-choice, push-button labels that test the visitor's understanding of the exhibit, and questionnaires prepared as zoo "treasure hunts."[8] In the future, zoos may even provide micro-sound recordings that will allow visitors to hear the wings of a hummingbird or the "heartbeat" of an insect.

Perhaps the most dramatic difference between zoos of the past and those of today is the modern zoo's extensive effort to conserve and protect endangered species. Earlier zoos replenished and expanded their stock by animal-collecting expeditions to the far corners of the world and made little effort to breed new animals within the confines of the zoo. As one expert explains:

Skip three lines between text and long quotation.

> Male and female animals usually lived in separate cages. Offspring from mated animals gladdened zoo officials' hearts but a captive breeding program was considered unnecessary as it was thought the wild would always offer new specimens.[9]

Skip three lines between quotations and text.

Unfortunately, the number of animals existing in the wild has steadily declined, and many species are now threatened with extinction. By 1975 the International Union for Conservation of Nature and Natural Resources listed 1,000 threatened species—over 100 of those were native to the United States. Legal hunting, illicit poaching, the pet trade, and pesticides are in part responsible, but the greatest threat comes from the ever-increasing use of natural habitat for industrial and agricultural purposes. Approximately 100,000 acres of wild habitat are destroyed by humans every day.[10]

Emily Hahn, the noted animal expert, believes that as late as the mid-sixties zoo directors were still somewhat selfishly concerned with expanding their own collections and, therefore, were unwilling to further the breeding of rare species by involving one of their own animals. Then, she adds:

Indent paragraph of long quotation ten spaces from left-hand margin.

Indent each succeeding line of long quotation five spaces.

> The changes came swiftly. Today, rare captive animals are shipped back and forth between even the most widely separated zoos in the hope that the rarities will produce offspring. For example, a female mountain gorilla from Tel Aviv was flown to Oklahoma City on permanent breeding loan just in case she might be able to stir up the libido of Oklahoma's obese male, M'Kubwa. Nothing came of it, but both zoos deserve praise for trying.[11]

Current statistics support the accuracy of one zoo director's prediction that zoos would gradually become "producers instead of consumers of wildlife."[12] In 1979 the National Zoo alone had over 450 specimens involved in breeding loans. In 1969 when only 250 golden marmosets existed in Brazil, their native habitat, the National Zoo began a breeding program with four of these animals. By 1978 the zoo had recorded the births of one hundred new marmosets.[13] Some species, most notably Père David's deer, Prezewolski's horse, and the wisent, are extinct in their native habitats and exist only in zoos where careful conservation programs have saved them. Breeding programs are now so extensive that American zoos have created a computerized inventory cataloging system called ISIS (International Species Inventory). This program, almost a computerized dating system for animals, provides detailed information about specific animals and helps zoo directors avoid the problems of inbreeding that can occur when a species dwindles to a small number.[14]

Zoos' conservation efforts are often hampered by lack of space and funds to care for the increasing populations of endangered species. The problems of maintaining species in captivity can be understood by looking at a single species—the Siberian tiger. This beautiful cat, the world's largest, is an endangered species but has been bred so successfully in zoos that the captive population of 750 animals now exceeds the population in the wild. However, one zoo expert estimates that over $1 million is spent every year just to feed these animals and $2½ million when veterinary care, heat, light, and other expenses are added. At that rate maintaining this endangered population until the year 2000 will require almost $50 million dollars.[15]

One solution is to return animals to the wild, as zoos are doing whenever possible. Rare Hawaiian geese bred in captivity have been returned to the island of Maui; the scimitar-horned oryx has been reestablished in the Middle East; and a French zoo outside Paris now exports lion cubs back to a game reserve in Africa. However, William Conway estimates that returning 750 Siberian tigers to the wild would require an area four times the size of Yellowstone National Park.[16] Also, reintroducing animals to the wild is not an easy or inexpensive process. Hand-rearing and training a captive cat to hunt is a time-consuming, sometimes unsuccessful process. One wildlife expert calculates that reintroducing ten tigers to the wild could take over five years and cost half a million dollars.[17]

Unfortunately, these problems have forced another new role on the modern zoo—one not relished or welcomed by zoo officials. At the 1980 World Conference on Endangered Species in Captivity, Thomas Lovejoy, chairman of the Wildlife Trust International, addressed zoo directors as the Noahs of the future who must realize that "a place in tomorrow's biota, or in the ark that zoos can provide will be by invitation only." He added that it is now "necessary to decide which species zoos should undertake to breed and save and which will have to be allowed to totter or fly into the sunset of extinction."[18]

While modern zoos will display animals in improved naturalistic exhibits, educate the public more effectively, and conserve species whenever possible through captive breeding, they will not save all the world's animals. Sadly, that African sand cat sleeping listlessly in the barren cage of yesterday's zoo may have no place at all in tomorrow's zoo. If tomorrow's children know him at all, it may be only as a stuffed artifact, a fossil of the earth's richer past, housed behind glass.

Footnotes

[1]Desmond Morris, as quoted in Barbara Ford, "Creature Comforts at the Zoo," *Saturday Review*, 5 Aug. 1972, p. 48.

[2]Bernard Livingston, *Zoo: Animals, People, Places* (New York: Arbor House, 1967), p. 148.

[3]Livingston, pp. 272–73.

[4]Personal interview with Thomas J. Brennan, Curator of Education and Coordinator of Information for Brookfield Zoo, 9 March 1981.

[5]Livingston, p. 235.

[6]Roger Caras, "Zoos of the Future," *Wildlife International*, Feb. 1975, p. 17.

[7]Alfred, Meyer, ed., *A Zoo for All Seasons: The Smithsonian Animal World* (Washington, D.C.: Smithsonian Exposition Books, 1979), p. 66.

[8]William G. Conway, *Zoo Education: Recent Interpretations*. Report for First Conference of New York State Zoological Parks and Aquariums, Nov. 1974 (New York: New York State Council on the Arts, 1974), p. 6.

[9]Meyer, p. 35.

[10]"Wildlife in Danger," *Newsweek*, 6 Jan. 1975, p. 36.

[11]Emily Hahn, "Eleventh Hour," *The New Yorker*, 1 Sept. 1980, p. 37.

[12]Livingston, p. 187.

[13]Meyer, p. 111.

[14]Personal interview with Thomas J. Brennan.

[15]Hahn, p. 69.

[16]Hahn, p. 68.

[17]Meyer, p. 125.

[18]Lovejoy as quoted in Hahn, p. 64.

Bibliography

Brennan, Thomas J., Curator of Education and Coordinator of Information for Brookfield Zoo. Personal Interview. 9 March 1981.

Caras, Roger. "Zoos of the Future." *Wildlife International*, Feb. 1975, pp. 12–17.

Conway, William G. *Zoo Education: Recent Interpretations*. Report for First Conference of New York State Zoological Parks and Aquariums. Nov. 1974. New York: New York State Council on the Arts, 1974.

Ford, Barbara. "Creature Comforts at the Zoo." *Saturday Review*, 5 Aug. 1972, pp. 41–48.

Hahn, Emily. "Eleventh Hour." *The New Yorker*, 1 Sept. 1980, pp. 37–69.

Livingston, Bernard. *Zoo: Animals, People, Places*. New York: Arbor House, 1967.

Meyer, Alfred, ed. *A Zoo for All Seasons: The Smithsonian Animal World*. Washington, D.C.: Smithsonian Exposition Books, 1979.

Perry, John. *The World's Zoo*. New York: Dodd, Mead, and Company, 1969.

"Wildlife in Danger." *Newsweek*, 6 Jan. 1975, pp. 36–41.

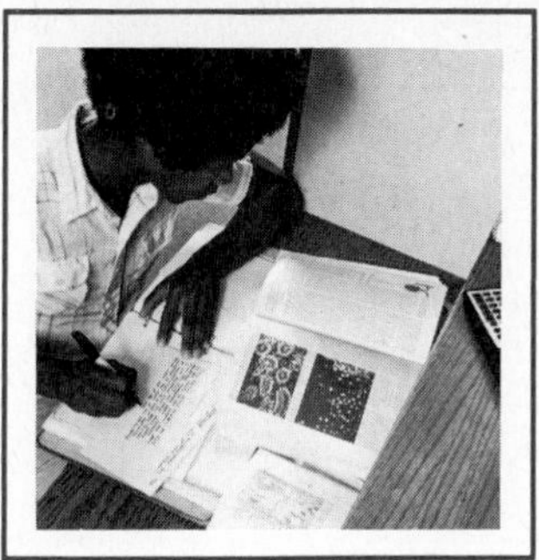

7 Logic and Writing

Uses of Logic

Logic means "clear and orderly thought."

In everyday conversation the word *logical* is used to refer to something that makes sense or seems reasonable. Actually, logic is an ancient science, a branch of philosophy. Writing on the laws and principles of how to think logically dates back to the Greek philosopher Aristotle, who lived almost 2,500 years ago. If you go to college and major in science, philosophy, math, or pre-law, you will probably take a logic course before you graduate. The purpose of the course is to train you in ways of thinking clearly. The purpose of this chapter is the same.

The ability to reach sound conclusions and to evaluate arguments is a skill that you will use in discussing ideas with friends and teachers, in thinking about problems and solutions, and in making decisions. In writing, logic is necessary to support an argument in any kind of persuasion, in answering an essay question, and in supplying evidence to support an opinion. Suppose, for example, that in an essay test in history, you are asked to refute or support the following statements.[1]

> If the American Revolution had produced nothing but the Declaration of Independence, it would have been worthwhile. The bill of wrongs against George III and Parliament, naturally, is exaggerated. Facts will not sustain many of the alleged "injuries and usurpations." But the beauty and cogency of the preamble, reaching back to the remotest antiquity and forward to an indefinite future, have lifted the hearts of millions of men and will continue to do so. . . .

[1]From *Oxford History of the American People* by Samuel Eliot Morison. Copyright © 1965 by Samuel Eliot Morison. Reprinted by permission of Curtis Brown, Ltd.

Based on your knowledge, experience, and reading, do you think that these statements are true or false? When you write the answer to the question, you will have to decide how best to support your position. What evidence or reasons are the strongest? How will you organize your answer? You should aim to present a tightly knit, strong argument that your reader will find both logical and convincing.

Deductive Reasoning

Experts in logic usually talk about two kinds of logical thought: deductive and inductive reasoning. The word *deductive* comes from Latin and means "leading down."

Deductive reasoning begins with a general statement, adds a related statement, and ends with a conclusion that is necessarily drawn from the two statements.

The three-statement argument in deductive reasoning is called a *syllogism.*

Major Premise:	All seniors at Shaw High School must take a course in government.
Minor Premise:	Floyd Kregenow is a senior at Shaw High School.
Conclusion:	Floyd Kregenow must take a course in government.

In a deductive argument the statements move from the general *(all seniors at Shaw High School)* to the specific *(Floyd Kregenow).* You can see that if the first two statements in the syllogism are true, the conclusion must necessarily be true.

Truth and Validity

A syllogism may look like a perfectly good argument, and yet the conclusion may be false. In order for the conclusion to be true, both of the following requirements must be met.

1. The major premise and the minor premise must both be true.
2. The argument must be valid—that is, the argument must follow the rules of logic.

Consider the following syllogism.

Major Premise:	All red flowers are roses.
Minor Premise:	This geranium is red.
Conclusion:	This geranium is a rose.

You can see immediately that the major premise of the preceding syllogism is false: it is *not* true that all red flowers are roses. Therefore, the conclusion drawn from the premises is necessarily false. You cannot arrive at a true conclusion when one or both of the premises are false. Even though the conclusion in this argument is false, the argument itself is said to be valid; that is, it follows the rules of logical reasoning. An argument may be valid, as in the red-geranium syllogism, yet result in a false conclusion if one of the premises is false.

In the following syllogism, is the conclusion true or false? Can you tell why?

All members of the Supreme Court are appointed by the President.
Greta Garbo is a member of the Supreme Court.
Greta Garbo was appointed to the Supreme Court by the President.

Someone living in another country or a thousand years from now might not be able to tell as easily as you that the conclusion is false because the second premise is false. Greta Garbo is a movie star, not a Supreme Court judge.

The second requirement for a sound deductive argument is that the argument must follow the laws of logic. First, no conclusion can be drawn unless the major premise states a universal. This means that the major premise must state (or imply) the words *all*, *every*, *no*, or *none*. The statement made in the major premise must be true of every person or thing that is being discussed. The following are some examples of premises that make universal statements.

All suns are stars.
No mammals have gills.
All insects have six legs.

In deductive reasoning a statement that contains a limiting word (such as *many*, *some*, *several*, *few*, *usually*, or *sometimes*) cannot lead to a valid conclusion. For example, the following non-universal statements cannot be used as either a major or minor premise in a syllogism.

Most commercial breads contain preservatives.
Some spiders have four eyes.
Professional musicians usually play more than one instrument.
Many Kiowa live in California.

The following syllogism has a non-universal major premise.

Premise: Most freshmen take four courses.
Premise: Julie Sizuki is a freshman.
Conclusion: ?

Both of the premises in the preceding syllogism are true, yet no valid conclusion is possible because the major premise contains the limiting word *most*. You do not know whether Julie Sizuki is one of the "most freshmen" who are taking four courses or one of the other freshmen who are taking three or five courses.

A second principle of deductive reasoning is violated in the following syllogism. Can you tell why the conclusion is not valid?

Premise:	All members of the Key Club visited the Northeast Nursing Home on Saturday morning.
Premise:	Jeffrey Ruiz visited the Northeast Nursing Home on Saturday morning.
Conclusion:	Jeffrey Ruiz is a member of the Key Club.

Jeffrey Ruiz may have visited the nursing home for any number of reasons. Perhaps a friend or relative is a patient there, or perhaps he had decided to volunteer some time to visiting patients in the nursing home. The fact that Jeffrey's visit coincided with that of the Key Club does not necessarily mean that he is a member of that club. This syllogism is not valid because the conclusion does not necessarily follow from the two premises.

In the following syllogism, is the conclusion valid or not? Why?

Premise:	All sixteen-year-olds who pass a written test can obtain a learner's permit from the Motor Vehicle Bureau.
Premise:	Katrina Radd has just gotten a learner's permit.
Conclusion:	Katrina Radd is sixteen.

Just because Katrina has a learner's permit does not mean that she is sixteen. Katrina Radd could be twenty-seven or sixty-seven and just learning how to drive. The syllogism is not valid because the conclusion cannot be logically and necessarily drawn from the premises. In fact, no conclusion is possible from the premises as stated.

Consider the following syllogism.

Premise:	All sixteen-year-olds are eligible to obtain a learner's permit from the Motor Vehicle Bureau.
Premise:	Katrina Radd is sixteen.
Conclusion:	Katrina Radd is eligible to obtain a learner's permit from the Motor Vehicle Bureau.

The preceding argument is valid because the conclusion must necessarily be true if the first two premises are true.

Exercise 1

Write the logically valid conclusion that can be drawn from each of the following sets of premises. Then decide whether the conclusion is true or false. If the conclusion is false, examine the premises to see whether one or both of the premises are false.

1. Premise: All horses can fly.
   Premise: Pegasus is a horse.
2. Premise: People who pilot airplanes must have a pilot's license.
   Premise: Janice pilots an airplane.
3. Premise: All water is made up of two molecules of hydrogen and one molecule of oxygen.
   Premise: Ice is water in its frozen, or solid, state.

4. Premise: All apples contain seeds.
   Premise: This is a Granny Smith apple.
5. Premise: All children can walk and talk before they are a year old.
   Premise: Sarah Jane is a year old.

Exercise 2

Write the conclusion that follows from the two premises of each of the following sets. Then tell whether the argument is valid and the conclusion is true. If no conclusion is possible, tell why.

1. Premise: All violins have four strings.
   Premise: This instrument is a violin.
2. Premise: A person who serves as President of the United States must have been born in the United States.
   Premise: Franklin D. Roosevelt was the thirty-first President of the United States.
3. Premise: Applications to the University of Cincinnati must be received by February 1.
   Premise: Jeanette Valentino is applying to Kenyon College.
4. Premise: In order to register to vote, a person must be eighteen and must have lived in an election district for six months.
   Premise: Juan Rivera has just registered to vote.
5. Premise: According to the Surgeon General, smoking is detrimental to your health.
   Premise: Katie smokes a pack of cigarettes a day.
6. Premise: All tuna are related to the mackerel family.
   Premise: The albacore is a type of tuna.
7. Premise: Many of the counselors at Hi-Y Camp have attended the camp as campers.
   Premise: Ron Chin is a counselor at the Hi-Y Camp.
8. Premise: All frogs are animals.
   Premise: All fish are animals.
9. Premise: Few people who live in this neighborhood have children.
   Premise: Mr. and Mrs. Cerrailla live in this neighborhood.
10. Premise: Since 1964 no quarter contains all silver.
    Premise: This quarter was minted in 1958.

Evaluating a Deductive Argument

Whenever you read, write, or listen to an argument, you should question whether the argument is valid and the conclusion is true. A long argument, as in a speech or an essay, usually does not have the neat three-step makeup of the syllogisms you have been studying. It may list several reasons to support the conclusion and may contain a lot of padding. Some of the premises may not even be directly expressed; the writer or speaker may simply make assumptions that the reader or listener will have to identify. In evaluating a deductive argument, always try to pare the argument down to its barest bones by asking questions such as the following ones:

1. What is the conclusion of the argument?
2. Does the argument contain a universal statement? If so, what is it?
3. What reasons are given to support the conclusion?
4. Are all of the reasons true? How can I find out whether or not they are true? (If the reasons are factual, check the facts in reference books. Your librarian can help you to locate books that will tell you whether the statements are true or not. If the reasons are opinions, decide on the basis of your experiences and what you have read and heard from others whether you think the opinions are true or not. Talk over the opinions with friends, relatives, and teachers to see what they think of them.)
5. What, if any, assumptions are made but not stated directly?
6. Does the conclusion necessarily follow from the premises? That is, does the argument follow the laws of logical reasoning?
7. Does the argument contain any fallacies? (See pages 162–167 for a discussion of fallacies.)

Exercise 3

Use the list of questions above to evaluate the following arguments.

1.

You know, I just don't understand why anyone would want to run for the office of County Commissioner. I really think that all politicians must be ego-maniacs: they like to be in the spotlight and to have power. Why would anyone work practically full time as a County Commissioner and have a lot of aggravation and get paid only $10,000 a year? Commissioners have to work a lot of evenings and weekends, too. A lot of politicians are rich and don't need to earn any money. But take, for example, a candidate who is not rich and has no big income, like Peter Bendix. Bendix is running for his third term as Commissioner, so he knows all about the hard work and little pay. I guess that Bendix is just as power-hungry and fame-hungry as the rest of the politicians.

2.

The newsroom of the *Daily Planet* has just received an anonymous letter saying that Joan Xavier, the city's mayor, has been seeing a psychotherapist for the past six months. The letter contains a photograph of the mayor leaving the therapist's office and a detailed log of her visits. Lew Ryan, the city editor, tosses the letter and photograph into the wastebasket and decides not to print the story. "Every individual has a right to privacy, even public officials," he says, "and whether or not someone is seeing a therapist is strictly a personal matter."

3.

Besides the money they must spend on tuition, room, and board, all college students need extra money for books, entertainment, clothing, extra food, transportation, and sundries. Most students have to live within a strict budget, and many work part-time to try to earn as much as they can during the summer. Gina Lombard and George Washburn and many of their friends at Great Western College have been unable to find part-time jobs and really need the extra money they would like to earn. The college should have a placement bureau that will help students like Gina and George find part-time work.

4.

"I'm going to die someday anyway," says Cheryl. She has been smoking a pack of cigarettes a day since she was fifteen. "So what," she says of the Surgeon General's warning on the cigarette package. "They say that everything we eat and drink causes cancer."

5.

Everyone can use all the help and training he or she can get on how to cope with life's problems. *Psychology* is the study of human beings from the viewpoint of child development, personality theory, learning theory, and abnormal behavior. *Anthropology* is the study of groups of people and their different cultures. Jefferson High has excellent courses in psychology and anthropology, but they are electives, and few people get the benefits of these courses. I think that these courses help students become better parents and have more respect for themselves and for others. I think that psychology and anthropology should be required courses so that everyone graduating from Jefferson has a better idea of what it means to be human and how there are different ways of solving life's problems.

Exercise 4

Use your powers of deductive reasoning to solve the following logic problem.

1. Jim, Perry, Wendy, and Terri all went to different colleges: the University of Michigan, Vanderbilt University, New York University, and Georgia Tech. Who went where?
   a. Perry's roommate was Fred.
   b. Wendy and Jim wrote letters often while Perry and Terri used the phone and never wrote letters.
   c. Jim didn't go to New York University.
   d. Wendy and Terri used to be roommates until Terri transferred to her new school.
   e. Terri called her friend at New York University, but he wasn't home, and Terri got a date with his roommate.
   f. Terri's old school wasn't Vanderbilt or the University of Michigan.
   g. Jim wrote a letter to his friend at the University of Michigan but never got an answer from her.

Inductive Reasoning

In *inductive reasoning* a general conclusion is reached at the end of a process in which a whole series of facts or evidence is gathered and weighed.

In effect, inductive reasoning begins at the opposite end from deductive reasoning.

DEDUCTIVE REASONING	INDUCTIVE REASONING
Generalization	Specific fact
+	+
Related fact	Specific fact
↓	+
Conclusion (specific instance)	Specific fact
	+
	Many more specific facts
	↓
	Generalization

Assume, for example, that Jenny Gagarin was trying to decide how cacti are different from other kinds of plants. Jenny visited several florist shops and plant nurseries and made the following observations.

Evidence: The ball cactus has spines.
The prickly pear cactus has spines.
The Indian fig cactus has spines.
The crown of thorns cactus has spines.
The tuna cactus has spines.

On the basis of what she saw, Jenny made the following generalization: "All cacti have spines." This is an example of inductive reasoning. The argument begins with a series of specific facts and moves to a general conclusion. In this example, the evidence is a series of personal observations. Evidence may also be made up of facts gathered from books or statements made by experts in a particular field. Often an inductive argument contains a mixture of personal observations, published statistics, and opinions of authorities. In the case of the cactus argument, the conclusion is unfortunately a false one. Jenny may have visited two florist shops and three nurseries, but she should also have checked a reference book because not all cacti have spines. In the following section you will learn how Jenny went wrong.

Defining Terms

In inductive reasoning, the word *population* is used to refer to the group or class of things that is being studied.

Jenny's population is "all cacti." Anything in the world—from seventeenth-century English poetry to white dwarf stars to Americans living in Tokyo today—may be the population (or subject under study) in an inductive argument.

The conclusion in an inductive argument is reached only after making what is called the *inductive leap*.

This jump is the process of moving from the specific evidence to a generalization about the entire population. The inductive leap from the evidence to the conclusion requires both caution and courage, as you will see, because you can never study every single member of the population before making the generalization.

The *sampling* is the number of specific cases of the population that are examined as evidence.

In order to ensure a sound inductive argument, the sampling must be large enough, and it must be taken at random. When a sampling is too small, as in the case of Jenny's cacti study, you cannot reach an accurate conclusion. How much of a sampling is enough? Surely not one or two or five or six. (On page 163 you will see that a too-small sampling is a fallacy called a *hasty generalization*.) If Jenny had gone on to examine perhaps forty or fifty different kinds of cacti, she would probably have discovered that some species of cacti do not have spines.

The randomness of a sampling ensures your chances of gathering accurate evidence. If you sample only the top layer in a basket of strawberries, for example, how can you tell whether the ones on the bottom and in the middle are ripe or hard and green? You should examine some from all parts of the basket before you buy the strawberries. People involved in public opinion polls, television ratings, or market research are especially concerned about getting a random sampling of the population. Assume that you were taking a poll of students in your high school about issues that concern them. How could you ensure that you were getting a random sampling? How large a sampling would you take?

Exercise 5

The following lists show the results of a poll taken of 300 students and 26 administrators in a high school of 3,000 students. Those who took the survey were asked to rank in the order of importance what they felt were the most common and serious problems that occurred among students in the school. What conclusions would you reach on the basis of the poll? What questions about the sampling would you ask?

Write a story for your school newspaper based on the information given.

STUDENTS

1. Drug abuse
2. Depression
3. Parent-teen communication
4. Alcoholism/drinking age
5. Individuality versus peer pressure
6. Work versus school attendance
7. Teens and violence/crime
8. Teen marriages/pregnancies
9. Students' rights
10. Shoplifting

ADMINISTRATORS

1. Drug abuse
2. Work versus school attendance

3. Individuality versus peer pressure
4. Depression
5. Parent-teen communication
6. Teens and violence/crime
7. Dealing with divorce
8. Runaways
9. Alcoholism
10. Race discrimination

How the Evidence Supports the Conclusion

The evidence in an inductive argument can never be considered as absolute proof that the conclusion is true. Consider the following example.[1]

> Eleven minutes after Flight 629 took off from Denver at 6:52 P.M., November 1, it crashed on farm land north of Denver. Wreckage was strewn over an area five miles long and two miles wide. The tail section and nose section were found virtually intact, far apart, but the engines, wings, and main cabin section were destroyed. Many bits of metal looked like shell fragments. Some remnants of the plane had the acrid smell of gunpowder. A thorough investigation turned up no indication of malfunction of the plane or of the crew. Farmers in the area told of hearing loud reports just before the crash. Officials of the Civil Aeronautics Board and the FBI properly concluded that a bomb had been placed in the luggage compartment and that its explosion had caused the crash.

All of the evidence supports the conclusion, but you cannot say for certain that this is exactly what happened. In this argument the conclusion is probably true and strongly supported by the evidence, but the evidence in an inductive argument cannot be considered as absolute proof. You must still make the inductive leap—and hazard the chance of being wrong.

The conclusion in an inductive argument is often worded to reflect exactly the evidence that has been presented and to show that the conclusion is suggested, not proved, by the evidence. Limiting words and expressions, such as the following, are used.

> *On the basis of this survey, it seems that* workers prefer job security over chances for advancement.
>
> *The evidence suggests that* the number of stray cats in the city *has probably* increased threefold over the past year and a half.
>
> *According to conversations with representative legislators, approximately* thirty per cent of the legislators have made up their minds on how they will vote.

The Inductive Method

How do you know that the sun rises in the east and sets in the west? Repeated experiences and observations enable you to reach this conclusion inductively.

---

[1] From *Thinking Straight: Principles of Reasoning for Readers and Writers*, 4th Ed., by Monroe C. Beardsley, p. 24. © 1975. Reprinted by permission of Prentice-Hall, Inc., Englewood Cliffs, N. J.

You use the inductive method when you make generalizations based on your own experiences and on what you read and learn from others. The scientific method is often called the *inductive method* because it, too, uses the inductive approach in its three basic steps:

1. Gather the data.
2. Weigh the evidence carefully.
3. State the conclusion.

It is easier said than done. Research scientists know that it is difficult to discover new "truths" that everyone will acknowledge as true. A scientist, for example, may run the same experiment over and over again, amassing thousands of figures over a course of several years. Cautiously, the scientist makes a generalization based on the evidence. Is the conclusion sound? Is it true? Before others are willing to accept the scientist's conclusion as a sound one, the following requirements must be satisfied.

1. The explanation (or conclusion) must account for all the facts.
2. The evidence must be observable by others and reproducible by others.
3. The evidence must strongly support the conclusion.
4. All plausible other explanations must be excluded.

Evaluating an Inductive Argument

When you read or listen to an inductive argument, you should question the soundness of the conclusion and the evidence leading up to it. Sometimes, especially in a long speech or essay, it is not easy to identify the conclusion and reasons. A good speaker or writer emphasizes these points, but sometimes the argument gets muddled. The following words are often clues that a conclusion will follow: *therefore, in conclusion, hence,* and *consequently*. Reasons are sometimes signaled by the words *first, second, since, because, for,* and *as shown by*. One way to find the main points of an inductive argument is to outline it briefly.

The following checklist may be helpful.

1. What is the conclusion of the argument?
2. What evidence is offered to support the conclusion? List each main reason (or type of evidence) separately.
3. What is the source of the evidence? Is the sampling random?
4. How much evidence has been gathered? Is the sampling sizable?
5. Does the evidence lend strong support to the conclusion, or is the evidence weak?
6. Is the conclusion carefully worded to reflect the evidence, or does it seem to make a statement for which there is no adequate evidence?
7. Does the argument contain any fallacies? (See pages 162–167.)

Exercise 6

Choose the word from the following list that you think will make each of the following generalizations into a true statement.

All Several Some Many Most No Few

Then think about what kind of evidence, and how much, you could gather to support each generalization. Note that some of the statements are opinions, not facts.

1. _______ children need love and discipline.
2. _______ automobile drivers must have licenses.
3. _______ women are capable of becoming good scientists, engineers, and doctors.
4. _______ mothers go back to working full time when their children are a few months old.
5. _______ green plants contain chlorophyll.
6. _______ people care about helping others.
7. _______ dogs can talk.
8. _______ teenagers respect their parents.
9. _______ people need to spend some time alone.
10. _______ people take criticism well.

Fallacies—Errors in Logical Thinking

Being aware of common errors that people make in logical thinking will help you to evaluate the soundness of arguments you hear and read, as well as those you write. These errors in reasoning are called *fallacies.* The following fallacies are found in deductive and inductive arguments.

1. *Post Hoc, Ergo Propter Hoc*

The Latin name for this fallacy means, "After this, therefore because of this." This fallacy occurs when one event is said to be the cause of a second event because the two events occurred in sequence. The following is an example of *post hoc* reasoning.

Evidence: On Tuesday afternoon I got my hair cut.
On Tuesday evening my goldfish died.
Conclusion: My goldfish died because I got my hair cut.

It is obvious that the preceding two events are unrelated; therefore, one cannot be considered the cause of the other, and the conclusion is ridiculous. However, *post hoc* reasoning is not always so apparent. Remember that a cause-effect relationship is usually quite difficult to establish. Whenever something is said to be a cause, the argument should be examined carefully.

2. *Only-Cause Fallacy*

Human beings seem to have a tendency to believe that everything has a cause and to want to identify causes. It is an oversimplification to name a single cause for a complex situation. Consider the following example of the only-cause fallacy.

> We can keep peace in the world only if every other country is afraid of being destroyed by our superior nuclear power. All we would have to do to ensure world peace is to drop a nuclear bomb—just once—on a country that gets out of line and invades another country. That would teach the whole world that we mean business and that they'd better keep the peace.

In the preceding argument only one thing causes the absence of peace in the world: the lack of fear of destruction by nuclear force. Look for the only-cause fallacy whenever the causes—and solutions—of complicated problems (such as inflation, unemployment, and injustice) are discussed. None of these complex problems has a single cause or a single solution.

3. *Non Sequitur*

This Latin expression means, "It does not follow." Whenever a conclusion does not logically and necessarily follow from the premises or evidence, a *non sequitur* occurs.

Premise:	All living things require water.
Premise:	An automobile requires water.
Conclusion:	An automobile is a living thing.

An inductive conclusion may also be a *non sequitur* if the evidence given is not sufficient to support the conclusion. Look at the following argument.

Evidence:	Lisa has chicken pox.
	Wendy has chicken pox.
	Charlie has chicken pox.
Conclusion:	The schools should be closed because there is an epidemic of chicken pox in the city.

4. *Hasty Generalization*

A conclusion based on inadequate sampling is called a *hasty generalization.* Unfortunately, this is one of the most widespread fallacies, appearing frequently in arguments as well as in individuals' thinking. Assume, for example, that your cousin took you to your first Mexican restaurant, where she suggested you order tacos. You thought the tacos were too spicy and refused to try any other Mexican food. If you spent the rest of your life avoiding Mexican food as too spicy, you would be guilty of a hasty generalization based on a single experience. Suppose you read two science fiction books and did not like them. If you concluded that all science fiction writing is trashy, you would be making a hasty generalization. Remember that generalizations should only be made after an adequate and random sampling.

5. *Stereotype*

A hasty generalization about groups of people is called a *stereotype.* Stereotypes are almost always negative. Unfortunately, racial, religious, and ethnic stereotypes continue to exist in this culture. Some people are biased against whole groups of people because of fixed ideas about what that group is like. The way to combat stereotypes is, first of all, to recognize them when they appear in advertising, in jokes, and in everyday speech. A second way is to get to know and respect individuals from every kind of racial, religious, and ethnic background. When people learn to see each other as individual human beings—not primarily as members of one group or another—stereotypes tend to be destroyed.

6. *Unreliable Authority*

Sometimes, a person will quote an authority in order to strengthen an argument. If the authorities are qualified experts with respected credentials, their opinions may be useful as evidence—provided that the experts are talking about the field in which they are experts. For example, the head of a tax-accounting firm should be listened to seriously when he or she is talking about income tax tips. A movie star, however, is not a qualified expert on income tax, nor is a baseball player a qualified authority on the nutritional value of cereals. *Ipse dixit,* meaning "He said it," is the fallacy of citing an unreliable authority, a person who is not an expert in the field being discussed. The *ipse dixit* fallacy appears in the following advertisement for an adult condominium community.

> According to Don Xenophon, world-renowned comedian, "Life is a lot of laughs at Sunshine Village. If you've worked hard all your life and now it's time for you to have fun full time, buy a condominium at the place where you'll be happiest—Sunshine Village. Folks who live at the Village say they're busy all day long and happy 85 per cent of every day. So when were you ever 85 per cent happy before?"

7. *Irrelevance or Distraction*

A sound argument has the same kind of unity found in a well-written paragraph. Every reason contributes meaningfully to the argument; none of the reasons are unrelated or distracting. In any argument look out for reasons or facts that are not really related to the argument. Such reasons, when they occur, are irrelevant and distracting, and weaken the argument. Often the fallacies of irrelevance or distraction involve emotional appeals, which have no place in a logical argument.

Assume, for example, that a woman lawyer has written a letter to the President. She argues that too few women judges have been appointed by the President to federal judgeships and that the number of female judges should reflect the number of female lawyers. Which of the following would be irrelevant to her argument?

a. The opinion of a member of the Supreme Court on having more women appointed as federal judges

b. The opinion of members of her family on having more women as federal judges
c. The present number of women and of men holding positions as federal judges
d. The percentages of women lawyers and men lawyers in the nation as a whole
e. The percentage of women judges on various state, county, and local levels
f. Biographical data about a woman who has served as a federal judge for the past ten years

The opinion of an expert (Item *a*) and the relevant figures (Items *c*, *d*, and *e*) are sound evidence to support the writer's conclusion, but Items *b* and *f* have no place in that argument.

8. *Attacking the Person and Not the Issue*

This fallacy also has a Latin name, *ad hominem*, which means "against the man." *Ad hominem* arguments often appear in election campaigns and in debates, when one person has to respond to the statements and criticism of another person.

> Candidate Y: We have heard Candidate X speak eloquently on the issue of inflation and on his specific proposals to curb inflation. Yet I ask you to take a look at Candidate X's personal situation. Inflation doesn't affect him—he's a millionaire. His financial disclosure form reveals that he's got nothing to worry about—no matter how expensive hamburger and gasoline get to be. And according to his last year's income tax return, Candidate X has found so many tax shelters that even though he's very rich, he paid less taxes last year than the average hard-working citizen.

A strong personal attack such as the preceding one is often called *poisoning the well.* No matter how sound or how reasonable Candidate X's proposals are, the audience has been turned against him by Candidate Y's attack.

9. *Argument by Analogy*

An *analogy* is a comparison in which two things are shown to have at least one quality in common.

> The human brain is like a computer. Because the brain can be programmed to think in a certain way, whoever controls the input into the human brain has tremendous power to shape the individual. Psychologists have told us that a child's first five years are the most crucial in the development of personality and mind. Therefore, children should start going to public schools at age three—before their brains are programmed too rigidly and finally by their parents and their community.

The brain is indeed like a computer in many ways. In fact, the first computer was developed by a scientist trying to imitate the workings of the human brain, so the analogy is a good one. However, even if several similarities are pointed out in an analogy, the comparison itself *proves* nothing. The argument about school for three-year-olds is weak because it is supported only by an analogy, and arguing by analogy is a fallacy.

10. *False Analogy*

A comparison that is shown, on close examination, to be farfetched is called a *false analogy*.

> An ideal human society would be like the society of the bees. Every individual has a job to do and knows what the job is and performs it well. There is no waste, no doubt, no insecurity.

An ideal human society cannot be compared meaningfully to life in a bee colony, where individuals have no choice of the kind of role they will perform. The colony is dominated by a single individual—the queen bee—and worker bees live for only six weeks. Is there happiness or creativity or fulfillment in a bee colony? Would people want an ideal human society in which these things did not exist? Can a bee colony and an ideal human society really be compared? False analogies are often found in arguments. Whenever you hear or read an argument containing an analogy, think about the comparison carefully. Is it really a sound comparison? Does it help in any way to make the writer's or speaker's argument clearer?

11. *Begging the Question, or Circular Thinking.*

Both of these names identify the same fallacy: arguing that a conclusion is true without providing any evidence or reasons.

> The law requiring students to attend school until the ninth grade is unjust because it keeps students in school who do not want to be there. I think the law should be changed because it is unfair to those students who want to drop out of school and can't do it legally.

The writer here is arguing that students be allowed to leave school before the ninth grade—but her position is not clear. When should the students be allowed to leave: Eighth grade? Seventh grade? Fourth grade? What reasons does the writer offer to support the call for a change? If you examine the argument carefully, you will see that no reasons are given. The writer simply restates in other words the fact that she desires a change. Not providing any reasons to support a conclusion is the fallacy of *circular thinking*.

12. *A Priori*

Similar to circular thinking is *a priori* reasoning, in which the person stating the argument assumes that a statement is true and expects the reader or listener to believe that it is true simply because the writer or speaker says that it is so.

> I'm absolutely sure that Maria is the best-qualified candidate for the Student Senate.

I feel confident that Solution B is the only solution that can solve our problem.

Both of these statements would be perfectly acceptable as a summary conclusion, offered at the end of an argument in which reasons were given to support the conclusion. However, if they are offered alone, without any reasons or evidence, the writer or speaker is guilty of *a priori* reasoning. Look for assumptions in arguments, and question whether or not the assumptions are true.

13. *Excluded Middle, or* Either-or

When this fallacy occurs, the person who is arguing claims that only two alternatives are possible in a given situation. All other possible choices or actions are ignored. Can you see the *either-or* fallacy in Jeff's argument?

Jeff: Marcia, we've been dating for a month now, and I really like you a lot. But I don't like your going out with other guys, too. Either you and I go steady or we have to stop seeing each other completely.

Marcia points out the fallacy:

Marcia: Jeff, I like you a lot, too, but we're just getting to know each other. We shouldn't have to choose between going steady and not seeing each other at all. I'd hate to lose your friendship, but I'm not ready to commit myself to just dating one person. We could see each other often—maybe more often—and continue to date others. Or we could just be friends and stop dating. Or maybe we could keep on getting to know each other and talk about how we feel and see if things change as time passes. I just don't see why it has to be one or the other of the choices you suggested—and no other possibilities.

Exercise 7

Choose six of the following fallacies and make up arguments containing the fallacy. Circulate the arguments among your classmates and see if they can identify the fallacy in each argument. Be ready to identify all of the fallacies mentioned in this section.

Post hoc, ergo propter hoc
Only cause
Non sequitur
Hasty generalization
Unreliable authority
Irrelevance
Ad hominem
Arguing by analogy
False analogy
Begging the question
A priori
Either-or

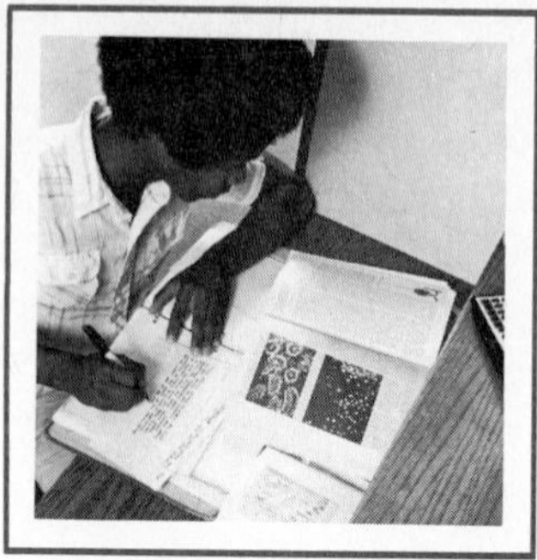

8 Persuasive Writing

The Purpose of Persuasion

The basic purpose of exposition is to give readers information. The purpose of persuasive writing, on the other hand, is to bring about either changes of opinion or actions in the reader.

When you write exposition, you give information so that your readers can form opinions and draw conclusions. When you write persuasion, you may also give information, but your main purpose is to change minds and bring about actions. For example, each of the following passages is about the eruption of Mount St. Helens in 1980. (The first is from Richard L. Williams' article, "Phenomena, Comments and Notes," in *Smithsonian* magazine.[1] The second is a passage such as a student might write.) As you read, decide whether the articles meet the definition of exposition or persuasion.

1.

> The other day I went out to George Mason University in northern Virginia to hear Dr. David W. Johnson, an ecologist (he also had been on the Smithsonian panel), talk about what survived and what did not. On leave from the University of Florida to direct ecological studies at the National Science Foundation, he has coordinated research at St. Helens, and has visited it three times since May.
>
> To me, the most interesting thing he talked about was not trees (200 billion board feet of lumber worth more than $500 million, looking today "like a giant game of pickup sticks" which could have built 200,000 homes "or a billion bluebird boxes") but the bees.

---

[1] From "Phenomena, Comments and Notes" by Richard L. Williams from *Smithsonian* Magazine, January 1981. Reprinted by permission.

"Honey bees," he said, "spend a great deal of their time grooming themselves; ash fell on their wings and bodies as well as on everything else, and when they brushed themselves clean the abrasive ash took away their protective cuticle. Also, ash clogged their tracheas, and they died." Whether more bees will be around in the spring to pollinate any plants they find is anybody's guess.

2.

The senior senator from this state has said that he will vote against a bill to provide funds for the cleaning up and rehabilitation of the area around Mount St. Helens. Everyone who is concerned with ecology and with the national economy should write to the senator, urging him to change his stand and support the bill.

With the funds appropriated, the federal government could salvage a large portion of the 200 billion board feet of lumber that now lie around the mountain like giant pickup sticks. The value of this lumber is estimated to be $500 million.

Aside from the economic value of the lumber, the government needs to do something to restore the ecological balance of the area. The plight of the honey bees is an example. Like many other insects, honey bees spend much time grooming themselves. When Mount St. Helens erupted, their wings and bodies were covered with abrasive volcanic ash. When they groomed themselves, the ash removed their protective cuticle and clogged their tracheas, and they died. Without these bees, how will the plants be pollinated in the spring?

From both the economic and ecological standpoint, the bill to provide funds for rehabilitating the Mount St. Helens area makes good sense. So don't postpone. Write to the senator today.

In the preceding examples the article from the *Smithsonian* is exposition. It gives information about Mount St. Helens, but it does not urge or suggest any action. The second passage is also informative, but it uses its data as reasons for taking action. This difference in purpose is the real difference between exposition and persuasion.

In this chapter you will study the art of persuasive writing. First, you will learn two basic approaches to persuasion: appeals to emotion and appeals to logic. Then, you will learn to write a persuasive essay based both on appeals to emotion and appeals to logic. Finally, you will examine a particular kind of persuasion called *propaganda*.

Appeals to Logic

The chapter "Logic and Writing" discusses inductive reasoning, deductive reasoning, and logical fallacies (see pages 151–167). A persuasive essay usually uses a combination of inductive and deductive reasoning. You can see that in constructing an argument (a series of reasons and facts) designed to support a conclusion, persuasive writing follows the basic procedures of inductive reasoning. However, the reasons given to support the writer's position may include general principles, which the writer may apply to a specific situation, as in deductive reasoning. For example:

> I think that we would all agree that human beings should have the right to determine their own destinies. Unless you live a totally isolated existence far from any form of civilization—perhaps high on a mountaintop or alone on a vast desert—you are part of a society. To a considerable extent the society and the government that it institutes affect each individual's life. As we can see in dictatorships and oppressed countries, government can and does determine human destinies. So when qualified citizens ignore elections and refuse to cast votes, they are in effect giving up part of the right to determine their own lives. Voting is not a right—it is an obligation.

In persuasive writing, the writer's challenge is to build a logical, tightly knit argument with enough evidence to be convincing. This means defining terms, giving clear reasons, supporting reasons with facts and data, and citing authorities.

Unfortunately, many persuaders use techniques that seem to appeal to logic, but that are really fallacious. The fallacies of hasty generalization, argument by analogy, and false analogy are discussed in the chapter "Logic and Writing." Avoid these fallacies in your writing and watch for them whenever someone tries to persuade you.

Appeals to Emotion

Appeals to emotion are not, in themselves, bad. In fact, persuasive writing at its best often combines appeals to logic and appeals to emotion. However, important decisions should be made rationally—not emotionally—so it is necessary for you to be able to recognize emotional appeals when they occur.

Television and magazine advertisers want to persuade you to buy a certain product or to think well of their company. Because advertisers know that they have only a few seconds or a quick glance to convince you, they rely primarily on emotional appeals. Advertisers have learned from psychologists that besides the basic physiological needs (such as food, drink, and shelter), everyone has powerful psychological needs. These include the need to be loved, the need to feel attractive, the need to feel well-liked and respected, the need to feel successful, the desire to be like everyone else, and the desire to remain young-looking. Advertisers plan their messages and visuals carefully to appeal to these needs and convince you to buy their products. For example, can you identify the emotional appeals in the following ad?

> A beautiful young woman is standing in a lush green meadow filled with wildflowers: "I feel confident and know I look my best when I use SPRING-FRESH soap."

Most women want to look like, and most men want to be with, the beautiful young woman (need to feel attractive; need to feel young-looking). Most people would like a guarantee of self-confidence (need to be well-liked), and most people would like to get away from problems and stand in a meadow filled with wildflowers (need to play and relax; need to stop worrying). The words *spring* and *fresh* are loaded words (see page 172), signifying rebirth, joy, newness, youth, and innocence.

Other emotional appeals are directed toward distinct emotions, such as love, guilt, loyalty, and fear. This type of appeal occurs more frequently in political campaign speeches—for example, as an appeal to patriotism or an appeal to fear. You can also find such emotional appeals whenever one person is trying to persuade another. Listen to Brenda, who is trying to convince her friend Debbie to help her study for a biology test.

> You know that we've been best friends since the sixth grade [appeal to love, appeal to pride] and that we've always been able to trust and depend on each other [appeal to loyalty]. I mean, who else can we trust more than each other? Remember the time that I helped you when you couldn't memorize your lines for the class play [appeal to guilt]? And would you ever have made it through algebra without my help [appeal to guilt]? I need your help now, Debbie. Can't you spend just a few hours helping me study for the biology exam, or are you too busy [appeal to guilt]?

Exercise 1

Most advertisements try to persuade the reader to buy the advertised product. Some ads, however, try to persuade readers to change their opinions about companies or products. (These are called public relations ads.) In a magazine or newspaper, find an example of a product advertisement and a public relations advertisement, and bring them to class. Use the following questions to analyze each ad.

1. What exactly does the ad try to persuade the reader to do?
2. What sort of reader is the ad aimed at? (Where you found the ad will provide a clue to the audience for which the ad is intended.)
3. What devices does the ad use to persuade? Promises? Bribes? Appeals to emotion?
4. What visual appeals does the ad make? (Consider the use of photographs, colors, design, and typography.)

Propaganda

Persuasive materials put out by an organized group to further its purpose are called *propaganda.*

The word *propaganda* usually has negative connotations because propagandists sometimes use devices that deceive the reader or distort the truth. However, propaganda is not all bad. For example, the United States government broadcasts propaganda daily in its Voice of America programs directed to Europe and Asia. Also, letters to state representatives, a visit to the state capitol to meet with legislators, television and newspaper editorials, lobbying by mental health experts and doctors—all of these can be part of a propaganda campaign for a good cause.

You should be able to recognize the following propaganda devices, used by advertisers and persuaders of all kinds.

1. *Loaded Words*

Besides having dictionary meanings, many words arouse feelings—either positive or negative. Such feelings are called *connotations.* Words such as *freedom, democracy, friendship,* and *justice* have strongly positive connotations; *evil, dishonest,* and *unethical* have negative connotations. For example, how many loaded words can you find in the following paragraph?

> My opponent's claim is utterly dishonest. I have had the utmost loyalty to my government, putting the interests of each and every citizen far above my own personal interest. I have sacrificed daily by working long hours above and beyond the call of duty. The evidence that my opponent purports to have gathered is as malicious as it is false, and his accusation is completely unethical.

POSITIVELY LOADED WORDS (for the speaker)	NEGATIVELY LOADED WORDS (against the speaker's opponent)
utmost loyalty	utterly dishonest
each and every citizen	purports
sacrificed daily	malicious
long hours	false
above and beyond the call of duty	completely unethical

2. *Glittering Generality*

A *glittering generality* is a loaded word or phrase with strong positive connotations, such as *the American Dream, mother love,* and *ethnic pride.* Patriotism and family or group loyalty are usually appealed to in these vague yet powerful devices for persuasion.

Exercise 2

Identify all of the loaded words in the following passages.

1. Does your house smell moldy and stale? Can you smell dust, grime, and yesterday's dinner? Are you ashamed and worried when friends come over? Try using OZONE fresh-air spray. OZONE makes your house smell like a spring morning—with sunshine and buds in bloom. Yet the scent is light and natural. All winter long OZONE makes you remember fresh, clean air, sunny breezes, and a spring day.
2. Anyone who believes in decency, justice, and the American way will vote for this bill. It gives every American citizen an equal opportunity to a decent education. Free college education will in turn provide better educated, proud, and self-supporting Americans.

3. *Card-Stacking*

Withholding pertinent information in order to persuade an audience is called *card-stacking.* For example, suppose that you were trying to sell a house and knew, but did not tell prospective customers, that in five years an expressway would be built in front of the house. That would be card-stacking. Or suppose that an advertisement for a new novel quotes only reviews that praise the novel, while negative reviews are omitted. That is another example of card-stacking—one that happens frequently in publishers' advertisements.

In any argument it is rare that all of the facts in the case will support a single point of view. Instead of omitting evidence that does not support your argument, deal with such contradictory evidence directly. Try to point out why the apparently contradictory evidence still does not defeat or negate your argument:

> Those who oppose my point of view claim that the plan to restore national parks to their natural state will limit the number of people who will have access to the park. Because private vehicles will be banned from the parks, as in some national parks in Alaska, fewer people will be able to enjoy the scenery and wildlife of the national parks. This is true. However, we must acknowledge that this loss of accessibility is far offset by the knowledge that the parks will not be spoiled by overuse of their facilities or by overbuilding of motels and campsites, restaurants, and grocery stores. We must keep in mind that the original purpose of national parks was to preserve forever the natural beauty of these areas, and that means limiting public access. You may be able to take a day trip into a national park on a park-run bus, but you must leave the park at night to the wildlife that lives there.

4. *The Bandwagon*

The *bandwagon* appeal is an emotional appeal to the need to be like everyone else. When "everybody else" is doing something, most people will join in. Advertisers use this appeal in ads such as the following:

> Don't be the last person in the world to try new Delicioso Potato Chips!
>
> Ninety per cent of all dog owners keep their dogs happy and comfortable with Magic Dust Flea Powder.
>
> Hurry, hurry, hurry! All but 8 of the 500 new cars on the lot have been sold to people who know a good buy when they see one.

5. *Plain Folks*

Political candidates and advertisers know that people tend to like and trust others who seem "just like" themselves. That is why images of middle-class, healthy-looking, cheerful people in ordinary clothing and everyday surroundings appear so often in television commercials and print media advertisements. In Florida a millionaire campaigned his way to governor by working for a day at a time at many different blue-collar jobs, such as waiter, cab driver, and garbage collector. His plain folks approach was a successful attempt to convince the voters that he knew and understood their problems because he had experienced them himself and had talked to other workers on his jobs.

6. *Snob Appeal*

You must have seen many ads showing "the beautiful people"—obviously wealthy, well-dressed, driving expensive cars and wearing expensive jewelry. The desire to be like these carefree, beautiful men and women helps sell things like perfume, automobiles, vacations, credit cards, and watches. The unstated sales pitch goes like this: "If you buy what these people own, your life will be happier, better, and more romantic." Snob appeal, the opposite of the plain folks approach, arouses the desire to achieve status and wealth, the desire to be superior to most people. For obvious reasons snob appeal is not used often in political campaigns, since most campaign material is aimed at the average voter—"the common man and woman."

7. *Transfer*

Advertisers hire popular sports figures and entertainment stars to persuade people to buy their products. Such advertisements are effective because viewers and readers transfer their feelings about the star to the product itself. For example, in a series of television ads, a respected actor who plays the part of a doctor in a long-running television series endorses a brand of decaffeinated coffee. Not only does the actor lend his prestige as an actor to the product he is selling, but he also lends his fictional authority as a doctor, established in the minds of his series' viewers. Sometimes, the transfer device is used for a good purpose, as when a sports star or well-known entertainment figure urges the public to contribute to a charity.

Exercise 3

In each of the following arguments, identify the appeals to emotion.

1. Author of a nationally acclaimed, best-selling book on running: "I eat Wholesome Brand cereal every morning. It's the best way to start my day."
2. All over the world people are starving to death every day. A contribution of less than three cents a day—a little more than ten dollars a year—can mean the difference between a child's life or death. You have so much—won't you share a bit of your food with those who have nothing at all? Send a contribution for any amount to this food relief agency.
3. A student candidate for city council in a university town speaks to a rally on campus: "For the past fifteen years, no one under fifty has served on the city council. We really need someone who can represent your interests, who can introduce legislation and look out for student concerns. For example, if you've tried to live off campus, you know that rents are out of sight. This city needs a strong rent control law. And what about more city parking lots around campus? Vote for me for city council, and I'll take care of you."
4. The city has offered to subsidize the cost of shade trees on the right of way in front of homes provided that eighty per cent of the residents on any given block agree to pay for, plant, and care for two trees on their property. "On our block, seventy-five per cent of the homeowners have already signed a statement agreeing to plant the trees. Don't be the one who will stop our block from becoming beautiful. Sign here please."

Evaluating an Argument

A group of citizens from an organization called GASP is trying to pass an ordinance that will limit smoking in public places. You read their brochure, which tries to convince you to vote for the law.

An organization to save the seals tries to persuade you to become a member or to donate money to promote its cause. The organization is lobbying against the killing of baby seals for fur.

An editorial in your local newspaper tries to persuade you that a certain viewpoint on a community issue is the "right" viewpoint.

How can you evaluate arguments such as the preceding ones? How can you know whether or not to be persuaded? You must practice being a critical thinker. That means asking questions such as, "How do you know?" "What proof do you have?" "Who says so?" "What do you have to gain by this?" In short, do not believe everything you read and hear.

In evaluating an argument in a persuasive essay, your first step should be to determine the writer's position. What is he or she trying to persuade you to do? Then you should be able to identify all of the reasons given to support the writer's position. What evidence is offered to support each reason?

Be sure to keep in mind those aspects of persuasive writing that you have been studying. Be aware of how language is used to appeal to your emotions. Do the reasons used to support the writer's position appeal to your reason or to your emotions? Be alert to fallacies—flaws in the reasoning process—and to the use of persuasive devices such as card-stacking and glittering generalities. Are terms clearly defined? Is the author's language easy to understand? What questions do you have about the issue that the writer does not answer? Before you decide whether or not to be persuaded, what other information do you need?

Reading a Persuasive Essay

Using what you know about evaluating an argument, read the following persuasive essay by Gloria Steinem, which first appeared in *Ms.* magazine. As you read, try to determine the writer's position and the reasons she uses to support that position. Look also for evidence she uses to support each reason. Be prepared to discuss the questions that follow.[1]

> (1) Almost every week now, we open our newspapers and read the story of an exceptional woman, some courageous "token" who has survived all odds and become the first woman vice-president of a large company, the first rabbi or priest, the first commercial pilot, truck driver, opera conductor, or TV anchorwoman. While we celebrate, extend support (which any "token" will no doubt need), and hope that some image-breaking results in the minds of readers who might have thought females couldn't do such things, we are also painfully aware of a fact that the newspaper reports never reflect. These invasions of "male" professions have no impact on the lives and economic problems of most women.

[1]From "Where the Women Workers Are: The Rise of the Pink Collar Ghetto" by Gloria Steinem in *Ms.* Magazine, 1977.

(2) In fact, the motive for printing the story sometimes seems to be an updated version of the motivation for covering some huge, atypical alimony settlement: if women can be convinced that we already have power, or the chance of power, as individuals, then perhaps we'll stop agitating on the issues of women as a group.

(3) Unfortunately, the media emphasis on tokenism probably does give us some false sense of well-being, even those of us who should know better. Many women have a vague sense that "things are getting better," even though a look at the growing female unemployment rates, the number of women and dependent children on welfare, and the increasing male-female salary differential shows clearly that—while token victories are important for raising aspirations—the economic situation of women as a group is remaining constant, or even getting worse.

Ghettoized means "kept separate and apart in inferior conditions."

Intrinsic means "essential, belonging to the very nature of the thing itself."

(4) A major reason for this uncomfortable truth is that the great majority of women workers are ghettoized in traditionally female occupations. In those areas, "equal pay for comparable work" and "equal chance for advancement" have very little meaning. Equal to whom? Advancement to where? These giant pools of cheap female labor—whether they are sales work or food service; typing for corporations or for government agencies—share many characteristics. First, they are paid according to the social value of the worker, not the intrinsic nature of the work. (A barber, for instance, performs less complicated tasks than a beautician, just as an assembly-line worker usually needs fewer skills than a secretary; yet the first two groups are paid and honored more, simply because they are men.) Second, the work areas traditionally occupied by women are usually nonunionized. Even existing unions that should or could organize such workers are rarely helpful. Third, the female work force is encouraged to be temporary by lack of advancement, pension, and sometimes even full-time opportunities. (Though women are said to be less employable because of family responsibilities, the subterranean truth seems to be that employers encourage the part-time worker, the young woman who leaves to care for children, and the older woman coming back into the labor force in an entry-level job.)

(5) Fourth, even the few men who are in traditionally female work areas are at the high end of the pyramid, leaving women workers still ghettoized at the bottom. (Here, too, there's no logic to job divisions. High-tip restaurants employ white males, while women, as well as minority men, are confined to cheaper restaurants, though the trays are just as heavy. Women sales personnel sell men's underwear while men sell kitchen ranges: the crucial difference is the higher commission, not who uses the product.)

(6) In an important new book called *Pink Collar Workers*, Louise Kapp Howe exposes this ghettoization of women workers. The sobering statistical analysis is all there; for instance, that there is at least as much restriction of women to poorly paid "female" jobs now, with many more women in the salaried work force, as there was in the 1900s. But the unique feature of the book is the long, in-depth, and intimate interviews with women in these professions; interviews that make clear the need for a massive movement to honor and humanize the "female" occupations, as well as to form unions that can force employers to pay decent salaries, even at the expense of high profits. The chapter on beauticians . . . as well as Louise Kapp Howe's subsequent chapters on salesworkers, waitresses, officeworkers, and housewives, are the personal expressions of a deep political caste system that tokenism cannot change, and

that women workers everywhere will recognize. An additional analysis is provided by economist Juanita Kreps, a longtime expert on women in the work force and currently Secretary of Commerce, who suggests that changed work patterns for both women and men may help to break down the female job ghetto, and change the social definitions of work.

(7) In a patriarchy, even suffering is valued according to the identity of the sufferer. We have heard a great deal about the plight of the blue-collar worker, for instance, in part because most of those workers are males. The few women in blue-collar professions are actually better paid than many if not most of their salaried sisters. But to raise the concerns of women working in traditionally female jobs is not to denigrate the problems of male workers. In fact, the threat of competition and absorption by women's cheap labor is a crucial factor in keeping many male workers in their place. For the sake of all workers, we need to look at the problems of that majority of women now working in the pink collar ghetto; a number of us that is growing more numerous, better educated but less well paid as the service sector of the economy increases.

(8) The work revolution we need isn't the toleration of a few women in "male" professions. It will begin with the rise of the pink collar worker.

(Paragraph numbers added)

For Discussion

1. Describe the audience for whom the essay is intended. Would you say the audience is likely to be hostile or sympathetic (or something in between) to Gloria Steinem's message?
2. What is the problem that the writer discusses? Which sentences state the problem most clearly? Do you agree that the problem exists, or do you disagree? Tell why.
3. What would you say is the purpose of the first paragraph?
4. Which paragraphs give analysis of the reasons for the problem? State the four reasons the author gives to explain the existence of the problem. Do you agree or disagree with these reasons?
5. What is the writer's proposed solution? Which sentences state the proposed solution most clearly? What reasons does the writer give to support her proposed solution?
6. What purpose does the book *Pink Collar Worker* play in the writer's argument? If you had a chance to look at this book, what information would you want to read in it?
7. In Paragraph 3 the writer states that "the economic situation of women as a group is remaining constant, or even getting worse." What evidence does she give to back up this statement?
8. What does the phrase "ghettoization of women workers" mean in Paragraph 6?
9. How effective do you think Gloria Steinem's essay is? How might it have been made even more effective?
10. What would you say is the purpose of the essay?

Writing a Persuasive Essay

Writing a persuasive essay is similar in many ways to writing an expository essay or a research paper. In the remaining sections of this chapter, you will study the following steps in writing a persuasive essay.

1. Choose a topic or proposition.
2. Gather evidence to support your proposition.
3. Outline your argument.
4. Write a first draft.
5. Revise and then write the final draft.
6. Proofread.

Choosing a Proposition

Developing a proposition is also discussed in the chapter "Improving Your Speaking and Listening Skills."

In persuasive writing the term *proposition* refers to the statement of the writer's position—that which the writer wants the reader to believe or to do.

A proposition, which is equivalent to a thesis statement in expository writing, must meet both of the following requirements.

1. The proposition must be arguable.
2. The proposition must be uncertain.

An arguable proposition is a specific statement that can be debated by people with opposing viewpoints.

For example, you can see that people may either agree or disagree with each of the following propositions.

1. Laws should be passed severely limiting the import of foreign cars.
2. The United States government should offer a voluntary national health insurance plan, available to citizens of all ages.
3. The President and Vice President of the United States should be elected by direct popular vote, and the Electoral College should be abolished.

Besides being debatable, each of the preceding propositions is specific. One cannot debate vague, general statements, such as, "People should be kinder to each other." Neither can one debate factual statements, such as "One hundred centimeters make a meter." By definition a fact is something that has been proved to be true and is therefore not arguable.

Each of the preceding three propositions is an opinion, not a fact. Notice the verb *should* in each. What *should be* is a matter of opinion, and opinions are arguable.

Which of the following is more suitable as a proposition for a persuasive essay? Why?

1. High school students should choose the most useful courses.

2. Students in career education should be required to take at least six literature courses.

The first proposition is too vague and too general. Which students? What courses? It is impossible to build an argument to support such a nonspecific statement. The second proposition, however, names specific students (those in career education) and a specific number (six) of a specific type of course (literature). This proposition is arguable and specific.

The second requirement is that the proposition have uncertainty.

With few exceptions (such as determining causes for major historical events), it is useless to be persuasive about the past. To be meaningful an argument must deal with an issue that is yet to be decided or one that involves changing an existing condition. Which of the following propositions meet the requirement of uncertainty?

1. Each of the states in the United States should be represented by a star on the flag.
2. If the draft is reinstated, young women should be drafted as well as young men.
3. Gasoline should be rationed in the United States.

Propositions 2 and 3 meet the requirements of uncertainty and are also arguable. Proposition 1 states an existing condition and is therefore unsuitable as the topic for a persuasive essay.

Exercise 4

Some of the following topics are arguable and uncertain, and some are not. Decide which of the statements might serve as a proposition for a persuasive essay. Be ready to explain your decisions.

1. Many items in a supermarket are too expensive.
2. The federal government should establish a panel of nutrition experts to define minimum food values for products. Those products that fall below the minimum level should be classified as "junk food" and be heavily taxed.
3. Since we are all responsible for our well-being, everyone should be required by law to demonstrate a knowledge of the basics of health care before completing high school.
4. Neil Armstrong stepped onto the surface of the moon in July of 1969.
5. The money spent putting a human being on the moon should have been spent to improve living conditions of humans on earth.
6. Capital punishment should be permanently abolished throughout the United States.
7. A fully equipped current model of the Super Packillac automobile lists at $12,500.

8. In comparison with other automobiles in its class, the Super Packillac is a poor value.
9. Certain courses should be required of most students.
10. A course in auto mechanics should be required of all students except those who obtain written permission from their parents to substitute another course.

Writing Practice 1

For each of the following topics, write an arguable proposition that meets the requirement of uncertainty. Your proposition may propose a solution or a way of dealing with a problem. Word your proposition carefully in order to be specific.

1. Capital punishment
2. Mandatory school attendance laws
3. Energy shortage
4. Inflation
5. Mandatory seat belt laws
6. School dropouts and teenage unemployment
7. Growth of nuclear energy
8. Increases in defense budget
9. Legalized gambling
10. Longer jail sentences for convicted criminals

Gathering Evidence to Support Your Position

Once you have chosen an issue and defined your views by stating a proposition, you are ready to begin gathering evidence to build your argument. For some kinds of persuasive essays, you can come up with all the evidence you need by simply thinking about your proposition. This might be true especially of essays that concern school situations with which you are very familiar. Most topics, however, will require you to do some research in order to assemble the facts and evidence you will use to support the proposition. Television and radio shows, the daily newspaper, current magazines, recent books, and pamphlets are all rich sources of material.

Ideally, the evidence that you gather will contain both factual evidence as well as opinions of authorities. Consult your librarian for the best sources for the kind of data you need. Take notes as you read recent books and magazine articles. It will be helpful in organizing your essay to outline arguments that you read or hear—even those that oppose your views. Always be sure to use more than a single source for your research, since a book or magazine may have some bias that you are not able to detect.

Discussing your topic with relatives, teachers, and friends may also be helpful. Find out what others think about the issue—and why. You will discover that people give a variety of reasons to support their opinions. These discussions may provide you with reasons for your essay and help you to clarify your own views as well. If you have already formulated some clear reasons to support your proposition, try convincing someone of your view. An informal discussion—and immediate feedback from the person with whom you are talking—will give you an idea of the effectiveness of your argument.

Exercise 5

Tell what sources you would consult and what kind of evidence you would look for if you were writing a persuasive essay on one of the following topics or on one of your own choosing.

1. Continuing the national speed limit at 55 miles per hour
2. Prohibiting the advertising of cigarettes in the print media
3. Making public school mandatory for twelve months of the year
4. Prohibiting the sale of junk food in school
5. Making one year of national service a requirement for all eighteen-year-olds

---

Outlining Your Argument

Before you begin your essay, you need a clear idea of your audience. How much background information you present and which reasons are most effective depend in large part on the particular makeup of your audience. For example, assume that you were writing an essay on the need for government-subsidized day-care centers for working mothers. Your argument would be quite different if you were addressing a group of working mothers (who would be favorably disposed) or if you were addressing a group of nonworking mothers (who may be hostile to the idea). A group of legislators addressed on this issue would probably need more convincing than either of the groups of mothers.

Go back over your notes and choose the reasons and opinions that you think are the strongest. You should have at least three reasons to support your proposition, and each of these should be supported with specific examples, statistics, illustrations, and quotations. The more evidence you give to support your statements, the more convincing you will be.

Outlining your argument will not only help you to decide what reasons to include in your essay, but will also help you to decide in what order to present them. You may want to present the strongest reason first or save the strongest argument for last. There is no single right order. Try out different combinations until you find the one that seems most effective.

At this point examine your reasons critically to be certain that you have not included any that weaken your argument. A good essay, like a unified paragraph, should have no wasted words, no rambling, no vagueness. If a reason does not provide strong support for your proposition, drop it and look for a better one.

Exercise 6

Outline the argument that you would use to persuade someone you know to do each of the following. Decide on your audience first and then list at least three reasons for each item. Make up any details that you need.

1. Read a newspaper every day.
2. Stop smoking cigarettes.
3. Stop eating junk food.
4. Lend you a car.
5. Lend you ten dollars.
6. Change a final grade from *C* to *B*.
7. Give you a summer job.
8. Come with you to a concert.
9. Contribute to a local charity.
10. Give up a Saturday to help in a clean-up drive at your school.

Writing the First Draft

In writing the first draft of your persuasive essay, you should consider especially its tone and its introduction, body, and conclusion.

Tone

Tone is also discussed on pages 99–100 of the chapter "Writing Exposition."

Before you begin to write, keep in mind that the tone of a persuasive essay should be formal. Informal usage, slang, and even contractions are inappropriate. Avoid highly technical terms, unless they are absolutely necessary. If they are, be sure to define the terms. Loaded words can be used for effect, especially when trying to motivate an audience to take some action. However, make sure that your argument is not based on emotional appeals alone. In general, the tone of a persuasive essay should be factual and objective, depending much more on appeals to logic than on appeals to emotion.

Introduction

Writing introductory paragraphs is also discussed on pages 96–97 of the chapter "Writing Exposition."

The beginning of a persuasive essay should capture the reader's attention. When you try to persuade someone, it is always a good idea to find a point of agreement as a place to begin. For example, suppose that Angela is writing a paper in support of the proposition that the school year should be extended through the summer with only two weeks for vacation. Her essay will appear as an editorial in the school newspaper. Since she knows that most students oppose the idea of a twelve-month school year, Angela knows her readers will be hostile at the outset. Before presenting her argument, she finds a common meeting ground:

> Life in the 1980s is much more complicated than it was in the '50s or even in the '60s and '70s. For example, computers are becoming as common as adding machines and typewriters once were. Ordinary citizens must under-

> stand basic economic theory or run the risk of having their savings depleted by fluctuations in the economy. Only informed people can take advantage of advances in medicine and health care. The list of examples could go on and on, but the point is this: As life becomes more and more complex, citizens need more and more "basic training" in order to cope. On this point we can all agree.
>
> Among several possibilities for teaching modern "survival skills," one stands out as the most economical, least complicated, and most effective: extending the school term through the summer, with two weeks for student vacations.

Angela begins her editorial tactfully by noting a common problem and common concerns. She wins over the audience enough to get them to listen to her argument, which she proceeds to develop in the body of her essay. Contrast Angela's approach with Mark's:

> Most high school graduates in America today are so ignorant that they don't understand computers, they know nothing about economics, and they can't make intelligent decisions about their own health care. Any intelligent person knows that the only way to remedy this problem is by extending the school year through the summer, giving students only a two-week vacation.

Because Mark likes to consider himself direct and honest, he launches headlong into the proposition. At the same time, Mark insults the reader by calling "most high school graduates" ignorant and stating that they are unable to make intelligent decisions. Even if the rest of Mark's essay were a model of sound logic, chances are he lost his readers completely in the opening sentences.

Besides capturing the reader's interest and establishing some common point of agreement, the introduction must clearly state your proposition or thesis statement. Readers should know your point of view from the outset so that they can judge the merits of your argument.

Body

For more information about developing the body of an essay, see page 97 in the chapter "Writing Exposition."

The body of a persuasive essay contains the argument. You will not be able to use all of the material that you have collected, but you should cover all of the major points in your outline in the order in which you have decided to present them. In general you should devote a paragraph to each of your reasons. Be sure to state each reason clearly and develop it with specific details and examples. Remember that every statement you make in a persuasive essay—unless it is blatantly obvious—needs to be supported. Offer proof to back up your claims, cite sources for your facts, and identify authorities whom you quote.

To be most effective a persuasive essay should deal with the opposing point of view in a serious and respectful way. It is inappropriate to say, "The people who oppose this view do not know what they are talking about." Choose two or three of the opposition's main arguments and try to refute them logically. Again, use evidence, facts, and quotations to support your statements.

Conclusion

For more information about writing conclusions, see page 97 in the chapter "Writing Exposition."

The concluding paragraphs should summarize your argument, repeating the proposition and each of the main reasons. Keep the summary brief by omitting the details and statistics that you have used to support each reason. Avoid the temptation to go on and on; remember that the argument in a persuasive essay should be tightly knit—without wasted words.

If you want your readers to perform a certain action, your final paragraphs should tell specifically what you want them to do—providing, of course, that they agree with your viewpoint. At this point many writers use appeals to emotion to overcome the readers' inertia and move them to action.

Writing Practice 2

Using a topic of your choice, write a persuasive essay. First, decide on the audience for whom you want to write. Then follow the steps outlined in this chapter: choose a proposition, gather evidence to support your position, outline the argument, and write the first draft. If you like, use the Gloria Steinem essay on pages 175–177 as a model for your own.

Writing the Final Draft

As in any kind of writing, allow yourself enough time to let at least half a day pass before writing the final draft. Being away from your paper for a while will give you a fresh perspective and enable you to read it critically. As you reread the first draft, use the following checklist to improve your essay.

Checklist for a Persuasive Essay

1. The beginning captures the reader's interest.
2. The proposition is clearly stated.
3. The reasons used to support the argument are clearly stated.
4. Each reason is backed up with facts, examples, illustrations, or some other kind of supporting detail.
5. Only reasons that will strongly support the proposition are included; weak reasons have been deleted.
6. The reasons are arranged in the most effective order.
7. The argument does not contain any logical fallacies. It does not use emotional appeals that distort the truth or deceive the reader.
8. The argument deals directly with the opposing viewpoint.
9. There is a clearly worded summary.
10. If the reader is meant to perform a specific action, that call to action is clearly stated.
11. Each paragraph has unity. There are no sentences or paragraphs that do not contribute meaningfully to the argument.
12. The tone of the essay is appropriately formal. The argument is geared toward the audience for which it is intended.

Writing Practice 3

Using the checklist in the preceding section, revise your persuasive essay. (Your teacher may wish to see it first.) Make changes on the first draft by adding, deleting, rearranging, or substituting words, phrases, and paragraphs. When you finish, rewrite the first draft for a final copy. As a last step check your writing for features that do not conform to Edited Standard English against the Checklist for Proofreading on page 14.

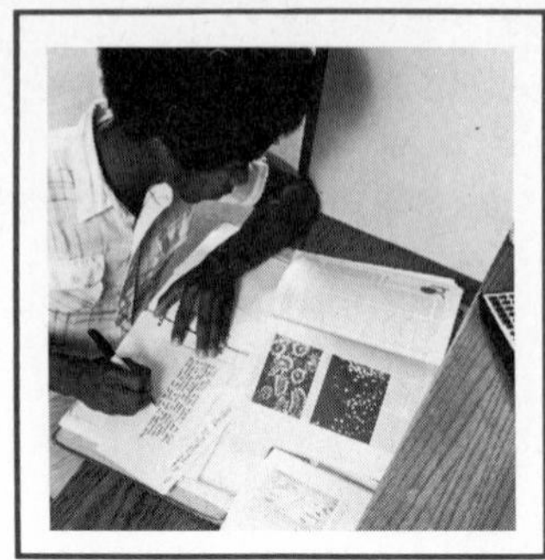

9 Business Letters and Forms

Business Writing

In this chapter you will review some of the basic skills for writing business letters. You will also practice writing letters to the editor, letters requesting information, consumer complaints, and letters to elected officials.

If you are like the average worker in the United States, you will apply for several different jobs during your lifetime. Whether you look for a job right after you graduate from high school or whether your job hunting is postponed until you receive further education or training, you will need to know how to present yourself to a prospective employer so that you will be seriously considered for a job. In this chapter you will also practice writing letters of application and a résumé.

Checkup Quiz: Form of a Business Letter

Number a separate sheet of paper 1–10 and write the correct answers to the items that follow.

1. Unlike a friendly letter, a business letter must always contain (a) a salutation, (b) a heading, (c) an inside address.
2. A business letter should be written on (a) plain, white paper, (b) colorful stationery, (c) ruled paper to keep the lines even.
3. In a business letter the salutation is followed by a (a) comma, (b) semicolon, (c) colon.
4. Between the name of the state and the ZIP code, there should be (a) no punctuation, (b) a comma, (c) a colon.
5. An appropriate closing for a business letter is (a) As always, (b) Yours truly, (c) Respectfully I remain yours sincerely.

6. The signature in a business letter appears directly below the (a) salutation, (b) body of the letter, (c) closing.
7. The return address on the envelope belongs (a) just below the middle of the envelope and slightly to the right, (b) in the upper right-hand corner, (c) in the upper left-hand corner.
8. If you are writing a business letter to Mrs. Katie Daniel, Director of Admissions at Metropolis University, the salutation should read: (a) Dear Katie: (b) Dear Mrs. Daniel: (c) To whom it may concern:
9. The third line of the heading contains (a) the writer's city, state, and ZIP code, (b) the city, state, and ZIP code of the person who will receive the letter, (c) the date on which the letter is written.
10. If a business letter is more than one page long, the second page should (a) begin on a new page, (b) be written on the back of the first page, (c) be deleted so that the letter fits on a single page.

The answers to this checkup quiz are on page 210. If you answered all the questions correctly, you may (with your teacher's permission) skip the next part of this chapter, on the forms of a business letter. Turn to page 194 for the section Writing a Consumer Complaint Letter. However, if you missed even one question, take the time to read the section on business letters and to do the exercises. Your business letters must be perfect, with no mistakes at all, if you want them to have the best possible results.

Reviewing the Form of a Business Letter

Appearance

A business letter should be written on standard-sized, plain, white paper (8½ by 11 inches or 5 by 7 inches). Use a typewriter if possible, making sure that the typewriter ribbon prints type that is dark enough to be easily read. If you cannot type your letter, write legibly in blue or black ink.

The margins of a business letter should frame your letter with white space. Your left margin should be absolutely straight, and the right margin should be as even as possible. The margins above and below the letter should be equal.

Never write on the back of a business letter. If your letter has a second page, always begin a new page. Across the top of the second page, write as a single-line heading the name of the person you are writing to, the page number 2, and the date:

Ms. Georgia Owolski 2 May 9, 1984

Proofread your letter carefully to make sure that you have avoided all mistakes in punctuation, grammar, and spelling. If you must make one or two corrections, use correction fluid and make the corrections neatly so that they are not obvious. A smudged, messy letter with many obvious corrections is not acceptable.

Form

A business letter has six parts: heading, inside address, salutation, body, closing, and signature.

See the model letter on page 196.

1. The three lines of the *heading* contain the following information.
   a. The writer's street address and apartment number (if any)
   b. The writer's city, state, and ZIP code
   c. The date on which the letter is written

    16902 Birchwood Avenue Apt. 203
    St. Paul, MN 55110
    June 5, 1984

Notice that in the heading commas are used only between the name of the city and state, and between the day of the month and the year. Do not make the mistake of putting commas at the end of each line of the heading or between the name of the state and the ZIP code.

2. The *inside address* contains the name and/or title of the person you are writing to and the company name, street address, city, state, and ZIP code.

    Mr. John Chin
    Director, Summer Programs
    American Youth Hostels, Inc.
    132 Spring Street
    New York, NY 10012

If you do not know the name of the person who will read your letter, you may address it to a title (such as *Director of Admissions* or *Personnel Manager*) or to a department (such as *Customer Service Department* or *Credit Department*). The inside address always begins at the left margin about four spaces below the heading.

3. In a business letter the *salutation* (or greeting) is always followed by a colon.

If you are writing to a specific person, the salutation should include that person's name and title:

    Dear Dr. Lorenzo:
    Dear Miss O'Neal:
    Dear Professor Orlinsky:
    Dear Mayor McLaughlin:
    Dear Mr. Kutun:

In recent years the abbreviation *Ms.* has become acceptable in addressing a woman when you do not know whether she is married or single.

    Dear Ms. Simond:

When you do not know the name of the person who will be reading your letter, you may repeat the title used in the inside address:

Dear Credit Manager:

You may also use *Dear Sir:* or *Dear Madam:* or *Gentlemen:* as your salutation.

4. The *body* of the business letter begins two spaces below the salutation.

Paragraph your letter as you would an essay, beginning a new paragraph when you begin a new topic or thought. In block form all paragraphs begin at the left-hand margin. In semiblock form, however, paragraphs are indented five spaces.

5. The *closing* is a phrase that appears at the end of the letter just before the signature.

The following closings are appropriate for business letters: *Very truly yours, Yours truly, Respectfully yours,* or *Sincerely yours.* Notice that the closing is followed by a comma and that only the first word is capitalized. The closing is always aligned with the heading.

6. Your *signature* should always be written in ink.

If you are typing your letter, type your name below your signature, just to make sure that the person reading the letter can see the correct spelling of your name. Notice that a title may be typed below the typewritten name but is not used as part of the signature.

Very truly yours,

Robert D. Ingraham

Dr. Robert D. Ingraham

Yours truly,

Elaine Thompson

Elaine Thompson
Senior Editor

Writing Practice 1

On a sheet of paper, set up forms for two of the following business letters. Draw lines to symbolize the body of the letter and write all of the other parts in their proper places according to the information provided. Use today's date or a future date.

1. Mrs. Olivia Hawthorne, who lives at 2869 Palo Alto Drive in Albuquerque, New Mexico 87112, is writing to Miss June Warshaw, Vice President, Olympic Sporting Goods Company, 104 Scaneatles Avenue, Hempstead, New York 11552.
2. Mr. Giorgio D'Allessandro, 5211 Derita Road, Charlotte, North Carolina 28213, is writing to the Customer Service Manager, Lionel Leisure, Inc., Philadelphia, Pennsylvania 19114. (Note that the company has no street address.)
3. Ms. Carole Ryan, 411 Sandpiper Avenue, Canton, Ohio 44718, is writing to Mr. K. J. Searles, President, M & M Upholstery Company, 500 East Texas Road, Allentown, Pennsylvania 18106.
4. Mr. Kevin Weiss, 21 East Burningtree Road, Charleston, South Carolina 29412, is writing to Mrs. Sarita Vasquez, Director, Island Tours, Inc., 4301 Villa Andalucia, San Juan, Puerto Rico 00926.

Folding the Letter

A business letter is customarily folded in a certain way, according to accepted practice. If you are using a long envelope for a letter on 8½ by 11 inch paper (or a short envelope for 5½ by 8 inch paper), the first step is to fold the letter in thirds (first, fold the bottom third of the letter toward the top; next, fold the top third down). Then insert the letter into the envelope with the open end of the letter at the top of the envelope.

If you are using a small envelope with 8½ by 11 inch paper, first fold the letter in half, bringing the bottom half up. Next, fold the right third of the letter toward the left, and then fold the left third over the right third. Insert the letter into the envelope with the open end of the letter at the top of the envelope.

Addressing the Envelope

An envelope must contain two addresses: the address of the person to whom the letter is sent and the return address of the sender. Begin by writing the return address in the upper left-hand corner of the envelope. Write three lines, using (1) your first and last name but no title, (2) your street address and apartment number, and (3) your city, state, and ZIP code. A return address enables the post office to return your letter in case it cannot be delivered as addressed.

See page 192 for a list of state abbreviations for use with ZIP codes.

Just below the middle of the envelope and slightly to the right, write the name, title, company name, address, city, state, and ZIP code of the person (or department) you are writing to. Always use a title *(Miss, Mrs., Ms., Mr., Dr.)* before the name of the person you are addressing. If you do not know the ZIP code, learn to use the ZIP code directory found in every post office and public library. A letter without a ZIP code may be delayed several days or more.

```
Alice Morikame
562 Arroyo Drive
Amarillo, TX  79107




                        Mrs. Grace Winover
                        Manager, Credit Department
                        Connors Department Store
                        428 Old Point Avenue
                        Hampton, VA  23669
```

Abbreviations

The United States Post Office has approved two-letter abbreviations for states, possessions of the United States, and Canadian provinces to be used with ZIP codes. (See the list on page 192.)

Writing Practice 2

On a sheet of paper, draw outlines for four envelopes. Address all of the envelopes for the following letters, using your name and address for the return address.

1. You are writing to Lois Moran, editor of *American Craft* Magazine, 22 West 55th Street, New York, New York 10019.
2. You are writing to the Box Office Manager, Superjet Stadium, 3920 Navaho Avenue, Spokane, Washington 99208.
3. You are writing to Frank Beale, Director, Institute of Natural Resources, 309 West Washington Street, Chicago, Illinois 60606.
4. You are writing to Mrs. Donna Tully, Manager, Discount Stereo, 2500 Whalen Lane, Madison, Wisconsin 53713.

Content of a Business Letter

A business letter may look perfect and yet fail to accomplish its purpose. The content and tone of a business letter are very different from that of a friendly letter or an essay. You must sharpen your focus to keep your writing clear, simple, and to the point.

Before you begin writing, ask yourself the following three questions:

1. What do you want the reader to do? (In other words, what is the purpose of your letter?)
2. What does the reader have to know in order to do this? (What information do you need to include in your letter?)

Alabama AL

Alaska AK

Arizona AZ

Arkansas AR

California CA

Colorado CO

Connecticut CT

Delaware DE

Florida FL

Georgia GA

Hawaii HI

Idaho ID

Illinois IL

Indiana IN

Iowa IA

Kansas KS

Kentucky KY

Louisiana LA

Maine ME

Maryland MD

Massachusetts MA

Michigan MI

Minnesota MN

Mississippi MS

Missouri MO

Montana MT

Nebraska NE

Nevada NV

New Hampshire NH

New Jersey NJ

New Mexico NM

New York NY

North Carolina NC

North Dakota ND

Ohio OH

Oklahoma OK

Oregon OR

Pennsylvania PA

Rhode Island RI

South Carolina SC

South Dakota SD

Tennessee TN

Texas TX

Utah UT

Vermont VT

Virginia VA

Washington WA

West Virginia WV

Wisconsin WI

Wyoming WY

Canal Zone CZ

District of Columbia DC

Guam GU

Puerto Rico PR

Virgin Islands VI

Alberta AB

British Columbia BC

Manitoba MB

New Brunswick NB

Newfoundland NF

Northwest Territories NT

Nova Scotia NS

Ontario ON

Prince Edward Island PE

Quebec PQ

Saskatchewan SK

Yukon Territory YT

Labrador LB

3. How can you get the reader to do this? (What is the best way of wording what you want to say?)

If you spend a few minutes thinking about purpose, information, and presentation before you begin writing, you will find it easier to write an effective business letter.

In any kind of business letter, three rules govern the content:

1. *Be complete.* Include all of the information the person reading your letter needs to know, such as dates, places, sizes, prices, account numbers, and so on. You may want to include photostat copies of bills or other relevant documents. Never send the original of any important document.
2. *Be clear and concise.* Say everything that you need to say as clearly and briefly as you can.
3. *Be courteous.* You should always create a pleasant tone in your business letter if you want to get results from the letter.

Writing Practice 3

Rewrite the following letter, correcting all errors in form. You may reword the letter as much as you think is necessary, deleting unnecessary information and creating any details you need to supply missing information.

7569 West Honey Creek Parkway
Milwaukee, Wisconsin 53219

Wisconsin Bell Telephone Company
14995 West Central Street
Milwaukee, Wisconsin 53218

Dear Customer Service Representative,

My telephone bill arrived today, and it has three long-distance telephone calls that I never made. Nobody else made those calls either. I live with my sister and her husband, but I have my own phone.

I refuse to pay my telephone bill until this matter is taken care of.

As always,

Wendy Ryan

Wendy Ryan

Proofreading a Business Letter

Before you mail a business letter, proofread it carefully to be certain that it is complete, follows standard form, and is free from errors. Use the following checklist as a guide in proofreading your business letters.

Checklist for Proofreading Business Letters

FORM AND APPEARANCE

1. The letter is neatly written in ink or typed with no smudges or obvious corrections.
2. The letter is centered on the page, with each part having the correct amount of spacing above and below.
3. The left-hand margins are exactly even. The left-hand margin of the heading aligns with the left-hand margin of the closing and signature. The left-hand margin of the inside address aligns with the left-hand margin of the salutation.
4. The right-hand margin of the body of the letter is fairly even.
5. Your signature is legible and written in ink.

PUNCTUATION

1. In the heading and inside address, a comma comes between the city and state. There should be no comma between the state and ZIP code.
2. A comma comes between the day of the month and the year in the heading.
3. A colon follows the salutation.
4. A comma follows the closing.

CAPITALIZATION

1. Capitalize the names of streets, cities, and states in the heading and inside address.
2. Capitalize the name of the month in the heading.
3. Capitalize the title of the person to whom you are writing and the names of the department and company listed in the inside address.
4. Capitalize the word *Dear* and all nouns in the salutation.
5. Capitalize only the first word of the closing.

Writing a Consumer Complaint Letter

Unless you are very lucky, you may have to write some letters of complaint about merchandise or services that you have purchased. You can protect yourself by checking the following facts before you sign a contract or pay for merchandise.

A Checklist for Consumers

1. Do the advertiser's claims seem unbelievably good? If so, beware.
2. Have you compared prices from several different companies?
3. Have you checked the company's complaint record with your local Better Business Bureau? If there are many complaints registered against the company, find another company to deal with.

4. If you are consulting a doctor, lawyer, or therapist, have you asked about fees, qualifications, and licenses?
5. Have you checked a consumer magazine to see if the product you are buying has been tested and evaluated? You can find several reliable magazines in your public library.
6. Do you fully understand the contract and all of its conditions? Read the fine print! Make sure that any additional promises that a salesperson makes are put into writing.
7. Is there a guarantee or warranty?
8. If you are dissatisfied with the product or service, how does the company handle complaints and refunds?

Suppose that even though you were cautious before you bought a product, something goes wrong and you are stuck with a defective product or have a legitimate complaint. Do not just sit back and say, "Oh well." Do something. Proceed according to the following steps.

1. Decide what you think would be a fair settlement of the problem. Do you think the company should replace the product or repair it? Do you think you should get your money back?
2. Go back to the salesperson who sold you the product. Take with you all your receipts (canceled check, repair slip, warranty). State the problem calmly and tell that person how you think the problem should be solved.
3. If you are not satisfied with the salesperson's response, ask to see the department manager or store manager. Repeat the facts and state what you want. Keep calm.
4. If you are not satisfied with the store manager's response and the company is a national one, write to the company president. You can obtain the name of the company president and the address of the company by calling the company's local office and asking for the information. Or you may go to the public library and consult a reference book called *Standard & Poor's Register of Corporations, Directors, and Executives,* which lists more than 37,000 American businesses. If you know only the product's name but have no idea of the name of the manufacturer, you can look up the name and address of the company in a book called the *Thomas Registry.*
5. Write a letter to the company president, stating your problem calmly and clearly, giving all necessary information. Enclose photocopies of important documents, such as the sales slip and warranty. Ask the company president for a solution to your problem (the action you want the company to take) within a reasonable period of time. Keep a copy of your letter.

A sample consumer complaint letter is on page 196.

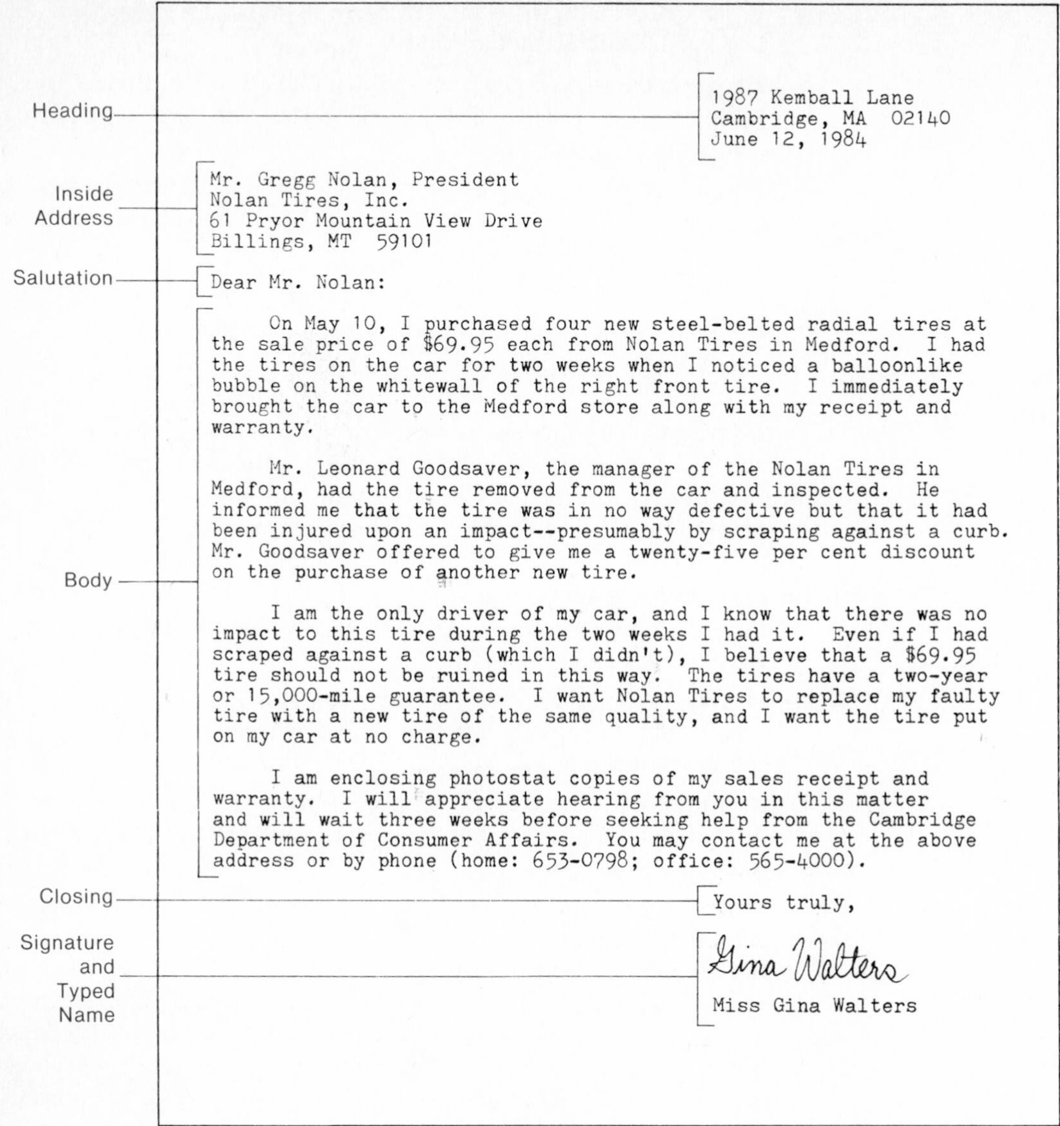

1987 Kemball Lane
Cambridge, MA 02140
June 12, 1984

Mr. Gregg Nolan, President
Nolan Tires, Inc.
61 Pryor Mountain View Drive
Billings, MT 59101

Dear Mr. Nolan:

On May 10, I purchased four new steel-belted radial tires at the sale price of $69.95 each from Nolan Tires in Medford. I had the tires on the car for two weeks when I noticed a balloonlike bubble on the whitewall of the right front tire. I immediately brought the car to the Medford store along with my receipt and warranty.

Mr. Leonard Goodsaver, the manager of the Nolan Tires in Medford, had the tire removed from the car and inspected. He informed me that the tire was in no way defective but that it had been injured upon an impact--presumably by scraping against a curb. Mr. Goodsaver offered to give me a twenty-five per cent discount on the purchase of another new tire.

I am the only driver of my car, and I know that there was no impact to this tire during the two weeks I had it. Even if I had scraped against a curb (which I didn't), I believe that a $69.95 tire should not be ruined in this way. The tires have a two-year or 15,000-mile guarantee. I want Nolan Tires to replace my faulty tire with a new tire of the same quality, and I want the tire put on my car at no charge.

I am enclosing photostat copies of my sales receipt and warranty. I will appreciate hearing from you in this matter and will wait three weeks before seeking help from the Cambridge Department of Consumer Affairs. You may contact me at the above address or by phone (home: 653-0798; office: 565-4000).

Yours truly,

Gina Walters

Miss Gina Walters

A Research Project

If your efforts to solve a problem directly with the manufacturer fail, you may seek help or advice from a government agency or private group that deals with consumer problems. Find out the addresses and phone numbers of the following organizations.

1. Department or Bureau of Consumer Affairs (state, county, or city government). Look in your phone book under state, county, or city government listings. If you cannot find a listing, call the office of your local

government's district attorney for help in locating a government consumer agency.

2. Better Business Bureau. In many cities local and national businesses sponsor this nonprofit organization, which attempts to settle consumer disputes.
3. Small Claims Court. This division under the city or county justice system handles claims from $100 to roughly $3,000. Generally you do not need a lawyer.
4. Legal Aid and Legal Services. Free legal advice and services may be available to people who cannot afford to hire a private lawyer.
5. Private Consumer Groups. A number of nonprofit organizations staffed by volunteers exist in all fifty states. You can obtain a list of the organizations in your state by writing to the Division of Consumer Organizations, U.S. Office of Consumer Affairs, Washington, D.C. 20201.

Writing Practice 4

Write one of the following consumer complaint letters, making up any details that you need.

1. Two weeks ago you bought a pair of Viking sneakers for $31.95 from Lombard's Sporting Goods store at 81 Nugget Court, Boulder, Colorado 80302. The rubber at the tips of the soles and heels has completely worn through, but the store manager refuses to replace the shoes. Write to the president of Viking Shoes, Inc., 3480 Calle Corta, Bakersfield, California 93309.
2. You have purchased an electric baseball game for your young nephew. When you examine the game closely, you discover sharp pieces of metal in the batter's box that you believe make this a dangerous game for children. Write to the Director of the Consumer Product Safety Commission, Washington, D.C. 20207.
3. You feel that you have been discriminated against when you tried to rent an apartment at 1680 Netherwood Avenue, Memphis, Tennessee 38106. The manager of the apartment told you that all of the apartments were rented, but a couple whom you know rented an apartment half an hour after you were told that no apartments were available. Write details to the Director, Fair Housing and Equal Opportunity Department, Department of Housing and Urban Development, Washington, D.C. 20410.

Writing Practice 5

Rewrite the letter of complaint on page 198. What details, information, and documents will you need to provide?

Writing Practice 6

Assume that a month has gone by and that your rewritten letter to Speedy Airlines has not been answered or acknowledged. Write a letter explaining

699 North Plum Grove Road
Roselle, IL 60164
October 6, 1984

Consumer Affairs Manager
Speedy Airlines
2268 Tantalus Drive
Honolulu, Hawaii 96813

Dear Consumer Affairs Manager:

I had a paid ticket to New York City, but when I got to the airport, I was told that my flight had been overbooked, and I could not have a seat on it. A representative of your airlines told me that I could fly free on the next available Speedy Airlines flight, but since your next flight was not until the following day, I flew on Potomac Airlines, which left at 2 P.M.

Please refund my money for the Speedy Airlines ticket for the flight from which I was bumped and for the Potomac Airlines ticket, which I had to pay for.

Yours truly,

Harold Wishma

Harold Wishma

your problem to the Director, Bureau of Consumer Protection, Civil Aeronautics Board, Washington, D.C. 20428.

Writing Requests for Information

Suppose that you are planning a camping trip in Colorado during your summer vacation. You might write to the Office of Tourism, asking for free information. (See page 199.)

As with all kinds of business writing, requests for information should be brief, clear, and specific. The person who reads your letter must understand exactly what you want to know before he or she can provide the information you want.

Writing Practice 7

Write one of the following requests for information. Make up any details that are necessary.

1. You have a relative in another country who wants to immigrate to the United States. Write to the Office of Immigration and Naturalization, Western Region, Terminal Island, San Pedro, California 90731. You want to know exactly what procedure must be followed for your relative to come to the United States to live permanently.

16954 East State Road 38
Lafayette, Indiana 47905
April 22, 1984

State of Colorado Office of Tourism
1313 Sherman Street, Room 500
Denver, Colorado 80203

Dear Office of Tourism:

I am planning a backpacking trip in Colorado during the month of June. I would appreciate your sending me any free information that you have about Colorado's national and state parks. Do you have maps that show hiking trails? If you have a guide to special events in the month of June, I would like to have a copy. I have never been to Colorado and would appreciate any booklets or brochures that give general information about the state so that I can choose the area for my backpacking trip.

Thank you very much.

Yours sincerely,

Karen Holberg

Karen Holberg

2. You and two of your friends are thinking about starting a small business. Write to the Small Business Administration, Regional Office, 60 Batterymarch Road, Boston, Massachusetts 02110. Tell what kind of business you are planning and what kind of information you need.
3. You are writing for information about national parks in your area. You want to know about camping, boating, hiking, and restaurant facilities. Find the names of four nearby national parks and write to the National Park Service, 1100 Ohio Drive, S.W., Washington, D.C. 20242.
4. You are writing to Northwestern University, 636 Clark Street, Evanston, Illinois, 60201, to find information about their summer programs for high school students. Ask for information about course offerings, tuition, room and board, and registration requirements.

Writing Letters to the Editor

In a letter to the editor, you can express your opinion on issues you think are important. Keep informed by reading the daily newspaper or watching the television news. If you think something is wrong, do not keep your ideas to yourself. Speak up. By writing a letter to the editor of your local or school newspaper, you may find that others who agree with you will work together to change what you think is wrong.

Since most letters to the editor are quite short, conciseness and clarity are essential. Express your opinion clearly in the first sentence or two and then give reasons to support your opinion. If your letter suggests a solution to a problem, tell how you would go about implementing that solution. Be sure to sign your name and address, since most newspapers will not print anonymous letters. Follow the standard business letter form in writing a letter to the editor.

Newspapers receive far more letters than they can print. One way to increase your chances of having your letter published is to think of some way to grab the reader's attention.[1]

Curb the Regulators

It is written in my will that when I die the cost of my funeral is going to be dirt cheap. I would like to be placed in a plastic garbage bag and deposited six feet under.

In this way the public will be protected, as I will not be a health hazard, and I will save my family a bundle of money. The only trouble is that, according to the Florida Funeral Regulatory Board, I can't select my own method of burial. Funeral homes must do it for me, at their price.

All funeral directors, doctors, architects, bankers and many others are controlled by people belonging to regulatory boards. These boards are supposed to protect the public from harm. But the sad fact is that often they only protect the interests of the professions and businesses they represent.

They can stifle competition and issue permits as they see fit. They can discourage advertising, set prices—even make and break their own rules. They can be unjust and inflationary. We absolutely do not need some of these boards. Would you believe there is a Frozen Dessert Regulatory Board?

Now, for the first time, we can do something about it. The Legislature now has the power to change the rules and makeup of the boards. It is a huge task with so many boards up for review. The professions and businessmen have been busy for months getting their acts together to ensure that they will not be put out of business or tampered with in any way.

Will citizens, the consumers, step forward and testify in behalf of themselves? Will retired professional people or businessmen testify against their own agencies?

The alternative is a big rubber stamp for another seven years—without a change in the direction of reform. And I will have to buy that padded, brass-and-mahogany coffin against my will.

Susie Guber, Miami

The writer of this letter wants to get the reader interested in the state legislature's review of professional and business regulatory boards. What device does she use to interest the reader at the outset? How would you describe the tone of the letter? What exactly do you think the writer's purpose is? How well do you think she accomplishes this purpose?

---

[1] Letter titled "Curb the Regulators" by Susie Guber, written February 5, 1979 to the editor, *The Miami Herald.* Reprinted by permission of Susie Guber.

The tone of a letter to the editor is important. Which do you think is more effective: an angry and outraged tone, or one that is reasonable and temperate? When appropriate, a letter to the editor can be lively and laced with humor; such letters are more often read and remembered.

Letters to the editor can be positive, too. They do not always have to criticize. People who work hard for the benefit of others are too often taken for granted. If you think something or someone deserves praise, write a letter to the editor.

Writing Practice 8

1. Read today's newspaper. Choose one article or editorial or letter to the editor and then decide what you think about the incident or situation the article describes. Write a rough draft of a letter to the editor, outlining your opinion and reasons. Think of a good attention-getting beginning. Then write a letter and mail it to the editor of your local newspaper.
2. What would you like to see changed in your school and community? How would you go about making the change? Choose one issue and suggest a solution and a way to implement the solution. Write a letter and mail it to the editor of your school or local newspaper.

Writing to an Elected Representative

A sample letter to an elected representative is on page 202.

When you write a letter to the editor, you are expressing your opinion to readers of the newspaper or magazine—the public in general. You can express your opinion even more effectively, however, when you write to your elected representatives: your city or county commissioner, mayor, governor, state senator and representative, United States senators and members of the House of Representatives. All of these people respond to mail they receive from their constituents, the people who live in their election district.

Letters about laws that are soon to be voted on carry a good deal of weight. The staffs of senators and representatives tally such letters carefully to see "how the public feels" on any bill. If you are writing to an elected representative about a bill, try to time your letter so that it arrives before the vote is taken. Express your opinion clearly. Tell how the proposed law (or change in law) will affect you personally, your community, and the people that you know. If you know the name of the legislation or the number of the bill, state it. As a voter, you are entitled to know your representative's opinion on the issue you are writing about. Ask your representative to tell you his or her position on the issue.

Everyone—especially a public official—likes to have hard work acknowledged and appreciated. Take the time to write a letter of thanks to your representative for a job well done or for specific work on a particular issue. For the rest of your life you can directly affect the quality of your government by voting in every election and by writing regularly to your elected representatives.

6021 LaTijera Blvd.
Los Angeles, CA 90056
February 11, 1984

The Honorable S. I. Hayakawa
United States Senate
Washington, D.C. 20510

Dear Senator Hayakawa:

I know that the Senate will soon be considering a bill to lower the cost-of-living increase in Social Security payments. I have followed news reports about the proposed bill and have read some magazine articles about it. I urge you strongly to vote against this bill.

My grandparents, who are in their early seventies, are having a hard time making ends meet with their Social Security checks. Given the present inflation rate, they would find it impossible to maintain their own home if there were a cutback in Social Security payments. They would probably have to ask for some kind of public assistance or even go into a nursing home, paid for by Medicare and Medicaid. This would cost the taxpayers more money than keeping up their Social Security payments.

Many of the elderly persons I talk to--neighbors and relatives--have had to cut back more and more on essentials like food, clothing, and heating. They just can't seem to manage. I think we owe these elderly citizens the feeling of security that they can get with cost-of-living increases in the Social Security system. I would appreciate knowing your views on this issue.

Sincerely yours,

Cynthia Talbot

Cynthia Talbot

For names and addresses of your local government officials, check your telephone book for listings under city, county, and state governments. It is customary to address a mayor, governor, senator, or representative by the title *The Honorable:* The Honorable Mayor Dianne Feinstein.

The following are addresses and salutations for the President and for members of the Senate and House of Representatives.

The President The White House Washington, D.C. 20015	The Honorable [*first and last name*] United States Senate Washington, D.C. 20015
Dear Mr. President:	Dear Senator [*last name*]:

The Honorable [*first and last name*]
House of Representatives
Washington, D.C. 20015

Dear Representative [*last name*]:

Writing Practice 9

1. Read the front section of your local newspaper every day for several days. Choose an issue that is currently being discussed by government officials—either on a local, county, state, or national level. Before you decide what your views on the issue are, you may need to do some additional research. Consult your librarian for recent articles on the issue. Find the name and address of your representative and write a letter expressing your views. Mail your letter to your representative.
2. Choose an issue that concerns you and write a letter to one of your representatives, asking how he or she stands on that issue.

Writing a Letter of Application

A sample letter of application is on page 204.

A letter of application should follow business letter form perfectly and contain no errors. If you can, find the name of the specific person who is responsible for interviewing and hiring, and address your letter to that person. In a large company you can call and obtain the name of the personnel manager; in a small company address your letter to the president.

Your letter should contain the following information:

1. Tell what job you are applying for and how you heard about the job—from an advertisement or from a relative or friend.
2. Give personal data (age, health, grade in school, grade average) that will enable the prospective employer to know something about you.
3. Tell what your qualifications for the job are, such as special skills or training, knowledge, and experience. If you have had no experience in the field, mention any skills and experiences you have had that might be related to the job.
4. As references give the names and addresses of two or three adults who are not relatives. Be sure to ask for permission to use their names as references.
5. Request an interview at the employer's convenience. Give your telephone number and tell when you can be reached.

Writing Practice 10

Think of a full-time or summer job that you would like to have. Locate the name and address of a company for which you might work and the name of the person in charge of hiring employees. Write a letter of application, following the guidelines in this section.

65 Ebony Road
Shreveport, Louisiana 71107
February 28, 1984

Mrs. Edna Printz
Director of Summer Programs
Camp Howard
1702 Peachtree Road, N.E.
Atlanta, Georgia 30309

Dear Mrs. Printz:

I would like to apply for a job as counselor in Camp Howard this summer. My friend Jerry Fleminger, who has been a counselor in your camp for the past two years, told me that several positions are available.

For the past three years I have worked part-time at the McDonald Center, an after-school day-care center, with seven- to ten-year-old boys. I have also been an assistant coach with the Little League teams for several years.

I am especially interested in a position as counselor in nature lore, since that is my special field of interest. I am an Eagle Scout and a member of the Audubon Club and Sierra Club. I am experienced as a canoe trip leader and have led several bird walks with younger scouts. This spring I am taking a six-week course on Saturdays at Shreveport Community College to learn to teach botany to young children.

The following persons can tell you more about my work with young people and my qualifications for a job as counselor:

Mrs. Gloria Lerner, Director, McDonald Center,
3548 Reisor Road, Shreveport, Louisiana 71118

Dr. Julie Rosecranz, Instructor, Shreveport Community College,
4028 Virginia Ave, Shreveport, Louisiana 71103

I would appreciate an interview at your convenience. I know that you will be in the city sometime next month at a reunion for Camp Howard campers. You can reach me at the above address, or you can call me at 790-4611. I work after school four afternoons a week and attend classes on Saturday but am usually home on Friday afternoon and in the evenings.

Sincerely yours,

John Stack

John Stack

Writing a Résumé

A sample résumé is on page 206.

A sample cover letter is on page 205.

A résumé is a summary of personal data, background, and experience in an outline form. Many prospective employers prefer to receive a résumé, which is easier to read than a long letter of application. Once you have prepared a résumé, you should be able to use it many times, updating it as needed.

A brief covering letter should accompany your résumé, telling what job you are applying for and asking for an interview. Do not repeat in the covering letter information that is found in the résumé.

11802 Edgewater Drive
Lakewood, Ohio 44107
March 8, 1984

Mr. Jonathan Scalley
Director, Marine Life Research Laboratory
2640 West 147th Street
Cleveland, Ohio 44111

Dear Mr. Scalley:

I would like to apply for a job as a lab assistant in the Marine Life Research Laboratory during the coming summer. I would also be interested in after-school work and work on Saturdays if such a job were available.

I an enclosing a résumé of my skills and background. I am very interested in pursuing a career in marine biology and have applied to several colleges where I can specialize in this field.

Whenever it would be convenient for you, I would be happy to come to the laboratory for an interview. You can reach me at the above address or by phone, 831-6098.

Very truly yours,

Robert Gordon

Robert Gordon

Writing Practice 11

Write your own résumé and covering letter for the job that you chose in Writing Practice 10 (page 203). Write a rough draft first and proofread both your letter and résumé carefully. Remember to include everything about yourself that is relevant to your qualifications for the job.

Filling Out Forms

A sample application form is on pages 207–209.

From now on, you will be filling out many important forms: applications for jobs, college, loans, credit, licenses, insurance, and so on. Before beginning to fill out any form, read the directions carefully and then follow them exactly. Be sure to fill out the form completely; do not leave any spaces blank except those designated for office use. Print neatly in ink or use a typewriter so that the information you write is legible.

A sample form is included on pages 207–209. It is similar to many college application forms and applications for financial aid. Use the information on the form to answer the questions that follow.

Sample résumé

Robert Alan Gordon

Address: 11802 Edgewater Drive
Lakewood, Ohio 44107

Telephone: 831-6098

Personal: Born May 17, 1967, in Akron, Ohio
Marital status: Single
Health: Excellent
Height: 5'8" Weight: 160 pounds
Social Security number: 085-44-3290

Education: Senior at Lakewood High School, college preparatory course
Grade point average: 3.5 (B+)
Member Community Lab Program of Cuyahoga County school for two years
Attended two-week program for gifted science students, summer 1982

Extracurricular activities:
President, Science Club
Member, debating team
Captain, swimming team
Member, National Honor Society

Skills: Can handle laboratory animals
Can compile and analyze results of laboratory experiments
Can operate centrifuge and other lab equipment
Can program computer

Work experience:
Mt. Sinai Medical School
Cleveland, Ohio

Lab assistant in study of lung diseases, using animals for research
Summer 1982, after school 1982-83

Corner Book Shop
Shaker Square, Ohio

Clerk on Saturdays
From 1983 to date

References: Mr. Larry Wyzckowski, Lab Director, Mt. Sinai Hospital, Cleveland, Ohio, 795-6000

Mrs. Jenny Owens, owner of Corner Book Shop
Shaker Square, Ohio, 442-8756

Writing Practice 12

1. Which section of the form may you choose to fill out or to leave blank?
2. Which tests are required or suggested for application and acceptance to these colleges?
3. Information about education should begin at what grade?

Agnes Scott • Alfred • Allegheny • American University • Antioch • Bard College • Bates • Beloit • Bennington • Boston College • Boston University • Bowdoin
Brandeis • Bucknell • Carleton • Case Western Reserve • University of Chicago • Clark • Coe • Colby • Colby-Sawyer • Colgate • Colorado College • Davidson
Denison • University of Denver • DePauw • Dickinson • Drew • Earlham • Eckerd • Elmira • Emory • Fairfield • Fisk • Fordham • Franklin and Marshall
Furman • Gettysburg • Goucher • Hamilton • Hampshire • Hartwick • Haverford • Hobart • Hood • Kalamazoo • Kenyon • Knox • Lafayette
Lawrence • Lehigh • Lewis and Clark • Linfield • Macalester • Manhattan
Manhattanville • Mills • Mount Holyoke • Muhlenberg • Newcomb College
New York University • Oberlin • Occidental • Ohio Wesleyan • Pitzer

COMMON APPLICATION

Pomona • University of Puget Sound • Randolph Macon Woman's College • University of Redlands • Reed • Rice • University of Richmond • Ripon
University of Rochester • Rollins • St. Lawrence • Salem • Sarah Lawrence • Scripps • Simmons • Skidmore • University of the South
Stephens • Stetson • Susquehanna • Texas Christian University • Tulane • Valparaiso • Vanderbilt • Vassar • Washington College
Washington University • Washington and Lee • Wesleyan • Western Maryland • Wheaton • Whitman • Willamette • William Smith • Williams

5311

APPLICATION FOR UNDERGRADUATE ADMISSION

These colleges and universities encourage the use of this application. The accompanying instructions tell you how to complete, copy, and file your application to any one or several of the colleges. Please type or print in black ink.

Legal name: ____ ____________
Last First Middle (complete) Jr., etc. Sex

Prefer to be called: ____________________(nickname) Former last name(s) if any: ____________________

Are you applying as a freshman ☐ or transfer student ☐ ? For the term beginning: ____________________

Permanent home address: ____
Number and Street

____ State of legal residence ____________________
City or Town County State Zip

If different from the above, please give your mailing address for all admission correspondence:

Mailing address: ____
Number and Street

____
City or Town State Zip

Telephone at mailing address: ________/____________ Permanent home telephone: ________/____________
Area Code Number Area Code Number

Birthdate: ____________________
Month Day Year

The following items are optional: Social Security number, if any: ☐☐☐ ☐☐ ☐☐☐☐

Place of birth: ____________ Marital status: ____________ Height: ________ Weight: ________

Of what country are you a citizen? ____________ Type of Visa ________ Visa Number ____________

How would you describe yourself? (Please check one)

- ☐ American Indian or Alaskan Native
- ☐ Asian or Pacific Islander (including Indian subcontinent)
- ☐ Black (non-Hispanic)
- ☐ Hispanic (including Puerto Rican)
- ☐ White, Anglo, Caucasian American (non-Hispanic)
- ☐ Other (Specify) ____________________

EDUCATION

Please list all the secondary schools, including summer schools, programs, and institutes you have attended since 8th grade.

Schools attended, present school first:

Name of School	Location (City, State, Zip)	Dates Attended

Present secondary school ACT/CEEB code number: ____________ Date of secondary school graduation: ____________

Is your school public? ________ private? ________ parochial? ________

College advisor: ____________________ School telephone: ________/____________
Name Position Area Code Number

Common Application/Application for Undergraduate Admissions. Reprinted by permission of the National Association for Secondary School Principals.

Please list all colleges at which you have taken courses for credit and list names of courses on a separate sheet. Please have a transcript sent from each institution as soon as possible.

Name of College	Location (City, State, Zip)	Degree Candidate?	Dates Attended

If you are not attending school at the present time, please describe what you are doing: __________

Probable area(s) of academic concentration / major: __________

Special college or division if applicable: __________

Probable career or professional plans: __________

Will you be a candidate for financial aid? Yes _____ No _____ If yes, the appropriate form(s) was/will be filed on: __________

TEST INFORMATION Be sure to note the tests required for each institution to which you are applying. The appropriate test scores must be submitted to each institution as soon as possible. Please list your test plans below.

	Scholastic Aptitude Test (SAT)	Achievement Tests (ACH)	Subjects	American College Test (ACT)
Dates taken or				
to be taken				

FAMILY

Father's full name: __________ Is he living? _____

Home address if different from yours: __________

Occupation: __________ *(Describe briefly)* __________ *(Name of business or organization)*

Name of college (if any): __________ Degree: _____ Year: _____

Name of professional or graduate school (if any): __________ Degree: _____ Year: _____

Mother's full name: __________ Is she living? _____

Home address if different from yours: __________

Occupation: __________ *(Describe briefly)* __________ *(Name of business or organization)*

Name of college (if any): __________ Degree: _____ Year: _____

Name of professional or graduate school (if any): __________ Degree: _____ Year: _____

If not with both parents, with whom do you make your permanent home: __________

Please give names and ages of your brothers or sisters. If they have attended college, give the names of the institutions attended, degrees, and approximate dates:

____

____

ACADEMIC HONORS

Briefly describe any scholastic distinctions or honors you have won since the eighth grade: 5313

EXTRACURRICULAR AND PERSONAL ACTIVITIES

Please list your principal extracurricular, community, and family activities and hobbies in the order of their interest to you. Include specific events and/or major accomplishments such as musical instrument played, varsity letters earned, etc. Please (V) in the right column those activities you hope to pursue in college.

Activity	Grade level or year of participation 9	10	11	12	Approximate number of hours spent per week	Positions held or honors won	Do you plan to participate in college?

WORK EXPERIENCE

Please list any job (including summer employment) you have held during the past three years.

Specific nature of work	Employer	Approximate dates of employment	Approximate no. of hours spent per week

4. Which years of extracurricular activities are the colleges interested in? Write your extracurricular and personal activities on a separate sheet of paper.
5. How would you fill out the section entitled "Work Experience"?
6. Is writing in blue ink acceptable?
7. If you are applying for financial aid, where on the form do you indicate this? What do you have to do if you are applying for financial aid?

Writing Practice 13

All college entrance applications have some kind of essay question to give the admissions officer an idea of how well you write and how your mind works. Choose one of the following essay questions and write an essay of 300 to 500 words.

1. Write a self-appraisal, stressing one aspect of your personality that you would like to change and how you would go about it. (Tufts University)
2. Describe your twenty-five-year high school reunion. (Tufts University)
3. Describe a problem that faces your home, school, city, region, or nation. How did the problem originate, and how might it be solved? (Cornell University)
4. To what prominent person (past or present) would you like to apprentice yourself? Why? (Dartmouth University)
5. Describe a meaningful experience that you have had, however brief or long-lived, that has affected your perspective on life. (Boston University)
6. Tell us more about you as a person. Share with an admissions officer something about the experiences that have shaped your personal development, or you may want to discuss your goals, values, or ideals. We seek a response which will help us to know you better. (Princeton University)

Answers to quiz on pages 186–187

1. c 2. a 3. c 4. a 5. b 6. c 7. c 8. b 9. c 10. a

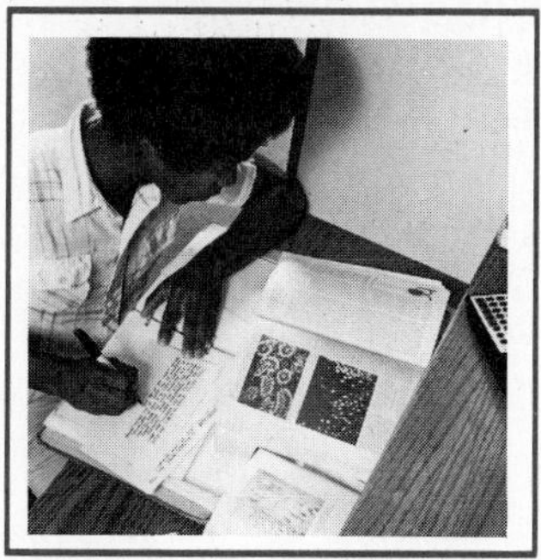

10 Imaginative Writing

Defining Imaginative Writing

The term *imaginative writing* encompasses stories, novels, plays, and poetry.

In imaginative writing, elements from the real world (such as actual places, character traits, and experiences) combine with elements that the writer invents. Imaginative writing takes these real and invented elements and combines them in a new way. This new creation—whether it is a story, play, novel, or poem—gives the reader an experience of the world through the mind of the writer.

In this chapter you will learn about some important aspects of short stories, plays, and poetry. You will also learn how to apply your own imagination to exploring your experiences through writing.

Writing a Short Story or Play

Short fiction and plays share many of the same basic elements. Both are constructed by combining *characters*, the people involved in the action; *setting*, the place or places of the action; *plot*, the action itself; and *conflict*, the element of struggle in the plot. The way in which these elements work together, plus other choices the writer makes about the language, ideas, and feeling conveyed in the short story or play, all constitute the writer's individual *style*.

Establishing Characters

The opening of a short story, like the first scene of a play, is especially important, because it is at this point that the reader will either become involved and read further or decide that the story is not interesting.

One way that short stories involve the reader from the beginning is by presenting the characters in a compelling way.

The paragraphs that follow are the opening paragraphs of a short story by Katherine Mansfield titled "Mr. Reginald Peacock's Day." Instead of describing her main character to the reader, Katherine Mansfield begins this story in the middle of the character's train of thought as he wakes up in the morning. As you read, notice what the character Reginald says about being wakened up by his wife and also notice the way that he expresses himself.[1]

> If there was one thing that he hated more than another it was the way she had of waking him in the morning. She did it on purpose, of course. It was her way of establishing her grievance for the day, and he was not going to let her know how successful it was. But really, really, to wake a sensitive person like that was positively dangerous! It took him hours to get over it—simply hours. She came into the room buttoned up in an overall, with a handkerchief over her head—thereby proving that she had been up herself and slaving since dawn—and called in a low, warning voice: "Reginald!"
>
> "Eh! What! What's that? What's the matter?"
>
> "It's time to get up; it's half-past eight." And out she went, shutting the door quietly after her, to gloat over her triumph, he supposed.
>
> He rolled over in the big bed, his heart still beating in quick, dull throbs, and with every throb he felt his energy escaping him, his—his inspiration for the day stifling under those thudding blows. It seemed that she took a malicious delight in making life more difficult for him than—Heaven knows—it was, by denying him his rights as an artist, by trying to drag him down to her level. What was the matter with her?

A story's *point of view* is the way its information is presented to the reader.

In the preceding paragraphs, Katherine Mansfield does not tell the reader about Reginald directly. Instead, she tells the story from Reginald's *point of view;* everything that happens is seen through Reginald's eyes. Reginald's train of thought—what he observes, and how he feels—all these inform the reader about him. For example, Reginald believes that his wife deliberately wakes him up abruptly because she knows he hates being awakened that way. He imagines her "gloat over her triumph" of making him miserable. What other thoughts does Reginald have about his wife's attitude?

When Reginald says, "But really, really, to wake a sensitive person like that was positively dangerous! It took him hours to get over it—simply hours," the reader can imagine him speaking in a fussy, excited tone of voice. What does Reginald's manner of speaking tell you about him as a character?

By beginning in the middle of a character's train of thought, Katherine Mansfield pulls her readers into the story through curiosity. A reader might want to know, for example, what sort of artist Mr. Peacock is, whether or not his feelings about his wife are justified, and what his feelings for her will cause him to do.

---

[1]Excerpt from "Mr. Reginald Peacock's Day" in *Collected Stories of Katherine Mansfield* by Katherine Mansfield.

Writing Practice 1

Use the Preparing to Write section that follows to help you with ideas for your paragraph.

Imagine that you are writing a short story from a character's point of view. The first paragraph of your story will follow that character's train of thought about something: perhaps your character's reaction to another person, as in the Katherine Mansfield story, or a reaction to a specific situation. Select one of the following characters and situations, or use one of your own, and write an opening paragraph from that character's point of view.

1. A young child, usually very practical and rational, wakes up at night and starts seeing or hearing strange things.
2. A waiter setting up tables before work remembers being yelled at the day before by the boss.
3. A young man who thinks very well of himself is walking to his next class thinking about asking a popular girl for a date.
4. A young woman at a party, angry at being taken for granted by her boyfriend, imagines what she would like to say to him.
5. A humanoid on a long journey from one space station to another fantasizes about what it would be like to be a respected human being.

Preparing to Write

When you write from the point of view of a character, you need to imagine exactly what your character is like. Appearance, personality, childhood background, activities—all these elements combine to make a real character. Even though you will not use all of these elements in your paragraph, thinking about them will help make your character seem real to you.

Take a few moments and imagine that you are the character you want to write about. You can get ideas for your character from many different sources: observation of people you know, details you notice about people you pass in the street, stories about your childhood or other people's childhoods, and any other sources that prove useful. On a separate sheet of paper, write the name you choose for your character at the top and jot down your responses to the following questions about the character. Use these notes to help get a complete sense of your character's identity before beginning the paragraph.

1. What was my childhood like? (Do I come from a large family, or am I an only child? Do I get along well with my family? Was there anything unusual about my childhood: for example, was I extremely poor or rich? What did my parents do for a living? What did they want me to be when I grew up?)
2. Where did I grow up? (What do I remember most about my childhood? Walking through the woods in the snow? Sitting on a hobbyhorse in a dusty attic? Getting in trouble by turning on the water hydrants in the summer?)

3. Where do I live now, and what do I do? (What brought me to this place? Do I still live in the town where I grew up, or have I traveled many places to arrive here? What do I do during the day? Do I have a job, am I unemployed, am I a student? How do I feel about what I do? Would I do something else if I could? How does my family feel about what I do?)
4. How do I feel about myself? (What do I look like? Do I feel pleased with my appearance? What is my most noticeable physical trait: a facial feature, the way I walk, the way I speak?)
5. What is the most important thing in my life? (What am I committed to: my work, another person, being successful? Do others think of me as a dedicated person, as an energetic person, or as a drifter? What would happen to me if I had to give up the most important thing in my life?)

Once you have your character clearly in mind, begin your paragraph in the middle of an activity. Katherine Mansfield focuses on her character waking up because it is a significant time for him. He detests the way his wife wakes him up. Imagine your character in the middle of a significant activity and begin by writing what is going on in your character's mind as it is happening.

Setting

In "Mr. Reginald Peacock's Day," the main focus is on the character Reginald rather than on the setting of the story. Many short story writers, however, weave in descriptions of the setting with character descriptions. In the opening paragraphs of the story "The Wheelbarrow" by V. S. Pritchett, the writer introduces the main characters and the setting together. He presents them from the general, or *omniscient*, point of view. As you read, notice how V. S. Pritchett combines descriptive details of the setting, the bonfire in particular, and the characters.[1]

Omniscient means "all-knowing."

> "Robert," Miss Freshwater's niece called down from the window of the dismantled bedroom, "when you have finished that, would you mind coming upstairs a minute? I want you to move a trunk."
>
> And when Evans waved back from the far side of the rumpled lawn where he was standing by the bonfire, she closed the window to keep out the smoke of slow-burning rubbish—old carpeting, clothes, magazines, papers, boxes—which hung about the waists of the fir trees and blew towards the house. For three days the fire had been burning and Evans, red-armed in his shirt sleeves and sweating along the seams of his brow, was prodding it with a garden fork. A sudden silly tongue of yellow flame wagged out: some inflammable piece of family history—who knew what?—perhaps one of her Aunt's absurd summer hats or a shocking year of her father's day dream accountancy was having its last fling. She saw Evans pick up a bit of paper from the outskirts of the fire and read it. What was it? Miss Freshwater's niece drew back her lips and opened

---

[1] From "The Wheelbarrow" from *Selected Stories* by V. S. Pritchett. Copyright © 1978 by V. S. Pritchett. Reprinted by permission of Literistic, Ltd. and Random House, Inc.

her mouth expectantly. At this stage all family privacy had gone. Thirty, forty, fifty, years of life were going up in smoke.

Evans took up the wheelbarrow and swaggered back with it across the lawn towards the house, sometimes tipping it a little to one side to see how the rubber-tyred wheel was running and to admire it. Miss Freshwater's niece smiled. With his curly black hair, his sun-reddened face and his vacant blue eyes, and the faint white scar or chip on the side of his nose, he looked like some hard-living, hard-bitten doll. "Burn this? This lot to go?" was his cry. He was an impassioned and natural destroyer. She could not have found a better man. "Without you, Robert," she said on the first day and with real feeling, "I could never have faced it."

The preceding paragraphs open in the middle of an interesting activity: Miss Freshwater's niece and her helper, Robert Evans, have built a bonfire to destroy the "old carpeting, clothes, magazines, papers, boxes" that the niece does not want to save from her aunt's house. The setting is the house itself and the lawn in front, where the fire has burned for three days.

V. S. Pritchett describes the bedroom the niece calls from as "dismantled." What does that one word tell you about the scene? How does Pritchett describe the lawn where Evans tends the fire? The writer also tells specific items that the niece imagines burning in the fire. What do these details, such as the "absurd summer hat," tell you about the niece's family and her attitude toward them? Evans himself is described as he "swaggered back" across the lawn. The word *swaggered* tells the reader a good deal about Evans' character: someone who swaggers is proud, conceited, sure of himself or herself. What other descriptive phrases tell about Evans' character?

Writing Practice 2

Imagine that you are writing a short story and that your opening paragraph or paragraphs will introduce the setting and main character. First, decide if you are going to write from a character's point of view, as in the passage by Katherine Mansfield, or from a general point of view, as in the passage from V. S. Pritchett. (You may want to write from the point of view of the character you created for Writing Practice 1.) Next, read the following suggestions to help imagine your setting and character, and on a separate sheet of paper, write down the details that come to you. Then select the most important details and write a one- or two-paragraph description introducing your main character and the setting of your story.

1. A young man sits at a window and looks into the street below. (Where does this scene take place—in a small town, a city? Does the man live in this room? Imagine what objects in the room might tell you about his personality. What is his mood as he looks into the street? Is he looking for someone or just watching the passersby? What does he look like? If someone walking by on the street noticed the man, what impression would he make?)
2. A woman standing in the middle of a room suddenly flies into a rage and starts breaking everything in sight. (Where does the action take

place—in the woman's home, the home of a friend, a public place? What is the first thing she picks up to break? Does she look at it before she breaks it? Why is she suddenly enraged? Is she alone, or did someone say something to her? What time of day is it? What is passing through her mind as she tears the room apart? Does she enjoy what she is doing? Think of five other items that she smashes. How old is the woman?)

3. An older man walks down the road to the place where he lives; he walks slowly because he has just been fired. (What does the man look like as he walks along? Could a passerby tell that something was wrong by looking at him, or does he contain his feelings? Where does he walk? Does he notice anything around him, such as lines in the pavement, snow beginning to fall, familiar shop windows? Does anyone speak to him as he walks along? What does he think of—what has happened, or what is going to happen to him in the future? Is the man married? What work did he do? Was he justly or unjustly fired? What time of day is it?)

Characters and Setting in Plays

When you read a play, you first learn about characters and setting by the notes the playwright makes at the beginning of the play. These notes describe where the action of the play will take place and also give brief descriptions of the characters involved. The following notes are taken from the beginning of a play by Tom Stoppard titled *Enter a Free Man.* As you read, notice the specific details given about the setting and about each character.[1]

Act One

> Stage Right is the living-room of RILEY's home . . . a dining-table with chairs, a settee, a grandfather clock, a portrait of the Queen, a transistor radio (the only thing that does not look vaguely out of date). Everything is spick and span. There are lots of potted plants, on sills, shelves and tables, and almost everywhere where there is a plant there is some plumbing above it, quite discreet. Stairs to the bedrooms can be seen beyond the door.
>
> PERSEPHONE is responsible for the tidiness. She is matronly, plump, plain, nice, vague, usually vaguely distracted. She is a great duster and emptier of ashtrays. Her daughter LINDA is in pyjamas. She is eighteen, self-assured, at least on the surface, and can be as cruel or warm as she feels like being. She is *never* sentimental, and often anti-sentiment: sharp, abrasive, cool, when her guard is up, and rather childlike when it drops.
>
> Stage Left is the bar, the public bar of a slightly old-fashioned unfashionable pub in what is probably a seedy urban suburb. . . .
>
> RILEY is a smallish untidy figure in a crumpled suit (when he appears)—a soiled fifty with a certain education somewhere in the past: it gives him a tattered dignity now. He is certainly not mad but he is definitely odd. Unsinkable, despite the slow leak.

The preceding descriptions help the reader to envision how the characters will interact. The tidy character of Persephone is set against the "untidy

---

[1]From *Enter a Free Man* by Tom Stoppard. Reprinted by permission of Faber and Faber Ltd. and Grove Press, Inc.

figure" of her husband Riley, and when their daughter Linda is described as "sharp, abrasive, cool," the reader can imagine that she will not be in harmony with either of her parents. What other descriptive details does Stoppard give as clues to the nature of the play? For example, the setting is given as two distinct places: the living room and the "old-fashioned unfashionable pub." The action of the play will shift between these two places. What specific details does Stoppard use to describe each place?

Dialogue

Dialogue is conversation between characters.

In plays, and in much short fiction as well, the reader learns about characters mainly through *dialogue.* Dialogue can be used to reveal the personality of characters by showing how they speak, how they interact with others, and by showing what others say about them.

The following dialogue from *Enter a Free Man* takes place between George Riley, the main character, and a casual acquaintance named Harry. Riley is an unsuccessful inventor, who believes that some day he will make it big. Harry is around thirty, "flashy, sharp, well-dressed." Earlier in the scene Riley announced that he has walked out on his family, but no one takes him seriously. As you read, notice how Stoppard uses conversation to give information about each character.[1]

RILEY: A man must resist. A man must stand apart, make a clean break on his own two feet! Faith is the key—faith in oneself. *(Producing out of his pocket an envelope which he waves about.)* I have in here a little idea—one of many—that will take me away from all this. I'm saying good-bye to it all, Harry, just as I said good-bye to Persephone.

HARRY: It rings a bell. Let's have a look at it.

RILEY: What the creative mind needs is respect for its independence.

HARRY: Exactly! Respect. That's what we've got for you. We all have. Right, Carmen?

Carmen, a man, is the pub owner.

CARMEN: What?

HARRY: You see—respect. You've been coming in here, and we like it. Raises the tone. Right, Carmen?

CARMEN: Eh?

HARRY: Because of what? Because we're common. I mean, what have we got to give the world? Nothing. But you're—well, you're a genius! An inventor! You're a clever bloke, sitting there in your workshop, pioneering you might say, from your blood and your sweat for the lot of your fellow man.

RILEY: The lot of my fellow man!

HARRY: It's people like you who made this country great.

RILEY: You've got something here, Harry. That's very good.

HARRY: I had to say it.

RILEY: Thank you, Harry.

HARRY: *Able* thinks you're somebody—don't you?

Able is a sailor.

ABLE: What?

---

[1]From *Enter a Free Man* by Tom Stoppard. Reprinted by permission of Faber and Faber Ltd. and Grove Press, Inc.

HARRY: Don't you think George here is a clever bloke?

ABLE: 'Course he's a clever bloke. He's an inventor, isn't he?

HARRY: My very point. An inventor. That's your job. Amazing. I don't know if you've ever thought, George, but if you took away everything in the world that had to be invented, there'd be nothing left except a lot of people getting rained on.

RILEY *(excitedly)*: You're right! Progress is the child of invention! . . . *(Soberly.)* Harry, I have been touched by what you have said. *(He brandishes his envelope.)* My own resources are limited, but simplicity is the hardest thing to achieve—the simple idea that is a revolution. And I have achieved it, Harry. I would like you to have the honour of being the first to see it.

HARRY: Oh, I'm very honoured, George. I'll remember this. *(*RILEY *opens the envelope and takes out a smaller, ordinary letter-envelope. He hands this to* HARRY, *who inspects it and turns it over dumbly.)* Yes. . . . Yes, I can see this going over very big. A lovely job. A nice piece of work. An envelope. But—well, George, I must confess to a slight sense of—how should I put it?—

CARMEN: Disappointment—

HARRY: Disappointment. Yes, disappointment. An envelope—oh, I'm not saying it's not good, but it's not new, George, not new. An invention is better if it's new.

RILEY: You haven't noticed. Look at it. Something's different. You see? Gum on both sides of the flap! You see what that means?

HARRY: Yeah, yeah . . . what?

RILEY: You can use it twice.

*(*HARRY *stands up. Walks round his stool, speechless with admiration and wonder.* RILEY *watches him expectantly.)*

HARRY: Genius . . . genius . . .

RILEY: You've got it. An envelope you can use twice. For instance, I write you a letter. I use one side, and then *you*—turn it inside out, write my address on it—and there's your gum on the flap!

HARRY *(almost beyond words)*: Simplicity. The simplicity of it. First the wheel, now this.

The preceding conversation shows two characters with completely different attitudes. The reader learns very early that Harry does not take Riley seriously, that Harry is quietly mocking him. For example, when Harry exaggerates about Riley's labors, "your blood and your sweat for the lot of your fellow man," he is obviously poking fun. Riley, however, is totally serious. From this dialogue the reader learns that Riley wants to believe in himself so much that he does not see the way Harry makes fun of him. What else do you learn about Riley's character from the conversation? What sort of person is Harry? What do you think his reason is for making fun of Riley?

Writing Practice 3

Use the Preparing to Write suggestions on pages 213–214 for help in creating a character.

Imagine that you are writing a play and that you will begin with a brief description of the scene and the main characters. You may use a realistic setting, like the one described by Tom Stoppard on page 216, or you may use a fantasy or science fiction setting. Using a separate paragraph for the setting and for each character, write a brief description telling where the play takes place and what each character is like.

Writing Practice 4

Imagine that you are writing a play and that you want to create a dialogue between two characters. You may use the characters you described for Writing Practice 3 or work with other characters of your choice. At the top of a sheet of paper, write the name of each character with a one- or two-sentence description of each. Then write at least one page of dialogue, indicating when each character speaks by writing the name on a new line as the dialogue on page 217 shows. The following suggestions may help you find ideas for your dialogue situation.

1. The scene is a bus station, train station, or airport. A girl is leaving for college, saying goodbye to her parents (or to one parent).
2. The scene is a front porch or stoop. Two people are saying goodnight after a date; one of them has had a great time, the other has been waiting all evening for the date to end.
3. The scene is a restaurant. Two people who used to be friends are meeting after several years. Each wants to impress the other with what he or she has done, but both feel insecure about themselves.
4. The scene is a deserted castle in the Carpathian Mountains. Viola Lovejoy, the heroine, is about to learn a terrible secret about Count Vladimir from the old gypsy.

For Your Journal

Good imaginative writing relies on the writer's powers of observation to make scenes and characters come alive for the reader. You can practice your own skills of observation by writing descriptions of places and people you encounter in daily life. (They do not have to be strange or unusual to be interesting.) Select one place or one person to observe closely. Then write a description, using specific details to record your impressions of the place: its sounds, tastes, smells, and textures as well as its visual details. Write a description of the person, noting important details of appearance and behavior.

Plot and Conflict

A *plot* is a story-line: a plan of action that centers on a conflict and that is brought to some kind of resolution.

The element of struggle between opposing forces in a plot is called *conflict*. Without conflict a plot becomes simply a series of connected events, with nothing special to compel the reader's attention. For example, the story "Mr.

Reginald Peacock's Day" begins with the main character in conflict with his wife, or rather in conflict with his wife as he imagines her to be. Without the conflict the character would simply wake up, conduct his singing lessons, give a successful concert, go to dinner, and return home. The story might have interesting descriptive passages, but without conflict it would not have a true plot. Conflict helps create tension; within a story it makes the reader ask, "How will this be resolved?"

Although there are several types of conflict, conflict most often occurs between characters. For example, Mr. Peacock is in conflict with his wife because he feels she does not understand his needs as an artist. Conflict can also refer to a character's struggle against external circumstances or to a character's inner battle. In the story "The Wheelbarrow" the real conflict in the story takes place within the mind of Miss Freshwater's niece. She feels that she has no attachment to her past and wants to burn it all in the huge bonfire. When she comes upon an old trunk with her private things in it, however, the sight of her old diary and letters and dresses overwhelms her. V. S. Pritchett describes her emotion: "The house, so anonymous, so absurd, so meaningless and ghostless, had suddenly got her." In the following passage from the story, notice the specific details the writer uses to describe the scenes in the album. How does the niece feel about the pictures she sees?[1]

> . . . She was looking painfully through the album, rocking her head slowly from side to side, her mouth opening a little and closing on the point of speech, a shoulder rising as if she had been hurt, and her back moving and swaying as she felt the clasp of the past like hands on her. She was looking at ten forgotten years of her life, her own life, not her family's, and she did not laugh when she saw the skirts too long, the top-heavy hats hiding the eyes, her face too full and fat, her plainness so sullen, her prettiness too open-mouthed and loud, her look too grossly sly. In this one, sitting at the café table by the lake when she was nineteen, she looked masterful and at least forty. In this garden picture she was theatrically fancying herself as an ancient Greek in what looked like a night-gown! One of her big toes, she noticed, turned up comically in the sandal she was wearing. Here on a rock by the sea, in a bathing dress, she had got thin again—that was her marriage—and look at her hair! This picture of the girl on skis, sharp-faced, the eyes narrowed—who was that? Herself—yet how could she have looked like that! But she smiled a little at last at the people she had forgotten. This man with the crinkled fair hair, a German—how mad she had been about him. But what pierced her was that in each picture of herself she was just out of reach, flashing and yet dead; and that really it was the *things* that burned in the light of permanence—the chairs, the tables, the trees, the car outside the café, the motor launch on the lake. These blinked and glittered. They had lasted and were ageless, untouched by time, and she was not.

Turning through the leaves of the photo album, Miss Freshwater's niece discovers "ten forgotten years of her life." Remembering them is painful to her. She sees herself critically, and even her prettiness as a girl seems "too open-mouthed and loud." What other details describe her in the photographs?

---

[1]From "The Wheelbarrow" from *Selected Stories* by V. S. Pritchett. Copyright © 1978 by V. S. Pritchett. Reprinted by permission of Literistic, Ltd. and Random House, Inc.

When the niece observes that the *things*, rather than herself in the photos, are what seem real and permanent, what does that tell you about her character? How do you imagine that she feels about having burned up all the many things from her past?

Writing Practice 5

The following suggestions are for conflicts between two characters in a play or short story, or conflict within a character. Select one of these conflicts, or substitute one of your own, and write a paragraph or play dialogue that sets forth the conflict.

1. Two friends walk home together from school. That day one noticed the other cheating on an important test in class, a test he/she had studied hard for all weekend. They argue.
2. Two brothers (or sisters) talk together on Saturday morning. The older one tells the younger one not to tag along during the day, and the younger one is hurt.
3. A clerk and a customer in a department store argue about merchandise the customer wants to return.
4. A mother is driving her son to school in the morning. He wants to tell her he is big enough to take care of himself and does not want the ride, but cannot bring himself to say anything directly.
5. A player walks home alone after a badly played game that his/her team lost. The player has doubts about his/her abilities in the game.

Resolving the Conflict

In fables and fairy tales, conflicts are usually resolved by a single simple action, and the characters live happily ever after. The Prince wakes Sleeping Beauty with a kiss, and the enchanted castle awakes; Jack kills the evil giant and saves his family from poverty. Conflict in most plays and short stories requires a more complex resolution. There are many different ways to resolve a struggle, but all depend on a number of factors rather than on one simple act, and most leave the reader with a sense of what will happen to the characters in the future.

The word *resolution* does not necessarily mean that the conflict will end. Sometimes, the characters are involved in a conflict they will not be able to change. In this case the resolution is the understanding that the nature of the struggle in the future will remain the same. For example, in "Mr. Reginald Peacock's Day" by Katherine Mansfield, the story ends with Mr. Peacock still unable to break through his negative feelings about his wife and treat her like a human being.

The most clear-cut type of resolution occurs when a character makes a major change. Something happens in the plot to make the character change behavior or point of view. This change can be the result of a personal realization, the efforts of another character, or a combination of the two.

Writing Practice 6

Write a short story or a short one-act play, using the elements of character, setting, dialogue, plot, and conflict. You may draw from material you wrote in another writing practice or use any of the suggestions for characters and situations in the Writing Practice exercises in this chapter.

Writing Poetry

The term *poetry* covers a wide range of imaginative writing. Although much poetry follows formal patterns of rhyme and rhythm, poetry can also be written with no formal patterns and can even be composed in paragraph form like prose. What do these highly different forms have in common?

The British poet Gerard Manley Hopkins described poetry as speech that was framed "to be heard for its own sake and interest even over and above its interest of meaning." In all poetry, then, the reader is aware not only of what the poet is saying but also of the special language being used to say it. The special language of poetry is in general more musical and rhythmic than everyday speech or even than the language of stories and plays. In this section you will learn about the elements that make the language of poetry distinct from other imaginative writing and also learn how to compose different types of poems yourself.

Sound patterns in poetry are similar to the sound patterns of repeated notes and phrases in music. The musical elements of poetry are so important that the British writer Thomas Carlyle once described poetry as "musical thought." In poetry the pattern of repeating sounds is called *rhyme,* the pattern of repeating rhythm is called *meter,* and the patterns of repeating lines are called *stanzas.*

The Element of Rhyme

Words *rhyme* when they share similar sounds.

Words can rhyme exactly, as in the rhyme *light/sight,* or words can rhyme approximately, as in *light/parasite, light/time,* or *light/out.* The first type of rhyme is called *exact,* or *perfect, rhyme.* The second type is called *half,* or *slant, rhyme.*

The following poem by the British poet Stevie Smith uses exact rhyme in combination with half rhyme. The combination gives a musical feeling to the poem, and the rhymes help knit the lines of poetry together. Identify the exact and half rhymes after reading the poem.

Not Waving but Drowning[1]

Nobody heard him, the dead man,
But still he lay moaning:
I was much further out than you thought

[1]"Not Waving but Drowning" in *Selected Poems of Stevie Smith* by Stevie Smith. Copyright © 1964 by Stevie Smith. Reprinted by permission of New Directions Publishing Corporation and James MacGibbon. (VERBAL PERMISSION from MacGibbon)

And not waving but drowning.

Larking means "playing."

Poor chap, he always loved larking
And now he's dead.
It must have been too cold for him his heart gave way,
They said.

Oh, no no no, it was too cold always
(Still the dead one lay moaning).
I was much too far out all my life
And not waving but drowning.

—*Stevie Smith*

The exact rhyme in "Not Waving but Drowning" is *dead/said.* The half rhyme is *moaning/drowning.* Notice that each stanza uses the same rhyming pattern, with the rhyme on the final word of the second and fourth lines.

The type of half rhyme used in Stevie Smith's poem is called *consonance. Consonance* is the repetition of final consonant sounds, but not vowel sounds, in a pair of rhyming words. *Wing/song, right/out, moaning/drowning*—all are examples of consonance. Another type of half rhyme is called *assonance. Assonance* is the repetition of vowel sounds in a poem. Whereas *seethe* and *breathe* are exact rhymes, *seethe/he* is an example of assonance. *Light/time, boat/shone,* and *half/apple* are all examples of assonance.

In formal rhyming patterns the words at the end of each line rhyme. It is also possible for words within a poem to rhyme exactly or to make a half rhyme. When repeating sounds occur within a poem, the effect is called *internal rhyme.* For example, Stevie Smith uses internal rhyme to emphasize meaning in the line "Oh, no no no, it was too cold always." The repeating *o* sound has a moaning quality that emphasizes the importance and the meaning of the line. Name other examples of internal rhyme that you find in "Not Waving but Drowning."

Another rhyming pattern that occurs within a poem is called *alliteration.* Words *alliterate* when they begin with the same sound rather than end with the same sound. The phrase "Oh, no no no," then, is an example of alliteration, but alliteration usually applies to different words that begin with the same sound.

Writing Practice 7

Use the Preparing to Write section that follows to help you with ideas for your poem.

Write a poem of at least eight lines, using the musical effects of exact rhyme, half rhyme, alliteration, or a combination of these. Do not use the same rhyming sound for the last word in each line. Instead, alternate rhymes in a pattern you choose throughout the poem.

Preparing to Write

When you write a poem using a formal element such as rhyme, it is important to think about the subject of the poem first rather than to think of the rhymes. When you write down a group of rhymes and then try to make a poem from them, the result is usually stilted and artificial. Rhyme should be an essential part of the poem, not an effect imposed upon it.

In her poem "Not Waving but Drowning" Stevie Smith writes about an impossible speech. A dead man speaks to the living, who do not understand him, and says in effect, "All my life I have been just beyond your reach, calling for help, and no one heard me." The other speakers in the poem think he was too far out in the cold water, that he had a heart attack: "Oh, no no no," the dead man answers. Still they do not understand him.

You might want to use an impossible speech as the subject of your poem; give voice to someone or something that cannot speak. This speech can come from a person who would like to express a thought or feeling but cannot, or it can come from something that has no voice. For example, you might imagine what the wind or rain would say if it had a human voice, or the ocean, the moon, the winter, a fire, death, or a long highway.

Suppose, for example, that you want to write about the voice of the snow. Imagine yourself in a particular place, looking at a snowy field or street, or watching the snow come down. Stevie Smith begins her poem, "Nobody heard him, the dead man." You may begin your poem in a similar fashion: "Nobody heard the snow," or some phrase to tell the reader that the snow will speak. Next, think about the snow itself. The snow is speaking because it is not understood, like the drowned man in Stevie Smith's poem. Why is it not understood? What does it want to say to people or to the earth? What does it feel? How does it envision itself? Think about all these questions as they apply to your subject. What your subject has to say is the heart of the poem.

As you think about what your subject has to say, jot down the ideas that come to you on a piece of paper. Then use brainstorming or a rhyming dictionary to create rhymes for some of the words you have chosen. For example, if you find many words that rhyme with *snow*, use *snow* as one of your end rhymes. You can rhyme every other line, as the Stevie Smith poem shows, or rhyme every line with another, like the Ted Hughes poem on page 231.

When you have finished your poem, give it a title.

The Element of Meter

Meter is a formal rhythmic pattern of sound in a poem.

There are many different ways to organize patterns of sounds into formal meters. The meter most commonly used in English poetry is called *accentual-syllabic* meter. To understand accentual-syllabic meter, look at the following line by the Irish poet William Butler Yeats.

When yóu are óld and gréy and fúll of sléep

In the preceding line the marked syllables are the ones your voice would emphasize as you read. The line makes a pattern. An unaccented syllable (starting with *When*) is followed each time by an accented syllable (starting with *you*). You can hear the same pattern in these words: *reléase, enjóy, deceíve, allów*. This unaccented/accented pattern is the metrical unit most common to English: the *iamb*.

The line by Yeats follows a second pattern of organization: the number of syllables used adds up to ten, so there are five accented syllables in each line. As you read the rest of the poem, "When You Are Old," notice how the two patterns work in each line. Read the poem aloud or listen to it read so that you can hear the basic sound pattern.

When You Are Old[1]

When you are old and grey and full of sleep,
And nodding by the fire, take down this book,
And slowly read, and dream of the soft look
Your eyes had once, and of their shadows deep;

How many loved your moments of glad grace,
And loved your beauty with love false or true,
But one man loved the pilgrim soul in you,
And loved the sorrows of your changing face;

Bars here means "bars of the fire grate."

And bending down beside the glowing bars,
Murmur, a little sadly, how Love fled
And paced upon the mountains overhead
And hid his face amid a crowd of stars.

—*W. B. Yeats*

Each line of the preceding poem follows the iambic pattern of an unstressed syllable followed by a stressed syllable. There are a few variations, to add emphasis or to prevent the poem from becoming too regular. For example, in the second line, the phrase "take down this book" is a variation. Usually you would not say "take dówn this bóok." The words *take down* are both accented, which emphasizes the meaning of the words. There is no variation, however, in the number of syllables used in each line. In accentual-syllabic meter the syllable pattern remains the same throughout the poem.

"When You Are Old" also follows a regular rhyming pattern throughout the poem. Does Yeats use exact rhyme or half rhyme at the end of each line? Name examples of internal rhyme that you find.

When you read a formal poem, always think about how the formal pattern of rhyme and meter fits the meaning of the poem. For example, in Yeats' poem the speaker addresses a woman he loves as he imagines her in the future, as an old woman. The regular, steady meter gives a quiet feeling to the poem that enhances its meaning; it is a poem about memory. What do you learn from this poem about the poet who loves the woman? What does the woman feel about him? What specific words does the poet use to describe the woman? How does he want her to think of him in the future?

---

[1]"When You Are Old" from *Collected Poems* of William Butler Yeats. (New York: Macmillan, 1956) Reprinted by permission of Macmillan Publishing Co., Inc., M. B. Yeats, Anne Yeats, and Macmillan London Limited.

Writing Practice 8

Write a poem that uses regular meter in each line. You may use the pattern of five accented syllables to a line or choose another number. It may be helpful to reread the Yeats poem on page 225 before you begin. You may include rhyme in your poem if you wish. The following ideas can be used as suggestions for the subject of your poem.

1. Write a poem to someone in the future, as Yeats does in "When You Are Old." Imagine what the person will be like then. It will help to visualize the person in a definite setting, as Yeats imagines the woman nodding by her fire over a book. Tell this person what you would like him or her to remember of earlier times. You could also write a poem to someone who has not been born yet and tell that person what he or she should know of the earth as it is now, when you are living. For example, you could talk about sights and sounds that are beautiful or pleasurable to you, experiences that a future person might not share.

2. Imagine two characters as the subject of your poem. One is in love with the other, but this love is not returned. Write the love poem that one would write to the other, using descriptive details as Yeats does when he speaks of the woman's appearance and her "pilgrim soul."

3. Imagine that you yourself are old and write a poem about an important memory that you have kept all your life. You might want to begin your poem by envisioning yourself in a particular place: sitting in a chair, staring out the window, walking through the park, or being someplace quiet where you can call up your memories. Include details about where you are and what you see in the present as well as what it is you remember.

The Element of Structure

When the lines of a poem are divided into groups, each grouping is called a *stanza*.

The number of lines in each stanza forms a pattern that usually repeats throughout the poem. For example, both the Stevie Smith poem on pages 222–223 and the Yeats poem on page 225 use three stanzas of four lines each. The way a poem is divided into stanzas is part of its overall form or structure. As with rhyme and meter, the structure should reflect and enhance the meaning of the poem.

Poets may also divide their poems into stanzas of unequal length. Usually this indicates a grouping of ideas, with each stanza devoted to one major idea. In the first two stanzas of "Dover Beach" by Matthew Arnold, for example, the stanza breaks serve a definite purpose. What is the subject of the first stanza? Of the second?

[from] Dover Beach

The sea is calm tonight,
The tide is full, the moon lies fair
Upon the straits;—on the French coast the light
Gleams and is gone; the cliffs of England stand,
Glimmering and vast, out in the tranquil bay.
Come to the window, sweet is the night-air!
Only, from the long line of spray
Where the sea meets the moon-blanched land,
Listen! you hear the grating roar
Of pebbles which the waves draw back, and fling,
At their return, up the high strand,
Begin, and cease, and then again begin,
With tremulous cadence slow, and bring
The eternal note of sadness in.

Sophocles long ago
Heard it on the Aegean, and it brought
Into his mind the turbid ebb and flow
Of human misery; we
Find also in the sound a thought,
Hearing it by this distant northern sea.

—*Matthew Arnold*

Matthew Arnold uses the stanza structure to indicate a change of thought and setting. In the first stanza a contemporary speaker watches and listens to the sea on a moonlit night from a window overlooking Dover Beach in England. In the second stanza the scene and time both change. The setting is ancient Greece in the time of Sophocles. Sophocles, too, thinks about life's sadness, "the ebb and flow/ Of human misery."

Two other important elements of structure in poems are *line length* and *line breaks.* The choices that poets make about the length of line to use in a poem, and where to break off each line and start another, have an important influence on their poems. The following poem by British poet Ken Smith uses short lines to give the effect of a list jotted down. As you read, notice how the short lines fit the meaning of the poem.

Inventory/Itinerary[1]

Illinois, Iowa
Dead grass & maize stalks
Miles, miles, 4½ thousand
Timeshift 7 hours
2 continents, 1 ocean

---

[1] "Inventory/Itinerary" from *Work, Distances* by Ken Smith. Copyright © 1973 by Ken Smith. Originally published by Swallow Press, Chicago. Reprinted by permission of the author.

Travelling, 4 days
1 good time, much being quiet
200 cigarettes, 1 bottle brandy
1 arrive in Iowa City
March 25th 1969, 6:00 pm
$3.38¢ in my pocket
1 cab-ride into the clapboard wilderness
1 return on foot carrying 2 bags
9 phone calls, 2 wrong numbers, 1 reply
Waiting, waiting
Hunger, loneliness, weariness, silence
1 poem written quickly holding things down
The durations of wind, cold, grainfields
Endless helpfulness, cheerfulness, on the nail
The bland faces, America America
And silence. And night
And wind blowing, right through the heart

—*Ken Smith*

The title of the preceding poem, "Inventory/Itinerary," tells you that the poem will be a kind of list, a record of things the poet takes with him and the places he goes. The short lines emphasize these items and places by focusing the reader's attention on one thing at a time. Notice that when Ken Smith starts writing about emotions and observations in America the line length grows. The longer lines give a flowing, continuous effect. For example, the final line would have a very different feeling if it were written in the following way.

And wind blowing
Right through the heart.

The line break would create a pause that interrupts the flow of thought. Look for other instances in the poem of the importance of line length. What other subjects or feelings do you think would be appropriate for short lines of poetry?

Writing Practice 9

Write an unrhymed poem, paying close attention to structure. If you write in traditional stanzas, be sure to make them all the same length. If you write using the shape of the poem for effect, make the content appropriate to the structure and the length of your lines. The following suggestions may help you find ideas for your poem.

1. Write a poem about a conflict between two people. Focus on one element of the conflict, as John Daniels does when he focuses on his wife's complaints. As you think about this conflict, try to use as many descriptive words as possible to make the two different views clear. You may treat

your subject humorously or seriously. Use the structure of your poem to emphasize the difference between the two people.

2. Write a poem about a journey. Like Ken Smith, you can emphasize the short, staccato quality of the experience by listing things you took, people you saw, things you said, observed, and so on.

Figurative Language in Poetry

Another element that makes the language of poetry distinct is its extensive use of figurative language. The purpose of figurative language is to go beyond the literal meaning of words in order to create a sense of identity or correspondence between dissimilar things. This discovery—the correspondence between things that are apparently different—can help you experience the world in a new way, through the poet's imagination.

Simile and *metaphor* are two widely used types of figurative language. You will find simile and metaphor in prose and even in daily speech, but in poetry figurative language is often the primary means of expression.

A *simile* states a comparison between two unlike items by using words such as *like*, *as*, *than*, *seems*, and *appears*.

The opening stanza of the following poem by British poet Charlotte Mew uses a simile to make an emotional comparison.

[from] To a Child in Death

You would have scoffed if we had told you yesterday
Love made us feel—or so it was with me—like some great bird
    Trying to hold and shelter you in its strong wing;—

—Charlotte Mew

Charlotte Mew, in talking to the dead child, compares herself to a "great bird" protecting the child as it would protect its young. This simile tells you that the poet felt protective toward the child. Similes can also create surprising comparisons, as in the following stanza by Scottish poet Hugh MacDiarmid.

[from] Esplumeoir[1]

'It was an amazing discovery, like the inside of your head
being painlessly scraped out. There was an amazing clarity,
like the brilliant moon falling into it and filling it neatly.'

—Hugh MacDiarmid

Hugh MacDiarmid begins his poem with a startling description of a discovery so amazing that he compares it to "the inside of your head/being

---

[1] From "Esplumeoir" from *Collected Poems of Hugh MacDiarmid*, Rev. Edn. © Christopher Murray Grieve 1948, 1962. Copyright © 1967 by Macmillan Publishing Co., Inc.

painlessly scraped out." What is the second simile in the poem? How does it relate to the first?

A *metaphor* is an implied comparison between two unlike items.

A metaphor is stated without the linking words used by similes. Poets use metaphor to create an expanded sense of experience by showing resemblances in more concentrated language than that of similes. Look for the metaphor in the following excerpt of a poem by Stevie Smith.

[from] Black March[1]

I have a friend
At the end
Of the world.
His name is a breath

Of fresh air.
He is dressed in
Grey chiffon. At least
I think it is chiffon.
It has a
Peculiar look, like smoke.

It wraps him round
It blows out of place
It conceals him
I have not seen his face . . .

—*Stevie Smith*

The metaphor about the strange friend ("His name is a breath/Of fresh air.") has a more concentrated effect than if Smith had written it as a simile: "His name is like a breath of fresh air." "Black March" also contains a simile in its description. What is the simile?

Of the many variations of metaphor, one of the most frequently used is called *personification*.

Personification is a metaphor attributing human appearance, emotion, or other qualities to nonhuman subjects.

In "When You Are Old," Yeats personifies the emotion love, describing it as if it were a person who "paced upon the mountains overhead/And hid his face amid a crowd of stars." This personification expresses in concentrated language how Yeats imagines lost love.

The following poem by Ted Hughes uses personification to describe the experience of inspiration. You have probably shared the experience of trying to write something, waiting for the right idea, and then suddenly having it come into your head. Hughes portrays the thought he is waiting for as a fox, "The Thought-Fox." As you read, notice how the identification of the thought with the fox continues through the poem.

---

[1] From "Black March" in *Collected Poems by Stevie Smith.* Copyright © 1976 by James MacGibbon. Reprinted by permission of Oxford University Press, Inc. and James MacGibbon.

The Thought-Fox[1]

I imagine this midnight moment's forest:
Something else is alive
Beside the clock's loneliness
And this blank page where my fingers move.

Through the window I see no star:
Something more near
Though deeper within darkness
Is entering the loneliness:

Cold, delicately as the dark snow,
A fox's nose touches twig, leaf;
Two eyes serve a movement, that now
And again now, and now, and now

Sets neat prints into the snow
Between trees, and warily a lame
Shadow lags by stump and in hollow
Of a body that is bold to come

Across clearings, an eye,
A widening deepening greenness,
Brilliantly, concentratedly,
Coming about its own business

Till, with a sudden sharp hot stink of fox
It enters the dark hole of the head.
The window is starless still; the clock ticks,
The page is printed.

—*Ted Hughes*

How does Hughes imagine the fox approaching him as the poem progresses? What descriptive words does he use to convey the appearance and movement of the fox? "The Thought-Fox" uses many other poetic devices besides personification, such as a formal stanza pattern. What types of rhyme do you find in the poem? Name the simile and the object that Hughes personifies in the poem.

Writing Practice 10

Write a poem based on simile, metaphor, and/or personification. You may use internal rhyme, but do not use rhyme at the ends of your lines. As you write, remember to fit the structure of the poem to its content. The following suggestions may be helpful in writing your poem.

1. In "Esplumeoir" Hugh MacDiarmid begins with two unusual similes to describe an experience. Write a poem about an experience by making a list of unusual similes. You may want to write about an action, such as

---

[1] "The Thought-Fox" from *Selected Poems, 1957–1967* by Ted Hughes. Copyright © 1957 by Ted Hughes. Reprinted by permission of Harper & Row, Publishers, Inc. and Faber and Faber Ltd.

ice skating, or jumping into a cold river; or you may want to write about a mental activity, such as looking at a painting or listening to music or daydreaming. This poem can be humorous or serious. Include a simile in each line.

2. In "The Thought-Fox" Ted Hughes links an animal with the human attribute of thought. Write a poem making another link between an animal and a human attribute. For example, you might want to write about dreaming: What animal do you associate with the act of dreaming? Thoughts seem to come into the mind instantly, while dreams have a slower, more gradual quality. What animal do you associate with that quality? Write a poem describing a dream coming to you by personifying it as an animal, or a poem linking human or animal qualities in another way.

PART

2 Resources for Writing

11 Library Resources

Using the Library A library is more than a collection of books; it is an ordered collection of information—books, magazines, pamphlets, records, perhaps films and microfilms—arranged so that users may easily find whatever sort of material they seek. In this chapter you will become more familiar with the following important items in the library:

1. The card catalogue
2. Fiction books
3. Nonfiction books
4. The *Readers' Guide*
5. Periodicals
6. Specialized reference books
7. The vertical file
8. Reserved books
9. New books
10. Rare books or special collections
11. Records, tapes, films, microfilms

A working knowledge of the various parts of your library will help you track down many sorts of information with ease and efficiency.

The Card Catalogue

When seeking information, you will find one of the most helpful places to begin looking is the *card catalogue,* a file of cards listing books and other reference material.

This file tells you if the library has a certain book or material on a certain subject, gives you basic information about the book, and indicates where you can find it. The file cards for fiction and nonfiction differ, since these two types of books are shelved separately from each other and are arranged according to different systems.

Catalogue Cards for Fiction

The card catalogue contains two cards for each work of fiction: a title card and an author (or editor) card.

In most libraries fiction works are arranged alphabetically according to the author's last name. Therefore, if you know a book's title, but not its author, you will need to consult the card catalogue. If the library has more than one book by an author, these books will be alphabetically arranged according to the first *main* word in each title. Novels by Elizabeth Bowen, for instance, would be arranged as follows:

The first main words in the title are underlined.

The Death of the Heart
The Heat of the Day
The Last September
A World of Love

Collections of short stories are alphabetized by the author's last name, if one author wrote all of the stories; or by the editor's last name if the collection contains stories by different authors. Short story collections may be shelved with novels, or they may be gathered in a group and placed at the end of the fiction section. Since practices may vary from library to library, check with your librarian on the placement of such collections.

Nonfiction and the Card Catalogue

Each nonfiction book or reference has three cards in the catalogue: one for the title, one for the author or editor, and one for the subject of the book. (See the sample title, author, and subject cards on page 236.)

Nonfiction books are shelved apart from fiction books and are arranged not by title, but by a *call number*, which appears in the upper left-hand corner of the cards.

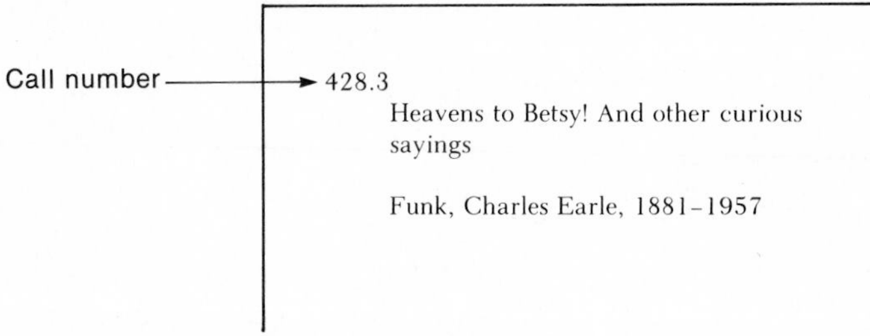

Call number
428.3
Heavens to Betsy! And other curious sayings
Funk, Charles Earle, 1881-1957

The call number of each book is stamped on its spine, and books are arranged in numerical order according to the *Dewey decimal system*, or in larger libraries according to the *Library of Congress system*.

Title card

590.744
ZOO

A zoo for all seasons : the Smithsonian animal world. — Smithsonian Institution, 1979.
192 p. : illus. — (Smithsonian exposition books)

ISBN 0-89599-003-2 ; LC 79-52492

1. National Zoological Park.
2. Zoological gardens. I. Smithsonian Institution.

Author card

Smithsonian Institution.

590.744
ZOO

A zoo for all seasons : the Smithsonian animal world. — Smithsonian Institution, 1979.
192 p. : illus. — (Smithsonian exposition books)

Subject card

ZOOLOGICAL GARDENS

590.744
ZOO

A zoo for all seasons : the Smithsonian animal world. — Smithsonian Institution, 1979.
192 p. : illus. — (Smithsonian exposition books)

The Dewey Decimal System

The Dewey decimal system was created by American librarian Melvil Dewey. In this system nonfiction books are assigned a number according to their subject matter. Subject matter is divided into the following ten general categories.

000–099 General Works:	Includes encyclopedias, periodicals, book lists, and other reference books.
100–199 Philosophy:	Includes the fields of psychology, conduct, and personality.
200–299 Religion:	Includes Bibles and other religious texts, theology books, and mythology.
300–399 Social Sciences:	Includes economics, education, etiquette, fairy tales, folklore, legends, government, and law.
400–499 Language:	Includes grammars and dictionaries of different languages, including English.
500–599 Science:	Includes animals, astronomy, biology, botany, chemistry, geology, general science, mathematics, anthropology, and physics.
600–699 Technology:	Includes agriculture, aviation, business, engineering, health, home economics, manual training, and television.
700–799 The Arts:	Includes movies, painting, photography, sculpture, recreation, and sports.
800–899 Literature:	Includes poetry, drama, essays, criticism, and history of literature.
900–999 History:	Includes geography, travel, history, and collective biography.

The Dewey decimal system contains 999 numbers for various subjects, but classification is expanded with decimal subdivisions. For instance, the subject *Judaism* falls within the 200–299 category of religion and is assigned the number *296*. However, Judaism is a complex subject, so decimal numbers are used to indicate books on specific aspects of the religion:

296.3	Judaic doctrinal theology
296.4	Public service, rites, traditions
296.8	Sects and movements

By using these numbers and decimal points, cataloguing agencies and libraries can assign a book its number and classify it correctly according to general and specific subject.

Exceptions to the Dewey Decimal System

One group of nonfiction books in the Dewey decimal system is not arranged numerically on the shelves: biographies and autobiographies. Collections of biographies, called *collective biographies,* are usually classified under *920,* then arranged alphabetically according to the writer or editor's last name. *The Kings and Queens of England* by Jane Murray would be catalogued as $\frac{920}{M}$, the *M* signifying the initial of the author's last name.

Biographies and autobiographies are usually classified under number *921* and arranged alphabetically according to the *subject's* last name. For instance, Cornelia Otis Skinner's biography of Sarah Bernhardt would be alphabetized under *B* for "Bernhardt." Libraries often stamp the spine of a biographical work with a *B* for biography, then place the last initial of the subject's name beneath. A biography of Pancho Gonzales, for example, might be stamped $\frac{B}{G}$. Check your school or public library to see how biographical works are labeled.

In many libraries books containing specialized information are taken from their usual place on the shelf and put in a special *reference section.* Encyclopedias, atlases, biographical dictionaries, and so on are frequently kept in reference sections. If you look up a book in the card catalogue and see the abbreviations *R* or *Ref.* above the call number, you will know you must consult the reference section, rather than the shelves containing general nonfiction.

The reference section is like a mini-library, with books arranged in order according to their Dewey decimal numbers. Many libraries do not allow reference books to be checked out, so you must use them only in the library.

The Card Catalogue: Cross-References

You may be looking for a book on a certain subject, but be unable to find it in the card catalogue on the first try. If you are interested in becoming a lawyer, for instance, and find no books on that subject, check under *attorney, legal careers,* and so forth. Some card catalogues contain aids called *see* cards; these cards direct you to look for information under another subject heading.

Another card you may encounter is the *see also* card; it means that there is information under that subject heading, but that additional information may be found under other headings.

Catalogue Cards: Other Information

The catalogue card contains more information than a book's subject, title, and author. You may use this additional information to decide how helpful the book will be to you.

1. The card states facts about the author or editor, such as birth and death dates; it also lists joint authors and illustrators, if any exist.
2. The card gives publication facts, such as the publisher's name.

Some publishing houses are more reputable than others, and sometimes a publisher may have a bias that will render information in the book unsuitable or useless. If you are writing a report on geology, for instance, you should probably avoid publications by the Hollow Earth Society, a group convinced that the earth is hollow and populated by unseen hordes of subterranean creatures. On the other hand, if you are writing about the Hollow Earth Society, their publications would be valuable.

Another crucial fact may be the date of the book's publication. In many fields where recent progress and discoveries have been made, an older book may be sadly outdated. Conversely, in an age of instant journalism, some books on important events are written quickly and with little research, and thus may contain errors.

3. The card states whether the book has diagrams, maps, illustrations, and so forth, and how many pages it has. These factors may influence your decision about whether the book will be useful to you.

The Library of Congress System

Although the Dewey decimal system is used in many libraries, another classification system, the Library of Congress system, is spreading and is widely used in college and university libraries. It is more complex and comprehensive than the Dewey decimal system, containing twice as many general subject classifications. Each classification is assigned a capital letter; *the social sciences*, for instance, are classified under *H*. A second capital indicates a subdivision of the classification; *economic theory*, a subdivision of social science, is labeled *HB*. Numbers are added to make more specific distinctions about subject matter. Call numbers *HB3711–HB3840* deal with economic crises of various sorts.

The following is a general outline of the Library of Congress classification system.

A GENERAL WORKS

- AE Encyclopedias (general)
- AI Indexes (general)
- AY Yearbooks (general)

B PHILOSOPHY—RELIGION

- B– BJ Philosophy
  - B Collection. History.
  - BC Logic
  - BF Psychology
  - BJ Ethics

	BL–BX	Religion
	BP	Christianity
	BS	Bible and Exegesis
	BX	Special sects
C	HISTORY—AUXILIARY SCIENCES	
	CB	History of civilization
	CC	Antiquities (general). Archaeology.
	CT	Biography
D	HISTORY AND TOPOGRAPHY (except America)	
	D	General History
	DA	Great Britain
	DK	Russia
	DS	Asia
	DT	Africa
E–F	NORTH AND SOUTH AMERICA	
G	GEOGRAPHY—ANTHROPOLOGY	
	G	Geography (general)
	GN	Anthropology
	GV	Sports and amusements. Games.
H	SOCIAL SCIENCES	
	H	Social sciences (general)
	HA	Statistics
	HB– HJ	Economics
	HB	Economic theory
	HF	Commerce
	HM–HX	Sociology
	HQ	Family, marriage, home.
	HT	Communities. Races.
	HX	Socialism. Communism.
J	POLITICAL SCIENCE	
	JC	Political science
	JF–JX	Constitutional history and administration
K	LAW	
L	EDUCATION	
	LA	History of education
	LB	Theory and practice of education. Teaching.
	LD– LT	Universities and colleges
M	MUSIC	
	M	Music
	ML	Literature of music
	MT	Musical instruction and study
N	FINE ARTS	
	NA	Architecture

ND	Painting	
NK	Art applied to industry	

P LANGUAGE AND LITERATURE

PA	Classical languages and literatures
PB– PH	Modern European languages
PJ– PL	Oriental languages and literatures
PN– PZ	Literature
PN	Literary history and collections (general)
PR	English literature
PS	American literature
PZ	Fiction and juvenile literature

Q SCIENCE

Q	Science (general)
QA	Mathematics
QC	Physics
QD	Natural history. Biology.
QL	Zoology

R MEDICINE

RA	Hygiene
RT	Nursing

S AGRICULTURE—PLANT AND ANIMAL INDUSTRY

SD	Forestry
SK	Hunting sports

T TECHNOLOGY

TA– TH	Engineering and building group
TL	Motor vehicles. Aeronautics.

U MILITARY

V NAVAL SCIENCE

Z BIBLIOGRAPHY

Exercise 1

Use your library to answer the following questions.

1. What system of classification does your library use: Dewey decimal or Library of Congress?
2. Look in the biography section of your library. How are biographical books marked by the librarian? What numbers or letters are used?
3. Where are collections of short stories kept in your library? Are they marked in any way to distinguish them from other fiction?
4. Does your library have a reference section? If so, where? Where are the encyclopedias located in your library?
5. Does your card catalogue contain any cross-referencing; that is, does it contain *see* or *see also* cards?

Exercise 2

Use your card catalogue to see if your library has the following books. If it does, write down the book's title, author, and (if it is nonfiction) its call number.

1. A work by Katherine Mansfield
2. A nonfiction work by James Baldwin
3. A biography of Ho Chi Minh
4. A copy of *Black Elk Speaks*
5. A book on data processing
6. A work by Gwendolyn Brooks
7. A work on running or jogging
8. A work about the War Between the States
9. A copy of *All the President's Men*
10. A copy of *The Dragons of Eden*

Exercise 3

Review the Dewey decimal system on pages 237–238. Using those classifications, write down the category and number series under which you think each of the following books might be found.

Examples

a. The poems of Langston Hughes
a. The poems of Langston Hughes
Literature (800–899)

b. A book on hunting and trapping
b. A book on hunting and trapping
The Arts (700–799)

1. A biography of Eva Peron
2. A book on cartooning
3. A book on whales
4. A book on home repairs
5. A book about *The New York Times*
6. A Latin grammar book
7. A book about women's rights
8. A book about abnormal psychology
9. A play by Lorraine Hansberry
10. A book about Chinese history

Abbreviations Used in Reference Material

You may encounter the following common abbreviations while doing research. Familiarize yourself with them so you can use them as aids.

anon.	author unknown
c.	copyright
cm.	centimeters (The catalogue card states the size of a book in centimeters.)
diagrs.	diagrams
ed.	editor or edition
et al.	and others (indicates several authors or editors)
illus.	illustrated or illustrator
mounted pl.	mounted plates: full page illustrations fastened to page
pseud.	pen name
rev.	revised (material has been updated)
tr. *or* trans.	translated or translator
v., vol., vols.	volume, volumes

Parts of a Book

The following terms refer to books or parts of books.

Appendix or Appendices:	Supplementary material at the end of the book that presents relevant information, such as statistics, quotations, tables
Bibliography:	A list of either (1) books and references the author consulted in writing the work, or (2) works the author recommends for further research on the subject
Copyright:	Copyright information is given on the back of a book's title page. It tells who copyrighted the book and when. Several copyright dates indicate that the book has been revised.
Glossary:	A list of key terms and definitions
Index:	An alphabetized list of people, places, and subjects treated in the book, with the number of the pages on which they appear
Introduction, Foreword, Preface:	Introductory material before a book's first chapter. The author or other writer may comment on the book's content, significance, and so forth.
Gazetteer:	A list of geographical places with brief descriptions of them or statistics about them
Text:	The main body of the book
Title Page:	A page at the book's beginning, stating title, author, and publication facts

Exercise 4

Find the catalogue cards for the following books. (For some questions, you will need to find the book as well.) Answer the following questions, including the title of each book you describe.

1. Find a book of poems by Emily Dickinson. Who is the editor? Is there a preface or introduction? How many pages does it have?
2. Find a book by Alexandre Dumas. Who is its translator? What is its publication date? Does it have any illustrations?
3. Find a book about Pablo Picasso. Are there photographs or illustrations? Are there any mounted plates? Is there an introduction?
4. Find a book by Adam Smith. Is there an appendix? Is there a bibliography? Who is the publisher?
5. Find a book on automotive repair. Are there diagrams and illustrations? When was it copyrighted? Has it ever been revised?
6. Look up *The Oxford Companion to English Literature.* Who is its editor? Does it have prefaces? If so, how many? Does it have appendixes? If so, how many?
7. Look up *The Annals of America.* How many volumes comprise it? Are there maps? Are there illustrations?
8. Find a copy of *Bulfinch's Mythology.* Is there a preface and, if so, by whom? Are there illustrations?
9. Find *The Amy Vanderbilt Complete Book of Etiquette.* Has it been revised or expanded since its first publication? If so, by whom? Are there illustrations?
10. Find a book by Lewis Carroll. Lewis Carroll is a pseudonym; what is the author's real name? Does the book have an introduction? Is it illustrated? If so, by whom?

Using Reference Works

Books that may be used to locate information or to find the answers to questions are called *reference books.* The *Readers' Guide*, encyclopedias, almanacs, and atlases are reference books found in the special reference section of most libraries. In the following sections you will learn how to use these and other reference works to locate specific information.

The *Readers' Guide*

Periodicals (magazines and newspapers) often contain information that may be valuable to your research. Periodicals dating back as far as a year are probably kept in a special section of your library. After a certain time, issues of one magazine or paper are bound into a volume and shelved with other volumes of past years. Your library probably displays a list of the periodicals it keeps, so you can know if the particular magazine or newspaper you seek is available.

Because so many periodicals are published, containing so much diverse information, guides to their contents are regularly published. These are called *periodical indexes*, and the most famous is the *Readers' Guide*. The *Readers' Guide* indexes the contents of over a hundred widely read magazines and is published twenty-one times a year. Each new issue contains an index of the most recent copies of the magazines. So that the library will not be burdened by a flood of small indexes, the *Readers' Guide* frequently publishes cumulative indexes, compiling information for recent months into one volume. At the year's end a one-volume index containing all information is compiled, and every two years a two-year index is issued, so the researcher can cover many months of publishing information by using only the single-volume cumulative indexes.

All issues of the *Readers' Guide* index authors and subjects in alphabetical order. Beneath each subject heading is a list of recent articles on that subject and where they can be found.

The *Readers' Guide* uses many abbreviations. These are explained in special keys in the front of the index. Using the Key to Periodicals Listed and the Key to Abbreviations, you can easily decipher an entry. Consider, for example, the following entry.

> **Fading fall season [effects of actors' strike] H. F. Waters and J. Huck. il Newsweek 96: 72 Ag 18 '80**

The preceding entry is for an article titled "Fading Fall Season," by H. F. Waters and J. Huck, in the August 18, 1980, issue of *Newsweek* magazine (volume 96, page 72). The illustrated article is about the effects of the actors' strike. (Notice that only the first word of the article's title is capitalized in the entry; this is a special style used by the *Readers' Guide*.)

On page 246 you will find a sample page from the *Readers' Guide*.

Exercise 5

Answer the following questions in complete sentences.

1. a. Where is the *Readers' Guide* located in your library?
   b. How far back does your library's collection of *Readers' Guides* extend?
   c. Where is the list of periodicals to which your library subscribes?
2. a. To which of the following periodicals does your library subscribe: *Monthly Labor Review*, *Foreign Affairs*, *Car and Driver*, *Congressional Digest*, *Consumer Reports*?
   b. Does your library keep back issues of any of these magazines? If so, how far back do the issues go?
3. Using copies of the *Readers' Guide*, find at least two recent articles on the following topics: automotive repair, astronomy, nuclear reactors,

WOOD pulp paper products. See Paper products
WOOD rats. See Rats
WOOD sculpture. See Wood carving
WOOD stove pollution. See Smoke
WOOD stoves. See Stoves
WOOD working. See Woodworking
WOODBURY, Robert S.
Yen for a yacht [excerpt] [cont] il Motor B & S 147:76-7+ F; 67+ Mr '81
WOODCARVING. See Wood carving
WOODCHUCK hunting
Chuck hunting is alive and well in Pennsylvania L. Atwill. il Outdoor Life 167:77-80 Ap '81
WOODCOCK, Leonard
Friendly relations, but no U.S. alliance with Peking [interview by J. Wallace] por U.S. •News 90:34 F 9 '81
Inside China [interview by J. Flint] il por Forbes 127:31-2 Mr 16 '81
WOODEN dolls. See Dolls
WOODENWARE
See also
Cutting boards

Lehn ware [reprint from February 1947 issue] V. M. Paul. il Antiques J 36:36+ F '81
WOODHOUSE, R. Y.
Equality faces a dangerous decade [address, November 18, 1980] Vital Speeches 47:242-6 F 1 '81
WOODLANDS, Goochland County, Va. See Plantations
The WOODLANDS, Tex.
Nobody's laughing now. il por Forbes 127:84+ Mr 2 '81
WOODS, Craig
Spring trout shortcut. il Outdoor Life 167:81-2 Ap '81
WOODS, James
James Woods' guilty pleasures. il por Film Comment 17:60-3 Mr/Ap '81
WOODSIDE, William S.
Why American Can is unloading so much. Bus W p48 Ap 13 '81 •
WOODSON, Carter Godwin
I knew Carter G. Woodson. B. E. Mays. Negro Hist Bull 44:21 Ja/F/Mr '81 •
Legend and legacy [excerpts from address, October 17, 1980] J. R. Picott. Negro Hist Bull 44:6-8 Ja/F/Mr '81 •
Philippine challenge. A. Scally. bibl Negro Hist Bull 44:16-18 Ja/F/Mr '81 •
WOODWARD, Bob
They were wrong about The brethren. R. M. Kaus. il Wash M 13:32-6+ Mr '81 •
WOODWORKING
See also
Carpentry
Joints (carpentry)
Miter boxes, gages, etc.
Saws and sawing
Wood carving

Projects

See also
Tables

Weekend workshop [cont] il Pop Mech 155:140-2+ F; 26-7+ Mr '81

Terminology

Words woodworkers use. M. Algozin. il Pop Mech 155:28 Ja '81
WOODWORKING machinery
See also
Lathes
Routing machines
WOODWORKING tools. See Tools
WOODY plants
See also
Shrubs
WOOL, Harold
Coal industry resurgence attracts variety of new workers [excerpt from Labor outlook for the bituminous coal mining industry] bibl f il M Labor R 104:3-8 Ja '81
WORCESTER Art Museum, Worcester, Mass. See Art galleries and museums—Massachusetts
WORD of God. See Logos (theology)
WORD processing
Word machines for word people [authorship use] G. Courter. il por Pub W 219:40-3 F 13 '81
WORD processing equipment industry
See also
Harris Corporation

Word processing: a road to management. B. Scala. Work Wom 6:24+ F '81
Word-processing boom. L. Glynn and others. il Newsweek 97:75 Ap 6 '81
WORDINESS. See Verbosity

entry by author

entry by title

title, issue, and date of magazine

subject heading

secondary subject heading

page numbers of article

"see" cross reference

cancer research. Copy the title, author, and page number of each article and write down the issue of the periodical in which it appears.

4. Pick a topic from among the following: fashion, popular music, wildlife conservation, budgeting, computers. Using the *Readers' Guide*, find an article on your topic. Write down the title, author, and issue of the magazine in which the article appears. Then locate the article itself and write a one-paragraph summary of it.

The Dictionary

Dictionaries are usually classified as one of two kinds: abridged and unabridged. An *abridged dictionary* is the shorter of the two; it does not attempt to define all of the hundreds of thousands of words in the language. An *unabridged dictionary* is more comprehensive, containing many more entries, plus examples of usage; consequently, the unabridged dictionary may be a huge volume or, as in the case of the monumental *Oxford English Dictionary*, as many as twelve hefty volumes.

A good dictionary will contain certain basic information: the word, its syllabication, pronunciation, and definition or definitions. In addition, it will supply a word's etymology, or origins, as well as variant spellings the word may have, and its inflections—for instance, if the word forms a plural or participle irregularly. The dictionary should also give *restrictive labels*, indicating whether the word has special meanings in different disciplines or instances (for example, the same word may mean one thing in chemistry and another in biology, or have another meaning that is slang or a colloquialism). The sample dictionary page on page 248 of this textbook shows how this information is arranged. The numbers and boxes on the sample dictionary page correspond to the numbered explanations of each feature on page 249.

The most complete unabridged dictionary is the twelve-volume *Oxford English Dictionary*. It is also available in a two-volume version with miniaturized print, an interesting work that comes supplied with a magnifying glass; as well as a two-volume *Shorter Oxford English Dictionary* with regular-sized print but fewer entries. A fine one-volume unabridged dictionary is *Webster's Third New International Dictionary*.

Good abridged dictionaries include the following:

Funk and Wagnalls New Standard Dictionary of the English Language
American Heritage Dictionary of the English Language
Random House College Dictionary
Webster's New Collegiate Dictionary
Webster's New World Dictionary

In addition to general dictionaries, there are specialized dictionaries on many subjects, such as *Black's Law Dictionary* and *Grove's Dictionary of Music and Musicians*, to name but two.

Using the Dictionary

Use this guide in conjunction with the sample page from *Webster's New World Dictionary* that is reprinted on this page. The numbers in the following

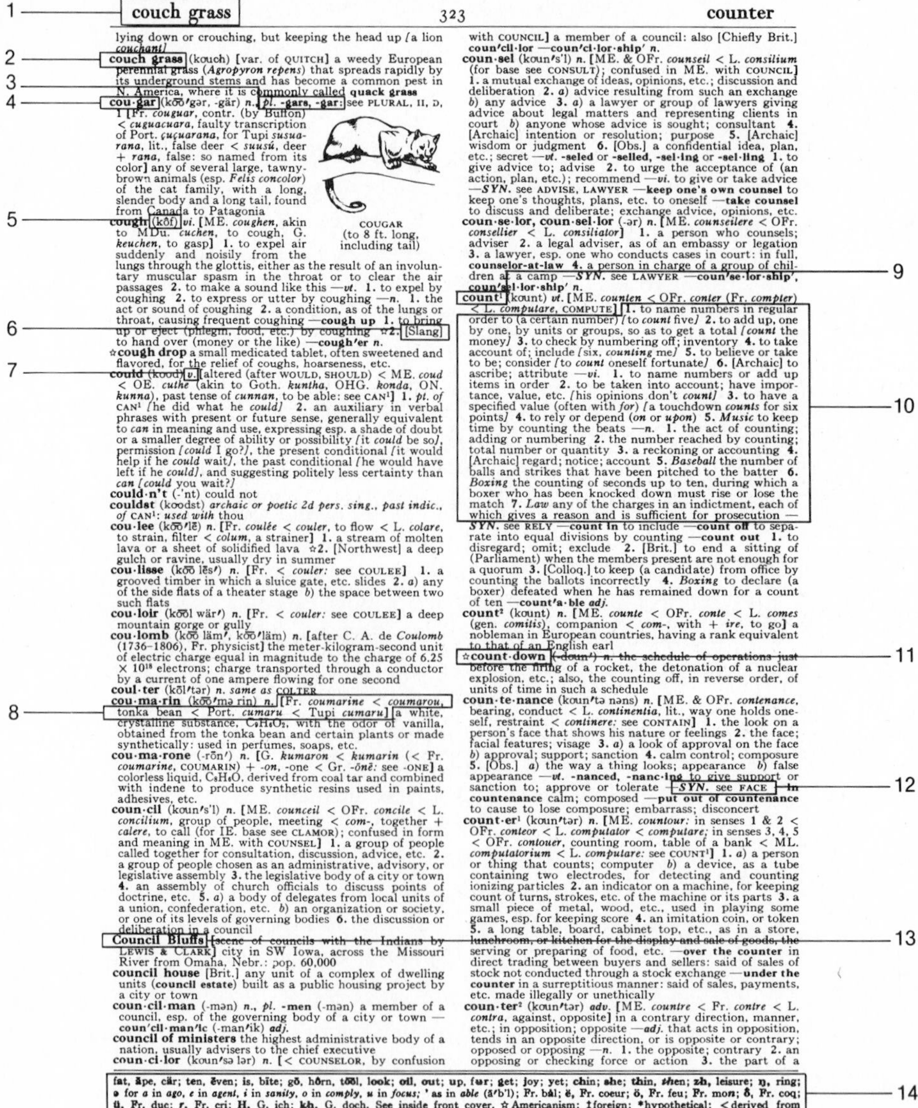

1 **couch grass** 323 **counter**

lying down or crouching, but keeping the head up *[a lion couchant]*

2 **couch grass** (kouch) [var. of QUITCH] a weedy European perennial grass (*Agropyron repens*) that spreads rapidly by its underground stems and has become a common pest in
3 N. America, where it is commonly called **quack grass**

4 **cou·gar** (kōō′gər, -gär) *n.*, *pl.* **-gars, -gar:** see PLURAL, II, D, 1 [Fr. *couguar*, contr. (by Buffon) < *cuguacuara*, faulty transcription of Port. *çuçuarana*, for Tupi *susuarana*, lit., false deer < *suusú*, deer + *rana*, false: so named from its color] any of several large, tawny-brown animals (esp. *Felis concolor*) of the cat family, with a long, slender body and a long tail, found from Canada to Patagonia

COUGAR (to 8 ft. long, including tail)

5 **cough** (kôf) *vi.* [ME. *coughen*, akin to MDu. *cuchen*, to cough, G. *keuchen*, to gasp] **1.** to expel air suddenly and noisily from the lungs through the glottis, either as the result of an involuntary muscular spasm in the throat or to clear the air passages **2.** to make a sound like this —*vt.* **1.** to expel by coughing **2.** to express or utter by coughing —*n.* **1.** the act or sound of coughing **2.** a condition, as of the lungs or throat, causing frequent coughing —**cough up 1.** to bring
6 up or eject (phlegm, food, etc.) by coughing ☆**2.** [Slang] to hand over (money or the like) —**cough′er** *n.*

☆**cough drop** a small medicated tablet, often sweetened and flavored, for the relief of coughs, hoarseness, etc.

7 **could** (kood) *v.* [altered (after WOULD, SHOULD) < ME. *coud* < OE. *cuthe* (akin to Goth. *kuntha*, OHG. *konda*, ON. *kunna*), past tense of *cunnan*, to be able: see CAN¹] **1.** *pt. of* CAN¹ *[he did what he could]* **2.** an auxiliary in verbal phrases with present or future sense, generally equivalent to *can* in meaning and use, expressing esp. a shade of doubt or a smaller degree of ability or possibility *[it could be so]*, permission *[could I go?]*, the present conditional *[it would help if he could wait]*, the past conditional *[he would have left if he could]*, and suggesting politely less certainty than *can [could you wait?]*

could·n't (-'nt) could not

couldst (koodst) *archaic or poetic 2d pers. sing., past indic., of* CAN¹: *used with* thou

cou·lee (kōō′lē) *n.* [Fr. *coulée* < *couler*, to flow < L. *colare*, to strain, filter < *colum*, a strainer] **1.** a stream of molten lava or a sheet of solidified lava ☆**2.** [Northwest] a deep gulch or ravine, usually dry in summer

cou·lisse (kōō lēs′) *n.* [Fr. < *couler:* see COULEE] **1.** a grooved timber in which a sluice gate, etc. slides **2.** *a*) any of the side flats of a theater stage *b*) the space between two such flats

cou·loir (kōōl wär′) *n.* [Fr. < *couler:* see COULEE] a deep mountain gorge or gully

cou·lomb (kōō läm′, kōō′läm) *n.* [after C. A. de *Coulomb* (1736–1806), Fr. physicist] the meter-kilogram-second unit of electric charge equal in magnitude to the charge of 6.25 $\times 10^{18}$ electrons; charge transported through a conductor by a current of one ampere flowing for one second

coul·ter (kōl′tər) *n. same as* COLTER

8 **cou·ma·rin** (kōō′mə rin) *n.* [Fr. *coumarine* < *coumarou*, tonka bean < Port. *cumaru* < Tupi *cumaru*] a white, crystalline substance, $C_9H_6O_2$, with the odor of vanilla, obtained from the tonka bean and certain plants or made synthetically: used in perfumes, soaps, etc.

cou·ma·rone (-rōn′) *n.* [G. *kumaron* < *kumarin* (< Fr. *coumarine*, COUMARIN) + *-on*, -one < Gr. *-ōnē:* see -ONE] a colorless liquid, C_8H_6O, derived from coal tar and combined with indene to produce synthetic resins used in paints, adhesives, etc.

coun·cil (koun′s'l) *n.* [ME. *counceil* < OFr. *concile* < L. *concilium*, group of people, meeting < *com-*, together + *calere*, to call (for IE. base see CLAMOR); confused in form and meaning in ME. with COUNSEL] **1.** a group of people called together for consultation, discussion, advice, etc. **2.** a group of people chosen as an administrative, advisory, or legislative assembly **3.** the legislative body of a city or town **4.** an assembly of church officials to discuss points of doctrine, etc. **5.** *a*) a body of delegates from local units of a union, confederation, etc. *b*) an organization or society, or one of its levels of governing bodies **6.** the discussion or deliberation in a council

13 **Council Bluffs** [scene of councils with the Indians by LEWIS & CLARK] city in SW Iowa, across the Missouri River from Omaha, Nebr.: pop. 60,000

council house [Brit.] any unit of a complex of dwelling units (**council estate**) built as a public housing project by a city or town

coun·cil·man (-mən) *n.*, *pl.* **-men** (-mən) a member of a council, esp. of the governing body of a city or town —**coun′cil·man′ic** (-man′ik) *adj.*

council of ministers the highest administrative body of a nation, usually advisers to the chief executive

coun·ci·lor (koun′sə lər) *n.* [< COUNSELOR, by confusion with COUNCIL] a member of a council: also [Chiefly Brit.] **coun′cil·lor** —**coun′ci·lor·ship′** *n.*

coun·sel (koun′s'l) *n.* [ME. & OFr. *counseil* < L. *consilium* (for base see CONSULT); confused in ME. with COUNCIL] **1.** a mutual exchange of ideas, opinions, etc.; discussion and deliberation **2.** *a*) advice resulting from such an exchange *b*) any advice **3.** *a*) a lawyer or group of lawyers giving advice about legal matters and representing clients in court *b*) anyone whose advice is sought; consultant **4.** [Archaic] intention or resolution; purpose **5.** [Archaic] wisdom or judgment **6.** [Obs.] a confidential idea, plan, etc.; secret —*vt.* **-seled** or **-selled, -sel·ing** or **-sel·ling 1.** to give advice to; advise **2.** to urge the acceptance of (an action, plan, etc.); recommend —*vi.* to give or take advice —***SYN.*** see ADVISE, LAWYER —**keep one's own counsel** to keep one's thoughts, plans, etc. to oneself —**take counsel** to discuss and deliberate; exchange advice, opinions, etc.

coun·se·lor, coun·sel·lor (-ər) *n.* [ME. *counseilere* < OFr. *consellier* < L. *consiliator*] **1.** a person who counsels; adviser **2.** a legal adviser, as of an embassy or legation **3.** a lawyer, esp. one who conducts cases in court: in full, **counselor-at-law 4.** a person in charge of a group of children at a camp —***SYN.*** see LAWYER —**coun′se·lor·ship′**, **coun′sel·lor·ship′** *n.* 9

count¹ (kount) *vt.* [ME. *counten* < OFr. *conter* (Fr. *compter*) < L. *computare*, COMPUTE] **1.** to name numbers in regular order to (a certain number) *[to count five]* **2.** to add up, one by one, by units or groups, so as to get a total *[count the money]* **3.** to check by numbering off; inventory **4.** to take account of; include *[six, counting me]* **5.** to believe or take to be; consider *[to count oneself fortunate]* **6.** [Archaic] to ascribe; attribute —*vi.* **1.** to name numbers or add up items in order **2.** to be taken into account; have importance, value, etc. *[his opinions don't count]* **3.** to have a specified value (often with *for*) *[a touchdown counts for six points]* **4.** to rely or depend (*on* or *upon*) **5.** *Music* to keep time by counting the beats —*n.* **1.** the act of counting; adding or numbering **2.** the number reached by counting; total number or quantity **3.** a reckoning or accounting **4.** [Archaic] regard; notice; account **5.** *Baseball* the number of balls and strikes that have been pitched to the batter **6.** *Boxing* the counting of seconds up to ten, during which a boxer who has been knocked down must rise or lose the match **7.** *Law* any of the charges in an indictment, each of which gives a reason and is sufficient for prosecution — 10
SYN. see RELY —**count in** to include —**count off** to separate into equal divisions by counting —**count out 1.** to disregard; omit; exclude **2.** [Brit.] to end a sitting of (Parliament) when the members present are not enough for a quorum **3.** [Colloq.] to keep (a candidate) from office by counting the ballots incorrectly **4.** *Boxing* to declare (a boxer) defeated when he has remained down for a count of ten —**count′a·ble** *adj.*

count² (kount) *n.* [ME. *counte* < OFr. *conte* < L. *comes* (gen. *comitis*), companion < *com-*, with + *ire*, to go] a nobleman in European countries, having a rank equivalent to that of an English earl

☆**count·down** (-doun′) *n.* the schedule of operations just before the firing of a rocket, the detonation of a nuclear explosion, etc.; also, the counting off, in reverse order, of units of time in such a schedule 11

coun·te·nance (koun′tə nəns) *n.* [ME. & OFr. *contenance*, bearing, conduct < L. *continentia*, lit., way one holds oneself, restraint < *continere:* see CONTAIN] **1.** the look on a person's face that shows his nature or feelings **2.** the face; facial features; visage **3.** *a*) a look of approval on the face *b*) approval; support; sanction **4.** calm control; composure **5.** [Obs.] *a*) the way a thing looks; appearance *b*) false appearance —*vt.* **-nanced, -nanc·ing** to give support or sanction to; approve or tolerate —***SYN.*** see FACE —**in** 12
countenance calm; composed —**put out of countenance** to cause to lose composure; embarrass; disconcert

count·er¹ (koun′tər) *n.* [ME. *countour:* in senses 1 & 2 < OFr. *conteor* < L. *computator* < *computare;* in senses 3, 4, 5 < OFr. *contouer*, counting room, table of a bank < ML. *computatorium* < L. *computare:* see COUNT¹] **1.** *a*) a person or thing that counts; computer *b*) a device, as a tube containing two electrodes, for detecting and counting ionizing particles **2.** an indicator on a machine, for keeping count of turns, strokes, etc. of the machine or its parts **3.** a small piece of metal, wood, etc., used in playing some games, esp. for keeping score **4.** an imitation coin, or token **5.** a long table, board, cabinet top, etc., as in a store, lunchroom, or kitchen for the display and sale of goods, the serving or preparing of food, etc. —**over the counter** in direct trading between buyers and sellers: said of sales of stock not conducted through a stock exchange —**under the counter** in a surreptitious manner: said of sales, payments, etc. made illegally or unethically

coun·ter² (koun′tər) *adv.* [ME. *countre* < Fr. *contre* < L. *contra*, against, opposite] in a contrary direction, manner, etc.; in opposition; opposite —*adj.* that acts in opposition, tends in an opposite direction, or is opposite or contrary; opposed or opposing —*n.* **1.** the opposite; contrary **2.** an opposing or checking force or action **3.** the part of a

fat, āpe, cär; ten, ēven; is, bīte; gō, hôrn, tōōl, look; oil, out; up, fur; get; joy; yet; chin; she; thin, *th*en; zh, leisure; ŋ, ring; 14
ə for *a* in *ago*, *e* in *agent*, *i* in *sanity*, *o* in *comply*, *u* in *focus;* ' as in *able* (ā′b'l); Fr. bál; ë, Fr. coeur; ö, Fr. feu; Fr. mon; ô, Fr. coq; ü, Fr. duc; r, Fr. cri; H, G. ich; kh, G. doch. See inside front cover. ☆ Americanism; ‡foreign; *hypothetical; < derived from

list of information to be found in the dictionary correspond with the numbered items on the sample dictionary page.

1. Guide words are printed at the top of the page to show the first and last words on that page.
2. Word entries are printed in **boldface** type. Words are in alphabetical order.
3. Other forms of the word are also given. These forms may include plurals, principal parts of verbs, and comparative forms of adjectives and adverbs.
4. Syllables are indicated in word entries with a raised dot between them. These syllable markers show where words may be divided at the end of a line of writing.
5. Pronunciation is shown with diacritical marks and simplified spellings. These follow the word entry and are in parentheses.
6. Usage markers show whether or not the word is used in formal English. Meanings of abbreviations for usage labels can usually be found in the front of the dictionary.
7. The part of speech is shown by an abbreviation. The meanings of part-of-speech abbreviations are also listed in the front of the dictionary.
8. Word origins are shown in brackets after the part-of-speech abbreviation. Look in the front of the dictionary for help in reading the history of a word.
9. When one entry has exactly the same spelling as the one that follows it, the two are distinguished by raised numbers.
10. Definitions of the words are numbered with Arabic numbers, with the oldest meanings having the lowest numbers. When a word has many definitions, the definitions are grouped according to the part of speech.
11. Phrases and compound words appear as entries.
12. Synonyms (words that have nearly the same meaning) often appear after definitions. *See* means "see the dictionary entry for the word."
13. Information about people, places, and events is often given.
14. A pronunciation key is often found at the bottom of every other page. A more complete key can be found in the front of the dictionary.

Encyclopedias

Like dictionaries, encyclopedias are a basic research tool, and like dictionaries, most encyclopedias list their entries in alphabetical order. However, whereas the ordinary dictionary confines itself primarily to words and their meanings, the encyclopedia tries to present accurate information from all fields of learning. It is a condensation of human knowledge in all fields of general interest. In addition to articles on various subjects, most encyclopedias contain illustrations, maps, charts, graphs, and (most important) cross-references and bibliographies. One article may contain a cross-reference to other articles that will aid your research, as well as a bibliography of other reference works you may consult.

The modern age is in the midst of what is often called "an explosion of learning"; new information is constantly emerging. Encyclopedias keep up to date in three ways. First, many publish a yearly supplement that updates information and presents new developments. Second, each time the encyclopedia is reprinted, minor revisions are made. Third, at certain intervals the encyclopedia is completely revised and a new edition brought out.

The following encyclopedias are those found most frequently in libraries.

Collier's Encyclopedia, composed of twenty-four volumes, is known for its readable style.

Compton's Encyclopedia and Fact Index, also twenty-four volumes, is written for the younger student, but adults may find its simple style and organization helpful as an introduction to many subjects. *Compton's* is profusely illustrated, containing charts, graphs, and maps. Bibliographies follow the articles, and cross-references are given. The fact index lists all articles pertinent to a certain subject, and a yearbook is published.

Encyclopedia Americana, thirty volumes, is the first encyclopedia published in America, its first edition appearing in 1829. It is also justly noted for its fine articles on science, technology, history, and biography. Containing illustrations, maps, glossaries, cross-references, and bibliographies, the encyclopedia is kept up to date through its yearbook, *Americana Annual.*

Encyclopaedia Britannica, thirty volumes, originally published in England, is now published in the United States. The most recent edition, in thirty volumes, orders information in a new way. The first volume, *Guide to the Britannica*, is introductory. It breaks human knowledge into different divisions, then lists articles pertaining to each subject, indicating where these articles are to be found in the other volumes. The next ten volumes, the *Micropaedia*, contain brief articles on many subjects. If a subject is too lengthy or complex for full treatment in the *Micropaedia*, it is summarized, and a cross-reference is made to relevant articles in the *Macropaedia*. The *Macropaedia* is composed of nineteen volumes of articles that treat subjects in depth. At the end of *Macropaedia* articles, extensive bibliographies of further references are given. Noted for its treatment of historical subjects, the *Encyclopaedia Britannica* is thorough, comprehensive, and scholarly. It is illustrated and contains maps, charts, and tables; it also includes a yearbook.

World Book Encyclopedia, twenty-two volumes, is designed for younger students although adults may find it a helpful reference early in research. It contains a research guide and index in Volume 22 and provides study aids on important subjects. A colorful work with many illustrations, the *World Book* provides lists of cross-references to related articles.

One- and Two-Volume Encyclopedias

"Desk encyclopedias," as one- and two-volume encyclopedias are sometimes called, are useful as introductions to subjects or for quick reference. Far less extensive than larger encyclopedias, they nevertheless present basic facts on a multitude of subjects. Compact and readable, they can be a useful aid to both research and general learning.

The Columbia Encyclopedia, two volumes, contains articles on numerous subjects and supplies bibliographies for further research. It is not illustrated.

The Columbia-Viking Desk Encyclopedia, a one-volume abridgment of the *Columbia Encyclopedia*, is a reference that omits bibliographies. It does, however, have illustrations and charts.

The Lincoln Library of Essential Information is a single-volume work that organizes its information under twelve basic subject headings. It contains an index but supplies no bibliographies.

Exercise 6

Although modern researchers take encyclopedias for granted, these resources have not always been so widely accepted. In the following excerpt from an article in *The New Yorker* on the Eleventh Edition of the *Encyclopaedia Britannica*, Hans Koning describes early reactions to an encyclopedia. After reading the selection, complete the activity that follows.[1]

> The age of the modern encyclopedia began in August of the year 1751, in France, with the delivery of the first volume of the Encyclopédie to its subscribers. When, twenty-one years later, the work was completed, in seventeen volumes of text and eleven volumes of illustrations, a number of its original editors and contributors either had resigned in disgust, like Jean Le Rond d'Alembert, or had spent time in jail, like the chief editor, Denis Diderot, and the printer, André François Lebreton. On one occasion, some of the volumes were locked in the Bastille like criminals, and throughout those years police agents were running around Paris with orders to burn the manuscripts and impound the books. At one point, subscribers were instructed to hand in their sets at the nearest police post. But the Encyclopédie survived—because, according to Voltaire, during a supper in the Trianon Louis XV got into an unceremonious argument over the composition of gunpowder, and his Mme. de Pompadour said she did not know how such things as silk stockings and face rouge were made. The assembled company found that there was no way out but to have a servant chase down a copy of the banned Encyclopédie, which the King had never laid eyes on until that moment. After that evening, Louis was supposedly halfhearted about the proscription of the work, whose main enemy was his clergy.
>
> Perhaps no other book, or set of books, has ever had the impact in its century of those twenty-eight volumes. They were called a War Machine, a Tower of Babel, the Gospel of Satan. Seventeen years after completion of publication, and as an unmistakable sequel, came the French Revolution.

After reading the selection, use your school library's encyclopedias and other sources to prepare a report on the history of encyclopedias. In your report answer the following questions.

1. What accounts for the hostile reaction to early encyclopedias?

---

[1]From "Onward and Upward With the Arts" by Hans Koning; © 1981. Originally in *The New Yorker.*

2. Other than increasing in size, encyclopedias have changed in what other ways over the years?

Yearbooks and Almanacs

New editions of yearbooks and almanacs are published annually because these works present much information that is subject to change, such as population statistics, and new information, such as election results. In addition, such works may contain information of general interest: state mottoes, historical events, and transcripts of famous documents and speeches. Almanacs and yearbooks always present information about the preceding year, so if you wished statistics on Canadian rainfall in 1978, you would look in the 1979 almanac. The following are important yearbooks and almanacs.

Information Please Almanac
The New York Times Encyclopedic Almanac
The Official Associated Press Almanac
Statesmen's Yearbook
Statistical Abstracts of the United States
World Almanac and Book of Facts

Atlases

An *atlas* is a book of maps that may also contain charts and tables on such information as climate, population, industry, resources, and so on. A standard atlas contains maps of all the countries of the world. Since boundaries change and governments rise and fall at a rather rapid rate today, check the copyright date of any atlas you consult. Major atlases are the following:

The Encyclopaedia Britannica Atlas
Goode's World Atlas
Hammond Contemporary World Atlas
National Geographic World Atlas
The New York Times Atlas of the World
Rand McNally New Cosmopolitan World Atlas

Historical Atlases

Since boundaries and governments do change, some atlases devote themselves to presenting maps of the world as it was; they contain maps showing countries in various periods of history. Such collections dramatically demonstrate the changing shape of the world's countries, the rise and fall of empires, the growth and dwindling of religions, languages, and populations. Major historical atlases are the following ones.

Historical Atlas of the United States
Shepherd's *Historical Atlas*
Heyden's *Atlas of the Classical World*
Rand McNally Atlas of World History

Biographical Reference Works

Biographical reference works contain information about the lives of famous people, both living and dead.

Biographical References to Living People

Current Biography, published monthly, deals with people in the news. Biographies are one to two pages long, and at the end of the year, the pamphlets are bound together with a cumulative index for easy reference.

International Who's Who is a biographical dictionary, published annually, that contains brief biographies of internationally prominent people in government, science, and the arts.

Who's Who, published annually, contains biographies of prominent British subjects, including those who live in British commonwealths, such as Australia. Entries are brief, giving only essential information.

Who's Who in America, revised every two years, gives concise information on prominent living Americans.

Biographical References to People Living and People Deceased

Biographical Index is published four times a year. It is an index to biographical material that has appeared in books and magazines.

Webster's Biographical Dictionary contains short biographies of famous people.

Biographical References to People Deceased

Dictionary of American Biography, twenty volumes plus indexes, is noted for its objectivity and its depth.

Dictionary of National Biography, twenty-two volumes and supplements, offers extensive biographical data on British subjects.

Who Was Who, published at intervals, contains biographies of people once listed in *Who's Who*, distinguished British subjects now deceased.

Who Was Who in America, the American counterpart of *Who Was Who*, contains biographies of people formerly listed in *Who's Who in America*.

Reference Works on Literature and Language

The following works can be helpful to you in your study of literature and language.

Books About Writers

American Authors, 1600–1900 (about 1,300 entries)
British Authors Before 1800 (about 650 entries)
British Authors of the Twentieth Century (about 1,000 entries)
Cyclopedia of World Authors (about 750 entries)
Twentieth Century Authors (about 1,850 entries)
The Writer's Directory (about 2,000 entries). This volume of short biographies is published every two years.

Index to Short Works and Plays

Single poems, short stories, and short plays can be located by using the following indexes.

Granger's Index to Poetry
Index to One-Act Plays
Index to Plays
Index to Short Stories

Exercise 7

Name a reference work you would use to find the following information.

1. A biography of Martin Luther King, Jr.
2. A quotation by Queen Elizabeth I of England
3. A book containing the one-act play *Hello Out There*
4. Information about twentieth-century British author E. M. Forster
5. A discussion of early American poet Phillis Wheatley
6. Information about the correct usage of *will* and *shall*
7. Where to locate the short story "The Monkey's Paw"
8. A brief biography of the current Vice President of the United States
9. Where to locate the poem "Medusa" by Louise Bogan
10. Information about the mythological figure Clotho

Finding Quotations

Sometimes, you may wish to track down a specific quotation; other times, you may want to look for quotations on certain subjects or by certain authors. The following books are good aids in finding quotations.

Bartlett's Familiar Quotations
Peter's Quotations, Ideas for Our Time
Oxford Dictionary of Quotations
Stevenson's Home Book of Quotations and *Home Book of Proverbs, Maxims, and Familiar Phrases*

General Reference Books and Periodicals on Literature and Language

American Authors and Books
Book Review Digest
Bulfinch's Mythology
The New Century Classical Handbook
Oxford Companion to American Literature
Oxford Companion to Classical Literature
Oxford Companion to English Literature

Reference Books for Questions About Grammar, Usage, and Style

A Dictionary of Contemporary American Usage by Bergen and Cornelia Evans

Words Into Type

Elements of Style by E. B. White and William Strunk, Jr.

American Usage: The Consensus by Roy H. Copperud

Writer's Guide and Index to English by Porter G. Perrin

Other General Reference Books

Your library probably contains numerous other reference works on a multitude of subjects. Some standard references in fields of general interest are as follows:

Addresses

Education Directory (American colleges and universities)

International Handbook of Universities (foreign colleges and universities)

Encyclopedia of Associations (organizations)

Ayer's Directory of Newspapers and Periodicals

American Book Trade Directory (book publishers)

Official Congressional Directory (Senators and Representatives)

Current Events

Facts on File

Science and Mathematics

Mathematical Dictionary, James Glenn and Robert C. James, ed.

Von Nostrand's *Scientific Encyclopedia*

Music and Art

Grove's *Dictionary of Music and Musicians*

Harvard Dictionary of Music

McGraw-Hill Encyclopedia of World Art

Oxford Companion to Music

Oxford History of Music

Pelican History of Art

Larousse Encyclopedia of Prehistoric and Ancient Art

Larousse Encyclopedia of Byzantine and Medieval Art

Larousse Encyclopedia of Renaissance and Baroque Art

Larousse Encyclopedia of Modern Art

History and Social Studies

Dictionary of American History by James T. Adams

Encyclopedia of American History by Richard B. Morris

Encyclopedia of World History by William L. Langer

Oxford Companion to American History by Thomas H. Johnson
Annals of America Encyclopaedia Britannica
Encyclopedia of Social Sciences

Colleges and Universities

American Universities and Colleges
Lovejoy's College Guide
New American Guide to Colleges by Gene R. Hawes

Exercise 8

On a sheet of paper numbered 1–10, write the title of a book or books you might consult to learn the information requested.

1. The address of Howard University
2. The population of Puerto Rico in 1982
3. The definition of the musical term *fugue*
4. The address of the National Basketball Association
5. The names of several prominent medieval works of art
6. A discussion of major battles of the American Revolution
7. The definition of the mathematical term *google*
8. The address of a Chinese university
9. The address of *Time* magazine
10. The date of the Greek Battle of Thermopylae

Other Reference Sources

The Vertical File

The *vertical file* is a filing cabinet or series of filing cabinets for storing information that cannot be put on the shelves. Such information includes news clippings, pamphlets, brochures, and small booklets. Recent news articles, as well as those of local interest, are kept and filed alphabetically, by subject. The vertical file is also the storehouse for the many pamphlets that are published on multitudinous subjects by federal, state, and local governments, businesses, colleges and universities, health organizations, and so on.

Rare Books and Special Collections

Some libraries have rare books; these may be anything from ancient manuscripts to first editions to books of which only a few copies still exist. Because of their rarity, such books are separate from the main collection and generally cannot be checked out, but rather must be used within the library.

A special collection may be a group of rare books or a particularly good collection of books on a certain subject or of a certain type. Many libraries have a special collection of books about state and local matters and by writers of the region. Sometimes, because some of the books may be old or hard to replace, and because the collection as a whole is considered as reference, parts of the collection may not be checked out, but must be used in the library.

Reserved Books

When a teacher wants many students to make use of one book, that book may be put on *reserve.* That is, it is kept at the librarian's desk instead of in its usual place. You must ask the librarian for the book on reserve, and usually use the book within the library, then return it to the desk. This method is used so that all students have an equal chance to use the book. Occasionally a reserved book can be checked out overnight if it is returned the next morning as soon as the library opens. If you cannot find a book on the shelves and it has not been checked out to someone else, ask your librarian if someone has placed it on reserve.

New Books

Many libraries reserve certain shelves, prominently displayed for new acquisitions. This is so library patrons will be aware of books that have been recently purchased. Since new books may be in demand—whether they are best-selling novels or nonfiction—they may generally be checked out for a shorter period of time than other books.

Records, Tapes, Films, Microfilms

This century has seen the emergence of many new ways to record and store information; thus, in addition to books and magazines, the modern library may also boast records, tapes, films, microfilm, and even computers. Record albums and tapes may contain more than the latest Top 40 songs: language lessons, famous speeches and newscasts, plays, authors reading from their works, and classical and folk music as well.

A library may have films and slides, and even small libraries are discovering the convenience of microfilm, a special film for reducing and storing print. A complete collection of local newspapers, for example, is space consuming, hard to handle, and subject to deterioration. With microfilm enormous amounts of material can be stored in a small space: back issues of newspapers and magazines, for instance. In addition, since microfilms are easily duplicated, libraries can now order copies of works that would otherwise be rare, expensive, or unavailable. Microfilm viewers are easy to operate, and your librarian can teach you to use one.

12 Vocabulary

Importance of Vocabulary

ses·qui·pe·da·li·an (sĕś-kwi-pe-dā′-lē-en) *adj.* 1. long and ponderous; polysyllabic 2. given to using long words.

You do not need a hoard of *sesquipedalian* words to have a good vocabulary. Indeed, using a three- or four-syllable word where a shorter one will do is often the mark of a writer or speaker who is more interested in showing off than in communicating. All words, long and short, have their uses and their times to be used. Having a good vocabulary means having a large number of words at your command and knowing how and when to use them.

Your command of language affects your command of your own thoughts and may affect your future as well. Vocabulary tests are a common device for measuring the aptitude of job applicants, college students, and entrants in training programs and the armed forces. The following sections on vocabulary building will help you to gain mastery over words.

Meaning Through Context

The *context* of a word is its environment—the other words that surround it.

Frequently a word's context gives clues to its meaning. Suppose, for instance, that a new word came into the English language: *fless.* By studying the contexts in which *fless* occurs, you could begin to understand its meaning:

> I hope it snows this weekend because I want to *fless.*
>
> Mona broke her leg while she was *flessing.*
>
> *Flessing* is more fun than skiing, and the equipment is less expensive than ski gear.

I was going to *fless* this weekend, but I broke my flessboard in a bad jump yesterday.

From the preceding contexts you know that *fless* means some sort of snow sport, rather dangerous, involving a board, perhaps something like a surfboard.

Words can also have different meanings in different contexts:

In geometry we learned about *obtuse* angles.
[An obtuse angle is greater than 90 degrees, but less than 180 degrees.]

I was too *obtuse* to learn much else in geometry.
[An obtuse person is dull, stupid.]

Exercise 1

Write down the *italicized* word in each of the following sentences and a definition for the word that you derive by looking at its context. If you cannot decide what the word means, look it up in your dictionary and write down the definition that seems most appropriate.

1. The dogs were howling, the cat was yowling, and the starlings were squawking; it was complete *cacophony*.
2. The book went on forever, it seemed; I thought it the most *prolix* work I have ever struggled through.
3. At the *lapidary* exhibit we saw many precious and semiprecious stones that had been cut, polished, and set.
4. People used to think there was a *plenitude* of energy and that we would never run out.
5. The fire inspector thought the *propinquity* of the cleaning fluids to the heating vents was a potential hazard.
6. Mr. Washington was his usual *taciturn* self, sitting there all evening without saying a word.
7. The movie critic hated that particular movie and wrote a particularly *vitriolic* review of it.
8. Some people cannot stand even the sight of a snake, and even a picture of one is *anathema* to them.
9. There were no people on the sidewalks, no cars in the streets; the town seemed *devoid* of people.
10. Walking around as he did while conducting lessons, Aristotle was the original *peripatetic* teacher.

Exercise 2

Read the following passage from a review by Brendan Gill of a recent production of *Macbeth.* Then write a brief definition of each of the underlined words. If you cannot deduce the meaning of a word from its context, consult your dictionary and supply an appropriate definition.

> *Macbeth* is a gory thriller written in exquisite verse. Blood gushes up at every turn of the plot, and so does poetry. The disparity between the barbaric story and the lyricism of language in which it is told provides a series of pleasing shocks to the ear. During the course of the play, we may be only half conscious of the commingling of vile deeds and melodious imagery, but as an aesthetic device the commingling is always poignantly, thrillingly at work, at once concentrating and magnifying our attention and causing us to feel an unexpected sympathy for the most contemptible of murderers—one who murders not out of jealousy or spite, or to avenge some grave social wrong, but simply in order to gain greater personal importance. At first, the villainous Macbeth and his wife appear to have little more on their minds than that they are Smiths and would like not only to keep up with the Joneses but to surpass them as well. Macbeth's ambitions are as loutish as they are commonplace, and yet in seeking to attain them he speaks some of the most ravishing lines ever written.[1]

Meaning and Shades of Meaning

Words have meanings, and the explicit meaning of a word is called its *denotation.* The best-known denotation of *lemon* is "a small, egg-shaped, edible citrus fruit with a pale-yellow rind and a juicy, sour pulp, rich in vitamin C." In another context *lemon* might be "a person or thing that is defective or undesirable," as in "The car that I bought turned out to be a lemon."

Words, however, can convey more than ideas; they can also convey attitudes and emotions. An *inexpensive canine* expresses an altogether different attitude from *cheap mutt,* and being a *sanitation engineer* sounds more dignified than being a *trash collector.* The associations of this sort that go with words are called *connotations.*

Two words that denote nearly the same thing are called *synonyms.*

Even though two words have nearly the same meaning, they may have different connotations, and it is important to understand these differences. Connotations may be very close to one another, as in *car* and *auto,* but they may also be very far apart, as in *car* and *jalopy.*

A *thesaurus,* which is a dictionary of synonyms, is a valuable reference tool. When choosing a synonym, however, be sure that you choose one with appropriate connotations. As Mark Twain said, "There is as much difference between a right word and an almost right word as there is between lightning and a lightning bug."

Antonyms are words whose meanings are nearly opposite; *hot* is the antonym of *cold; up* is the antonym of *down.*

Many words form their antonyms with a prefix or a suffix; thus, *happy* can be turned into an antonym, *unhappy; guilty* into the antonym *guiltless.* Other antonyms are not related in form, and a word may have more than one antonym: *guilty's* antonym, for instance, could be either the related word *guiltless* or the unrelated word *innocent.* Knowing a word's synonyms and antonyms helps you better to understand the word itself.

---

[1]From "Supping on Horrors" by Brendan Gill in *The New Yorker,* February 2, 1981, p. 62. © 1981 by Brendan Gill. Reprinted by permission.

Exercise 3

For each of the following words, write three words that have the same denotation but different connotations. Be prepared to discuss what kinds of connotations these words have.

Examples

a. food

a. food—snacks, eats, chow

b. house

b. house—cottage, mansion, abode

1. said
2. street
3. frightened
4. unhappy
5. thin
6. walk
7. clothing
8. talkative
9. thrifty
10. horse

Exercise 4

Sportswriters and sportscasters need many synonyms to keep their stories from being too repetitive; thus, the *football* becomes the *pigskin* or the *spheroid,* and "The Tigers *beat* the Vikings" becomes "The Tigers *trounced* the Vikings." Rewrite the following scores, replacing the word *beat* with one more lively. Then rewrite the sports story that follows, using synonyms and fresh phrases for the underlined words.

Springdale beat Fayetteville
The Bucks beat the Hawks
The Warriors beat the Wombats
DePaul beats Indiana
The Terriers beat the Mounties
Nebraska beat Oklahoma
The Bunnies beat the Bears
New York beat Philadelphia
Silverlake beat Aims
Texas beat SMU

The Charleston Patriots beat the Winslow Wildcats tonight, 70–60. The Wildcats led by twelve points at the half, but a rally led by Willie Washington and Greg Forster tied the game. Then Clark Whitewater stole the ball and ran down the court to make a basket. Fouled on the play, he made another basket. The Wildcats turned over the ball, and Whitewater made another three-point play. In an incredible series of steals and turnovers, Washington made another basket, Forster made another basket, and Whitewater made another basket. The Patriots play the Buckingham Bucks next Friday night, in what promises to be an exciting game.

Examining Words

By examining the parts of words—their roots and affixes—you can often determine the meanings of the words themselves.

A *root word* is one from which others have been derived.

The words *meter, metric, metronome,* and *speedometer* are all derived from the root word *metron,* a Greek word meaning "measurement." One root may have many descendants, some bearing great family resemblance, some less. One way in which roots are transformed into new words is by the adding of *affixes.*

Prefixes and suffixes are discussed on pages 265–267.

An *affix* is a word element, such as a prefix or suffix, that is added to the root and changes its meaning.

Some roots and affixes come from early English words; others have been borrowed from other countries, especially Greece and Rome. Familiarity with common roots and affixes can help you better to understand new words, as well as those you already know.

The following list contains the most common Greek roots used in the English language, their definitions, and examples of derived words.

GREEK ROOTS

ROOT	DEFINITION	ENGLISH DERIVATIVE
-agog-	leader	demagogue
-anthrop-	man, human	anthropoid
-arch-	ancient, chief	archaeology
-aster-, -astr-	star	astronaut
-auto-	self	automatic
-bibl-	book	bibliography
-bi-, -bio-	life	biography
-chrom-	color	chromatic
-chron-	time	chronology
-cosm-	order, world	cosmos
-crac-, -crat-	govern	democrat
-crypt-	hidden	cryptogram
-cycl-	wheel	bicycle
-dem-	people	democracy
-derm-	skin	dermatology
-dox-	belief	orthodox
-dyn-	power	dynamite
-erg-	work	energy
-gam-	marry	monogamy
-gen-	kind, source	genealogy
-geo-	earth	geography
-gon-	corner	hexagon
-gram-	write	grammar
-graph-	write	telegraph
-gyn-	female	misogynist
-hem-	blood	hemoglobin
-hetero-	other	heterogenous
-homo-	same	homogenize
-hydr-	water	hydrant
-lith-	stone	monolith
-log-	word, reason	logic
-mega-	large	megaton

ROOT	DEFINITION	ENGLISH DERIVATIVE
-metr-, -meter-	measure	perimeter
-mono-	one	monogram
-morph-	shape	amorphous
-nom-	law	economic
-orth-	straight	orthopedist
-pan-	all	pantheism
-path-	feeling, sufferer	sympathetic
-phil-	love	philanthropy
-phos-, -phot-	light	photo
-poly-	many	polyhedron
-pyr-	fire	pyre
-soph-	wise, wisdom	philosophy
-theo-	god	theology
-therm-	heat	thermometer
-tom-	cut	atom
-zo-	animal, life	zoologist

Exercise 5

On a sheet of paper numbered 1–10, write down each of the following words and the Greek root or roots from which it is derived. Using your knowledge of the root, supply a definition for the word and then check your definition with that in a dictionary. Some words may be formed from more than one root.

1. polymorphous
2. protozoa
3. autocratic
4. orthography
5. lithography
6. monotheistic
7. synergy
8. pyromania
9. cryptic
10. bibliophile

Exercise 6

List and define two words drawn from each of the following Greek roots. Do not give words previously used as examples in the chapter.

1. -anthrop-
2. -dyn-
3. -path-
4. -mega-
5. -theo-
6. -arch-
7. -cycl-
8. -gen-
9. -log-
10. -hydr-
11. -auto-
12. -bio-
13. -phot-
14. -poly-
15. -mono-
16. -crac-, -crat-
17. -dem-
18. -graph-
19. -gram-
20. -aster-, -astr-

The following list contains the most commonly used Latin roots in the English language, their meanings, and examples of words derived from them.

LATIN ROOTS

ROOT	DEFINITION	ENGLISH DERIVATIVE
-ag-, -act-	do	action
-cap-	seize	captive
-cede-, -ceed-	go	exceed
-clud-, -clus-	close	conclusion
-cur-	run	excursion
-dic-	say	dictate
-duc-	lead	conduct
-fac-, -fec-	make	factory
-fid-	faith	fidelity
-fin-	limit	finite
-form-	shape	formation
-gress-	go	regress
-junct-	join	junction
-pend-, -pens-	hang	pendant
-reg-, -rig-, -rect-	straight	regiment, rigor
-sent-, -sens-	feel	sensitive
-sequ-, -secut-	follow	sequence, consecutive
-spec-	look	speculate
-ten-, -tent-	hold	detention
-tract-	pull	traction
-vert-, -vers-	turn	divert, diversion
-volv-, -volu-	roll	revolve

Exercise 7

On a sheet of paper numbered 1–10, write down the following words and the Latin root from which each is derived. Using your knowledge of the root, supply a definition for the word. Look in your dictionary to check and, if need be, revise your definition.

1. preclude
2. perfidious
3. rectitude
4. ductile
5. sentience
6. precursor
7. aversion
8. convoluted
9. subsequent
10. tractable

Exercise 8

Using your dictionary or drawing on your own vocabulary, list and define two words drawn from each of the following Latin roots. Do not give words previously used in the chapter as examples.

1. -ag-
2. -fac-
3. -fin-
4. -pend-
5. -reg-
6. -gress-
7. -vers-
8. -volv-
9. -sent-
10. -ceed-

Prefixes

Affixes are syllables added before or after a root word; they change or modify the meaning of the root.

Affixes that are put before the root are called *prefixes.*

The following is a list of common prefixes. Some have more than one spelling so that they can combine more easily with different root words.

PREFIX	MEANING	EXAMPLE
ab-, a-	from, away	abstain
ante-	before	antecedent
anti-	against	antidote
auto-	self	automobile
bi-	two, twice	bicycle
circum-	around	circumstance
com-, con-	with	companion, contract
de-	down, from, away	depart
demi-	half	demitasse
dis-	negation, lack	distrust
en-, em-	in, among	engage
eu-	good, true	eulogy
ex-, e-	from, out of	expire
extr-, extro-	beyond	extraordinary, extrovert
fore-	previous	forecast
hemi-	half	hemisphere
hyper-	excessive	hyperbole
hypo-	under, below	hypothesis
in-, il-	not, against	invisible, illiterate
im-, ir-	not, against	impossible, irreplaceable
in-, il-	in, into	infest, illuminate
im-, ir-	in, into	immigrate, irritate
inter-	between, among	international
meta-	changed, later	metamorphosis
mis-	wrong, not	mismatch
para-	beyond, beside	paramedic
peri-	around, near	perimeter
post-	after	postpone

PREFIX	MEANING	EXAMPLE
pre-	before	prepare
pro-	for, forward	promote
re-	back, again	recount
retro-	back	retrospect
se-	away	secede
semi-	half	semicircle
sub-	under, beneath	substandard
trans-	across	transplant
un-	not	unwise
ultra-	beyond, excessive	ultraviolet

Exercise 9

On a sheet of paper numbered 1–10, write down the following words, underlining the prefix in each word. Then use each word correctly in a sentence, checking with your dictionary if necessary.

1. abjure
2. euphemism
3. paradox
4. periscope
5. excoriate
6. ultramodern
7. transgress
8. prognosis
9. subsume
10. immolate

Suffixes

An affix that attaches to the end of a root word is called a *suffix.*

Sometimes, a suffix changes not only the meaning of the root word but its part of speech as well.

luck	[noun]	achieve	[verb]
lucky	[adjective]	achievement	[noun]
luckily	[adverb]	achiever	[noun]

The following list of suffixes is arranged according to the parts of speech they form.

NOUN-FORMING SUFFIXES	MEANING	EXAMPLE
-age	rank, process, state	bondage
-ance, -ancy	being, condition of	hesitance, hesitancy
-ation	action, state of	federation
-dom	state, condition	serfdom
-eer	doer, maker	auctioneer
-er	doer, action	reader
-ery	state	treachery
-hood	state, rank	motherhood
-ice	state	malice
-ine	dealing with	feline
-ism	act, doctrine	barbarism

NOUN-FORMING SUFFIXES	MEANING	EXAMPLE
-ist	doer, believer	guitarist
-ition	action, state	rendition
-ment	means, result, action	judgment
-mony	result, condition	alimony
-ness	quality, state	quietness
-or	doer, state	donor
-ory	pertaining to	memory
-tion	state	creation
-tude	quality, state	latitude
-ty	quality, state	scarcity
-ure	result, state	pleasure
-y	result, state	injury

ADJECTIVE-FORMING SUFFIXES	MEANING	EXAMPLE
-able	able to, able to be	washable
-en	made of	oaken
-ful	having qualities of	delightful
-ish	like	foolish
-less	without	careless
-like	similar	lifelike
-some	apt to, showing	troublesome
-ward	in the direction of	windward

VERB-FORMING SUFFIXES	MEANING	EXAMPLE
-ate	become, form, treat	separate
-en	cause to be	shorten
-esce	become, continue	convalesce
-fy	make, cause	liquify
-ish	do	finish
-ize	make, cause to be	fertilize

Exercise 10

Write out each of the following words and underline the suffix. Define the word and then use it correctly in a sentence.

Example

a. novice

a. novice—a person new to a particular activity or occupation
Being a novice at surfing, I spent more time under the waves than on them.

1. rectify
2. pulchritude
3. winsome
4. anarchist
5. acquiesce
6. parsimony
7. bellicosity
8. coercion
9. sanctimonious
10. porcine

Review Exercise A

The following sentences contain words whose meanings you should be able to deduce either by context clues or by your knowledge of word roots and affixes. Number a sheet of paper 1–20 and supply a definition for each *italicized* word.

Example

a. My sister didn't get her own way, so she sat around all evening looking *petulant.*

a. petulant—peevish, ill-tempered

1. The movie star didn't like to be recognized, so he often traveled *incognito.*
2. Our Saint Bernard and our old tomcat manage to live in quiet *amity.*
3. Ms. Washington, the new principal, doesn't believe in *corporal* punishment.
4. The confession was ruled invalid because it was obtained under *duress.*
5. A disc jockey has to be a fairly *loquacious* person to fill up air time.
6. A few senators thought the issue was *moribund,* but many fought to keep it alive.
7. The coach punished the *malefactors* by benching them for the rest of the season.
8. Richard Pryor is noted for the *alacrity* of his wit.
9. "H'm," said my brother, peering into the refrigerator, "it seems we are experiencing a shortage of *comestibles.*"
10. My sister's favorite record is the Fifth Dimension's *ebullient* "My Beautiful Balloon."
11. I dislike shopping in that store because the salesclerks are so *unctuous;* their main sales technique is flattering customers.
12. Ms. Smith is a *meretricious* poet, but that doesn't stop her from publishing book after book at her own expense.
13. The treasurer passed out copies of the club's expenditures to help *elucidate* her report.
14. I think deep, philosophical thoughts and do not worry about such *mundane* matters as how to pay the rent.
15. We won the basketball game after three overtimes; I was totally *enervated* by the experience.
16. The game warden wasn't sure if the attack had been made by a wolf or by a *feral* dog.
17. Never try to *obfuscate* your thoughts with sesquipedalian words.
18. Juanita says she can't go to the movies; she's absolutely *impecunious.*
19. The pond out in the field is too *fetid* to swim in.
20. The fame of many a recording artist has been *ephemeral.*

Dictionary Definitions

If the context and analysis of the word's parts do not help you to determine its definition, consult a good dictionary.

In most dictionaries the various definitions for a word are numbered and grouped according to the parts of speech a word may be. For example, in the following entry for the word *reach*, there are twenty-one definitions.[1]

> **reach** (rēch) *vt.* [ME. *rechen* < OE. *rǽcan*, akin to G. *reichen* < IE. base **rēiĝ-*, to stretch out, extend the hand] **1.** to thrust out or extend (the hand, etc.) **2.** to extend to, or touch, by thrusting out, throwing something, etc. **3.** to obtain and hand over [*reach* me the salt] **4.** to go as far as; attain [to *reach* town by night] **5.** to carry as far as; penetrate to [the news *reached* him late] **6.** to add up to; come to [to *reach* thousands of dollars] **7.** to have influence on; affect; impress **8.** to get in touch with, as by telephone —*vi.* **1.** to thrust out the hand, foot, etc. **2.** to stretch, or be extended, in amount, influence, space, time, etc. [power that *reaches* into other lands] **3.** to be added; amount (with *to* or *into*) **4.** to carry; penetrate, as sight, sound, etc. **5.** to try to obtain something; make an attempt **6.** to try too hard to make a point, joke, etc. **7.** *Naut.* to sail on a reach —*n.* **1.** the act of stretching or thrusting out **2.** the power of stretching, obtaining, etc. **3.** the distance or extent covered in stretching, obtaining, influencing, etc. **4.** a continuous, uninterrupted extent or stretch, esp. of water ☆**5.** a pole joining the rear axle to the forward part of a wagon **6.** *Naut.* a tack sailed with the wind coming more or less from abeam: it may be a **close reach,** with the wind forward of the beam; a **beam reach,** with the wind abeam; or a **broad reach,** with the wind abaft the beam —**reach′er** *n.*
>
> ***SYN.***—**reach,** the broadest of these terms, implies an arriving at some goal, destination, point in development, etc. [he's *reached* the age of 60]; **gain** suggests the exertion of considerable effort to reach some goal [they've *gained* the top of the hill]; **achieve** suggests the use of skill in reaching something [we've *achieved* a great victory]; **attain** suggests a being goaded on by great ambition to gain an end regarded as beyond the reach of most men [he has *attained* great fame in his profession]; **accomplish** implies success in completing an assigned task [to *accomplish* an end] See also RANGE

The first set of eight definitions is for *reach* as a transitive verb *(vt.)*; the second set of seven definitions is for *reach* as an intransitive verb *(vi.)*; and the last set of six definitions is for *reach* as a noun.

In most hardcover dictionaries you will find a special section in the front explaining how definitions are numbered and grouped. In *Webster's New World Dictionary* the oldest meaning for each set of definitions is listed first and the most recent last. Thus, the first meaning for *reach* as a transitive verb, "to thrust out or extend (the hand, etc.)" is closest to the original meaning. Definition 8 for *reach* as a transitive verb, "to get in touch with, as by telephone," is the furthest removed from the sense of the word as it came into the English language.

Specialized uses for the word (uses not found in general speaking and writing) are included and labeled. In the main entry for *reach*, two definitions are included for *reach* as a nautical *(Naut.)* term. In many instances a phrase is included in brackets after the definition to illustrate how the word is used in that sense. For example, after Definition 4 for *reach* as a transitive verb is the phrase "to reach town by night."

---

[1]With permission. From *Webster's New World Dictionary*, Second College Edition. Copyright © 1982 by Simon & Schuster, Inc.

Until you know the context of a word, you usually cannot determine its definition. Consider the following sentence.

> Unfortunately for the world, Adolf Hitler's message reached into all parts of the German nation.

In the preceding sentence the word *reached* is used as an intransitive verb (it does not take an object). However, in this sentence the word does not carry the most common meaning of "thrusting out the hand, foot, etc." Instead, the context of the sentence suggests Definition 2 for *reach* as an intransitive verb: "to stretch, or be extended, in amount, influence, space, time, etc." Also, the use of *reach* in the example sentence is the same as that in the sample phrase that follows Definition 2.

Exercise 11

Look up each of the *italicized* words in the following sentences and write a definition that fits the context in which the word is used. Then use each word in an original sentence of your own, underlining the word.

Example

a. My little sister looks *seraphic,* but she certainly doesn't act it.

a. seraphic—angelic
After Mr. Chang heard the good news, he sat with a seraphic smile on his face.

1. In the summer the blackflies become *profuse.*
2. The congresswoman said too many people were fearful of *chimeras* in the new amendment.
3. The temple was surrounded by *effigies* of gods and goddesses.
4. The buggy whip is almost *obsolescent,* so don't buy stock in that buggy whip factory.
5. Shirley Jackson wrote a number of *macabre* stories and novels.
6. Many *scurrilous* tales were told about Mary Todd Lincoln.
7. After his illness Ricardo looked like a *wraith.*
8. Several Indian tribes have been forced to *litigate* in order to preserve their lands.
9. We could not attend the wedding but sent our *felicitations.*
10. Daisy Bates was an *intrepid* champion of civil rights.
11. Roberto denounced the report as *fallacious.*
12. The horses were *chary* of crossing the rickety bridge.
13. Riko listened to the speaker's *diatribe,* then left the meeting in disgust.
14. Frankly, I thought all of Georgette's tears and protestations were merely *histrionic* gestures.
15. Students who are *indolent* usually have poor grades.

16. One must never *prevaricate* on the witness stand; the penalty is severe.
17. Crazy Horse was an *enigmatic* figure.
18. Carlotta thought she heard a prowler in the house, and moved *surreptitiously* toward the phone.
19. A *superannuated* dog met us at the gate, his growl revealing his few remaining teeth.
20. Muhammad Ali has been many things, but he has never been *diffident*.

Mastery Exercise A

Read each of the following passages carefully, then list the underlined words on a sheet of paper. Using context clues, your knowledge of roots and affixes, or a dictionary, determine the meaning of each word that fits its context. Write this definition next to the word on your paper.

A. From "The Living Spirit of the Indian—His Art"[1]

> The spiritual health and existence of the Indian was maintained by song, magic, ritual, dance, symbolism, oratory (or council), design, handicraft, and folk-story.
>
> Manifestly, to check or thwart this expression is to bring about spiritual decline. And it is in this condition of decline that the Indian people are today. There is but a feeble effort among the Sioux to keep alive their traditional songs and dances, while among other tribes there is but a half-hearted attempt to offset the influence of the Government school and at the same time recover from the crushing and stifling régime of the Indian Bureau.
>
> —*Chief Standing Bear*

B. From "Is There an American Stock?"

> Every traveler in the tropics comes away with an unforgettable sense of the pervasive jungle enclosing him. America's jungle is its ethnic environment of a myriad of peoples. In such a tropical luxuriance every ethnic type is present, everything grows fast and intertwines with everything else, anything is ethnically possible.
>
> —*Max Lerner*

C. From "Tears, Idle Tears"[2]

> Frederick stumbled along beside her, too miserable to notice. His mother seldom openly punished him, but often revenged herself on him in small ways. He could feel how just this was. His own incontinence in the matter of tears was as shocking to him, as bowing-down, as annulling as it could be to her. . . .
>
> Crying made him so abject, so outcast from other people that he went on crying out of despair. His crying was not just reflex, like a baby's; it dragged up all unseemliness into view. No wonder everyone was repelled.
>
> —*Elizabeth Bowen*

---

[1]From Chief Standing Bear: "What the Indian Means to America" from *A Nation of Nations* edited by Theodore L. Gross. Copyright © 1971 The Free Press, a Division of Macmillan Publishing Co., Inc.

[2]"Tears, Idle Tears" in *Look At All Those Roses* by Elizabeth Bowen. Reprinted by permission of Alfred A. Knopf, Inc., Curtis Brown Ltd., London, literary executors of The Estate of Elizabeth Bowen and Jonathan Cape Ltd.

D. From "The Schartz-Metterklume Method"[1]

A loud, angry screaming from the direction of the lawn drew Mrs. Quabarl thither in hot haste, fearful lest the threatened castigation might even now be in process of infliction. The outcry, however, came principally from the two small daughters of the lodge-keeper, who were being hauled and pushed towards the house by the panting and disheveled Claude and Wilfrid, whose task was rendered even more arduous by the incessant, if not very effectual attacks of the captured maidens' small brother. —*Saki*

A Vocabulary List

The words in the following list are not graded according to difficulty; instead, they have been selected because of their use in "real life" situations. Many of them are multiple-meaning words; that is, they have a number of different meanings. Some of these meanings are very familiar to you; other meanings are "specialized," related to a particular topic. As you consider the words, pay particular attention to their specialized meanings. Discover what they mean in the real-life materials related to banking, applications, medicine, family relationships, legal situations, consumer information, work situations, and so on.

A
abrasion
accountable
accrue
actuary
adjudicated
adjusted
affidavit
alien
anticipatory
anticipated
antidote
applicable
applicant
application
appraisal
aptitude
assessed
assets
attorney
authorized
authority

B
bankruptcy
beneficiary
benefits
budget
bureau

C
cancel
cancellation
capital
carcinogen
certify
certificate
certification
chronic
civil
clientele
code
collateral
combustible
commensurate with
compensation
competitive
compute
concurrent
confidential
consecutive
consumer
consumerism
contract
cosigner
countersign
creditor
currency
current

D
data
debit
deceased
deductions
deficit
defraud
dependent
deposit
depositor
depreciate
designate
designation
digit
directory
disability
domestic
domicile

---

[1]From "The Schartz-Metterklume Method" in *The Complete Short Stories of Saki* (H. H. Munro).

dosage

E
eligible
eligibility
emigré
employee
employer
employment
endorse
equity
estate
eviction
exemption
expire
expiration

F
falsification
finance
financial
fiscal
flammable
forfeiture
franchise
fraudulent

G
gainfully
generic name
graduated
gratuity
gross income
guarantee
guardian

H
heirs
hemophiliac
hereinafter

I
immerse
immoderate
impersonation
implied contract
incinerate
income
incurred
indigent
infraction
ingredient
initial
insurable
intent
issue
item
itemized

J
joint
judiciary

L
lease
legend (map)
legible
liable
liability
licensee
lien
loitering

M
maintenance
malfunction
manual
marital status
maternity
median
menu
merchandise
merge
miscellaneous
monetary
mortgage
municipal
mutilate

N
negotiable
net weight
nontransferable
notary public
notarized
null

O
obituary
offspring
opinion (second)
overdrawn

P
paraplegic
paraprofessional
participatory
payee
payor
payable
payment
pedestrian
per
perishable
perjury
personable
plea bargaining
populace
post-secondary
potential
preface
preferred
premises
premium
principal
proficiency
prosecuted

Q
qualified
quarterly

R
real estate
receipt
reconcile
redemption
reference
relocate
render
repossess
reside
residence
residential
restrictions
resume
résumé
revenue
revoke

S
scale (map)
schedule
security

settlement
sibling
solvent
spindle
spouse
status
statutory
stipulations
subject to
surname

T
taxable
tenant
terminal
terminate
timetable
transaction

U
unit price
utility

V
valid
validate
verification
veteran
vicinity
vita
void
voided
voucher

W
warranty
withholding

PART

3 Reading

13 Reading for Yourself

Reading to Find Entertainment

This society is filled with possibilities for entertainment—books, movies, television, records, magazines, concerts, art exhibits, and so on. In fact, you could probably spend all of your waking hours being entertained by the performances and artistic endeavors of others.

Since most people have neither the time nor the money to partake of all this entertainment, it is important to make choices, to decide which books to read, which movies to see, which art exhibits to visit. To help you make these choices, the publishers of most magazines and newspapers have on their staffs a reviewer whose job it is to make critical judgments about movies, books, television shows, and other sources of entertainment. If you are able to critically evaluate these reviews, they can help you to make good choices for spending your entertainment time and dollars.

In this chapter you will learn how to use your critical-reading skills to evaluate reviews.

Learning from Reviews

A *review* (sometimes *revue*) is a critical report or evaluation of a book, movie, play, television show, or art exhibit.

Although there are different types of reviews, most usually contain brief information about the subject and a critical analysis of it. The purpose of the review is to pass judgment on the subject's merit.

Successful reading of reviews requires the use of a variety of reading skills at several levels. Your purposes for reading the reviews will also determine the kind of review you will want to read and the information you will want to acquire. For example, if you have only enough money to see one of two currently showing movies, you may want to read a longer review or one by a reviewer you trust more completely than another. On the other hand, if you have been invited to go to a certain movie, and you just want an idea of what to expect, you may be less particular in the source of the review you read and less careful in your reading of the review.

Reading reviews requires you to read at the literal, interpretive, and applied levels.

At the literal level you identify information directly stated in the review. You may be directly told by the reviewer that (1) the movie is in color, (2) the novel is about an intergalactic war, (3) the exhibit is dull, (4) the album is the first of its kind, (5) the film is a Disney production, (6) the play is guaranteed to have you dancing in the aisles, (7) the choreography of the ballet is masterful.

At the interpretive level, you use your intuition, the directly stated information, and your previously learned store of information to make inferences and interpretations. You might determine that the movie will be a science fiction movie, that it is appropriate for a younger child, that the reviewer likes or dislikes the work being reviewed, or that the album will be different from the artist's previous works.

At the applied level, you make judgments based on the literal and interpretive information you have acquired. For example, you may decide that the movie sounds like a waste of your time and money, that the reviewer is being sarcastic when he or she says that the choreography is masterful, that you do not yet know whether the movie is worth seeing, or that the reviewer does not like any horror movie, well done or not.

To read reviews successfully, you must do more than identify what has been directly stated. You must also (1) identify the writer's (the reviewer's) purpose, (2) note the difference between fact and opinion, (3) understand the reviewer's word choice, (4) recognize the reviewer's tone, (5) identify the reviewer's biases or prejudices, and (6) identify and understand the reviewer's selection of materials to be included or omitted from the review.

Facts and Opinions in Reviews

Facts are pieces of information that can be verified.

Opinions are beliefs, views, judgments, or appraisals based on an interpretation of facts.

In reviews, the reviewers have viewed, read, or listened to the work being discussed and have made their own decisions about its merits and demerits. In their reviews they present not only facts about the work but also their evaluations and opinions.

Sometimes, reviewers may give their judgments directly; other times, however, their feelings are implied. For this reason it is important to know when the reviewer is using words that *evaluate* rather than give factual detail about a work.

Activity 1

The following are statements that might appear in entertainment reviews. On a numbered sheet of paper, identify each statement as either fact or opinion. Be prepared to discuss your answers.

1. The Eagles album, *Eagles: Their Greatest Hits 1971–1975*, contains "Take It Easy," "Desperado," and "Lyin' Eyes."
2. Waylon Jennings is the greatest country-and-western singer alive today, as this album demonstrates.
3. Dolly Parton made the original recording of the song "Workin' 9 to 5."
4. Humphrey Bogart and Ingrid Bergman starred in *Casablanca.*
5. *Casablanca* is in black and white.
6. Disco music is better than country-and-western music.
7. *The Empire Strikes Back* continues the story begun in *Star Wars.*
8. *The Dukes of Hazard* is infantile.
9. This disaster movie is certainly in the right genre. It is a complete and total disaster from beginning to end.
10. This book is guaranteed to put the worst insomniac to sleep.
11. Emily Brontë's *Wuthering Heights* is a powerful novel that remains the best of its kind.
12. This story, although not original or especially distinguished, is an interesting moral odyssey.
13. The dialogue is insipid, the plot totally predictable, and the characters one-dimensional.
14. The special effects in this movie are the most expensive and detailed in any film to date.
15. This television series is a strong contender for the worst I have ever seen.
16. Originally assigned an R rating, this movie has been reedited and assigned a PG rating.
17. This movie contains some violence and nudity.
18. John Travolta's performance in this movie is more convincing, if somewhat overplayed in places, than his earlier efforts.
19. *Watership Down* is a modern classic.
20. *Apocalypse Now* received eight Oscar nominations, including Best Picture.

Word Choice in Reviews

In reading reviews, it is important to be aware of the reviewer's word choice. You need to know the denotations (dictionary definitions of words), as well as the connotations (the additional meanings suggested by the words). In addition, you need to know when words are used ironically, so that they have a meaning opposite the usual meaning, and what the variations in meaning are among very similar words.

For example, a story about the settling of the American West might be described in a variety of ways, and each way would suggest something different. Consider the following descriptions.

A *yarn* set in the old West
A *thriller* set in the old West
A *saga* set in the old West
A *study* set in the old West

The use of the word *yarn* in the preceding list probably suggests an entertaining story without great fidelity to truth or reality. A *thriller*, on the other hand, suggests that the story contains a great deal of action and suspense, more than you would expect in a *yarn*. *Saga*, however, suggests more than just an entertaining story, no matter how much action or suspense. *Saga* suggests a long story covering a number of years and events.

To describe a book or movie as a *study* has still other implications. *Study* suggests a more detailed, perhaps sophisticated, account of life in the old West, perhaps demonstrating social issues of the times. Often in a *study* movie or book, the *times* or the theme is more important than the individual characters.

Activity 2

The following are some descriptive terms or phrases frequently found in book and movie reviews. On a sheet of paper, write down what you would expect from a movie or a book described by each word. (It may be necessary for you to look up some of the terms in a dictionary.)

1. Propaganda piece
2. Romance
3. Melodrama
4. Farce
5. Outdoor yarn
6. Crime-caper
7. Lampoon
8. Satire
9. Terror tale
10. Cops and robbers
11. Spoof
12. Documentary
13. Real-life story
14. True-to-life account
15. Gothic tale

Most of the time, reviewers are not satisfied with merely labeling a book or movie or television show according to type. Usually, they add additional descriptions. Some descriptions suggest positive or negative qualities; whereas others provide additional information or interpretation without making value judgments about the work's quality. For example, to call a comedy a *light* or *dark* comedy does not say if it is good or bad, but rather if it is a pleasant or disturbing comedy. However, to describe a comedy as a *trifle* (meaning "insignificant") or as *hard-hitting* carries a value judgment about the quality of the work.

Sometimes, words that could be used simply to provide additional information carry with them certain connotations for the readers of the review. For example, the term *avant-garde* is sometimes used to describe a work in which the writer, director, or someone has invented or applied new techniques or used unorthodox, nontraditional techniques. The resulting work is experimental, different in form or format from traditional works. While the term simply adds information about the work, many readers might make judgments about the work because they have strong feelings about experimental works. One reader might "read into" the review that the movie will be good because it is avant-garde. Another reader might "read into" the review that the movie will be bad because he or she "hates avant-garde movies."

Reviews usually give the plot of a book or movie considerable attention, and the words selected to describe it can be very important. For example, if a plot is described as *tortuously complex*, the reviewer is telling you that the story line is very difficult to follow, but he or she does not say if the effort required to follow the plot is or is not worth it. However, if the reviewer describes the plot as *tedious*, meaning "boring," a value judgment is made. Once again, it is important to consider connotation. *Easy*, for example, does not necessarily mean "good," and *hard* does not necessarily mean "bad."

Activity 3

The following is a review of the horror movie *Without Warning*. In it the reviewer does more than just tell you what the movie is about; he also tries through various word choices to help you make a decision about whether or not to see the movie. Read the review and then answer the questions about it that follow.[1]

> It takes a film like "Without Warning" to make you appreciate "Fade to Black." "Without Warning" is technically a science fiction movie, since a balloon-headed alien is involved, but the creature is simply a convenient monster. It likes to throw objects resembling floppy Frisbees with bloodsucking tentacles that ooze mustard and ketchup. They attach themselves to humans (inspiring the audience to groan "Oh, gross!") and, like the more expensive Frisbees, they glow in the dark.
>
> Martin Landau plays a crazed ex-Army sergeant who ends up shooting the local sheriff instead of the alien. He's not very believable, but then, Landau never is. On the other hand, it's fun to watch Jack Palance play a crusty old mountain man, even though his lines don't make much more sense than Landau's.
>
> Compared to the plot, however, the dialogue sounds better. The four people who wrote this thing left so many holes in the plot you begin to wonder if the alien didn't eat a few pages of the script during the filming.

1. How is the alien's head described?

---

[1]From James Calloway's review of the movie, "Without Warning" (*The News and Observer*, January 20, 1981). Reprinted by permission of *The News and Observer*, Raleigh, North Carolina.

2. When you think about balloons, which of the following do you also think about? (Select more than one.)
   a. Monsters
   b. Parties
   c. Blood
   d. Spring days
   e. Happy children
   f. Haunted houses
   g. Guns
   h. Spring
3. The alien throws some type of weapon. How is the weapon described?
4. Are you frightened by Frisbees?
5. When you think of ketchup, you think of which of the following things?
   a. Hot dogs
   b. Blood
   c. Good food
   d. Monsters
   e. Tornadoes
   f. Special effects —realistic
   g. Special effects in cheap movies—unrealistic
   h. Showoffs
   i. Sporting events
   j. Picnics
6. Do you want to sit through a horror movie in which the audience (a) screams, (b) groans, (c) sits with closed eyes, (d) says, "Oh, gross!"
7. In a movie or story, what is dialogue?
8. Should the dialogue make sense?
9. According to the review, does the dialogue in *Without Warning* make sense?
10. According to the review, is the plot carefully constructed?
11. Does the reviewer think this movie is worth seeing? Why or why not?
12. What words or phrases does the reviewer use to make fun of the movie?
13. Reread the first sentence of the review. Knowing what you do now, do you think the reviewer liked the movie *Fade to Black?*
14. Does the reviewer think Martin Landau is a good actor?
15. Did the reviewer directly state whether or not the movie was worth seeing or whether or not Martin Landau is a good actor or whether or not he liked *Fade to Black*, or did you have to interpret information and decide what the reviewer thought for yourself?

Evaluating Opinions

Pieces of information presented as facts are fairly easy to deal with—you can identify them and then either prove or disprove them. Opinions, however, may be more difficult. It is important to notice, for example, (1) if the reviewer has a built-in bias, (2) if the reviewer gives reasons for his or her opinions, and (3) if reasons given by the reviewer for opinions expressed are sufficient, appropriate, and convincing. These points are particularly important in reading reviews for some fairly obvious reasons.

First, consider bias. *Bias* is the coloring of events or descriptions from a particular point of view.

Someone who does not like raw fish, for example, will not be on the lookout for qualities that make one Japanese restaurant's raw fish better than another's. Similarly, if a reviewer dislikes detective novels, he or she is not likely to begin a new detective novel with an open mind.

The ability to recognize bias can help you in making better decisions. Sometimes, you may have to read a number of reviews or pieces of writing by a certain author (reviewer) in order to discover his or her biases. Exposure to a number of reviews helps you come to "know" the writer and gives you more information for interpreting what you read. Just as you have some friends whose opinions you value on certain subjects but not on others, so you may find some reviewers whose opinions you value more than others. You also need to be aware of your own biases and how they affect interpretations of what you read.

Second, consider whether or not the reviewer has given examples to support his or her opinions. Just knowing if a reviewer thinks a movie is good or bad may not help you make your own decisions unless you are willing to take the reviewer's word. However, if the reviewer can give specific examples or reasons for his or her opinion, you might be convinced.

Finally, consider the examples used by the reviewer to support his or her opinions. Do they actually support the point being made? Are they one-sided? Are there enough to convince you? Obviously you are more likely to find out a reviewer's biases and reasons for opinions in longer, rather than shorter, reviews.

Activity 4

After reading the following reviews about the novel *Firestarter*, answer the questions that follow on a sheet of paper.

REVIEW #1[1]

King's particular talent in the eerie-scary realm goes beyond the frightening. He makes us care about his beset human beings as people to whom we can relate. From *Carrie* to *Firestarter* this has been true. We open here with a man and his little girl, Charlie, fleeing down the streets of New York. Both are terrified. She is about to be forced in desperation to use a talent of which she has only a little knowledge and no understanding: she can start fires by thinking about and wishing them—pyrokinesis. In flashbacks we learn how it all began. Charlie's parents were students when they participated in a government-sponsored drug experiment. Step by step, we follow what has happened since then. At this point King introduces The Shop, a government agency altogether evil and, unfortunately for plot terms, altogether predictably so. Nevertheless, it is not so much the murderous machinations of The Shop that fascinate us as it is the desperate hope that Charlie and her dad will escape as they flee out of the city. Charlie's mother has already been killed. Their possible nemesis is a

---

[1] Review of *Firestarter* by Stephen King, reprinted from the July 25, 1980 issue of *Publisher's Weekly*, published by R. R. Bowker Company, a Xerox company.

scarred killer. . . . Along the way King brings in interesting and lively secondary characters, and he has us rooting for Charlie right up to the climactic last moment.

REVIEW #2[1]

An *archetype* is an ancient story pattern or character, found in the myths and literature of many cultures, throughout time.

My mailbox is a creature of habit. Fatigued by its daily obligation to disgorge perhaps a dozen new books, it has for some years now offered me each day the same novels it produced for me the day before. One of these invariably has a picture of a pretty young thing in a Regency dress on its jacket. Another sports a swastika. The third displays an ominous-looking child with weird eyes. . . . Usually I find my mailbox's assembly-line productions eminently resistible, but last week I succumbed to curiosity. These fearful children, for instance: surely there is some archetypal myth at play here? The oldest story in Western civilization is that of the usurping child. Though it did him little good, Kronos acted prudently when he chose to swallow his children.

Odd Powers: Stephen King has made a lot of money from such children. In his first novel, *Carrie*, a young girl with odd mental powers sets fire to a building full of people who have abused her. In his new novel, Charlie, a younger girl with odd mental powers, sets fire to several buildings full of people who have abused her. The essence of a good myth is that it stays essentially the same.

Charlie's lot, however, is more desperate than Carrie's. At 8 years old, she is the child of parents who participated in an alarming drug experiment conducted by a ruthless government agency called "the Shop." The experiment left her father with the ability to "push" people—that is, an ability to make others see and do what he wants. Her mother, as befits domesticated women, can only shut a refrigerator door from across the kitchen. Charlie's inheritance is more disturbing: not only can she will fires to start, she can't entirely control the force within her. The mad villains at the Shop fear that as she matures her talent will achieve nuclear, perhaps doomsday proportions. Hit men are sent in pursuit of the family. Imprisoned at the Shop's headquarters, prefatory to the novel's great climactic conflagration, Charlie is put through her paces incinerating steel and burning up cinder-block walls.

Dictum means "a formal statement or pronouncement."

Dare you ask how the story ends? Come, now: what chance has a government agency that couldn't give Castro an exploding cigar against a third-grader who can raise 30,000 degrees of heat? I can say only that Coleridge's dictum about the willing suspension of disbelief takes a merciless beating in the course of these many pages. And yet, says Stephen King, "There is nothing in *Firestarter* that isn't documented or based on actuality." Indeed. The key to successful trashy fiction lies in its author's belief that it is truly the genuine article.

—*Peter S. Prescott*

1. The word(s) that describe the tone of Review #1 is/are
   a. straightforward
   b. sarcastic
   c. negative
   d. positive
   e. enthusiastic
   f. objective
   g. biased
   h. indifferent

---

[1]"Hot Tot" by Peter S. Prescott from *Newsweek*, October 6, 1980.

2. The word(s) that describe the tone of Review #2 is/are
   a. straightforward
   b. sarcastic
   c. negative
   d. positive
   e. enthusiastic
   f. objective
   g. biased
   h. indifferent

3. In the opening two paragraphs of Review #2, the reviewer expresses the opinion that *Firestarter* is
   a. an original idea
   b. a poor retelling of a familiar story
   c. a good retelling of a familiar story
   d. an old idea
4. The first two paragraphs of Review #2
   a. tell you about the author's taste in books
   b. tell you about the novel
   c. both *a* and *b*
   d. neither *a* nor *b*
5. In Review #1 which of the following information is used to describe the novel?
   a. good secondary characters
   b. realistic setting
   c. predictable plot
   d. weak plot
   e. flashbacks are used to reveal events that took place before the novel opens
   f. realistic dialogue
   g. suspenseful story
6. Reviewer #1 says that the novel is suspenseful and that the reader roots for Charlie to escape; however, the other review suggests that there is no suspense. What is the reason for Reviewer #2's opinion?
7. Which review refers to the novel as "an assembly-line production"?
8. By using the phrase "an assembly-line production," what is the reviewer saying about the book?
9. Which review tells you how the novel ends?
10. According to the review, how does the novel end?
11. Why do you think one review tells you how the novel ends?
12. Throughout the review, Reviewer #2 makes it clear that he does not think much of the novel; yet he calls it "successful trashy fiction" in the last paragraph. Words like *successful* and *trashy* are usually not found together. What do you think the author means to imply with the use of these two words?
13. If you have read the book, which review do you think is more in line with your own assessment? Explain.
14. In Review #2 there is a mention of the mythical Greek god Kronos.

Using an encyclopedia of mythology or a book on classical mythology, find out who Kronos is and why he behaved as he did with his children.

15. In Review #2 Samuel Taylor Coleridge's statement about "willing suspension of disbelief" is mentioned. Using a reference book on literary terms, find out what is meant by the "willing suspension of disbelief."

The Review as a Whole

The review should be taken as a whole. Isolated negative or positive statements should not be used alone in evaluating a work. Sometimes, for example, a reviewer might be critical of certain aspects of a book or movie, while still admiring the work as a whole. Such is the case in Michael Bishop's review of Poul Anderson's fantasy novel *The Merman's Children.* A portion of the review follows. Read the excerpt and the following discussion about it.[1]

Venerable means "worthy of respect or reverence by reason of age or dignity."

> Anderson has been tweaked before about wrapping himself in the cloak of the venerable saga-spinner, and he has done that here, too, I'm afraid. Such archaisms as "belike," "bedight," "erelong," and "naught save," especially when they occur in exposition rather than dialogue, often reek of midnight oil rather than the sweat of smithies and the perfume of courtiers. Anderson uses these terms correctly, of course, but I wish that he had refrained. I hasten to add that my quibble is a minor one. *The Merman's Children* pretty much overcomes this idiosyncratic failing and unrolls a genuinely moving story against the rich and well-wrought backdrop of fourteenth-century Europe. If I further state that this may be Anderson's best novel, and undoubtedly his best fantasy, you will comprehend the full extent of my praise.

In the preceding excerpt the reviewer, Michael Bishop, criticizes the writing style of Poul Anderson, specifically his word choice. The intent of this negative criticism is not to prevent a reader of the review from reading the novel; in fact, the criticism seems to be directed at Poul Anderson himself. It almost seems as if Michael Bishop is saying something like the following: "Look, Poul, you write good stories, so in the future, don't mess up on your word choice like you did here."

This type of criticism, directed more at the artist than at the reader of the review, is of little use to the person who is trying to decide whether or not to read the novel. However, it is important to note that a reviewer's comments can frequently help someone who is going to read a book or see a movie to further enjoy the work. The review can do this by calling the reader's attention to important aspects of the movie or book. (Reviews can also help someone who has already read or viewed a work to increase his or her understanding and enjoyment of the work.)

An example of such useful information is found in the following review of the made-for-television spy movie *Tinker, Tailor, Soldier, Spy,* a BBC production of the best-selling novel by John le Carré.

---

[1]From a book review of Poul Anderson's *The Merman's Children* by Michael Bishop. © 1980 by Mercury Press, Inc. Reprinted from *the Magazine of Fantasy and Science Fiction* by permission of Mercury Press and the author.

Activity 5

Read the following review and then write the answers to the questions that follow on a sheet of paper.[1]

BBC is the British Broadcasting Company.

The denouement is the outcome.

Anatoly Karpov is a Russian chess master

Viewers who are into James Bondage, or who actually believe that real spies behave like Charlie's angels, should be warned away from this six-part adaptation of John le Carré's best-selling thriller. Its hero is a dumpy, bookish and melancholy middle-ager, forever fiddling with his spectacles or brooding about his adulterous wife. There are no car chases, no kung fu demolitions. The hideously complex plot is as demanding as a London Times crossword. Yet anyone who sticks with this BBC import will discover the most mesmerizing, ingeniously crafted whodunit ever designed for the small screen.

Sir Alec Guinness plays George Smiley, a retired British spy who is recalled to duty to ferret out a "mole"—a Russian double agent who has infiltrated the top echelons of British intelligence. Smiley's suspects number four, all old colleagues. The maze through which we follow him teems with false exits, ambiguous flashbacks and claustrophobic menace. Almost everyone could be someone else, an effect le Carré mischievously enhances by giving his operatives such innocent trade labels: "baby-sitters" [for bodyguards], "lamplighters" [surveillance experts] and "bad boys" [professional muscle men]. The series' denouement, in which the mole reveals the chilling rationale for his treachery, may be the most subtly nuanced of this genre.

Memory: Public TV has commissioned Robert MacNeil to serve as a sort of plot-decoder for the American audience. Even so, each episode presents a maddening memory test; at least readers of the novel could flip back the pages. Turn away for just a few minutes—or what it takes to write a check to PTV—and you'll be as lost as Smiley when he takes the case. Still, none of that miffed British viewers; the which-one's-the-mole mystery was debated in pubs almost as hotly as the who-shot-J.R. Perhaps that's because the story is based, in part, on that of Kim Philby, Donald Maclean and Guy Burgess, the notorious British spies who defected to Moscow during the cold-war period but whose duplicitous legacy is still making headlines.

Once again, Alec Guinness turns in an elegantly effortless performance, playing George Smiley almost as if he had invented him. The role calls on Guinness to spend almost all of his time listening to others. Only his eyes, and an occasional offhand gesture or sign, convey a mind that is sifting and connecting with computerlike ease. The closest Guinness comes to histrionics is in the climactic scene, when he confesses to his wife . . . that he had momentarily considered shooting his quarry. "Poor George," she dryly scolds. "Life is such a puzzle to you, isn't it?"

"Tinker, Tailor" is chess played with human pieces, the lights off and the opponent unknown. Viewers patient enough to figure out the moves, however, will come away feeling like winners over Anatoly Karpov.

—*Harry F. Waters*

1. The reviewer cautions certain people against watching this spy movie. Who are they?

---

[1]Column on "Tinker, Tailor, Soldier, Spy" by Harry F. Waters in *Newsweek*, October 6, 1980.

2. Do you think the reviewer begins the review with a caution in order to dissuade certain people from watching the movie or to let the viewer know what to expect?
3. The review describes the plot as "hideously complex." What behavior does this phrase suggest will be required of the viewer to understand the movie? For example, could you do homework or do work around the house while you watched?
4. According to the review, the plot is a *maze*, or "intricate puzzle." What does the review say that the plot consists of?
5. Look at your answer to the previous question. In your answer you have included both fact and opinion words. Which are which?
6. The reviewer defines some words in the second paragraph. What words does he define? Why and how are the definitions of the words helpful to the prospective viewer?
7. This review uses contemporary allusions. In other words, it makes references to and comparisons with current events and shows. Sometimes, it explains references, but other times it does not. If someone were to read this review 150 years from now, which comparisons/references might not mean anything to him or her?
8. Suppose you wanted to find out more about the real spies mentioned in the review. How might you go about finding information concerning them? Go to the chapter in this textbook on using the library, and outline possible sources and steps you could take to find the information.
9. What is the reviewer's opinion of Sir Alec Guinness's performance as Smiley?
10. The reviewer tells the prospective viewer indirectly to note certain aspects of Guinness's performance. What are those aspects?

Finding Reviews

Thus far in this chapter, you have been asked to read reviews already selected. To find your own reviews, look back in the chapter on using the library and review what you learned about locating information. Major sources of reviews are newspapers, news and other magazines, and guides to viewing, such as *TV Guide*. The *Readers' Guide to Periodical Literature* provides a current index of articles found in many different publications. Using what you have learned about reading reviews and what you know about using library resources, complete the following activity.

Activity 6

Select a book, movie, or television program that you have recently seen or read or that you have considered seeing or reading. Then locate at least two reviews of the work, using the *Readers' Guide* or other resource material. Read the reviews and then compare them on the following points: (1) facts presented, (2) opinions expressed, (3) purpose of reviewer, (4) tone of the reviewer, (5) examples of word choice, (6) extent of support for opinions expressed, and (7) degree of agreement or disagreement between reviews.

PART

4 Sentence Combining

14 Joining Sentences

Fluent Writing

What is wrong with the following passage?

> The forests were somber. The forests were dull. They stood motionless and silent. They stood on each side of a stream. The stream was broad. Nipa palms stood at the foot of trees. The trees were big and towering. The nipa palms were trunkless. They rose from the mud of the bank. They rose in bunches of leaves. The leaves were enormous. They were heavy. They hung unstirring over the brown swirl of eddies.

Certainly the preceding passage is well edited, with no errors in mechanics, usage, or spelling, and is descriptive and imaginative. However, the author Joseph Conrad might be shocked at reading these altered sentences from his short story "The Lagoon." Each sentence seems to stand alone, unconnected to the next. The passage lacks the unity and fluency that characterize the prose of this master of English fiction. When the sentences are recombined into Conrad's original form, you can see how important the arrangement of ideas in sentences is in writing:

> The forest, somber and dull, stood motionless and silent on each side of the broad stream. At the foot of big, towering trees, trunkless nipa palms rose from the mud of the bank, in bunches of leaves enormous and heavy, that hung unstirring over the brown swirl of eddies.

Creative ideas alone do not make for good writing; the combination and arrangement of the ideas in sentences, and sentences in paragraphs, are equally important. Through arranging and combining sentences, you give to your writing the variety and fluency that appeal to readers. In this chapter you will learn several ways to combine sentences for variety and fluency.

Using Connectors to Join Sentences

Several groups of words can be used to join sentences of equal importance. This process, called *coordination*, is used more frequently than any other pattern.

Single words called *connectors* make up the first group of coordinators. Each connector signals a relationship between ideas:

Connectors are also called *coordinating conjunctions*. See page 463.

CONNECTOR	RELATIONSHIP
and	similarity
but	opposition or contrast
yet	opposition or contrast
or	choice
nor	negation
so	cause and effect
for	an explanation

In the following sentence sets, a word in parentheses, called a *signal*, indicates which coordinator is to be used to join the sentences. Notice that joining sentences with the negative word *nor* requires a change in word order and the deletion of the word *not* in one of the sentences. Study the following examples to learn how the combinations work.

Notice that a comma precedes the joined sentences.

Sentences: Michael ordered the concert tickets.
Jason picked them up. (AND)

Combined: Michael ordered the concert tickets**,** and Jason picked them up.

Sentences: Luis received a scholarship to nursing school.
Anna's request was denied. (BUT)

Combined: Luis received a scholarship to nursing school**,** but Anna's request was denied.

Sentences: We did not feel comfortable sitting in the elegantly furnished room.
We could not decide how to eat the delicate cucumber sandwiches. (NOR)

Combined: We did not feel comfortable sitting in the elegantly furnished room**,** nor could we decide how to eat the delicate cucumber sandwiches.

Exercise 1

After studying the examples, combine the following sentence sets. The first five sets are signaled; for the last five choose the connector you think works best.

Examples

a. Michael wants to attend one of the community colleges next year. First he must explore the programs each offers. (BUT)

a. Michael wants to attend one of the community colleges next year, but first he must explore the programs each offers.

b. The recruits did not have the time to write long letters home.
They did not have the energy to do much more than fall exhausted into bed. (NOR)

b. The recruits did not have the time to write long letters home, nor did they have the energy to do much more than fall exhausted into bed.

1. Should we harvest the grapes now?
Should we take a chance on fair weather next week? (OR)
2. The Democratic party has traditionally appealed to organized labor.
The Republican party has traditionally appealed to the interests of big business. (AND)
3. The audience anticipated a rousing musical.
The acoustics in the theater were bad. (BUT)
4. Striking workers voted to accept the proposed contract.
It was in their best interests. (FOR)
5. We wanted to see the movie before it closed.
We were reluctant to drive on the icy roads. (YET)
6. The doctors did not prescribe special drugs.
They did not offer any other avenue to a cure.
7. Lisa was not satisfied with her performance.
She knew she could have done much better.
8. Using credit cards requires some caution.
The results could be financial disaster.
9. Elizabeth did not want to marry Mr. Collins.
She did not want to marry Mr. Darcy.
10. Long before kickoff a large crowd filled the stadium.
We knew our chances of getting last-minute tickets were remote.

Using Connectors to Join Parts of Sentences

Connectors can be used to join one sentence with parts of one or more other sentences. In the following example notice that repeated words are left out when the sentences are joined. Notice also that no comma is necessary and that the verb in the combined sentence is changed to its plural form.

Sentences: In the Bradbury Building is elaborate wrought-iron decoration throughout the interior.
In the Bradbury Building is a soaring skylight to brighten the entire area. (AND)

Combined: In the Bradbury Building are elaborate wrought-iron decoration throughout the interior and a soaring skylight to brighten the entire area.

If you join more than two sentences, you create a series. In that case you will need to use commas or conjunctions to separate each part. The signals

The use of commas and conjunctions with a series is also discussed on page 553.

(,) or (,AND) or (,OR), or (,BUT) and so on tell you how to join the sentences, as the following example shows:

Sentences: Ancient Greece gave the world the foundations of democracy.
It gave the world an unsurpassed architecture. (,)
It gave the world great works of literature and music we study yet today. (,AND)

Combined: Ancient Greece gave the world the foundations of democracy**,** an unsurpassed architecture**,** and great works of literature and music we study yet today.

Sentences: Mrs. Donato was unable to decide whether to order the seafood salad.
She was unable to decide whether to order the cannelloni with tomato sauce. (,)
She was unable to decide whether to order the special turkey dinner. (,OR)

Combined: Mrs. Donato was unable to decide whether to order the seafood salad**,** the cannelloni with tomato sauce**,** or the special turkey dinner.

Exercise 2

After studying the examples, join the sentences in each of the following sets. The first five sets are signaled; for the last five, you must decide how to make the combinations.

Examples

a. The family gathered around the little grave.
The family joined hands to pay silent tribute to the one they had lost. (AND)

a. The family gathered around the little grave and joined hands to pay silent tribute to the one they had lost.

b. Should I spend my vacation sunning in my yard?
Should I spend my vacation hiking in the mountains? (,)
Should I spend my vacation exploring the city? (,OR)

b. Should I spend my vacation sunning in my yard, hiking in the mountains, or exploring the city?

1. Requirements for this job include the ability to read two languages other than English.
Requirements for this job include extensive travel experience. (AND)

2. Whenever Zachary feels depressed, he goes for long walks along the levee down by the Mississippi River.
Whenever Zachary feels depressed, he hums quietly to himself.(,)
Whenever Zachary feels depressed, he tries to think of cheerful, pleasant things. (,AND)

3. The people were desperately poor.
The people had little food in storage for the winter. (,)

The people could find no way to make the soil they tilled more productive. (,AND)

4. Rushing back and forth in its cage consumed the wild animal's entire day.
   Searching for bits of food under rock ledges consumed the wild animal's entire day. (,)
   Screaming occasionally at gaping visitors consumed the wild animal's entire day. (,AND)
5. The speaker's eyes searched the crowd.
   They tried to spot the heckler. (,)
   They could not find the source of the noise. (,BUT)
6. This new book will surely become a best seller.
   This new book will make its author justly famous.
7. Snow fell from ominously dark clouds.
   It drifted across roads and fields.
   It blocked homeward-bound commuters from their destinations.
8. Marianna's ambition would not allow her to waste time in frivolous pursuits.
   Marianna's ambition would not allow her to expend her energy on worthless projects.
9. Visitors to the factory may park in the visitors' lot.
   They may park in the vacant lot next to the power plant on Ninth Street.
10. If the weather is favorable, the class picnic will be held in Central Park.
    If enough students sign up to attend, the class picnic will be held in Central Park.
    If we can find suitable transportation, the class picnic will be held in Central Park.

Using Paired Connectors to Join Sentences

These connectors, also called *correlative conjunctions*, are discussed on page 463.

Two sets of paired connectors—*either . . . or* and *not only . . . but also*—can be used to join sentences of equal importance. The paired connector *either . . . or* suggests a choice between alternatives; *not only . . . but also* indicates an additional idea in the second sentences.

In the following examples notice that words or word order may change slightly when the combination is made.

Sentences: You will have to turn up the heat in this building.
I will be forced to complain. (EITHER . . . OR)

Combined: Either you will have to turn up the heat in this building, or I will be forced to complain.

Sentences: The scholarship offered her a chance to attend the college of her choice.
It did a world of good for her self-esteem. (NOT ONLY . . . BUT ALSO)

Combined: Not only did the scholarship offer her a chance to attend the college of her choice, but it also did a world of good for her self-esteem.

Exercise 3

After studying the examples, use paired connectors to join the following sentence sets. The first five sets are signaled; for the last five decide for yourself which of the two paired connectors to use.

Notice that a comma precedes the second sentence.

Examples

a. Reduce the number of calories you consume.
Increase the time you spend exercising. (EITHER . . . OR)

a. Either reduce the number of calories you consume, or increase the time you spend exercising.

b. This new diet will do wonders for your health.
It will make you look and feel better. (NOT ONLY . . . BUT ALSO)

b. Not only will this new diet do wonders for your health, but it will also make you look and feel better.

1. New sources of revenue will have to be found.
Local governments will have to increase taxes. (EITHER . . . OR)
2. Studying for a test is important.
It is a good idea to get plenty of sleep the night before. (NOT ONLY . . . BUT ALSO)
3. The weather forecasters made a huge mistake in their forecast.
What I see falling from the sky isn't snow. (EITHER . . . OR)
4. We will have to find a new system for keeping the books.
This company faces financial ruin. (EITHER . . . OR)
5. Computer crimes are increasing.
This form of white-collar crime is expected to continue climbing in the future. (NOT ONLY . . . BUT ALSO)
6. We have the kitchen left to clean up.
Someone has to find a good way to get the kitten out from behind the refrigerator.
7. Michelangelo was a great painter.
He was a sculptor, poet, and architect.
8. I did not get the job I wanted.
The personnel manager is waiting a long time to notify me to come to work.
9. We must find a way to feed the world's growing population.
We must face the prospect of worldwide famine.
10. We will have to raise money through car washes, bake sales, and the like.
We will have to ask each band member to pay his or her own expenses.

Using Adverbs to Join Sentences

The last group of words that join sentences of equal importance is more formal than those you have studied in the previous sections. These coordinators are called *conjunctive adverbs*, and they require a semicolon between the joined sentences; in addition, they are followed by a comma. The most frequently used adverb connectors are the following ones.

CONJUNCTIVE ADVERB	RELATIONSHIP
however instead on the other hand nevertheless	connect opposite ideas
therefore thus consequently hence	indicate that a conclusion or result follows
besides furthermore moreover in addition	indicate that an additional idea follows
indeed in fact	indicate emphasis

Notice how the signals work in the following sentence sets.

Sentences: Six inches of snow fell last night.
Chris and I will have to shovel the walkway this morning. (CONSEQUENTLY)

Combined: Six inches of snow fell last night; consequently, Chris and I will have to shovel the walkway this morning.

Sentences: The price of housing has risen sharply in the last decade.
The interest rates on home mortgages have also kept the upward pace. (MOREOVER)

Combined: The price of housing has risen sharply in the last decade; moreover, the interest rates on home mortgages have also kept the upward pace.

Exercise 4

Join the following sets of sentences with a semicolon and the conjunctive adverb indicated by the signal. Study the examples before you begin. Write each combined sentence on a sheet of paper.

Examples

a. Danielle had insufficient funds in her checking account.
Her check bounced. (CONSEQUENTLY)

a. Danielle had insufficient funds in her checking account; consequently, her check bounced.

b. Nuclear war is the greatest threat to humans.
Its potential effects are more devastating than any recorded natural disaster. (INDEED)

b. Nuclear war is the greatest threat to humans; indeed, its potential effects are more devastating than any recorded natural disaster.

1. Ian Fleming was the author of the James Bond novels.
He wrote a novel for children titled *Chitty-Chitty-Bang-Bang*. (IN ADDITION)
2. Rosie argued that she wasn't going over thirty.
The officer gave her a ticket. (NEVERTHELESS)
3. The apartment building is an old firetrap.
The city will condemn it. (THEREFORE)
4. Hamlet suspected Claudius of murdering his father.
Claudius was now his stepfather. (ON THE OTHER HAND)
5. Dinh believed the course would be a snap.
He had all of his brother's notes from the previous year. (BESIDES)

Exercise 5

The following sets of sentences have no signals. Join them, choosing the conjunctive adverb that best expresses the relationship between the ideas presented. (Refer to the list of conjunctive adverbs on page 296.) Study the example before you begin.

Example

a. The Hispanic population of California is a major economic, social, and cultural influence.
More Hispanics of Mexican descent live in Los Angeles than in any city in Mexico except Mexico City.

a. The Hispanic population of California is a major economic, social, and cultural influence; in fact, more Hispanics of Mexican descent live in Los Angeles than in any city in Mexico except Mexico City.

1. Robert put up all the storm windows.
He was ready for the storm.
2. The officials assessed a fifteen-yard penalty against the team.
They threw the coach out of the game.
3. A good résumé can be a door opener in the job market.
Good interview skills are probably most important to the job hunter.
4. Comparative shopping often results in a tremendous savings.
Comparative shopping also costs time and money.
5. The horror film was billed as the scariest ever.
It was so poorly scripted and acted that it was laughable.

Joining Sentences with the Semicolon

If two sentences are of equal importance *and* are closely related in thought, they can be combined with a semicolon, as the following examples show.

Sentences: The 1980 national census shows that the most dramatic population increases are in the Southern and Western states.
Collectively, these states are called the Sun Belt. (;)

Combined: The 1980 national census shows that the most dramatic population increases are in the Southern and Western states; collectively, these states are called the Sun Belt.

Sentences: Pham completed all the assignments for the course.
Tomorrow he takes the final exam. (;)

Combined: Pham completed all the assignments for the course; tomorrow he takes the final exam.

Exercise 6

Each of the following sets of sentences can be combined with a semicolon. Some of the sentences can also be combined with a connector and a comma. After studying the example, combine the sentence sets, deciding which method is best.

Example

a. Polio is a very rare disease today.
Only a few cases are reported each year.

a. Polio is a very rare disease today; only a few cases are reported each year.

1. Our basketball team made the final round of the playoffs.
Our opponents, last year's champs, are favored to win.
2. Esperanza wants to buy a car.
She begins driving lessons tomorrow.
3. Robert never puts onions and lettuce on his hamburgers.
Sally loves everything on hers.
4. I need a ride home after school.
My sister can't pick me up today.
5. Mr. Gonzales was promoted to plant manager.
He had been the production foreman.
6. Jennifer wants to study law.
Her friend Maria wants to be a social worker.
7. Many of Charles Dickens' novels deal with the working class of industrialized England.
He was very concerned with the living conditions of the common people.
8. Michelle's cousin lives in Dallas.
She plans to visit her there next summer.
9. The gray whale is an endangered species.
Several countries still hunt the animals commercially.

10. Daniel is entering the army in June.
He will train in California.

Joining Sentences with a Dash, Colon, and Parentheses

Certain marks of punctuation can be used to join sentences with special relationships. You can use a colon to join two sentences when one of them explains or restates the idea of the other, as the following example shows.

Sentences: The contract settlement was acceptable to both sides. Management held down the wage increase to 8 per cent, and the workers received improved medical benefits. (COLON)

Combined: The contract settlement was acceptable to both sides**:** management held down the wage increase to 8 per cent, and the workers received improved medical benefits.

The dash can also be used to connect two sentences when one explains or restates the idea of the other.

Sentences: The officials should have thrown a flag on the play. They could have penalized our team ten yards. (DASH)

Combined: The officials should have thrown a flag on the play—they could have penalized our team ten yards.

Parentheses can also be used to join sentences when one sentence explains the other. However, with the parentheses, the explanatory information is usually incidental to the idea of the sentence.

Sentences: Ambassador Okimi presented the resolution to the General Assembly. He is from Japan. (PARENS)

Combined: Ambassador Okimi **(**he is from Japan**)** presented the resolution to the General Assembly.

Exercise 7

Combine the following pairs of sentences, using a dash, a colon, or parentheses. Because these punctuation marks are frequently interchangeable, you must choose the one you think works best. Study the examples before you begin.

Examples

a. Fewer people voted in the recent Presidential election than in the previous ten.
Refer to Diagram A for the figures.

a. Fewer people voted in the recent Presidential election than in the previous ten (refer to Diagram A for the figures).

or

a. Fewer people voted in the recent Presidential election than in the previous ten—refer to Diagram A for the figures.

b. Jason could have prevented the accident.
He should have checked his brakes last week.

b. Jason could have prevented the accident: he should have checked his brakes last week.

or

b. Jason could have prevented the accident—he should have checked his brakes last week.

1. The sunset over the mountains was spectacular.
The yellow and orange sky was a beautiful backdrop to the snow-capped peaks.
2. The referee stopped the fight too late.
Thompson was already seriously injured.
3. Senator McCarthy will chair the new committee.
He is a liberal Democrat.
4. The use of metaphors in Hopkins' poetry often makes it difficult to understand.
A discussion of metaphors in lyric poetry begins on page 243.
5. The long-forgotten trunk contained many of Grandmother's personal things.
It contained letters, a diary, her wedding dress, and a collection of dolls.
6. Jennifer got the job at the bank.
She was ecstatic.
7. The new synthetic material will last longer than nylon.
It is colorfast and resistant to high heat.
8. Nicole was very upset after the swimming meet.
Her team performed badly.
9. The general ordered our troops to advance.
The enemy was retreating.
10. Most department stores hold regular, seasonal sales.
The sales include back to school, after holidays, and summer clearance.

Joining Parts of Sentences with a Colon, Dash, or Parentheses

A colon, dash, or parentheses can be used to join parts of one sentence to another. A colon can join the part of a sentence that explains, gives an example or illustration, or provides a list to the end of another sentence. The following example illustrates how this combination works.

Sentences: The overseas cargo carrier brought goods from all over the world.
It brought spices, footwear, heavy machinery, and rattan furniture. (COLON)

Combined: The overseas cargo carrier brought goods from all over the world**:** spices, footwear, heavy machinery, and rattan furniture.

A part of a sentence that explains or restates the idea of another or that adds information can be attached with a dash or paired dashes.

Sentences: My tendency to be lazy prevents me from finishing homework on time.
My tendency to be lazy is a trait I would like to be rid of. (DASHES)

Combined: My tendency to be lazy—a trait I would like to be rid of—prevents me from finishing homework on time.

When a list or illustration precedes the main part of a sentence, it is followed by a dash and a summary word, such as *such, these,* or *all.*

Sentences: These were the only objects the rescue team found on the frozen body.
The objects were a ration of beef jerky, a pocket knife, a pair of binoculars, one wet match.

Combined: A ration of beef jerky, a pocket knife, a pair of binoculars, one wet match—these were the only objects the rescue team found on the frozen body.

Parentheses can also join part of a sentence to another sentence.

Sentences: Martha Yvonne Carruthers became head of a large corporation before she was thirty-nine years old.
Martha Yvonne Carruthers was a naturalized citizen. (PARENS)

Combined: Martha Yvonne Carruthers (a naturalized citizen) became head of a large corporation before she was thirty-nine years old.

Exercise 8

Combine the following pairs of sentences using a dash, a colon, or parentheses. (Choose the punctuation you think works best.) Study the examples.

Examples

a. On the line hung three quilts my grandparents had made years ago.
The quilts were a blue and white crisscross pattern, a rose bouquet on a white background, and a patchwork design with bright red borders.

a. On the line hung three quilts my grandparents had made years ago: a blue and white crisscross pattern, a rose bouquet on a white background, and a patchwork design with bright red borders.

b. I hope that a good mechanic will be able to diagnose what is wrong with my car and repair it quickly.
My car is definitely a lemon.

b. I hope that a good mechanic will be able to diagnose what is wrong with my car (definitely a lemon) and repair it quickly.

or

b. I hope that a good mechanic will be able to diagnose what is wrong with my car—definitely a lemon—and repair it quickly.

1. Dell's interest in movies began when he was a child watching Disney films and has grown ever since.
   The Disney films were *Snow White*, *Bambi*, and *Pinocchio*.
2. Behind her on the wall were posters of her favorite entertainers.
   The entertainers were the Beatles, Roberta Lynn, and Charlie Daniels.
3. An adequate diet should contain some fiber-rich bran as well as foods that provide protein, fats, and carbohydrates.
   Fiber-rich bran is available in bran cereals or in bulk at some health food stores.
4. These activities helped Melissa maintain her good health and trim figure.
   Swimming fifty laps every day, bicycling several miles on weekends, and playing volleyball after school were the activities.
5. In writing a comparison essay, it is a good idea to choose two items that share some elements and then show their similarities and differences.
   The items are perhaps two poems on death.
6. Senta was attracted to the young man as soon as she saw his superb skill on the ice.
   The young man was a wonderful, graceful skater!
7. Take this letter to the front office for confirmation of your employment.
   There are no signatures needed.
8. These were the traits that made her so likable.
   A good sense of humor, a warm personality, and a sensitivity to the needs of other people were the traits.
9. Five vehicles suffered front- or rear-end damage when they ran into each other in the swiftly moving expressway traffic.
   The five vehicles were all late model cars.
10. The visitors had to smile when they saw the animals in the zoo nursery window.
    The animals were a two-week-old spider monkey nursing on a doll-sized bottle, a baby cheetah trying to chew off a bandage on its paw, and a newborn African kudu that pressed its nose softly against the glass.

Connecting Sentences of Unequal Importance

Words called *subordinators* can be used to join two sentences of unequal importance.

Subordinators connect a sentence of lesser importance (the subordinate sentence) to a major sentence (the base sentence) by indicating the relationship between the two sentences. The following are the most common subordinators.

These words are also called *subordinating conjunctions*. See page 463.

after	before	until
although	even though	when
as if	just as	whenever
as long as	just when	where
as soon as	since	wherever
as though	so that	whether
because	unless	while

By placing a subordinator in front of a sentence, you create a *subordinate clause* that cannot stand alone but is dependent on the base sentence. For example, when the subordinator *although* is added to the sentence *He began life as a slave,* the resulting clause, *Although he began life as a slave,* is no longer an independent sentence.

Sentence: He began life as a slave. (ALTHOUGH)
Booker T. Washington became president of the first Negro college.

Combined: Although he began life as a slave, Booker T. Washington became president of the first Negro college.

In the preceding example the subordinate clause is attached to the beginning of the base sentence, but you can also attach clauses to the end of a base sentence. A subordinate clause is usually separated from the base sentence with a comma when the clause is attached to the beginning of a sentence. A subordinate clause at the end of a sentence usually does not require a comma. The following example illustrates the options.

Sentences: The barbecue was ready.
The kids returned from the lake. (WHEN)

Combined: The barbecue was ready when the kids returned from the lake.
or When the kids returned from the lake, the barbecue was ready.

Exercise 9

Combine the following pairs of sentences by using subordinators. In signaled examples and problems the signal appears immediately *after* the sentence that will become the subordinate clause. When no signal is given, choose the subordinator you think is appropriate, remembering that the subordinate clause may be placed before or after the base sentence for variety and style. Punctuate your combined sentences correctly.

Examples

a. The mountain residents are evacuating.
The volcano may erupt at any time. (BECAUSE)

a. The mountain residents are evacuating because the volcano may erupt at any time.

or

a. Because the volcano may erupt at any time, the mountain residents are evacuating.

b. The personnel manager called me for an interview.
   She read my application.

b. The personnel manager called me for an interview as soon as she read my application.

or

b. As soon as she read my application, the personnel manager called me for an interview.

1. The camera crew arrived at the fire.
   The helicopters arrived to rescue people from the roof. (JUST AS)
2. Shoplifting is really a serious crime. (ALTHOUGH)
   Some people consider it little more than an innocent game.
3. Some species of whale may become extinct.
   Many countries refuse to ban whale hunting. (BECAUSE)
4. In his writing Geoffrey Chaucer captured the spirit of medieval England.
   He lived at the close of the Middle Ages. (EVEN THOUGH)
5. Members of Congress can ill afford to give themselves a substantial pay raise.
   The government is asking the public to hold down wages and prices. (WHEN)
6. The winters remain dry.
   The New England states will have to conserve water.
7. Andy will not graduate.
   He passes the proficiency tests.
8. Vitamin supplements probably are not necessary.
   You maintain a well-balanced diet.
9. She turned fifteen.
   Christine got a Social Security card.
10. No part of the United States is immune from tornadoes.
    They usually occur in the Midwest.

Review Exercise A

As a review of the sentence-combining strategies you have studied, follow the signals to combine the following sentence sets in the order they appear. Before you begin, study the example sentences on this page and page 305 and the paragraph that resullts. After you have combined the sentences in the exercise, write out your sentences as a complete paragraph.

Examples

(Adapted from "To Build a Fire" by Jack London)

a. He plunged in among the big spruce trees.
   He found a faint trail. (AND)

a. He plunged in among the big spruce trees and found a faint trail.

b. A foot of snow had fallen.
The last sled had passed over. (SINCE)

b. A foot of snow had fallen since the last sled had passed over.

c. He was glad he was without a sled.
He preferred to travel light. (BECAUSE)

c. He was glad he was without a sled because he preferred to travel light.

d. He left his pack at camp yesterday. (AFTER)
He now carried nothing but the lunch wrapped in the handkerchief.

d. After he left his pack at camp yesterday, he now carried nothing but the lunch wrapped in the handkerchief.

e. He rubbed his numb nose and cheekbones with his mittened hand. (JUST AS)
He concluded that it certainly was cold.

e. Just as he rubbed his numb nose and cheekbones with his mittened hand, he concluded that it certainly was cold.

f. He was a warm-whiskered man.
The hair on his face did not protect the high cheekbones and the eager nose. (BUT)
They were thrust so aggressively into the frosty air. (SINCE)

f. He was a warm-whiskered man, but the hair on his face did not protect the high cheekbones and the eager nose, since they were thrust so aggressively into the frosty air.

PARAGRAPH FORM

He plunged in among the big spruce trees and found a faint trail. A foot of snow had fallen since the last sled had passed over. He was glad he was without a sled because he preferred to travel light. After he left his pack at camp yesterday, he now carried nothing but the lunch wrapped in the handkerchief. Just as he rubbed his numb nose and cheekbones with his mittened hand, he concluded that it certainly was cold. He was a warm-whiskered man, but the hair on his face did not protect the high cheekbones and the eager nose, since they were thrust so aggressively into the frosty air.

1. Life is complex.
Life is also fun. (YET)

2. It is complicated. (BECAUSE)
Think of life in this way.

3. Life is not a lot of happy endings and somewheres.
It is a long, never-ending pathway stretching out ahead of you. (BUT)

4. You are on one pathway now. (JUST AS . . . SO)
There are many other pathways leading off to either side.

5. The pathway you are on now represents the life style you are now living.
The side pathways represent new directions you might take. (;)
You will find new jobs, new hobbies, new places to live. (DASH)

6. One pathway might be labeled "be a cartoonist."
   You might choose to start down that pathway. (AND)
7. Soon you will reach a fork.
   One branch would be labeled "free-lance cartoonist," and the other, "regularly employed." (WHERE)
8. You will have to choose.
   Your choice will have considerable influence on your future options. (AND)
   The side pathways leading off the two branches will not always be the same. (BECAUSE)

Review Exercise B

The following sentence sets have no signals. Combine each set into one sentence, using the connectors you have studied. (Remember that some sets can be combined several ways.) When you have combined the sentences, write them in paragraph form.

(Adapted from "The Necklace" by Guy de Maupassant)

1. She came to know the heavy work of the house.
   She came to know the hateful duties of the kitchen.
2. She washed the plates.
   She wore out her pink nails on the coarse pottery and the bottoms of pans.
3. She washed the dirty linen, the sheets, and dish cloths.
   She hung them out to dry on a string.
4. Every morning she took the dustbin down into the street.
   She carried up the water.
5. She held tightly to the basket on her arm.
   She went to the fruiterer, to the grocer, and to the butcher.
6. She was dressed as a poor woman.
   She fought, haggled and insulted for every wretched halfpenny of her money.

Writing Exercise A

Most people have childhood memories that will always remain important—family vacations, visits to Grandma's, a close friend, a first pet, a birthday party, and so on. Choose from your childhood a moment or experience you cannot forget—possibly one that you would like to live over again. Then think about the memory and the places, people, and events that were involved. Now write about the experience so vividly that someone else can understand what happened and how you felt. Remember that you are taking your reader through unfamiliar territory, so you must write clearly and with plenty of detail. Use your senses—all the sights, sounds, smells, touches, and tastes of your memory. As you write, use some of the sentence-combining strategies you have studied.

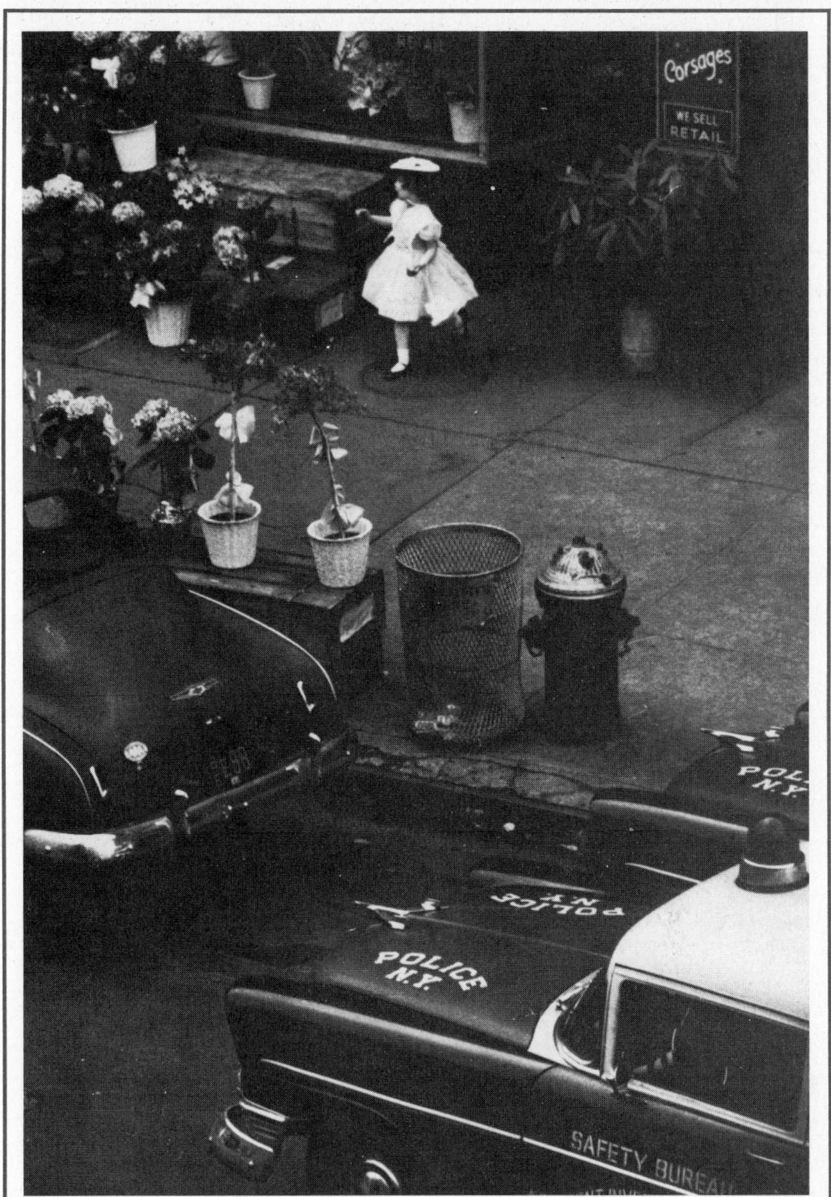

Writing Exercise B

What careers interest you now? As you near the end of high school, career planning and decision making probably occupy a great deal of your thoughts. A career decision is not something that must come with graduating from high school, but you will have to make some decisions about immediate directions soon. As you plan for your immediate future, one question should always play a part in the decision-making process: What do you really want?

If you had to make a career goal decision now, what would it be? Write a paper in which you select a career and explain how your choice answers the question, "What do I really want?" Ask yourself the following questions as you make the decision and prepare your response.

1. Would I be happy doing a job that calls for a lot of math? Or history? Or science?
2. Would I prefer to work alone or with other people?
3. Which people do I admire? Why? What do I like about them?
4. Do I want to be like them? Could I learn to be like them?
5. Where do I want to work?
6. Do I want to move around a lot or stay in one place?
7. Would I like a quiet job or a job with lots of excitement?
8. Would I like to be famous, or am I the kind of person who would be happy just quietly earning a good living?

As you write, use some of the sentence-combining techniques you have studied.

Writing Exercise C

Using some of the sentence-combining skills you have learned, write a description of the photograph on page 307. If you prefer, write a short story or play, using the situation in the photograph.

15 Inserting Sentences

Inserting Modifiers

Another strategy writers use to achieve sentence variety and fluency is to expand a *base sentence* by inserting modifiers from other sentences, called *insert sentences.*

Modifiers are adjectives, adverbs, prepositional phrases, and other words used to describe. Several modifiers can be inserted into a base sentence as long as each is clearly connected to the word it modifies.

Base Sentence: Rosie's explanation of the traditional dance was interesting and informative.
Insert: Rosie's explanation was lively.
Insert: The dance was from Mexico.
Combined: Rosie's lively explanation of the traditional dance from Mexico was interesting and informative.

Because the word *lively* and the phrase *from Mexico* modify (or describe) words in the base sentence, they can be inserted into the base sentence without altering its meaning. In fact, the combined sentence is more interesting and economical than the original sentences.

Frequently two or more modifiers describe the same word. In this situation the modifiers usually can be reversed, and they may be separated by a comma or the word *and.* The following example illustrates reversible modifiers that are separated by a comma and the word *and.* Watch for the signals (,) or (AND) or (,AND) at the end of the insert sentences. These signals will appear in the exercises.

Base Sentence: Early joggers run along the sea's edge.
Insert: The joggers run effortlessly.
Insert: The joggers run gracefully. (,)

Insert:	The joggers run silently. (,AND)
Combined:	Early joggers run effortlessly, gracefully, *and* silently along the sea's edge.
or	Early joggers run gracefully, effortlessly, *and* silently along the sea's edge.

Although modifiers can be inserted into different places in the base sentence, they must be clearly attached to the words they modify so that readers correctly understand the writer's meaning. The first example that follows illustrates how modifiers can be correctly inserted in different places, while the second illustrates how misplaced modifiers change or confuse meaning.

Base Sentence:	We drove cousin George to the bus station.
Insert:	We drove through the fog.
Insert:	The fog was dense.
Insert:	The fog was dangerous. (AND)
Combined:	Through the dense and dangerous fog, we drove cousin George to the bus station.
or	We drove cousin George to the bus station through the dense and dangerous fog.
Base Sentence:	The coach jumped up from the bench to protest the foul, and the referee threw her out of the game.
Insert:	The coach was irritated.
Insert:	The referee threw the coach out of the game without a warning.
Combined:	Irritated, the coach jumped up from the bench to protest the foul, and the referee threw her out of the game without a warning.
but not	Without a warning, the coach jumped up from the bench to protest the foul, and the referee threw her out of the game irritated.

In the second combination *irritated* cannot be moved to the end of the sentence because it describes how the coach felt; it should be placed next to the word it modifies. Also, the phrase modifier *without a warning* cannot be inserted at the beginning of the sentence because these words describe the referee's actions.

Sometimes, an insert sentence can be made into a modifier by changing it to a "with . . ." phrase. The following examples show how this combination works.

Base Sentence:	The girl is my cousin.
Insert:	The girl has long hair.
Combined:	The girl with long hair is my cousin.
Base Sentence:	The peacock strutted around the yard.
Insert:	Its long, flowing tail trailed behind.
Combined:	With its long, flowing tail trailing behind, the peacock strutted around the yard.

Exercise 1

Using the first sentence in the set as the base sentence, combine the following sets of sentences. Some of the sets have signals in parentheses; some of the sets are unsignaled, and you must use your own judgment. Study the examples before you begin.

Examples

a. Winds chased the leaves from the branches.
The winds were autumnal.
The leaves were brown.
The leaves were dry. (,)
The branches were bending.

a. The autumnal winds chased the brown, dry leaves from the bending branches.

b. A man was sleeping on the park bench.
The man was dirty.
The man was ragged.
The man was hungry.
The park bench was in the playground.

b. A dirty, ragged, and hungry man was sleeping on the park bench in the playground.

1. The boys failed to recognize the nature of Uncle Jeffrey's comments about the water shortage.
The boys were giggling.
The boys were talking. (AND)
The nature of Uncle Jeffrey's comments was serious.
The water shortage is imminent.

Note: Change *an* to *a* in the combined sentence.

2. The rescuer of the child received an award.
The rescuer was brave.
The rescuer was persistent.
The child was small.
The reward was well-deserved.

3. The car stalled, leaving John alone in a town.
The car was old.
The car stalled on a street.
The street was dark.
The street was deserted.
The town was strange.

4. A farmer digging a well found several pieces of pottery and a stone weapon, a discovery that led to the excavation of a burial site.
The farmer was from California.
The farmer found the pottery and stone weapon in 1978.
The pieces of pottery were broken.
The stone weapon was carved.

The carvings were intricate.
The burial site was Indian.
The burial site was important.

5. Heroes have achieved an immortality as constellations.
The heroes are ancient.
The heroes are mythological.
The constellations are brilliant.
The constellations are majestic. (AND)
The constellations are in our night skies.

6. Although the city sprayed every neighborhood and treated swamps, the mosquitoes continued to swarm.
The city sprayed routinely.
The swamps were treated chemically.
The swamps were nearby.
The mosquitoes were pesky.
The mosquitoes were dangerous. (AND)

7. Even though historians credit the Vikings with the discovery of America, some feel that an Irish expedition to this continent was possible and even likely.
The historians are American.
The historians are European.
The discovery was the first.
The discovery was Western.
The Irish expedition was legendary.

8. During the reign of Charles I, the peace was shattered.
The reign of Charles I lasted twenty-five years.
The peace was of the Elizabethan era.
The peace was shattered by a civil war.
The civil war was long-threatened.
The civil war was devastating.

9. The dentist probed her mouth, looking for plaque deposits.
The dentist was concerned.
The dentist probed carefully.
The dentist probed thoroughly.
Her mouth was wide open.
The plaque deposits are destructive.
The plaque deposits are between the gums and teeth.

10. Awaiting her arrival, Carlos arranged the bouquet.
Carlos was awaiting her anxiously.
Her arrival was from the office.
Carlos arranged the bouquet tenderly.
Carlos arranged the bouquet nervously.
The bouquet was of a dozen roses.
The roses were red.
He arranged the bouquet in a vase.
The vase was antique.

Inserting Participial Phrases as Modifiers

Participial phrases are discussed on page 521.

Writers often create vivid and compact images by using participial phrases to modify words in a base sentence. The present participle is made by adding *-ing* to the basic verb form. The past participle is the verb form used with *has* or *have.* A participle is often supported by additional words built around it, making a *participial phrase.* The following example illustrates how an insert sentence can be added to a base sentence by forming a participial phrase.

Base Sentence:	The Reverend Jesse Jackson directs a successful program that develops a positive self-concept among young black students.
Insert:	The Reverend Jesse Jackson works mainly with inner-city high schools. (ING)
Combined:	Working mainly with inner-city high schools, the Reverend Jesse Jackson directs a successful program that develops a positive self-concept among young black students.

Notice that the verb *work* from the insert sentence is changed to its *-ing* form when added to the base sentence as a participial phrase. The signal (ING) indicates that the verb must be changed to this form. The underlining signal shows what part of the insert sentence will be added to the base sentence.

The signal (ING) is not used when a past participial phrase is inserted, although changes in the verb may be necessary. The following example illustrates how a past participial phrase is inserted into a base sentence.

Base Sentence:	I was late for my appointment
Insert:	I was delayed by heavy traffic.
Combined:	Delayed by heavy traffic, I was late for my appointment.

In the preceding set notice that the helping verb *was* from the insert sentence is not used in the combined sentence.

When two or more participial phrases are added to the base sentence, they are separated by commas, by a conjunction, or by a comma and a conjunction. The signal will indicate how to join the phrases.

Notice the comma separating the participial phrases.

Base Sentence:	The President prepared the State of the Union Address.
Insert:	The President is confined to the Oval office.
Insert:	The President read the advice of his counselors. (,ING)
Combined:	Confined to the Oval Office, reading the advice of his counselors, the President prepared the State of the Union Address.

Notice that *and* joins the participial phrases.

Base Sentence:	The young woman broke her wrist.
Insert:	She fell in her haste. (ING)
Insert:	She threw out her arms to protect herself. (ING + AND)
Combined:	Falling in her haste and throwing out her arms to protect herself, the young woman broke her wrist.

You may insert participial phrases at the beginning, in the middle, or at the end of the sentence. However, the phrases should be closely attached to the word or words they modify in order to avoid confusing or nonsensical statements, as the following example shows.

Base Sentence: The woman slowly reeled in the prize marlin.
Insert: The woman was strapped to the swivel chair at the stern.
Combined: Strapped to the swivel chair at the stern, the woman slowly reeled in the prize marlin.
or The woman, strapped to the swivel chair at the stern, slowly reeled in the prize marlin.
but not The woman slowly reeled in the prize marlin strapped to the swivel chair at the stern.

The use of commas with participial phrases is also discussed on page 530.

As the preceding example illustrates, participial phrases inserted at the beginning of a sentence are usually followed by a comma. Those appearing at the end or in the middle of the sentence are set off by a comma or paired commas only when they provide information not essential to understanding the sentence's meaning. Phrases essential for an understanding of the sentence's meaning are not set off by commas when the phrases appear at the end or in the middle of the sentence.

Exercise 2

Combine each of the following sentence sets by inserting the underlined participial phrases into the base sentence. Remember to insert the phrases where they will make the best sense and to add commas where necessary. Study the examples before you begin.

Examples

a. We watched the lead guitarist.
He twisted and jumped on the stage. (ING)
He was singing our favorite cut.

a. We watched the lead guitarist, twisting and jumping on the stage, singing our favorite cut.

b. The cat ran across the yard.
The cat heard us coming. (ING)

b. Hearing us coming, the cat ran across the yard.

1. The satellite passed over the city.
The satellite shined brightly. (ING)
2. The fire fighters found a gasoline can in the charred hallway.
The fire fighters conducted an arson investigation. (ING)
3. Robert walked into the manager's office.
Robert straightened his tie. (ING)
Robert buttoned his coat. (ING + AND)
4. Robert Louis Stevenson also wrote poetry.
He is remembered first as a writer of adventure novels.
5. The students waited for the teacher to begin the exam.
The students thought they were prepared. (ING)
The students crammed to the last minute. (ING + BUT)

6. The mother robin searched for her baby.
   The mother robin flew down from her nest. (ING)
   She looked around the grass below. (ING)
   She wondered if the cat was about. (ING + AND)
7. The artist spread black paint over the canvas.
   The artist realized that the original idea would not work out. (ING)
8. Thomas Alva Edison enjoyed the company of fellow inventor Henry Ford.
   Edison never realized the financial success of his friend. (ING)
9. Karen began planning her wedding for early July.
   She thought about the guest list. (ING)
   She remembered the relatives out west. (ING + AND)
10. The quarterback staggered off the field.
    He was sacked by the defensive cornerback.
    He gasped for air as he reached out for the oxygen mask. (ING)

Exercise 3

Combine each of the following unsignaled sentence sets by inserting participial phrases. In this exercise you must decide which sentence works most effectively as the base. Remember that you may have to change the verb form to *-ing* or add commas or connectors when you insert a phrase. Study the examples before you begin.

Examples

a. The cabbie pulled over to the curb.
   The cabbie noticed a man frantically waving and yelling.

a. Noticing a man frantically waving and yelling, the cabbie pulled over to the curb.

b. The labor market is swollen with members of the postwar baby boom.
   The labor market is depressed by high inflation and tight money.
   The current labor market reflects a very high unemployment rate.

b. Swollen with members of the postwar baby boom and depressed by high inflation and tight money, the current labor market reflects a very high unemployment rate.

1. Ella Grasso was the first woman to govern a state who did not succeed her husband.
   She was elected governor of Connecticut in 1974.
2. He was born in poverty.
   George Washington Carver is especially known for his research on industrial uses of the peanut.
3. Patches was covered with mud.
   Patches was shivering.
   Patches sat curled up on the doormat.

4. Sidney Poitier was nominated for his role in *Lilies of the Field.*
   Sidney Poitier was the first black performer to receive an Oscar for best actor.
5. Joe and his son prepared for the cold winter.
   They chose mature trees near the cabin.
   They cut down the oldest ones.
   They chopped the wood.
   They piled it near the door.
6. The parachutist descended rapidly.
   The parachutist pulled the cord.
   The parachutist opened the parachute.
7. The coroner did not know the victim.
   The coroner suspected foul play.
   The coroner began to examine the body.
   The coroner looked carefully at the two puncture marks on the neck.
8. They congratulated each other.
   They knew their opponents had conceded.
   They anticipated the next match.
9. Kiyo decided to apply to medical school.
   She realized that it would be very expensive.
   She made an appointment with the financial aide's office.
10. Tommy noticed an old horse.
    Tommy turned as he heard an odd noise.
    An old horse was drawing a rickety wagon.
    The old horse was breathing with difficulty.

Inserting Adjective Clauses

Inserting adjective clauses is another strategy for adding specific information to a base sentence. An *adjective clause* contains a subject and verb, but it cannot stand alone as a sentence. The adjective clause is dependent on the noun or pronoun it modifies in the base sentence.

Adjective clauses are also discussed on pages 538–539.

An adjective clause usually begins with a relative pronoun, an adjective, or an adverb that replaces a word in the insert sentence. The following example shows how a clause containing additional information about Albert Einstein is inserted into the base sentence. The relative pronoun *who* replaces the words *Albert Einstein* from the insert sentence to form the adjective clause. In the combined sentence *who* attaches the clause to the noun it modifies: *Albert Einstein.*

Base Sentence: Albert Einstein profoundly changed and deepened basic concepts of space, time, matter, and energy.

Insert: Albert Einstein was also a philospher and humanitarian (WHO)

Combined: Albert Einstein, who was also a philosopher and humanitarian, profoundly changed and deepened basic concepts of space, time, matter, and energy.

The following words usually mark the beginning of adjective clauses.

who, whom, that	relate to people
whose	relates to possessives
which, that	relate to things
where	relates to place
when	relates to time
why	relates to a reason

The preceding words replace a noun or pronoun from an insert sentence and relate the inserted clause to a base sentence. The following examples show that the signal word introducing the adjective clause is clearly attached to the noun or pronoun it modifies in the base sentence.

Base Sentence: The SAT/ACT tests do not measure real intellectual ability.
Insert: Colleges and universities use the tests to screen applicants for admission. (WHICH)
Combined: The SAT/ACT tests, which colleges and universities use to screen applicants for admission, do not measure real intellectual ability.

Base Sentence: The club officers will meet in the room.
Insert: They met in the room last week. (WHERE)
Combined: The club officers will meet in the room where they met last week.

When the adjective clause is not essential to the meaning of a sentence, it is set off by a comma or paired commas. However, when a clause is essential to the meaning of a sentence, as in the preceding example, it is not set off by commas.

Exercise 4

Following the signals, combine each of the following sentence sets by adding adjective clauses to the base sentence. (Remember to use commas when the adjective clause gives nonessential information.) Study the examples before you begin.

Examples

a. Sir W. Arthur Lewis received the Nobel Prize for Economics in 1979. Sir W. Arthur Lewis was the first black person to win a Nobel award other than the Peace Prize. (WHO)

a. Sir W. Arthur Lewis, who was the first black person to win a Nobel award other than the Peace Prize, received the Nobel Prize for Economics in 1979.

b. The Space Shuttle was transported from California to Cape Canaveral.

The space shuttle will make its first flight from Cape Canaveral. (WHERE)

b. The Space Shuttle was transported from California to Cape Canaveral, where it will make its first flight.

1. Mary was admitted to the hospital yesterday.
   Mary has a history of severe headaches. (WHO)
2. Anna applied for a job at Zion National Park.
   Anna has a degree in archaeology. (WHO)
   She hopes to work on some Indian digs at Zion National Park. (WHERE)
3. The cleaning deposit must be paid with the first month's rent.
   The cleaning deposit may be refunded when you move. (WHICH)
4. Some say John Wayne was the last American hero.
   John Wayne's real name was Marion Morrison. (WHOSE)
5. Chinese New Year is celebrated by the Chinese, Korean, and Vietnamese people.
   Chinese New Year is based on a lunar calendar. (WHICH)
6. Langston Hughes was one of the foremost interpreters to the world of the black experience in the U.S.
   Langston Hughes is remembered as a major American Poet. (WHO)
7. Henry told a joke.
   Henry is usually very serious. (WHO)
   I had not heard the joke before. (THAT)
8. Services from the Library of Congress are available to many schools and institutions.
   The Library of Congress has over 1,000 employees. (WHICH)
   The Library of Congress is the largest repository of information in the U.S. (AND + WHICH)
   Schools and institutions subscribe to its services. (THAT)
9. The pizza had anchovies.
   We ordered the pizza. (THAT)
   Few people like anchovies. (WHICH)
10. The river was rising rapidly yesterday afternoon.
    The river flooded last winter. (WHICH)
    The rains stopped yesterday afternoon. (WHEN)

Inserting Appositives

Another strategy for adding information to a base sentence is inserting an appositive or appositive phrase. An appositive, with or without additional modification, is used as a noun and placed near another noun or pronoun to further explain it.

Appositives are also discussed on page 525.

The appositive phrase *the league's leading scorer* in the following example renames and further explains the noun *Melissa Johnson.*

Base Sentence: Melissa Johnson just received a scholarship from Oregon State.
Insert: Melissa Johnson is the league's leading scorer.
Combined: Melissa Johnson, the league's leading scorer, just received a scholarship from Oregon State.

In this lesson underlining identifies the word or phrase you will insert in the base sentence.

For emphasis and variety, an appositive is sometimes placed at the beginning of the base sentence, in front of the word it explains or identifies.

Base Sentence: Alaska contains America's largest oil and gas reserves.
Insert: Alaska was once a booming gold rush territory.
Combined: Once a booming gold rush territory, Alaska contains America's largest oil and gas reserves.
or Alaska, once a booming gold rush territory, contains America's largest oil and gas reserves.

Appositives are set off by commas when they express information not essential to understanding the meaning of a sentence.

Exercise 5

Combine each of the following sets of sentences by inserting appositives or appositive phrases into the base sentence. Follow the underlining signals in the first five sets; the last five sets are unsignaled. For variety remember that you can shift some appositives to the beginning of a sentence. Study the examples before you begin.

Examples

a. The *Concorde* was the world's first supersonic passenger plane.
The *Concorde* is a British and French project.

a. The Concorde, *a British and French project, was the world's first supersonic passenger plane.*

b. "Sir Duke" is a tribute to Duke Ellington.
"Sir Duke" is a popular song by Stevie Wonder.

b. A popular song by Stevie Wonder, "Sir Duke" is a tribute to Duke Ellington.

1. Mr. Yee came to this country only three years ago.
Mr. Yee is the new plant manager.
2. The surgical team will be led by Dr. Cynthia Meyers and Dr. Jason Mathews.
Dr. Cynthia Meyers is a renowned heart specialist.
Dr. Jason Mathews is the inventor of the artificial valve.
3. His new book received complimentary reviews.
His new book is a review of the American economy today.
4. The house was designated a historical landmark.
The house is perhaps the oldest in the state.

5. Yesterday I went ice-skating.
   That's <u>something I hadn't done for ten years.</u>
6. Four American Presidents have been assassinated.
   They are Lincoln, Garfield, McKinley, and Kennedy.
7. The ancient Chinese gave the world many important tools and machines.
   The ancient Chinese were a people of inventors and discoverers.
8. The Amazon flows almost 4,000 miles across northern Brazil.
   The Amazon is the second largest river in the world.
   Brazil is the largest country in South America.
9. The Super Bowl is the championship game between the National and American Football Conferences.
   The Super Bowl is the most watched of any sports event.
   The National and American Football Conferences are both part of the National Football League.
10. Spaghetti was originally brought to Europe from the Orient by Marco Polo.
    Spaghetti is a type of pasta popular all over the Western world.
    Marco Polo was an explorer who made the first official European contact with China.

Review Exercise A

Combine each of the sentence sets in this exercise into a single sentence by following the signals. When you have finished, write the sentences in the order they appear so that they form a paragraph. Study the example before you begin. In these sets underlining serves as a signal to tell you which words to include in the combined sentence.

Examples

a. Susan asked the career counselor for the name of the store manager.
   Susan <u>decided to apply.</u> (ING)
   The application would be for the job.
   The counselor had helped her write a résumé last month. (WHO)

a. Deciding to apply for the job, Susan asked the career counselor, who had helped her write a résumé last month, for the name of the store manager.

b. The counselor suggested Susan call for an appointment tomorrow.
   The counselor <u>gave her the information.</u> (ING)
   The information was necessary.
   The appointment was for an interview.
   She could submit the application tomorrow. (WHEN)

b. Giving her the necessary information, the counselor suggested Susan call for an interview appointment tomorrow, when she could submit the application.

c. Susan answered the questions.
She picked up the application that afternoon. (ING)
She answered the questions carefully.
The questions asked for much of the information. (WHICH)
The information was in her résumé. (THAT)

c. Picking up the application that afternoon, Susan carefully answered the questions, which asked for much of the information that was in her résumé.

d. Susan dropped off the application.
Susan dropped it off before school the next morning.
The application was completed.
Susan made an appointment to see the store manager. (AND)
She would see the store manager at 3:00.

d. Before school the next morning, Susan dropped off the completed application and made an appointment to see the store manager at 3:00.

PARAGRAPH FORM

Deciding to apply for the job, Susan asked the career counselor, who had helped her write a résumé last month, for the name of the store manager. Giving her the necessary information, the counselor suggested Susan call for an interview appointment tomorrow, when she could submit the application. Picking up the application that afternoon, Susan carefully answered the questions, which asked for much of the information that was in her résumé. Before school the next morning, Susan dropped off the completed application and made an appointment to see the store manager at 3:00.

1. Sacajawea won recognition and appreciation.
Sacajawea was honored as one of the greatest women in American history.
Sacajawea is also known as Bird Woman.
She won recognition and appreciation for her assistance.
Her assistance was valiant.
She guided a group of explorers. (ING)
She guided explorers to the Pacific Ocean.

2. This was the Lewis and Clark expedition.
The Lewis and Clark expedition crossed America. (THAT)
The Lewis and Clark expedition crossed America in the years 1804–1806.
The Lewis and Clark expedition then came back to report its findings. (AND)
The Lewis and Clark expedition reported its findings to President Jefferson.

3. Sacajawea was purchased as a slave by another Indian guide to Lewis and Clark.
Sacajawea was a member of the Shoshone tribe.

The other Indian guide later went mad. (WHO)
The other Indian guide left the jobs of translator and guide to Sacajawea. (ING)

4. Sacajawea made a contribution to the development of the young United States.
She used diplomacy in dealing with other Indians. (ING)
She used survival skills in managing the expedition camps. (,)
She used a sense of direction in leading the men. (,AND)
Her sense of direction was uncanny.
Sacajawea's contribution was invaluable.
She became a symbol of all the virtues of frontier women. (AND)
The virtues were unsung.
The virtues were unrewarded. (,)

5. Sacajawea kept on traveling.
She lived to more than one hundred years of age. (WHO)
She traveled after the expedition, too.

6. She crossed the country many times as an old woman.
She used passes. (ING)
The early stagecoach companies provided her with the passes. (WHICH)
She promoted goodwill between whites and Indians. (ING)

7. Sacajawea's fame has grown steadily.
She died in 1884. (SINCE)

8. The monuments raised in her honor salute the intelligence, courage, and kindness of an Indian woman.
The monuments were raised in far Western towns.
She played a part in saving for the United States the riches and beauties of the territories. (WHO)
The riches and beauties of the United States were great and natural.
The territories later became the states of Montana, Idaho, Washington, and Oregon. (THAT)

Writing Exercise A

If you have ever struggled to read the directions accompanying a game, here is your chance to do a better job. Write directions for the game tic-tac-toe for someone who has never played it. Explain how to draw the board as well as exactly how to play the game. (If you prefer, choose another simple game to write directions for.) As you write a clear and detailed set of directions, remember to use the sentence-combining techniques you have practiced.

Writing Exercise B

For a number of years social and political commentators have said that America lacks, or has lost, the ability to foster heroes. Some say the American hero may have died with John Kennedy, Martin Luther King, Jr., or even John Wayne. At best, the idea of an American hero is not as clear as it may have been twenty years ago. Think of someone who you think might be a modern hero. It need not be someone well known or someone who has performed an outstanding feat; some of the people most admired are known to only a few people. What qualities make that person heroic in your personal estimation? As you write, remember to use the sentence-combining skills you have studied.

Inserting Noun Clauses

Noun clauses are also discussed on pages 542–543.

Inserting noun clauses into a base sentence is another sentence-combining strategy. A *noun clause* contains a subject and verb, but when inserted into a base sentence cannot stand alone as a sentence. The noun clause functions as a noun in the combined sentence. In this lesson the base sentence contains the signals SOMETHING or SOMEONE, which are replaced by a noun clause made of all or part of the insert sentence.

Base Sentence: Henry thought SOMETHING.
Insert: Her advice about the proposal was wrong.
Combined: Henry thought her advice about the proposal was wrong.

The signals (WHO), (WHAT), (WHEN), (WHERE), (WHY), (THAT), and (HOW) indicate how to attach the noun clause to the base sentence. The following examples illustrate these signals.

Base Sentence: This booklet by the Internal Revenue Service explains SOMETHING.
Insert: You are to prepare your tax return. (HOW)
Combined: This booklet by the Internal Revenue Service explains how you are to prepare your tax return.

Base Sentence: SOMETHING was as much a mystery as SOMEONE.
Insert: The airplane crashed somewhere. (WHERE)
Insert: Someone was the pilot. (WHO)
Combined: Where the airplane crashed was as much a mystery as who the pilot was.

As in the second example, notice that the word order may change when a noun clause is inserted.

Other signals such as (IT . . . THAT), (THE FACT THAT . . .), (HOW LONG), or (HOW FAR) are sometimes used to insert noun clauses. In the following examples notice that the word order of a sentence may change when it is inserted as a noun clause.

Base Sentence: SOMETHING was strange.
Insert: All the whales beached themselves without apparent injury or disease. (IT . . . THAT)
Combined: It was strange that all the whales beached themselves without apparent injury or disease.

Base Sentence: SOMETHING didn't seem to affect their relationship.
Insert: He had been away. (HOW LONG)

Combined: How long he had been away didn't seem to affect their relationship.

The signal (JOIN) indicates that you should insert the noun clause directly into the SOMETHING slot. The following example illustrates this combination.

Base Sentence: We thought SOMETHING.
Insert: It was a good idea. (JOIN)
Combined: We thought it was a good idea.

Exercise 6

Combine the following sets of sentences by inserting noun clauses into the base (first) sentence. The first five sets have signals; the last five sets are unsignaled, and you must decide the best way to combine them, using a noun clause. Study the examples before you begin.

Examples

a. The doctor suggested SOMETHING.
I slow down and not worry so much. (JOIN)
a. The doctor suggested I slow down and not worry so much..

b. SOMETHING was certain.
The hotel disaster was a result of arson. (IT . . . THAT)
b. It was certain that the hotel disaster was a result of arson.

1. Before leaving on their trip, our neighbors told us SOMETHING and SOMETHING.
The dogs should be fed. (HOW MUCH)
They should run every day. (HOW LONG)
2. José quickly learned SOMETHING.
The new computer terminal worked. (HOW)
3. SOMETHING is frustrating to Europeans.
Americans are reluctant to learn foreign languages. (WHY)
4. SOMETHING suggests Carolyn will get the promotion.
The supervisor has asked her to handle the special projects. (THE FACT THAT . . .)
5. A good résumé should tell SOMETHING, SOMETHING, and SOMEONE.
You have studied and worked. (WHERE)
You have studied. (WHAT)
Someone can attest to your performance. (WHO)

Note: *Where* replaces the word *something* when you combine the sentences; *who* replaces the word *someone*.

6. You should bring warm clothing, but SOMETHING is not necessary.
You bring a raincoat and umbrella.
7. Scientists are trying to determine SOMETHING.
The escape of radon gas from the ground relates to earthquakes.
8. SOMETHING didn't seem to influence the judge's decision.
Cindy slipped once on the ice.

9. The newscaster explained SOMETHING.
   The hostages were not released after the ransom was paid.

10. SOMETHING must be decided before SOMETHING.
    We can take our vacation sometime.
    We can take our vacation somewhere.

Inserting Absolute Phrases

Another strategy for adding variety and detail to your sentences is to use the *absolute phrase.* An absolute phrase adds related meaning to a sentence, but it does not modify a specific word. Form absolute phrases by omitting the *to be* verb from the insert sentences, as in the following example.

Base Sentence:	The young child still refused to sleep.
Insert:	All the dolls were positioned on the bed.
Insert:	The hall light was on. (AND)
Combined:	The hall light on and all the dolls positioned on the bed, the young child still refused to sleep.

For sentence variety and emphasis, absolute phrases can go at the beginning, middle, or end of a sentence. They are always set off by a comma or paired commas.

Exercise 7

Combine each of the following sets of sentences by inserting absolute phrases. The first five sentence groups have underlining signals; the last five are unsignaled. Remember that absolute phrases are set off by commas and that they can be attached to the beginning, middle, or end of a sentence. Study the examples before you begin.

Examples

a. Standing at the pulpit, the minister began the ceremony.
   A glass of cool water was on her right.
   A spray of flowers was on her left. (AND)

a. Standing at the pulpit, the minister began the ceremony, a glass of cool water on her right and a spray of flowers on her left.

b. The city razed the old apartment building.
   Its lower floors were gutted by looters.
   Its facade was tired with age. (,)

b. The city razed the old apartment building, its lower floors gutted by looters, its facade tired with age.

1. The newspaper was shut down by a strike.
   The workers were angry over the new automation program.

2. The photographer caught the winner just as she crossed the finish line.
   His camera was focused.
   His body was stretched out over the rail. (AND)

3. The judge gave instructions to the jury.
   The closing arguments were over.
4. The cat waited for the mouse to appear.
   Its body was hunched in the striking position.
   Its eyes were fixed on the small opening. (,)
5. From on the hill, the neighborhood looked deserted.
   All the houses were dark.
   No one was stirring about. (AND)
6. Jim was nervous as he entered the principal's office.
   His palms were sweaty.
   His legs were wobbly.
7. Jenny finished the report without interruption.
   The office was closed.
   The phone was off the hook.
8. A few hours later I made my way back to the car.
   Packages were under my arm.
   My feet and legs were aching.
9. The farmer sat on the ground and smiled.
   The last truck was loaded.
   The trees were bare.
10. Chris walked confidently up to Sarah.
    An anxious smile was on his face.
    Two tickets to the concert were in his hand.

Inserting Gerunds

When the *-ing* form of a verb is used as a noun, called a *gerund,* it can be inserted into a base sentence. In the following example, the verb *leaves* is changed to the gerund *leaving* and is inserted with its modifiers into the base sentence.

Base Sentence: SOMETHING was a good idea because the rains came that afternoon.
Insert: We left the campground early. (ING)
Combined: Leaving the campground early was a good idea because the rains came that afternoon.

In the preceding example, the subject of the insert sentence is not included in the combined sentence. In many sentences, however, the subject is changed to a possessive and inserted directly in front of the gerund. Both possessives and gerunds are used in the following sentence combinations. The signal (POS) directs you to make a noun or pronoun in the insert sentence possessive.

The use of possessives before a gerund is also discussed on page 396.

Base Sentence: SOMETHING gave strength and intelligence to an otherwise weak production.

Insert: Maria acted in the play. (POS + ING)
Combined: Maria's acting in the play gave strength and intelligence to an otherwise weak production.

Base Sentence: SOMETHING definitely annoyed the concert promoters.
Insert: We waited in line all night. (POS + ING)
Combined: Our waiting in line all night definitely annoyed the concert promoters.

Notice in the last example that the pronoun *we* was changed to the possessive *our*. The following list contains all of the possessive pronouns.

PRONOUN	POSSESSIVE PRONOUN
I	my
she	her
he	his
it	its
we	our
you	your
they	their

Both possessive pronoun and gerund changes are made in the following example.

Base Sentence: Tony's downfall was SOMETHING.
Insert: He studied all night before the exam. (POS + ING)
Combined: Tony's downfall was his studying all night before the exam.

An additional change allows you to insert an adverb from the insert sentence into the base sentence as a gerund modifier. The signal (~~LY~~) tells you to drop the *ly* ending from words such as *carelessly*, *happily*, and *slowly*. The following example illustrates how this combination works.

Base Sentence: SOMETHING impressed the audience.
Insert: She skated gracefully. (POS + ~~LY~~ + ING)
Combined: Her graceful skating impressed the audience.

An (OF) signal also works with (POS), (ING), and (~~LY~~) to produce the following combination.

Base Sentence: SOMETHING was pitiful.
Insert: The woman mourned her loss ceaselessly. (POS + ~~LY~~ + ING + OF)
Combined: The woman's ceaseless mourning of her loss was pitiful.

Exercise 8

Combine each of the following sets of sentences into one sentence. Signals for inserting possessives and gerunds are given in the first five sentences; the last five sentences lack signals but can also be combined with possessives and gerunds. Study the examples before you begin. (There may be more than one way to make a combination.)

Examples

a. Melissa made it to class on time by SOMETHING.
She ran across the football field. (ING)

a. Melissa made it to class on time by running across the football field.

b. I was irritated by SOMETHING.
She threw the ball constantly against the wall. (POS + ~~LY~~ + ING + OF)

b. I was irritated by her constant throwing of the ball against the wall.

c. SOMETHING was the only way Clover could get any food.
She waited patiently for the large German shepherd to finish eating.

c. Her patient waiting for the large German shepherd to finish eating was the only way Clover could get any food.

1. Your mistake was SOMETHING.
You sent cash through the mails. (ING)

2. The teacher forbids SOMETHING.
We talk during class. (POS + ING)

3. Researchers feel that someday it may be possible to replace destroyed brain cells with healthy brain cells by SOMETHING.
They will carefully transplant cells from a healthy human brain into a brain with neurological disorders. (POS + ~~LY~~ + ING + OF)

Note: *Were* is the past tense of the verb *be;* its *-ing* form is *being.*

4. SOMETHING kept you out of trouble.
You were honest. (POS + ING)

5. SOMETHING changed his entire life.
He read the book *Roots.* (POS + ING + OF)

6. By SOMETHING, Dr. Don Young solved two ecological problems, SOMETHING and SOMETHING.
He removed sulfur from gasoline.
He reduced the pollutants emitted when gasoline is used as fuel.
He created a soil additive that greatly improves the productivity of alkaline soil.

7. SOMETHING was the gift the ancient Phoenicians gave to the world.
They created an alphabet in which each letter represented a sound rather than a word or an idea.

8. SOMETHING costs billions of municipal dollars each year.
The city removes garbage.

9. SOMETHING is an unfortunate but necessary part of life in California.
Commuters drive on the freeways.

10. SOMETHING and SOMETHING are her favorite pastimes.
She watches movies avidly.
She eats popcorn constantly.

Inserting Infinitives

One sentence can be inserted into another as an *infinitive phrase.* An infinitive phrase is the word *to* plus a verb. To combine two sentences with an infinitive phrase, the (TO + VERB) combination replaces the signal SOMETHING in the base sentence, as in the following example.

Base Sentence: SOMETHING is good exercise.
Insert: Jogging is exercise. (TO + VERB)
Combined: To jog is good exercise.

If there is a helping verb in the insert sentence, remove it when you form the infinitive.

Base Sentence: During his visit to the college, Frank wants SOMETHING and SOMETHING.
Insert: Frank will inquire about dorm rooms. (TO + VERB)
Insert: Frank will talk to the athletic director about a tennis scholarship. (TO + VERB)
Combined: During his visit to the college, Frank wants to inquire about dorm rooms and to talk to the athletic director about a tennis scholarship.

Sometimes, the verb will change form when it is inserted into the base sentence as an infinitive phrase. In the next example *fishes* becomes *to fish.*

Base Sentence: Her favorite sport is SOMETHING.
Insert: She fishes for marlin.
Combined: Her favorite sport is to fish for marlin.

In some base sentences you will see the words *(to do)* in parentheses. They appear simply to help you understand the meaning of the base sentence. When you insert an infinitive phrase, remove the words *(to do).*

Base Sentence: The twins felt they would have (to do) SOMETHING in order to develop their own personalities.
Insert: They would attend different colleges. (TO + VERB)
Combined: The twins felt they would have to attend different colleges in order to develop their own personalities.

Base Sentence: For Estella (to do) SOMETHING is quite unlikely.
Insert: She gives up her dream of becoming a film set designer. (TO + VERB)
Combined: For Estella to give up her dream of becoming a film set designer is quite unlikely.

Exercise 9

Combine each of the following sentence sets into a single sentence by following the (TO + VERB) signal. In the first five sentences the signals are included; in the last five sentences no signals are given, and you must decide how to combine the sentences by inserting infinitive phrases. Study the examples before you begin.

Examples

a. SOMETHING was Simon's goal.
He becomes a fire fighter. (TO + VERB)

a. To become a fire fighter was Simon's goal.

b. For the United States (to do) SOMETHING or (to do) SOMETHING is a dilemma facing us today.
The United States initiates a national medical services program. (TO + VERB)
The United States maintains its present mix of private and public medical services coverage. (TO + VERB)

b. For the United States to initiate a national medical services program or to maintain its present mix of private and public medical services coverage is a dilemma facing us today.

1. SOMETHING was the dream of Martin Luther King, Jr.
He ensured equality for all Americans. (TO + VERB)
2. A good citizen does not refuse SOMETHING.
A good citizen votes in elections and serves on juries. (TO + VERB)
3. For you (to do) SOMETHING is wasteful.
You throw away empty cans and bottles. (TO + VERB)
4. My brother prefers SOMETHING because he is afraid of heights.
He sleeps on the bottom bunk. (TO + VERB)
5. Would you choose SOMETHING or SOMETHING?
You take the summer off. (TO + VERB)
You earn money for the fall semester. (TO + VERB)
6. If Josie wants SOMETHING, she will have (to do) SOMETHING.
She attends cosmetology school.
She sends in her application now.
7. Traveling allows us SOMETHING.
We better understand peoples from different countries and cultures.
8. Sky divers like SOMETHING.
They live dangerously.
9. SOMETHING is SOMETHING.
(People) consider the experiment a failure.
(People) admit the failure of the entire project.
10. For people (to do) SOMETHING requires endless patience.
People train parrots.
Parrots talk.

Review Exercise B

In the following paragraph exercises, use absolutes, noun clauses, gerunds, and infinitives to combine each group of sentences into a single sentence. Follow the signals, combining the sentences in the order they appear. Write out the combined sentences as complete paragraphs when you finish.

PARAGRAPH A

1. SOMETHING and SOMETHING helped Carlotta become aware of her own abilities and interests at an early age.
   She knew the kind of work her parents did. (ING)
   She came into contact with people in different occupations. (ING)
2. (To do) SOMETHING, Carlotta spent the first years of school acquiring basic skills, such as reading and writing.
   Carlotta prepared for an eventual career. (TO + VERB)
3. She learned SOMETHING and SOMETHING.
   She disciplined herself. (TO + VERB)
   She followed the necessary rules. (TO + VERB)
4. Carlotta's career development continued as she moved into the upper elementary grades.
   Her interests were becoming more focused.
5. At this point she started SOMETHING.
   She compared herself to people working different jobs. (TO + VERB)
6. SOMETHING began SOMETHING.
   She was similar to or different from a hairdresser, a secretary, a flight attendant, or a plumber. (HOW)
   It aroused her curiosity and attention. (TO + VERB)
7. She began SOMETHING.
   She valued work as a useful activity. (TO + VERB)
   Her self-discipline was continuing to develop.
   Her knowledge about and interest in workers in various jobs was growing. (AND)
8. SOMETHING and SOMETHING occupied Carlotta as she prepared to enter junior high school.
   She saw various life styles. (ING)
   She discovered the changing roles of women in the world of work. (ING)
9. SOMETHING was also a rich reward during these years.
   She developed an awareness of herself and the ability to get along better with others. (THAT)

PARAGRAPH B

1. A turning point came sometime.
   Carlotta entered high school. (WHEN)
2. SOMETHING was an important discovery for her.
   She became aware of her values and their relationship to jobs. (ING)
3. She realized SOMETHING.
   She was a unique, independent individual. (THAT)
4. SOMETHING excited her.
   She saw and understood the life styles of people in the business world. (ING)

5. As a result Carlotta decided SOMETHING.
   She took business courses in senior high school. (TO + VERB)
6. As Carlotta's career development continued, she began SOMETHING.
   She tested herself as a person working in the business world. (TO + VERB)
7. SOMETHING gave her valuable experience.
   She tried several part-time and temporary jobs. (ING)
8. After graduation from high school, she decided SOMETHING.
   She attended a local business college for a year to get further training. (TO + VERB)
9. During her year at business college, Carlotta decided SOMETHING.
   She wanted to work in accounting. (THAT)
10. SOMETHING was Carlotta's first step to a rewarding and successful career in business.
    She accepted a job as an accounting clerk. (ING)

Writing Exercise C

You often hear and read about the changing role of women in American society. The stereotype of the housewife and mother has given way to working mothers, increasing numbers of women in the professions, and a growing awareness of sexual equality. Today you even hear of a new role for men—the "househusband." To be sure, the changing role of women has a significant effect on all men and women today. Write a paper in which you discuss how the changing role of women has affected you as a teenager, as a date, as a member of a family, as you consider a future career, or as you think about marriage sometime in the future. As you write, use some of the sentence-combining skills you have learned.

Writing Exercise D

Americans spend many hours each week watching television. Some critics blame television for the decline in literacy among students; others say that it exposes the population to too much violence and sex; still other critics argue that television is the greatest educational tool since the printed word. Whatever your point of view, you cannot ignore the impact of television on this society. Discuss one important way television has changed the lives of modern Americans. Explain whether this change has been good or bad, and tell why you feel that way.

PART

5 Language

16 How Language Means

Language as Abstraction

Language itself is symbolic. The letters *s-u-n*, for example, are not the gaseous sphere around which the earth revolves; instead, those letters symbolize, or represent, the object that provides light and heat to this planet. In addition to representing objects such as the sun, words also represent ideas: *democracy*, *justice*, *peace*, *beauty*, and so on.

The word *abstract* means "removed from material reality." As symbols that represent objects and ideas, all words are to an extent abstract. Some words, however, are further removed than others, and it is these words with higher levels of abstraction that are likely to cause problems in communication. For example, consider the Jones' family dog, Rover. Petted, fed, walked, and occasionally bathed by members of the Jones family, Rover presents no problems in communication. If one family member posts a note on the bulletin board saying "Please walk Rover," the other family members know exactly who Rover is. Even two-year-old Melissa Jones calls Rover by name. The word *Rover* is not far removed from reality, since the thing it represents can be seen, heard, touched, and smelled.

At a slightly higher level of abstraction is the word *dog*. It is at a higher level because the word does not refer to any one thing; instead, it represents a class of animals that share many of Rover's characteristics. For very young children a word such as *dog* sometimes causes problems until they are able to sort out the characteristics represented by the word. They might, for example, refer to a cat or a pony as a dog. Most older children and adults, however, have few problems communicating at this level of abstraction.

Most problems in communication are caused by words that have little or no grounding in reality.

Such abstract words do not represent anything that can be seen, touched, tasted, smelled, heard, or felt; nor do they represent a class of such things that share common characteristics. For the most part these words represent ideas or qualities, such as *democracy*, *peace*, *femininity*, *masculinity*, *courage*, *patriotism*, and so on. Speakers and writers are more likely to disagree about the meanings of such words because they do not have concrete referents. For example, one speaker might feel that freedom is the total absence of all laws, another that freedom is the right to elect representatives who make the laws we all must obey. One person could believe that being feminine means dressing and behaving a certain way, someone else that dress and behavior have nothing to do with femininity.

Language Activity 1

In the following excerpt from *Gulliver's Travels*, Jonathan Swift shows how difficult it would be to communicate without the symbolism of language. Discuss the alternative Swift proposes to using words as symbols. What are the problems with the proposals?

Diminution means "lessening."

> . . . and this was urged as a great advantage in point of health as well as brevity. For it is plain that every word we speak is, in some degree, a diminution of our lungs by corrosion, and consequently contributes to the shortening of our lives. An expedient was therefore offered that since words are only names for things, it would be more convenient for all men to carry about them such things as were necessary to express a particular business they are to discourse on. . . . Many of the most learned and wise adhere to the new scheme of expressing themselves by things, which has only this inconvenience attending it, that if a man's business be very great, and of various kinds, he must be obliged, in proportion, to carry a greater bundle of things upon his back, unless he can afford one or two strong servants to attend him. I have often beheld two of these sages almost sinking under the weight of their packs, like peddlers among us; who, when they meet in the street, would lay down their loads, open their packs, hold conversation for an hour, and then put up their implements, help each other to resume their burdens, and take their leave.

Language Activity 2

From the following list select those statements that are likely to cause problems in communication because of abstract language. Discuss the problems the speaker and listeners are likely to have and the specific words that are likely to cause the problems.

1. A stock clerk has just finished cleaning out a storeroom. After checking the work, the boss tells the clerk, "You didn't do a good job; you'll have to do it again."
2. Two friends are sitting in a movie theater. One friend says, "I don't like sitting this close to the screen. Let's move back a couple of rows."
3. A community resident speaks out against a proposed ordinance at a local meeting. The moderator then rises and says, "What kind of American citizen are you? How dare you criticize our government like that!"

4. Two friends are walking through a museum. One pauses before an abstract painting and says, "Now that's what I call art! What a beautiful painting!"
5. A teenager says to a parent, "It's time I became responsible for myself. I need a $25-a-week allowance so that I can buy my own groceries."
6. A salesperson at a used-car lot says to a customer, "You can't go wrong with this one. We offer our own Friendly Freddy guarantee."
7. The mayor of a small town speaks before a group of concerned citizens: "The crime rate is entirely too high. It's time we passed a curfew law for teenagers."
8. A newspaper headline announces that, on the day of a summit conference, Russia has referred to the United States as a "war-mongering nation."
9. A Northern community passes a new ordinance that reads: "After snowfalls of two inches or more and until the streets have been plowed, you may not park on streets with the special blue and red 'Snow Route' signs."
10. At the end of the school day, the principal announces to students and faculty, "If the weather is bad tomorrow, we will not have classes."

How Words Change as Symbols

Jargon When a group of people from a particular profession or type of work talk about their job, they sometimes use a specialized language called *jargon.*

Jargon has a real purpose when members of a profession or of a particular group speak with one another. Jargon can be a common vocabulary, a type of shorthand speech used to point out special features of work, such as tools, instruments, actions, procedures, and concepts.

Sports are well known for their jargon:

soccer:	heading, save, sweeper, wall, marking, centering
baseball:	RBI, twin bill, two-bagger, pinch hitter, steal
basketball:	lay-up, foul, dribble, travel, shot clock

Professions and occupations also have their jargon:

editor:	copy, green sheets, galleys, boards
NASA employee:	hold, systems, countdown, lox, shutdown
builder:	foundation, frieze, bridging, flashing

The media of television, film, and newspapers have been influential in making the specialized language of jargon more familiar. In fact, many words that are considered jargon by some groups have become a part of everyday language, such as the following examples.

WORD	JOB	JOB MEANING	GENERAL MEANING
feedback	computers	return of data	reactions between people; answers to questions
score	all sports	to make points	to be successful at something; to complete a goal
strikeout	baseball	to miss hitting the ball and not get on base	to get nowhere
third degree	police	harsh questioning of suspects	any harsh questioning
zoom in	film	to focus on something	to direct your attention to something in particular
grandstand	baseball	seating for spectators	to show off before people
hurdle	track	a frame to be jumped over while running in an event	a barrier; an obstacle
pawn	chess	a chess piece that has the least power	a person who is unknowingly used by another person

Most jargon words that have become a part of everyday language are considered *slang* words that are only appropriately used in informal speech situations. Using jargon can cause problems in communication. When jargon excludes people from a conversation, it sets up a barrier that prevents understanding.

Language Activity 3

Choose one of the following occupations or professions and make a list of ten words that are a normal part of the jargon this group of people would use in speaking to each other.

realtor	lawyer	law enforcement officer
architect	electrician	building contractor
swimmer	mechanic	stockbroker
pilot	cook	journalist

Gobbledygook

Jargon that is used to confuse and exclude people is generally called *gobbledygook* or *doublespeak.*

Gobbledygook, also known as *bafflegab, officialese*, and numerous other insulting names, pretends to be impressive and sophisticated. In its long, wordy phrases, it manages to conceal thought rather than reveal it. Can you understand what the following sentences are trying to communicate?

1. The realistic operational breakthrough produced a uniform growth reaction.
2. Global research dialogues are cost-benefit incentives for classified departmental commitments.
3. Optimal priority applications determine compatible maintenance dynamics for authoritative security parameters.

Sentences such as the preceding ones destroy the symbolic nature of language in their attempt to be impressive. You can avoid this confusing use of jargon by making your language as clear and direct as possible.

GOBBLEDYGOOK	DIRECT LANGUAGE
He rendered a positive acclamation on the matter of my interrogation.	He said "Yes" to my question.
We proceeded to the dry cleaning facility where the proprietor acknowledged our presence.	We went to the dry cleaners where the owner greeted us.
I utilized your idea to finalize my project.	I used your idea to finish my project.
The usage of shinguards offers protectional advantages to players during the game.	The use of shinguards gives protection to the players during the game.

Euphemisms

Another form of language that causes confusion is the *euphemism.*

Euphemisms are words that are substituted to make something that is offensive or unpleasant sound more agreeable or inoffensive.

In some cases euphemisms are harmless forms of courtesy used to avoid language that is offensive to many people. Euphemisms for swearing, for example, first developed in this country when Puritan laws prohibited the use of profanity. Such words as *darn, drat, doggone, blasted,* and *heck* are common euphemisms used to avoid swearing.

Euphemisms have been traditionally used to avoid such "taboo" subjects as personal hygiene, parts of the body, articles of clothing, and death. Today's words *coffin* and *casket,* which appear to be synonymous, were once thought to be quite different in acceptance. In *Our Old Home* (1863) Nathaniel Hawthorne commented, " 'Caskets!' —a vile modern phrase which compels a person . . . to shrink . . . from the idea of being buried at all." Similarly, awkwardness is lessened for some people when they use the words *washroom, bathroom, lavatory, restroom, comfort station, powder room, ladies' room,* and *men's room* for "toilet."

Some forms of euphemism, however, go beyond courtesy and misrepresent the meaning of language. To call the janitor of a building a *maintenance facilitator* is misleading and deceptive, especially if that person is limited to sweeping floors. Elevating social status is becoming a common misuse of euphemism, but an even greater offense occurs when euphemisms are used to avoid the frightening facts of reality, such as in war. In 1977, for instance, the neutron bomb was described as a *radiation enhancement weapon.* Using the pleasant-sounding word *enhancement* with the destructive words *radiation* and *weapon* conceals the fact that such a bomb *kills* people within forty-eight hours.

Language Activity 4

Cut out an editorial from the newspaper or find an article in a news magazine and list or underline the phrases and words that you think conceal meaning behind gobbledygook and euphemism.

Clichés

When euphemism confuses and misinforms people, it becomes a dishonest use of language that conceals the real meaning of words. In a similar way the meaning of words is also concealed in *clichés.*

A *cliché* is an overused, stale term that no longer conveys a real sense of meaning.

Regular use of clichés represents dull, unimaginative language. How many clichés do you recognize in the following sentences?

> Steve was just as cute as a button when he arrived on the first day of school all bright-eyed and bushy-tailed.
>
> If I put my nose to the grindstone, I can probably sell these boxes of light bulbs for the band.
>
> Silence is golden, and I finally learned my lesson; better late than never, I always say.
>
> Burning the midnight oil will probably get me an *A* in physics, but I guess I shouldn't count my chickens before they hatch.

Clichés lack the original thinking that is needed to keep language alive and changing. In fact, some clichés even have a harmful effect when they are used to stereotype people and insult them.

> Didn't you bring the little lady with you?
> A woman's place is in the home.
> You throw the ball like a girl.
> Stop crying like a little girl.

Language Activity 5

Copy the following phrases on a sheet of paper, filling in the blanks to illustrate some of the common clichés in the English language. Next to each cliché write a word or phrase that conveys the same meaning more originally.

apple of ______ ______	sow wild ______
birds of ______ ______	mountains out of ______

hook, line, and ________
blind as a ________
strong as an ________
cool as a ________
happy as a ________
wise as an ________
timid as a ________

raining ________ and ________
boys will be ________
sober as a ________
lock, stock, and ________
busy as a ________
cold as ________
gentle as a ________

17 Language Change and Variation

The Origin of Language

Language experts, called *linguists*, still disagree about the origin of language. The disagreement between two noted scholars, Noam Chomsky and B. F. Skinner, is often called the *nature-nurture controversy*. In his book *Verbal Behavior* B. F. Skinner suggests that language is an outgrowth of the cultural development of human beings and not an inborn capability of the human mind. Skinner believes that, initially, language was nurtured by humans' observation of sounds in the environment and developed as a set of habits that were handed down in the same way that humans learn other skills, such as knitting, swimming, or driving.

Noam Chomsky, on the other hand, does not accept Skinner's ideas and suggests that language is natural to humans in the same way that barking is natural for dogs and pecking for chickens. Chomsky suggests that language originated because the human brain contains a special capacity for language—a model or pattern that is present in the mind at birth.

Research studies have not solved this controversy. The fact that a normal child will always acquire language skills but may not master other skills, such as guitar playing or clear handwriting, supports Chomsky's theory. On the other hand, the fact that children raised in isolation do not develop language casts some doubt on his theory. A number of studies have been made of children who grew up completely free from human contact, but even when two children were isolated together, there was no evidence of a language developing between them.

Experiments in which researchers have successfully trained apes and dolphins to communicate seem to support Skinner's idea. However, none of these animals has developed the understanding of word order and use that seems a natural talent of the young child. While a child may fail at learning to swim or play the piano, skills acquired by imitating and learning from adults, the normal child always acquires a native language. Also, Chomsky's theory suggests that language, like other human skills, would become more and more refined and sophisticated as does civilization, but that is not the case. In fact, some ancient languages are as complex and as rich in vocabulary as modern languages.

For the moment the truth about the origin of language is still shrouded in mystery. It may be that modern linguists, psychologists, and researchers will find the answer to this in some combination of the nature versus nurture theories.

Families of Language Development

In the same way that children of the same family may share a common characteristic inherited from their parents or grandparents (freckles or curly hair, for instance), modern languages share certain characteristics inherited from older parent languages. For example, from their study of the similarities of English, Swedish, Russian, Italian, Greek, and Sanskrit, linguists have learned that these languages and several other European and Asian languages belong to the same language family; they are all modifications of an older parent language called *Indo-European*, which was spoken by groups of people living in central Europe around 4000 B.C.

Notice the similarities between the forms of the word *mother* in the following list. The languages in the list are all part of the Indo-European family.

Sanskrit: matar	Swedish: moder
Latin: mater	Danish: moder
Greek: meter	Dutch: moeder
Persian: mader	German: mutter
Icelandic: mōdhir	French: mère
Old Irish: mathir	Spanish: madre
Russian: mati	Portuguese: mae
Polish: matka	Italian: madre

Among the Indo-European languages, English is a western Germanic language closely related to Dutch, German, Flemish, Yiddish, Afrikaans, and Frisian.

Linguists are still in the process of positively identifying all language families. While the Indo-European family spread over a large geographic area as the original tribes moved east and west about 2000 B.C., some language families are confined to smaller areas. For example, there are over one hundred American Indian language families, and at least three families (Sudanese-Guinean, Bantu, and Hottentot-Bushman) can be found on the African continent.

The Old English Period (450 to 1066)

The history of English as a separate language begins around A.D. 410, when the Romans, who had invaded Britain 400 years earlier, abandoned their colony there and left the island's native inhabitants, the Celts, unprotected. Helpless, the Celts sought protection from three fierce Germanic tribes—the Angles, Saxons, and Jutes. Instead of protecting the Celts, these three tribes from northern Europe crossed the North Sea about A.D. 450 and conquered the Celts' homeland. These invaders brought with them their own West-Germanic language. This Anglo-Saxon dialect, soon referred to as "Angleish," developed into Old English.

The following example of language from the Old English (OE) period is a portion of the epic poem, *Beowulf.*

OLD ENGLISH

De ā waes wundor micel/ Dæt se winsele.
Wiotæfde headodērum,/ Dæ hē on hrūsan ne fēal,
Fæger foldbold; . . .

TRANSLATION

It was a marvel that the wine hall withstood the battlers,
that it did not fall to the ground, beautiful building; . . .

Although the preceding example may seem as strange as a foreign language, so many basic, modern English words began in Old English that this language is often known as the backbone of modern English. Common prepositions *(under, to, with, from),* the conjunction *and,* the adverb *where,* and some pronouns *(his, I, we, your)* were all part of Old English. Some aspects of modern English grammar are also related to Old English; *was* and *were,* for example, are much like their Old English counterparts *waes* and *waere.* Even the words for certain weekdays, drawn from the names of Anglo-Saxon gods, are remnants of this time period: *Tuesday* comes from Tiw, the god of war; *Wednesday* comes from Woden, the chief god; *Thursday* from Thor, the god of thunder; and *Friday* from Frigga, the goddess of the home.

Three other languages also contributed to the English vocabulary during the Old English period. The native Celts retreated as the Anglo-Saxons invaded, but they left behind such place-names as Kent, Dover, and Thames. The early Romans, who left Britain in 410, and missionaries under St. Augustine, who brought Christianity to the Anglo-Saxon population around 597, introduced Latin words such as *altar, shrine, school,* and *paper.*

Finally, Viking invaders who settled in northern England provided everyday terms, such as *guess, leg, loose,* and *window,* that are still part of the English language.

Language Activity 1

Using library resources, prepare a brief report on one of the following topics related to the development of Old English.

1. The Celts and their culture
2. The Angles, Saxons, and Jutes and their invasion of Great Britain
3. King Alfred
4. *Beowulf*
5. The runic alphabet
6. Celtic place-names in Britain such as Bryn Mawr or Dover
7. The Vikings and their influence on English
8. St. Augustine
9. *Anglo-Saxon Chronicle*
10. The historian called "the Venerable Bede"

The Middle English Period (1066 to 1450)

The Old English period, which had begun with an invasion, also ended with an invasion in 1066 when William the Conqueror, also the Duke of Normandy, defeated the King of England at the Battle of Hastings. Under these Norman invaders (from Normandy in northwest France) the English way of life changed. For 200 years two languages coexisted in Britain—the French spoken by the ruling class and the English spoken by common people. After 1250, when the invaders' ties with the continent were severed, the Normans began to think of themselves as English. However, by the end of the Middle English (ME) period, over 10,000 French words had become a part of the English language. As a result Modern English often has two words, one French and one from the older English, for the same item. For example, the French *village* has the same meaning as the English *borough.* In some cases a French word replaced an English one; the French *people,* for example, replaced the English *leod.*

These borrowed French words were not the only changes that marked the Middle English period. While it might be logical to assume that English would grow more complex as time passed, exactly the opposite was true. English grammar became simpler. In old English a noun might have twelve different forms, six singular and six plural; during the Middle English period these forms were gradually eliminated until most nouns had only two singular forms and one plural form. Also, around 1400 a standard written language was developed. Before this time residents of different geographical areas in England who spoke different dialects spelled words as they were pronounced in their locale. After 1400, however, all English writers tended to use the dialect of London as a standard, making written communication clearer and easier.

As you read the following example of Middle English, a passage about King Arthur's death, notice the changes in spelling and grammar that make it easier to understand than the Old English passage from *Beowulf.*

After was it monthes two,
    As frely folke it undyrstode,
Or ever Gawayne myght ryde or go,
    Or had fote upon erthe to stonde;
The thirde tyme he was full thro
    To do batayle with herte and hande,
But than was word comen hem to
    That they muste home to Yngland.
Suche mesage was hem brought,
    There was no man that thought it goode;
The kynge hym selfe full sone it thought
    —Full moche mornyd he in hys mode
That suche treson [in Ynglond] shuld be wroght—
    That he moste nedys over the flode.
They brake sege and homward sought,
    And after they had moche angry mode.
That fals traytour, sir Mordreid—
    The kynges sostersone he was,
And eke hys owne sonne, as I rede—
    Therefore men hym fo[r] steward chase—
So falsely hathe he Yngland ledde,
Wete yow wele, withouten lese,
Hys eme is wyffe wolde he wedde,
    That many a man rewyd that rease.
Festys made he, many and fele,
    And grete yiftys he yafe also;
They sayd with hym was joye and wele,

Modern English Period (1500 to Present)

Students are often surprised to learn that writing such as the following passage from Shakespeare's *Macbeth* is considered Modern English.

SEYTON: The queen, my lord, is dead.
MACBETH: She should have died hereafter;
    There would have been time for such a word.
    Tomorrow, and tomorrow, and tomorrow,
    Creeps in this petty pace from day to day
    To the last syllable of recorded time,
    And all our yesterdays have lighted fools
    The way to dusty death. Out, out, brief candle!
    Life's but a walking shadow, a poor player
    That struts and frets his hour upon the stage
    And then is heard no more. It is a tale
    Told by an idiot, full of sound and fury,
    Signifying nothing.

Although Shakespeare's plays often contain unfamiliar words, the language in his work is closer to that used by English writers today than it is to Middle English. One reason for this similarity is the Great Vowel Shift of the late 1400s, which altered the pronunciation of many words. For instance, in the Middle English period *care* sounded like *car*, *sheep* like *shape*, and *boat* like *bought*. In the early years of the Modern Period, vowel sounds changed, and words acquired the pronunciation used today.

William Caxton's invention of the printing press also affected language during this period. Printing made books available to more and more people and increased the tendency toward standardized spelling. Print impresses a particular spelling on the mind, and once a word appeared in print spelled in a particular way, new writers felt constrained to adopt that spelling.

The invention of the press and the birth of the Renaissance also prompted more writing. In the Middle English period much writing was still done in Greek and Latin; however, the Renaissance fostered nationalism and a pride in the language of one's native country that promoted writing in English. When authors found the English language inadequate, they borrowed words from Latin and Greek, sometimes adding English endings. Words such as *education*, *esteem*, *theocracy*, and *dexterity* all found their way into English in this way. Increased trade and exploration of new lands also added more words to the English vocabulary, and as scientific knowledge expanded, new words were coined for the new inventions and technology that made life easier.

Language Activity 2

Using a reliable dictionary, look up the following words to determine the period of language development in which each word entered the English language. To record your findings, use the abbreviations *OE*, *ME*, and *Mod. E.* For help in reading word histories, consult the front of your dictionary under the heading "Etymology."

abbot	verdict	psalm
they	aesthetic	landscape
geology	poetry	mayor
druid	liberty	leg
martyr	hostage	meditate

American English

Since the early days when parts of colonial America were settled by the English, some noticeable differences have developed between British and American uses of the same language.

These differences in spelling, vocabulary, and pronunciation have resulted in a distinct American English.

Some of these differences originated when Noah Webster, a young American schoolteacher simplified the spelling of some English words for his *American Spelling Book* (1783) and the *American Dictionary of the English Language* (1828). Not all of Webster's changes were accepted, but today many American words have simpler spellings than their British counterparts.

BRITISH	AMERICAN
cheque	check
humour	humor
programme	program
kerb	curb
defence	defense

Many words are also pronounced differently by British and American speakers.

	BRITISH	AMERICAN
clerk	klärk	klərk
schedule	shed′-yü (ə)l	skej′-ü(ə)l
laboratory	lə-bär′-ə-t(ə-)rē	lab′-(ə)rə-tōr-ē
lieutenant	le(f)′-ten-ənt	lü-ten′-ənt

Even greater differences in vocabulary exist between British and American English.

BRITISH	AMERICAN
lift	elevator
petrol	gasoline
biscuit	cookie
chemist	druggist
underground	subway
flat	apartment

Language Activity 3

Use a dictionary to find the American English equivalents for the following British terms.

draughts	wireless
spanner	pram
lorry	post
torch	trunk call
queue up	boot

Language Activity 4

Because of differences in meaning the vocabulary in American novels must sometimes be changed to make words understood by British readers. The following passage is from the British edition of Sinclair Lewis' American novel *Babbitt*. On a separate sheet of paper, list five words or phrases that are British rather than American. Then write the American equivalent for each one.[1]

> The first white cherry blossoms flickered down a gully and robins clamoured.

[1]From *Babbitt* by Sinclair Lewis. Reprinted by permission of the Estate of Sinclair Lewis, Jonathan Cape Ltd. and Harcourt Brace Jovanovich, Inc.

Babbitt . . . driving a good motor . . . stopped . . . to have the petrol tank filled.

The familiar rite fortified him; the sight of the tall red-iron petrol pump, the hollow-tile and terra-cotta garage, the window full of the most agreeable accessories—shiny casings, sparking-plugs with immaculate porcelain jackets, tyrechains of gold and silver. . . .

Later he shouted at a respectable-looking man who was waiting for a tramway car, "Have a lift? . . . it's a fellow's duty to share the good things of this world with his neighbours. . . ."

Babbitt fell into a great silence and devoted himself to the game of beating tramway cars to the corner: a spurt, a tail-chase, nervous speeding between the huge yellow side of the tram and the jagged row of parked motors, shooting past just as the tram stopped . . . past groceries and laundries and chemist shops. . . . Hoardings with crimson goddesses nine feet tall advertising cinema films. . . . Then the business centre, the thickening darting traffic, the crammed trams unloading, and high doorways of marble and polished granite.

Growth in Language

One thousand years ago dictionaries of the English language contained only 37,000 words. Today English dictionaries often contain over half a million entries. During the Old English, Middle English, and early Modern Period, new words added to the language were usually borrowed from other languages. Although borrowing still adds some new words to the language, in recent years other processes have accounted for more than half of the new words added to English dictionaries.

Compounds

One of the easiest ways to make a new word is to use two or more old words as one expression. Such words as *downtown, football,* and *alongside* are common compounds used in daily conversation. Compounds are either written as one or two words or are hyphenated, as is *brother-in-law.*

Language Activity 5

When people speak, it is sometimes difficult to determine whether an expression is a compound written as one word or hyphenated, or if the expression is actually two separate words. Look up the following expressions in a dictionary and rewrite each in its correct form: one word, hyphenated, or two separate words.

back yard	news paper
book keeper	next door
butcher knife	out doors
court martial	out of date
forty two	study hall

Blends

Blends, or *portmanteau words*, are created by combining two words and eliminating the unneeded letters to form a new word.

The following blends are extremely old; the dates in parentheses indicate when the words were used separately and the time of the blend's entrance into the language.

bat (1205) + *marsh* (1000) = *bash* (1641)
clap (1375) + *crash* (1400) = *clash* (1500)
flame (1377) + *glare* (1400) = *flare* (1632)
gleam (1000) + *shimmer* (1100) = *glimmer* (1400)

More recent examples of blending are *motel (motor + hotel)* and *smog (smoke + fog).*

Language Activity 6

List each of the following portmanteau words on a sheet of paper. Then, beside each word, write the two older words that have been blended to create the new word. Use your dictionary if you need help.

1. telethon
2. squiggle
3. moped
4. paratroop
5. motorcade
6. brunch
7. splotch
8. chortle
9. splurge
10. whodunit

Clipped Words

Speakers of English have a tendency to shorten long words by using only a part of the original. These partial or *clipped words (auto* for *automobile, fan* for *fanatic)* occur so frequently that speakers often forget the original longer form of the word.

Language Activity 7

The following list contains clipped words formed from longer words. Copy the list on a sheet of paper and beside each clipped word write the original longer form of the word. Use your dictionary for extra help.

1. gym
2. flu
3. dorm
4. bus
5. champ
6. lab
7. exam
8. lunch
9. sub
10. ad

Eponyms

The word *sandwich* was created to describe the special snack frequently requested by the Earl of Sandwich. The word *lynch* is believed to have originated when John Lynch of South Carolina was hanged as a horse thief without the benefit of a fair trial. These words, called *eponyms*, are derived from the names of people. After years of use, the capital letters used with a proper noun are often dropped from the eponym.

Language Activity 8

Copy the following list of eponyms on a sheet of paper. Using a dictionary for information about each word's origin, write the name of the person or place from which the word originated beside the eponym.

1. Ferris wheel
2. bloomers
3. maverick
4. pompadour
5. boycott
6. diesel
7. hamburger
8. cardigan
9. tuxedo
10. pullman car
11. Braille
12. watt
13. bowdlerize
14. silhouette
15. leotard

Acronyms

Acronyms are formed from the initials of a group of words.

Some short acronyms are pronounced by saying each letter separately (*UN* for *United Nations*), but most acronyms are pronounced as one word (*NOW* for the *National Organization for Women* or *radar* for *radio detecting and ranging*). Notice that the letters in some acronyms are all capitals. As more and more agencies and organizations are formed and as more scientific and legal terminology become part of the general vocabulary, more acronyms are formed. In fact, there are now over 12,000 acronyms in the English language.

Language Activity 9

Copy the following list on a separate sheet of paper and beside each acronym write out the words it represents.

1. SALT
2. NASA
3. CARE
4. WAC
5. CORE
6. NATO
7. VISTA
8. HUD
9. laser
10. SEATO

New Meanings for Old Words

As the population of a nation grows and new discoveries occur, and different life styles arise, word meanings change. For example, the word *eavesdrop* originally referred only to the ground beside a house, on which water from the eaves dripped. Later, used as a verb, *to eavesdrop* meant "to stand beneath the eaves and spy on a house." Today this verb refers to any situation in which one person secretly listens to another's conversation. The following list shows how the meanings of common words have changed.

WORD	FORMER MEANING
closet	private room
girl	a child of either sex
villain	farm worker
silly	fortunate
carriage	things carried

Language Activity 10

Look up each of the following words in a dictionary that provides information about word origin and change. On a sheet of paper, write the oldest definition for each word and its current meaning.

1. marshal
2. cousin
3. nice
4. astonishing
5. skeleton
6. bravery
7. conceit
8. admirable
9. footmen
10. meat

Variations in Language

In addition to the many ways language changes over time, it also varies in the way it is used at any one time. Some of these variations are the result of dialects—ways of speaking shared by people in a particular area, economic level, or occupation. Language also varies according to the occasion for which it is used—more formally on some occasions and less so on others.

Regional Dialects

A resident of New England may speak of bringing home groceries in a *sack* and buying a *bag* of feed for livestock, while a Midwesterner carries a grocery *bag* and purchases a *sack* of feed. These differences in vocabulary, along with differences in pronunciation and grammar, occur because residents of one geographical area share a regional dialect.

A regional dialect is a variation of English shared by people in a particular part of the country.

As John Steinbeck illustrates in the following passage from the novel *Grapes of Wrath*, individuals quickly recognize a dialect different from their own.

> "I knowed you wasn't Oklahomy folks. You talk queer kinda—That ain't no blame, you understan'."
>
> "Ever'body says words different," said Ivy. "Arkansas folks says 'em different, and Oklahomy folks says 'em different. And we seen a lady from Massachusetts, an' she said 'em differentest of all. Couldn' hardly make out what she was saying'."[1]

The character Ivy understands an important concept about dialects: no one dialect is more correct than another, but one dialect is different from another.

American dialects did not come about from the corruption of an originally pure language; in fact, there was no standard for written or spoken English in colonial America. Instead, regional dialects grew from the haphazard circumstances that governed settlement, transportation, and communication in early America.

For example, the earliest residents of New England continued the pronunciations typical of their southern English dialect *(caht* for *cart, fahm* for *farm)* when they came to this country. Later immigrants from northern England and Europe pronounced their *r*'s more distinctly but tended to settle farther west on the frontier rather than in the populated New England area. The few immigrants who settled in New England learned English from the more numerous original settlers and, therefore, adopted their speech habits. However, on the western frontiers of Ohio and Indiana, the new immigrants' strong *r* sounds won out, and pronunciations such as *ahnt* for *aunt* or *bahn* for *barn* gradually faded.

Ironically, some dialects result not from change in language, but from the absence of change. For instance, the Appalachian dialect is actually very similar to Elizabethan English. Because the early settlers of Appalachia's mountainous, isolated areas had little contact with the outside world, some linguists believe their dialect changed very little.

Often accidents of transportation and settlement created strange patterns of dialect. In Illinois distinct Northern and Southern dialects exist side by side—a circumstance that dates back to the early 1800s when discontented residents from Kentucky, Tennessee, and St. Louis, sharing a similar Southern dialect, moved into the lower half of the state. Several decades passed before large numbers of New Englanders, lured by rumors of fertile land, used the newly completed Erie Canal to move west into northern Illinois. As a result of this pattern, travelers in Illinois today still notice a distinct change from Northern to Southern dialect as they reach the center of the state.

In many areas of the West, no such clear pattern of settlement occurred; Southerners, New Englanders, Midwesterners, and European immigrants lived side by side. As a result there is no one Western dialect.

The following chart shows some of the differences in dialect in three large geographical areas: the South, the Midwest, and the North. As you read the chart, keep in mind that it lists only broad, general variations of dialect

---

[1] From *The Grapes of Wrath* by John Steinbeck.

and does not apply to all speakers; within each area there are smaller dialect pockets, such as Appalachia, Boston, and Brooklyn.

VARIATIONS IN VOCABULARY

SOUTHERN DIALECT	MIDLAND DIALECT	NORTHERN DIALECT
skillet	frying pan	spider
corn pone	corn bread	johnnycake
cherry seed	cherry pit or seed	cherry pit
chicken pulley	wishbone	
polecat	skunk	wood pussy
a poke	paper *sack*, but *bag* of potatoes	grocery *bag*, but *sack* of potatoes

VARIATIONS IN PRONUNCIATION

SOUTHERN DIALECT	MIDLAND DIALECT	NORTHERN DIALECT
his'n, her'n	his, her	his, her
greasy with a *z* sound	*greasy* with a *z* or *s* sound	*greasy* with an *s* sound
warsh for *wash*	*warsh* for *wash*	
coop and *hoop* may have the sound in *book*		
fellow and *yellow* pronounced as *feller*, *yeller*		
	mourning and *morning* are pronounced the same	
	merry and *marry* are pronounced the same	
		car sounds like *cah*, *farm* sounds like *fahm*
		idea pronounced *idear*

VARIATIONS IN GRAMMAR

SOUTHERN DIALECT	MIDLAND DIALECT	NORTHERN DIALECT
Y' all	you	you
few pair, several bushel, ten pound	few pairs, several bushels, ten pounds	few pair, several bushel, ten pound
	quarter till six, quarter of six	quarter to six
We might could do that.		
sick at one's stomach	sick at/to/in one's stomach	sick to one's stomach
	I'm leaving. Do you want to come with?	
	He give me a dollar. I seen that movie.	

Language Activity 11

Use the dialect chart in the preceding section for the following activities.

1. Write out the lyrics from two different kinds of songs, such as a country-and-western song and a folk ballad. Using the dialect chart as a reference, underline the words and expressions that you think indicate a particular dialect.
2. Choose a member of your class to interview on the subject of regional dialect. If you are both from the same region, make a list of words that you both feel represent the region in which you live. If you are originally from different regions, listen closely to each other's speech and list the differences in your dialects.

Black English

Black English, a major American dialect, is not limited to a specific geographical region; instead, it is a way of speaking shared by many black people living in the United States today.

Some linguists believe that the long and rich history of Black English began in Africa when individuals from many different African villages were brought to coastal slave markets. In order to communicate with one another, they developed a *pidgin language*, a simplified mixture of several African languages. Slaves brought this pidgin language to Southern plantations where it blended with aspects of English to form Black English.

Some researchers believe that even urban Black English still reveals traces of its West African origins. One researcher traces the words *hip, hipster,* and *hippie* back to the African *hipi,* "to open one's eyes" or "to be aware of what is going on." Long before the word *heavy* became popular American slang, a linguist recorded the use of the word *hibi* by African dancers to mean "strong, difficult, or dangerous." Many other terms *(buckra, gumbo, jazz)* of African origin are now part of Standard English.

Some pronunciations characteristic of Black English may also have their roots in Africa. West African languages contain few long vowels, and two vowels are often used together. These features may account for Black English pronunciations such as *tat* for *tight, fond* for *find,* and *tahm* for *time.* Consonant sounds of Black English are also different. At the beginning of a word, *th* may sound like a *d* (as in *dey* for *they*); in the middle of a word, the *th* may become a *v* or *f* (as in *faver* for *father* or *mouf* for *mouth*).

Another interesting aspect of Black English involves the use of verb tense. The statement "My sister is sick" is limited in the information it gives, since a listener cannot tell if the illness is only a slight, temporary case of the flu or a long continuing condition. However, Black English includes sentence structures that provide this information. "My sister sick" means that this is true only at the moment; the condition is temporary. "My sister be sick" indicates a continuing or long-term condition.

Black English, like every other dialect, developed from the history of the people who use it and is not the result of mispronunciation or misuse of language. As the author Ishmael Reed makes clear in the following passage, the use of Black English does not indicate either a lack of education or an inability to communicate in Standard English.[1]

> You not gone make me give up Black English. When you ask me to give up my Black English you askin me to give up my soul. But for reasons of commerce, transportation hassleless mobility in everyday life, I will talk to 411 in a language both the operator and I can understand. I will answer the highway patrolman who stops me, for having a broken rear light, in words he and I both know. The highway patrolman, who grew up on Elvis Presley, might speak Black English at home, because Black English has influenced not only Blacks but whites too.

Language Activity 12

In 1949 Lorenzo Dow Turner published the results of a fifteen-year study of Gullah, the dialect spoken in the coastal region around Charleston, South Carolina, and Savannah, Georgia. This study was very important to the understanding of Black English. Use a language reference encyclopedia to try to find out in what specific ways the Gullah study was important.

---

[1]From "How Not to Get the Infidel to Talk" by Ishmael Reed in *The State of the Language,* Leonard Michaels and Christopher Ricks, editors.

English as a Second Language

Throughout American history immigrants born in countries as diverse as Germany, Russia, China, and Cambodia have struggled with the irregularities of pronunciation, spelling, and grammar that make English difficult even for professional translators and linguists.

The problems that students face in learning English as a second language result from the differences between English and their native tongue. For example, although both English and Spanish were influenced by Latin and share some similarities, the differences between the two create difficulties for Spanish-speaking immigrants and children born here but raised in families where Spanish is used at home.

For example, differences in pronunciation create difficulties for the Spanish speaker. Because the contrasting sounds *ch* and *sh* in English do not exist in Spanish, the words *chore* and *shore* may sound alike for Spanish speakers. In Spanish each vowel *(a, e, i, o, u)* has only one sound. As a result words such as *mitt* and *meat* sound alike, and the native speaker of Spanish may pronounce "Sit with me, please" as "Seet weeth me, pleece."

In Spanish, adjectives often follow the nouns they describe:

Es un chico rubio de ojos azules.
He's a boy redheaded with eyes of blue.

Even this brief example of how Spanish and English differ illustrates the difficulty non-native speakers of English have encountered in learning to speak English at various points in American history.

Language Activity 13

If you are taking a foreign language, make a list of some of the differences in pronunciation, word order, and vocabulary between the foreign language and English.

Language Activity 14

Several linguists have invented "universal languages" so that people all over the world might understand one another. Some of these languages are *Esperanto, Interlingua*, and *Novial.* Choose one of the languages and in a report describe that language and tell where it is used.

Levels of Usage

The term *levels of usage* refers to the way speakers vary their language according to the degree of formality of the situation.

For conversations with close friends and relatives, an informal level of usage is appropriate. In other situations, however, such as job interviews, public presentations, and business meetings, speakers find a more formal level of usage to be suitable. For example, to a close friend a student might comment, "Man, this booking it every weekend is a drag. What's the scoop on Monday's chem exam, anyway?" However, if the student's employer asks about school, the same student might respond, "I plan to study several hours this weekend because I have a chemistry test next Monday."

One difference between formal and informal English is that speakers using formal English generally avoid slang, while informal English is often characterized by such language.

Slang is a highly informal language consisting of words and phrases that carry a special meaning for members of a group.

Age groups, especially teenagers, often have a special slang vocabulary that identifies the users as members of the group. Occupational groups, such as the military, police, plumbers, and so on may also have a common slang vocabulary, although such vocabulary is often referred to as "jargon" or "shoptalk." Sometimes, words that begin as slang become an accepted part of formal usage. Words such as *fireworks*, *fretful*, and *clumsy*, for example, were once considered slang. More often, however, slang becomes dated, and its use is gradually discarded. How many of the following words, once popular slang, would you use today: "23, skiddoo," "it's the bees' knees," "on the beam," "oh, you kid," "that's groovy, man," "far out," and so on?

Colloquial expressions also mark informal English. These words and phrases, such as *chicken* for "coward," *bucks* for "dollars," and *hold your horses* for "wait a minute," are used by most speakers, but only in very informal situations.

Formal and informal English differ also in sentence structure, grammar, and vocabulary. At the formal level, sentences are likely to be longer and more complex. The grammar of formal English usually closely follows the features of Edited Standard English, and the speaker's vocabulary tends to consist of longer words with few contractions and little or no slang or colloquial expressions. When using informal English, on the other hand, speakers use shorter sentences, frequently broken by interruptions in conversation, features of regional dialects, and slang and colloquial expressions.

Levels of usage vary widely, from very formal language in ceremonies, such as bar mitzvahs and weddings, to slightly less formal for public speeches to very informal for conversations among friends. Generally the more formal the situation and the more distant the speaker from his or her audience, the more formal the language. Levels of usage do not carry with them labels of "right" and "wrong." Deciding which levels to use is a matter of appropriateness, and speakers frequently move from one level to another, depending on the situation.

Language Activity 15

Write out the meaning conveyed by each of the following colloquial expressions on a sheet of paper. Beside each expression write a phrase that has the same meaning but that would be more suitable in formal English.

1. Hold your horses.
2. Cat got your tongue?
3. A heart of gold

4. Fall flat on your face
5. Chicken-hearted
6. To be a big wheel or a big shot
7. Fly off the handle
8. Put your finger on it
9. To break even
10. Give me a break.
11. Carry a chip on your shoulder
12. Bright-eyed and bushy-tailed
13. Get in on the ground floor
14. To let the cat out of the bag
15. To cry over spilt milk

Language Activity 16

With your classmates compile a dictionary of slang expressions used by members of your generation, writing each expression and its meaning in an alphabetical list. If possible, interview a parent and grandparent, or other older relative, to find out what slang expressions were popular during their teenage years.

Language Activity 17

In the following excerpt from an interview published in Studs Terkel's book *Working*, a waitress describes her job and her feelings about it. As you read the selection, look for features of sentence structure, grammar, and vocabulary that mark it as informal English.[1]

> It's not the customers, never the customers. It's injustice. My dad came from Italy and I think of his broken English—*injoost.* He hated injustice. If you hate injustice for the world, you hate more than anything injustice toward you. Loyalty is never appreciated, particularly if you're the type who doesn't like small talk and are not the type who makes reports on your fellow worker. The boss wants to find out what is going on surreptitiously. In our society today you have informers everywhere. They've informed on cooks, on coworkers. "Oh, someone wasted this." They would say I'm talking to all the customers. "I saw her carry such-and-such out. See if she wrote that on her check." "The salad looked like it was a double salad." I don't give anything away. I just give myself. Informers will manufacture things in order to make their job worthwhile. They're not sure of themselves as workers. There's always someone who wants your station, who would be pretender to the crown. In life there is always someone who wants somebody's job.

---

[1]From "Delores Dante" in *Working: People Talk About What They Do All Day and How They Feel About What They Do* by Studs Terkel. Copyright © 1972, 1974 by Studs Terkel. Reprinted by permission of Pantheon Books, a Division of Random House, Inc. and Wildwood House Ltd.

I'd get intoxicated with giving service. People would ask for me and I didn't have enough tables. Some of the girls are standing and don't have customers. There is resentment. I feel self-conscious. I feel a sense of guilt. It cramps my style. I would like to say to the customer, "Go to so-and-so." But you can't do that, because you feel a sense of loyalty. So you would rush, get to your customers quickly. Some don't care to drink and still they wait for you. That's a compliment.

There is plenty of tension. If the cook isn't good, you fight to see that the customers get what you know they like. You have to use diplomacy with cooks, who are always dangerous. (Laughs.) They're madmen. (Laughs.) You have to be their friend. They better like you. And your bartender better like you too, because he may do something to the drink. If your bartender doesn't like you, your cook doesn't like you, your boss doesn't like you, the other girls don't like you, you're in trouble.

And there will be customers who are hypochondriacs, who feel they can't eat, and I coax them. Then I hope I can get it just the right way from the cook. I may mix the salad myself, just the way they want it.

Maybe there's a party of ten. Big shots, and they'd say, "Delores, I have special clients, do your best tonight." You just hope you have the right cook behind the broiler. You really want to pleasure your guests. He's selling something, he wants things right, too. You're giving your all. How does the steak look? If you cut his steak, you look at it surreptitiously. How's it going?

Carrying dishes is a problem. We do have accidents. I spilled a tray once with steaks for seven on it. It was a big, gigantic T-bone, all sliced. But when that tray fell, I went with it, and never made a sound, dish and all (softly) never made a sound. It took about an hour and a half to cook that steak. How would I explain this thing? That steak was salvaged. (Laughs.)

Edited Standard English

While American dialect added an interesting color and richness to the language, it also created some problems. For example, in the early 1900s a major mail-order catalogue described one catalogue item as a *coal hod*, a *coal bucket*, *coal pail*, and *coal scuttle*, so that every potential customer, regardless of his or her regional dialect, would be reached. The need for a standard form for written English became apparent as businesses, newspapers, magazines, and literature developed. Such a form, called *Standard English*, developed to meet these needs.

In the United States today, Standard English is often referred to as the "language of the marketplace" because it is the English most accepted in business, industry, and commerce.

As the English most often used by television and radio commentators, standard English has reached into every part of the United States, including previously isolated areas. For some Americans, perhaps those who speak a regional dialect or Black English, Standard English is a second dialect. They may speak in an Appalachian dialect or in Black English at home and among friends and then switch to Standard English in school and on the job.

In the "Using Grammar" part of this textbook, you will learn the written features of Standard English: subject-verb agreement, pronoun reference, and so on. Since in writing you have the opportunity to proofread, making changes that bring your writing into conformity with Standard English, the written form of Standard English is referred to by the authors of this textbook as "Edited Standard English."

PART

6 Using Grammar

18 The Parts of Speech

Classifying Words into Parts of Speech

English words can be classified into the following eight *parts of speech: noun, pronoun, verb, adjective, adverb, preposition, conjunction,* and *interjection.*

In this chapter, you will study all eight of these parts of speech. There are two sections for each part of speech: an *Understanding* section and a *Using* section. The Understanding sections will help you to identify the parts of speech as they occur in sentences and paragraphs. The Using sections will help you to learn to use the parts of speech according to Standard English usage. In the exercises in the Using sections, you will practice using each part of speech correctly in sentences and in longer pieces of writing.

Understanding Nouns

Nouns are words that name—people, places, things, and even ideas. In this section you will learn three ways to identify nouns: by their definition, by the classes into which they can be divided, and by the features that distinguish them from other parts of speech. In addition to working through this section now, you might want to use it later as a handy reference on common usage problems with nouns when you work in the section Using Nouns.

Defining a Noun

A *noun* is often defined as the name of a person, place, thing, or idea.

Tina wants to go to law school. [name of person]
On our vacation we went to *Dallas.* [name of place]

Ricardo jogs a *mile* around the *track*. [names of things]
The statue symbolizes *truth, justice,* and *liberty*. [names of ideas]

Exercise 1

Write out the following sentences and underline all nouns. Above each noun write whether it names a person, place, thing, or idea.

Example

a. Leontyne Price was considered a great singer both in the United States and in Europe.

person *thing* *place*
a. Leontyne Price was considered a great singer both in the United States
place
and in Europe.

1. Della keeps a journal in which she writes down her thoughts and emotions.
2. Zeke the hound snored in the shade, the picture of perfect peace.
3. The politician spoke about law and order in England and about how police there carry no firearms.
4. The area of the United States that first emerged from beneath prehistoric seas is the Ozark Plateau, a section of land rich in fossils.
5. Two sparrows sat on the fence, ruffling their feathers to protect themselves against the chilly wind and freezing drizzle.
6. The phoenix is a mythical bird that dies in flames but springs reborn out of its own ashes.
7. The villain claimed to be interested only in truth and justice, but she really loved only power, money, and fame.
8. Terry yearned to buy the old convertible and restore it to its former glory; such a car would be a rare antique.
9. The Sweetwater River earned its name when an explorer's mule slipped while crossing it and lost several bags of sugar to the rushing waters.
10. Mary Teresa Norton was the first woman to be chairperson to the Democratic party in New Jersey.

Classifying Nouns

Nouns fall into several general classifications. First, nouns are either proper or common.

Proper nouns name specific persons, places, things, or ideas; nouns that are not specific names are called *common nouns.*

PROPER NOUN	COMMON NOUN	
Sarah Vaughan	singer	[person]
Alaska	state	[place]
Brooklyn Bridge	bridge	[thing]
the Four Freedoms	freedom	[idea]

Proper nouns are capitalized; common nouns are not.

The *building* is immense.	[common noun]
The *World Trade Center* is immense.	[proper noun]
The *doctor* performed the operation.	[common noun]
Dr. Rosa Diaz performed the operation.	[proper noun]

Nouns may be classified as either concrete or abstract.

Concrete nouns name objects that can be perceived by the senses—seen, touched, tasted, heard, or smelled. *Abstract nouns* name ideas, qualities, feelings, and so forth, entities that cannot be seen, touched, etc.

concrete *abstract* *concrete*
The *United States Constitution* stresses the legal *equality* of all *citizens.*

concrete *abstract* *abstract*
All *people* are endowed with the *right* to pursue *happiness*.

Every noun may be classified as either common or proper, concrete or abstract. *Ethel Kennedy*, for instance is a proper noun and a concrete noun. *Motherhood* is a common noun and an abstract noun.

Two or more words joined to name one person, place, thing, or idea are called a *compound noun.*

Many proper nouns are compound nouns: *Diana Ross, Nitty Gritty Dirt Band, Boston Celtics, Empire State Building, Boy Scouts of America.*

Not all compound nouns are proper, however; many common nouns are compound as well. They may be spelled as one word, two separate words, or a hyphenated word. If you are unsure whether a compound noun should be written as two separate words or hyphenated, use a dictionary to find the accepted spelling.

One Word:	landlady, motorboat, shinbone, searchlight
Two Words:	minus sign, relay race, saddle horse, outer space
Hyphenated Word:	sister-in-law, self-control, merry-go-round

Some compound nouns have more than one acceptable spelling:

rock 'n' roll, rock-and-roll
drug store, drugstore

A final classification of nouns is the collective noun class.

A *collective noun* names a group.

choir	committee	group
class	crowd	organization
club	jury	team

Exercise 2

Write out the following sentences, underlining each noun. Then beneath each sentence, list the nouns and the classes to which they belong: *proper* or *common*, *concrete* or *abstract*, *compound*, *collective*. Remember that a noun may belong to several different classes.

Example

a. O.J. Simpson, famous for his ability in football, was well liked by the team.

a. O.J. Simpson, famous for his ability in football, was well liked by the team.

O.J. Simpson—proper, concrete, compound; ability—common and abstract; football—common, concrete, compound; team—common, concrete, collective

1. The yucca, a kind of cactus, is sometimes called "Adam's needle" because of its long, sharp thorns.
2. Aunt Carol has a large collection of old records, including boogie-woogie, rhythm and blues, and early rock.
3. A *cat's-eye* is a semiprecious stone, but a *cat-o'-nine-tails* is a type of whip.
4. The most dramatic moments of a launch are the countdown and the takeoff, the moment the great rocket finally rises into the air.
5. *A Raisin in the Sun*, a play by Lorraine Hansberry, was a success on Broadway and later a critically acclaimed motion picture.
6. The lawyer for the defense conducted a brilliant cross-examination of the witness, and the courtroom was filled with excitement.
7. Anglo-Norman was the language spoken by the Scandinavians who invaded and settled in early England; Anglo-French was a dialect spoken by French settlers.
8. Uncle Smedley makes a terrible dish he calls chili; he uses chickpeas, chili sauce, garlic powder, and ground liver.
9. A "bread-and-butter" letter is a note written to thank a person who has been your host, whether for a meal or an extended visit.
10. Stories of spies and intrigue are especially popular among young adults.

Finding a Noun by Its Features

Nouns have four characteristics that help you distinguish them from other parts of speech. Not all nouns have all four characteristics, but most nouns will have at least one of the following identifying features.

1. Nouns often follow determiners.

Determiners signal that a noun will soon follow. The most common determiners, the words *a*, *an*, and *the*, always indicate a noun will soon appear; these specialized words are sometimes called *articles.* Besides the articles, other words may sometimes work as determiners as well, words like *her, his, many, my, this, that, these,* and *some.*

a village	*many* cars
an apple	*some* countries
her sweater	*these* problems

Sometimes, the determiner and noun will be separated by one or more words. The determiner still signals that a noun is on its way and will eventually arrive.

the battered, old guitar
an unripe apple
a large Hopi village
her comfortable old gray sweater
many European cars
some newly emerged African countries

2. Nouns are singular or plural.

Rules for forming the plurals of nouns are on pages 368–373.

Another feature of nouns is that they show number. Most nouns have a form to show they are singular and another form to show they are plural. A few nouns, however, do not have different forms for singular and plural.

SINGULAR	PLURAL
one toad	two toads
a doghouse	several doghouses
an octopus	eleven octopuses or octopi
the goose	two geese
a deer	many deer

3. Nouns may change form to indicate possession or ownership.

To form the possessive of a noun, you usually add an apostrophe (') and an *-s* or an apostrophe alone. A noun's possessive form shows that the possessive noun has a special relationship to another noun:

Amy's trumpet	Muhammad's beliefs
the city's problems	the pitcher's handle

4. Nouns may be formed with certain *noun suffixes*, such as *-ance, -ation, -ence, -ism, -ment,* and *-ness.*

When a noun suffix is added to a word, the resulting word is a noun. You can recognize a number of nouns by learning these suffixes.

guide + ance = guidance	national + ism = nationalism
invite + ation = invitation	place + ment = placement
confer + ence = conference	sick + ness = sickness

Exercise 3

Many of the nouns in the following paragraph are preceded by a determiner. Write out the paragraph and draw a circle around each determiner. Then underline the noun that follows the determiner.

Example

a. Sharon Washington is helping a group of people in her town work on the special centennial project.

a. Sharon Washington is helping (a) group of people in (her) town work on (the) special centennial project.

The centennial marks the town's one-hundredth anniversary, and the group Sharon is helping is a genealogical society. A genealogical society is an organization composed of people who have an interest in tracing their ancestors and preserving the records of the past. Sharon is taking part in a special project that involves many hours of work and some traveling as well. This project involves visiting the county cemeteries, recording the locations of the graves and the names on the stones, and noting the stones that are illegible and those graves that have never been marked. This information will be put into order and printed in a special booklet. Sharon is glad to be involved with the project; her interest in genealogy was sparked by Alex Haley's book *Roots.*

Mastery Exercise A

The following passage about working conditions during the 1800s is from the book *The Good Old Days—They Were Terrible* by Otto L. Bettmann. Using what you have learned about identifying nouns, find the nouns in the selection and list them on a sheet of paper in the order they appear.[1]

For this exercise do not count dates or figures (*1 percent,* etc.) as nouns.

History offers a yardstick by which to measure the status of the American worker. Today he has dignity and protection; less than a hundred years ago he was poor, debased and unprotected. Industrialists of the period regarded labor as a commodity—a raw material like ore or lumber to be mined of its vitality and flushed away. Profits were enormous against meager wages—"Never before have the rich been so rich and the poor been so poor"—an imbalance that helped 1 percent of the population by 1890 to own as much as the remaining 99 percent put together. Marshall Field's income was calculated to be $600 an hour, while his shopgirls, at a salary of $3 to $5 a week, had to work over three years to earn that amount. Virtually unopposed by any organized front—by 1900 only 3.5 percent of the work force was unionized—employers hired and fired at will. A New England shoe manufacturer sacked outright all of his workers and replaced them with Chinese laborers he brought from the West Coast who were willing to work for $26 a month. To survive in the absence of social benefits, workers endured wretched conditions. The huge labor pool, augmented by a massive influx of foreigners, created a rivalry for even the most repugnant jobs. And if labor unrest caused an occasional stir, industrialist Jay Gould was confident he had the solution for it: "I can hire one half of the working class to kill the other half."

---

[1]From *The Good Old Days—They Were Terrible!* by Otto L. Bettman.

Mastery Exercise B

From a favorite poem, short story, or piece of nonfiction, select a passage about the length of that in Mastery Exercise A. Then using your knowledge of the definition, classes, and features of nouns, find the nouns in the selection and list them on a sheet of paper in the order they appear. (Your teacher may ask you to explain how you identified each noun.)

Using Nouns

In this section you will practice using nouns: forming noun plurals, both regular and irregular; forming possessives; and using concrete and proper nouns to add clarity and life to your writing.

Forming the Regular Plurals of Nouns

Most nouns form their plurals by adding *-s* or *-es* to their singular forms. These nouns form *regular plurals.*

Form the plural of most nouns by adding the suffix *-s.*

SINGULAR	PLURAL
one jacket	ten jacket**s**
one tire	a dozen tire**s**
one movie	two movie**s**

Form the plural of nouns ending in *s, sh, ch, x,* or *z* by adding the suffix *-es.*

SINGULAR	PLURAL
a hiss	several hiss**es**
one crash	two crash**es**
a switch	a number of switch**es**
one hex	three hex**es**

Form the plural of nouns ending in *o* preceded by a vowel by adding the suffix *-s.* Form the plural of nouns ending in *o* that have to do with music by adding the suffix *-s.*

SINGULAR	PLURAL
one stereo	two stereo**s**
one solo	three solo**s**
one arpeggio	two arpeggio**s**

Form the plural of most nouns ending in *o* preceded by a consonant by adding the suffix *-es.*

SINGULAR	PLURAL
hero	hero**es**
potato	potato**es**

Exception: Some nouns that end in an *o* preceded by a consonant form the plural by adding either *-s* or *-es*. If you are unsure how a certain plural should be formed, check your dictionary. The following entries tell you that both spellings are acceptable for *hobo, mosquito,* and *zero.*

> **ho·bo** n., pl. **hobos, hoboes**
> **mos·qui·to** n., pl. **mosquitos, mosquitoes**
> **ze·ro** n., pl., **zeros, zeroes**

Exercise 1

Write out the following sentences, changing each *italicized* noun to its plural form by adding either *-s* or *-es*. Underline the nouns that you make plural.

Example

a. The *chemist* had been startled by the loud *hiss* and strange *fizz* of the *mixture.*

a. The chemists had been startled by the loud hisses and strange fizzes of the mixtures.

1. The *cargo* consisted of the *box* of *metal*, the *burro*, and the pack *saddle.*
2. The student wrote about the *hero* of the *rodeo*, the *clown* who save the *rider* from the *bull.*
3. In the store *window* were the *stereo, piano, radio, guitar,* and *tuba* that were on sale.
4. The show was rather strange; for instance, the *soprano* sang the big *solo* in the *silo* at the back of the stage.
5. The *box* containing the *switch*, the *watch*, the *lantern*, and the *key* to the *church* had been misplaced.
6. The *crunch* and *crash* told us that the *burro* and *mule* must be escaping from their *stall.*
7. Weird *moss* hung from the *arch* that formed the *entryway* to the *tower* on which the *witch* had cast the *hex.*
8. The *chef* felt outraged when the *swatch* of *chintz* had been discovered in the stewed *tomato.*
9. The *flash* of light from the *match* helped us open the *latch* of the *gate* that led into the cemetery.
10. The *screech* of the *owl* and the *buzz* of the *mosquito* kept the *camper* awake and uncomfortable until the first *ray* of dawn came over the *hill.*

Forming the Irregular Plurals of Nouns

Some nouns do not form a plural with the addition of *-s* or *-es;* their plurals are formed through changes in their basic spelling. Such plurals are called *irregular plurals.*

For most nouns that end in *y*, change the *y* to *i* before adding the suffix *-es*.

SINGULAR	PLURAL
one story	two stor**ies**
a democracy	several democrac**ies**
one artery	a number of arter**ies**

For nouns that end in *y* preceded by a vowel, add the suffix *-s* to the singular form.

SINGULAR	PLURAL
a donkey	many donkey**s**
one Tuesday	four Tuesday**s**

Form the irregular plurals of some nouns by changing an internal vowel sound.

SINGULAR	PLURAL
foot	f**ee**t
goose	g**ee**se
man	m**e**n
tooth	t**ee**th
woman	wom**e**n

For many nouns ending in *fe* or *f*, change the *f* to *v* before adding the suffix *-es.*

SINGULAR	PLURAL
calf	cal**ves**
elf	el**ves**
half	hal**ves**
hoof	hoo**ves**
leaf	lea**ves**
life	li**ves**
loaf	loa**ves**
self	sel**ves**
sheaf	shea**ves**
thief	thie**ves**
wife	wi**ves**
wolf	wol**ves**

For some nouns ending in *fe* or *f*, simply add the suffix *-s.*

SINGULAR	PLURAL
belief	belief**s**
dwarf	dwarf**s**
puff	puff**s**
roof	roof**s**

Some nouns have the same form for both singular and plural. Many of these nouns name fish, game birds, or other animals.

SAME SINGULAR AND PLURAL FORMS

shrimp	pike	grouse
elk	salmon	quail
fish	sheep	carp
moose	trout	deer

Some nouns that name nationalities also use the same form for both singular and plural.

SINGULAR	PLURAL
one Chinese	10,000 Chinese
a Japanese	several Japanese
one Portuguese	three Portuguese
a Swiss	a million Swiss
one Vietnamese	a hundred Vietnamese

Form the plural of some nouns by a change in spelling.

Many words from Old English or from Latin and Greek form plurals with a spelling change.

SINGULAR	PLURAL
alumnus	alumn**i**
basis	bas**e**s
crisis	cris**e**s
datum	dat**a**
louse	**lice**
hypothesis	hypothes**e**s
index	index**es** *or* ind**ices**
medium	medi**a**
ox	ox**en**
parenthesis	parenthes**e**s
radius	radi**i** *or* radius**es**

If you are in doubt about the plural form of any noun, check your dictionary. If the dictionary gives no plural form, it means the noun forms its plural regularly.

Exercise 2

The *italicized* nouns in the following sentences all have irregular plurals. Write out each sentence, changing the *italicized* noun to its plural form. If you are unsure how the plural is formed, check your dictionary. Underline the nouns you change.

Example

a. The *foot* of the *calf* showed some *injury*, but the *sheep* seemed unharmed.

a. The feet of the calves showed some injuries, but the sheep seemed unharmed.

1. The scientist wanted *datum* on the *life* of the *grouse*, *quail*, and *ostrich* in the zoo.
2. The *alumnus* of the college awarded the *child* the *trophy*.
3. The *man* could not explain the *phenomenon* of the mysterious disappearance of the *tooth* of the *ox*.
4. The *Swiss* and the *English* met with the *Vietnamese* and the French *woman*.
5. On Wednesday the zoo keeper bathes the monkey, the *wolf*, the *goose*, and the *grouse*.
6. The *basis* of the *crisis* had been discovered, and the *man* and *woman* had saved the *life* of the *child*.
7. The Thanksgiving decorations were the *loaf* of bread, the *sheaf* of grain, and the colored *leaf*; the Christmas decorations were the *elf* and the angel with the *halo*.
8. The *moose* and the *elk* grazed peacefully beside the *deer* and the *buffalo*.
9. The *thief* stripped the *shelf* of the *battery*, the rare *dictionary*, and the valuable *penny*.
10. I hated the book because it was about the little *fairy*, the adorable *dwarf*, the cute little *elf*, and the disgustingly sweet little *pixie*.

Forming the Plurals of Compound Nouns

Form the plurals of compound nouns written as one word by adding the suffix *-s*.

SINGULAR	PLURAL
one *cupful*	two *cupful**s***
a *doorknob*	three *doorknob**s***
the *stronghold*	the *stronghold**s***

Exception: passerby, passersby

Follow the appropriate rule to form the plural of a compound noun written as one word that ends in a word with an irregular plural.

SINGULAR	PLURAL
a *chairwoman*	several *chairwom**en***
the *grandchild*	four *grandchild**ren***
one *werewolf*	several *werewol**ves***

Form the plurals of compound words written as separate or hyphenated words by making plural the most important word.

SINGULAR	PLURAL
one *merry-go-round*	two *merry-go-round**s***
the *hound dog*	the *hound dog**s***
a *brother-in-law*	seven *brother**s**-in-law*

If you are unsure how to form the plural of a compound noun, check your dictionary.

Exercise 3

Each of the following sentences contains one or more compound nouns in their singular forms, as well as other nouns with irregular plurals. Rewrite the sentences, changing each *italicized* noun to its plural form. Underline the nouns you make plural.

Examples

a. The *apple blossom* were in bloom, and the *jack-in-the-pulpit* were up.

a. The apple blossoms were in bloom, and the jack-in-the pulpits were up.

b. The worst *enemy* of *king cobra* are *mongoose.*

b. The worst enemies of king cobras are mongooses.

1. The poem "Beowulf" is about one of the *hero* of a tribe called the *Spear-Dane* who aids another tribe called the *Ring-Dane.*

2. The king of the *Ring-Dane* built the largest of *mead-hall,* a large building to house himself and his warriors, his family and *in-law.*

3. *Elf* and other supernatural creatures lived in the *swampland* near the hall; the most fearsome of these was Grendel, the marsh-stalker, most savage of *blood drinker.*

4. Grendel terrorized the *Ring-Dane* until Beowulf came, braving the *sea-current* with his fellow *hero,* garbed in their *mail coat* and carrying their *battle spear.*

5. No *war-shield* were strong enough to protect the *man* from the *tooth* of Grendel, stealer of *life.*

6. Beowulf, best of *warrior-prince,* must defeat Grendel without *battle spear* or *war sword,* for the monster had cast *magic spell* on all weapons.

7. Beowulf killed Grendel with his bare hands but then had to fight Grendel's mother, the most savage of *monster-wife,* cruelest of the *water dweller,* one of the creatures called *mere-woman.*

8. He pursued her underwater and seized *handful* of her slimy hair; she struck out at him with *fingernail* like *knife.*

9. The *seafarer* celebrated when Beowulf emerged from the lake; he had slain both *water monster* and brought back *trophy* of his *success.*

10. The king rewarded Beowulf and his fellow *swordsman* with *trunkful* of treasure: *war weapon,* gold, and *heirloom.*

Forming the Possessives of Nouns

A noun's possessive form may show ownership or possession:

The film was about Harriet *Tubman'**s*** career.

The *dog'**s*** new collar has an identification plate on it.

A noun's possessive form may show origin or relationship.

The *neighbor'**s*** noisiness was getting on our nerves.

*Amelia Earhart'**s*** disappearance remains a mystery.

Form the possessive of a singular noun by adding an apostrophe (') and an *-s*.

SINGULAR NOUN	POSSESSIVE FORM
the death of the *tree*	the *tree'**s*** death
an edge on the *box*	the *box'**s*** edge
the speech by *Standing Bear*	*Standing Bear'**s*** speech

When a singular noun ends in *s* and has more than one syllable, the possessive may also be formed by adding only the apostrophe. Dropping the *s* after the apostrophe eliminates the second *-s* sound, which is sometimes difficult to pronounce.

the *mattress'* cover

Gwendolyn *Brooks'* poem

the *abyss'* depth

Paris' streets

Note: It is also considered correct to add both an apostrophe and an *s*: *mattress'**s*** cover, Gwendolyn *Brooks'**s*** poem, *abyss'**s*** depth, *Paris'**s*** streets.

Form the possessive of a plural noun ending in *s* by adding only an apostrophe.

the team of the *girls*	the *girls'* team
the den of the *lions*	the *lions'* den

Form the possessive of a plural noun that does not end in *s* by adding an apostrophe and *s*.

the honking of the *geese*	the *geese'**s*** honking
the liberation of *women*	*women'**s*** liberation
the hardness of the *teeth*	the *teeth'**s*** hardness
the nest of the *mice*	the *mice'**s*** nest

Exercise 4

Write out the following sentences, supplying the possessive form of each noun given in parentheses. (Before you form the plural, check whether the noun is singular or plural.) Then underline the possessive nouns.

Examples

a. The ______ fragrant blossoms drew swarms of foraging bees. (bushes)

a. The bushes' fragrant blossoms drew swarms of foraging bees.

b. The ______ honking disturbed the young ______ sleep. (geese) (woman)

b. The geese's honking disturbed the young woman's sleep.

1. The ______ violence was unexpected, and the rains caused some damage to the ______ facilities. (storm) (zoo)

2. The ______ den was flooded, and in the eastern part of the zoo, the water was as high as the tallest ______ knees. (wolves) (giraffe)

3. The ______ cage had a foot of water in it, and the beast kept filling its trunk and squirting water in the ______ faces. (elephant) (rescuers)

4. The ______ pond was also flooded, but the creature didn't notice; the ______ disgust was evident, though, as they gingerly trod the spongy soil and avoided puddles. (hippopotamus) (camels)

5. The ______ pen was a muddy mess, with muck and water up to the ______ belly; the ______ legs were caught in the mire. (rhinoceros) (rhino) (beast)

6. In the Australian exhibit the ______ pen and the ______ yards were damaged, but the ______ field was unhurt. (kangaroos) (wallabies) (ostriches)

7. In the polar exhibits the ______ den and the ______ pool were unhurt, but the ______ pen and the old bull ______ cage received slight flooding. (bear) (penguins) (arctic foxes) (walrus)

8. In the monkey house the cage that was most seriously flooded was the spider ______; the ______ cage was filled with water but was easily drained, and the ______ dwellings were undisturbed. (monkey) (rhesus) (chimpanzees)

9. In the insect and reptile house the ______ exhibit was slightly damaged, the ______ more seriously damaged, and the ______ glass case was completely destroyed; the ______ cage was undamaged, so its disappearance was a mystery. (butterflies) (praying mantises) (tarantulas) (daddy longlegs)

10. The most tragic occurrence was the giant ground ______ death; the ______ name was Cosmo, and ______ innate laziness kept him from climbing out of the ______ path. (sloth) (animal) (Cosmo) (water)

Using Specific Nouns

Good writers use nouns to present a clear, specific picture to the reader, ordinarily avoiding dull or general nouns, such as *stuff, junk, things, elements.* Instead, such writers use concrete nouns that add vitality and clarity:

My brother's room is full of *stuff.* [vague]

My brother's room contains one *bed*, one *dresser*, one *lamp*, five *aquariums*, two *radios*, a complete electric *train layout*, a life-sized *poster* of *Dracula*, a *unicycle*, a *pogo stick*, and a *set* of *stilts*. [improved]

Proper nouns also help to make writing more precise and informative.

Several women were pioneers of blues music. [vague]
Bessie Smith and *Ma Rainey* were pioneers of blues music. [improved]

Writing Exercise A

Rewrite each of the following sentences, replacing the vague nouns in *italics* with concrete or proper nouns. Underline the nouns you supply.

Examples

a. My favorite television shows are *comedies.*
a. My favorite television shows are Happy Days, Barney Miller, *and* Laverne and Shirley.
b. There were only *leftovers* in the refrigerator.
b. There were only a few withered carrots*, half of an old* pork chop*, and a dab of* applesauce *in the refrigerator.*

1. The book was helpful to us because it covered *many subjects.*
2. The fire was caused by *several factors.*
3. On the wall were pictures of *several recording stars.*
4. On my dream vacation I would like to visit *a couple of places.*
5. I like *some kinds of food*, but I dislike *others.*
6. At the museum we saw the skeletons of *some animals* and fine artwork by *several Indian tribes.*
7. There is a huge pile of *junk* behind the garage.
8. At summer camp my little sister learned how to make *several things.*
9. I want to see *some movies* this weekend.
10. At the scene of the crime, the detectives discovered *several clues.*

Review Exercise A

Rewrite the following sentences, making each of the nouns in parentheses plural. Underline the plurals that you form.

Example

a. The (hoof) of the (sheep) showed (trace) of disease.

a. The hooves of the sheep showed traces of disease.

1. The (child) opened the (box) of (toy).
2. All the news (medium) covered the (story) about the prehistoric (tooth) discovered in the volcanic (ash).
3. By the (bush) a group of (jack-in-the-pulpit) grew, and at the (edge) of all the (flower bed), ornamental (moss) grew.
4. Linda's mother lives with her (sister-in-law) and her two (teenager), Linda and Jody, as well as with two (four-year-old) who are her twin (niece).
5. When we go to (rodeo), sometimes we meet the (Valdez), who also like to watch the (rider) on the (bronco) and the (Brahman bull).
6. On (Saturday) we go fishing for (bass), (trout), (bluegill), and (bull-head).
7. In the polar exhibit at the museum, there are stuffed (seal), (walrus), (polar bear), and (wolf).
8. In the (lobby) of the (office) were (bench), (sofa), and low (table).
9. The (basis) of the (hypothesis) were drawn from (datum) on a certain strain of (bacterium).
10. When the (concerto) reached their (crescendo), the (alumnus) of the college shouted their (bravo).
11. (Moose), (elk), (buffalo), and (coyote) were once plentiful on the plains.
12. The (Vietnamese) joined the (Korean) and the (Japanese) in their protest of the (treaty).
13. The (Jones) and the (Washington) like having their (breakfast) on their (patio).
14. The (wife) of the (cattleman) collected money for (shelf) and (supply) for the small neighborhood (library).
15. Both (attorney) got their (degree) from (university) in the (Dakota).
16. The (dish) and (glass) were set in (china cabinet) along with the silver (knife).
17. During (tornado) (object) as heavy as (piano) and (tractor) may blow away as lightly as down from (goose).
18. The (man) and (woman) waited expectantly for the (child) to return from (class).
19. Once the (sky) were darkened by (mass) of flying (passenger pigeon); now all these beautiful (bird) are extinct.
20. The (bird dog) were trained to hunt for (grouse), (pheasant), and wild (turkey).

Review Exercise B

Rewrite each of the following sentences, putting each of the nouns in parentheses into its possessive form. Underline the possessive nouns you form.

Examples

a. (Charles) brother cleaned the (cockatoo) cage.

a. Charles' brother cleaned the cockatoo's cage.

b. The (children) favorite program was not shown so that the (politicians) speeches could be broadcast.

b. The children's favorite program was not shown so that the politicians' speeches could be broadcast.

1. It is said that (geese) cries alerted Romans of their (enemy) approach.
2. A (goose) honk is as loud and effective as a (watchdog) bark.
3. The (gas) distinctive odor made (Mavis) eyes water.
4. In a (year) time they might forget the mistake; in a hundred (years) time they will certainly not remember it.
5. (Cheech and Chong) new comedy album isn't nearly as funny as (Joan Rivers) new one.
6. The (Mayberry Accordion Company) president is also the president of the (world) largest kazoo company.
7. (Women) liberation put an end to the notion that a (woman) place is in the home and nowhere else.
8. (Ray Charles) recording of that song is better than the (Beatles) original version.
9. The Steinberg (family) Hanukkah party was a huge success; it's too bad all (families) reunions can't be so perfect.
10. (Ross) answer to the problem came out differently than (Corliss) did.
11. In an (hour) time we had spent two (weeks) allowance.
12. (James Earl Jones) voice was dubbed onto the *(Star Wars)* soundtrack; he provided (Darth Vader) deep, frightening tones.
13. The (mongoose) fury will repel even the (king cobra) attack.
14. The (shepherdess) sleep was poor because all night long she heard twenty (sheep) coughs and bleats.
15. Through the (magnifying glass) lens we could see the (tarantula) unusual eyes.
16. All the (seniors) pictures were in the yearbook, but one (junior) photo was missing.
17. The (mice) nest was discovered in (Mrs. McNeatly) sugar bowl.
18. The (oxen) yoke was made of oak, and the (cart) wheels were made of ash.
19. (Miss Harris) shop is right next to (Mrs. Foss) restaurant.
20. The (media) coverage of the (volcano) eruption was excellent.

Writing Exercise B

Write at least two well-developed paragraphs on any one of the following topics, being as specific as possible in your use of proper and concrete nouns.

1. Imagine that you are the eyewitness to some famous historical event, such as the eruption of Mount St. Helens or the first moon landing. Describe the event as vividly as possible, giving details about the sights and sounds and about your feelings as you experience the event.
2. An eccentric millionaire has just announced that you will be given the house of your dreams. Describe the house you will have—its location, features, and furnishings.

3. Describe an ordinary coin in as great detail as possible. In addition to describing the features it shares with other coins like itself—size, shape, inscription, and so on—describe how it differs from those other coins. These latter details could include any distinctive marks, such as scratches or nicks and the amount of wear it has suffered. Based on your description, you should be able to mix the coin with similar coins and then be able to identify it again.
4. The photograph on page 379 is of a lithograph by the artist M. C. Escher. Using concrete nouns, describe the man who is the subject of the lithograph. In your description include such details as his facial features, hair, clothes, and hands.

Understanding Pronouns

Generally thought of as words that take the place of nouns or other pronouns, pronouns are a helpful way for writers to avoid unnecessary repetition and to add variety to writing. In this section you will learn three ways to identify pronouns: by their definition, by the classes into which they can be divided, and by the features that distinguish them from other parts of speech.

Defining Pronouns

A *pronoun* is often defined as a word that takes the place of a noun or another pronoun.

The noun or pronoun that the pronoun replaces and refers to is called the *antecedent* of the pronoun. In the following examples the pronouns are in *italics*, and an arrow points to the antecedent.

Mari Sandoz spent *her* youth in Nebraska.

Cochise was the leader of *his* people.

Here is the picture *that* Mary painted.

A single noun may be the antecedent of several pronouns.

Cammy wondered if *she* should take *her* jacket with *her*.

The antecedent of a pronoun may also appear in a preceding sentence.

Julio stared at the snake. *It* was a natrix, a harmless water snake.

Sometimes, a pronoun may take the place of another pronoun.

A few of the customers complained about *their* dinners.

Exercise 1

Write out the following sentences, underlining the pronouns. (Some sentences have more than one pronoun.) Then draw an arrow from each pronoun to its antecedent.

Examples

a. Maria found the lost book, which had fallen behind the sofa.

a. Maria found the lost book, which had fallen behind the sofa.

b. The camel stared at the people with a superior expression on its face.

b. The camel stared at the people with a superior expression on its face.

1. The worst thing about the movie was its inconclusive ending.
2. The shamrock is the plant that people connect with Ireland.
3. There are many people who have allergic reactions to milk or who lack the enzymes to digest milk properly.
4. The first woman physician in America was Elizabeth Blackwell. She and her sister helped train nurses during the Civil War.
5. Helen Keller and Anne Sullivan were remarkable women; many people have read about their inspiring story.
6. Carbon, nitrogen, oxygen, and hydrogen are the most numerous elements in the universe; they make up ninety-nine per cent of all matter, and they are the basic matter of stars.
7. Bobby Leech was the man who survived going over Niagara Falls in a barrel, but he later died when he slipped on a banana peel.
8. The first woman who was elected to the Senate was Hattie Caraway, who was a Democrat from Arkansas.
9. *The Mousetrap* is a play that Agatha Christie wrote for Queen Mary of England. It became the longest-running play in the world.
10. Larry Doby, Jackie Robinson, and Roy Campanella played their first All-Star game together in 1949.

Classifying Pronouns

The largest group of pronouns can be divided into several smaller classes: personal, relative, interrogative, demonstrative, and indefinite pronouns.

Personal Pronouns

Personal pronouns are used to refer to one or more persons or things.

Except for the pronoun *you*, personal pronouns have separate singular and plural forms.

	SINGULAR	PLURAL
First Person:	I/me/my/mine	we/us/our/ours
Second Person:	you/your/yours	you/your/yours
Third Person:	he/him/she/her/it his/hers/its	they/them/their/theirs

The *person* of a pronoun indicates the relationship of that pronoun to the speaker.

First-person pronouns (I, me, we, us) refer to the speaker or to a group of which the speaker is a part.

I sat on *my* lunch accidentally.	[the speaker]
We finished *our* assignment.	[the speaker and others]

The *second-person pronouns* refer to the person or persons being spoken to.

Notice that the singular and plural forms of the second-person pronouns are the same.

You are the only person to get the answer right.	[one person]
You have succeeded because all of *you* have worked together.	[more than one person]

The *third-person pronouns* are used to refer to persons or things other than the speaker or the speaker's listeners.

She is an excellent tennis player.
They have the best spaghetti in town at this restaurant.
Marcia poured a glass of milk and drank *it*.

Personal pronouns have reflexive forms that are formed with the suffix *-self* or *-selves* added to the pronoun base.

SINGULAR	PLURAL
myself	ourselves
yourself	yourselves
himself	themselves
herself	
itself	
oneself	

Note: The words *hisself* and *theirselves* are not a feature of Edited Standard English.

The reflexive forms of personal pronouns may be used in two ways. In one way they may be used to refer to the person or thing named as the subject, showing the subject doing something to itself.

I cut *myself* on the letter opener.

Carlotta asked *herself* how she could have forgotten such an important appointment.

The reflexive forms may also be used to show emphasis.

Queen Elizabeth *herself* made this request.

This football was autographed by Mean Joe Green *himself*.

Exercise 2

On a sheet of paper, list the personal pronouns in the following paragraphs from "That Brings to Mind" by R. L. Marquard. (Remember that in contractions such as *I'd* and *you're*, only the pronouns *I* and *you* need to be listed.)

There are more than twenty personal pronouns, and the first four are underlined for you.[1]

> George Bernard Shaw was constantly being pressed into reading newly written plays or into attending debuts of plays by unknown authors who thought he could give them advice. A story is told of a not-very-talented woman playwright who somehow persuaded Shaw to witness the opening of her first play.
>
> The matron guided Shaw to a seat behind her in a box and told him firmly, "Now, you naughty man, you're not to sneak out in the middle of my drama." So Shaw resigned himself to a long evening and began looking around.
>
> The play began, and Shaw found his view blocked by the woman's hat. So he sat forward in his seat in order to see better. As he did so, he happened to see a stray curl fall from the playwright's elegant coiffure.
>
> More interested in the hair than in the play, Shaw watched as the curl began to irritate the neck of its owner. Finally, she reached back and felt for the hair; then she pinned it in place with a jab of her hatpin.
>
> "Ouch!" Shaw whispered loudly, feeling strangely prankish. "Madame," he hissed, "if you will kindly take my beard out of your hair, I promise I won't budge out of this seat until your confounded play is over!"

Relative Pronouns

Subordinate clauses are discussed on pages 535–544.

A *relative pronoun* introduces a subordinate clause, connecting it to some other word in the sentence.

> My cousin is the girl *who* is wearing the yellow sweater.
>
> The three-toed sloth, *which* is native to South America, has a much better disposition than its cousin the two-toed sloth.

When the following words are used to introduce subordinate clauses, they function as relative pronouns.

which who whose that whom

Interrogative Pronouns

Interrogative pronouns are used to introduce a question.

The following words function as interrogative pronouns when they stand alone to introduce a question.

who whose what whom which

When one of the words in the preceding list modifies a noun, however, it is no longer considered an interrogative pronoun but rather a modifier. The words *what, which,* and *whose* may function as either interrogative pronouns or as modifiers.

What is a quark?	[interrogative pronoun]
What vitamins are water soluble?	[modifier]

---

[1] From *That Brings to Mind* by R. L. Marquard, Editor, copyright 1975 Hart Publishing Company, Inc.

Which is the right answer?	[interrogative pronoun]
Which color looks best?	[modifier]
Whose is this?	[interrogative pronoun]
Whose coat is that?	[modifier]

Demonstrative Pronouns

A *demonstrative pronoun* is used to point out a specific person, place, thing, or idea.

This is a recording by Roberta Flack.
That is Mount Rainier in the distance.
These are the peach trees we planted.
Those are mockingbirds.

There are only four demonstrative pronouns:

this that these those

When one of these words is used before a noun, it is no longer considered a demonstrative pronoun but a modifier.

These were my great-grandfather's cuff links.	[demonstrative pronoun]
These papers are illegible.	[modifier]
Have you noticed *this?*	[demonstrative pronoun]
Would you hold *this* carton?	[modifier]

Indefinite Pronouns

An *indefinite pronoun* does not refer to a specific person or thing.

Indefinite pronouns may take the place of a noun in a sentence, but they frequently have no antecedents.

Somebody will probably call about the lost watch.
Both of us knew what we had to do.

Pronoun/verb agreement is discussed on pages 423–424.

Most indefinite pronouns are either singular or plural.

SINGULAR INDEFINITE PRONOUNS

anybody	everyone	no one
anyone	much	one
each	neither	somebody
either	nobody	someone
everybody		

Everybody *is* here.
One of these pens *is* yours.

PLURAL INDEFINITE PRONOUNS

both few many others several

Both *are* here.
Several of these pens *are* yours.

A few indefinite pronouns can be either singular or plural, depending on how they are used in a sentence.

INDEFINITE PRONOUNS THAT ARE SINGULAR OR PLURAL

all any most none some

None of the book *was* very interesting.	[singular]
None of the articles *were* very interesting.	[plural]
Some of the land *is* swampy.	[singular]
Some of the berries *were* ripe.	[plural]

Exercise 3

On a sheet of paper, write out the following sentences, underlining the relative, interrogative, demonstrative, and indefinite pronouns. Beneath each sentence identify the class to which each pronoun belongs.

Examples

a. The first native American woman who was a candidate for sainthood was an eighteenth-century woman of the Mohawk nation.

a. The first native American woman who was a candidate for sainthood was an eighteenth-century woman of the Mohawk nation.
who—relative

b. Are these the pictures that all of the controversy is about?

b. Are these the pictures that all of the controversy is about?
these—demonstrative; that—relative; all—indefinite

1. This is Max, who is from Switzerland, and who is our exchange student this year.
2. These are the election results that everyone has been waiting to hear.
3. What is the name of the girl who checked out all of these books?
4. Everyone who heard the news was stunned, but nobody was sure yet that the information was true.
5. Which of these is the one that Lydia wants?
6. Who was the astronomer who predicted the existence of the planet Pluto long before anyone else suspected it was there?
7. Many of the people who saw the incident gave conflicting accounts; this was not unusual.
8. These are the documents that contain most of the information that the report calls for.
9. "What is this?" the archaeologist asked. "None of these bones look like any that have ever before been seen."
10. Someone who has a warped sense of humor has put goldfish in most of the office's water coolers.

Finding a Pronoun by Its Features

Pronouns have three features that distinguish them from other parts of speech. Most of the personal pronouns exhibit all three features; most other kinds of pronouns have at least one of the features.

1. A pronoun may be singular or plural.

Personal, reflexive, demonstrative, and indefinite pronouns have singular and plural forms.

SINGULAR	PLURAL
I	we
he, she, it	they
myself	ourselves
himself, herself, itself	themselves
this, that	these, those
each, neither, everybody	both, many, several
anybody, no one, one	few, others

Relative pronouns and interrogative pronouns do not show number; the same forms are used with both singular and plural antecedents.

2. Pronouns may change form to show their function in a sentence.

Only personal pronouns and the relative and interrogative pronoun *who* have this characteristic. The personal pronouns and *who* have both subject forms and object forms.

SUBJECT FORMS	OBJECT FORMS
I, we	me, us
you	you
he, she, it, they	him, her, it, them
who	whom

The *subject form* is used when the pronoun functions as the subject or complement of a clause. (For a more detailed discussion of when to use subject and object forms, see pages 392–396.)

Subject: *She* will be elected mayor.
Complement: The mayor will be *she*.
It is *I*.

The *object form* is used when the pronoun functions as a direct object, indirect object, or object of a preposition.

Direct Object: The sudden noise startled *them*.
Indirect Object: My aunt gave *me* a Confederate dollar bill.
Object of Preposition: When you see Dawn, give this note to *her*.

In addition to subject and object forms, the personal pronouns and *who* have possessive forms as well.

POSSESSIVE FORMS

my, mine, our, ours
your, yours
his, her, hers, its, their, theirs
whose

3. Pronouns may have gender.

Personal and reflexive pronouns may be masculine, feminine, or neuter.

Masculine:	he, him, his, himself
Feminine:	she, her, hers, herself
Neuter:	it, its, itself

Pronouns like *I*, *me*, and *myself* can be either masculine or feminine, depending on the user. Words like *they*, *them*, *we*, and *us* may refer to either sex or to mixed groups of both sexes, depending on the context.

Exercise 4

Use your knowledge of the classes of pronouns and their features to locate at least twenty-five pronouns in the following passage from Graham Greene's "Across the Bridge." List the pronouns on a sheet of paper in the order they appear; beside each pronoun identify the class to which it belongs: *personal*, *relative*, *interrogative*, *demonstrative*, or *indefinite*.[1]

Hint: The first two pronouns are *they* and *he* (in *he's*). Both are personal pronouns.

"They say he's worth a million," Lucia said. He sat there in the little hot damp Mexican square, a dog at his feet, with an air of immense and forlorn patience. The dog attracted your attention at once; for it was very nearly an English setter, only something had gone wrong with the tail and the feathering. Palms wilted over his head, it was all shade and stuffiness around the bandstand, radios talked loudly in Spanish from the little wooden sheds where they changed your pesos into dollars at a loss. I could tell he didn't understand a word from the way he read his newspaper—as I did myself, picking out the words which were like English ones. "He's been here a month," Lucia said. "They turned him out of Guatemala and Honduras."

You couldn't keep any secrets for five hours in this border town. Lucia had only been twenty-four hours in the place, but she knew all about Mr. Joseph Calloway. The only reason I didn't know about him (and I'd been in the place two weeks) was because I couldn't talk the language any more than Mr. Calloway could.

Review Exercise A

Write out the following sentences, underlining the pronouns. Beneath each sentence indicate the class to which each pronoun belongs.

Examples

a. Which of the whales that the scientists studied was the most intelligent?

---

[1]From "Across the Bridge" in *Collected Stories* by Graham Greene. Copyright 1947, © renewed 1975 by Graham Greene. Published by The Bodley Head and William Heinemann. Reprinted by permission of Viking Penguin Inc. and Laurence Pollinger Limited as agent for the author.

a. *Which of the whales that the scientists studied was the most intelligent?*
which: interrogative; that: relative

b. Sheila bruised herself when she was putting the steer back into its stall.

b. *Sheila bruised herself when she was putting the steer back into its stall.*
herself: personal, reflexive; she: personal; its: personal, possessive

1. Oberlin College, which is in Ohio, was the first American college that granted women the same education as men.
2. My scientific friend says that there were several serious scientific errors in the movie *Star Wars*, but I don't know what they were.
3. This is the essence of the new law: anyone who burns trash within the city limits will be fined.
4. Only a few of the trees that we planted last spring survived the long winter with its abnormally low temperatures.
5. The Republic of San Marino honored someone unusual on one of its commemorative stamps when it pictured Mickey Mouse on a special issue.
6. One of the extraordinary things about the camel is the number of noises it can make.
7. When O. Henry began publishing short stories, few of his readers knew that he was writing while serving a prison term.
8. Queen Elizabeth I of England was a strong monarch who could be ruthless if she had to be; most of her subjects appreciated her courage and strength.
9. The aloe vera and the garlic are plants that have had miraculous healing powers ascribed to them—but nobody ever says much in the defense of stinkweed.
10. "You won't catch many fish today," the guide told her clients. "The heavy rains that fell last night might have roiled the water and made it too muddy for the fish to bite."
11. The sonnet, which was invented by the Italian poet Petrarch, is a form that English writers quickly adopted because they liked both its beauty and economy.
12. Both of the dogs I walk insist on entangling themselves and their leashes in every bush and shrub along our way.
13. Others may disagree with the senator's stand on this issue, but I myself believe that she is 100 per cent correct.
14. The only lake in the world that is deep enough to have deep-sea fish is one that is located in Siberia.

15. We have a recording by Miriam Makeba on which she sings a song that is in the African Click language.
16. Several of the swimmers made themselves sick because they stayed in the sun too long; they complained of headaches and nausea.
17. "These are succulent mushrooms," said the professor to his daughter, "but those are toadstools that are deadly."
18. We thought someone must have been prowling around last night because both of our dogs were barking.
19. Each of the students taught himself or herself a few words of a different language.
20. The four Brontë children, who entertained themselves by inventing a mythical kingdom, all grew up to be writers.

Mastery Exercise A

On a sheet of paper, list the pronouns in the following paragraphs from Paul Roberts' "Considering the Reader." Your teacher may ask you to explain which of the following means you used to identify the pronouns.

1. Definition: the pronoun takes the place of a noun or another pronoun.
2. Classes: the pronoun can be classified as *personal, relative, interrogative, demonstrative,* or *indefinite.*
3. Features: the pronoun is singular or plural; the pronoun changes form to show its use as either subject or object; the pronoun has gender.

> Writing implies reading, and in whatever writing community one finds oneself, one must consider not only the message one has to convey but also the reader who is going to receive the message. Writing communities are much less complicated and various than speech communities, but the nature of writing makes it possible, and inevitable, to pay more attention to the differences that do exist. In speech situations we must react fast, get on with it, and necessarily we rely chiefly on more or less automatic response. In writing we have the opportunity to choose, to weigh words, to consider consciously the reader's reaction.
>
> Not always do we want to please the reader. If you are writing advertising copy, you obviously want above all things to avoid offense. On the other hand, in a letter of resignation to a tyrannical employer, you may want to be as offensive as all get out. The point is that the writer can control the reader's reaction, whatever he wants it to be, through his knowledge of the reader's language experience, his likes and dislikes and capacities and expectations.
>
> Students often complain of inconsistencies between teachers, particularly English teachers. "Miss Smithfield wanted us to make our compositions breezy and colloquial, and Mr. Osborne said he'd mark us down if we used colloquialisms. What kind of system is that?" It isn't any kind of system; it's just the way it is. You adapt.[1]

---

[1]Excerpt from pp. 326–327 in *Understanding English* by Paul Roberts. Copyright © 1958 by Paul Roberts. Reprinted by permission of Harper & Row, Publishers, Inc.

Mastery Exercise B

From an essay or other piece of writing you have recently completed, select a passage about the length of that in Mastery Exercise A. Using your knowledge of the definition, classes, and features of pronouns, identify the pronouns in the selection and list them on a sheet of paper in the order they appear.

Using Pronouns

One of the characteristics of Edited Standard English is the way in which pronouns are used. In this section you will learn to use pronouns in conformity with ESE—pronouns that agree with their antecedents in number and gender and pronouns with the proper subject or object forms. You will also learn to increase the clarity of your writing by avoiding ambiguous, general, and indefinite pronoun reference. As you work through this section, refer to the preceding section, Understanding Pronouns, for any help you may need in identifying or classifying pronouns.

Agreement with Antecedent

A pronoun must agree with its antecedent in number.

When the antecedent is singular, the pronoun used to refer to it must be singular.

Even if the antecedent is followed by a prepositional phrase containing a plural noun, the antecedent remains singular and a singular pronoun is used.

A list of singular and plural indefinite pronouns is on page 384.

Neither of the boys has memorized *his* part.

Everyone in the girls' locker room has found *her* place.

When the antecedent is plural, a plural pronoun is used to refer to it.

Many of the representatives answer *their* mail faithfully.

Both of the calves had broken *their* halters.

The pronouns *all, any, some,* and *none* may be either singular or plural in meaning, depending on their use in a sentence.

Singular: None of the diet had lost *its* appeal.

Plural: None of the students liked *their* test scores.

When two or more singular antecedents are joined by *and,* they take a plural pronoun.

Mrs. Highwater and her son enjoyed *their* tour of New York.

Bill and I looked mournfully at *our* lunches.

When two or more singular antecedents are joined by *or* or *nor*, a singular pronoun is used to refer to them.

Neither Kim nor Juanita has gotten *her* pictures back yet.

Imat or Malcolm must have left *his* sweater here.

A pronoun must agree with its antecedent in gender.

When a singular antecedent is clearly masculine, use the pronouns *he, him,* or *his.* When a singular antecedent is clearly feminine, use the pronouns *she, her,* or *hers.* When the antecedent is neuter, use the pronouns *it* or *its.*

The man stood with *his* hand in *his* pocket.

The girl finished *her* lab experiment.

The tree was losing *its* leaves.

Formerly, students were taught to use a singular masculine pronoun when the antecedent is an indefinite singular pronoun.

Everybody has *his* own problems.

Some critics believe that such use of language is unfair to women, since the indefinite pronoun often refers to a mixed group of both men and women. In such sentences it may be better to use the expression *his or her* or else reword the sentence so that the problem is avoided.

Everybody has *his or her* own problems.
All people have *their* own problems.
Everybody has problems.

Exercise 1

For more practice in making pronouns agree with antecedents, see exercises 13–14 on pages 485–486.

Write out the following sentences, choosing the pronoun in parentheses that agrees with its antecedent or antecedents. Underline the pronoun you have chosen and be prepared to point out the antecedents of all pronouns.

Examples

a. Each of the girls makes (their, her) own clothes.
a. Each of the girls makes her own clothes.

b. Neither Carlos nor Eddie had cast (their, his) vote yet.
b. Neither Carlos nor Eddie had cast his vote yet.

1. Either Ms. Washington or Miss Gold will lend you (their, her) keys.
2. Each of the young men groomed (their, his) animals before the livestock show began.
3. Nobody in the senior class had received (their, his, his or her) yearbook yet.
4. Neither the pine nor the larch loses (their, its) foliage in the winter.
5. Everyone is responsible for (their, his or her) own property.
6. Both glass and brick employ sand as (their, its) basic ingredient.

7. All of the speakers in the debate contest waited politely for (their, his) turn to come.

8. Neither Mike nor Max has heard anything about (their, his) job application yet.

9. Some of the streets had large sycamores along (their, its) borders.

10. One of the full-time members and several of the part-time members presented (their, his) reports.

Using Subject Pronouns

The following personal pronouns are subject form pronouns, or pronouns in the nominative case.

SUBJECT FORM (NOMINATIVE CASE)

SINGULAR	PLURAL
I, you, he, she, it	we, you, they

The subject form of the personal pronoun cannot be used in positions where the object form is required. The subject form performs certain specific functions in a sentence.

When a pronoun is the subject of a group of words, use the subject form.

The Washingtons and *they* are coming late.
Karen and *I* will be there early.

When a pronoun follows a linking verb (such as a form of the verb *be*) and renames or describes the subject, use the subject form.

It is *I*.
The winners are Julio and *she*.

In informal speaking the expression "It's me" is acceptable. In formal situations or in Edited Standard English, however, the subject form is used.

It is *they* who must deal with this problem.

"I know the perpetrator of this crime," said Holmes, his eyes gleaming, "and it is *he!*"

Most problems in using the subject form of the pronoun occur when the pronoun is part of a compound subject or complement. Which pronoun is correct in the following sentence?

Mollie and (she, her) watched the program.

Try each pronoun alone as the subject of the sentence to see which sounds "right."

An asterisk (*) indicates a sentence with a feature that is not part of ESE.

She watched the program.	[sounds correct]
*Her watched the program.	[sounds unnatural]

Try this method to find the correct pronoun in the following sentence.

Have you and (I, me) got the assignment down correctly?
Have I got the assignment down correctly? [sounds correct]
*Have me got the assignment down correctly? [sounds unnatural]
Have you and I got the assignment down correctly?

Exercise 2

Write out the following sentences, choosing the pronoun from the pair in parentheses that correctly completes each sentence. Underline the pronoun you select.

Examples

a. Dawn and (I, me) are in the forensic society.
a. Dawn and I are in the forensic society.

b. The leads in the play will be Imat and (her, she).
b. The leads in the play will be Imat and she.

1. Neither Renaldo nor (her, she) will be able to attend the meeting.
2. The yearbook editors will be Pat Whitefeather and (me, I).
3. Either Ms. Washington or (me, I) can take your ticket money.
4. You and (her, she) are invited over to our place tonight.
5. The police chief and (she, her) talked to our civics class about careers in crime prevention.
6. In spite of the doctor's apparent innocence, in the end the villain was (he, him) after all.
7. Are Sonia and (they, them) still planning to sign up for VISTA?
8. (Her and me, She and I) are going to the Halloween party dressed as Tweedledum and Tweedledee.
9. The winners of the art contest are (her and him, he and she).
10. Mr. Chavez and (us, we) discussed energy conservation in class.

Using Object Pronouns

The object form of the personal pronoun is sometimes called the *objective case.*

OBJECT FORM (OBJECTIVE CASE)

SINGULAR	PLURAL
me, you, him, her, it	us, you, them

Use an object form when a personal pronoun is a direct object.

The college interests Clair and *me.*
The mechanic phoned *us* about the carburetor.

Use an object form when a personal pronoun is the indirect object.

The college sent Clair and *me* copies of the student handbook.
The mechanic sent *us* the bill.

Use an object form of a personal pronoun when the pronoun is the object of a preposition.

The Washingtons sent postcards to *her* and *me*.
The Lings live across the street from *us*.

Use the object form when the personal pronoun is the subject, object, or predicate pronoun of an infinitive. The *infinitive* is the form of the verb that begins with the word *to: to go, to search, to find, to keep.* Infinitive phrases may have subjects, objects, and complements, just as sentences do. (See pages 523–525 for a full discussion of the infinitive phrase.)

Marv asked *me* to lend him five dollars.
[*Me* is the subject of the infinitive *to lend.*]

We were just coming to see *him*.
[*Him* is the object of the infinitive phrase.]

Everyone expected the high scorer to be *her*.
[*Her* is the predicate pronoun following the infinitive *to be;* it renames the subject of the phrase, *high scorer.*]

Confusion over using the object form usually occurs when the pronoun is part of a compound construction. Try using the pronoun alone to see which form sounds better.

An asterisk (*) indicates a sentence with a feature that is not a part of ESE.

Raoul met Pam and (me, I) at the game.	
*Raoul met I at the game.	[sounds wrong]
Raoul met *me* at the game.	[sounds right]
Raoul met Pam and *me* at the game.	[correct]

Exercise 3

Write out the following sentences, choosing the pronoun from the pair given in parentheses that correctly completes each sentence. Underline the pronoun you select.

Examples

a. Vlad explained the story of the ballet to Carol and (me, I).
a. Vlad explained the story of the ballet to Carol and me.

b. Bring Davis and (her, she) to the party when you come.
b. Bring Davis and her to the party when you come.

1. Sharon called Glenn, Lola, and (me, I) about the class election.
2. The wrong grades were mistakenly sent to Franklin and (her, she).
3. Whenever Sarah and Malcolm are at one of our parties, we always ask (they, them) to sing.
4. The paintings on display were by Romare Beardon and (her, she).
5. Ms. Washington gave Irv and (me, I) our make-up assignments.

6. Roger invited the Wongs and (we, us) to a baseball game.
7. The practical jokes were attributed to Carla and (he, him).
8. We spent all afternoon waiting for Bill and (she, her) to arrive.
9. Jill sent the Orlandos and (they, them) thank-you notes.
10. We are anxious for Lisa and (she, her) to return from the airport.

Using Pronouns Correctly

When you must decide between using the subject or object form of a pronoun, the following general rules apply.

1. Decide how the pronoun functions in the sentence.
2. If the pronoun is used as the subject or predicate pronoun in a clause, use the subject form.
3. If the pronoun is used as an object (direct object, indirect object, object of a preposition, part of an infinitive clause), use the object form.

The pronouns *who* and *whom* follow these same principles.

Use *who* when the pronoun is used as a subject; use *whom* when the pronoun functions as an object.

Who and *whom* are interrogative pronouns when they introduce a question. Although *whom* is not often used in informal conversation, it is still used in formal speech and in Edited Standard English.

Subject Function: *Who* wrote this essay?
[*Who* is the subject of the sentence.]

Aphrodite was *who?*
[*Who* is the predicate pronoun.]

Object Function: *Whom* have you told about this?
[*Whom* is the direct object of the verb phrase *have told.*]

To *whom* shall I make out this check?
[*Whom* is the object of the preposition *to.*]

Who and *whom* are relative pronouns when they are used to introduce a subordinate clause. To decide which pronoun to use, first determine the pronoun's function within the clause. (See pages 535–544 for a full discussion of subordinate clauses.)

Subject Function: Sarah Hale is the woman *who campaigned to make Thanksgiving a national holiday.*
[*Who* is the subject of the *italicized* subordinate clause.]

Object Function: We exchanged addresses with some people *whom we met on the train.*
[*Whom* is the object of the verb *met* in the *italicized* subordinate clause.)

Use *we* before a plural noun if the noun functions as a subject. Use *us* before a plural noun that functions as an object.

Subject Form:	*We* stamp collectors held our meeting last week. The winners were *we* seniors.
Object Form:	The rumor gave *us* science fiction fans a jolt. Here is a new magazine for all of *us* jogging addicts.

When a pronoun is an appositive, its form is determined by the function of the noun with which it is in apposition.

An *appositive* renames or explains a nearby noun or pronoun. If the noun or pronoun functions as a subject, use the subject form of the pronoun. If it functions as an object, use the object form of the pronoun.

Subject Form:	The soloists—Lee and *I*—were getting nervous. [The pronoun *I* is in apposition with the noun *soloists*, which functions as the subject of the sentence.]
Object Form:	The coach sent the guards—Liebnitz and *me*—back to the bench. [*Me* is in apposition with the noun *guards*, which functions as a direct object in the sentence.]

Gerunds are discussed on page 522.

Use the possessive form of a personal pronoun before a gerund—a noun formed from a verb ending in *-ing*.

Two kinds of words formed from verbs end in *-ing:* participles and gerunds. Gerunds are nouns; participles are modifiers. The possessive form of the personal pronoun is always used when a pronoun precedes a gerund.

My singing sounds like the gargling of a bullfrog.
The coach criticized *our* catching.

Exercise 4

Rewrite the following sentences, correcting pronoun usage that does not conform to Edited Standard English. Underline the corrections you make.

Examples

a. Whom is calling, please?
a. Who is calling, please?

b. Mr. Allingworth decided to give we French students a test.
b. Mr. Allingworth decided to give us French students a test.

1. For who did he say the package was left?
2. Us banjo players can be identified by the calluses on our fingers.
3. The two runners-up—Bonnie and him—received plaques.
4. The clerk asked the last customers—Robb and she—to check out.
5. These are the neighbors for who we bought the Chinese mushrooms.
6. I don't mind them playing the radio; I mind them keeping the volume so high.

7. "Who do you wish to visit?" asked the nurse, who obviously disapproved of us skipping by the desk.
8. Anyone who scores well on the test will help the rest of we students in special study sessions.
9. The judge sent the speeders—Judy and I—to a two-hour class designed to prevent her and me from repeating the offense.
10. When us film fanatics, who would never leave in the middle of a screening, heard about his leaving, we couldn't believe it.

Review Exercise A

Write out the following sentences, choosing the correct pronoun from the pair given in parentheses. Underline the pronoun you choose.

Examples

a. The attendants at the wedding were Pat and (I, me).
a. The attendants at the wedding were Pat and I.

b. Give these order slips to (she, her) or Mr. Medina.
b. Give these order slips to her or Mr. Medina.

1. Dawn, Carol, and (I, me) went to the All Night Monster Marathon and Creature Feature Film Fest together.
2. Please call Kim or (I, me) when you get back from your vacation.
3. We congratulated the policewoman to (who, whom) the city had given its most highly prized medal.
4. "Why is it always Eddie and (I, me) who have to do the dishes?" grumbled Marcus.
5. The two backpackers—Laura and (he, him)—swore they saw a huge, hairy creature that left enormous, apelike footprints.
6. "When is somebody going to give (we, us) poor taxpayers a break?" groaned my father, rolling his eyes upward.
7. I appreciate (you, your) telling me about this problem.
8. Cassie and (them, they) are going for job interviews at the television station.
9. No one had expected (she, her) to react the way she did.
10. Marv asked both Carla and (she, her) for dates on the same night.
11. This is Terry, the cousin with (who, whom) I grew up.
12. The set designers for the play were Jim and (me, I).
13. The coach glared sternly at the two linebackers—Dan and (he, him).
14. (We, Us) seniors can take a few community college classes for credit.
15. The Snobsons keep bragging about (them, their) ordering a pearl-encrusted limousine with platinum hubcaps.
16. Mayor Byrne is the one (who, whom) ordered that this part of the budget be slashed.

17. "I'm looking for Mrs. Stein," said the delivery person. "Are you (she, her)?"
18. By the third act of the play the heroine no longer knew (who, whom) she could trust.
19. "It is (me, I), the Scarlet Pimpernel," he cried, brandishing his sword at the evil Marquis de Zut.
20. (We, Us) hikers were footsore and half-starved by the end of the first day.

Making Pronoun Antecedents Clear

To write clearly, make sure your pronouns have clear antecedents. Three kinds of unclear pronoun reference should be avoided: the *ambiguous*, the *general*, and the *indefinite*.

Reword sentences in which the antecedent of the pronoun is ambiguous.

An *ambiguous* statement is one that can have more than one meaning. Ambiguous pronoun references mean that a pronoun seems to have more than one possible antecedent. Such ambiguous pronoun references can usually be remedied by rewording the sentence or by replacing the pronoun with a noun.

Ambiguous: Marcia told Lisa *her* ride was going to be late. [Whose ride, Marcia's or Lisa's, will be late?]
Clear: Marcia said that Lisa's ride would be late.
Marcia told Lisa that Lisa's ride would be late.

Ambiguous: Jack went to see Phil and worked on his car. [Whose car—Jack's or Phil's—was worked on?]
Clear: Jack went to see Phil and worked on Phil's car.

Reword sentences in which the pronouns *which, this, that,* and *it* refer to ideas that are vaguely expressed.

The antecedent of a pronoun may be a whole series of ideas. If the pronoun's antecedent is not clear, the sentence should be rephrased.

General: My sister had borrowed my backpack without asking, had taken it for the weekend to the lake, and had brought it home sopping wet; she never explained or apologized, *which* made me angry.
Clear: My sister had borrowed my backpack without asking, had taken it for the weekend to the lake, and had brought it home sopping wet; she never explained or apologized. Her total lack of consideration made me angry.

General: The windows were shut, the room was overheated, and weird smells were seeping in from the chemistry lab next door. *It* kept me from studying.
Clear: The shut windows, the overheated room, and the weird smells seeping in from the chemistry lab next door kept me from studying.

Reword sentences in which the pronouns *it*, *they*, or *you* do not have a clear antecedent.

Speakers and writers often use expressions such as "It says . . ." or "They say . . ." to refer to some indefinite authority. Avoid such indefinite pronoun references by specifically naming who or what is the source of the information.

Indefinite: It says that the buffalo hunters and railroads destroyed the economy of the Plains tribes.
Clear: Our American history text states that the buffalo hunters and railroads destroyed the economy of the Plains tribes.

Indefinite: They say this restaurant has very good trout.
Clear: Jim and Peggy say this restaurant has very good trout.

Indefinite: You can tour President Truman's house in Independence, Missouri.
Clear: Visitors to Independence, Missouri, can tour President Truman's house.

Writing Exercise A

Rewrite the following sentences to eliminate ambiguous, indefinite, and overly general pronoun reference.

Examples

a. If you shop carefully, you yourself can save money.
a. Shoppers who are careful save themselves money.

b. They say that lightning often strikes twice in the same place.
b. Our science book says that lightning often strikes twice in the same place.

1. What did it say on the radio about the election returns?
2. They say that the new park will cost the city over a million dollars.
3. Howard told Dan he had won the science fair's top prize.
4. They are having a mammoth closeout at Dreeson's Department Store.
5. You can get a good pet quite cheaply at the animal shelter.
6. Lisa told Kim the news about her sister.
7. Out at the Horseshoe Bend Marina, they have some tame carp that stay near the dock, waiting for food to be tossed to them.
8. Pete was practicing his tuba, Stacie had her radio blaring, and the twins were trying to see if they could master yodeling. It was deafening.
9. On television it said that there was the possibility of flash floods in the area tonight.
10. Last night my dog ran off. This morning I lost the filling out of my tooth. This afternoon I discovered my car had two flat tires. This depressed me.

Review Exercise B

Rewrite each of the following sentences, changing any pronouns that do not conform to Edited Standard English or that have ambiguous, general, or indefinite pronoun reference.

Examples

a. Nobody in the girls' choir had their robe yet.
a. Nobody in the girls' choir had her robe yet.

b. Gina and her sister worked on her art project.
b. Gina and her sister worked on Gina's art project.

1. Somebody on the boys' swimming team left their books in the locker room.
2. Rubin told Scott he had lost his car keys.
3. In Omaha, Nebraska, they have the headquarters of the Union Pacific Railroad.
4. Each of the elephants in the zoo has their teeth checked twice a year by a dentist.
5. Everybody who sat at the game with the band members wore their "Beat Benton High" badge.
6. They say that the temperature may drop to freezing tonight.
7. Neither Raoul nor his brother wanted to quit their job.
8. Both Dena and Carrie wore her mittens to the skating party.
9. They can now perform miracles with plastic surgery.
10. None of the dogs would stop its frantic barking.
11. Nobody who sent for that record album has received their order yet.
12. In the newspaper it said that Indira Gandhi is not related to Mahatma Gandhi.
13. Either Hester or Gina can lend you their skills.
14. To build a truly good doghouse, you should put in at least one layer of insulation.
15. Somebody had left their catcher's mitt on the park bench.
16. Both Madame Curie and her daughter won her Nobel Prizes in the field of science.
17. None of the witnesses wanted his name mentioned in the newspapers.
18. If you get your hair cut at Fantastic Fred's, you get a free pass to the Saturday afternoon movie at the mall.
19. Don never changes the oil in his car, never checks the water in his radiator, and never changes his filters. This will eventually ruin his motor.
20. I have to mow the lawn, trim the shrubs, burn a tree stump, weed the garden, and pick raspberries, which depresses me deeply.

Writing Exercise B

Choose one of the following topics and write a short paper on it as directed. When you have finished your first draft, check your pronoun usage carefully. Have you used subject and object forms correctly? Are the antecedents of all pronouns clear? When you are certain you have used pronouns according to ESE, write your final draft.

1. Write a narrative and descriptive scene in which two characters perform some action. They may be meeting for the first time, having an argument, shooting the rapids in a canoe, or making plans for some event. Describe each character and his or her actions as vividly as you can.
2. Compare and contrast two figures in history, literature, or current politics. Describe their characters or contributions or drawbacks fully and clearly.
3. Based on your own experiences, what do you think are some important guidelines for rearing a child? What essential information should a prospective parent have about the physical and emotional needs of a young child? What determines whether or not someone will be a good parent? Write several paragraphs in which you explain your ideas on this subject.
4. The photograph on page 402 shows the kind of place to which many Americans, caught up in the stresses of modern life, feel they would like to escape. Do you think that you could make a life for yourself in such a place? Could you live comfortably without modern conveniences and comforts? What would you miss most about your present life? Least? Write a description of what your life in such a place might be like.

Understanding Verbs

In this section you will learn three ways to identify verbs: by their definition, by the classes into which they can be grouped, and by the features that distinguish them from other parts of speech.

Defining a Verb

A *verb* is often defined as a word describing an action or a state of being.

Buffy St. Marie *composes* and *sings* songs.	[action]
The gorilla *glowered* at the teasing children.	[action]
The brown recluse spider *is* highly poisonous.	[state of being]
Something *seemed* peculiar about the old house.	[state of being]

Verbs that describe states of being usually assert that something *is* or *exists*, or they describe something's *condition*. The most frequently used verbs that describe a state of being are *am, are, is, was,* and *were*.

Exercise 1

Write out the following sentences, underlining the verbs. (A sentence may have more than one verb.)

Example

a. The explosion of Mount St. Helens scattered volcanic ash over four states and halted tourism for several weeks.

a. The explosion of Mount St. Helens scattered volcanic ash over four states and halted tourism for several weeks.

1. Lisa Lu and Kam Tong were costars on popular television series in the 1950s.
2. Loretta Lynn married at the age of fifteen and became a grandmother at twenty-nine.
3. Josh Gibson of the American Negro League hit 800 home runs in his career; he once knocked the ball out of Yankee Stadium.
4. In World War I British sailors rescued a fox terrier from the wreckage of a German ship; the dog became the mascot of the British Navy.
5. Palindromes are words or sentences that read exactly the same forward and backward; an example of a palindrome is "Was it a car or a cat I saw?"

6. Myth says that Pegasus, the winged horse, sprang from the blood of the gorgon Medusa.
7. Comedian Flip Wilson created a number of memorable characters; my favorites were Geraldine and Reverend Leroy, who were both comic masterpieces.
8. Calypso music swings and sparkles, and one of its most famous composers was Rupert Grant, who called himself "Lord Invader."
9. Sequoya was the Indian name of George Guess, the Cherokee who invented the first American Indian syllabary.
10. The comic strip "Pogo" contained many amusing characters, but the one with the most unusual name was the bloodhound who was called "Beauregard Chaulmoogra Frontenac de Montmingle Bugleboy"—with a name like that, it is no wonder he always looked bewildered and sad.

Classifying Verbs

Within the large category of verbs, there are four smaller classes: action and linking verbs, main and helping verbs.

Action Verbs

Action verbs describe physical or mental activity.

Most action verbs show some kind of physical movement, but a number of them describe mental or emotional activity that cannot be seen by others.

The horses *thundered* around the curve.	[physical action]
Mrs. Reisman *laughed* at the birthday card.	[physical action]
Marsha *believed* the story.	[mental action]
Mort *wondered* about the time.	[mental action]

Linking Verbs

A *linking verb* joins the subject of a sentence to a noun or adjective that identifies or describes it.

Her name *is* Lana Valdez.
[*Is* is a linking verb because it links the subject, *name*, with a proper noun that identifies the name.]

The record *sounded* scratchy.
[*Sounded* is a linking verb because it links the subject, *record*, with the adjective, *scratchy*.]

The most commonly used linking verbs are forms of the verb *be: am, are, is, was, were, been,* and *being.* Other verbs may also be used as linking verbs:

appear	look	sound
become	remain	stay
feel	seem	taste
grow	smell	turn

Verbs in the preceding list may be either action or linking verbs, depending on their use in the sentence.

The puppies *looked* frightened.
[*Looked* is a linking verb in this sentence because it links the subject, *puppies*, to an adjective describing them: *frightened.*]

The puppies *looked* at the lizard with curiosity.
[*Looked* is an action verb in this sentence because it does not link the subject *puppies* to a word that describes or identifies it; rather, it names an action of the puppies.]

Main Verbs and Helping Verbs

Verbs may be either single words or verb phrases.

Verb phrases consist of two or more verbs acting as a single unit. The last verb in the verb phrase is called the *main verb.* The other verbs in the verb phrase are called *helping verbs* or *auxiliary verbs.*

The following is a list of common helping verbs.

is	do	should
are	does	would
was	did	have
were	can	has
am	could	had
be	will	may
been	shall	might

We *are going* to Montana this summer.
The baby-sitter thought the children *should have been* asleep hours ago.
We *will be playing* Tech High in the semifinals.

Sometimes, a main verb is separated from its helping verb or verbs by other words, such as *always, ever, never, not,* or the contraction *n't.* Such modifiers are not part of the verb phrase. In questions another word may occur between parts of the verb phrase.

Have you *seen* Sheila's tennis racket?
Mr. Whitewater *has* always *lived* in South Dakota.
The lost watch *may* never *be found.*
The dog *does*n't always *come* when it is called.

In some sentences a helping verb may be contracted:

She*'ll be coming* around the mountain.
[*She'll* is a contraction of *she will.*]

Priborski has the ball; he*'s running* past the ten-yard line.
[*He's* is a contraction of *he is.*]

Exercise 2

Write out the following sentences, underlining the verb phrases. (Be careful not to underline any other words that may modify the verb phrase or that occur between its parts.)

Examples

a. A single drop of water may contain 50 million bacteria cells.
a. A single drop of water may contain 50 million bacteria cells.

b. Saturn's rings are not always seen, due to the planet's tipping.
b. Saturn's rings are not always seen, due to the planet's tipping.

1. Plant life could not exist without lightning.
2. Nitrogen is required by plants.
3. Earth's atmosphere is formed of almost 80 per cent nitrogen.
4. This nitrogen, however, is in a form that plants can't use; it is insoluble.
5. Lightning is always accompanied by intense heat.
6. High temperatures will force nitrogen to combine with oxygen.
7. Nitrogen oxides are formed by the lightning; these oxides can be dissolved in water.
8. The nitrogen oxides are mixed with rain, and a dilute nitric acid is formed.
9. This acid is mixed with minerals in the earth and becomes the nitrates that the plants must have to live.
10. If electrical storms did not occur, the world's vegetation would most certainly perish, and the world would become an unlivable desert.

Finding a Verb by Its Features

Most verbs have three distinct features.

1. Verbs show tense.

Every verb has three forms called the *principal parts.* These principal parts are the *present,* the *past,* and the *past participle.*

PRESENT	PAST	PAST PARTICIPLE
trim	trimmed	(have) trimmed
teach	taught	(has) taught
ring	rang	(had) rung

The third principal part of the verb can be used with a number of helping verbs. Together, the principal parts and helping verbs can form all the different tenses in English, describing a wide variety of times.

Present:	I *trim* the bushes.
Past:	I *trimmed* the bushes.
Future:	I *will trim* the bushes.
Present Perfect:	I *have trimmed* the bushes.
Past Perfect:	I *had trimmed* the bushes.
Future Perfect:	I *will have trimmed* the bushes.

In addition to the tenses formed by the principal parts of the verb, another sense of time can be conveyed by the *progressive forms* of the tenses. The progressive forms of the tenses use the *-ing* form of the verb. This *-ing* form, called the *present participle*, is used with a form of the verb *be* in the progressive forms of the tenses.

PRESENT PARTICIPLES

trimm**ing** teach**ing** ring**ing**

PROGRESSIVE FORMS OF THE TENSES

Subject-verb agreement problems are discussed on pages 421–429.

Present Progressive:	I *am trimming* the bushes.
Past Progressive:	I *was trimming* the bushes.
Future:	I *will be trimming* the bushes.
Present Perfect:	I *have been trimming* the bushes.
Past Perfect Progressive:	I *had been trimming* the bushes.
Future Perfect Progressive:	I *will have been trimming* the bushes.

2. Verbs change form to agree in number with the subject of a sentence.

Every present tense verb has two different forms, one to agree with a singular subject, and one to agree with a plural subject.

SINGULAR FORM

Alice *drives.*
The train *arrives* on time.
The woman *works* at the plant.
[The singular form ends in *-s* or *-es*.]

PLURAL FORM

Alice and Lana *drive.*
The trains *arrive* on time.
The women *work* at the plant.
[The plural form does not add an ending. It is simply the present form of the principal parts.]

The singular form of the verb is used with the pronouns *he*, *she*, and *it* and with a singular noun.

He *drives.*
She *arrives.*
It *works.*
The battery *works.*

The plural form of the verb is used with the pronoun subjects *I*, *you*, *we*, and *they* and with a plural noun.

I *drive.*
You *drive.*
We *work.*
The girls *work.*

3. Verbs show mood.

Problems in using the three moods are discussed on pages 418–421.

Verbs may express three different moods: the *indicative*, the *imperative*, and the *subjunctive*.

The *indicative mood* asserts something as a factual statement. Most of the verbs you use in speaking and writing are in the indicative mood.

> The bus *stops* at this corner.
> A meteor shower *will occur* tonight.
> Queen Guinevere's love for Sir Lancelot *destroyed* the kingdom of Camelot.

The *imperative mood* is used to make commands or requests.

> Please *pass* the yogurt, Marsha.
> *Show* me your driver's license and registration.

The *subjunctive mood* expresses a wish or makes a statement that is opposed to fact, usually following the words *if* or *as though.*

> I wish this corn fritter *were* a piece of cherry pie.
> If wood ticks *were* worth money, our land would be unbelievably valuable.

Exercise 3

Using what you have learned about the features of verbs, identify the verbs and verb phrases in the following sentences. Write out the sentences, underlining the verbs and verb phrases. Be prepared to explain how you identified each verb. (A sentence may have more than one verb or verb phrase.)

Example

a. The original Harlem Globetrotters were known as the Saucy Big Five because they had played games at the Saucy Ballroom.

a. The original Harlem Globetrotters were known as the Saucy Big Five because they had played games at the Saucy Ballroom.

1. Sports promoter Abe Saperstein organized the team in 1927.
2. Because they did not have a hometown sponsor, they toured the country in Saperstein's car.
3. They played exhibition games and were soon known for their skill on the court.
4. The Globetrotters weren't just excellent ball players, however; they were proving themselves great entertainers as well.
5. Their clowning and fantastic ball handling endeared them to audiences, and the Globetrotters were beginning to be famous.
6. Their early years were filled with hardships and offered them little financial reward.
7. They truly became "Globetrotters" when their fame spread to other countries and they were playing exhibition games abroad.
8. The team has drawn crowds as large as 75,000, and their audiences are always pleased.

9. The players simply amaze people; they make impossible and flamboyant shots; they dribble and pass with dazzling skill; and somehow they always manage to perform antics as spectacular as those of the best comics.
10. Although the team had a humble beginning, it has now performed on all seven continents of the world.
11. A movie has been made about them, and they have starred in television specials.
12. Even a Saturday morning cartoon series was created about them; books have been written; and a series of comic books has been published featuring them.
13. Some of the team's greatest stars have been "Goose" Tatum, Marques Haynes, Clarence Wilson, "Meadowlark" Lemon, and Wilt "the Stilt" Chamberlain.
14. Chamberlain has also been called "The Big Dipper" and will go down in sports history as one of basketball's greatest players.
15. When he played for the Philadelphia Warriors, he once scored 100 points in a single game; the Warriors trounced the New York Knicks 169 to 147.
16. The previous record of points by a single player was broken that night—but Chamberlain had broken his own record—78 points in a single game.
17. Only three white men have ever played for the Globetrotters, and one of these was their manager Abe Saperstein.
18. The other two white players were Bunny Levitt and Bob Karstens, but the Globetrotters have primarily been a showcase for great black talent.
19. By 1970 the Globetrotters had played 10,000 exhibition games and had won 9,678 of them.
20. Other teams that imitate the Globetrotters' combination of skill and comedy have sprung up, but there will always be only one Globetrotters team; they have always been and will always be the great originals.

Mastery Exercise A

Using what you have learned about the definition, classes, and features of verbs, identify the verbs and verb phrases in the following selection about the artist Georgia O'Keeffe by Mary Lynn Kotz. List the verbs and verb phrases on a sheet of paper in the order they appear and be able to explain how you identified each one.[1]

Hint: The first two verbs are *is* and *drive.*

It is noon and I drive O'Keeffe to her other house, at Ghost Ranch, part of a spread that she first discovered 50 years ago. She knows every inch of the way, every mesa, curve and vista, and points them all out to me—including "the first

[1]From "Georgia O'Keeffe: An American Original" by Mary Lynn Kotz. © *ARTnews* 1977.

Hint: *To paint* and *to have* are infinitives; do not list these as verbs in this exercise.

hill I ever painted here. I drove my Model A out here," she says, "took my canvas and sat in the back seat to paint." She tells me that she drove across the United States, almost everywhere. "I'd leave home in an open car, with paint and canvases. When I had some paintings, I'd come back."

Her face has taken on a new light. There is something especially exciting for her about this world that she has painted so many times. . . .

I ask her when she realized that she had a great gift.

"I don't think I have a great gift," she replies. "It isn't just talent. You have to have something else. . . . It is mostly a lot of nerve, and a lot of very hard work."

Mastery Exercise B

From a convenient source, such as a newspaper, magazine, or textbook, select a passage about the length of that in Mastery Exercise A. Then, using what you have learned in this section, identify the verbs and verb phrases in the selection and list them on a sheet of paper. If you like, use a recently written paper of your own as the basis for this assignment.

Using Verbs

The features of verbs—that they show tense, that they have singular and plural forms, and that they show mood—cause some usage problems. In this section of the textbook, you will learn how to use verbs in Edited Standard English. As you work, you may wish to refer to the section Understanding Verbs for any questions you have about the definition, classes, and features of verbs.

Forming Verb Tenses

Verbs show tense, or time, with their three principal parts; the *present*, *past*, and *past participle*.

The wind *howls* up in these hills.	[present]
The sirens *howled* in warning.	[past]
He *had howled* in protest.	[past participle with helping verb *had*]

Verbs are classified as either *regular* or *irregular*, depending on the formation of their principal parts.

The past and past participle parts of regular verbs are formed by adding *-d* or *-ed* to the present form.

PRESENT	PAST	PAST PARTICIPLE
enjoy	enjoyed	enjoyed
ignore	ignored	ignored
hop	hopped	hopped

rent	rented	rented
apply	applied	applied

Rules about spelling changes are discussed on pages 609–614.

Notice that some verbs, such as *hop* and *apply*, have spelling changes when *-ed* is added to the present form.

The past and past participle of *irregular verbs* are not formed in regular ways. For this reason, principal parts of irregular verbs must be memorized. The following list gives the principal parts of the most common irregular verbs.

IRREGULAR VERBS

PRESENT	PAST	PAST PARTICIPLE (*has*, *have*, or *had*)
become	became	become
begin	began	begun
break	broke	broken
bring	brought	brought
build	built	built
burst	burst	burst
buy	bought	bought
catch	caught	caught
choose	chose	chosen
come	came	come
cost	cost	cost
dive	dived or dove	dived
do	did	done
draw	drew	drawn
drink	drank	drunk
drive	drove	driven
eat	ate	eaten
fall	fell	fallen
fly	flew	flown
forget	forgot	forgotten
freeze	froze	frozen
give	gave	given
go	went	gone
grow	grew	grown
hit	hit	hit
keep	kept	kept
know	knew	known
lay	laid	laid
lie	lay	lain
ride	rode	ridden
ring	rang	rung
rise	rose	risen
run	ran	run
see	saw	seen
shake	shook	shaken
shrink	shrank	shrunk
sing	sang	sung

sink	sank	sunk
slay	slew	slain
speak	spoke	spoken
spend	spent	spent
spring	sprang	sprung
steal	stole	stolen
strive	strove	striven
swear	swore	sworn
swim	swam	swum
take	took	taken
teach	taught	taught
think	thought	thought
throw	threw	thrown
wear	wore	worn
write	wrote	written

If you are not sure how the principal parts of a verb are formed, check your dictionary, which uses the present form as the entry for all verbs. Some dictionaries do not list the principal parts of regular verbs. This means that the verb forms its principal parts in the usual way, with *-d* or *-ed* added to the present form. All dictionaries list the principal parts of irregular verbs:

grind (grīnd) vt. **ground, grind′ing**
par·take (pär tāk′) vi. **-took′, -tak′en, -tak′ing**

When dictionaries list the principal parts of irregular verbs, the forms are listed in the same order as they are on the chart on pages 410–411. In addition, some dictionaries list the present participle, or *-ing* form. Up to four forms may be listed:

PRESENT FORM	PAST FORM	PAST PARTICIPLE	PRESENT PARTICIPLE
write (rīt), v.t.	**wrote**	**written**	**writing**

When only three forms are listed, the past and past participle are the same:

PRESENT	PAST AND PAST PARTICIPLE	PRESENT PARTICIPLE
spend (spend) v.t.	**spent**	**spending**

Sometimes, a dictionary will list alternate past or past participle forms. Either form is acceptable, but the one listed first is preferred.

PRESENT	PAST	ALTERNATE PAST	PAST PARTICIPLE	PRESENT PARTICIPLE
dive (dīv) v.i.	**dived** or	**dove**	**dived**	**diving**

Exercise 1

Each of the following sentences contains an irregular verb. Write out the sentences, supplying the appropriate principal part of the verb given in

For more practice in using irregular verbs, see exercises 1–9 on pages 479–484.

parentheses. (Remember that the past participle form is always used with the helping verbs *has*, *have*, or *had*.) Underline the verb or verb phrase.

Examples

a. LaDonna had ______ about soccer practice after school. (forget)

a. LaDonna had forgotten about soccer practice after school.

b. Rita, Nicki, and Rosa all have ______ on jumbo jets. (fly)

b. Rita, Nicki, and Rosa all have flown on jumbo jets.

1. Lily has ______ her horse in the barrel races at the rodeo ever since she was twelve years old. (ride)
2. We weren't sure exactly what we had ______, but we thought it might have been a UFO. (see)
3. The dripping water had ______, and the icicles had ______ marvelously long. (freeze) (grow)
4. Mrs. Lewington has ______ her famous banana bread to every reunion her family has ______. (bring) (hold)
5. The forest fire had ______ their courage badly and had ______ some of them nightmares for weeks afterwards. (shake) (give)
6. The boat had first ______ a leak, and finally it had ______. (spring) (sink)
7. He had ______ to see the log cabin that Josie and Ed ______. (go) (build)
8. The children accidentally ______ the baseball through Mrs. McGrouchly's picture window and then ______ in terror. (throw) (run)
9. The defendant has ______ that he has never ______ anything in his life, and you know he is a man who has always ______ the truth. (swear) (steal) (speak)
10. Have you ______ what Margo has ______ to school? It is a poem that Gwendolyn Brooks has ______ in her own handwriting. (see) (bring) (write)

Using Verb Tenses

In this section you will learn to avoid common usage problems with verb tenses.

Simple Tenses

The three simple tenses are the *present tense*, *past tense*, and *future tense*.

1. *Present Tense*

Verbs in the *present tense* express an action happening at the present moment or an action that occurs repeatedly.

Billie Jean King *returns* the serve.	[present action]
The calf *kicks* and *bellows.*	[present action]
The sun *rises* in the east.	[habitual action]
My pet tortoise *eats* tomatoes and lettuce.	[habitual action]

Progressive verb forms are discussed on page 406.

The *present progressive* form of the verb also shows action happening in the present or action occurring repeatedly.

The ice *is melting* in the lemonade.	[present action]
We *are saving* our money to buy a houseboat.	[habitual action]

2. *Past Tense*

Verbs in the *past tense* express action or a state of being that occurred in the past.

Marcie *studied* for the math test.	[past action]
The old cat *dozed* in the afternoon sunlight.	[past action]
Karen *was* upset about the party.	[past state of being]
We *were* champions for two years in a row.	[past state of being]

The *past progressive* form of the verb expresses an action in the past that was ongoing.

We *were fishing* for crawdads in the lagoon.
My mother *was working* in a law office then.

3. *Future Tense*

The *future tense* is formed with the helping verb *shall* or *will* added to the present form of the verb.

Verbs in the future tense express an action that will occur in the future. Future tense verbs may also give orders or make predictions.

We *will hold* the next meeting three weeks from tonight.	[future action]
You *will study* harder from now on.	[order]
Little green people from space *will* soon *land* on earth.	[prediction]

The *progressive* form of the future tense also describes future action.

Next week we *will be swimming* in the Pacific.
If those dogs keep barking, the neighbors *will be calling* up.

Perfect Tenses

The three perfect tenses are the *present perfect*, the *past perfect*, and the *future perfect*.

4. *Present Perfect Tense*

The *present perfect tense* is formed with *has* or *have* and the past participle of the verb.

Verbs in the present perfect tense may describe an action that began in the past and continued to the present.

Marcia *has had* a cold all week.
We *have wondered* what is wrong with the reception on our television.

The present perfect tense may also be used to describe an action completed at an unspecified time in the past.

Lisa *has seen* every episode of *Star Trek.*
The club members *have collected* over a thousand dollars for the Red Cross.

Like other tenses, the present perfect tense has a progressive form. The progressive form expresses an action begun in the past and continuing into the present.

My Uncle Ebenezer *has been saving* string for forty-eight years.
The girls' tennis team *has been practicing* all week.

5. *Past Perfect Tense*

The *past perfect tense* is formed with the helping verb *had* and the past participle.

Verbs in the past perfect tense describe either an action that was completed before another action was begun or one that was completed before a certain specified time.

Linda called, but you *had left* for work.
We *had finished* our project the day before it was due.

The past perfect tense also has a progressive form. The progressive form of the past perfect tense describes an action that was ongoing in the past.

Leslie *had been mowing* the lawn when the company arrived.

The coach was angry because the players *had been missing* too many free throws.

6. *Future Perfect Tense*

The *future perfect tense* is formed with *will have* or *shall have* and the past participle of a verb.

Verbs in the future perfect tense describe a future action that will be completed before another future action.

In December we *will have completed* work on the house.
My grandparents *will have been married* forty-five years this April.

There is a future perfect progressive form of the verb, but it is used less often than the other progressive forms.

This month Marcie *will have been dating* Tony for five years.

By the time you get this letter, we *will have been fishing* in Minnesota and will have returned home.

Conjugation of the Verb See

To conjugate a verb means "to show its different forms according to voice, mood, tense, number, and person."

In the following conjugation, the verb *see* is conjugated in the active voice, indicative mood. The verb is conjugated in each of the six tenses, singular and plural, as used with first, second, and third person. The progressive form of the verb in each tense is shown in *italics*. Use the conjugation as a study aid as you learn the tenses.

Voice is discussed on pages 504–505, mood on pages 418–420.

Principal Parts

PRESENT	PAST	PAST PARTICIPLE
see	saw	seen

Present Tense

		PROGRESSIVE FORM (present form of *be* + *-ing* form of verb)	
SINGULAR	PLURAL	*SINGULAR*	*PLURAL*
I see	we see	*I am seeing*	*we are seeing*
you see	you see	*you are seeing*	*you are seeing*
he / she / it } sees	they see	*he / she / it } is seeing*	*they are seeing*

Past Tense

		PROGRESSIVE FORM (past form of *be* + *-ing* form of verb)	
SINGULAR	PLURAL	*SINGULAR*	*PLURAL*
I saw	we saw	*I was seeing*	*we were seeing*
you saw	you saw	*you were seeing*	*you were seeing*
he / she / it } saw	they saw	*he / she / it } was seeing*	*they were seeing*

Future Tense

(*will* or *shall* + present form of verb)

		PROGRESSIVE FORM (future form of *be* + *-ing* form of verb)	
SINGULAR	PLURAL	*SINGULAR*	*PLURAL*
I will see	we will see	*I will be seeing*	*we will be seeing*
you will see	you will see	*you will be seeing*	*you will be seeing*
he / she / it } will see	they will see	*he / she / it } will be seeing*	*they will be seeing*

Present Perfect Tense

(*have* or *has* + the past participle)

		PROGRESSIVE FORM (present perfect form of *be* + *-ing* form of verb)	
SINGULAR	PLURAL	*SINGULAR*	*PLURAL*
I have seen	we have seen	*I have been seeing*	*we have been seeing*
you have seen	you have seen	*you have been seeing*	*you have been seeing*
he / she / it } has seen	they have seen	*he / she / it } has been seeing*	*they have been seeing*

Past Perfect Tense

(*had* + past participle)

		PROGRESSIVE FORM (past perfect form of *be* + *-ing* form of verb)	
SINGULAR	PLURAL	*SINGULAR*	*PLURAL*
I had seen	we had seen	*I had been seeing*	*we had been seeing*
you had seen	you had seen	*you had been seeing*	*you had been seeing*
he / she / it } had seen	they had seen	*he / she / it } had been seeing*	*they had been seeing*

Future Perfect Tense

(*will* [or *shall*] *have* + past participle)

		PROGRESSIVE FORM (future perfect form of *be* + *-ing* form of verb)	
SINGULAR	PLURAL	*SINGULAR*	*PLURAL*
I will have seen	we will have seen	*I will have been seeing*	*we will have been seeing*
you will have seen	you will have seen	*you will have been seeing*	*you will have been seeing*
he / she / it } will have seen	they will have seen	*he / she / it } will have been seeing*	*they will have been seeing*

Note: In formal English *shall* is used with the first person in future tenses.

Exercise 2

Write out the following sentences, supplying the verb in the tense indicated in parentheses. Underline the verbs or verb phrases you supply.

Examples

a. My sister ______ to night school for six years and ______ in August. (*go*, present perfect; *graduate*, future) *a. My sister <u>has gone</u> to night school for six years and <u>will graduate</u> in August.*

b. The newspaper office _______ the type for our yearbook, but another company _______ it. (*set*, past perfect; *print*, past)

b. The newspaper office <u>had set</u> the type for our yearbook, but another company <u>printed</u> it.

1. By the time you _______ to New York, we _______ to go home. (*get*, present; *leave*, future perfect)
2. The detectives _______ that the butler _______ the crime. (*believe*, past; *commit*, past perfect)
3. We _______ Ms. Winnetka if she _______ the French Club. (*ask*, present perfect; *sponsor*, future)
4. After we _______ Alaska, we _______ every state in the Union. (*visit*, present perfect; *see*, future perfect)
5. The Olsens _______ a complaint to the company, and the vice president herself _______ to investigate the matter. (*write*, past perfect; *come*, past)
6. In this novel a young writer _______ to a small town in Maine and _______ supernatural happenings. (*come*, present; *discover*, present)
7. The debate team _______ first place in every tournament this year; they _______ only one debate last year. (*win*, present perfect; *lose*, past perfect)
8. My sister _______ in every store in town, and she finally _______ a dress for the dance. (*look*, present perfect; *find*, present perfect)
9. Juliet _______ a sleeping potion, but Romeo _______ that she had poisoned herself. (*take*, past perfect; *believe*, past)
10. The Jackson twins _______ every scholastic award that the school _______ by graduation time. (*win*, future perfect; *give*, present)

Review Exercise A

Write the following sentences, choosing the correct form of the verb from the pair given in parentheses. Underline the verb you supply.

Examples

a. I have (know, known) Clair for six years.

a. I have <u>known</u> Clair for six years.

b. The deflated beach ball slowly (sank, sunk) beneath the waves.

b. The deflated beach ball slowly <u>sank</u> beneath the waves.

1. The kudzu vine (grew, growed) so thickly that it choked out all other vegetation.
2. During the rodeo Sarah Darkmoon has (rode, ridden) the bucking horses as well as any man.

3. The plot of the book took an improbable turn because the heroine had (ate, eaten) a bad hot dog.
4. When Pat drove to Pea Ridge, she (seen, saw) a number of deer and a blue heron standing in a farm pond.
5. The ferret (sprung, sprang) from its hiding place and seized the mouse in its jaws.
6. We have (wrote, written) to our representative about the gun control laws.
7. All the leaves had (fell, fallen) from the old oak tree.
8. Ellen Swallow Richards had (striven, strove) hard to become the first woman to graduate from an American school of science.
9. Booker T. Washington (knew, knowed) the value of education.
10. That abominable laundry (shrank, shrunk) my shirts again!
11. Leah (sang, sung) the solo in the pageant just as her sister had (sang, sung) it four years before her.
12. The bubonic plague that (sweeped, swept) through Europe in the fifth century killed tens of thousands of people.
13. In the Pacific native American soldiers had (spoke, spoken) Navaho during radio transmissions in World War II, thus foiling the enemy.
14. The bad news had visibly (shook, shaken) the family.
15. Arctic terns have been (knowed, known) to have (flew, flown) over 18,000 miles in one round-trip migration.
16. A woolly mammoth in perfect condition was found by scientists; it had been (freezed, frozen) by a freak storm.
17. A gust of wind wrecked the Wright brothers' airplane after they (flew, flown) it only four times.
18. According to reports only seven people have been (struck, striked) by falling meteorites.
19. Explorers were surprised to discover that high winds have (keeped, kept) patches of Antarctica bare of snow.
20. Maria Mitchell had been (teached, taught) astronomy by her father; she (become, became) the first woman to discover a new comet.

Using the Different Moods of Verbs

The word *mood* in grammar refers to the speaker's attitude toward his or her statement—whether the statement is made as fact, as contrary to fact, as a wish, or as a command. In English all verbs are said to be used in one of three moods: the *indicative,* the *imperative,* or the *subjunctive.*

Indicative Mood

Statements in the *indicative mood* are statements that are expressed as facts.

Statements in the indicative mood assert that something happened, is happening, or will happen. Most of the verbs you use in speaking and writing are in the indicative mood.

The banjo *is* an instrument invented in America.
Mr. Jefferson *walks* his St. Bernard every night.
The La Fleshe sisters *advocated* Indian rights.

Imperative Mood

The *imperative mood* is used to express direct commands and requests.

The imperative mood is used when a speaker or writer gives an order or makes a request. Even when the word *please* is used, the verb is still considered to be in the imperative mood.

Get out of Mr. Fudd's carrot patch right now.
Stop making that noise.
Please *do* the dishes.

Most native speakers of English have little trouble using the indicative and imperative moods. The subjunctive mood, however, may be troublesome for speakers and writers, even those who have used English all their lives.

Subjunctive Mood

The *subjunctive mood* is used to express wishes, possibilities, statements contrary to fact, and indirect commands, especially after such words as *insist*, *request*, *recommend*, and *urge*.

When English was a young language, uses of the subjunctive and rules concerning it were clearer. Although the passing of years and the changing of the language have blurred many of the distinctions between the indicative and subjunctive moods, a few of these distinctions still remain.

Most verbs show only one difference in the present tense between the indicative and subjunctive moods. This difference occurs in the forms used with *he*, *she*, *it*, or a singular noun.

Indicative:	he *obeys*	she *goes*	it *stops*	Lisa *sings*
Subjunctive:	he *obey*	she *go*	it *stop*	Lisa *sing*

The third-person subjunctive form is most frequently used in stating commands or requests not addressed directly to a listener or reader.

The teacher insisted that Herb *obey*.
We urged that she *go* with us.
When my mother heard the loud music, she insisted that it *stop*.
Ms. Moffat requested that Lisa *sing* the solo in the Thanksgiving program.

In the present tense of the subjunctive, the verb *be* does not change form.

Indicative:	I *am*	you *are*	she *is*	we *are*	they *are*
Subjunctive:	I *be*	you *be*	he *be*	we *be*	they *be*

The use of *be* for the present tense of the subjunctive mood is usually encountered in only two places: older literature and rather formal statements.

If this *be* treason, make the most of it. —Patrick Henry
If music *be* the food of love, play on. —William Shakespeare

I move that the amendment *be* approved.
I ask that I *be* excused.

In the past tense the only subjunctive verb whose form differs from the indicative form is *be*. The differences occur only with *I*, *he*, *she*, and *it*.

Indicative:	I *was*	*she was*	it *was*
Subjunctive:	I *were*	he *were*	it *were*

This form of the subjunctive is often used to make statements contrary to fact or expressing a wish.

If I *were* President, I would cut taxes. [contrary to fact]
If she *were* here, we could get this meeting started. [contrary to fact]
I wish I *were* at the beach. [wish]
I wish she *were* going with us. [wish]

Exercise 3

Write out the following sentences, supplying the appropriate form of the verb given in parentheses. Underline the verb that you supply.

Examples

a. ________ quiet, or else please leave the theater. (*Be*, imperative)

a. Be quiet, or else please leave the theater.

b. Queen Victoria ________ monarch of England for over fifty years. (*be*, indicative)

b. Queen Victoria was monarch of England for over fifty years.

1. Steve Martin advised his audience: "________ pompous, obese, and eat cactus." (*Be*, imperative)
2. We ________ down at the pond, fishing, when we heard the commotion. (*be*, indicative)
3. If I ________ rich, the first thing I'd buy would be a ticket to Paris. (*be*, subjunctive)
4. We requested that she ________ . (*stay*, subjunctive)
5. Debbie ________ home in the evening to study because she wants a scholarship. (*stay*, indicative)
6. When Mrs. Highwater cleans house, she zooms about as if she ________ a whirling dervish. (*be*, subjunctive)
7. My cousins insisted that my aunt ________ to school to finish her degree. (*return*, subjunctive)
8. A boomerang is a hunting stick that ________ to you if you throw it correctly. (*return*, indicative)
9. The landlord demanded that Inez ________ raising chinchillas in her apartment. (*stop*, subjunctive)

10. The entire bus rattles and shakes every time the vehicle ______. (*stop*, indicative)

Making Verbs Agree with Subjects

A verb must agree with its subject in number.

One feature of verbs is that they have tense. Another is that the verb in a sentence agrees with its subject. Subjects are either singular or plural.

Singular subjects take a singular form of the verb; plural subjects take a plural form.

SINGULAR	PLURAL
Pete leaves.	Pete and Stacey leave.
Cheese contains protein.	Fish and cheese contain protein.
Marcia does the dishes.	Marcia and Lance do the dishes.

In the present tense the singular form of the verb ends in *-s* or *-es*.

The toaster work**s**.

he work**s**, she work**s**
it work**s**
that work**s**, this work**s**

(The verb *be* is an exception to this rule because it has two singular tense forms—*am* and *is*—as well as two past forms—*was* and *were*. See pages 429–430 for a discussion of the special verb *be*.)

Past and future tense verbs use the same form for both singular and plural subjects.

PAST		FUTURE	
I voted you voted he, she, it voted	singular	I will vote you will vote he, she, it will vote	singular
we voted you voted they voted	plural	we will vote you will vote they will vote	plural

Agreement problems occur only when either the main verb or the helping verb of a verb phrase is in the present tense.

SINGULAR	PLURAL
Sharon plays piano.	Sharon and I play piano.
Sharon has studied four years.	Sharon and I have studied four years.
Lila does not jog.	Lila and Malcolm do not jog.

The verb or verb phrase must agree with the true subject of the sentence.

Sometimes, the subject and verb of a sentence may be divided by a group of words. In such a case, special care must be taken to make the verb agree with the true subject of the sentence rather than with some intervening noun or pronoun.

One of the puppies has a patch over its eye.

[*One*, not *puppies*, is the subject of the sentence.]

The box that has the eggs in it has disappeared.

[*Box*, not *eggs*, is the subject of the sentence.]

When word order is inverted, as in questions, be sure to locate the true subject in order to make the verb agree with it in number.

Has the call of whooping cranes ever been recorded?

[*Call*, not *cranes*, is the subject.]

Where does he take his photographs to be developed?

[*He*, not *photographs*, is the subject.]

The subject also follows the verb in sentences beginning with the expletives *here* or *there*.

Here is a recipe for buttered snails.

[*Recipe* is the subject, not *here*.]

There were several old license plates nailed to the walls of the garage.

[*License plates*, not *there*, is the subject.]

There was an exhibit of Zuñi silverwork at the museum.

[*Exhibit*, not *there*, is the subject of the sentence.]

Exercise 4

Write out the following sentences, choosing the verb that agrees with the subject from the pair of verbs given in parentheses. Underline the subject once and the verb or verb phrase twice.

Example

a. The technology of printing presses ______ advanced greatly in recent years. (has, have)

a. The technology of printing presses has advanced greatly in recent years.

1. Only one of the file cabinets ______ saved from the fire. (was, were)
2. Where ______ the San Andreas Fault? (is, are)
3. There ______ several good reasons why you should wear a seat belt while driving. (is, are)
4. That collection of folk songs ______ recorded by Odetta. (was, were)

5. There _______ some people known as the Dogon tribe who have a surprising knowledge of modern astronomy. (is, are)
6. The stories written by Rudyard Kipling about India _______ a special place in my mother's library. (has, have)
7. Several types of exotic food _______ available at the new restaurant. (is, are)
8. Where _______ frogs, toads, and salamanders go in the winter? (do, does)
9. The books of Maya Angelou _______ exceptionally well-written. (is, are)
10. The presence of sharks _______ only one of the many reasons why I don't like swimming in the ocean. (is, are)

Subject-Verb Agreement with Indefinite Pronouns

A group of words known as the *indefinite pronouns* may cause speakers and writers some difficulty in subject-verb agreement.

The following indefinite pronouns are always singular and take the singular form of the verb.

anybody	everybody	no one
anyone	everyone	one
each	neither	somebody
either	nobody	someone

Anybody who needs a library pass can get one from Miss Garcia.

Each of the twins has her own distinct set of likes and dislikes.

Somebody among the students is clicking a ballpoint pen.

Five indefinite pronouns are always plural and take the plural form of the verb.

both	many	several
few	others	

Several of my ancestors are Choctaw Indians.

Few of the old Model T Fords are left.

Many are called, but few are chosen.

The last five indefinite pronouns may be either singular or plural, depending on how they are used in a sentence.

all	most	some
any	none	

This is the *only* situation in which a group of words coming between a subject and verb may help determine the correct form of the verb. When these indefinite pronouns refer to a singular noun, they take the singular form of the verb.

All of the meatloaf has been eaten.
[*All* refers to the noun *meatloaf*, which is singular.]

Most of the flood damage was minor.
[*Most* refers to the noun *damage*, which is singular.]

None of the milk is left.
[*None* refers to the noun *milk*, which is singular.]

When these five indefinite pronouns refer to a plural noun, they take the plural form of the verb.

All of the aces were gone from the deck.
[*All* refers to the noun *aces*, which is plural.]

Most of the tomato plants were ruined by the hail.
[*Most* refers to the noun *tomato plants*, which is plural.]

None of the people named Jones were related to one another.
[*None* refers to the noun *people*, which is plural.]

Exercise 5

Write out each of the following sentences, choosing the correct form of the verb from the pair given in parentheses. Underline the subject once and the verb or verb phrase in each sentence twice.

Examples

a. Neither of the girls (was, were) able to come to the party.
a. Neither of the girls was able to come to the party.

b. Most of the book (move, moves) quickly, but the ending (seem, seems) a bit slow.
b. Most of the book moves quickly, but the ending seems a bit slow.

1. Either of those parking places (is, are) all right for you to use during the weekend.
2. Some of the students (was, were) taking the advanced test.
3. Both my sister and my cousin Coretta (is, are) going to the art museum on Saturdays for drawing lessons.
4. Each of the suspects (was, were) capable of the crime, and each of them had an excellent motive.
5. Someone in those lines of marching players (is, are) quite out of tune with the rest of the band.
6. Looking for a midnight snack, I discovered all the milk (was, were) gone, and most of the bagels (was, were) eaten.
7. Any of the ponds (seems, seem) good for fishing around here, but most of the river (yield, yields) few catches at this time of year.
8. Nobody among the students in the classes (know, knows) the answer to that problem.

9. None of the critics (like, likes) the movie, but all of the public (enjoy, enjoys) it nevertheless.
10. Both of the farms (cost, costs) a great deal, but one of them (seem, seems) an excellent buy.

Subject-Verb Agreement with Compound Subjects

Two or more subjects joined by the word *and* always take the plural form of the verb.

Clea and Erin are the outstanding students in science.

The sleet and snow make the roads hazardous tonight.

Mrs. Washington and Miss Garcia were both officers in the League of Women Voters.

Roses and raspberries are members of the same plant family.

Jackals and wolves are the ancestors of the modern dog.

When two or more singular subjects are joined by the words *or* or *nor*, the singular form of the verb is used.

Either Clea or Erin is the lab assistant.

Sleet or snow makes the mountain pass dangerous.

Neither Mrs. Washington nor Miss Garcia was in charge.

When two or more plural subjects are joined by *or* or *nor*, the plural form of the verb is used.

Lizards or turtles are good pets for apartment dwellers.

Either bees or wasps seem to be living in the old barn.

Neither trains nor planes have as many accidents as automobiles do.

When one part of a compound subject is plural and one part is singular, and the subjects are joined by *or* or *nor*, the verb agrees with the subject closest to it.

Either cheese or nuts are a good source of protein.

Either nuts or cheese is a good source of protein.

Neither I nor my brother likes rhubarb.

Neither my brother nor I like rhubarb.

Either you or Sharon still has the car keys.

Either Sharon or you still have the car keys.

Exercise 6

Each of the following sentences contains a compound subject. Write out the sentences and choose the correct verb from the pair given in parentheses. Then underline the subject once and the complete verb or verb phrase twice.

Examples

a. Both the monkeys and the parrot (screech, screeches) when the door to the pet shop is opened.

a. Both the monkeys and the parrot screech when the door to the pet shop is opened.

b. Neither Cindy nor her sisters (attend, attends) public schools.

b. Neither Cindy nor her sisters attend public schools.

1. The chickens and the rooster (is, are) huddled on their perches in the dark henhouse.
2. Neither the shamrock plant nor the ferns (need, needs) much sunlight.
3. Either the students or the teacher (was, were) confused about what the assignment had been.
4. Tusks, warts, and bristly hair (distinguish, distinguishes) the wild swine called the wart hog.
5. Either the Ling sisters or Gary (is, are) going to design the stage set.
6. Mrs. Hubbard and her daughters (was, were) horrified to discover that four baby skunks had taken up residence under their porch.
7. The moon and planets (shine, shines) with light reflected from the sun.
8. Neither my parents nor I (am, are) happy about our upcoming move.
9. Either the camera's shutter or batteries (is, are) not working properly.
10. Neither my brothers, my sisters, I, nor the family dog (like, likes) the woodchuck casserole Uncle Rufus made.

Some Common Problems in Subject-Verb Agreement

Collective Nouns

Words such as *committee, team, crowd, class, audience,* and *group* are called *collective nouns* because they name a collection, or group, of persons or things. Collective nouns may be either singular or plural in meaning.

When a collective noun is used to describe a unit acting together, the noun has a singular meaning and takes the singular form of the verb.

The band practices on the football field every morning.

The jury agrees unanimously.

When the collective noun refers to the individual members of the group, the plural form of the verb is used.

The band were wearing plumed hats and white boots.

The jury disagree among themselves and with the judge.

Singular Nouns with Apparently Plural Forms

Use the singular form of the verb for nouns that are singular in meaning even though their form appears to be plural.

athletics	genetics	news
civics	mathematics	physics
economics	measles	politics

No news is good news.

Nouns that have only plural forms take only plural verbs. Some nouns have no singular forms:

jeans	pants	slacks	tweezers
pliers	scissors	trousers	

The pliers were old and rusty and badly in need of oil.

If the word *pair* precedes one of these nouns, however, use the singular form of the verb.

The pair of pliers is missing.

This pair of jeans has seen better days.

Titles and Names of Countries

Use the singular form of the verb for titles of works of art or for the names of countries.

Bolts of Melody is a collection of poems by Emily Dickinson.

The Union of Soviet Socialist Republics contains the vast area known as Siberia.

Amounts

Use a singular form of the verb for words and phrases that express time and amounts (money, fractions, weight, volume).

Two quarts is approximately the same as two liters.

Three-quarters is equal to 75 per cent.

When such amounts are thought of individually and not as a unit, the plural form of the verb may be used.

The last three days have been long and dreary because of the rain.

Eleven dollars were hidden between the pages of the book.

Predicate Nominatives

When the subject and the predicate nominative are different in number, use a verb that agrees in number with the subject.

Leon's most prized treasure is his rare coins.

[*Coins* is the predicate nominative.]

Maintenance and repairs are the duty of the janitor.

[*Duty* is the predicate nominative.]

Every and *Many a*

Use the singular form of the verb when the words *every* or *many a* precede the subject.

Every student knows about prefinal jitters.

Many a person has suffered the pangs of love.

Every nook and cranny was investigated.

Doesn't and *Don't*

Use *doesn't* with singular nouns and third-person singular pronouns. Use *don't* with plural nouns and pronouns and with the pronouns *I* and *you*.

the cat he she it this that	doesn't	the cats I you we they these those	don't

Exercise 7

Write out the following sentences, choosing the form of the verb that agrees with the subject. Underline the subject once and the verb you have chosen twice.

Examples

a. Our girls' basketball team (was, were) the state champion last year.

a. Our girls' basketball team was the state champion last year.

b. The United States (has, have) serious energy problems that need solving.

b. The United States has serious energy problems that need solving.

1. Physics (offers, offer) the scientist many paradoxes.
2. The soccer team (has, have) a chance for the district tournament.
3. The majority of taxpayers (want, wants) lower taxes and simpler tax forms.
4. One-eighth (is, are) the equivalent of twelve and a half percent.
5. Many a mountaineer (has faced, have faced) the challenge of Everest, and every climber and guide (has faced, have faced) hardships on its cold steeps.
6. I (don't, doesn't) want to go; you (don't, doesn't) want to go; she (don't, doesn't) want to go; so it (don't, doesn't) seem we ought to go.
7. The audience always (listen, listens) appreciatively when the choir (sing, sings).
8. The scissors (is, are) lost; the pliers (is, are) misplaced; and the only pair of tweezers (have, has) disappeared.

9. *The Frogs* (is, are) a play by Aristophanes; *Seven Against Thebes* (is, are) a play by Aeschylus.
10. Three hours (is, are) the usual time it takes to fly to Chicago from here, but four hours (is, are) not unusual if there is fog or turbulence.

Using the Verb *Be*

Be is the most irregular verb in English. It has three present tense forms and two past tense forms. Since *be* is also the most commonly used verb, it is important that you learn to use it in accordance with Edited Standard English (ESE).

PRESENT TENSE

SINGULAR	PLURAL
I am	we are
you are	you are
he/she/it is	they are

Notice that the word *be* itself is not listed as a present tense form. Although it is used in some spoken dialects, it is not used in Edited Standard English.

An asterisk (*) indicates a sentence with a feature that is not part of ESE.

*I be sorry to hear that.
I *am* sorry to hear that.

*You be right about that problem.
You *are* right about that problem.

*She be asleep right now.
She *is* asleep right now.

PAST TENSE

SINGULAR	PLURAL
I was	we were
you were	you were
he/she/it was	they were

Avoid using *was* with the pronouns *you, we,* and *they,* or with plural nouns.

*You was a member of the rifle team, wasn't you?
You *were* a member of the rifle team, *weren't* you?

*We was in a hurry when we left.
We *were* in a hurry when we left.

*They was anxious to start the game.
They *were* anxious to start the game.

*Weevils was in the cotton.
Weevils *were* in the cotton.

The past participle of *be* is *been*, which is used with a helping verb in Edited Standard English.

> *I been sick.
> I *have been* sick. [or] I'*ve been* sick.

Exercise 8

Rewrite the following sentences, choosing the form of the verb in parentheses that is used in Edited Standard English. Underline the verb you select.

Examples

a. You (been, have been) rather cool toward Cheryl lately.
a. You have been rather cool toward Cheryl lately.

b. The Platters and The Supremes (was, were) two popular recording groups.
b. The Platters and The Supremes were two popular recording groups.

1. Someone (been, has been) telephoning for you all afternoon.
2. The Sioux, Cheyenne, and Pawnee (was, were) all tribes of the Great Plains.
3. "The Great Bear" (be, is) another name for the constellation usually called "The Big Dipper."
4. We (was, were) late, but you (was, were), too.
5. Arturo (been, has been) to California several times and says his trips (was, were) all pleasant.
6. I (be, am) sleepy today because all last night two cats (was, were) yowling beneath my window.
7. You (is, are) sure that they (was, were) invited, aren't you?
8. (Wasn't, Weren't) the Yankees the winners of the Series in 1978, and (wasn't, weren't) there some dissension on the team?
9. The cars (was, were) bigger in the 1950s because the gasoline prices (wasn't, weren't) so high.
10. The McCoys (be, are) our neighbors, and the Hatfields (was, were) our neighbors before.

Verbs That Are Frequently Confused

Three pairs of verbs are frequently confused because they sound alike and have similar meanings. These verbs, however, are not interchangeable. To write Edited Standard English, you need to know the principal parts of these verbs and the differences in their meanings.

lie/lay

Lie and *lay* are probably the most confusing pair of verbs because they not only have similar meanings, but also share a common form.

PRESENT	PAST	PAST PARTICIPLE
lie	lay	(had) lain
lay	laid	(had) laid

Notice that the word *lay* is the present of the verb *lay*, but is also the past form of the verb *lie.*

Lay means "to put something down" or "to place something."
Lie means "to recline" or "to be in a horizontal position."

When you use the verb *lay*, tell what object is being put down or placed.

Hens *lay* eggs.
Masons *lay* bricks.
Each night we *lay* out our clothes for the next morning.

If you are confused about whether to use a form of *lay* or *lie* in a sentence, decide precisely what you are trying to say. If you can substitute the word *put* in the sentence, use the verb *lay.*

Lay: Marcia *laid* (put) her books on the table.
Darrin *had laid* (had put) out the cards for a game of solitaire.

Lie: The cow *lay* in the deep meadow grass chewing her cud.
The dollar bill *had lain* near the sidewalk all day.

sit/set

In some dialects the word *set* means "sit down." In Edited Standard English, however, *sit* and *set* have distinctly different meanings.

Sit means "to occupy a seat" or "to rest."
Set means "to put down or place something."

When you use *set* in a sentence, tell what object is being placed or put somewhere.

The principal parts of *sit* and *set* are not difficult to memorize.

PRESENT	PAST	PAST PARTICIPLE
sit	sat	(had) sat
set	set	(had) set

Sit: The houses *sit* on a crest overlooking the river.
The cockatoo *sat* on its perch.

Set: Dawn *set* down her packages.
I thought I *had set* my book on the hall table.

rise/raise

Rise means "to go up" or "to get up."
Raise means "to move something upward."

The principal parts of *rise* are irregular, but the principal parts of *raise* are regular.

PRESENT	PAST	PAST PARTICIPLE
rise	rose	(had) risen
raise	raised	(had) raised

Rise: The audience *rose* to its feet, cheering.
Farmers *rise* early in the morning to begin their chores.

Raise: The scout troop *raised* the flag at the Memorial Day ceremony.
The cobra *had raised* its body and begun to sway.

Exercise 9

Choose the correct verb in parentheses to complete each of the following sentences. Write out the sentences and underline the verb that you supply.

For more practice in using these verbs, see exercises 10–12 on pages 484–485.

Examples

a. Ginger (lay, laid) out in the sun on her beach towel.
a. Ginger lay out in the sun on her beach towel.

b. Ira Hayes was one of the men who (rose, raised) the flag on Iwo Jima.
b. Ira Hayes was one of the men who raised the flag on Iwo Jima.

1. Alex didn't feel well, so he (lay, laid) down.
2. A huge copper-colored harvest moon (rose, raised) in the sky.
3. Marcia (had set, had sat) the basket too near the edge of the table.
4. Please (sit, set) down and fill out these forms.
5. My Aunt Consuela (had risen, had raised) early for the trip.
6. Doris couldn't remember where she (had lain, had laid) her glasses.
7. For centuries the pirate treasure (had lain, had laid) beneath the sea.
8. The smoke from the signal fire (rose, raised) high above the trees.
9. We (have sat, have set) in this bus so long it seems like forever.
10. The setter (lay, laid) down the pheasant, then (lay, laid) by its master's feet.

Review Exercise B

Write out the following sentences, choosing the form of the verb in parentheses that agrees with the subject. Underline the word you have chosen.

Examples

a. Sheila (don't, doesn't) like to play outfield.
a. Sheila doesn't like to play outfield.

b. Eleven days (is, are) slightly less than 1 million seconds.
b. Eleven days is slightly less than 1 million seconds.

1. The elephant (don't, doesn't) fear mice as the stories say.
2. Fifty-two cards (is, are) the number in an ordinary deck.
3. Both Phillis Wheatley and Anne Bradstreet (was, were) early American poets.
4. A carton containing boxes of seeds (was, were) left at the post office.
5. All of the breads (was, were) baked too long.
6. None of the flood water (has reached, have reached) our area yet.
7. Neither Rosa nor Kim (have seen, has seen) the final test scores yet.
8. A swarm of locusts (was, were) one of the Biblical plagues.
9. Everybody in all of the city's volunteer groups (was, were) eager to help.
10. Either the pliers or the tweezers (is, are) necessary for this job.
11. A pair of scissors (is, are) in the desk drawer.
12. Neither Shana nor her sisters (like, likes) sharing a room.
13. Either Miss Wallabee, Mr. Diaz, or the Johnson twins (is, are) going to be in charge of selling tickets.
14. Only a few of the team (was, were) graduating that spring.
15. As the gates are opened, the crowd (surge, surges) forward.
16. None of the lost treasure (has, have) ever been located.
17. None of the lost diamonds (has, have) ever been located.
18. After their boat tipped over, Nancy's jeans (was, were) wringing wet, and Pat's pair of shorts (was, were) ruined.
19. Either mayonnaise or yogurt (is, are) necessary for this recipe.
20. Economics (is, are) a complex science, and so (is, are) physics.
21. *Little Women* (is, are) a novel by Louisa M. Alcott.
22. We (did, done) what we could for the wounded eagle; then a team of veterinarians (was, were) called in.
23. Neither the United States nor the Netherlands (is, are) in support of the new treaty.
24. Saving and budgeting money (is, are) my biggest problem.
25. Fifty thousand dollars (is, are) a great deal to pay for a painting, but Mary Cassatt's *Woman with a Dog* (is, are) certainly worth it.

Writing with Verbs

In an article in *Writer's Digest*, written by Bill Kirtz, the historian Barbara Tuchman describes the effect that well chosen verbs can have on a piece of writing: "I hate sentences that begin, 'There was a storm!' Instead, write, 'A storm burst!' " As an example of Barbara Tuchman's skill in using action verbs, Bill Kirtz cites the following lines from her book about World War I, *The Guns of August:*

> The slaughter at Morhange snuffed out the bright flame of the doctrine of the offensive. It died on a field in Lorraine where at the end of the day nothing was visible but corpses strewn in rows and sprawled in the awkward attitudes of sudden death as if the place had been swept by a malignant hurricane.[1]

Barbara Tuchman brings a distant event into clear focus by using precise, vivid verbs: a doctrine is "snuffed out" and dies. Bodies are strewn and sprawled. The place seems as if it "had been swept by a malignant hurricane."

Limp, vague verbs result in limp, vague writing:

There *was* the sound of thunder.	[vague]
Thunder *mumbled* and *rumbled.*	[stronger]
The dog *came* down the street.	[vague]
The dog *bounded* down the street.	[stronger]
Leslie *looked* displeased.	[vague]
Leslie *frowned* and *wrinkled* her nose in distaste.	[stronger]
The humidity *seemed* oppressive to us.	[vague]
The humidity *pressed* us down and *drained* our energy.	[stronger]

Writing Exercise A

The following sentences are dull because they employ lifeless, vague verbs. Rewrite the sentences, replacing *italicized* verbs with more precise and vivid ones. You may change other words in the sentence besides the verbs and add other details as well.

Examples

a. The cars on the street *were* noisy.
a. The cars chugged, wheezed, honked, rattled, and shook the pavement as they lumbered down the street.

b. There *were* garbage stains in the sink.
b. Garbage stains mottled and streaked the sink.

1. The guests at the party *were* loud.
2. There *was* an explosion at the plant.
3. After the bell the students *were* in the halls.
4. The bird *made* a sound, then *flew* away.
5. The man *looked* frightened.
6. The fire *began* to burn.
7. There *was* movement in the trees caused by the storm.
8. The drum major *came* down the street.
9. The dogs *were* asleep in the sun.
10. The woman *seemed* very excited.

---

[1]From *The Guns of August* by Barbara W. Tuchman. Copyright © 1962 by Barbara Tuchman. Reprinted by permission of Macmillan Publishing Co., Inc. and Russell & Volkening as agents for the author.

Writing Exercise B

Choose one of the following assignments and write several well developed paragraphs. Check your first draft to make sure that you have used the verb forms correctly and that you have chosen exact and vivid verbs to make your paper readable and effective.

1. Imagine that you have a pen pal in a distant country and that he or she has never seen many things that Americans take for granted. Describe, so that your reader will understand and be able to picture, one of the following processes:

   Going to a drive-in restaurant and ordering a meal
   Going to an automatic car wash
   Taking a subway ride
   Riding a roller coaster
   Shopping in a supermarket
   Attending a dance
   Beginning the day in a typical American high school

2. Write a description of what you think the United States will be like one hundred years from now. What will be changed and how? Will some things remain unchanged? What will be the greatest advances that have been made? What will be the biggest problems?

3. Describe the physical sensations you experience during some grueling or demanding activity, such as finishing a race, participating in an active game, or walking home through intense heat or cold. Choose verbs that will make your reader feel the same sensations you experienced.

4. Using precise, vivid verbs, describe the scene in the photograph on page 436. Your purpose is to re-create the setting for the readers.

Understanding Adjectives

Adjectives allow writers to describe colors, tastes, shapes, sizes, and a multitude of other qualities; they can add important details to a sentence.

> The man with the mustache wore a suit and vest.
>
> The *large* man with the *handlebar* mustache wore a *checkered* suit and a *shabby* vest.

The adjectives in the second sentence supply details that make the description clearer and easier to picture.

In this section you will learn how to identify adjectives through their definition, the classes into which they can be grouped, and the features that distinguish them from other parts of speech.

Defining an Adjective

An *adjective* is usually defined as a word used to modify a noun or pronoun.

Adjectives limit or qualify nouns or pronouns by telling *what kind*, *which one*, *how many*, or *how much*.

What Kind:	an *old* car, a *brick* building, a *heavy* package, a *red* rose
Which One:	*this* street, *that* boat, *these* plants, *those* books
How Many:	*three* cats, *ninety* years, *many* insects, *few* dollars
How Much:	*little* time, *more* intelligence, *less* gasoline

Exercise 1

Write out the following sentences, underlining the adjectives. (*A*, *an*, and *the* are always adjectives.) Do not count the possessive pronouns, such as *mine*, *our*, *his*, as adjectives; they are considered pronouns.

Examples

a. The hottest temperature on record occurred in the African country of Libya.

a. The hottest temperature on record occurred in the African country of Libya.

b. An ear of corn has an even number of rows due to its genetic formula.

b. *An ear of corn has an even number of rows due to its genetic formula.*

1. During the American Revolution many brides wore red gowns as a symbol of political rebellion.
2. The first nation to give women the right to vote was New Zealand, a member of the British Empire.
3. A French astronomer suggested the existence of black holes two centuries ago.
4. Handsome Dan is a bulldog, the famous canine mascot of Yale.
5. The first Congressional Medals of Honor were given to Union soldiers who hijacked a Confederate locomotive.
6. A memorial statue was erected to Balto, the lead dog of a team of huskies that braved a savage blizzard to deliver serum to fight a deadly epidemic among Alaskan Eskimos.
7. In the nineteenth century few people realized that a shy, reclusive woman, Emily Dickinson, would become a famous poet.
8. Pamela, a poor but virtuous servant, was the heroine of the first English novel, a great popular success.
9. "Blooper" is the name of a gold statuette presented to broadcasters that make the best—or worst—mistakes on the air.
10. The seven wonders of the ancient world included the Egyptian pyramids and the gigantic statue known as the Colossus of Rhodes.

Classifying Adjectives

Although many common adjectives (such as *hot, cold, happy, sad*) belong to no special class, others can be classified as articles, proper adjectives, predicate adjectives, pronouns used as adjectives, and nouns used as adjectives.

Articles

The most common adjectives are the articles *a*, *an*, and *the*.

A and *an* are called *indefinite articles* because they do not point out a definite person, place, or thing. *The* is called a *definite article* because it points out a specific person, place, or thing.

Indefinite Article:	We'll have to take *a* bus.
Definite Article:	Here comes *the* bus.
Indefinite Article:	*An* aardwolf is not really a wolf.
Definite Article:	*The* aardwolf at the zoo is named Aaron.

A is used before words that begin with a consonant sound; *an* is used before words that begin with a vowel sound.

a busy schedule	*an* impossible task
a rugby team	*an* airline attendant
a history exam	*an* honest answer

Proper Adjectives

Adjectives formed from proper nouns are called *proper adjectives.*

A proper adjective begins with a capital letter.

Mexican artists	**C**hinese checkers
Ethiopian history	**G**uatemalan Indians
Korean restaurant	**S**outh **A**frican novelist

Predicate Adjectives

Adjectives usually precede the nouns they modify.

Sasha is an *extraordinary* and *beautiful* animal.

Some adjectives, however, are separated from the word they modify. An adjective that follows a linking verb and modifies the subject of the sentence is called a *predicate adjective.*

The table was *dusty.*

The hiking boots were too *tight.*

The cat seemed *nervous.*

Pronouns as Adjectives

Some words may function as either pronouns or adjectives, depending on how they are used in a sentence. The following words are adjectives when they modify a noun or pronoun. When they stand alone, however, they are considered pronouns.

all	few	one	this
another	many	other	those
any	more	several	what
both	most	some	which
each	much	that	
either	neither	these	

Pronoun: *Which* was correct?
Adjective: *Which* one was correct?
Pronoun: A *few* of the boats were damaged by the storm.
Adjective: A *few* boats were damaged by the storm.
Pronoun: Tomorrow we'll pick *more* of the raspberries.
Adjective: Tomorrow we'll pick *more* raspberries.

Nouns Used as Adjectives

A noun that modifies another noun is considered an adjective. Nouns used as adjectives always come directly before the nouns they modify.

I hate hoeing the *vegetable* garden.

Did you see the *hockey* game last *Friday* night?

There are some *news* magazines on the top *closet* shelf.

Nouns used as adjectives can be easily confused with compound nouns that are written as two separate words. In the phrase *closet shelf*, for example, *closet* (a noun) modifies *shelf*: closet shelf. *Closet drama*, however, is a compound noun meaning "a play written mainly to be read, not staged." If you are uncertain about the classification of a word, consult a dictionary where you will find compound nouns listed as separate entries.

Exercise 2

On a sheet of paper, write out the following sentences, underlining the adjectives. Beneath each sentence identify the class to which each adjective belongs. You will also find adjectives that belong to none of these classes. (Do not count possessive pronouns as adjectives.)

Example

a. Charles Fort was a newspaper reporter who liked to collect accounts of strange events that science could not explain.

a. Charles Fort was a newspaper reporter who liked to collect accounts of strange events that science could not explain.
a—article; newspaper—noun used as adjective; strange—adjective

1. Fort's relentless research and his wry wit attracted a number of followers.
2. Many Fortean Societies now exist, and events that science cannot explain are called "Fortean phenomena."
3. Such phenomena are numerous; some are comic, but others seem spooky and sinister.
4. Examples include such bizarre events as falls of red, blue, and black rains; Roman coins found in American Indian mounds; and sworn testimonies that large numbers of fully grown frogs have fallen out of an empty sky.
5. Some of Fort's theories were wild; he suggested, for instance, that certain animals were capable of traveling by mind power alone and crossing vast spaces in short periods of time.
6. This theory seemed sensible to Fort because it explained apparently unexplainable facts such as crocodiles that appeared suddenly in English gardens and the mysterious presence of swarms of adult African snails in Ceylon.
7. Many of Fort's findings read like science fiction; but his work, he claimed, was factual.
8. Some theories he proposed were fantastic, and a few were most certainly jokes, for Fort was a humorous man; nevertheless, he was serious about his main theory: modern science tends to ignore unexplainable phenomena.

9. Fort has been dead for fifty years now, but a large and strong American Fortean Society still exists and still investigates those unexplained events that Fort loved to fling in the face of science.
10. The society publishes a news and opinion magazine and collects data on such matters as sea serpents, the abominable snowman, flying saucer reports, and animal oddities.

Finding an Adjective by Its Features

Adjectives can be identified by certain features that distinguish them from other parts of speech.

1. Adjectives may change form to show degrees of comparison.

There are three degrees: *positive*, *comparative*, and *superlative*. The *positive degree* describes a quality or characteristic; it is the "plain form" of the adjective. The *comparative degree* is used to compare two persons or things. The *superlative degree* is used to compare three or more persons or things.

Positive:	Lisa is *tall.*
Comparative:	Lisa is *taller* than Sharon.
Superlative:	Lisa is the *tallest* member of the basketball team.
Positive:	This novel is *suspenseful.*
Comparative:	This novel is *more suspenseful* than the last one I read.
Superlative:	This novel is the *most suspenseful* that I've ever read.

The comparative and superlative forms of adjectives are formed in two different ways.

Most adjectives of one syllable, and a few adjectives of two syllables, add *-er* to form the comparative degree and *-est* to form the superlative degree.

POSITIVE	COMPARATIVE	SUPERLATIVE
large	larger	largest
hot	hotter	hottest
kind	kinder	kindest
heavy	heavier	heaviest

Many adjectives of two syllables, and all adjectives of more than two syllables, form the comparative degree with the word *more* and the superlative with the word *most.*

POSITIVE	COMPARATIVE	SUPERLATIVE
bashful	more bashful	most bashful
essential	more essential	most essential
abundant	more abundant	most abundant

The words *less* and *least* are used before all adjectives to indicate less or least of a quality.

POSITIVE	COMPARATIVE	SUPERLATIVE
high	less high	least high
necessary	less necessary	least necessary

A few common adjectives form their comparative and superlative degrees irregularly. (See page 444.)

2. Adjectives may follow intensifiers.

Words like *extremely*, *quite*, *rather*, and *very* are called intensifiers. (See page 450.) They qualify the word that follows by telling "to what extent."

The job was *very* demanding.

The play was *quite* good.

The music was *rather* loud.

3. Adjectives may be formed with suffixes.

Certain suffixes, such as *-able*, *-en*, *-ful*, *-ish*, *-less*, *-like*, and *-ous*, are used to form adjectives. These suffixes signal that the word is an adjective.

dutiful	wooden	selfish
capable	industrious	penniless
lifelike	usable	mysterious

Exercise 3

Use your knowledge of adjectives to identify all the adjectives in the following passage from the short story "The New Dress" by Virginia Woolf. (Remember to count the articles *the*, *a*, and *an*.) Write at least twenty-five adjectives on a sheet of paper in the order in which they appear.[1]

> "I feel like some dowdy, decrepit, horribly dingy old fly," she said, making Robert Haydon stop just to hear her say that, just to reassure herself by furbishing up a poor, weak-kneed phrase and so showing how detached she was, how witty, that she did not feel in the least out of anything. And, of course, Robert Haydon answered something quite polite, quite insincere, which she saw through instantly, and said to herself, directly he went (again from some book), "Lies, lies, lies!" For a party makes things either much more real or much less real, she thought; she saw in a flash to the bottom of Robert Haydon's heart; she saw through everything. She saw the truth. This was true, this drawing room, this self, and the other false. Miss Milan's little workroom was really terribly hot, stuffy, sordid. It smelled of clothes and cabbage cooking; and yet, when Miss Milan put the glass in her hand, and she looked at herself with the dress on, finished, an extraordinary bliss shot through her heart.

Mastery Exercise A

Write out the following paragraphs from a condensed version of *Broca's Brain* by Carl Sagan and underline at least forty-five adjectives. To determine

---

[1]From "The New Dress" in *A Haunted House and Other Stories* by Virginia Woolf. Reprinted by permission of Harcourt Brace Jovanovich, Inc., the Literary Estate of Virginia Woolf and The Hogarth Press Ltd.

if a word is an adjective, ask yourself whether it modifies a noun or a pronoun or whether it has any of the features of adjectives. Be sure to classify as adjectives any nouns or pronouns that modify nouns. In this selection Carl Sagan discusses the popular interest in unexplained phenomena such as the Bermuda Triangle, UFO's, and ancient astronauts.[1]

> The extraordinary should certainly be pursued; but extraordinary claims require extraordinary evidence—the burden of proof should fall squarely on those who make the proposals. In the meantime, the best antidote for pseudoscience lies, I believe, in the documented wonders of science itself:
>
> —There is an African freshwater fish that is nearly blind. It generates an electric field that enables it to distinguish between predators and prey and communicates in a fairly elaborate electric language with other fish of the same species. This involves an organ system and sensory capability unknown to pretechnological human beings.
>
> —Pigeons are now found to have a remarkable sensitivity to magnetism, evidently using this sensory capability for navigation and to sense their surroundings—a sensory modality never glimpsed by any human.
>
> —Quasars seem to be violent galactic explosions that destroy millions of worlds, many of them perhaps inhabited. . . .
>
> Such a list could be continued almost indefinitely. I believe that this smattering of findings in modern science is far more compelling and exciting than most of the doctrines of pseudoscience. Science is more intricate and subtle, reveals a much richer universe and powerfully evokes our sense of wonder. And it has the additional and important virtue of being true.

Mastery Exercise B

For this assignment select two or three advertisements from your local newspapers or from magazines. Clip out the ads and tape them to a sheet of paper. Then beneath the ad list the adjectives used to describe the product or service. Finally, look at your lists of adjectives and decide why those particular ones were selected for that audience. For example, if the ad is for nail polish, do the words give the ad a different tone from that of a coin advertisement? To what audience is each ad directed? In what way are the adjectives suitable for that audience?

Using Adjectives

In this section you will practice using both regular and irregular forms of comparative and superlative adjectives. You will also practice writing with adjectives that provide exact descriptions and evoke sensory details.

---

[1]Excerpt from "Astral Projection and the Horse Could Count" by Carl Sagan condensed in *Reader's Digest*, July 1979 from *Broca's Brain*. Copyright © 1979 by Carl Sagan. Reprinted by permission of Random House, Inc. and The Reader's Digest.

Using Comparative and Superlative Degrees

When comparing only two things, use the comparative degree.

The kodiak bear is *larger* than the black bear.
This bicycle is *more expensive* than that one.

When comparing three or more things, use the superlative degree.

The kodiak bear is the *largest* of all bears.
This bicycle is the *most expensive* one in the shop.

Use the words *other* or *else* when comparing a person or thing with the rest of a group to which it belongs.

An asterisk (*) indicates a sentence with a feature that is not a part of Edited Standard English (ESE).

*Jupiter is larger than any planet in our solar system.
Jupiter is larger than any *other* planet in our solar system.

*Chrissy is a better athlete than anyone in her school.
Chrissy is a better athlete than anyone *else* in her school.

Avoid double comparisons in Edited Standard English. Do not use the *-er* or *-est* suffix with the words *more* or *most.*

*I bought the most ugliest mask in the store.
I bought the *ugliest* mask in the store.

*Lon is feeling more better today.
Lon is feeling *better* today.

Exercise 1

In some of the following sentences, adjectives are used in ways that do not conform to Edited Standard English. If a sentence has a feature that is not part of ESE, rewrite it so that it conforms to ESE. If a sentence is already in ESE, write *ESE* next to that number on your paper.

Examples

a. Which of these four brands is more economical?
a. Which of these four brands is most economical?

b. That reporter talks faster than anyone else on television.
b. ESE

1. Mo is a more smarter dog than Sophie.
2. Rhode Island is smaller than any state in the Union.
3. The cobra is one of the most deadliest snakes in the world.
4. We decided to sell the oldest of the two cars.
5. The house was more larger than we had expected.
6. Ross' poem was judged the best of the one hundred entries.
7. It is hard to say which of the three Brontë sisters was more remarkable.
8. Chico is the twin who is most outgoing.

9. Lucille Ball had a longer career than any comedienne on television.
10. Of all sports which is most safest?

Using Irregular Adjectives

Most adjectives form their comparative and superlative degrees either with the suffixes *-er* and *-est* or with the words *more* and *most.* A few common adjectives, however, have irregular comparative and superlative forms. To write Edited Standard English, you must memorize these forms.

POSITIVE	COMPARATIVE	SUPERLATIVE
bad	worse	worst
good	better	best
ill	worse	worst
little	less *or* lesser	least
many	more	most
much	more	most
well	better	best

I have *little* time and *less* money.
Married couples vow to take one another for *better* or *worse.*

Exercise 2

Write out the following sentences, using either the comparative or superlative degree of the adjective in parentheses. Underline your choice.

Example

a. In 1980 Texas experienced the (bad) heat wave in recent history.
a. In 1980 Texas experienced the worst heat wave in recent history.

1. Statistics show that (much) energy is consumed by industry than by citizens.
2. Booker T. Washington founded Tuskegee Institute so that black students could prepare themselves for (good) jobs than those available to them without education.
3. Sugar and honey are both sweeteners, but many people believe that honey is much (good) for your health.
4. Many people with allergies find pollen is their (bad) enemy.
5. Which has (few) calories—carrots or celery?
6. Sea travel makes me ill, and air travel makes me even (ill).
7. (Many) dogs are brown-eyed, but a few breeds have blue eyes.
8. Yesterday Carla didn't feel well, but today she is much (well).
9. Soybeans are much (little) expensive than meat and an excellent source of protein.
10. Many American rivers are treacherous, but the one that presents the (many) dangers is the Missouri.

Writing with Adjectives

Well-chosen nouns and verbs help to create a clear picture in the reader's mind. Adjectives, too, can add important specific details that make descriptions spring to life. Consider, for example, the following description.

> A *cold, greasy* egg stared up at me from the *cracked* plate; *two withered* sausages, *blackened* and *rock-hard,* flanked the egg. Next to them a *stiff* piece of *burnt* toast served as the *resting* place for a *moldy* dab of *calf's-foot* jelly.

Notice how the *italicized* adjectives add sensory details and specific information. How would you change the adjectives to transform this breakfast horror into something more tempting?

How would you describe getting into a hot car on a blazing summer day?

> I felt as if I had been shut in a box of *oppressive, blasting* air. The *sun-baked plastic* seat covers felt *searing,* and touching the *hot* steering wheel was like wrapping my fingers around a *fiery* rim.

Lack of adjectives may create writing that gives little detail of sight, smell, sound, taste, and touch. Using too many adjectives, however, can be equally damaging. As a rule avoid long strings of adjectives.

> Weak: A tall, white regal-looking, woolly, dark-eyed llama stood near the fence. It turned and looked at us.
>
> Better: A tall, white llama stood near the fence. It turned its regal head and looked at us with dark eyes.

Equally damaging to writing is the use of overworked adjectives. Words such as *great, nice, cute,* and *fantastic* are so vague and overused that they communicate little. Try to use specific, fresh adjectives to say what you mean.

Writing Exercise A

Rewrite the following sentences, adding details that make the description more specific and vivid. Try to avoid using overworked adjectives, but do use adjectives that evoke sensory details. Underline the adjectives that you supply.

Example

a. In the midst of the garden stood a statue of a horse.

a. In the midst of the <u>snow-covered</u> <u>tulip</u> garden stood a <u>bronze</u> statue of a <u>winged</u> horse.

1. A woman in a car parked in front of the building.
2. Charlotte went shopping and bought a nice sweater, some neat shoes, and a terrific coat.
3. A fish swam in the waters beneath the dock.
4. A rose lay on the grass near the grave.
5. For lunch I had a slice of pizza, a salad, and an apple.
6. Beyond the mountains, clouds were forming in the sky.

7. Around the house were drifts of snow.
8. A boy and a girl were sitting on a couch in the room.
9. A man in a hat and overalls was playing the fiddle.
10. Several chickens pecked around the yard of the house, and a pig slept beneath the porch.

Review Exercise A

In some of the following sentences adjectives are used in ways that do not conform to Edited Standard English. Rewrite these sentences, bringing them into conformity. If adjective use follows ESE in a sentence, write *ESE* next to that number on your paper. Underline any changes you make.

Examples

a. We looked over the two tents carefully and bought the one that was most durable.

a. We looked over the two tents carefully and bought the one that was more durable.

b. The first movie on the double feature was bad, and the second was even worse.

b. ESE

1. Of all the girls on the swimming team, Juanita has the more endurance.
2. Hydrogen is more common than any element.
3. For some reason the common cold is more commoner among well educated people.
4. The beautiful Mata Hari was the more famous of all spies during World War I.
5. Franklin D. Roosevelt served a longer term than any U.S. President.
6. Wild strawberries bear littler fruit than domestic strawberries.
7. The effects of smoking are more bad on the heart than on the lungs.
8. One of the most important figures in the early exploration of America was the Indian guide Sacajewa.
9. Insects are the more numerous species on earth.
10. The women of North Dakota have the most high life expectancy in the United States—slightly over eighty years.
11. Catherine the Great was certainly the more colorful of all the Russian empresses.
12. Broiling, baking, or frying—which is the better way to cook meat and retain the natural vitamins?
13. The Atacama Desert in Chili is drier than any desert in the world.
14. At twilight our radio reception gets worser and worser.

15. The injured race horse was not completely well, but it was weller than it had been.
16. President Andrew Johnson was probably the President with the littlest education—his wife taught him how to write.
17. Nutritionists say that whole wheat flour is more better for people than refined flour.
18. When Mars is most closest to earth, it is still over 34 million miles away.
19. One of these two engines has significantly least horsepower.
20. Jesse Owens, the track star, once demonstrated that he could run more faster than a race horse on a 100-yard course.

Writing Exercise B

Choose one of the following situations and write several well developed paragraphs of description. Use exact adjectives to make your description easy for readers to imagine. When you have finished writing, underline the adjectives.

1. Imagine that a very rich relative has just appeared and promised you that, after your graduation, you will be provided with your own luxurious apartment. Anything you desire will be granted. What will it be like—how large will it be, how will it be decorated, and what special features will it have?
2. Science fiction writers delight in creating beings from outer space, but two such fictional characters have become overused objects of ridicule: the little green man and the bug-eyed monster. Create and describe a new kind of extraterrestrial visitor: how does the visitor look, sound, feel, and how does its body suit it for life on its planet?
3. Food is or is not appealing for more reasons than taste—appearance, odor, and texture influence people as well. Using details that evoke all of the senses, describe a favorite (or a least favorite) food—how it looks, feels, smells, and tastes, and perhaps even sounds. Be as specific and vivid as possible.
4. Write a description of a place. It may be a place you see every day, a place you have never visited, or a place you have read about, seen in a movie, or even imagined for yourself, or it may be the place in the photograph on page 448. Use well chosen adjectives to describe its appearance, trying to write vividly enough so that a reader will be able to visualize the place clearly.

Understanding Adverbs

Like adjectives, *adverbs* are modifiers. In this section you will learn to identify adverbs by their definition, the classes into which they can be divided, and the features that distinguish them from other parts of speech.

Defining an Adverb

An *adverb* is often defined as a word that modifies a verb, an adjective, or another adverb.

Modifies a Verb: The dog barked *frantically*.
Modifies an Adjective: The land was *fairly* rocky.
Modifies an Adverb: The elms grow *very* quickly.

Adverbs answer the question *how? how often? when? where?* or *to what extent?*

How: The embers glowed *softly*.
How Often: The century plant blooms *infrequently*.
When: The package should reach you *tomorrow*.

Where: The mothballs are kept *downstairs.*

To What Extent: Our emergency supplies were *nearly* gone.

Exercise 1

Write out the following sentences, underlining the adverbs. Beneath each sentence write the question answered by each adverb. Then draw an arrow to the word or words the adverb modifies.

Examples

a. Sometimes, Hal wished that he could graduate immediately.

a. Sometimes, Hal wished that he could graduate immediately.
sometimes: how often?
immediately: when?

b. Carlie was very proud that she played well.

b. Carlie was very proud that she played well.
very: to what extent?
well: how?

1. Today we drove slowly because of the slick streets.
2. Kio can skate forward or backward with equal ease.
3. Lorenzo will call you later tonight.
4. The Pasternaks often go north for their summer vacations.
5. You should never approach a wild bear closely, even if it seems completely tame.
6. As the curtains slowly parted, the audience clapped loudly.
7. *We Have Always Lived in the Castle* is one of Shirley Jackson's highly suspenseful novels.
8. Billy Dee Williams is an extraordinarily gifted actor who still finds time for his favorite hobby, painting.
9. Too much Vitamin A can be very harmful to the body; an overdose can be fatal.
10. We seldom go into those woods because it seems poison sumac grows everywhere.

Classifying Adverbs

Many adverbs fall into no special class; they are simply adverbs. There are, however, four special kinds of adverbs as well. Knowing these classes will help you to understand adverbs in general.

Interrogative Adverbs

The adverbs *how, when, where,* and *why* are *interrogative adverbs* when they introduce a question.

How do you spell your name?
When is the news special going to be on?
Where is Timbuktu?
Why do stars seem to twinkle?

Negative Adverbs

Not (and its contraction *n't*), *never*, *seldom*, *scarcely*, *barely*, and *hardly* are called *negative adverbs*. They deny or invert the statement being made, or they qualify it in a negative way.

Positive:	He will be at play practice.
Negative:	He will *not* be at play practice.
Positive:	Rosa was through with her term project.
Negative:	Rosa was*n't* through with her term project.
Positive:	The governor makes long, boring speeches.
Negative:	The governor *never* makes long, boring speeches.

Intensifiers

Intensifiers are adverbs that modify adjectives or other adverbs, but not verbs. They immediately precede the word they modify. Common intensifiers are *extremely*, *rather*, *somewhat*, *really*, *too*, *more*, *most*, *quite*, and *very*.

Modifies Adjective:	Whooping cranes are *extremely* rare.
	A *very* old oak stands in our yard.
Modifies Adverb:	The storm arose *very* quickly.
	Don't drive *too* quickly.

In writing avoid overusing the intensifier *very*. When used too often, it loses its force.

Nouns Used as Adverbs

Just as nouns are sometimes used as adjectives, so some nouns may be used as adverbs. A noun that answers the adverbial question of *when? where? how much?* or *to what extent?* should be classified as an adverb.

Sheila went *home* after lunch. [where?]
Chico will leave *Sunday*. [when?]
The next ice age could last *centuries*. [how long?]

Exercise 2

Write out the following sentences, underlining the adverbs. If the adverb belongs to a special class, indicate that beneath the sentence.

Examples

a. Where did you go yesterday?
a. Where did you go yesterday?
where: interrogative; yesterday: noun used as adverb

b. We had not planned our trip very carefully.

b. We had not planned our trip very carefully.
not: negative; very: intensifier; carefully: adverb

1. How did the team do tonight?
2. Our oil reserves are not quite enough to meet an emergency.
3. My cousin worked in the desert a year, prospecting for uranium without success.
4. Marcia doesn't work evenings now; she works mornings.
5. "It rains here too much," grumbled the tourist. "I'm never coming back."
6. We are going downtown tomorrow. What is the best way to go—by bus or car?
7. The pirate map indicated we should walk forty paces south, twelve paces east, and then we would see an extremely large boulder.
8. When and where did the very largest volcanic eruption in history take place?
9. Sarah wasn't home, so we went to the park and found her there.
10. Today will be rather cool, with that extremely low pressure center moving north.

Finding an Adverb by Its Features

Adverbs and adjectives are both modifiers and share the same three features. In order to distinguish an adjective from an adverb, you must look to see what word it modifies. Remember that adverbs modify verbs, adjectives, and other adverbs; adjectives can modify only nouns or pronouns.

1. Adverbs may change form to show degrees of comparison.

Some—but not all—adverbs show degrees of comparison: positive, comparative, and superlative. Adverbs that end in *-ly* form their comparative and superlative degrees with the words *more* and *most.*

POSITIVE	COMPARATIVE	SUPERLATIVE
quickly	more quickly	most quickly
obviously	more obviously	most obviously
stubbornly	more stubbornly	most stubbornly

Most one-syllable adverbs form their degrees of comparison with *-er* and *-est* added to the positive degree. Most such adverbs may also function as adjectives.

POSITIVE	COMPARATIVE	SUPERLATIVE
far	farther	farthest
fast	faster	fastest

deep	deeper	deepest
hard	harder	hardest
late	later	latest
long	longer	longest
soon	sooner	soonest
wild	wilder	wildest

All adverbs that have degrees of comparison are compared in a negative way with the words *less* and *least. Less* is used to compare two items negatively, *least* to compare three or more items negatively.

POSITIVE	COMPARATIVE	SUPERLATIVE
quickly	less quickly	least quickly
obviously	less obviously	least obviously
far	less far	least far
soon	less soon	least soon

2. Adverbs may be used with intensifiers.

Intensifiers are a special class of adverbs that modify only other adverbs or adjectives. (A list of intensifiers is on page 450.) Intensifiers can be thought of as modifier signals because a modifier always immediately follows an intensifier. In the following sentences adverbs follow the intensifiers.

Dawn arrived *rather* late.

Malcolm finished *very* quickly.

3. Adverbs may be formed with suffixes.

The most common adverb suffix is *-ly*, which means "in a certain manner" or "at a certain time."

slowly recently nervously

Not all words that end in *-ly* are adverbs, however; some, such as *homely, friendly, lovely,* and *kindly*, are adjectives.

Other adverb-forming suffixes include *-ward (upward, forward), -ways, (sideways, always),* and *-wise (crosswise, sidewise).*

Exercise 3

Use your knowledge of the definition and features of adverbs to identify the adverbs in the following sentences. Write out the sentences, underlining the adverbs.

Example

a. The roof has been leaking rather badly lately.

a. The roof has been leaking rather badly lately.

1. Usually poison ivy occurs very rarely in this area.
2. We measured the fence wire lengthwise, then fastened it tightly.

3. Is it true that moss grows less thickly on the side of the tree that faces southward?
4. Because its orbit is quite eccentric, Pluto sometimes approaches nearer to earth than Saturn does.
5. The car hit the patch of ice too quickly, then skidded sideways.
6. Snails sleep more heavily than most animals; sometimes they may snooze for three years.
7. Scientists maintain that nothing moves more quickly than light, but science fiction writers frequently ignore this law.
8. The elevator moved downward quickly, and the many passengers stood silently.
9. Unfortunately, for short distances alligators can run more swiftly than people.
10. The sky rocket rose upward, then exploded most impressively into a shower of green stars.

Mastery Exercise A

On a sheet of paper, list all of the italicized adverbs in the order they occur in the selection. Next to each adverb write the verb, adjective, or adverb it modifies. These paragraphs are taken from *Walden* by the nineteenth-century American naturalist and writer Henry David Thoreau. (Not all of the adverbs are italicized.)

When I went to get a pail of water *early* in the morning I *frequently* saw this stately bird sailing out of my cove within a few rods. If I endeavored to overtake him in a boat, . . . he would dive and be *completely* lost, so that I did *not* discover him *again*, sometimes, till the latter part of the day. But I was more than a match for him on the surface. He *commonly* went off in a rain.

As I was paddling along the north shore one *very* calm October afternoon, for such days *especially* they [loons] settle on to the lakes, like the milkweed down, having looked in vain over the pond for a loon, *suddenly* one, sailing out from the shore toward the middle a few rods in front of me, set up his wild laugh and betrayed himself. I pursued with a paddle and he dived, but when he came *up* I was *nearer* than before. He dived again, but I miscalculated the direction he would take, and we were fifty rods apart when he came to the surface this time, for I had helped to widen the interval; and *again* he laughed *long* and *loud*, and with more reason than before. He maneuvered *so cunningly* that I could not get within half a dozen rods of him. Each time, when he came to the surface, turning his head this way and that, he *coolly* surveyed the water and the land, and *apparently* chose his course so that he might come up where there was the widest expanse of water and at the greatest distance from the boat. It was surprising how *quickly* he made up his mind and put his resolve into execution. He led me at once to the widest part of the pond, and could *not* be driven from it. While he was thinking one thing in his brain, I was endeavoring to divine his thought in mine. It was a pretty game, played on the smooth surface of the pond, a man against a loon.

Mastery Exercise B

From your community or school newspaper, select an article describing a recent sports event. Then using what you have learned about identifying adverbs, read the article to find the adverbs and list them on a sheet of paper. When you have finished, read the article to yourself, leaving out the adverbs. What effect did the adverbs have on the writing? On your perception of the event?

Using Adverbs

In this section you will practice using comparative and superlative forms of adverbs, both regular and irregular. Also, you will learn to distinguish between some adjective and adverb word pairs that are often confused, and you will learn that double negatives are not a feature of ESE.

Using Comparative and Superlative Forms of Adverbs

When two items are being compared, the comparative degree of the adverb is used.

Morty swims *faster* than Max does.
Morty swims *less fast* than Max does.

Kim studies *more often* than Maria.
Kim studies *less often* than Maria.

When three or more items are being compared, use the superlative degree of the adverb.

Morty swims *fastest* of all the competitors.
Morty swims *least fast* of all the competitors.

Kim studies *most often* of the sisters.
Kim studies *least often* of the sisters.

Exercise 1

Write out the following sentences, using the correct comparative or superlative form of the adverb given in parentheses. So long as it fits the sense of the sentence, the comparison may be either positive or negative. Underline the adverb you have used.

Example

a. Valery reads (frequently) than Pat.
a. Valery reads more frequently than Pat.
or
a. Valery reads less frequently than Pat.

1. Mercury moves around the sun (quickly) than Venus does.
2. Of all classes the seniors scored (high) on the achievement tests.

3. The cockroach has survived (successfully) than most other species.
4. Of all nineteenth-century novelists, Helen Hunt Jackson wrote (effectively) on behalf of native American rights.
5. Trains use fuel (efficiently) than planes.
6. Which breed of dogs learns tasks (easily)?
7. Some scientists claim that of all food additives, sugar (frequently) injures our health.
8. Our daily paper reports events (accurately) than the radio station does.
9. Of all European explorers the Vikings appear to have visited America (early).
10. The willow grows (swiftly) than the oak tree, but the oak endures (long).

Using Irregular Forms of Adverbs

Most adverbs ending in *-ly* use the words *more* or *most* to form their degrees of comparison, while one-syllable adverbs usually add *-er* or *-est*. A few common adverbs form their comparative and superlative degrees irregularly. These forms must be memorized.

POSITIVE	COMPARATIVE	SUPERLATIVE
badly	worse	worst
far	farther	farthest
little	less	least
much	more	most
well	better	best

Some of the words in the preceding list may also be used as adjectives. Remember that they are adverbs only when they modify a verb, adjective, or another adverb.

Adverb: We have to travel *farther.*
The car ran *worse* after we fixed it.

Adjective: This is the *best* score I've made yet.
Please give me *less* salt this time.

Exercise 2

Write out the following sentences, supplying the comparative or superlative degree of the adverb in parentheses. Then underline each adverb and draw an arrow to the word that it modifies.

Examples

a. These nails will work (well) for the job than those will.

a. *These nails will work better for the job than those will.*

b. Of all injuries burns hurt (much).

b. Of all injuries burns hurt most.

1. Of all NASA's rockets which has traveled (far) from earth?
2. Fish bite (much) when it is cool than when it is hot.
3. Of all chemicals I think sulphur stinks (badly).
4. Of all diets the one that works (well) is simply saying no to second helpings.
5. Nowadays, you have to make a dollar stretch (far) than you used to.
6. A body weighs (little) at the North or South Pole than it does at the equator.
7. The higher you are above sea level, the (little) easily water boils.
8. Magnets attract nickel somewhat, but attract iron (much).
9. Robins use their sight (little) than their hearing to find worms.
10. Poison ivy infection itches badly, but poison oak infection itches (badly).

Choosing Between Adjectives and Adverbs

In writing and speaking you often have to choose between an adjective or an adverb. If you are uncertain which modifier you should use, check to see what word is being modified.

Use an adverb to modify a verb, adjective, or another adverb; use an adjective to modify a noun or pronoun.

Adverb: The scientist watched the white rat *closely*. [modifies verb *watched*]

Adjective: The race was *close*. [modifies noun *race*]

In many cases you will have no difficulty deciding whether to use an adjective or an adverb in a sentence. Problems sometimes arise, however, when an adjective is so frequently misused that the wrong choice sounds natural. Three such adjective-adverb pairs are discussed in the following paragraphs.

bad/badly

Bad is an adjective that modifies a noun or pronoun. It is frequently used after linking verbs such as *feel, look, taste, smell.*

We felt *bad* about the mistake.

Mildew makes things smell *bad*.

Badly is an adverb that tells how an action is performed.

Tech High beat our team *badly* in the play-offs.

good/well

Good, an adjective, is not used as an adverb in ESE.

Good boots are essential to the hiker.

The apple blossoms smelled *good.*

Well is a troublesome modifier because it can be used as both an adjective and an adverb. *Well* is an adjective when it means "healthy," "attractive," or "satisfactory." It is an adverb when it tells how an action is performed.

Adjective: Marcia should be *well* by Friday.

Three days after it got the shot, the steer looked completely *well.*

Adverb: A "mudder" is a horse that runs *well* on a muddy track.

slow/slowly

Slow is an adjective that means the opposite of *fast.*

The traffic is *slow* during rush hour.

Because of its use on highway signs, however, *slow* has become accepted as an adverb in some situations:

Drive *slow.* Go *slow.*

The adverb *slowly*, however, should be used after action verbs other than *drive* and *go.*

The boat chugged *slowly* toward its destination.

The black snake crept *slowly* toward the robin's nest.

Exercise 3

Write out the following sentences, choosing the correct modifier from the pair in parentheses. Underline the modifier you have chosen.

Example

a. Terry had a serious operation, but she is almost (good, well) again.
a. Terry had a serious operation, but she is almost <u>*well*</u> *again.*

1. Freshly baked bread always smells (good, well).
2. I don't play tennis (good, well) because my reflexes are (slow, slowly).
3. The liquid trickled (slow, slowly) into the beaker; the experiment was going (good, well).
4. I felt (bad, badly) about forgetting to call Carol; I hope she doesn't take it (bad, badly).
5. The swordfish steaks tasted surprisingly (good, well), but the squid looks (bad, badly) to me.
6. Sharon is (good, well) at sports, sings (good, well), but makes friends (slow, slowly).
7. A rose smells (good, well), but a perfume tester smells perfume (good, well).
8. If you want to do (good, well) with your exercise program, begin (slow, slowly).

9. Sharon dresses (good, well), and she always smells (good, well)—she never goes out without squirting on a bit of cologne.
10. When they saw their test scores, Eddie felt (good, well) and Miriam felt (bad, badly).

Using Negatives

When two negative words are used where only one is needed, the construction is called a *double negative.*

Avoid double negatives in speaking and writing.

An asterisk (*) indicates a sentence with a feature that is not a part of ESE.

*I don't know nothing about it.
I don't know anything about it.
I know nothing about it.

*I don't have no pen.
I don't have a pen.
I have no pen.

Remember that the adverbs *barely*, *scarcely*, and *hardly* are also considered negative when used with other negatives.

*I was so confused, I couldn't hardly think.
I was so confused, I couldn't think.
I was so confused, I could hardly think.

The words *but* and *only* have negative meanings in such expressions as "haven't but," "can't help but," and "haven't only." Avoid these double negative expressions when speaking and writing.

*I don't have but two dollars left until payday.
I have but two dollars left until payday.

*When Gwen takes notes, she can't help but doodle in the margins of her notebook.
When Gwen takes notes, she can't help doodling in the margins of her notebook.

Exercise 4

Each of the following sentences contains a double negative. Rewrite each sentence so that it conforms to Edited Standard English.

Examples

a. We can't hardly change our minds at this point in the project.
a. We can hardly change our minds at this point in the project.

b. We haven't got hardly enough gas to get home.
b. We haven't got enough gas to get home.

1. No white person never knew where the grave of Crazy Horse is.
2. The store doesn't carry but one brand of seeds.
3. It seems some people can't help but talk too much.

4. The rickety bridge couldn't barely hold the weight of the truck.
5. My teacher claims I don't know nothing about double negatives.
6. It seems as if Grandmother's appearance hasn't scarcely changed since we were children.
7. We haven't got but enough supplies to get us to the next camp.
8. There's never hardly enough time in the day to finish my work.
9. We don't have but sixteen dollars in the fund; that's not scarcely enough.
10. Nothing can't be done about the problem unless citizens are willing to admit that a problem exists.

Writing with Adverbs

Just as adjectives help the reader to visualize a person, place, or thing, so adverbs help the reader visualize action. Consider the action described in the following sentences.

The fire burned *savagely.*
The fire burned *weakly.*
The fire burned *cheerfully.*

Use exact adverbs to help the reader visualize an action.

Writing Exercise A

Improve each of the following sentences by using one or more adverbs to describe the action precisely. You may also add verbs, adjectives, phrases, and concrete, specific nouns to make the sentences more vivid.

Example

a. The dachshund climbed the steps.
a. The dachshund struggled awkwardly up the steep stairs, its short legs scrambling furiously.

1. A judge should listen, consider, and decide.
2. The stereo played while the partygoers enjoyed themselves.
3. Carol put on her brakes and the car skidded.
4. The dog rose, looked out the door, and barked.
5. The wind blew, the rain fell, and the trees tossed.
6. The ambulance raced down the street, its siren screaming, cutting in and out of traffic.
7. The volcano rumbled, then shook; clouds appeared and lava flowed.
8. The actor overdid every emotion: he sobbed, laughed, gasped, and raged.
9. The house stood on the hill; weeds grew in the yard and vines climbed the walls.

10. The air conditioner purred, the fan rotated, but still heat filled the room.

Review Exercise A

Write out the following sentences, choosing the correct modifier from the pair in parentheses. Underline the word you have chosen.

Example

a. When the buzzer sounded, I gathered up my books (quick, quickly) and headed for my locker.

a. When the buzzer sounded, I gathered up my books quickly and headed for my locker.

1. The car's engine started (quick, quickly) even in winter.
2. Which of these three packages is the (better, best) buy?
3. Kevin didn't feel (bad, badly) about not making the first team.
4. Do you know which of Mars' two moons orbits the planet (more, most) swiftly?
5. Donna (has, hasn't) only fifty cents to buy lunch.
6. I don't (never, ever) want to eat parsnip pudding again.
7. The dead frog I had to work on in biology didn't smell very (good, well).
8. Carlos (can, can't) hardly wait to graduate.
9. There (is, isn't) but one aspirin left in the bottle.
10. After I broke the school record for eating dill pickles, I didn't feel too (good, well).
11. Things were going very (good, well) for our team until Tina tripped and hurt her ankle (bad, badly).
12. John grew (slow, slowly) until tenth grade, and then he shot up (quick, quickly).
13. "The fish you caught is starting to smell (bad, badly)," my sister complained.
14. Of all the people who addressed the convention, Barbara Jordan spoke (more, most) effectively.
15. I (have, haven't) got enough money to buy only one record album.
16. Ham and eggs always go (good, well) together.
17. The peaches looked (good, well), but they didn't sell very (good, well).
18. We (could, couldn't) hardly ignore the noise outside the classroom.
19. After I had read for six straight hours, I felt rather (bad, badly) and my eyes didn't focus (good, well).
20. I like Ms. Jackson (better, best) of the two candidates.

Writing Exercise B

Write a description or step-by-step directions telling someone how to perform one of the following actions. Use adverbs to communicate your instructions precisely and colorfully.

1. Doing the latest dance
2. Making a pizza
3. Changing a tire
4. Getting from your school to your home
5. Making the perfect sandwich
6. Postponing your homework assignment until the last possible minute
7. Giving an animal a bath
8. Preparing for a long run
9. Building a good fire
10. Controlling a younger brother or sister

Understanding Conjunctions

Conjunctions, like prepositions, join sentence parts together. In the lessons that follow, you will learn to recognize the three different kinds of conjunctions and how they are used.

Defining a Conjunction

A *conjunction* is usually defined as a word that connects words or groups of words.

Some of the smallest and most common words in English are conjunctions. Words such as *and, but, or, for, nor,* and *yet* may join either single words or groups of words.

Jane Austen and Emily Brontë were early English novelists.

Roberto will letter the place cards, and Marissa will make the centerpieces for the banquet.

Vonnegut's novels are funny but thought-provoking.

Milk contains important nutrients, but many people are allergic to it.

Conjunctions like *either . . . or, neither . . . nor, both . . . and,* and *not only . . . but also* work together as pairs.

Either hamburger or sausage may be used in this recipe.

Both Wyatt and Surrey influenced the development of the English sonnet.

Independent clauses are discussed on page 535.

Some conjunctions join groups of words to independent clauses. Conjunctions such as *after, because, before, when, since,* and *where* join dependent word groups to independent clauses.

> We left before the concert was over.
> Jerry always takes his first-aid kit when he goes backpacking.

Exercise 1

Write out the following sentences, drawing one line under the conjunctions. Be prepared to identify the words they connect. (Some sentences contain more than one conjunction; some have conjunctions that work in pairs.)

Examples

a. Working independently of one another, both Soviet and American scientists discovered the laser in the 1950s.

a. Working independently of one another, both Soviet and American scientists discovered the laser in the 1950s.

b. Lasers are one of our country's most versatile and awe-inspiring discoveries; they can be used for either good or evil.

b. Lasers are one of our country's most versatile and awe-inspiring discoveries; they can be used for either good or evil.

1. Ordinary light diffuses as it travels; laser beams neither dissipate nor lose their strength.
2. Unlike ordinary light, laser beams can be aimed and focused; they are the most powerful lights on earth.
3. Laser beams can be used by artists to create holographs or by doctors to perform delicate eye surgery.
4. They can be used both to transmit signals and to generate steam power.
5. Because of the laser's power, it can be used as a precision cutting tool for substances as dense as steel or concrete.
6. In addition, the geologist can use it to detect signs of impending earthquakes, and the meteorologist can use it to measure cloud covers.
7. The possibilities for the peaceful use of the laser are heartening, yet the laser as a weapon has produced possibilities that are frightening.
8. Because lasers can transmit extremely clear photos, the beams are used to transmit photos of enemy installations and movements.
9. Since the war in Vietnam, many laser weapons have been developed, including bombs and ballistic missiles.
10. Before the invention of the laser, a "death ray" existed only in science fiction; lasers may well make this devastating weapon not only possible, but also inevitable.

Classifying Conjunctions

Conjunctions can be divided into three classes: *coordinating conjunctions*, *correlative conjunctions*, and *subordinating conjunctions.*

Coordinating Conjunctions

The *coordinating conjunctions* are *and, but, or, nor, yet, so,* and *for.*

Coordinating conjunctions join single words, phrases, or clauses. When one or more sentence parts are joined by a coordinating conjunction, the parts should be of equal importance.

The recipes were economical, yet nutritious. [two adjectives]

Edna St. Vincent Millay or Sara Teasdale wrote that poem. [two nouns]

We subscribed to the news magazine, but not to the sports journal. [two prepositional phrases]

Cedar chips or pine needles in a doghouse will discourage occupancy by fleas. [two noun phrases]

I haven't heard Raphael's new joke, nor do I want to. [two independent clauses]

Correlative Conjunctions

Correlative conjunctions are used only in pairs:

either . . . or	not only . . . but also
neither . . . nor	whether . . . or
both . . . and	

Either mozzarella or provolone cheese is good on a pizza.

The wasps were not only numerous, but also unfriendly.

Both a drama and a musical have been based on the novel *I Am a Camera.*

Subordinating Conjunctions

See pages 540–542 for a complete discussion of adverb clauses.

Subordinating conjunctions are used to introduce adverb clauses.

A subordinating conjunction expresses the relationship of a subordinate clause to the main clause by showing time, place, cause, purpose, limitation, or condition. A list of the most common subordinating conjunctions follows:

after	before	since	though	whenever
although	how	so	till	wherever
as	if	so that	unless	whether
as much as	inasmuch as	than	until	while
as soon as	in order that	that	when	
because	provided that			

As much as I would like to, I won't be able to go with you to the beach.

The pageant will be held *wherever* the committee decides.

The reporters waited outside *while* the meeting was in session.

Exercise 2

Write out the following sentences, underlining the conjunctions. Beneath each sentence list each conjunction and the class to which it belongs: *coordinating (coor.)*, *correlative (cor.)*, or *subordinating (sub.)*.

Examples

a. Either the band or the orchestra will perform at graduation.

a. Either the band or the orchestra will perform at graduation.
either . . . or—cor.

b. Vera has planned on being a television reporter since she was a sophomore.

b. Vera has planned on being a television reporter since she was a sophomore.
since—sub.

1. Wolves are neither as destructive nor as dangerous as many people imagine.
2. Although everyone dreams, many people do not recall dreaming.
3. Both Sigmund Freud and his daughter were influential in the development of psychiatry.
4. Since my sister took up the drums, our household has had neither peace nor quiet.
5. Graduation exercises will be held out-of-doors provided that no rain is forecast.
6. Both magnesium and calcium aid the body in proper utilization of Vitamin C.
7. Neither age nor infirmity could deter actress Sarah Bernhardt; she continued to act although she was often unwell and after she had her leg amputated.
8. Let us know when the party will be, and we'll help you with the cleaning and refreshments.
9. Because fiberglass is tough, yet lightweight and flexible, it is often used for the bodies of speedboats and racing cars.
10. Although Pete wanted a pizza or a hamburger, he was too tired to cook, so he settled for a peanut butter sandwich and a glass of milk.

Mastery Exercise A

In the following paragraphs the contemporary American writer Ralph Ellison discusses his childhood bewilderment about being named for the poet and philosopher Ralph Waldo Emerson. Using what you have learned about conjunctions, identify the conjunctions in the passage and list them on a sheet of paper in the order they appear. Beside each conjunction write the class to which it belongs: *coordinating (coor.)*, *correlative (cor.)*, or *subordinating (sub.)*. Find at least fifteen conjunctions.

Hint: The first conjunction is *and*, a coordinating conjunction.

From the start I was uncomfortable with it, and in my earliest years it caused me much puzzlement. Neither could I understand what a poet was, nor why, exactly, my father had chosen to name me after one. Perhaps I could have understood it perfectly well had he named me after his own father, but that name had been given to an older brother who died and thus was out of the question. But why hadn't he named me after a hero, such as Jack Johnson, or a soldier like Colonel Charles Young, or a great seaman like Admiral Dewey, or an educator like Booker T. Washington, or a great orator and abolitionist like Frederick Douglass? Or again, why hadn't he named me (as so many Negro parents had done) after President Teddy Roosevelt?

Instead, he named me after someone called Ralph Waldo Emerson, and then, when I was three, he died. It was too early for me to have understood his choice, although I'm sure he must have explained it many times, and it was also too soon for me to have made the connection between my name and my father's love for reading. Much later, after I began to write and work with words, I came to suspect that he was aware of the suggestive powers of names and of the magic involved in naming.[1]

Using Conjunctions

Conjunctions help the writer to combine and connect ideas coherently. In the following lessons you will practice combining sentences with conjunctions and punctuating those sentences correctly.

Writing with Conjunctions

A series of short, choppy sentences can make writing seem childlike. By using coordinating, correlative, or subordinating conjunctions, you can combine such sentences and show the relationship between them.

The following sentences use coordinating conjunctions to connect ideas of equal importance.

For more practice in joining sentences with conjunctions, see the chapter "Joining Sentences."

We could order invitations. We could make them ourselves.
We could order invitations *or* make them ourselves.

Cattle and sheep sleep very little. Armadillos sleep up to twenty hours a day.
Cattle and sheep sleep very little, *but* armadillos sleep up to twenty hours a day.

The Oklahoma City Zoo has excellent facilities for wild canines. It has a superior reptile house.
The Oklahoma City Zoo has excellent facilities for wild canines *and* a superior reptile house.

Subordinating conjunctions express the specific relationship of a subordinate clause to a main clause.

[1]Excerpt from "Hidden Name and Complex Fate" in *Shadow and Act* by Ralph Ellison. Copyright © 1964 by Ralph Ellison. Reprinted by permission of Random House, Inc.

RELATIONSHIP	SUBORDINATING CONJUNCTION
Cause:	because, since, as, for, so
Purpose:	in order that, so that
Limitation:	though, although, in spite of the fact that, since
Time:	after, as, as soon as, before, since, until, when, while
Place:	where, wherever

Subordinate clauses are discussed on page 535.

The following sentences employ subordinating conjunctions to show the relationship of a subordinate clause to a main clause.

Salvador Dali is one of the most flamboyant twentieth-century artists. Many people are familiar with him.

Because Salvador Dali is one of the most flamboyant twentieth-century artists, many people are familiar with him.

Sandy decided she wanted to be a chemist. She had read about Madame Curie.

Sandy decided she wanted to be a chemist *after* she had read about Madame Curie.

We wanted to see Greenwich Village during our vacation. We didn't have time.

Although we wanted to see Greenwich Village during our vacation, we didn't have time.

Exercise 1

Combine the following short sentences by using appropriate conjunctions. Underline the conjunctions you have used.

Examples

a. None of the Brontë sisters lived very long. Each made a lasting mark on English literature.

a. Although none of the Brontë sisters lived very long, each made a lasting mark on English literature.

b. The store on the corner carries electronic supplies. It carries hobby items.

b. The store on the corner carries electronic supplies and hobby items.

1. Many people know about the disease of diabetes. Few are aware of a common, related disorder, low blood sugar.
2. We could not afford to have the literary magazine typeset. We typed it ourselves on the school typewriters.
3. I may go to the Halloween party as a vampire. I may go as a robot.
4. Coyotes are native to America. Raccoons are native to America.
5. I knew my answer must be right. Carrie had arrived at the same solution. Kim had arrived at the same solution.
6. Our national bird is the eagle. Benjamin Franklin wanted the turkey adopted as our nation's symbol. He felt eagles were nasty, predatory birds.

7. Some people felt Willie Stargell was too old to play in the 1979 World Series. He led his team to victory. He was chosen Most Valuable Player.
8. Calvin saw Sammy Davis, Jr., perform in Las Vegas. He wants to be a performer, too.
9. Siamese cats are beautiful. They are extremely noisy. They like a lot of attention.
10. I found it hard to study. My sister had her stereo going full blast. My brother was practicing on his drums.

Punctuating with Conjunctions

In a series of words, phrases, or clauses, a comma is used to take the place of each conjunction that is omitted. A comma also precedes the conjunction at the end of a series.

> The Oglala**,** Humkpapa**,** and Brule are all tribes of the Sioux.
>
> Our canoe trip will be on either the White**,** Mulberry**,** or Illinois River.

Commas are not necessary if no conjunctions are omitted, but this is not a frequently used construction.

> John *and* Dave *and* Shelley are the club's new officers.
> We could go water skiing *or* swimming *or* snorkeling.

A comma usually separates the subordinate clause from the main clause when the subordinate clause begins the sentence.

> Because California is located on the San Andreas Fault**,** it has frequent earthquakes.
>
> While Marcia typed the report**,** Cammy worked on the charts.

A comma is not usually necessary when the subordinate clause comes at the end of the sentence.

> California has frequent earthquakes because it is located on the San Andreas Fault.
>
> Cammy worked on the charts while Marcia typed the report.

Exercise 2

Write out the following sentences, adding commas wherever necessary. If the sentence is punctuated correctly, write *C* after it. Circle the commas you insert.

Examples

a. If you don't wear a seat belt in a car you substantially increase your chances of being hurt in an accident.

a. If you don't wear a seat belt in a car(,) you substantially increase your chances of being hurt in an accident.

b. When we think of colonial costumes we usually think of knee breeches tricornered hats and hoop skirts.

b. When we think of colonial costumes, we usually think of knee breeches, tricornered hats, and hoop skirts.

1. Since Mark was originally from Florida he didn't like driving in the Midwest during the winter.
2. Although everyone recognizes the actors who played Luke Skywalker Princess Leia and Hans Solo few recognize the actor who played Artoo Detoo, the android.
3. I would love to spend the whole summer loafing and reading and napping.
4. Tina bought a used car because she couldn't afford a new one.
5. Although many people are familiar with the phrase "blood sweat and tears" not many know that the original expression was "blood sweat toil and tears."
6. We couldn't leave to go shopping until the lawn was mowed the porch was cleaned and the mail had arrived.
7. The necklace was priceless because it contained flawless diamonds pearls and a huge star sapphire.
8. Because the sewing room was littered with needles and pins and scissors it was unsafe to sit down carelessly.
9. It was unsafe to sit down carelessly in the sewing room because it was littered with needles and pins and scissors.
10. Because drought continued for so long many cities began to ration water.

Writing Exercise A

For practice in using conjunctions, write two or three well-developed paragraphs on one of the following topics. When you have finished, underline the conjunctions you have used.

1. Names are very personal things. Write a short essay about your name: how you feel about it (whether you like it or not and why); how you came to receive your name; whether you would change it if you could. If you are female, would you change your name when you marry? Why or why not? If you are male, would you prefer your wife to take your name upon marriage or to keep her own? Why?
2. Summarize the plot of a favorite book or movie. Who are the major characters, and what are they like? Why do they act as they do? What key events trigger their actions, and how do they react to them? Have any

of the key characters changed by the end of the book or movie? If so, how have they changed?

3. Choose one problem facing Americans today about which you are especially concerned. Discuss why you think it is an important problem and why it must be solved. How do you think it will be best solved?
4. What kind of job would you like to have when you finish your schooling? What are the job's advantages and disadvantages? What kind of personality traits does such a job demand? How does your own personality match the requirements of the job?

Understanding Prepositions

Prepositions are one of the parts of speech that connect other words so that they work together in groups. By changing the preposition, a writer may radically change the meaning of a sentence.

A family of skunks lives *near* our house.
A family of skunks lives *under* our house.
A family of skunks lives *in* our house.

In the following lessons you will learn how to identify prepositions.

Defining a Preposition

A *preposition* is usually defined as a word that shows the relationship of a noun or pronoun to another word in the sentence.

The girl *with* the braids is Maureen.

In the preceding sentence the preposition *with* shows the relationship of the noun *braids* to the noun *girl.*

In Edited Standard English prepositions are not used alone. Instead, a preposition is part of a prepositional phrase that has two essential parts: the preposition *(P)* and the object of the preposition *(OP).* A prepositional phrase may also contain one or more modifiers.

P OP P OP
The opera singer stood **in** the *center* **of** the *stage.*
P OP P OP
On the album's *cover* was a picture **of** a silver *unicorn.*

A single preposition may also have a compound object.

P OP OP
The college is famous **for** its science *division* and drama *department.*
P OP OP
We had a fine breakfast **of** *eggs* and *steak.*

The object of the preposition is usually a single word, but it may also be a group of words.

P *OP*
Sell the car **for** *whatever you can get.*

P *OP*
After *seeing the double feature* we were all hungry.

The following is a list of commonly used prepositions.

about
above
across
after
against
along
amid
among
around
as
at
before
behind
below
beneath
beside
besides
between
beyond
but
by
concerning
down
during
except
for
from
in
into
like
of
off
on
over
past
since
through
throughout
to
under
underneath
until
unto
up
upon
with
within
without

Besides these one-word prepositions there are several compound prepositions that are made up of more than one word. Each of these should be considered as a single preposition.

according to
along with
aside from
as to
because of
by means of
in front of
in spite of
out of
owing to
subsequent to
together with

Some words that function as prepositions, such as *across, down, behind, in, under, up,* and so forth, may also function as adverbs. Remember that a preposition introduces a prepositional phrase. If you can find no object to the preposition, the word is probably used as an adverb.

Adverb: We had to go *on.*

P *OP*
Preposition: We had to go **on** the *bus.*

Adverb: The election results are *in.*

P *OP*
Preposition: The election results are **in** the *paper.*

Do not confuse the infinitive *to* with the preposition *to.* The infinitive is the verb form that begins with the word *to.* (See page 523.)

Infinitive: It takes persistence *to* succeed. [*to* followed by verb]

P *OP*
Preposition: Are you going **to** the *rally?* [*to* followed by noun]

P OP
Preposition: Please give this **to** *her.* [*to* followed by pronoun]

Exercise 1

Write out each of the following sentences, underlining the prepositional phrases. Above each preposition write *P*; above each object of the preposition, write *OP*. (Some sentences contain more than one prepositional phrase; some may have compound objects.)

Examples

a. In spite of the storm, we decided to go.

P *OP*
a. In spite of the storm, we decided to go.

b. When assembly was over, students poured through the aisles and halls.

P *OP*
b. When assembly was over, students poured through the aisles and
OP
halls.

1. Because of the heat our relatives won't be coming to visit.
2. On Tuesday the air raid sirens went off and nearly startled me out of my wits.
3. Mange is a common disease in dogs, caused by parasites in the animal's hair follicles.
4. Did you know that people with type A blood seem to be most susceptible to ulcers?
5. My brother always insists on practicing his tuba when I'm on the phone or trying to listen to the news.
6. Ms. Chavez has cast all the parts in the play except the part of the ballerina.
7. After all is said and done, writing is mostly a matter of persistence and of discipline.
8. When Dan was learning to play the banjo, all of us were subjected to his constant plinking and plunking.
9. The United States and a number of other countries did not send teams to the 1980 Olympics in the Soviet Union because they disapproved of Soviet activities in Afghanistan.
10. According to many sports writers, Muhammad Ali revived the ailing sport of boxing with his skill and flamboyant character.

Mastery Exercise A

Using what you have learned about prepositions, list the prepositional phrases on a sheet of paper in the order they appear. Find at least forty-five.[1]

Hint: The first two prepositional phrases are *from a lecture tour* and *at my typewriter.*

I had just returned home from a lecture tour, tired and not feeling very well, and here I was tapping away at my typewriter, sipping a cup of hot tea and humming to myself.

My wife said, "If you don't feel so good, why don't you go up to bed?" and I replied, quite truthfully, "It makes me feel better to sit here working."

This is the beauty of doing work you enjoy, so that while it is a chore in one respect, it is a pleasure in another. And I earnestly urge all young people contemplating their careers to keep in mind that nothing in work is finally rewarding unless it is work you would be willing to do for nothing if you could afford to.

This is the ultimate test for lifelong congeniality in a career, of no matter what sort. Money is not the most important thing; fame is fleeting and uncertain; even status is irksome and uncomforting after a time. All that remains at the end is satisfaction—and occasionally delight—in the performance itself.

Do not do what does not please you; it does not pay, no matter how beguiling the material rewards may seem to be. The pot of gold that appears to be gleaming at the end of the rainbow is less gratifying than the rainbow itself.

The best recipe for a long and happy life is to be able to approach each new morning with anticipation and zest for the job, whatever it may be. This does not mean, of course, that we are not sometimes disgruntled or frustrated or even bored; but, over the long haul, these disaffecting moments are washed away by the tide of contentment, the swell of gratification, at doing well what one does best.

If you are engaged in work you like, even the drudgery and tedium involved in it seems worthwhile. The talented woodcarver who works patiently for hours, and whistles at his work, is getting more out of life—and of himself—than the affluent stockbroker who needs three martinis to get through the afternoon.

The people I have known who seem to rest most easily within themselves are those who have found, by design or lucky accident, the niche made just for them, in whatever field it may be, lofty or humble, so long as it gives them a sense of being needed, of being purposeful and of doing it a little better than most others can.

And those who seemed most unhappy, whatever their degree of external success, were the ones to whom the job was a *means*, not an end, a way of earning a living rather than a way of living. All they can look forward to is retirement, as boring, in a different way, as their jobs are. When the heart goes, the hands should still be tapping away happily.

Mastery Exercise B

From a source such as a magazine, newspaper, or book, or from a paper you have recently written, select a passage about the length of that in Mastery

[1] "Whatever Kind of Job You Perform, You Should Love It or Leave It" from *Strictly Personal* by Sydney J. Harris, © 1981 Field Enterprises, Inc. Courtesy of Field Newspaper Syndicate.

Exercise A. Using what you have learned about prepositions, identify the prepositional phrases in the selection and list them on a sheet of paper in the order they appear.

Using Prepositions

In this section you will study several prepositions that frequently cause writers and speakers trouble. Learn to use these prepositions correctly and use the correct preposition when writing Edited Standard English.

beside/besides

Beside means "by the side of."
Besides means "in addition to," "moreover," or "except."

> The saltshaker is *beside* the napkins.
> *Besides* chemistry I am taking English, history, and art.
> There are few programs *besides* cartoons on Saturday morning television.

between/among

Between refers only to two persons or things.
Among refers to three or more persons or things.

> This information must be kept *between* you and me.
> The information was circulated *among* the five committee members.

Between is sometimes used to compare the items within a group when each is considered individually.

> What are the similarities *between* rock, country, and gospel music?

different from

Use the preposition *from* after the adjective *different* instead of *different than.*

> The program was *different from* what we had expected.
> One kitten was *different from* the others in the litter.

except/accept

Except is a preposition that means "excluding."
Accept is a verb meaning "to take" or "to receive." *Accept* should not be used as a preposition.

> Everyone could come to play practice *except* Rosita.
> That restaurant will not *accept* checks or credit cards.

in/into

In means "inside" or "within."
Into shows a movement from the outside to the inside of something.

A stained glass ornament was hanging *in* the window.
A sparrow flew *into* our open window.
We have red and white corpuscles *in* our bloodstreams.
The veterinarian injected the serum *into* the bloodstream.

Exercise 1

Write out the following sentences, choosing the word from the pair in parentheses that is used in ESE. Underline the word you have chosen.

Examples

a. The Rhodesians would not (accept, except) the terms of the treaty.

a. The Rhodesians would not accept the terms of the treaty.

b. Carla sits (beside, besides) Riko in biology class.

b. Carla sits beside Riko in biology class.

1. The petition circulated (between, among) the three classrooms.
2. Something about my band uniform seemed different (from, than) the others.
3. In the last furlong the race was (between, among) the bay horse and the gray.
4. What do you want for lunch (beside, besides) a hamburger?
5. There are a number of differences (between, among) insects and arachnids.
6. Linguists have noted distinct similarities (between, among) the English, German, and Danish languages.
7. Nobody preferred a skating party to a picnic (accept, except) Marie.
8. Was the Mayan culture very different (from, than) the Toltec?
9. Be sure that the life jackets are (in, into) the boat.
10. Be sure to put the life jackets (in, into) the boat.

Writing Exercise A

To practice in using prepositions in Edited Standard English, write one or two well developed paragraphs on one or more of the following topics.

1. The historic picture on page 475 shows Menachem Begin of Israel, Jimmy Carter of the United States, and Anwar El-Sadat of Egypt in 1979 when the Camp David Accords were made. Describe any similarities and differences you see in the photograph, using *between* and *among*.
2. Discuss the ways in which you expect a job or college to be *different from* high school. In your writing use the words *different from* several times.
3. Discuss the conditions under which you think a state university should be required to accept students. (Should students have to pass a college-

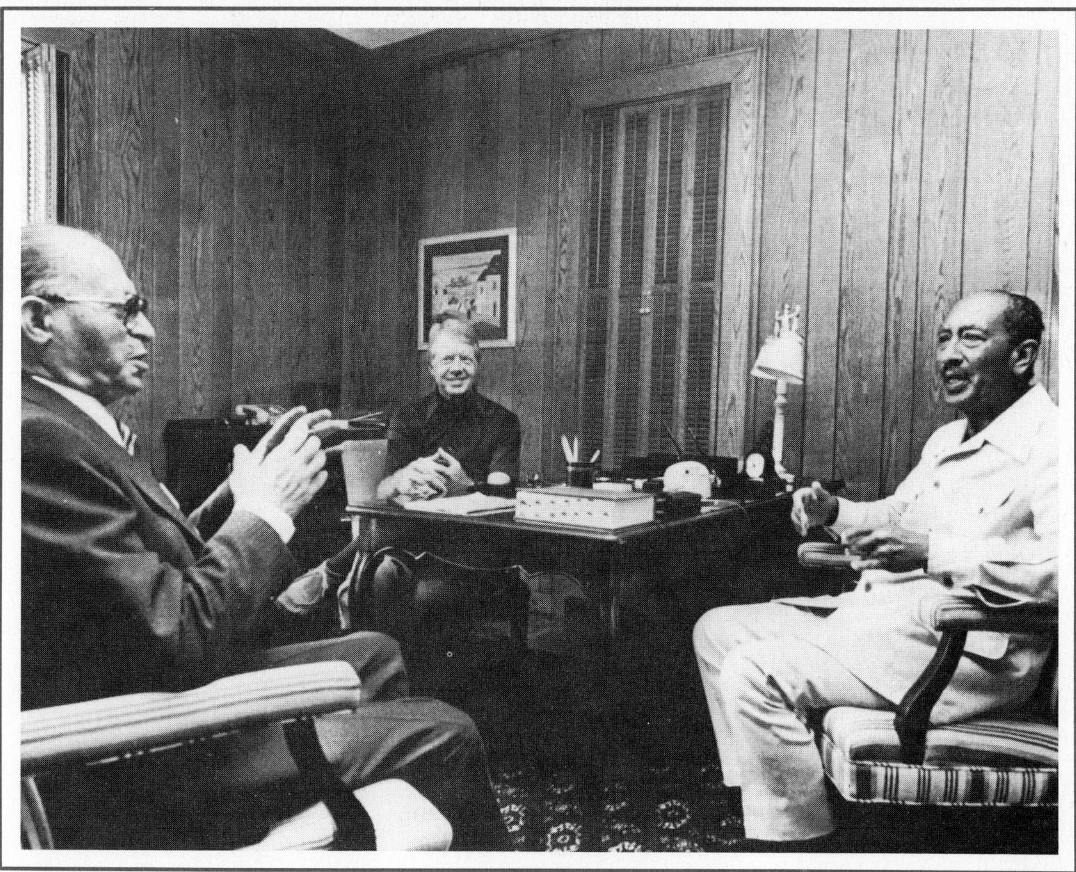

administered test, have a certain grade average in high school, and so on?) What exceptions should state universities have to make for students who do not meet these requirements? In your writing use the words *accept* and *except* two or three times each.

4. Imagine yourself walking or bicycling down this street. Tell what you do and what you see. In your writing use the words *in* and *into* two or three times each.

Understanding Interjections

Interjections are words that express strong feeling: surprise, pain, joy, anger.

Unlike other parts of speech, interjections have no grammatical relationship to the rest of the sentence. They stand apart, complete in themselves, as exclamations or expressions of emotion.

> "*Drat!*" the professor said, "I've forgotten my umbrella."
> *Ouch!* That handle is hot!

Some interjections express milder feelings, such as surprise or interest.

Well, look at that!
Oh, is this where you live?

The following is a list of some words commonly used as interjections.

ah	goodness	nonsense
aha	great	no way
alas	help	phew
congratulations	hey	ugh
dear me	hooray	whew
gee	hurrah	yippee
good grief	never	

Notice that some of the words in the preceding list may also be used as other parts of speech.

Goya was a *great* painter. [adjective]
You got an A? *Great!* [interjection]

Exercise 1

Write out the following sentences, underlining each interjection.

Example

a. Rats, I dropped the keys in the mud!

a. Rats, I dropped the keys in the mud!

1. Great Scott, Professor! A creature is emerging from the meteorite!
2. Oh, I didn't know anyone was in here.
3. We're having boiled parsnips for supper? Ugh!
4. The actress sobbed and wrung her handkerchief, "Alas, we will lose the farm unless we can pay the mortgage."
5. Hurray! I passed my driver's test!
6. Well, things could be worse, but not much worse.
7. Did you smell the sulphur in the chemistry lab today? Whew!
8. He's hit the ball. Wow! It's going to go over the fence!
9. Congratulations, you have just won a year's supply of cat food.
10. Aha! I think I see how to solve this problem.

Using Interjections

Interjections, more than any other part of speech, go in and out of fashion. Your grandparents might have said *grand* or *swell;* your parents *great* or *neat;* an older brother or sister *wild* or *out of sight.* Because interjections often have a meteoric rise and fall in popularity, be careful about using them in formal writing. They can sound foreign to some readers and in a few years may seem dated or quaint.

Punctuating Interjections

Interjections may be followed either by an exclamation mark or by a comma. An interjection followed by an exclamation mark shows strong feeling, while a comma indicates milder emotion.

Yippee**!** The weekend is finally here! [indicates strong feeling]
*Well***,** I suppose we should get started. [indicates milder emotion]

Notice that the word following the exclamation point is capitalized because it is the first word in a new sentence. When a comma is used after an interjection, however, the next word is not capitalized, for it does not begin a new sentence.

In a direct quotation use either a comma or an exclamation point, but not both.

"Wow!" Margaret said, "It's later than we thought."
"Mercy," said the trucker, "it looks like we've got ourselves a convoy."

Exercise 1

Write out the following sentences, underlining each interjection. Then place an exclamation point after an interjection that shows strong or sudden feeling. Use a comma after an interjection that expresses a milder emotion. Remember to capitalize the first word following an exclamation point if that word begins a new sentence. Circle the punctuation you insert.

Example

a. "Alas" cried the knight. "I wish I had never been born to see this tragic day."

a. "Alas (!) " cried the knight. "I wish I had never been born to see this tragic day."

1. Oh I don't know whether I'll go or not.
2. Yipe that's a black widow spider crawling up the wall!
3. "Help" cried the swimmer. "I've been stung by a jellyfish!"
4. The pitcher sighed and sat down wearily. "Gee I thought we were going to win."
5. Hey this is a one-way street!
6. The nurse regarded the patient coolly. "Nonsense you will take this medicine or else!"
7. Wow did you see the size of that shark?
8. Grandmother said, "Well I suppose we ought to get out and do the chores."
9. "Whoopee we've won the championship!" the fan cried, embracing his wife and pounding her on the back.
10. Aunt Frances set the table, then said, "Oh gracious I forgot the cream."

Writing Exercise A

As practice in using interjections, select one of the following situations and write a dialogue based on it. As you write, use appropriate interjections to make your characters' speeches seem realistic. If you prefer, think of a situation of your own. (Supply any details about the situation that you wish to.)

1. Two aliens from a distant galaxy have landed on earth for the first time. The first place they choose to visit is a roller-skating rink in your city or area on a Saturday evening.
2. Twins, either male or female, were separated at birth. Now, at age eighteen, each has learned that he or she has a twin. They are having their first meeting—in the form of a telephone conversation.

3. A young man or woman has let a friend convince him or her to join a skydiving club. Not fully persuaded about the safety of the sport, the young person is nevertheless in the plane about to make his or her first jump. The friend makes some encouraging remarks.
4. A football (track, soccer, baseball, etc.) star is injured during a crucial time in the game. Pleading that the injury is not serious, the player wants to remain in the game. The coach, however, argues that another player will be substituted.

More Practice Using the Parts of Speech

Using Irregular Verbs

Exercise 1

Study the present, past, and past participle forms of the following irregular verbs:

PRESENT	PAST	PAST PARTICIPLE
be	was	(had) been
become	became	(had) become
begin	began	(had) begun
break	broke	(had) broken
bring	brought	(had) brought

Then write out the following sentences, supplying the correct form of the verb in parentheses. Underline the verb you supply.

Example

a. We arrived at the theater a bit late, but the movie hadn't ______ yet. (begin)

a. We arrived at the theater a bit late, but the movie hadn't begun yet.

1. Surely I ______ in class for years, not just fifty minutes. (be)
2. That wretched cat has ______ another flowerpot. (break)
3. After we had hiked ten miles into the forest, we discovered nobody had ______ a can opener. (bring)
4. Mrs. Adams doesn't realize her darling little son Oliver has ______ a neighborhood pest. (become)
5. We ______ to suspect that the fire had been set deliberately. (begin)
6. The twins misbehaved until Uncle Osgood ______ so angry that he threatened to spank them. (become)
7. I'm trying to break the world's record; I've ______ sitting on this flagpole eighteen days. (be)
8. Lucy ______ the wrong notebook to class. (bring)
9. When the two players collided, Carlos ______ his glasses. (break)
10. And just where were you when all this trouble ______? (begin)

Exercise 2

Review the forms of the irregular verbs *buy, catch, choose, come,* and *dive.* (See page 410.) Then choose the word in parentheses that correctly completes each of the following sentences. Write out the sentences, underlining the word you choose.

Example

a. Kim hasn't (buyed, bought) her class ring yet.

a. Kim hasn't bought her class ring yet.

1. Who was (chose, chosen) for the team?
2. A bad strain of flu is going around, but I haven't (caught, catched) it yet.
3. Our neighbor (come, came) over last night to complain about my sister's dog.
4. When the starter fired the pistol, all the swimmers (dived, doved) into the water.
5. Have you (bought, boughten) your tickets yet?
6. The farmer finally (catched, caught) all the escaped cattle.
7. I (come, came) close to getting hit at that intersection.
8. I haven't ever (dived, dove) from the highest board at the pool.
9. Whoever (buyed, bought) that car made a terrible mistake.
10. Have you (chose, chosen) which sleeping bag you want?

Exercise 3

Review the forms of the irregular verbs *do, draw, drink, drive,* and *eat* on page 410. Then write out the following sentences, supplying the correct form of the verb in parentheses. Underline the verb you supply.

Example

a. The detective sighed, "I don't know who _______ it." (do)

a. The detective sighed, "I don't know who did it."

1. Has Margo _______ her biology homework yet? (do)
2. Mrs. Jaworski has _______ a map of the library. (draw)
3. I'll _______ clams, but I don't like them. (eat)
4. After Juliet _______ the potion, she appeared to be dead. (drink)
5. Lisa never _______ a foul for goal-tending. (draw)
6. Have you ever _______ prune juice? (drink)
7. Lady Macbeth's guilt had _______ her mad. (drive)
8. We have _______ at the new Korean restaurant. (eat)

9. The doctors ______ everything they could to repair the injured elbow. (do)
10. We ______ cautiously down the winding road. (drive)

Exercise 4

Review the forms of the irregular verbs *fall*, *fly*, *forget*, *freeze*, *give*, and *go* on page 410. Then write out the sentences, choosing the verb in parentheses that completes each sentence. Underline the words you choose.

Example

a. Have you ever (gone, went) to a Ray Charles concert?

a. Have you ever gone to a Ray Charles concert?

1. I felt as if my toes had (frozen, froze).
2. The reputation of that politician has certainly (fell, fallen).
3. We stopped at the office, but Ms. Garcia had already (went, gone) home.
4. The robins have all (flown, flew) south for the winter.
5. When I walked into the classroom, I (forget, forgot) everything I had studied.
6. I have never (forgotten, forgot) Chief Dan George's performance in that movie.
7. Suddenly a pheasant (flied, flew) up out of the brush.
8. The lake (freezed, froze) over, but not enough to skate on safely.
9. I have (gave, given) my decision to the coach.
10. Carey has (gone, went) to work for an oil company.

Exercise 5

Some of the following sentences contain errors in verb usage. Rewrite the sentences, making any necessary corrections. If the sentence is correct, write *C*. Underline any corrections you make. A list of irregular verb forms is on pages 410–411.

Examples

a. I knowed my irregular verb forms perfectly.

a. I knew my irregular verb forms perfectly.

b. Marcia kept the secret to herself.

b. C

1. Our cute puppy growed up into a huge, shaggy, obnoxious dog.
2. My little brother keeped peeking around the corner at us.
3. I hitted the ball with all my strength.
4. I've knew Dr. Arnez for three years.
5. Have you ever rode a Tennessee walking horse?

6. Hank Aaron has hit more home runs than any other American player.
7. Every time I've rid on the bus, I've got queasy.
8. You knowed better than to tease the bull; here's another bandage.
9. He has keep asking me for favors until I am tired of it.
10. Imat has growed a mustache.

Exercise 6

Review the forms of the irregular verbs *ring, run, see, shake,* and *shrink* on page 410. Then choose the correct form of the verb in parentheses to complete each sentence. Write out the sentences, underlining the correct forms.

Example

a. Have you ever ______ the Harlem Globetrotters play? (see)

a. Have you ever seen the Harlem Globetrotters play?

1. Someone has ______ the dismissal bell too early. (ring)
2. Not many Americans have ______ a live panda bear. (see)
3. The laundry ______ my favorite sweater. (shrink)
4. Denise wasn't hurt in the accident, only ______ a bit. (shake)
5. A raccoon got in our garbage, but the dogs ______ it off. (run)
6. Yesterday I ______ a great antique car. (see)
7. It seems that the buying power of a dollar has ______ drastically. (shrink)
8. The church bells ______ after the ceremony. (ring)
9. The cat stepped onto the dewy grass, then ______ its paw. (shake)
10. The television station had ______ the wrong commercial. (run)

Exercise 7

Review the forms of the irregular verbs *sing, sink, slay, speak,* and *spend* on pages 410–411. Then choose the word in parentheses that correctly completes each of the following sentences. Write out the sentences and underline your choices.

Example

a. Josephine Baker had (sung, sang) in America before she became a star in Paris.

a. Josephine Baker had sung in America before she became a star in Paris.

1. Our boat swamped and our fishing gear (sank, sunk) out of sight.
2. He was as proud as if he had (slayed, slain) a dragon.
3. We (sang, sung) some Osage songs at camp last summer.
4. I have (spoke, spoken) to the company about the problem.

5. Central didn't just beat us; they (slayed, slew) us.
6. I've (spend, spent) all my allowance and am poverty-stricken.
7. The congresswoman (speak, spoke) to the student body.
8. The tenor had (sung, sang) badly off-key.
9. The center had (sank, sunk) an almost impossible shot.
10. The golfer deftly (sunk, sank) the putt.

Exercise 8

Review the forms of the irregular verbs *spring, steal, strive, swear,* and *swim* on page 411. Some of the following sentences contain errors in verb usage. Rewrite the sentences, making necessary corrections. If the sentence is correct, write *C*. Underline any corrections you make.

Examples

a. Several women have swam the English Channel.
a. Several women have swum the English Channel.

b. The witness had sworn to tell the truth.
b. C

1. Lester sprung out of the shadows, trying to scare me.
2. I swum in the river, but the current was dangerously strong.
3. We have striven to win this championship.
4. Chief Joseph had swore to fight no more.
5. Moncrief stoled the ball and made a great stuff shot.
6. Have you ever swam in a heated pool?
7. We sprang a surprise party for Cassie.
8. The dogs strived to catch the fleeing fox.
9. My grandfather sweared he once saw a hoop snake.
10. Somebody had stole most of the apples from the tree.

Exercise 9

Review the forms of the irregular verbs *take, teach, think, throw, wear,* and *write* on page 411. Then write out the following sentences, supplying the correct form of the verb in parentheses. Underline the verb.

Example

a. Somebody must have ______ my jacket by mistake. (take)
a. Somebody must have taken my jacket by mistake.

1. I've ______ my term paper for history class. (write)
2. The tires on my car are almost ______ out. (wear)
3. Have you ______ your vitamin pill today? (take)

4. I haven't ______ of a solution yet. (think)
5. Leslie ______ a class in belly-dancing. (teach)
6. Pat had ______ the ball too hard. (throw)
7. Conchita had ______ a note of apology. (write)
8. I accidentally ______ out the wrong papers. (throw)
9. We ______ our parrot how to talk. (teach)
10. Marcia must have ______ her knee out of joint. (throw)

Using Verbs Often Confused

Exercise 10

Review the forms of the verbs *lie* and *lay* on page 431. Remember that *lie* means "to recline" and that *lay* means "to place something" or "to put something down." Complete the following sentences by choosing the correct verb in parentheses. Write the sentences, underlining the verb you choose.

Example

a. I was (lying, laying) on the couch reading a mystery.

a. I was lying on the couch reading a mystery.

1. You look horrible, Selma, perhaps you should (lie, lay) down.
2. The keys had been (laid, lain) on the mantel.
3. Mel was in the backyard, (laying, lying) in the hammock.
4. The poker player (lay, laid) his cards down in disgust.
5. My uncle (lay, laid) the bricks for our patio.
6. Would you (lay, lie) those coats across the bed?
7. Zounds! The hen has (laid, lain) a blue egg!
8. I (lay, laid) down the book I was reading.
9. The cat was (lying, laying) on the front porch, asleep.
10. If a bear wanders into camp, just (lie, lay) still.

Exercise 11

Review the forms of the verbs *sit* and *set* on page 431. Remember that *sit* means "to occupy a seat" or "to rest" and that *set* means "to put or place something." Complete the following sentences by choosing the correct verb in parentheses. Write out the sentences and underline the verb you choose.

Example

a. (Set, Sit) down and make yourself comfortable.

a. Sit down and make yourself comfortable.

1. The lion (set, sat) in its cage, yawning hugely.
2. Someone needs to (set, sit) down with him and have a talk.

3. She has (sat, set) in that chair all afternoon.
4. Just (set, sit) the groceries down on the counter.
5. Maureen will (set, sit) out some strawberry plants this spring.
6. I had just (sit, sat) down when the phone rang.
7. Marcia accidentally (set, sat) too many books on the desk.
8. A bird (set, sat) on the clothesline wire.
9. John was just (setting, sitting) down to write when you called.
10. Inez (set, sat) the trophy down with a thump.

Exercise 12

Review the forms of the verbs *rise* and *raise* on page 432. Remember that *rise* means "to go up." *Raise* means "to make something move up" and takes a direct object. Complete the following sentences by choosing the correct verb in parentheses. Write the sentences, underlining the verb you choose.

Example

a. A hand (raised, rose) up and fumbled at the window latch.
a. A hand rose up and fumbled at the window latch.

1. Prices have (risen, rose) again at the grocery store.
2. She (raised, rose) from her chair and went to the door.
3. Please (raise, rise) and salute the flag.
4. The Scouts (raised, rose) the flag for Memorial Day.
5. The snake (raised, rose) its head and flicked its tongue.
6. We'll have to (raise, rise) from our beds at dawn tomorrow.
7. Some questions have been (raised, risen) about the new school policies.
8. Miko's voice (raised, rose) with emotion.
9. The phone company's rates (raised, rose) last year by five percent.
10. The issue has been (raised, risen) and discussed already.

Making Pronouns Agree with Antecedents

Exercise 13

Review the list of singular and plural pronouns on page 423. Then choose the pronoun that correctly completes each of the following sentences. Write out the sentences and underline the pronoun you select.

Example

a. Neither of the girls had received (her, their) grades.
a. Neither of the girls had received her grades.

1. Each of the choir members purchases (his or her, their) own robe.
2. Several of the boys had parked (his, their) cars in the faculty lot.

3. Only one of the boys had (his, their) car ticketed.
4. Somebody left (his or her, their) lunch in the biology lab.
5. Some of the apple trees had blight on (its, their) leaves.
6. Either of the girls might have lent you (her, their) tape recorder.
7. Everyone on the girls' softball team has improved (her, their) batting average.
8. None of the Boy Scouts wore (his, their) merit badges at the meeting.
9. All of the seniors have made (his or her, their) yearbook payments.
10. Everybody will bring (his or her, their) own food for the picnic.

Exercise 14

Remember that when two or more singular antecedents are joined by *and*, a plural pronoun is used to refer to them. However, when two or more singular antecedents are joined by *or* or *nor*, a singular pronoun is used to refer to them. Complete the following sentences by choosing the correct pronoun in parentheses. Write out the sentences, underlining the pronoun you select.

Examples

a. Either Kim or Estralita will bring (her, their) records.

a. Either Kim or Estralita will bring her records.

b. Mr. Blanco and Mr. Washington have seen (his, their) children become doctors.

b. Mr. Blanco and Mr. Washington have seen their children become doctors.

1. Neither Karen nor her mother wore (her, their) gloves.
2. The shortstop and the catcher both broke (his, their) records in that game.
3. Either the shepherd or the shepherdess lost (his or her, their) sheep.
4. Both Kevin and Mark got (his, their) letters in track.
5. Neither Archie Bunker nor Fred Sanford merited any points for (his, their) politeness.
6. Neither the collie nor the poodle liked (its, their) yearly visit to the vet.
7. Marge or Amanda will lend you (her, their) history notes.
8. Fran and Ruby have finished (her, their) short stories for creative-writing class.
9. Neither Burt nor Rodney remembered (his, their) lines on opening night.
10. Carrie or Pat can use (her, their) artistic talents to help us.

19 English Sentence Structure

Understanding Sentences

If you have been around children who are learning to talk, you know that their first utterances are single words, such as *Mama*, *Daddy*, and *Kitty*. Gradually children learn to combine words to express more complex ideas. In their first few years they learn the rules for combining words to make sentences—no matter what language is their native one. It does not matter if you grew up speaking English, Spanish, or Chinese; you automatically learned how to put words into their proper order to make a statement or ask a question.

In this section you will learn about the structure of sentences. Even though you may have little trouble speaking in sentences, understanding sentence parts and how they work will help you to write more clearly and effectively.

Defining a Sentence

A *sentence* is often defined as a group of words that expresses a complete thought.

Incomplete: The woman in the hard hat.
[What about the woman? Who is she, or what did she do?]

Complete: The woman in the hard hat is the city's chief building inspector.

Incomplete: Scuttled after the fleeing hunter.
[Who or what chased the hunter?]

Complete: The large alligator scuttled after the fleeing hunter.

Incomplete: With the head of an eagle and the legs of a lion. [What?]

Complete: The griffin was a fearsome mythical beast with the head of an eagle and the legs of a lion.

Groups of words expressing incomplete thoughts leave you with unanswered questions, such as *who? did what? what about it?* or *what happened?* Whenever you have such questions, the group of words is not a sentence because it does not express a complete thought.

Exercise 1

Decide whether each of the following word groups expresses a complete thought. Then on a sheet of paper, write *S* for sentences and *NS* for non-sentences. If the group of words is not a sentence, add whatever words are needed to express a complete thought.

Examples

a. The songs from the musical *Hair* were strongly influenced by African rhythms and melodies.

a. S

b. Since her broken leg hadn't healed yet.

b. NS. Sandy couldn't ski in the race since her broken leg hadn't healed yet.

1. The girl over in the corner in the jeans and orange sweater.
2. Just when everyone was least expecting it.
3. Because the river was at flood stage and very swift.
4. A serigraph is a print made by a silk-screen process.
5. Hunting pythons in the jungles of Burma.
6. Groundhogs are also called "woodchucks."
7. Especially when I have to get up early the next morning.
8. While I was talking on the telephone to Pat.
9. A fern does not reproduce by seeds or shoots.
10. After eating six hot dogs with everything on them.

The Purposes of Sentences

Sentences may be classified in two ways—by their purpose or by their structure. (Classification by structure is discussed in the section on clauses, pages 536–537.)

Words can be joined to make a sentence for one of four different purposes.

1. A declarative sentence makes a statement and ends with a period.

Maxine Hong Kingston is an excellent writer.
All leprechauns have a hidden pot of gold.

2. An interrogative sentence asks a question and ends with a question mark.

   Are there really giant sharks?
   Have you read any of the novels of Frank Yerby?

3. An imperative sentence gives a command or makes a request and may be followed either by a period or an exclamation mark.

The subject of an imperative sentence is always *you*, the person or persons being addressed. Even if the word *you* does not appear in the sentence, it is considered to be the "understood subject."

   (You) Never stand under a tree during a lightning storm.
   (You) Abandon ship!

4. An exclamatory sentence expresses strong feeling and is usually followed by an exclamation mark.

   We won the talent contest!
   The dam has burst!
   How lucky you are!

Exercise 2

On a sheet of paper, write out the following sentences, ending each sentence with an appropriate punctuation mark. Then after each sentence indicate whether it is *declarative, interrogative, imperative,* or *exclamatory.* Circle the punctuation marks you insert.

Examples

a. Do you like Erica Jong's poetry
a. Do you like Erica Jong's poetry(?) interrogative
b. Run for your lives
b. Run for your lives(!) exclamatory

1. Did you know that Robert Redford was elected sewer commissioner of Provo, Utah
2. The dog's name "Fido" comes from the Latin word for "faithful"
3. What a disappointment that movie was
4. Please go through the metal-detecting apparatus before boarding the plane
5. Quasars are believed to be about 10 billion light years away from our planet
6. In what countries is cork grown
7. Don't touch that wire
8. Our motor is on fire
9. Does anyone know what started the great Chicago fire in 1871
10. The game of lacrosse is derived from an ancient Indian game called "baggataway"

The Parts of the Sentence

Every sentence has two essential parts: the *subject* and the *predicate*.

The *subject*, often a person or thing, is usually defined as that part of the sentence about which something is being said.

The *predicate* is usually defined as that part of the sentence that says something about the subject.

In the following sentences a slash divides the subject from the predicate:

Subject *Predicate*
Badminton / originated in India.

Subject *Predicate*
Mrs. Nancy Johnson / is credited with inventing the ice cream freezer.

Subject *Predicate*
The digestive system of the pig / is remarkably like that of a human.

In most English sentences the subject precedes the predicate. In some sentences, however, the subject follows all or part of the predicate.

Predicate *Subject*
Under the pile of papers was / the lost check.

Exercise 3

Write out each of the following sentences and draw a slash separating the subject from the predicate. Then label each part *Subject* or *Predicate.*

Examples

a. The coal miner's job is the most hazardous in America.

Subject *Predicate*
a. The coal miner's job / is the most hazardous in America.

b. In the Botanical Gardens in San Marino, California, is the world's largest collect of desert plants.

Predicate
b. In the Botanical Gardens in San Marino, California, is / the world's
Subject
largest collection of desert plants.

1. Harriet Beecher Stowe's *Uncle Tom's Cabin* was a novel of great social impact.
2. The ancient Greeks painted their marble statues in several colors for realistic effect.
3. Brief and tragic was the career of Anne Boleyn.
4. A parrot in a national park in New Zealand learned to let the air out of the tires of parked cars.
5. Very few types of germs and bacteria can survive the cold of the South Pole.
6. Pepi the Second of the sixth Egyptian dynasty reigned for ninety years.

7. The first female boxing match took place in 1876 and was won by Miss Nell Saunders.
8. Deep in the cave slept hundreds of hanging bats.
9. Our word *dandelion* comes from a French phrase meaning "tooth of the lion."
10. A medieval suit of armor might weigh as much as a hundred pounds.

Complete Subject and Simple Subject

The *complete subject* tells who or what the sentence is about.

In the following sentences the complete subject is *italicized.*

> *Four of the band uniforms* have to be replaced.
> *The actress playing the part of Nancy* was Pearl Bailey.
> *The turkey with chestnut dressing* looked delicious.

The *simple subject* is the main word or words in the complete subject.

The simple subject is never part of a prepositional phrase, nor does it ever include modifiers.

In the following sentences the complete subject is *italicized;* the simple subject is underlined.

> *Four of the band uniforms* have to be replaced.
> *The actress playing the part of Nancy* was Pearl Bailey.
> *The turkey with chestnut dressing* looked delicious.

When the simple subject is a proper name, it may be made up of more than one word.

> *Stevie Wonder* is an extraordinary musician.
> *Westminster Abbey* is the burial place of many great poets.

In discussions of the parts of the sentence, the word *subject* usually refers to the simple subject, not to the complete subject.

Exercise 4

Write out the following sentences, underlining the complete subject once and the simple subject twice.

Examples

a. An important figure in British legend and literature is King Arthur.
a. An important figure in British legend and literature is King Arthur.

b. Fiction, not fact, is the source of most Arthurian stories.
b. Fiction, not fact, is the source of most Arthurian stories.

1. Bits of information indicate the existence of a real King Arthur.
2. One of the ancient historians states that Arthur was a chieftain of the fifth or sixth century.

3. A very old manuscript in Latin states that Arthur died at the battle of Mount Badon in 518.
4. Several ancient poems, including the "Black Book of Carmathen," mention a King Arthur.
5. The Arthur of these ancient poems is a supernatural king, almost a god.
6. A few researchers on the subject claim there may have been two King Arthurs.
7. One of these kings was a figure from ancient British folklore and was completely fictional.
8. The second Arthur, however, may have been an actual hero and warrior.
9. The characters of the two figures may have merged over the years.
10. A dashing figure with supernatural powers emerged to become the King Arthur of Camelot.

Complete Predicate and Simple Predicate

The *predicate* is the part of the sentence that tells something about the subject.

The *complete predicate* is made up of the verb and all of its modifiers and complements.

In the following sentences the complete predicate is *italicized.*

> The hummingbird *swiftly darted in and out of the blossoms of the trumpet vine.*
> I *accidentally brushed my teeth with hair cream this morning.*
> Marcia *is playing bass bugle in the drum and bugle corps.*

The *simple predicate* is the verb or verb phrase, the main word or words in the complete predicate.

In the following sentences the complete predicate is *italicized;* the simple predicate is *underlined.*

> The hummingbird *swiftly <u>darted</u> in and out of the blossoms of the trumpet vine.*
> I *accidentally <u>brushed</u> my teeth with hair cream this morning.*
> Marcia *<u>is playing</u> bass bugle in the drum and bugle corps.*

In discussions of the parts of a sentence, the word *verb* or *verb phrase* is used more often than the term *simple predicate.*

Exercise 5

Write out the following sentences, underlining the complete predicate once and the simple predicate (verb or verb phrase) twice.

Examples

a. *Frankenstein* was written by Mary Shelley in 1817.

a. Frankenstein <u>*was written by Mary Shelley in 1817.*</u>

b. The book was originally subtitled *"or the Modern Prometheus."*
b. The book was originally subtitled "or the Modern Prometheus."

1. The name *Frankenstein* actually refers to the scientist and not to the monster he created.
2. Dr. Frankenstein has learned the secret of endowing matter with life.
3. The doctor is like the legendary Prometheus, bringer of light to humanity.
4. Prometheus was punished by the gods for his gift to humans.
5. Dr. Frankenstein, like Prometheus, must suffer for his breakthrough.
6. He creates human life, but of a monstrous sort.
7. The creation is filled with loathing for its creator.
8. The monster murders the doctor's brother and the doctor's bride.
9. The monster ultimately causes the destruction of the horrified Dr. Frankenstein himself.
10. The gift of life has turned into the curse of death for the ambitious doctor.

The True Subject

In most English sentences the subject appears before the verb. Speakers or writers first identify who or what they are talking or writing about, then complete the statement. (In the example sentences in this section, the subject is underlined once and the verb or verb phrase twice.)

The fly buzzed loudly against the windowpane.

Subject-verb agreement is discussed on pages 421–429.

In some sentences, however, all or part of the verb appears before the subject. Being able to identify the true subject of a sentence is essential in order to choose a verb that agrees with the subject in number.

The verb may precede the subject in a question.

Is there any peanut butter in the cupboard?

Will you kindly step into the principal's office?

Have you seen my civics books?

Does Karen like her job at the radio station?

Sometimes, sentences are inverted for effect. This means they are purposely written with the subject following the verb.

Under my lettuce leaf was a large insect.

Directly in our path was a large, brown bear.

In many sentences that begin with *there* and *here*, the subject follows the verb.

Here are my reasons for refusing.

There are few storms more powerful than a Pacific typhoon.

An *expletive* is a word that signals that the subject will follow the verb.

Sometimes, the word *it* is also used as an expletive.

It is hard to concentrate with that television blaring.

To find the true subject of a sentence, first find the verb and then ask to *whom* or to *what* the verb refers.

Another way of locating the subject of a sentence is to change the inverted sentence or question into a statement with the subject preceding the verb.

You will kindly step into the principal's office.
Karen does like her job at the radio station.
My reasons for refusing are here.
Few storms are more powerful than a Pacific typhoon.

Remember that the subject of an imperative sentence is always the word *you*, the person or persons being addressed. When the word *you* does not appear in the sentence, it is understood as the subject.

(You) Help me with this package, please.
(You) Have some more mashed potatoes.

One last obstacle to locating the true subject of a sentence is the prepositional phrase.

Several (of the choir members) were late for practice.
A number (of people in the area) saw the mysterious flash in the sky.

The subject of a sentence never appears in a prepositional phrase.

Exercise 6

Write out the following sentences, underlining the simple subject once and the verb or verb phrase twice.

Examples

a. Somewhere beneath the sea may lie Atlantis.
a. Somewhere beneath the sea may lie Atlantis.

b. Where is my physics notebook?
b. Where is my physics notebook?

1. There is a myth about how the bear got its short tail.
2. Far in the west was a vague rumble of thunder.
3. The fear of heights is a very common phobia.
4. Here is an instance of poor engineering.
5. When will the next leap year occur?
6. Call me about the homework assignments.
7. There is a mysterious red spot on the planet Jupiter.

8. Down the path came a stray dog without a collar.
9. A box of broken tools and old flower pots sat in the garage.
10. How many of the seniors can graduate in January?

Compound Subjects and Verbs

Compound means "having two or more parts." Subjects and predicates may be compound.

A *compound subject* consists of two or more simple subjects joined by a conjunction.

The parts of a compound subject share the same verb.

> Distemper, rabies, and parvovirus are serious canine illnesses.
>
> A carton of eggs and a quart of milk were in the cooler.

A *compound verb* consists of two or more verbs that are joined by a conjunction.

The parts of a compound verb have the same subject.

> The audience laughed, applauded, and cheered.
>
> The blizzard tied up traffic and brought all travel to a halt.

A sentence may contain both a compound subject and a compound verb.

> Mrs. Rinaldo and Miss Chavez collected the votes and counted them.

Exercise 7

Write out the following sentences, underlining the simple subject once and the simple predicate (verb or verb phrase) twice. Remember to look for compound subjects and verbs.

Example

a. Kim is a Korean-American and speaks two languages fluently.
a. Kim is a Korean-American and speaks two languages fluently.

1. Bacon, eggs, toast, and juice were set before the seasick passenger.
2. Hurricane Allen struck in 1980 and caused severe damage and flooding in the southern states.
3. A tank of tropical fish and a cage of finches stood in the pet shop.
4. Birds have no teeth and must use rocks and gravel to grind their food.
5. President Chester A. Arthur held a garage sale on the grounds of the White House and sold twenty-five wagonloads of furniture.
6. Susan B. Anthony was fined a hundred dollars for attempting to vote, but refused to pay.
7. In 1972 a baboon escaped, jumped onto a passing bus, looked at the passengers, then ran all the way back to its cage.

8. Dorothy Dandridge, Sammy Davis, Jr., and Sidney Poitier starred in the movie version of *Porgy and Bess.*
9. A bushel of tomatoes and a crate of chickens fell from the truck and bounced across the highway.
10. A mouse or rat got into the cabin and ruined our supplies.

Review Exercise A

Write out each of the following sentences, underlining the simple subject once and the verb or verb phrase twice. (Be sure to look for compound subjects and verbs.)

1. Margaret Mitchell of Atlanta, Georgia, wrote one of the most phenomenal best sellers of the century, *Gone with the Wind.*
2. Miss Mitchell was born and reared in Georgia.
3. She and her brother knew many older people and listened to their stories of Civil War times.
4. Margaret herself often went riding with a group of Civil War veterans.
5. She was a spirited girl and loved history, romance, and adventure.
6. She had a vivid imagination and a flair for language.
7. She became a newspaper reporter and was famous for her lively feature stories.
8. She and her husband lived in a tiny apartment in Atlanta.
9. Her husband and friends urged her to write a book.
10. She began but would show the pages to no one.
11. For years the stacks of paper grew and began to fill drawers and closets.
12. She used several chapters, piled high, to support the leg of a wobbly couch.
13. At last a New York editor visited Atlanta and heard about the book.
14. Miss Mitchell was unsure of its worth and did not wish to show it to anyone.
15. Besides, the manuscript was incomplete and had many revisions scribbled on the pages.
16. The book had no opening chapter, no title, and was scattered all through her home.
17. Nevertheless, the editor talked her out of the book, read it, and knew its worth instantly.
18. There have been few books that generated the excitement of *Gone with the Wind.*
19. It was a novel that both pleased critics and delighted readers.
20. Scarlett O'Hara and Rhett Butler became two of the most popular lovers in fiction.

21. The book was sold to Hollywood and made into an equally popular movie.
22. Both the book and the movie raised a question maddening to their audiences.
23. Would the spoiled and selfish heroine of the story find Rhett Butler again and regain his love?
24. Mrs. Mitchell and her family were bombarded by letters and pestered by phone calls and visitors demanding an answer.
25. Never did Mrs. Mitchell break her silence concerning this riddle, nor hint at its solution.

Sentence Patterns

A small number of sentence patterns form the basis of all English sentences.

The simplest sentence pattern is the pattern *Subject-Verb*, abbreviated *S–V*.

In the S–V pattern the verb is always an action verb or one that expresses a state of being. Linking verbs occur only in other sentence patterns.

S V
Jeans fade.

Modifiers do not affect the sentence pattern. Even though both the subject and the verb may have modifiers, the basic sentence pattern remains unchanged.

S V
Even expensive designer jeans often fade.

This sentence may be expanded still further without changing the S–V pattern:

S V
Even expensive designer jeans from the best stores often fade (after they are washed a few times).

Note: The group of words in parentheses is a subordinate clause (see page 535), which does not affect the basic pattern.

A verb phrase counts as a single verb.

S V
The roses *were wilting* swiftly.

S V
Miranda *had been dreaming.*

In any sentence pattern one or more of the elements may be compound.

S V V
Several passers-by stopped and stared.

S *S* *V* *V*
The goose and gander honked and hissed at the dog.

A sentence is still considered *S–V* even though the verb may appear before the subject, as in a question or inverted sentence.

V *S*
Where is Timbuktu?

V *S*
Out of the basket rose a swaying cobra.

Complements

Sentences express complete thoughts by means of a subject (who or what the sentence is about) and a predicate (what the subject is or does). Some sentences express a complete thought with only a subject and a verb. Many English sentences, however, contain a third necessary part—a complement.

A *complement* is usually defined as a word or group of words that completes the meaning of the verb and the subject.

S *V*
Incomplete: Carrie seems [seems what?]

S *V* *Comp.*
Complete: Carrie seems angry.

S *V*
Incomplete: José sent [sent what?]

S *V* *Comp.*
Complete: José sent his congratulations.

Complements, like subjects, are never found within a prepositional phrase.

S *V*
Barbara bounced into the room.
[*Into the room* is a prepositional phrase.]

S *V* *Comp.*
Barbara bounced the basketball.

In the following lessons you will learn to identify several kinds of complements: predicate nominatives, predicate adjectives, direct objects, indirect objects, and objective complements. You will also learn the sentence patterns associated with these complements.

Predicate Nominatives

A *predicate nominative* is a noun or pronoun that follows a linking verb and renames the subject.

A sentence containing a predicate nominative has the sentence pattern S–LV–PN.

S LV PN
"Fig-eaters" are beetles.

S LV PN
"Fig-eaters" are the ones destroying the garden.

Adding modifiers does not change the basic sentence pattern.

S LV PN
"Fig-eaters," a type of garden pest, are large beetles with iridescent wings.

Inverting sentence order to ask a question does not change the basic pattern:

LV S PN
Are "fig-eaters" large green beetles?

Exercise 8

Write out the following sentences, underlining and labeling each part of the sentence according to its pattern. (Not all sentences contain predicate nominatives.)

Examples

a. Tina was my locker mate for a semester.

S LV PN
a. Tina was my locker mate for a semester.

b. The lifeguard quickly swam to the struggling child.

S V
b. The lifeguard quickly swam to the struggling child.

1. Pit vipers are highly poisonous reptiles.
2. The last people in the band bus were Stacey and I.
3. The 1981 Scout Jamboree was held in Virginia.
4. Dorothy Sayers became one of the foremost mystery writers of our time.
5. "Nessie" is the nickname for the famous Loch Ness monster.
6. Our foreign exchange student this year is from Taiwan.
7. The actresses Margaux and Mariel Hemingway are the granddaughters of Ernest Hemingway, the novelist.
8. At last soccer is becoming a popular game in the United States.
9. Isn't "Heart" an all-female rock music group?
10. My sister is a graduate of the music department of Howard University.

Predicate Adjectives

Predicate adjectives, like predicate nominatives, are complements that follow linking verbs. Predicate adjectives, as the name implies, are always adjectives; predicate nominatives are always nouns or pronouns.

A *predicate adjective* is usually defined as an adjective that follows a linking verb and modifies the subject of the sentence.

Laura was *happy* about her scholarship.

The clerk became *impatient* with the customer.

The campers looked *tired* and *dirty*.

Sentences with predicate adjectives have the pattern *S–LV–PA*.

S LV PA
Laura was happy about her scholarship.

Exercise 9

Write out the following sentences, underlining and labeling each part of the sentence according to its pattern: S–V, S–LV–PN, or S–LV–PA.

Examples

a. This book is a serious examination of religious cults and cult leaders.

S LV PN
a. This book is a serious examination of religious cults and cult leaders.

b. The baby quail looked toylike and helpless.

S LV PA PA
b. The baby quail looked toylike and helpless.

1. The first woman candidate for the Presidency of the United States of America was Victoria Claflin Woodhull.
2. Sacajawea was a Shoshone woman and a guide for the explorers Lewis and Clark.
3. The Sahara desert is larger than any state and many countries.
4. The sun, moon, and stars appear larger when near the horizon.
5. Cheese is the oldest of all human-made foods.
6. A "red herring" is a slang term for a false or misleading clue.
7. Even in captivity zebras are wild and almost untrainable.
8. Soybeans are useful, versatile, and nutritious.
9. *Tess of the D'Urbervilles* is the tragic story of a young woman at the mercy of her environment.
10. In the tangled underbrush lurk many strange creatures of the night.

Direct Objects

Verbs are either linking verbs or action verbs. The complements used with linking verbs are the predicate nominative and the predicate adjective. In this and the next two sections you will study the complements used with action verbs. The first of these is the direct object.

A *direct object* is usually defined as a word or group of words that receives the action of the verb.

A direct object usually follows an action verb and answers the question *whom?* or *what?*

Conchita mailed the *invitations.*	[What did she mail?]
Jeff phoned his *sister.*	[Whom did he phone?]

Direct objects may be nouns, pronouns, phrases, or clauses.

Dan can ride a *unicycle,* but not very well.	[noun]
Marcia called *me* about the party.	[pronoun]
We liked *working with the movie equipment.*	[phrase]
Nobody wanted *to watch that program.*	[phrase]
Everyone knows *that germs cause disease.*	[clause]

Transitive and Intransitive Verbs

Action verbs are classified as either *transitive* or *intransitive.*

A *transitive verb* is an action verb that takes a direct object. An *intransitive verb* is an action verb that does not take a direct object.

Many English verbs may be either transitive or intransitive, depending upon their use in the sentence.

Intransitive:	The speaker *mumbled* unintelligibly.
Transitive:	Sharon *mumbled* an apology. [*apology* receives the action]
Intransitive:	The violinist *performed* at Carnegie Hall.
Transitive:	The violinist *performed* her own composition at Carnegie Hall. [*composition* receives the action]

Sentences with direct objects have the pattern *S–V–DO.*

S V DO
The governor released a statement to the press.

S V DO
(You) Remember your dentist's appointment at 9:30.

Exercise 10

Write out the following sentences, underlining and labeling each part of the sentence according to its pattern. (Not all sentences have direct objects; some may have more than one.)

Examples

a. Ursula LeGuin writes science fiction.

S V DO
a. Ursula LeGuin writes science fiction.

b. The trained seal could play the horns and the xylophone.

S V DO DO
b. The trained seal could play the horns and the xylophone.

c. Our physics teacher is Mr. Wang.

S LV PN
c. Our physics teacher is Mr. Wang.

For sentences with an understood subject, write *(you)* before the sentence.

1. The jets left vapor trails across the sky.
2. The 4-H Club members sold popcorn and peanuts at the football game.
3. Before entering politics, Ronald Reagan was a movie actor.
4. Kevin and Lucy can play either guitar or banjo.
5. Please buy a carton of eggs at the store.
6. In our creative writing class we wrote haikus, limericks, and ballads.
7. Melinda is studying German and French in Europe this summer.
8. Gwendolyn Brooks is poet laureate of the state of Illinois.
9. Sheila telephoned every member of the band and pep club about the changes in the schedule.
10. Japan has discovered the charms of American bluegrass music.

Indirect Objects

A sentence containing a direct object may also have an indirect object.

An *indirect object* is usually defined as a word that tells *for whom* or *to whom* the action of the verb is done.

The indirect object usually comes immediately before the direct object. (In sentence patterns indirect objects are labeled *IO.*)

S V IO DO
The cat brought her *kittens* a mouse.

S V IO DO
The gas station attendant drew *me* a map.

S V IO DO
We made *Rover* a two-story doghouse with pillars and a veranda.

Indirect objects, like other kinds of complements, are never found in a prepositional phrase. When the word *to* or *for* is used, the noun or pronoun that follows is the object of a preposition, *not* an indirect object.

S V DO
My father made a pizza for us.

S V IO DO
My father made us a pizza.

S V DO
Mrs. Bush told her opinion on the issue to the reporters.

S V IO DO
Mrs. Bush told the reporters her opinion on the issue.

Remember that a sentence must contain a direct object in order to have an indirect object. No sentence may have an indirect object alone. Not all sentences with direct objects, however, have indirect objects.

Sentences containing an indirect object have the pattern S–V–IO–DO.

S V IO DO
Carla gave her horse an apple.

S V IO DO
Marcia tossed Jimmy his car keys.

Exercise 11

Write out the following sentences, underlining and labeling each sentence part. (Not every sentence contains an indirect object.)

Examples

a. We bought Grandmother a new tennis racket.

S V IO DO
a. We bought Grandmother a new tennis racket.

b. The clerks showed the customers the new line of merchandise.

S V IO DO
b. The clerks showed the customers the new line of merchandise.

1. Cammie made her cousin a funny get-well card.
2. The director gave the cast a few final words of encouragement.
3. The United States has sent several missions to the moon.
4. The magician told us the secret of his rope trick.
5. The rangers taught the younger campers some essential survival skills.
6. The chimpanzee in the zoo gave me a strange look.
7. The court awarded the victim of the accident $10,000.
8. Will the college offer adults any special night classes this spring?
9. Al carved his sister an ivory pendant.
10. Nobody had told either Clare or Rita the change of plans.

Objective Complements

A special kind of complement that follows a direct object is called an *objective complement* because it describes or renames the object.

Objective complements follow only a few action verbs:

make	choose	appoint	voted	prove
consider	elect	name	think	find

Our joking made her *angry*.
We elected John *president*.

In order to have an objective complement, a sentence must also have a direct object. The sentence pattern for a sentence with an objective complement is S–V–DO–OC.

S V DO OC OC
Congress considered the bill poorly *executed* and poorly *timed.*

S V DO OC
Carmen appointed Nick *treasurer.*

Exercise 12

Write out the following sentences, underlining and labeling each part of the sentence according to its pattern. (Not all sentences contain objective complements.)

Examples

a. Riko considers math her best subject.

S V DO OC
a. Riko considers math her best subject.

b. The motion of the roller coaster made Pam sick.

S V DO OC
b. The motion of the roller coaster made Pam sick.

c. The chairwoman appointed B.J. to the vacant office.

S V DO
c. The chairwoman appointed B.J. to the vacant office.

1. We named our cocker spaniel Buffy.
2. Marcia considers soap operas stupid and boring.
3. The mayor thought the tax cut unwise at this time.
4. The team made Sherrie's English bulldog its mascot.
5. The detective proved Lady Tudberry the author of the crime.
6. Did we make Debby angry with our teasing?
7. Film critics have named that movie the best of the year.
8. The voters elected Ms. Johnssen and Mr. Olivetti delegate and alternate delegate.
9. The jury found the man and woman innocent of the charges.
10. The Nitty Gritty Dirt Band was selected to tour Russia.

Active and Passive Voice

Transitive verbs (those that take direct objects) may be either active or passive.

A verb is in the *active voice* when the subject of the verb performs the action. The verb is in the *passive voice* when the subject receives the action rather than performs it.

The following sentences illustrate the difference between active and passive voices.

Active: Ed *designed* the cover of the yearbook.
[The subject *Ed* performs the action.]

Passive: The cover of the yearbook *was designed* by Ed.
[The action is performed upon the subject *cover*.]

Form the passive voice of each verb tense with the appropriate tense of *be* and the past participle of the verb.

PRESENT
Active: Nipsey Russell *plays* the lead.
Passive: The lead *is played* by Nipsey Russell.
[present tense of *be* + *played*]

PAST
Active: Nipsey Russell *played* the lead.
Passive: The lead *was played* by Nipsey Russell.
[past tense of *be* + *played*]

FUTURE
Active: Nipsey Russell *will play* the lead.
Passive: The lead *will be played* by Nipsey Russell.
[future tense of *be* + *played*]

PRESENT PERFECT
Active: Nipsey Russell *has played* the lead.
Passive: The lead *has been played* by Nipsey Russell.
[present perfect tense of *be* + *played*]

PAST PERFECT
Active: Nipsey Russell *had played* the lead.
Passive: The lead *had been played* by Nipsey Russell.
[past perfect tense of *be* + *played*]

FUTURE PERFECT
Active: Nipsey Russell *will have played* the lead.
Passive: The lead *will have been played* by Nipsey Russell.
[future perfect tense of *be* + *played*]

The Retained Object

Transitive verbs may have indirect objects as well as direct objects. When either of these objects continues to function as a complement in the passive construction, the object is called a *retained object.*

S V IO DO
Active: Ms. Sosa gave the newspaper staff their assignments.

When the preceding sentence is put into the passive voice, either the direct object, *assignments,* or the indirect object, *staff,* may serve as the subject of the sentence.

S V RO
Passive: The assignments were given the newspaper staff by Ms. Sosa.
S V RO
Passive: The newspaper staff were given their assignments by Ms. Sosa.

Staff in the first sentence, and *assignments* in the second sentence are retained objects—objects of a verb in the passive voice.

Exercise 13

Rewrite each of the following sentences. If the verb is in the active voice, change it to the passive voice. If the verb is in the passive voice, change it to the active voice. Then identify the voice of the sentence that you have written. Finally, if there is a retained object, underline and label it *RO.*

Examples

a. The piece was recorded by the Preservation Hall Jazz Band.
a. The Preservation Hall Jazz Band recorded the piece.
active voice

b. The real estate agent showed the Lings the old mansion.
RO
b. The Lings were shown the old mansion by the real estate agent.
passive voice

1. "Irene, Goodnight" was written by the great folk artist Leadbelly.
2. The dust and mold in the old house gave Alison the sniffles.
3. Chief Red Cloud made an impassioned speech about Indian rights.
4. *Pride and Prejudice* was written by the English novelist Jane Austen.
5. Queen Elizabeth the First considered Mary Queen of Scots a threat to her power.
6. Madeline was presented a scholarship by the League of Women Voters.
7. The experiment proved the theory false.
8. The starring role in *The World, the Flesh, and the Devil* was played by Harry Belafonte.
9. The British elected Margaret Thatcher Prime Minister.
10. Nuclear power is considered unsafe by some people.

Mastery Exercise A

Write out each of the following sentences, underlining and labeling each part of the sentence according to its pattern.

Examples

a. The neoclassic period was a time of balance and harmony in literature.
S LV PN
a. The neoclassic period was a time of balance and harmony in literature.

b. The writers of the age admired careful structure and elegant language.

S V DO DO

b. The writers of the age admired careful structure and elegant language.

1. The world was a pleasant and orderly place to the neoclassic writers.
2. They considered the universe a perfectly ordered mechanism.
3. They gave reason and logic the utmost respect.
4. They were optimistic about the advances of science.
5. They admired the works of the ancient Greeks and Romans and patterned their own after them.
6. The height of the neoclassic period in England was in the eighteenth century.
7. Some people consider the poetry of this age cold and artificial.
8. A few young writers disliked the rules and formality of the period.
9. Critics call their revolt against the age "the Romantic Rebellion."
10. "Romantic" writers did not write about love necessarily.
11. The word is associated with imagination, adventure, and intense emotion.
12. Two important early romantic poets were William Wordsworth and Samuel Taylor Coleridge.
13. Wordsworth wrote about ordinary people, not ancient gods or heroes or nobles.
14. His language was simple and unaffected.
15. Coleridge gave us the unsurpassable "Rime of the Ancient Mariner."
16. This poem is not logical and orderly, but magical and imaginative.
17. Its form is simple.
18. Lord Byron was probably the most famous romantic poet.
19. He wrote passionate lyrics and long poems of high adventure.
20. His savage sense of humor gained him numerous enemies.

Using Sentences

In the following lessons you will learn how to avoid run-on sentences and sentence fragments, the two most common problems in writing sentences. You will also learn to improve your writing style by selecting appropriate words, by being concise, and by avoiding weak constructions.

Avoiding Run-On Sentences

When two closely related sentences are joined only by a comma or by no punctuation at all, the resulting group of words is called a *run-on sentence.*

Avoid using run-on sentences in your writing.

Run-On: Sally's favorite singer is Glen Campbell she has all of his albums.
Correct: Sally's favorite singer is Glen Campbell; she has all of his albums.

Run-On: Jan works for the police department, she is a dispatcher.
Correct: Jan works for the police department where she is a dispatcher.

Run-on sentences may be corrected by making separate sentences or by changing the punctuation and wording.

1. The clauses of a run-on sentence can be written as separate sentences.

   Run-On: Most poets cannot live on the income from their writing, they must have another job as well.
   Correct: Most poets cannot live on the income from their writing. They must have another job as well.

2. A semicolon can be used to separate the two clauses when they are closely related in meaning.

   Run-On: My little sister wants a special watch for her birthday it has a picture of Kermit the Frog on it.
   Correct: My little sister wants a special watch for her birthday; it has a picture of Kermit the Frog on it.

A list of conjunctive adverbs is on page 296.

3. A semicolon followed by a conjunctive adverb may be used to separate the parts of a run-on sentence. The adverb, which is always followed by a comma, shows the relationship of one part of the sentence to the other.

   Run-On: Ferrets have a strong odor, some people don't like them for pets.
   Correct: Ferrets have a strong odor; *therefore*, some people don't like them for pets.

4. A comma followed by a coordinating conjunction may be used to combine the two parts of a run-on sentence.

   Run-On: We will have a centennial celebration next year all men who don't grow beards will be fined.
   Correct: We will have a centennial celebration next year, *and* all men who don't grow beards will be fined.

5. One part of the run-on sentence may be changed to a subordinate clause or to a phrase.

   Run-On: My aunt is a translator at the UN, she speaks three languages fluently.
   Correct: My aunt, who is a translator at the UN, speaks three languages fluently.
   Correct: My aunt, a translator at the UN, speaks three languages fluently.

Run-On: We set off for the movie early, we knew there would be a long line.
Correct: We set off for the movie early because we knew there would be a long line.

Exercise 1

Using one of the methods discussed in the preceding section, correct each of the following run-on sentences. Write out the corrected sentence.

Example

a. *Rendezvous* is a French word, it means "to get together again," "to meet."

a. Rendezvous, which is a French word, means "to get together again," "to meet."

1. American fur trappers used the word *rendezvous* to describe their regathering in the spring, the members of the fur companies had gone their separate ways to trap throughout the winter.
2. Goods and furs were traded, there was much celebrating, eating, and drinking.
3. Today many people are still interested in the trapper's independent life style, they hold a modern rendezvous.
4. A rendezvous is an amazing sight you feel you have somehow traveled back in time to the previous century.
5. Those who attend the rendezvous obey strict rules, no modern tools, clothing, food, or shelter are allowed.
6. Most men dress in homemade buckskin clothing, women and children wear hand-sewn costumes of skins or cloth.
7. Participants live in tepees or wickiups, some of the shelters are brightly painted with designs and pictures.
8. All cooking is done over open fires with old-fashioned utensils, no canned food or refrigeration is allowed.
9. Furs, muzzle-loading rifles, and fine knives are traded, trade items are spread out on large hides before the shelters.
10. There are contests in tomahawk throwing and shooting with black powder rifles, the competition is as fierce as at the rendezvous of old.

Avoiding Sentence Fragments

Run-on sentences need to be divided or rewritten because they contain too much information crammed together. Fragments, on the other hand, contain too little information and need words added to them to make them complete. Remember the three requirements for a complete sentence:

1. A sentence expresses a complete thought.
2. A sentence has a subject.

3. A sentence has a predicate verb.

In a sentence fragment one or more of these three requirements is missing.

Avoid using sentence fragments in your writing.

Incomplete:	While we were dancing.
Sentence:	I lost my watch while we were dancing.
No Subject:	Snores like a defective chainsaw.
Sentence:	Our St. Bernard snores like a defective chainsaw.
No Predicate Verb:	The address written on the envelope.
Sentence:	The address written on the envelope was illegible.

Remember that participles (verbs ending in *-ing*, *-en*, and so on) must have a helping verb to function as a predicate verb. Used alone, they function as modifiers.

PARTICIPLE	VERB PHRASE
playing	is playing
chosen	has been chosen

Phrases as Fragments

A *phrase* has neither a subject nor a predicate nor does it express a complete thought. When a prepositional phrase, infinitive phrase, participial phrase, or gerund phrase is written as a sentence, it is a sentence fragment.

Phrases are discussed on pages 518–533.

Fragment:	I had left my term paper. In Stacey's car.
Sentence:	I had left my term paper in Stacey's car.
Fragment:	The tennis players were distracted by the sound of the jet. Roaring over the court.
Sentence:	The tennis players were distracted by the sound of the jet roaring over the court.

Clauses as Fragments

A *subordinate clause* contains both a subject and a verb, but does not express a complete thought. Subordinate clauses must be attached to an independent clause; they cannot stand alone.

Subordinate clauses are discussed on pages 538–543.

Fragment:	I am now the proud owner of a stuffed owl. Because I got carried away at an auction.
Sentence:	I am now the proud owner of a stuffed owl because I got carried away at an auction.
Fragment:	Although the repair crews examined all the lines and equipment and worked throughout the night. The source of the power failure wasn't found.
Sentence:	Although the repair crews examined all the lines and equipment and worked throughout the night, the source of the power failure wasn't found.

Appositives as Fragments

An *appositive* is a word or group of words that identifies a nearby noun or pronoun. An appositive cannot be punctuated as a sentence because it does not express a complete thought nor does it contain a subject and its verb.

Appositives are discussed on page 525.

Fragment: One of our family's favorite foods is kima. A spicy Indonesian dish of sauteed meat and vegetables.

Sentence: One of our family's favorite foods is kima, a spicy Indonesian dish of sauteed meat and vegetables.

Exercise 2

Write out the following sentences, correcting all sentence fragments.

Examples

a. We always attend the War Eagle Arts and Crafts Fair. The biggest such fair in the United States.

a. We always attend the War Eagle Arts and Crafts Fair, the biggest such fair in the United States.

b. Clement had to give up swimming. Because water gives him sinus difficulties.

b. Clement had to give up swimming, because water gives him sinus difficulties.

1. One evening last summer I decided to take a stroll with my sister. Down along the edge of the golf course.
2. It was a peaceful, pleasant evening with a faint breeze. A light mist forming on the green.
3. It seemed to us that there was a peculiar hush over everything. Because no birds were singing or crickets chirping.
4. We walked to our favorite spot. A large pond near the edge of the course.
5. Now, in the fading light, it looked rather sinister. With scarves of mist coiling over the dark water.
6. At almost the same moment we noticed bubbles boiling up in the water. Just a few yards away from us.
7. At first we thought a turtle or muskrat must be in the pond, but the bubbles became too large and violent. Far too large for any small animal to make.
8. Suddenly a huge, glistening black shape, as big as a person rose from the water, and we both yelled. Thinking somehow, against all logic, that we were seeing a monster!
9. We were embarrassed but relieved to find it was only a scuba diver. Who had been collecting lost golfballs from the bottom of the pond.
10. My sister and I still are a little ashamed to admit that for one terrible moment we truly believed that we were going to be chased. By the Creature from the Black Lagoon.

Review Exercise A

Write out each of the following sentences, correcting run-on sentences and sentence fragments.

1. There is a wealth of myth and legend about animals. Creatures that are both real and imaginary.
2. An old belief about geese was that a goose brought good luck to honest, innocent people, it brought bad luck to evil ones.
3. Germans believe that a stork nest on the roof brings good luck however Moroccans believe the opposite is true.
4. The Thebans thought crocodiles were sacred, they had pet crocodiles that wore bracelets and other jewelry.
5. A crocodile was supposed to weep as it devoured its prey, insincere crying is often referred to as "crocodile tears."
6. In the Renaissance it was thought that a toad's blood was lethal poison. Since toads were supposed to be venomous, like snakes.
7. Native American mythology sometimes shows the tortoise as the creator of the world. Which is similar to the Chinese legend of the tortoise and three other animals' bringing the world into existence.
8. Egyptian doctors carried snakes to the homes of ill people. To drive out disease or pain.
9. The snake figures in many stories of death it also is a central figure in stories about immortality.
10. Legends of India and China show great respect for the wisdom of apes, ancient Hebrews thought apes were unlucky.
11. The Greeks had a legend that the moon created the cat and that night-time clouds are mice. Fleeing from the catlike moon.
12. Cats were respected and worshipped in Egypt they were even mummified after death.
13. Medieval Europeans connected cats with witchcraft cats were often burned as demons.
14. In Islamic religion the cat is a good friend to the prophet Muhammad, Buddhist folklore says that Buddha and the cat were enemies.
15. The panther has been favorably associated with numerous religious figures. Greek gods, including Dionysus.
16. In medieval times the bear was associated with converting new believers to Christianity it was sometimes used as a symbol for the church.
17. Native American stories usually portray the coyote as well endowed with two attributes. High intelligence and an endless capacity for playing tricks.
18. St. Francis is said to have tamed a wolf people named it "Brother Wolf" or Fra Lupo.

19. The dog has always been renowned for faithfulness there are legions of stories recounting the loyalty of dogs.
20. Eskimo mythology portrays the raven as a powerful, creative god, but European folklore is less kind. Connecting the raven with the devil.

Writing Effective Sentences

Good writing entails more than a grasp of the principles of grammar; it also demands clarity, grace, and a sense of what is appropriate. The following lessons offer guidelines for improving writing style.

Improving Style with Diction

Diction, in writing, is your choice of words.

The words you choose should be appropriate to the subject and tone of your writing and to the reader for whom you intend the writing—the wrong word can ruin the effect of a sentence. Consider, for example, the unfortunate poet who compared those he loved to drops of his heart's blood, then addressed his sweetheart as "one of my most treasured drips."

Some writers think long, "ten-dollar" words are the mark of a mature style; they are mistaken. Do not use a long word where a short one will do, unless you have a special reason for doing so. Good writing is a vehicle for expressing thoughts clearly, not for displaying the longest words you know simply to display them. Notice in the following sentences how the impressive sounding words of the first example add up to a sentence that is distinctly *not* impressive.

Poor: Members of the populace who inhabit domiciles of a hyalescent character should eschew the propulsion of sedimentary, igneous, or metamorphic conglomerates.

Better: People who live in glass houses shouldn't throw stones.

The second sentence is clear, pointed, pithy—and justly famous. The first sentence, an awkward jawbreaker, manages to be both pompous and murky.

The words you choose should depend primarily on two considerations: the audience for whom you write and your purpose in writing. Even the most formal writing, however, should be simple and clear. To write simply is not to write in "Dick and Jane" sentences such as you find in a first-grade reader. To write simply means to use understandable words in clearly constructed sentences.

Poor: It is patently impossible to subjugate a human being without demeaning oneself as well.

Better: You can't hold a man down without staying down with him.

—Booker T. Washington

Other Diction Problems

The use of large, ponderous words is not the only error of diction. Equally offensive is the sudden intrusion of slang or trite, flabby words and phrases into serious writing. Each of the following examples has a word that is inappropriate because of its cheapness.

> Perhaps Adolph Hitler was a cunning but warped politician with unusual gifts for persuasion and leadership; on the other hand he may have been simply nutso.
>
> *Othello* is a remarkably constructed play with vital characters, a complex plot, and super language.
>
> The witches are intriguing figures in the tragedy of *Macbeth*. They are frightening, fascinating, but pretty gross.

Writing Exercise A

Each of the following sentences contains one or more problems in diction. Rewrite the sentences, changing the offending words or phrases to more appropriate ones. Use your dictionary for help with vocabulary.

Example

a. The arboreal growth about the edifice obfuscated it.

a. The trees around the house nearly hid it.

1. Several creatures of the bovine persuasion masticated the foliage in the bucolic area.
2. Historians still dispute whether Custer's strategy at Little Big Horn was brilliant but misguided, or if it was goofy.
3. Allow canines under the influence of Morpheus to remain recumbent.
4. Branwell Brontë had genius equal to any of his famous sisters; it is lousy that he wasted it.
5. He evinced emotions of the deepest and most passionate and amorous category for her.
6. This particular novel by Jane Austen has been called her most ambitious; it shows great promise in the opening chapters, but unfortunately, she blows it in the later ones.
7. When Cleopatra appeared on her barge, she was as pretty as pretty can be.
8. I will elucidate the import of the information to my youngest sibling.
9. My maternal parent frequently emphasizes the necessity of my restoring my abode to a locale of greater hygienic quality and order.
10. Dear Dr. Brady: Please excuse me for rushing from the biology lab without permission this afternoon, but when I started to cut open my frog, I felt I was going to puke.

Conciseness

Wordiness is the enemy of good writing. Some writers think that the more words they use, the more impressive their writing becomes. Other writers, minds boggled at the idea of writing 500 words on a subject, pad their sentences or repeat the same idea in different words. As a good writer you must make your point and not waste words in doing so.

Conciseness is the opposite of wordiness; a concise statement expresses a thought clearly and cleanly.

Most first drafts, even carefully written ones, need revision—the cutting of extra words, repeated ideas, and unnecessary statements. The following examples show how sentences can be made more concise.

Poor: This phenomenon we call life seems to me to go on and on forever, very much calling to mind the incessant gnawing of a small mouse.

Better: Life goes on forever like the gnawing of a mouse.

—Edna St. Vincent Millay

Poor: My advice would be to avoid the tendency to turn one's glance behind one. The reason is that something may very well be gaining on one.

Better: Don't look back. Something may be gaining on you.

—Satchel Paige

Writing Exercise B

Rewrite the following sentences to make them more concise.

1. In the modern world of today we must finally come to grips with the problems generated by the energy crisis.
2. We must resolve and end the crisis in the Middle East, and we must do so now, at this point in time.
3. In my opinion and my opinion only, for I am no expert on political matters, I would tend to believe the Electoral College should probably be replaced by another, more democratic process.
4. In this great country of ours, the United States of America, land of the free and home of the brave, there still exists, it is sad, perhaps even tragic, to say, poverty.
5. In the Civil War, or the War Between the States as some prefer to call the bloody ordeal, emancipation of the slaves, or those in bondage to the archaic institution of slavery, was but one of many, many issues.
6. The reason the color yellow is my favorite color of all is that it always tends to remind me of sunlight, summer flowers, and many other cheerful things of a similar nature.
7. When I take my pen in hand on occasions such as this, it is a frequent occurrence that I am incapable of finding anything in my mind that I can, in good faith, put down on paper.
8. In the novel the hero or protagonist, Carlos Garcia, is driving down a quiet, deserted road in his car when he suddenly sees before him a big, enormous spaceship hovering up in the air in front of him.

9. I like to play the game of "Dungeons and Dragons" because I can imagine a state of being in which I am one of a number of characters that I want to be: a big giant, an ugly monster, a magical wizard, or a fighting warrior.
10. Malcolm X has been perceived as a great and important leader by some people, but other people tended to think of him as a radical who was very dangerous.

Avoiding Weak Constructions

Action verbs have two voices: the active and the passive.

Active: The horse bucked off the rider.
Passive: The rider was bucked off by the horse.

Active: Tina bought an old silver bracelet.
Passive: An old silver bracelet was bought by Tina.

Active and passive voices are discussed on pages 504–505.

As the preceding examples show, the active voice is usually the shorter, more vigorous way of making a statement.

Use the active voice when you write unless you have a good reason for using the passive.

A second weak construction is the sentence beginning with an unnecessary expletive: "There is. . . ," "Here is. . . ," "It is. . . ," and so on.

If you can drop these phrases without hurting the meaning of your sentence or without creating an awkward construction, do so. The following examples show how such cutting can improve your writing:

Poor: There were several Holstein cows grazing in the meadow.
Stronger: Several Holstein cows grazed in the meadow.

The damage these two constructions (the passive voice and the "there is," "there are" constructions) can do is evident in the following passage.

Chinese Astrology—If You Were Born in the Year of the Rooster

Poor: Because dreaming is loved by him, the Rooster risks falling at times into laziness—though it is his nature to give everything to the job in hand once it is started by him, the reputation is had by him of being a hard worker. But there is the fact that he's forever biting off more than can be chewed by him, undertaking tasks that are beyond his strength. And if, after all his efforts, it still can't be made by him, there is nobody more disappointed than he.

Stronger:[1] Because he loves to dream, the Rooster risks falling at times into laziness—though his nature is to give everything to the job in

---

[1]From *Chinese Astrology* by Paula Del Sol. Reprinted by permission of Nat Sobel Associates, Inc.

> hand once he starts it, and he has the reputation of being a hard worker. But he's forever biting off more than he can chew, undertaking tasks that are beyond his strength. And if, after all his efforts, he still can't make it, nobody is more disappointed than he.

The first paragraph limps along under the weight of useless words and unnecessary constructions. The second paragraph, using the active voice and cutting unnecessary introductory phrases, moves quickly and clearly.

Writing Exercise C

Rewrite the following paragraph, eliminating weak constructions and making any other changes you feel will strengthen the style.

> There is a twisted, little-used road that leads to the town. It is seldom traveled by the residents of the county, almost never traveled by tourists. The town itself is situated in a valley that is green, gracious, and pleasant. There are ancient oaks and pines lining the hillsides, and there is a remarkably clear creek at the town's outer edge. But there are no people walking in the streets, sitting on porches, conversing in the deserted stores. Houses have been abandoned, store windows have been boarded up by the long-absent residents. The surrounding farms have been deserted by their farmers. There is only the motion of a tumbleweed being blown by the wind down the dusty main street.

Writing Exercise D

To practice using good, forceful sentences, write a rough draft on one of the following topics. Then proofread your first draft, checking your sentence structure and eliminating run-ons and fragments. If any of your sentences seem flat or ineffective, revise them; also revise any sentences that might not seem clear to a reader.

1. A friend of yours offers to sell you the car of your dreams for a mere $300 cash. Write a letter to your rich uncle (you acquire a rich uncle for the duration of this exercise) explaining the situation and asking to borrow the money.
2. Write a letter to the newspaper or the mayor complaining about a law or ordinance you think is unjust. Explain why you feel the way you do and how you think the law or ordinance should be changed.
3. You have just learned that a local television station is canceling your favorite show and replacing it with a series on how to speak French. Write a letter to the station in which you politely but firmly protest, explaining what you like about your favorite show and why you think the substitution is a poor idea.
4. The principal of your school has just issued an announcement that no more homecoming queens will be elected, since such elections are merely popularity contests at best, and at worst, teach people to prize and judge women on the basis of their looks. Write a letter in which you state your reasons for agreeing or disagreeing with your principal.

20 The Phrase

Understanding Phrases

Phrases, groups of words that work together as a unit, can add a great deal of information to a sentence:

The girl sat and wrote.

The girl *with the term paper assignment* sat *at the library table* and wrote *to the Agriculture Department, asking for information about beekeeping.*

In this section you will learn to identify the various kinds of phrases and to understand how they function in a sentence.

Defining a Phrase

A *phrase* is usually defined as a group of words, without a subject and its verb, that functions as a single part of speech.

A phrase may function in a sentence as a noun, verb, adjective, or adverb. *Noun phrases* are usually defined as a noun and its modifiers.

All students in the creative writing class must write *ten rhymed poems.*
DeKalb County in Illinois is known for *the fertility of its soil.*

A *verb phrase* consists of a main verb plus one or more helping verbs.

A recycling project *will be held* the second week in March.
New science equipment for the lab *has been needed* for several years.

In the following sections you will study two other kinds of phrases: *prepositional phrases* and *verbal phrases*.

Prepositional Phrases

Commonly used prepositions are listed on page 470.

A *prepositional phrase* is made up of a preposition, its object, and any modifiers the object may have.

The object of a preposition is the noun or pronoun (or group of words that function as a noun) that ends the prepositional phrase. In the following examples the prepositional phrase is in parentheses, and the object of the preposition is *italicized.*

We are going (to *Tulsa*) (on *Friday*) (for a field *trip*).
The otters cavorted and swam (in the stream's swift *water*).
A shaft (of *sunlight*) fell (on the brightly patterned *carpet*.)

Prepositional phrases cannot stand on their own; they are modifiers, functioning either as adjectives or adverbs.

Adjective Phrases

An *adjective phrase* is a prepositional phrase that modifies a noun or a pronoun. Like a single-word adjective, it tells *what kind, which one,* or *how many.*

Modifies Noun: The player *on the right* is Rosie Casales.
[The phrase *on the right* tells *which one.*]

Modifies Noun: The refrigerator contained only a box *of cheese.*
[The phrase *of cheese* tells *what kind.*]

Modifies Pronoun: One *of the baby jaguars* was in the petting zoo.
[The phrase *of the baby jaguars* tells *what kind.*]

In a series of prepositional phrases, an adjective phrase may modify the object of a preposition in the preceding phrase.

Sherry snapped a photo *(of the hippopotamus) (with the bird) (on its head).*

Adverb Phrases

An *adverb phrase* is a prepositional phrase that modifies a verb, an adjective, or another adverb.

Adverb phrases answer the question *where? when? how?* or *how much?*

Modifies Verb: Human beings have journeyed *to the moon.*
[The prepositional phrase *to the moon* answers *where?*]

Modifies Adjective: The coach became angry *in the afternoon.*
[The prepositional phrase *in the afternoon* answers *when?*]

Modifies Adverb: Our mail arrived late *in the afternoon.*
[The prepositional phrase *in the afternoon* answers the adverbial question *when?*]

Two or more adverb phrases may be used in succession to modify the same word.

> The fire roared *(through the forest) (toward the settlement).*
> [Both phrases modify the verb *roared*.]

Exercise 1

Write out the following sentences. Underline each prepositional phrase and write above it *Adj.* for adjective phrase or *Adv.* for adverb phrase. Then draw an arrow from the phrase to the word or words it modifies.

Examples

a. The strange animal in the cage was an armadillo from Texas.

Adj. *Adj.*
a. The strange animal in the cage was an armadillo from Texas.

b. We usually swim at the lake on weekends.

Adv. *Adv.*
b. We usually swim at the lake on weekends.

1. The classical physics of Isaac Newton went unchallenged for two centuries.
2. The house on the corner of Eleventh and Poplar burned to the ground.
3. The unicorn is a horselike beast of mythology with a horn in the center of its forehead.
4. Hugh Glass was a trapper wounded by a bear and left for dead by his companions; he crawled over 400 miles across the prairie, recovered, and resumed his trapping career.
5. The bottom of the skillet was covered with burnt chili; we had to soak it for several hours and scour it with sand.
6. For years my parents have wanted to buy an old Victorian house with stained glass windows, gables, and a cupola.
7. Birdcage Walk and Constitution Hill are two London streets near Buckingham Palace; Victoria Street leads to Victoria Station, which is close to Westminster Cathedral.
8. The game went on in spite of the drizzle, and the miserable but loyal fans huddled under umbrellas or held sodden newspapers over their heads.
9. The hurricane moved across the Gulf of Mexico toward the Texas coastal towns, and weather forecasters warned residents about the potential dangers.
10. Hinduism is one of the most ancient of religions and also one of the most complex; many of its adherents live in India.

Verbal Phrases

Verbals—participles, gerunds, and infinitives—are formed from a verb but do not function as a verb in a sentence. A *participle* is used as an adjective; a *gerund* functions as a noun; and an *infinitive* may function as a noun, adjective, or adverb.

When a verbal has a complement or a modifier, it becomes part of a *verbal phrase*. In the following sections you will learn to identify the three types of verbal phrases: *participial phrases*, *gerund phrases*, and *infinitive phrases*.

Participial Phrases

A *participle* is a form of the verb that is used as an adjective.

Participles have present, past, and perfect forms.

Present: The river, *rising* rapidly, threatened to overflow.

Past: The bread dough, *risen* to twice its original size, was ready to be kneaded.

Perfect: *Having risen* early to catch my plane, I napped for most of the flight.

A *participial phrase* consists of a participle and its modifiers and complements. A participial phrase always functions as an adjective, modifying a noun or pronoun.

In the movie *Love Happy*, Harpo Marx, *having hidden inside a giant mechanical penguin*, eludes his pursuers.

The governess, *wondering what the strange noises were*, slowly descended the staircase with a candelabra in her hand.

Buddhism, *originating first in India*, spread to China, Japan, Sri Lanka, Vietnam, and many other Eastern countries.

Exercise 2

Write out the following sentences. Underline the participial phrases and draw an arrow to the word each phrase modifies.

Examples

a. The mercury, already rising in the thermometer, indicated another scorching day was ahead of us.

a. The mercury, already rising in the thermometer, indicated another scorching day was ahead of us.

b. The vase fell to the floor, shattering into a hundred fragments.

b. The vase fell to the floor, shattering into a hundred fragments.

1. The diamond, seriously flawed, was not worth such a high price.
2. The dog, dreaming perhaps that it was chasing rabbits, barked and twitched its paws.

3. The truck, not having been used for two years, surprised us by starting immediately.
4. Searching for the mythical Bonaventura River, Jed Smith came upon the Great Salt Lake of Utah.
5. *Finnegan's Wake*, written over a period of thirty years, is one of the world's most complex novels.
6. The elephant, plagued by arthritis that kept it from lifting its feet from the damp straw, had to be outfitted with specially made boots.
7. We had to throw out the flour ruined by the mice and the corn meal infested with weevils.
8. The highways covered with sleet and snow made travel impossible, and a storm sweeping in from the northwest promised more bad weather.
9. Determined to get the best from his students, Mr. Boseman never settles for a mediocre performance.
10. Having studied English at a private school in Hong Kong, the exchange student surprised us with an excellent grasp of grammar.

Gerund Phrases

A *gerund* is a form of the verb that is used as a noun.

Gerunds may be used in the same way nouns are used—as subjects, objects, and predicate nominatives.

Subject:	*Dancing* is Joey's favorite recreation.
Object:	Marcia likes *fishing*.
Predicate Nominative:	Priborski's specialty was *punting*.

A *gerund phrase* is made up of a gerund and its complements or modifiers. In a gerund phrase the modifiers may be single words, phrases, or clauses.

Skipping breakfast is a bad habit.

We enjoyed *hearing that school would be let out a week early*.

Our art teacher demonstrated how to get some interesting effects by *painting with a goose quill*.

You will not confuse participial and gerund phrases if you remember how each phrase functions in a sentence.

1. A participial phrase always functions as an adjective.
2. A gerund phrase always functions as a noun.

Exercise 3

Write out the following sentences, underlining the gerund phrases. (Some sentences contain more than one gerund phrase.)

Examples

a. Some scientists credit animals with having ESP.

a. Some scientists credit animals with having ESP.

b. ESP, or extrasensory perception, is being able to know things beyond the range of our immediate senses.

b. ESP, or extrasensory perception, is being able to know things beyond the range of our immediate senses.

1. An example of ESP would be a dog's finding its way across many miles to be reunited with its owner.
2. There are many accounts of dogs and cats who have found distant owners by journeying for weeks or even months over strange territory.
3. Many people claim they first became aware of a supernatural event or a UFO by an animal's acting strangely.
4. A dog's eerie howling or a cat's sudden spitting and bristling are common devices in ghost stories.
5. Horses have often been credited with refusing to cross a bridge or stretch of road that offered unseen danger.
6. Even the great psychiatrist Sigmund Freud is on record as admitting a belief in animal ESP.
7. Duke University is one of the most famous institutions involved in experimenting with ESP.
8. Findings by Duke's scientists and researchers indicate such strange, extranormal powers do exist, in spite of the scoffing of cynics.
9. Serious Russian experimenting with ESP indicates that the Soviet Union considers it an important phenomenon.
10. Learning to use and control this power is the dream of many scientists, and continued researching in the field may someday yield the secrets of ESP.

Infinitive Phrases

The *infinitive* is a form of the verb preceded by the word *to.*

Infinitives may be used as nouns, adjectives, or adverbs.

Noun: *To err* is human.

Adjective: John's hayfever gives him a tendency *to sneeze.*

Adverb: The formula for that chemical is hard *to remember.*

An *infinitive phrase* is made up of an infinitive, its modifiers, complements, and subject.

An infinitive may be used as the subject of a sentence, the direct object, the predicate nominative, or as an adjective or adverb.

Subject: *To ski down a mountain at breakneck speed* is not my idea of fun.

Object: Tracey hopes *to win the tennis tournament.*

Predicate Nominative: The way to succeed is *to be honest and persistent.*

Adjective: That was the perfect movie *to give you nightmares.*

Adverb: The sled dog was too old *to be sent on another long, grueling expedition.*

Unlike other verbal phrases, the infinitive phrase may also take a subject, which is part of the infinitive phrase. The subject of the infinitive phrase comes after the main verb and immediately before the infinitive.

The state trooper advised *the motorist to take the alternate route.*
We reminded *Mickey to bring her cymbals to the pep rally.*
The operator told *me to dial the number again.*

The subject of an infinitive follows only action verbs such as *urge, order, ask, tell, persuade, warn,* and so on.

Notice also that pronouns that function as subjects or objects in an infinitive phrase are always in the object form *(me, him, her, us, them).*

Subject of Infinitive: The weather reports warned us *to drive slowly.*

Direct Object of Infinitive: We needed *to see her.*

Indirect Object of Infinitive: We have *to tell her the news.*

Exercise 4

Write out the following sentences and underline the infinitive phrases. (Be sure to include any subject an infinitive phrase may have.) Then beneath the sentence write how each phrase is used: subject, object, predicate nominative, adjective, or adverb.

Examples

a. It is amusing to read about some of the strange inventions registered with the U.S. Patent Department.

a. It is amusing to read about some of the strange inventions registered with the U.S. Patent Department.
adverb

b. One inventor, for instance, designed spectacles to be worn by chickens.

b. One inventor, for instance, designed spectacles to be worn by chickens.
adjective

1. A water-squirting alarm clock certainly persuades a person to wake up on time.
2. Such a clock, however, would also probably persuade the person to throw the contraption out the nearest window.

3. For those who like to fly in balloons, there was a perfectly amazing invention, a balloon to be guided by eagles or vultures.
4. The birds would have to wear specially designed little corsets.
5. Then there are suspenders designed to be turned into a rope to help you escape from a burning building.
6. Another ingenious device could be used to grate and slice food and also to trap mice and flies.
7. For the person who wants to work while relaxing, there is a rocking chair designed to churn butter.
8. A horrible-looking device resembling a carpenter's drill was supposed to produce dimples.
9. It might be easy to convince people you are mannerly if you wear a hat designed to tip itself.
10. For people needing to jump out of windows or to hurl themselves from cliffs, there is this handy double invention: a parachute to attach to the head, and elastic-sole shoes to absorb the shock of landing.

Appositive Phrases

An *appositive* is a noun or pronoun that identifies or explains a nearby noun or pronoun.

Appositives are discussed on page 511.

Irish folklore tells of the pookah, *a supernatural animal.*

Margaret Meade, *an anthropologist,* wrote an important book about adolescence in Samoa.

My dog *Destrey* loves to chase moths and June bugs.

An *appositive phrase* consists of an appositive and its modifiers, which may be single-word modifiers, phrases, or clauses.

The Sweet Adelines, *a singing group,* will perform at the fair.

The aspidistra, *a sturdy plant with long green leaves,* is also known as the "cast iron plant."

My car, *an old Edsel that is always needing repairs,* keeps me broke.

Exercise 5

Write out the following sentences and underline the appositive phrases. Then draw an arrow from the phrase to the noun or pronoun it modifies.

Examples

a. The Pea Ridge Battlefield, the scene of an important Civil War engagement, is now a national park.

a. The Pea Ridge Battlefield, the scene of an important Civil War engagement, is now a national park.

b. The Hollow Earth Society, a group that believes the center of the earth is not only hollow but also inhabited, has 400 members.

b. The Hollow Earth Society, a group that believes the center of the earth is not only hollow but also inhabited, has 400 members.

1. The tomato, a fruit often mistakenly classified as a vegetable, contains vitamin C.
2. Miss Piggy, the world's most glamorous swine, is my favorite Muppet character.
3. Alpha Centuri, the star that is nearest our own sun, often figures in science fiction stories.
4. The Sufis, a mystical sect of Persians, often used humorous stories to illustrate philosophical points.
5. *Paradise Lost*, an epic poem by John Milton, is about the fall of Lucifer from heaven and his temptation of Adam and Eve.
6. Pegasus, the winged horse of mythology, is the symbol of poetic inspiration.
7. One of Agatha Christie's most beguiling detectives is Miss Jane Marple, a deceptively innocent-seeming elderly woman who often knits while thinking out a murder case.
8. Sidney Moncreif, the highest scoring player in the game, won the "Most Valuable Player Award."
9. Phrenology, a pseudoscience that claimed a person's character was indicated by the bumps of the skull, flourished in the nineteenth century.
10. Updoc, an odious mixture of corn syrup and peanut butter, is the creation of my Uncle Basil, who slathers it generously on his pancakes.

Review Exercise A

Write out the following sentences, underlining the prepositional, participial, gerund, infinitive, and appositive phrases. Above each phrase write one of the following abbreviations:

Adj.	adjective phrase	Ger.	gerund phrase
Adv.	adverb phrase	Inf.	infinitive phrase
Part.	participial phrase	App.	appositive phrase

Examples

a. During the Renaissance the politics of England were often complex and brutal.

Adv. Adj.

a. During the Renaissance the politics of England were often complex and brutal.

b. Upon the death of Henry the Eighth (a powerful and scheming king) a long, relentless struggle for the throne began.

b. Upon the death [Adv.] *of Henry the Eighth* [Adj.] *(a powerful and scheming king)* [App.]
a long, relentless struggle for the throne [Adj.] *began.*

1. Edward, Henry's only son, took the throne at the age of nine.
2. Edward, having been weakened by illnesses, had a brief life and a brief reign, dying in his fifteenth year.
3. Before his death he had signed a will forbidding his two half-sisters to rule.
4. Parliament had to agree to this because Edward was quite capable of beheading anyone who opposed him.
5. He left the crown to his cousin, Lady Jane Grey, who became one of England's most pathetic victims in the long power struggle.
6. Jane Grey's "reign," lasting only nine days, ended in her imprisonment and death.
7. Edward's eldest half-sister, Mary of Scotland, seized the throne, accusing Jane Grey and her relatives of treason against the rightful heir.
8. Mary, later nicknamed "Bloody Mary," sent Jane Grey, only a sixteen-year-old girl, and all of her relatives to the executioner's block.
9. In addition, Mary, a religious fanatic, ordered 200 "heretics" to be burned at the stake.
10. Like her brother, Mary of Scotland was in ill health, suffering from a mysterious malady that caused her death in the fifth year of her reign.
11. Elizabeth, Mary's half-sister and the next queen, was no stranger to intrigue and violence.
12. Anne Boleyn, Elizabeth's mother, had been beheaded by Elizabeth's father primarily because she had been unable to produce a son for him.
13. During Bloody Mary's brief reign, she sent Elizabeth to prison, and Elizabeth narrowly escaped the fatal walk to the headsman's block.
14. Elizabeth, at the age of twenty-five, became queen, perhaps the strongest queen in English history.
15. Her subjects loved her, her ministers respected her, and her political enemies learned, to their sorrow, that they should not have tried to plot against her.
16. Condemning people to death was distasteful to Queen Elizabeth, but she was quite capable of it.
17. Seeing her power menaced by her cousin, Mary Queen of Scots, Elizabeth signed that unfortunate lady's death warrant.
18. Near the end of her long life, Elizabeth apparently fell in love with a much younger man, the Earl of Essex.

19. After a quarrel Elizabeth gave Essex a special ring, telling him to send it to her if he needed her help; she said she would forgive him for anything.
20. Essex committed the unpardonable sin, treason against the queen, attempting to seize power from her.
21. Elizabeth sent him to the tower prison and condemned him to death.
22. Many stories, based on Essex's ring, are told about Essex and the queen in those last days.
23. Some say Essex sent her the ring, begging pardon, but Elizabeth, wounded by his treason, did not reply.
24. Another version is that Essex refused to send the ring to her, hoping her love was strong enough to make her spare him and to share her power with him.
25. Elizabeth was a woman in love, but she was also a queen schooled by harsh realities.

Mastery Exercise A

Using what you have learned about identifying phrases, find the adjective, adverb, participial, gerund, infinitive, and appositive phrases in the following selection from *Adventures in English Literature.* List the phrases on a sheet of paper; beside each phrase indicate its type.[1]

> English literature begins with *Beowulf.* It is England's heroic epic, a proper beginning for a national literature, but it belongs to everyone because it is profoundly human. The poem shapes and interprets materials connected with the tribes from northern Europe, the Angles, Saxons, and Jutes, who invaded England after the Romans left in the fifth century. Their tribal history is in the poem . . . It is a history of festering pride, loud talk, and drunken violence, of spies, bloody borders, and raids. But against this dark background the poem presents another kind of history. It is a history in which a stranger comes openly to help rather than covertly to kill and loot, in which eating and drinking and speaking and gift-giving are natural ceremonies uniting young and old, in which heroic strength is wise and generous. It is a history of ideal possibilities . . .
>
> *Beowulf,* like all epic poems is about a hero who is leader of his people . . . The diction is stately and many of its scenes—the banquet, the battle, the boast, the voyage, and the funeral—are traditional. The general tone of the poem is somber, owing to a vision of evil in the world, a belief in the power of Fate . . . to rule human destiny, and resignation to the certainty of death.

Mastery Exercise B

From a paper you have recently written or from another source, select a passage about the length of that in Mastery Exercise A. Using your knowledge of the definition and types of phrases, identify the phrases in the selection and list them on a sheet of paper in the order they appear. Beside each phrase

[1]From "Anglo-Saxon Literature" in *Adventures in English Literature,* Heritage Edition, edited by Leopold Damrosch, et al., copyright © 1980 by Harcourt Brace Jovanovich, Inc. Reprinted by permission of the publisher.

identify its type: adjective, adverb, participial, gerund, infinitive, or appositive.

Using Phrases

You can combine ideas and avoid short, choppy sentences by using phrases.

The dog was barking. It was tied to the fence. It lunged futilely. It was lunging at the stray cat.

The barking dog, tied to the fence, lunged futilely at the stray cat.

In the following lessons you will review how phrases are punctuated. You will also practice placing phrases within a sentence so that they communicate their meaning clearly and effectively, and you will see how phrases can be used to give variety to your sentence structure.

Punctuating Phrases

A phrase is not a sentence, because it does not contain a subject and its verb; therefore, it cannot express a complete thought. A phrase should not be punctuated as if it were a sentence.

Avoid phrase fragments in your writing.

A phrase must be attached to the sentence to which it logically belongs.

Fragment:	I wrote a note in the dust on the coffee table. Reminding myself to clean up the house. One of these days.
Sentence:	I wrote a note in the dust on the coffee table, reminding myself to clean up the house one of these days.
Fragment:	To sum up my opinions. I am against the proposed budget cuts because they will hurt the educational system.
Sentence:	To sum up my opinions, I am against the proposed budget cuts because they will hurt the educational system.

In certain situations commas are used to set off phrases from the rest of the sentence.

1. Appositives are usually set off by commas.

Howard Hawks, *a Hollywood director*, was renowned for making great movies about the American West.

The long interval, *probably the best tactic in defensive driving*, can help you in many diverse situations.

Appositives are not set off when they are essential to the meaning of the sentence. Such appositives are usually a name or a one-word appositive.

My cousin *Dino* works at the hospital.
The conjunction *and* joins sentence parts together.

2. When introductory phrases are long or several introductory phrases are linked together, they are set off by a comma.

   Shortly after the ringing of the burglar alarm, a police car pulled up.
   To make matters worse, I accidentally dropped my car keys in the sewer.

A short introductory phrase that precedes the subject is *not* set off by commas.

   In July we are going to visit Mexico.
   During October the monarch butterflies migrate southward.

3. An introductory participial phrase that precedes the subject is set off by a comma.

   Gurgling horribly, the drain began to back up.
   Disgusted by the long line at the ticket window, we decided to skip the movie.

4. Nonintroductory phrases are set off by commas when they are not essential to the meaning of the sentence. (Such phrases are called *nonessential* phrases.) A phrase that is essential to the meaning of the sentence is not set off by punctuation.

Essential:	The artist *sketching with charcoal* is Rita Washington.
Nonessential:	The artist, *sketching with charcoal*, bent over her pad of paper in absolute concentration.
Essential:	All Americans are guaranteed the right *to pursue happiness.*
Nonessential:	His single desire, *to pursue happiness*, seemed shallow and immature.

Exercise 1

Write out the following sentences, correcting phrase fragments and errors in punctuation. If a sentence is correct as written, write *C*. Circle the punctuation you insert.

Examples

a. The principal wants to see you. In the office right now.
a. The principal wants to see you in the office right now.

b. Howling balefully, the Hound of the Baskervilles stalked the fog-shrouded moors.
b. C

1. The novel the story of a Polish girl who survived a Nazi concentration camp was nominated for the National Book Award.
2. A large snapping turtle, nearly a foot across, sat hissing and shaking its head back and forth. Right in our path.
3. Slipping from my hands the book dropped to the floor and bounced down the stairs.
4. The vegetable marrow, a type of large squash, is a favorite crop of British gardeners.

5. The musical comedy created in the nineteenth century is one of America's contributions to the world of theater.
6. Up until the very last second of the game with Texas A. & M. our team remained within one point of winning.
7. The actress playing the role of Suzie Wong was France Nuyen.
8. Bill Cosby the well-known comedian earned a doctor's degree in education.
9. Pedro trained for his ambitious goal. To compete in the 1984 Olympics.
10. At the high point of the third act in the school play, I suddenly forgot my lines completely.

Placing Phrases

When phrases are used as modifiers, they usually come as close as possible to the words they modify; otherwise, confusion may result. Two kinds of problems sometimes occur when using phrases as modifiers: *misplaced modifiers* and *dangling modifiers.*

Misplaced Modifiers

Occasionally a modifier is placed so that it seems to modify a noun or pronoun other than the one it was meant to modify.

Misplaced: I saw a moose *looking out of the cab of my truck.*
Corrected: *Looking out of the cab of my truck*, I saw a moose.

In your writing place a modifier as near as possible to the word it modifies.

Misplaced: Phyllis saw the Rocky Mountains *flying to Utah.*
Corrected: *Flying to Utah*, Phyllis saw the Rocky Mountains.

Misplaced: *Hanging by a long furry tail*, John watched the monkey eat the orange.
Corrected: John watched the monkey, *hanging by a long furry tail*, eat the orange.

Dangling Modifiers

A modifier is said to dangle when a sentence contains no word or words for it to modify.

Dangling: *Listening to the news flash*, it was hard to believe the story was possible.
[Who was listening to the news flash?]
Corrected: *Listening to the news flash*, we found it hard to believe the story was possible.

Place phrases so that they clearly modify a word or words within the sentence.

Dangling: *Straining his eyes*, the pilot's visibility was difficult.
Corrected: *Straining his eyes*, the pilot could barely see through the fog.

Dangling: *Waiting for the train to pass*, the streets were blocked.
Corrected: *Waiting for the train to pass*, the cars blocked the streets.

Exercise 2

Rewrite the following sentences, correcting misplaced and dangling modifiers.

Examples

a. Coiled up in the rain spout, Grandmother saw a small copperhead snake.
a. Grandmother saw a small copperhead snake coiled up in the rain spout.

b. Sprawled in the armchair, it felt relaxing at last.
b. Sprawled in the armchair, Morris felt relaxed at last.

1. In order to provide new students with essential information, a news sheet is sent to each one.
2. We ate a dessert made by my cousin called "Idiot's Delight."
3. Disgusted by poor grades, the test was given again.
4. I saw several ancient mummies touring the museum.
5. Lying ear-deep in mud and contentedly chewing garbage, I watched the hogs.
6. I luckily escaped injury when I hit a cow on my motorcycle.
7. Completely upsetting the sportscasters' predictions, the tournament was won by Marcia Redhawk.
8. Rummaging under the sofa cushions, a dime, two pennies, and four pencils were recovered.
9. By not reading the instructions on the box, the bicycle was put together incorrectly.
10. Looking through the microscope, the germs appeared large and ugly.

Writing Exercise A

Write several well developed paragraphs on one of the following topics. First write a rough draft and then check what you have written, paying special attention to the placement and punctuation of phrases. Try to improve your writing by using phrases that add detail, that allow you to combine sentences, and that give your sentences variety of structure.

1. You stroll over to your best friend's house for a visit, only to find no one is home. As you are leaving, you notice a car with two people in it pulling up in the alley behind the house. Suspicious, you take a good, long look at the car and its passengers. Later that evening you discover your friend's house has been robbed, just shortly after you left the scene. You telephone

the police, who believe you have seen the thieves. Give a detailed description of the car and its passengers.

2. Imagine you have an overseas pen pal who has never witnessed some common American event, such as a rodeo, carnival, homecoming parade, demolition derby, or Saturday night dance. Write a vivid description of one of these events or another of your own choosing so your friend can envision such an event and imagine the atmosphere.
3. Give a character sketch of your favorite character from a television show, movie, or book. Describe the character physically; then tell what this person's personality is like and what interests you about the character—why you find him or her appealing.
4. Choose an issue or problem in your school or community. Discuss this issue—the choices to be made or the problem to be faced. Then state how you think it should be dealt with. If there are two opinions about a solution, discuss why yours is the better solution.

21 The Clause

Understanding Clauses

In the following lessons you will learn to identify clauses through their definition and through the categories into which they can be divided. You will also learn to classify sentences according to the number and kinds of clauses they contain.

Defining a Clause

A *clause* is usually defined as a group of words containing a subject and a predicate that functions as part of a sentence.

Although the definition of a clause resembles that of a sentence (a clause and a sentence both have a subject and a verb, or predicate), a sentence differs from a clause in that a sentence must *always* express a complete thought. Some clauses, although they have both subjects and predicates, do not express a complete thought.

All of the following are clauses.

because the streets (S) were frozen (V)

although the game (S) was (V) on Friday

The bowling ball (S) fell (V) on my toe.

S V
The stars shone brightly down on the little town.

Clauses may be divided into two main categories: *independent clauses* and *subordinate clauses.*

Independent Clauses

An *independent*, or *main*, *clause* is one that can stand on its own as a sentence.

Every sentence must contain at least one independent clause. An independent clause can stand alone, expresses a complete thought, and contains a subject and its verb. It may also contain single-word modifiers, phrase modifiers, or both. Each of the following sentences is one independent clause that contains a subject and its verb.

S V
The main chamber of the castle was gloomy and dank.

S V
The riders had dismounted from their horses.

A sentence may contain two or more independent clauses connected by a conjunction or semicolon.

The apples were ruined by the hail storm, but most of the pear crop survived.

Emily Brontë was an English poet and novelist; Emily Dickinson was an American poet.

Subordinate Clauses

The word *subordinate* means "of lower rank." A subordinate clause is of lower rank than an independent clause because it cannot stand alone as a sentence. It needs to be attached to an independent clause in order for its meaning to be clear.

A *subordinate clause* is usually defined as a clause that cannot stand on its own as a sentence.

In the following examples the subordinate clauses are *italicized.*

Subordinate Clause: *whenever the meter reader comes*
Sentence: *Whenever the meter reader comes*, the dogs bark wildly.

Subordinate Clause: *that the tornado damaged*
Sentence: We saw the barns *that the tornado damaged.*

Subordinate Clause: *which was unusual*
Sentence: The pygmy rattlesnake ate well in captivity, *which was unusual.*

Exercise 1

On a sheet of paper numbered 1–10, write *S* if the *italicized* group of words in each of the following sentences is a subordinate clause. Write *I* if it is an independent clause.

Examples

a. *An Englishman went to a cemetery* because he wanted to visit the grave of a friend.

a. I

b. He brought a small bouquet *that he laid upon the grave.*

b. S

1. The man stood at the grave *while he remembered his old friend.*
2. *When he looked up,* he saw another visitor at a neighboring grave.
3. The other man was a Chinese, *who was placing a bowl of rice on a grave.*
4. *The Englishman was startled and amused* because he had never seen such a sight.
5. "When do you expect *that your friend will come up and eat the rice?*" he asked.
6. *After the Chinese gentleman bowed politely,* he spoke.
7. "He will come up about the same time *that your friend comes up to smell the flowers,*" he replied.
8. *Although this story is probably fictional,* it illustrates an important truth.
9. We often accept familiar customs without question, *whereas we are astonished by customs that are strange to us.*
10. Our own actions and beliefs may seem as strange to others *as theirs do to us.*

Classifying Sentences by Structure

Sentences may be classified according to the number of independent and subordinate clauses they contain. According to structure, there are four types of sentences: *simple, compound, complex,* and *compound-complex.*

A *simple* sentence contains one independent clause and no subordinate clauses.

All of the mice in the laboratory escaped.
I bought myself a new record album.

A simple sentence may have a compound subject, a compound verb, or both.

Hinduism and Taoism are both eastern religions and are very ancient.

The forward and the guard both went for the ball and collided.

A *compound sentence* is made up of two or more independent clauses but no subordinate clauses.

I had to study, but people kept interrupting me.

A slight dew was on the field, and a gentle breeze stirred the grasses.

Crazy Horse was one of the most important Indian chiefs, yet no photographs exist of him.

A *complex sentence* is composed of one independent clause and one or more subordinate clauses.

In the following examples the independent clauses are underlined once, the subordinate clauses twice.

We didn't go to the game because we lost our tickets.

Since I can't concentrate while the television set is on, I turn it off when I study.

If gasoline prices don't go down, I will have to travel on foot when I go to college.

A *compound-complex sentence* is composed of two or more independent clauses and one or more subordinate clauses.

In the following examples the independent clauses are underlined once, the subordinate clauses twice.

Because my sister likes to travel, she has been to Ireland and Hong Kong, but I prefer to stay home with a good book, since I hate planes and ships.

Although a small shark was found dead in the river, the authorities think that pranksters put it there, for this type of shark cannot live in fresh water.

Exercise 2

Write out the following sentences, underlining the independent clauses once and the subordinate clauses twice. After each sentence identify its type according to structure: simple, complex, compound, or compound-complex.

Examples

a. We saw that the river was up, but we didn't believe that it was nearing flood stage yet.

a. We saw that the river was up, but we didn't believe that it was nearing flood stage yet.

compound-complex

b. I let my brother borrow the car once, but I'll never do it again.

b. I let my brother borrow the car once, but I'll never do it again.

compound

1. Hypnosis, which is derived from a Greek word meaning "sleep," is familiar to most of us, but it is not well understood.
2. Hypnosis first began to be recognized in France, when the physician Mesmer began experimenting with magnets; he believed that magnets might have healing properties.

3. Although Mesmer seemed to heal some people with magnets, he soon began to believe that the power came from his own body.
4. He theorized that some people have a power, "animal magnetism," that could effect cures.
5. One of his followers who was performing experiments soon discovered that "animal magnetism" seemed to have nothing to do with magnetism.
6. By simply talking, he could put people into "trances."
7. Freud and other early psychologists experimented with hypnotism because they thought that it could open up the mind.
8. Today hypnotism is used in psychoanalysis, medicine, and in police work to help witnesses recall details.
9. Hypnotism exists and it often works, but we still do not know quite what it is or how it works.
10. Some experts say that there is no such thing as a "trance" and that the powers of suggestion and imagination bring about what we know as "the hypnotic state."

Adjective Clauses

According to their function in the sentence, subordinate clauses can be divided into three classes: *adjective, adverb, and noun.*

An *adjective clause* is a subordinate clause that modifies a noun or pronoun.

We saw the spot *where the tornado touched down.*

The Andrews Sisters, *whose first names were Pattie, Maxine, and LaVerne,* were the most popular singing group in the early 1940s.

We visited Red Cloud, Nebraska, *where Willa Cather lived.*

An adjective clause is usually introduced by a relative pronoun: *who, whom, whose, which, that,* and *where.*

Relative pronouns refer to the noun or pronoun in the sentence that the adjective clause modifies. Within the clause the relative pronoun may function as the subject of the clause it introduces.

S (who) *V* (has accomplished)

She is a woman *who has accomplished much.*

S (that) *V* (affects)

Air pollution is an issue *that affects us all.*

Relative pronouns may also serve as the object of the clause or as the object of a preposition within the clause.

DO (whom) *S* (we) *V* (met)

Daisy Bates, *whom we met at the convention,* is a well-known civil rights worker.

OP S V
I know someone *with whom I can ride.*

Where and *when* can also introduce adjective clauses.

I want to see the lake *where the sea serpent is supposed to live.*

The 1950s were the period *when rock-and-roll music became popular.*

Sometimes, a relative pronoun is omitted when the clause has its own subject and verb and the meaning is clear. In the following sentence the relative pronouns have been dropped.

The writer *I like best* is Maya Angelou.
[The relative pronoun *whom* has been dropped from the subordinate clause.]
I'll show you the truck *I want to buy.*
[The relative pronoun *that* has been dropped from the subordinate clause.]

Exercise 3
Write out the following sentences, underlining the adjective clause in each and drawing an arrow to the word the clause modifies. (A sentence may contain more than one adjective clause.)

Examples
a. Many young couples want a house that they can call their own.
a. Many young couples want a house that they can call their own.

b. They should find a reliable real estate agent on whom they can depend.
b. They should find a reliable real estate agent on whom they can depend.

1. Such an agent will not try to talk the customer into a house that is too expensive for him or her.
2. An agent who knows about houses can spot potential problems or hidden disadvantages in a certain home.
3. A pleasant-looking house may hide a number of flaws, of which termites, poor plumbing or wiring, and a leaky basement may be only a few.
4. The house a customer buys should be in a neighborhood that meets his or her needs.
5. A childless couple might not be happy in a neighborhood where a dozen preschoolers are playing noisily every day.
6. A house that is located far from the buyer's place of work or shopping may result in staggering gasoline bills.
7. The quiet soul who needs peace and calm should not move next door to the animal lover whose eight beagles yodel all night long.

8. Another point the buyer should keep in mind is energy; a low-priced house that has huge gas and electric bills is no bargain.
9. A person who can't hammer a nail should probably not tackle a house that needs extensive repairs.
10. Novice house-hunters need an agent whom they can trust and who has their best interests in mind.

Adverb Clauses

An *adverb clause* modifies a verb, an adjective, or an adverb.

Like adverbs and adverb phrases, an adverb clause may answer the questions *why? where? when? to what extent?* or *under what conditions?*

We always fish a lot *when we go camping.*
[The clause tells *when.*]

You can't go overseas *unless you take a series of inoculations.*
[The clause tells *under what conditions.*]

Like single-word adverbs, adverb clauses may modify verbs, adjectives, and other adverbs.

You will fail *unless you study.*
[The clause modifies the verb *will fail.*]

As soon as we left, the rain began.
[The clause modifies the verb *began.*]

Ms. Polanski was certain *that she had left the tests on her desk.*
[The clause modifies the adjective *certain.*]

We were afraid *that the canoe would tip over in the rapids.*
[The clause modifies the adjective *afraid.*]

Kim can solve algebra problems more quickly *than I can.*
[The clause modifies the adverb phrase *more quickly.*]

The magician shuffled the cards faster *than the eye could follow.*
[The clause modifies the adverb *faster*.]

An adverb clause always begins with a subordinating conjunction:

after	as though	since	when
although	because	so that	whenever
as	before	than	where
as if	if	though	wherever
as long as	in order that	unless	while
as soon as	provided that	until	

You may recognize some of the words in the preceding list as other parts of speech. For example, *since, until, before,* and *as* can be used as prepositions; *before* and *after* can be adverbs. In order to be classified as subordinating conjunctions, these words must introduce an adverb clause. Unlike the relative pronoun, the subordinating conjunction never functions as a subject or object within the clause.

The subordinating conjunction is important because it expresses the relationship of the ideas contained in the subordinate clause and the independent clause. Notice how changing the subordinate clause changes the meaning of the sentence:

> I'll go *because I have to.*
> I'll go *when I have to.*
> I'll go *as soon as I have to.*
> I'll go *wherever I have to.*
> I'll go *if I have to.*

When two ideas are combined into a single sentence, either one may be subordinated to the other, depending on which idea the writer thinks is more important. Notice that the meaning of the following two sentences is somewhat different.

> Although Linda didn't want to go to the party, she had a good time.
> Linda didn't want to go to the party, although she had a good time.

Adverb clauses may be elliptical.

An *elliptical clause* is one in which a word or words have been omitted.

In elliptical clauses the omitted words are understood by both the speaker and the listener or the writer and reader. Notice that the omitted words, shown in brackets, may be the subject of the clause or the verb, or both.

> *When* [*she was*] *visiting Utah*, Clare saw the Mormon Tabernacle.
> *When* [*I was*] *eating my dinner*, I thought I saw something moving in my salad.
> Georgia is a larger state *than Tennessee [is].*
> *When* [*you are*] *in Rome*, do as the Romans do.

Exercise 4

Write out each of the following sentences, underlining each adverb clause and circling the subordinating conjunction. If the clause is elliptical, write out the clause beneath the sentence and include the words that have been omitted in brackets.

Examples

a. The lake is lower than it has been for ten years.

a. The lake is lower (than) it has been for ten years.

b. When leaving, be sure to turn out the lights.

b. (When) [you are] leaving, be sure to turn out the lights.

1. Since the late movie wouldn't be over until three in the morning, we decided to skip it.
2. While running to answer the phone, I tripped, knocked over the chair, and landed in a heap on the living room rug.
3. Although Marcia loves cats, she can't have one because they make her sneeze constantly.

4. When the Blazers played the Bucks, Moncrief made one of his stunning slam dunks.
5. Trailers cost less than houses, but they depreciate faster as well.
6. Willows and elms grow more quickly than oaks, but they are less sturdy than many other trees.
7. Because we didn't believe in ghosts, we tried to find some other explanation for the weird sounds in our attic.
8. My little sister will get her driver's license in May, provided that she raises her grades in math.
9. A pound of feathers is heavier than a pound of gold, because a "pound" of gold is only fourteen ounces.
10. Catherine looked as though she weren't feeling well after she rode the roller coaster.

Noun Clauses

A *noun clause* is a subordinate clause used as a noun.

A noun clause may be the subject of an independent clause, the direct object, the indirect object, the predicate nominative, the object of a preposition, or an appositive. In short, a noun clause may serve any function a noun can.

What I need is an extra day in each week.	[subject]
I believe *that flying saucers really exist.*	[direct object]
She gave *whoever called* the same message.	[indirect object]
My invention is *just what the world needs.*	[predicate nominative]
We will give help to *whoever needs it.*	[object of preposition]
Her theory, *that all is futile,* is ridiculous.	[appositive]

Adjective clauses usually begin with relative pronouns, and subordinating conjunctions introduce adverb clauses. Some of these same words introduce noun clauses, but they are not considered relative pronouns or subordinating conjunctions when they do. When any of the following begin a noun clause, they are considered introductory words.

that	whatever	where	whoever
what	when	who	whomever

In noun clauses, as in adjective clauses, the introductory word is sometimes omitted. For example, direct quotations that follow an expression such as *he said*, or *she answered* are really noun clauses with the introductory word *that* omitted.

He said, [that] *"The Jones sisters are the best teachers in the city system."*
I thought [that] *he was right.*
Grandmother knew [that] *a snake must be in the henhouse.*
Coretta wishes [that] *she were at home.*

Exercise 5

Write out the following sentences, underlining the noun clause in each. (Some sentences may have more than one noun clause.) After the sentence indicate how each clause is used.

Example

a. Whoever sat next to me at assembly took my book by mistake.

a. <u>Whoever sat next to me at assembly</u> took my book by mistake.
subject

1. The trophy will be awarded to whoever climbs the greased flagpole first.
2. Whatever took my bait was very large and very fast.
3. We saw what appeared to be a large bluish light hovering over the swamp.
4. Sheila thought the bell would never ring.
5. For the party, dress in whatever costume expresses your secret fantasy.
6. More exercise and less rich food is what many Americans need.
7. Where I long to be is on a surfboard, riding the perfect wave.
8. Who the culprit must be suddenly flashed into the detective's mind.
9. A sudden thought, that I was not alone in the house, made me uneasy.
10. Give whoever needs extra paper one of these examination tablets.

Mastery Exercise A

Using what you have learned about identifying clauses, find the noun, adjective, and adverb clauses in the following paragraphs from *Adventures in English Literature.* List the clauses on a sheet of paper in the order they appear, labeling each clause *noun*, *adjective*, or *adverb.* For noun clauses identify the function of the clause in the sentence; for adjective and adverb clauses identify the word or words modified by the clause.[1]

> It is natural that we should be curious about the life of a writer who is almost unanimously considered to be the greatest figure in English literature. Fortunately, more facts are known about Shakespeare than about most Elizabethan playwrights. We know that he was born in Stratford-on-Avon in April (probably on the 23rd) 1564, and that his father John was a fairly prominent citizen of the town who eventually became an alderman and bailiff. Shakespeare was presumably educated at the local school in Stratford. He never attended a university. In 1582 he married Anne Hathaway. They had a daughter in 1583, and twins, a boy and a girl, in 1585. After this there is no factual information for seven years, but we know that by 1592 he was in London working as an actor and a playwright, for in this year he was attacked in writing by a resentful rival.

---

[1]From "William Shakespeare" in *Adventures in English Literature,* Heritage Edition, copyright © 1980 by Harcourt Brace Jovanovich, Inc. Reprinted by permission of the publisher.

In 1593 the London theaters were closed because of an outbreak of the plague, and Shakespeare, temporarily out of work, needed the support of a private patron. He got such support from the Earl of Southampton, a wealthy young nobleman to whom Shakespeare dedicated two rather long narrative poems: *Venus and Adonis* (1593) and *The Rape of Lucrece* (1594). When the theaters reopened, Shakespeare became a member of the most successful company of actors in London, the Lord Chamberlain's Men.

Mastery Exercise B

From a textbook or a paper you have recently written, select a passage about the length of that in Mastery Exercise A. Then follow the instructions for Mastery Exercise A.

Using Clauses

The next few lessons will give you practice using what you know about clauses to strengthen your writing. Helpful writing skills you will study are punctuating clauses correctly, knowing when to use *who* and *whom*, and combining sentences by using subordinate clauses.

Punctuating Clauses Correctly

1. Set off an introductory adverb clause from the rest of the sentence with a comma.

If you have any doubts, contact me.

After Washington struck out, we knew the game was lost.

A comma is usually unnecessary, however, when the adverb clause follows the main clause.

Contact me if you have any trouble.
We knew the game was lost after Washington struck out.

2. Do not use commas to set off an essential clause.

An adjective clause that is essential to the meaning of a sentence is called an *essential* (or *restrictive*) *clause*. Such a clause cannot be removed without changing or damaging the meaning of the sentence.

Essential: We saw a play *that won every award on Broadway*.
[Not just any play was seen; it was the play *that won every award on Broadway*.]

Essential: Every cabbage *that we've ever bought from Tudbury's Market* has been wormy.
[Not every cabbage in the world was wormy, not even every cabbage purchased was wormy; only those *that we've ever bought from Tudbury's Market* were inhabited.]

A *nonessential clause*, on the other hand, does not add essential information. It adds additional information, but the sentence would still mean the same if the clause were dropped. Commas are used to set off nonessential clauses.

Nonessential:	The mail is late today, *which is not unusual.*
Nonessential:	Mrs. Gomez, *who lives next door*, is a certified public accountant.

3. Avoid making sentence fragments from subordinate clauses by punctuating them as if they were sentences.

A subordinate clause cannot stand alone; it must be attached to an independent clause.

Fragment:	Until the final ballots are counted.
Sentence:	We won't know who the next dog catcher will be until the final ballots are counted.
Fragment:	Because he thinks the moon is made of green cheese.
Sentence:	Because he thinks the moon is made of green cheese, he is not a very good candidate for astronaut training school.

Exercise 1

Rewrite the following sentences, adding commas where necessary and correcting sentence fragments. If a sentence is punctuated correctly, write *C*. Circle the commas you insert.

Examples

a. Even if it rains or snows Ken jogs a mile each day.

a. Even if it rains or snows, Ken jogs a mile each day.

b. The cat ate the lamb chops that were defrosting on the counter.

b. C

1. The Zuñi who are a Southwestern nation are noted for their exquisite silverwork.
2. Of course, I can go with you to the movies. After I do my eighteen pages of geometry.
3. My biology teacher who is rather cynical says that soon human beings will have one large eye for watching television and one large finger for pushing buttons.
4. The student government wants to turn the area that was supposed to be for storage into a student lounge.
5. The crowd laughed at the hypnotist's willing subject. Who was convinced she was the world's greatest hula dancer.
6. Whenever we let Rover in the house he immediately races through the kitchen and leaps onto the couch.

7. The house which had been built before the Civil War was beautiful but had no central heating system.
8. Nebraska which is a completely landlocked state has a mythical navy and bestows the honorary title of "Admiral of the Nebraska Navy" on some people as a joking tribute.
9. Since the invention of the automobile courting practices have changed drastically.
10. Although John McClure is an excellent mystery writer few Americans are familiar with his work. Because he is a South African.

Using *Who* and *Whom* in Clauses

Who and *whom* are used to introduce adjective clauses and noun clauses. Simple rules govern the use of *who* and *whom* in Edited Standard English.

Who is always used as the subject of a clause. *Whom* is used to function as an object, usually either a direct object or an object of a preposition.

The woman *who came to the door* was Ms. Feinberg.
[*Who* is the subject of the adjective clause.]

Chris is the person *whom I'd recommend for the job.*
[*Whom* is the direct object in the adjective clause.]

Do not ask *for whom the bell tolls.*
[*Whom* is the object of the preposition in the noun clause.]

Whom the police suspect has not yet been made public.
[*Whom* is the direct object of the noun clause.]

Notice that you must determine the use of *who* or *whom* as it functions within the clause, not within the sentence.

The words *whoever* and *whomever* follow the same rules. *Whoever* is the subject form; *whomever* is the object form.

Use *whoever* as the subject of the clause. Use *whomever* for an object within the clause.

Whoever passed the test must have been a genius.
[*Whoever* is the subject of the noun clause.]

The scholarship will be given to *whomever the coach recommends.*
[*Whomever* is the direct object of the noun clause that serves as the object of the preposition.]

Exercise 2

Write out the following sentences, choosing and underlining the correct word from the pair in parentheses. Remember that you must first determine how the word is used within the clause.

Examples

a. Louis Armstrong is the singer (who, whom) made that song famous.
a. Louis Armstrong is the singer <u>who</u> made that song famous.

b. Give these old magazines to (whoever, whomever) you want to have them.

b. Give these old magazines to whomever you want to have them.

1. Mr. Mwangi is the teacher (who, whom) the students most respect.
2. (Whoever, Whomever) was trying to drive us from the castle would not succeed.
3. The housekeeper (who, whom) the agency recommended so highly was slovenly and ill-tempered.
4. We need to contact (whoever, whomever) is in charge of tickets.
5. The player (who, whom) was on second base made a sprint to steal third.
6. The donation will go to (whoever, whomever) is the most deserving recipient.
7. (Who, Whom) shall I say is calling, please?
8. The organization will give $10,000 to (whoever, whomever) breeds a hamster marked like a panda bear.
9. (Who, Whom) did the committee elect as president?
10. Nobody knows (who, whom) will be selected for Groundhog Queen this year.

Review Exercise A

Write out the following sentences, correcting any errors in punctuation or word choice. If a sentence is correct, write *C.* Circle the punctuation you insert and underline the corrections you make.

1. Send the announcements to whomever is on the membership list.
2. If John Keats had lived longer he might have been one of our very greatest poets.
3. Transporting the fish and newts from our aquarium was our biggest problem when we moved to Chicago.
4. Give whoever the committee elects copies of the minutes of past meetings.
5. Since our cat has the bad habit of stalking birds we put several bells on its collar.
6. Marlie's favorite television program is *Soul Train* which is hosted by Don Cornelius.
7. The person who I most admire is Mother Teresa of India.
8. The book that won top honors for a first novel was *Song of Solomon* by Toni Morrison.
9. If a lightning storm begins while you are outside you should not take shelter under a tree.
10. The manager of the jewelry store who had no sense of humor threatened to fire Pat because of the prank.

11. When the Studebaker Company closed down in South Bend, Indiana, the city suffered a grave unemployment problem.
12. Della finally found the person for who she was searching.
13. Whenever Uncle Waldo decides to cook one of his gourmet delights the kitchen ends up looking like a disaster area.
14. The restaurant that specialized in health food dishes was closed down by the Board of Health.
15. I was only halfway through my test when the bell rang.
16. In honor of the students' favorite basketball player, the bookstore sells T-shirts, that say "Eugene, Eugene, the Dunking Machine."
17. When my sister went to college last fall she took her most treasured possession: a mounted moose head.
18. The local newspaper always contains so many printing errors, that it's called "The Daily Mistake."
19. Free entry blanks are available for whomever wants to enter the contest.
20. Because the cold rain poured down all day the dogs stayed in their houses and looked forlorn.

Writing Exercise A

Using a mixture of noun, adjective, and adverb clauses, write a brief paper on one of the following topics. Use care in punctuating clauses and in choosing between *who* and *whom*, *whoever* and *whomever*.

1. What do you think would be the ideal job for you? Write a description of your version of the ideal job: the duties it entails, the advantages it offers, and why it would suit you.
2. Imagine that you are a television critic and describe the television show you think is the worst being shown. State all the reasons that you think it is terrible and should be taken off the air. Make your attack pointed and vivid.
3. Students in the 1950s were called the "Quiet Generation"; students in the 1960s and early 1970s were considered rebellious and daring. Young people in the late 1970s were called the "Me Generation," self-centered and pleasure-loving. How would you describe the generation of students to which you belong? What traits seem to characterize people of your age and time? What ideals, flaws, problems, concerns do they share?
4. The possibility of an Equal Rights Amendment raises many questions, including that of drafting women. Some critics maintain that women should never be drafted; others think it would be a good idea. What is your stand on the issue? Should women be drafted? Should they be placed in combat during time of war? Give specific reasons for your opinion.

PART

7 Mechanics

22 Punctuation

Using Punctuation

Marks of punctuation add meaning to your writing beyond what the words alone can convey. You rely, to an extent, on punctuation to transmit to your writing the tone or emotion that you might, if speaking, convey through changes in inflection and through body language. For example, by using an exclamation point instead of a period, you add excitement or a sense of urgency to your words. By inserting a comma, you slow readers down. If you were speaking, you might pause to achieve the same effect.

Punctuation also helps show the relationships between groups of words in writing. The period, for instance, clearly indicates where one sentence ends. It causes readers to stop for a second and assures that they read a particular group of words as one complete thought. Other marks of punctuation, such as the semicolon or colon, show that there is a relationship between a word or a group of words and those that follow.

By mastering the punctuation rules of Edited Standard English, you will be able to write more clearly and accurately.

The Period

The *period* marks the end of a sentence or an abbreviation.

1. A declarative sentence ends in a period.

   Conservationists voice concern about the pollution of our rivers by chemical wastes**.** Fortunately, many factories now have antipollution controls**.**

2. A mildly imperative sentence ends in a period.

   Please park your car across the street**.**
   Call home on Sunday**.**

3. A period follows many abbreviations.

Dr.	doctor	Capt.	captain
M.D.	doctor of medicine	Wm.	William
Inc.	incorporated	P.M.	post meridiem
Mr.	mister	A.M.	ante meridiem
Jr.	junior	Ave.	avenue
Sr.	senior	lb.	pound
U.S.	United States	i.e.	that is
B.C.	before Christ	cf.	compare

Some abbreviations, such as *Ms.* and *Mrs.*, cannot be spelled out. Some other abbreviations are not followed by a period; metric units *(10 ml, 2kg)*, postal abbreviations for states in addresses (*PA, NY, NJ*), most government agencies *(NASA, FBI)*, many large corporations *(CBS, NBC, IBM)*, and some common abbreviations such as *TV*, *AM*, *FM*, and *mph.*

Dr. Carter and Mrs. Clark both worked for NASA.
Approximately 4 oz. of flour equals 112 g of flour.
Did you watch last night's TV special on NBC?

The Question Mark

A *question*, or *interrogative sentence*, ends with a question mark.

When is the party? I can't be there until after 9:00.
Who wrote that book? Is it someone we know?

Note: When a question is part of a declarative sentence, it is an *indirect question* and ends with a period.

Why aren't we going?	[direct question]
I wondered why we weren't going.	[indirect question]

A question mark is placed inside quotation marks only if the quotation is a question.

For more information about the use of quotation marks, see pages 575–577.

"Where is Albania?" Noah asked.

If the entire sentence is a question, the question mark is placed outside the quotation marks.

Who wrote "The Black Cat"?

When an interrogative pronoun or adverb such as *who, what, where, when, why,* or *how* is used alone to ask a question, it is followed by a question mark.

You made this yourself? How?
What? I did not hear that last question.
You missed the concert last night. Why?

The Exclamation Point

1. A strong imperative sentence is followed by an exclamation point.

   Watch out!

   Come quickly; we're late!

2. An exclamation point follows an exclamation.

   How late I am!

   What a great idea!

Sometimes, the end mark you use is a matter of personal choice. Remember that a mildly imperative sentence can end with a period. Similarly, a mild exclamation at the beginning of a sentence can be followed by a comma. Use an exclamation point, rather than a period or a comma, when you wish to convey stronger feeling. Likewise, a polite request can be followed by a question mark, a period, or an exclamation point. The end mark you choose depends on the meaning and emotion you want to convey.

Exercise 1

Write out each of the following sentences and use periods, question marks, and exclamation points as necessary. Be prepared to explain why you used each mark of punctuation. Circle punctuation marks you insert.

Examples

a. That raccoon is adorable Will it forage through our garbage

a. That raccoon is adorable(!) Will it forage through our garbage(?)

b. Has Dr Garcia ever been to St Kitts I must ask her

b. Has Dr(.) Garcia ever been to St(.) Kitts(?) I must ask her(.)

1. Ms Allen, Mr Janex, and Dr Cottler are looking for artists for their new gallery Send inquiries to this address:
   Modern Space Gallery
   4333 E Roosevelt Ave
   Reno, NV 85305
2. Help Where is Dr Lance's phone number Oh, how I hate this disorganized phone book
3. H J Castillo asked why it was snowing when the CBS 7:00 PM report had predicted fair weather "Who knows" replied Mrs Castillo. "How can anyone really predict the weather"
4. "When did the SS *France* take its last voyage" Capt L Jacobs asked. "Wow I would like to have piloted that ocean liner"
5. Sgt J J Newsome, US Army, barked orders to the new recruits. "Attention About face Forward march"
6. Did you see the writer P D James interviewed on the PBS show *Mystery* at 10:00 PM last night

7. Were you stationed at Ft Riley or at Ft Dix, Pvt Singer Did you, by any chance, know Dr W W Barnes What a coincidence
8. Bravo Bravo What an exciting performance Don't you think that the cast of Players, Inc, puts on a professional show, Prof Cours
9. How exciting that you've won a trip to Europe, Mrs Alonzo When will you go If you need more information, write to Walton Travel, Ltd, Ft Lauderdale, Florida
10. Please call as soon as you arrive That road is so bumpy it could have been built in 1950 BC instead of in AD 1950

The Comma

The *comma* separates words, phrases, or clauses within a sentence. Sometimes, the comma is used where a pause would occur in speech; at other times the comma is used as custom dictates.

1. Use a comma to separate words or groups of words in a series.

Ilena sings, dances, and acts.

Walter designed the table, cut the wood, and assembled the pieces.

When items commonly go together, such as *bread and butter*, they can be paired as one item.

Jake added scallions, cheese, and salt and pepper to the omelet.

When the last two items in a series are joined by a coordinating conjunction *(and* or *but)*, a comma precedes the conjunction. However, when all the items in a series are joined by conjunctions, do not use commas.

We ate chicken, salad, and carrots.

We ate chicken and salad and carrots.

Notice that the use of commas helps make the meaning of a sentence clear. Commas help to avoid confusion about whether or not items are separate. In the following examples notice how the commas clarify the meaning of each sentence.

We ate chicken salad, potatoes, and carrots.	[three items]
We ate chicken, salad, potatoes, and carrots.	[four items]
Carlos invited Mary Beth, Sue Ann, and Kendra to the party.	[three people]
Carlos invited Mary, Beth, Sue, Ann, and Kendra to the party.	[five people]

2. Use a comma to separate two or more adjectives preceding a noun.

Eight hundred talented, enthusiastic applicants answered the ad for the job.

The high-paying, interesting, rewarding job was more than I had hoped for.

Note: Do not use a comma between the last adjective and the noun that follows it. Sometimes, you should not use a comma between adjectives preceding a noun. Use a comma if the word *and* would make sense in its place.

> The creaky wooden canoe seemed unsafe.
> [No commas are necessary between the adjectives.]
>
> The refreshing, salty air blew from the sea.
> [An *and* makes sense between the adjectives; therefore, use a comma.]

3. Use a comma to separate independent clauses that are joined by the coordinating conjunction *and, yet, but, or, nor, for,* or *so.*

> The house is inexpensive, but it requires a lot of repairs.
>
> Juan is a good tennis player, yet he rarely plays.
>
> I love warm weather, so I applied for a job in Hawaii.

Exercise 2

Write out each of the following sentences, using commas where necessary. Circle the commas you insert.

Examples

a. Alec Audrey and Carmen visited Austin San Antonio and Dallas.

a. Alec(,) Audrey(,) and Carmen visited Austin(,) San Antonio(,) and Dallas.

b. José used to work for the San Francisco *Chronicle* but now he writes a syndicated column.

b. José used to work for the San Francisco Chronicle(,) *but now he writes a syndicated column.*

1. During March April and May the weather became warmer the rains ceased the buds appeared.
2. Pablo eats neither fish nor meat nor will he even kill an insect.
3. My sentimental sensitive romantic sister has saved every letter card and note that her husband has ever written her.
4. Helena Maxine and Juanita chose green blue and beige fabric for their couch and chairs and draperies.
5. Hernando looked under the bed behind the dresser and in the closet for his favorite well-worn sneakers.
6. Fire is a constant hazard in Los Angeles County so the people post signs to warn visitors of the danger.
7. Every day Judy eats half a grapefruit before breakfast and lunch and dinner for she believes the grapefruits are healthful.
8. Tim and Jim and Kim live in the same apartment building but they work on different schedules and rarely see each other.

9. Janet designed the patterns bought the fabric and then sewed a skirt two shirts and a dress.
10. The narrow bumpy dirt road winds into the woods up the hill and around the reservoir; it must lead somewhere yet I have no idea where.
11. New Bedford has a large Portuguese population so many shopkeepers there speak both English and Portuguese.
12. Lydia claimed that her steamy ill-tasting herbal tea cured headaches backaches and stomachaches but not baldness poor eyesight or wrinkles.
13. In 1980 few people borrowed money for mortgages for the prime interest rate had soared to record-breaking levels.
14. Jill rented a small cozy one-room apartment and spent the summer there with her dog her cat and her canary.
15. The landlord and the tenants and a lawyer talked for three or four hours but they could not come to an agreement about rent increases.
16. Pamela had no use for the torn patchwork quilt but she had a sentimental fondness for it and couldn't throw it out.
17. The Monroes could no longer maintain their enormous house and no longer needed all the space so they decided to convert the building to an inn.
18. Campers may spend two four six or eight weeks at the camp but must leave by the end of August.
19. The Calders prepare for their challenging annual treasure hunt by writing cryptic clues cleverly hiding them around the grounds and burying the treasure.
20. Joey loved to sail so he sublet his apartment and sold his car and set out on his boat to see the world.

4. Use a comma to separate introductory adverb clauses, introductory participial phrases, and long introductory prepositional phrases from the rest of the sentence.

Adverb clauses are explained on pages 540–541.

INTRODUCTORY ADVERB CLAUSES

When the concert ended, thousands of people jammed the exits.

Before she accepted the job, Mary Anne went on several interviews.

Participial phrases are explained on page 521.

INTRODUCTORY PARTICIPIAL PHRASES

Running all the way, Janice reached the train station just in time.

Raised in Atlanta, Clarice never lost her Southern drawl.

Note: Be sure that a word ending in *-ing* is actually part of an introductory participial phrase and not the subject of the sentence.

Running is good exercise.
[*Running* is the subject.]

LONG INTRODUCTORY PREPOSITIONAL PHRASES

Prepositional phrases are explained on pages 519–520.

In a corner of the yard near the house, a beautiful lilac bush bloomed annually.

Without the benefit of a letter of introduction, Ken felt uncomfortable entering the personnel office of the large company.

Note: Use a comma with short introductory prepositional phrases only if the comma is necessary to make the meaning clear.

During May the company closes on Fridays.
[no comma needed]

By the sea, shore birds wade lazily.

[comma needed for clarity]

Interjections are explained on pages 475–477.

5. Use a comma to separate some short introductory elements from the rest of the sentence.

Use a comma after mild interjections and words such as *yes, no, well, why, still,* and *now* when they introduce a sentence or an independent clause.

No, I've never seen a cobra.

Why, it's pouring!

Bert lives in Chicago; still, he prefers living in the country.

Note: When these words are used as adverbs, they should not be followed by commas.

Now, I'm sure you'll enjoy studying in Mexico.

She now studies in Mexico.

Use a comma after a noun of direct address when it introduces a sentence or an independent clause. (When a noun of direct address occurs at the end of a sentence or clause, a comma precedes it.)

Marika, please call your brother.

I can't hear you, Rachel.

Governor, where is your office?

Use a comma after introductory transitional and parenthetical expressions such as *however, accordingly, thus, consequently, therefore, besides, in fact, on the other hand,* and *by the way.* (When these expressions appear at the end of a sentence, they are preceded by a comma.)

By the way, Ellen has finished writing her book; however, she has not yet sold it to a publisher.

Therefore, please call before midnight.

I'm moving to Detroit, in fact.

In general, use a comma after any introductory expression that would be followed by a pause if you were speaking.

6. Use a comma to separate contrasting words, phrases, and clauses introduced by the word *not.*

   Carmine is a shade of red, not blue.

   Jack starred in the stage production, not the movie.

Exercise 3

Write out each of the following sentences and use commas where necessary. Circle the commas you insert.

Examples

a. In fact Denise was born in Japan; however she speaks no Japanese.

a. In fact(,) Denise was born in Japan; however(,) she speaks no Japanese.

b. The New Deal was enacted by Franklin Roosevelt not Theodore Roosevelt.

b. The New Deal was enacted by Franklin Roosevelt(,) not Theodore Roosevelt.

1. Levi Strauss originally went west to seek gold Mabel.
2. Having traveled west with canvas to sell for tents and wagons Strauss sold the fabric for pants instead; people needed sturdier pants not sturdier tents.
3. Called *overalls* or *Levis* these pants were durable clothing for the miners and farmers.
4. Strauss soon stopped using canvas however; as a matter of fact he began using denim.
5. When the Civil War ended Levi shipped his pants to Texas; thus they soon became the standard garb of cowhands.
6. Well Strauss wanted all of his pants to be the same color; therefore he dyed them with indigo so they would all be blue.
7. During the early days of Levis people wore the pants into the water and kept them on until they dried; as a result the pants fit perfectly!
8. Margo the original jeans had copper rivets on the back pockets; however the rivets scratched saddles and furniture. Consequently the manufacturer eliminated the pocket rivets.
9. In the collection of the Smithsonian Institution in Washington there is a pair of Levis canvas dungarees I think.
10. Well Levi Strauss would certainly be surprised to learn that his dungarees became popular fashion not just sturdy work pants!

Review Exercise A

Write out the following sentences, using periods, question marks, and exclamation points where necessary. Circle the punctuation marks you insert.

Examples

a. Sri Lanka was formerly Ceylon not Siam; as a matter of fact Siam is now Thailand.

a. Sri Lanka was formerly Ceylon, not Siam; as a matter of fact, Siam is now Thailand.

b. Diana did you invite Duane Harris Jackie and Helga to dinner?

b. Diana, did you invite Duane, Harris, Jackie, and Helga to dinner?

1. Roberto those records are not appropriate for Rashid; he likes classical music not jazz.
2. Now where did I put my invitation to Dr Jackson and Ms Harker's wedding I think I left it at my office or I filed it in my appointment calendar.
3. What an incredible magician Marge that illusionist led an elephant onto the stage put the animal inside a cage and made it disappear How did it happen
4. By 10:00 AM on the morning of March 15 Jorge has to finish his thesis bring it to the university and present it to Dr J Ahern Prof L Lewis and Ms A Marcus.
5. Having taken every photography course available at her school Cassie applied to study with a professor, W J Yeng, Jr, at a nearby college.
6. Father you should have mailed the package to 100 St Clair Circle not 100 St Clair Avenue; since the box was delivered to the wrong address returned to the post office and sent out again it took four weeks to arrive at the right address.
7. Disguised as two helpless elderly women the police officers walked their beat After only a few hours they arrested several muggers.
8. What a rush of people Where is everyone running Is there a fire or is someone giving away money
9. Anita the museum is open on Tuesday evening not on Wednesday evening; by the way none of the museums or shops or galleries are open late on Wednesday.
10. Well here's Mrs Martin's address for the summer:
    Helen and Jack Martin
    ℅ Adm J Hanks, USN
    1400 Deer Park Rd
    Mt Kisco, NY 13705
11. Come quickly I'm afraid this shelf is going to collapse for it's sagging a lot in the middle.
12. Manuel didn't you used to work for either NBC or CBS You ought to call Joel Washington, Jr, about a job because he must produce a show and needs help.
13. During the ninth inning of the deciding game of the World Series our

television broke Can you believe it We did have a radio so we heard the end of the game.

14. "Where did you take that picture of the village and the mountain and the meadow" Benito asked. "Was it in Austria in Switzerland or in France"

15. Surprised by the steady sound of her own voice Carla challenged the mayor on the proposed budget cuts Without faltering Carla pointed out the problems offered an alternate plan and persuaded the mayor to reconsider the proposal.

16. In the summer Nellie Pamela and Amanda play baseball not basketball; in the fall and winter and spring they play basketball however.

17. Carmen here's your sweater hat and coat and gloves Unfortunately I can't find your umbrella.

18. No I don't think that I'm interested in that high-pressure low-paying job I don't necessarily mind either high pressure or low salary if the work is interesting but that job offers no advantages; consequently I'll keep looking for work.

19. Mr Alonzo that flight goes to O'Hare Airport in Chicago not New York. Isn't there another flight that goes to Kennedy Airport LaGuardia Airport or Newark

20. Maj R King had spent a long hot August in Ft Worth yet he decided to spend his vacation in Texas.

Paired Commas

Sometimes, words of direct address or transition appear within a sentence, rather than at its beginning or end. When this happens, enclose the interrupting word, phrase, or clause with commas, placing a comma both before and after the expression. These *paired commas* separate the expression from the rest of the sentence.

1. Use paired commas with nouns of direct address when they interrupt a sentence.

   I think, Anita, that your drawing is lovely.

   Why, Doctor, is my neck stiff all the time?

Parenthetical expressions are explained on page 556.

2. Use paired commas with transitional or parenthetical expressions that interrupt the sentence.

   We stayed, nevertheless, until the game had ended.

   The painter Georgia O'Keeffe, by the way, took up pottery late in life.

3. Use paired commas with contrasting expressions when they interrupt the sentence.

   Goats, not cows, graze on that hill.

   Fleming, not Pasteur, discovered penicillin.

Note: Before placing commas, make sure that a word or phrase is really an interrupter.

> Arthur Ashe, I think, has stopped playing tennis.
>
> I think that Arthur Ashe has stopped playing tennis.

Exercise 4

Write out the following sentences and place commas where necessary. Circle the commas you insert.

Examples

a. Mrs. Maggiore uses spinach flour not whole wheat flour to make her pasta.

a. Mrs. Maggiore uses spinach flour, not whole wheat flour, to make her pasta.

b. The Nile I think is the longest river in the world.

b. The Nile, I think, is the longest river in the world.

1. I believe that daffodils not roses are poisonous; I suggest however that you check with the botanical gardens.
2. Early movie entrepreneurs I believe moved west to escape legal problems in the East; Hollywood as a matter of fact became the home of the movie industry.
3. You know Sidney that Alfred Hitchcock not Anthony Perkins directed *Psycho;* Perkins on the other hand starred in the picture.
4. All the stores in London by the way will be closed on Thursday; Thursday it seems is the Queen's birthday.
5. Fares on the London subway Marika vary according to the length of the ride; a long ride therefore costs more than a short one.
6. It is possible I suppose to enjoy a toy poodle. I wish however that those little poodles would bark not yelp when they get excited.
7. Alice by the way rarely makes a phone call after 7 o'clock in the evening; I on the other hand could talk on the phone all night.
8. Have you ever Bernardo visited the Brooks' farm in the winter? Julio claims that winter not summer is the most beautiful season there.
9. Last fall's rains as a matter of fact lasted for weeks; many homes as a result were flooded or washed away.
10. Silver not gold tarnishes; gold believe it or not keeps its shine for many years.

4. Use paired commas to enclose nonessential phrases and nonessential clauses and to separate them from the rest of the sentence.

Essential and nonessential phrases are discussed on page 530.

Nonessential phrases and clauses are those that could be omitted from a sentence without changing its basic meaning. They are, in other words, not essential to the thought conveyed by the sentence.

Irene Warner, who lives across the street, is a physicist.

[*Who lives across the street* is a nonessential adjective clause; it does not affect the meaning of the sentence.]

Benito Juarez, panting and exhausted, just won the Boston Marathon.

[*Panting and exhausted* is a nonessential participial phrase.]

Essential and nonessential clauses are discussed on pages 544–545.

On the other hand, essential phrases and clauses are necessary to the meaning of a sentence. If eliminated, the meaning of the sentence would change; therefore, do not separate essential phrases and clauses with commas.

The woman who lives across the street just got a job with the Los Angeles *Times*.
[*Who lives across the street* identifies the woman and is essential to the sentence.]
The man standing there just won the Boston Marathon.
[*Standing there* identifies which man and is an essential participial phrase.]

Note: When a nonessential phrase or clause appears at the end of a sentence, only one comma precedes it.

We attended the debut performance of Ken's youngest sister, who is a singer.

Appositives are explained on page 525.

5. Use paired commas to enclose nonessential appositives that interrupt a sentence.

When an appositive merely explains the meaning of the noun or pronoun it refers to, it is nonessential and should be set off by paired commas. However, when an appositive distinguishes the noun or pronoun it explains from other people or things, it is essential and is not enclosed by commas.

I. M. Pei, the noted architect, has designed New York's new Convention Center.
Joanna Perkins, our accountant, just opened her own firm.

The appositives in both of the preceding sentences are nonessential. Since they do not affect the meaning of the sentences, they require commas. The appositives in the following sentences, however, are essential to the meaning of the sentences.

Barbara's brother Paul is a data processor.
[*Paul* identifies which brother.]

The documentary film *Number Our Days* captures the life of elderly Jews in Venice, California.
[*Number Our Days* identifies which film.]

Note: A nonessential appositive at the beginning of a sentence is followed by a comma. A nonessential appositive at the end of a sentence is preceded by a comma.

An opera fan, Cara attends every performance she can.

Marta studies at Reed College, a small school in Oregon.

Exercise 5

Write out the following sentences and use commas where necessary. Be prepared to explain your reason for using each comma. Circle the commas you insert.

Examples

a. Mary Lou Williams a jazz pianist and composer performed last week with the Alvin Ailey dancers.

a. Mary Lou Williams, a jazz pianist and composer, performed last week with the Alvin Ailey dancers.

b. That is a photograph of Clara Barton who founded the American Red Cross.

b. That is a photograph of Clara Barton, who founded the American Red Cross.

1. A talented singer and dancer Rita Moreno is now part of the cast of *The Electric Company* which is a television show for children.
2. Jack's dog Ken is a Saluki which is a nervous high-strung dog; however, Jack's other dog Luch is the sweetest mutt in the world.
3. The photographs that depict the earthquake were taken in 1886. That earthquake which occurred in South Carolina on August 31, 1886 was strong enough to derail locomotives!
4. A hat that has a wide brim offers good protection from the sun; on the other hand, a beret a brimless cap won't protect your face from the sun.
5. Margaret Corbin who fought bravely during the American Revolution is buried at West Point.
6. Did you know that Duke Ellington the composer and band leader used to live on West 106th Street in New York? In 1977, West 106th Street which runs between Riverside Drive and Central Park West was renamed Duke Ellington Boulevard.
7. Vermeil a mixture of gold and silver is frequently used to make jewelry instead of gold which has become very expensive.
8. In the Old West the chuck wagon a kitchen on wheels was the most popular vehicle on the trails; and the cook who often had to make much out of little was treated with a great deal of respect!
9. In a famous scene from *North by Northwest* a film by Hitchcock Cary Grant who starred in the film is chased by a crop-duster which is a small, two-winged propeller plane.

10. The woman who owns Kellogg Shoe Shop just wrote a book which will be published next spring; the book titled *Profits* is a well-written guide about managing a business.

Commas are also used to separate a variety of items that may or may not occur within a sentence. These conventional uses of the comma are dictated by custom and tradition.

6. Use a comma to separate parts of geographical names and dates.

   Jerry was born on Thursday, March 14, 1970, at 5:55 P.M.

   Meet me at Martin Luther King High School, 7503 Warwick Road, Detroit, Michigan 48233.

   Otters live off the coast of Monterey, California.

Note: In addresses do not use a comma between the street number and the street name, nor between the state and the ZIP code. In dates do not use a comma between the name of the month and the year. A comma is unnecessary when only a month and a year are given in a date *(September 4, 1888; September 1888.)*

When these items are joined by prepositions, commas are not necessary.

   The museum is on Main Street **in** West Chicago, Illinois.
   She was born in November **of** 1945.

7. Use a comma to separate a person's name (or a company's name) from the degree, title, or affiliation that follows it.

   We bought these lamps from Lightoleer, Inc., in New York.

   Connie Clark, M.D., is a pediatrician.

   Dan Dowd, USAF, is an expert computer analyst.

Note: When used in a sentence, the degree or title is also followed by a comma.

   Julio Perez, M.D., just became president of the American Medical Association.

8. Use a comma after the salutation and the closing of a friendly letter.

   Dear Bert,　　　　Sincerely yours,

Exercise 6

Write out the following sentences and use commas where necessary. Circle each comma you insert.

Examples

a. The Whartons drove from Denver Colorado to San Francisco California and back.

a. The Whartons drove from Denver, Colorado, to San Francisco, California, and back.

b. New bus fares will go into effect at 12:00 P.M. Saturday May 15 1981.

b. New bus fares will go into effect at 12:00 P.M., Saturday, May 15, 1981.

1. World Airlines Inc. announced a sale on flights between Newark New Jersey and Los Angeles California from April 15 1980 until May 15 1980.
2. If you're looking for a pet, go to the Best Pet Shop Ltd. 750 Wabash Road Bismarck North Dakota 58501.
3. Ann Miller M.D. consulted with Carl Rogers M.D. and Raina Fillipo M.D. regarding the injured patient.
4. On Thursday June 25 at 1:30 P.M. Colton Industries Inc. will announce the winner of their Employee of the Year Award.
5. Dear Aunt Helga

   I would like to order two plants from your catalogue of April 1981. Please send them to my friend Jonah Jakes Jr. 140 Walker Road Tampa Florida 31031.

   Fondly
   Kim
6. According to their ad, the Riviera Hotel at 333 Mission Drive San Diego California will lower its rates from May 15 1980 until February 1981.
7. Janis signed her complaint "Furiously yours" and sent it to Lance Lucky Sr. Sturdy Furniture Corp. 77 Park Avenue Jefferson Wisconsin.
8. Joel Yourk RAF and Bart Mars USAF owned a charter airline running flights between Boston Massachusetts and New Haven Connecticut.
9. The museum on the Parkway in Philadelphia Pennsylvania will have a special showing for its members on Tuesday May 13 from noon until 5:00 and on Thursday May 15 from 1:00 P.M. until closing.
10. Carolyn Mendez M.D. will lecture to medical students in Paris France and London England and Hamburg Germany; her tour will begin on Friday November 12 1982 and continue until January 1983.

Review Exercise B

Write out the following sentences and use commas where necessary. Circle the commas you insert.

Examples

a. Linda Ronstadt not Roberta Flack will perform on Tuesday January 4 in New Orleans Louisiana; Flack however will perform on Saturday in Baton Rouge.

a. Linda Ronstadt, not Roberta Flack, will perform on Tuesday, January 4, in New Orleans, Louisiana; Flack, however, will perform on Saturday in Baton Rouge.

b. Bermuda located off the coast of South Carolina has its busiest season between May and October.

b. Bermuda, located off the coast of South Carolina, has its busiest season between May and October.

1. There are I believe over 300,000 restaurants in the United States; this figure by the way includes all eateries from fancy urban restaurants to roadside diners that dot America's highways.
2. Although the design of nails has changed over the centuries, old-fashioned nails which were square were more efficient than round nails which we use today.
3. Over the years rose collectors have brought roses from all over the world back to England a country known for its roses; England as a result is filled with exotic varieties of roses from places as diverse as Peking China and Delhi India.
4. Clusius a Flemish botanist experimented with tulip bulbs and I think was responsible for their popularity in Europe; at one time in fact Europeans bought tulip bulbs which were as valuable as diamonds or pearls as financial investments.
5. Did you know Melania that saffron a yellow spice comes from the crocus? It takes I'm sad to say more than four thousand crocus flowers to produce one ounce of saffron!
6. According to the etiquette of the Old West, a nod of the head not a wave of the hand was an appropriate greeting; a wave which might unnerve a horse that was skittish was improper.
7. If you want to take a seminar with Harriet Towers Ph.D. register at 9:00 A.M. on either Tuesday September 10 or Thursday September 12 at Harris Hall 300 College Drive Madison Wisconsin.
8. The Persuasions singing without accompaniment drew rousing applause from their audience; the group's harmonies Doris were perfect.
9. I know that Julia not Fran is going to Carlton College a school in Minnesota next year; Fran I believe is going to Ohio State University in Columbus Ohio.
10. Tim who is a carpenter is an expert at dating early American buildings; he can tell for example a building's age by the type of nails that were used.
11. After 1846 it seems screws used in building were pointed at the tip; before 1846 the screws had blunt not pointed ends.
12. The Pilgrims who are usually considered New England's first settlers were not the first to arrive there; a man named Verrazano in fact had visited New England many years before the Pilgrims.
13. Yes I did know Martha that Pocahontas the native American who saved John Smith's life died in London England in 1617.
14. Abundant forests without doubt have always been one of America's richest resources; the tree consequently has always been an important American symbol which has adorned American money and flags.

15. On May 27 1980 the Whitney Museum which exhibits American art had a retrospective of the work of sculptor Louise Nevelson celebrating her eightieth birthday.
16. Paula and Luiz enjoyed watching Miriam Colon the founder of the Puerto Rican Traveling Theatre perform last Thursday evening May 15 at St. Peter's Hall 336 West 20th Street New York.
17. Vicki Gomez who owns Lark's Department Store in Plains Texas is going to marry the man who saved my oldest son Rob from drowning last summer in Miami Florida.
18. Dinosaurs were without doubt huge but unfortunately not too smart; for instance the stegosaurus which weighed nearly two tons had a brain that was the size of a walnut!
19. The London Bridge is I'm sure the biggest antique anyone has ever bought; I believe that in March 1968 a developer from Los Angeles California bought the bridge and moved it to Lake Havasu City Arizona.
20. My dear Aunt Fran

    Thanks Aunt Fran for your letter. I'm spending the summer by the way at Camp Canadensis Canadensis Pennsylvania 19113. Please write to me there after Thursday June 23 until August 23.

    With love
    Beth

The Semicolon

You might think of the *semicolon* as a cross between a comma and a period. Although the semicolon is a stronger mark of punctuation than the comma, it does not signal as strong a break as does the period.

Independent clauses are discussed on page 535.

1. Use a semicolon to separate independent clauses not joined by a coordinating conjunction when the clauses are closely related.

   José is an expert pianist**;** he has studied the piano since he was seven.
   Irene never eats fish**;** she is allergic to it.

2. Use a semicolon between independent clauses when the second clause begins with a transitional expression such as *still, moreover, furthermore, otherwise, therefore, however, besides, in fact*, and *for example*.

   The movie has already begun**;** besides, I'm too tired to go.

   Last night's storm knocked down power lines**;** as a result, we had no electricity this morning.

3. Use a semicolon to separate items in a series when one or more of the items contains commas.

   The awards read Alma Navarro, first place**;** Ken Yamah, second place**;** and Susie Castellano, third.

An Egyptian-Israeli peace settlement was negotiated by Jimmy Carter, President of the U.S.; Menachem Begin, Prime Minister of Israel; and Anwar Sadat, President of Egypt.

4. Use a semicolon between independent clauses when commas appear within the clauses.

Barbara Ling, who has relatives in Shanghai, will visit China next month; in addition to Shanghai, she'll travel to Peking and Manchuria.

For his aquarium Raoul bought snails, goldfish, angel fish, and guppies; but the angel fish, unfortunately, died within a week.

Exercise 7

Write out the following sentences and place semicolons where they are needed. Circle the semicolons you insert.

Examples

a. Bart, a well-known animal handler, trains large animals for television, he is currently training a bear for an insurance company's commercial.

a. Bart, a well-known animal handler, trains large animals for television(;) he is currently training a bear for an insurance company's commercial.

b. That book is filled with photographic firsts it includes the first photos ever taken of a dog begging, of the moon, and of a snowflake!

b. That book is filled with photographic firsts(;) it includes the first photos ever taken of a dog begging, of the moon, and of a snowflake!

1. Ramon has just published a best-selling book as a result, he constantly appears as a guest on TV talk shows.
2. Cats, they say, have nine lives my cat, I'm sure, has already used seven of them.
3. Use a comma between independent clauses joined by a coordinating conjunction however, use a semicolon if the clauses contain commas.
4. Elizabeth Blackwell, the first woman doctor in the United States, founded the New York Infirmary for Women and Children that hospital still functions today.
5. Early photographers in the American West used portable darkrooms in horse-drawn wagons there is, in fact, a famous photograph, taken in 1868, of a wagon darkroom traveling across the Nevada desert.
6. The evening lectures will be held in the following rooms: Art and Culture, Room 412 Hopi Architecture, Room 606 and Women of the '80s, Room 1000.
7. After George Washington Carver introduced the peanut to Southern farmers, they no longer had to depend solely on the cotton crop for income as a result, their economy boomed.

8. Everyone in the room had seen the UFO no one, however, had taken a picture!
9. The Banyons bought a camper for their cross-country drive still, they planned to stay with friends in Chicago, Illinois Denver, Colorado Winslow, Arizona and Sacramento, California.
10. Native Americans often made their canoes from the bark of large birch trees they sewed the pieces of bark together with white spruce roots.

The Colon

A *colon* calls attention to the word, phrase, or list that follows it.

1. Use a colon to separate a list of items from an introductory statement, which often contains the words *as follows, the following, these,* or a number.

   Monique speaks four languages: English, French, Spanish, and Dutch.

   Deciduous trees that fill Jake's yard are as follows: elm, maple, oak, and chestnut.

Note: The introductory statement that precedes a colon should be a complete sentence. Do not use a colon between a verb and its direct object or after a preposition.

An asterisk (*) denotes a sentence with a feature that is not a part of ESE.

*Kelly's dog eats only: liver and fish.
[Unacceptable use of colon between verb and direct object]

Kelly's dog eats only two things: liver and fish.

2. Use a colon to separate an introductory statement from an explanation, appositive, or a quotation.

   The crowd rose and yelled its cheer: "Bravo!"

   Martha's Boston accent rang clear when she read these words: "Park your car in Harvard Yard."

The colon should also be used in three conventional situations:

3. Use a colon after the salutation of a business letter.

   Dear Jane Coe: Dear Dr. Hart:

4. Use a colon to separate hour and minutes in expressions of time.

   11:30 A.M.   4:00 this afternoon

5. Use a colon to separate chapter numbers from verse numbers in reference to chapters from the Bible.

   Genesis 12:6   Matthew 2:10

Exercise 8

Write out the following sentences and place colons where necessary. Circle the colons you insert.

Example

a. Buses depart for Newark at these times 830 A.M., 215 P.M., and 326 P.M.

a. Buses depart for Newark at these times(:) 8(:)30 A.M., 2(:)15 P.M., and 3(:)26 P.M.

1. For her birthday Maureen received tickets to three Broadway shows *Barnum*, *West Side Story*, and *Children of a Lesser God.*
2. Which of these states has the largest population Texas, Massachusetts, or Illinois?
3. Before it was ravaged by civil war, Beirut had this nickname "Paris of the Middle East."
4. Having heard the concert, Julio had only one response wonderful.
5. Liane, the movie plays at several times 300, 500, 700, and 900.
6. The dance involves four basic steps shuffle, kick, turn, bend.
7. Read the following excerpts from the Old Testament Genesis 3 7, Genesis 10 9, and Exodus 2 3.
8. The tour bus will make three stops between 1000 and 1100 A.M. Hotel Regency, El Toro Palace, and the Western Court Inn.
9. This sums up Jack's baby's vocabulary *pa*, *ma*, and *hi*.
10. Having traveled around the country, novelist Emmett Grogan said this of the United States "Anything anybody can say about America is true."

The Dash

The *dash* calls attention to the word or group of words that precedes it.

1. Use a dash to separate an introductory series or thought from the explanation that follows.

   Lilacs and roses—those are my favorite flowers.
   A twelve-inning game—that's exciting!

2. Use a dash to separate a sudden change in thought.

   Dinner is ready—oh, I left my hat at the office.
   June's birthday party is on Friday at—oops, I've lost the invitation.

3. Use a dash to show the omission of words in dialogue.

   "It's thunderi—," Jack shouted.

When the elements separated by a dash occur within a sentence, use paired dashes to enclose the word or group of words and separate them from the rest of the sentence. Use dashes for parenthetical phrases that contain commas.

> Betty's dog—it's an Australian sheepdog—won first prize at the show.
> Some peppers—jalapenos, for instance—are very spicy!

Exercise 9

Write out the following sentences and place dashes where necessary. Circle the dashes you insert.

Examples

a. Carolyn's dictionary it's very old doesn't list the word *astronaut.*
a. Carolyn's dictionary⊖it's very old⊖doesn't list the word astronaut.

b. Blue cheese now that's strong cheese!
b. Blue cheese⊖now that's strong cheese!

1. Terrified it's the only word to describe how I felt before the match.
2. Max was charged with littering throwing papers on the street and fined fifty dollars.
3. "Is the train com?" Joanne asked.
4. The Martinez's house a ranch, I think has a staggering view of the sea.
5. Marian, I can't hear that barking is horrible a word you're saying.
6. Georgia Coles I think that's her name just opened a boutique on Columbus Avenue.
7. There's a monument to the boll weevil it's a very destructive insect in Enterprise, Alabama.
8. Photographers who worked for the FSA that's the Farms Security Administration documented American life during the Depression.
9. Proud and tired mostly tired, I think was how I felt after having finished first in the marathon last weekend.
10. Those enormous dogs they're either Great Danes or mastiffs, I believe live across the street.

Parentheses

Parentheses, like commas and dashes, are used to enclose elements that interrupt a sentence.

Parentheses indicate a strong break in thought. Elements in parentheses, in fact, are really additional information. If these words were omitted, the meaning of the sentence would in no way change.

> Estelle's mother (born in 1900) tells wonderful tales of her childhood.
> Dr. Michaels (our dentist) lives in Oakland.

Review Exercise C

Write out the following sentences and use colons, semicolons, dashes, and parentheses where necessary. In some instances more than one mark of punctuation could be used correctly, so be prepared to explain the reason for each of your choices. Circle the punctuation marks you insert.

1. Geronimo 1829–1909 was a well-known Apache chief my brother by the way has a wonderful old photograph of him.
2. The Elgin Film Festival will show these films tomorrow *Rear Window*, 1200 *Psycho*, 200 and *Frenzy*, 400.
3. The story of the prisoners' escape it's a really exciting tale will appear in three local papers tomorrow *The Herald*, *The Voice*, and *The Star*.
4. Because he was ill, James missed the history final accordingly the professor rescheduled his exam for Tuesday morning at 1100.
5. Dear Order Department

   I would like to order the following items one flannel shirt, size small one cotton shirt, size medium and one camp jacket, red. Enclosed is my check actually, a money order for the exact amount.

   Sincerely yours, Elie Gaines
6. W. C. Handy the W. C. stands for William Christopher is known as "The Father of the Blues." Included among his hits are these two songs "Memphis Blues" and "St. Louis Blues."
7. Warren G. Harding has the most memorable middle name of any President Gamaliel unfortunately, his career was not as memorable.
8. A home-cooked meal that's what Hal needed after a week of traveling he unpacked his suitcase and headed straight for his kitchen.
9. Didn't Lorraine Hansberry 1930–1965 write these dramas *A Raisin in the Sun*, 1959 and *The Sign in Sidney Brustein's Window*, 1964?
10. Tom's enormous cat it must weigh at least twenty pounds has a few annoying habits it scratches the furniture, eats the plants, and sheds.
11. Finally, the emcee made this announcement rains have caused local flooding and traffic jams nonetheless, the concert will still begin promptly at 800 P.M.
12. Have you read this quotation it sounds so familiar used recently in a candidate's speech "Wisdom is better than rubies" Proverbs 8 11?
13. "Please stop crying," Joan pleaded with the screaming child but her baby, it seems, had no intention of listening to her.
14. Library hours are from 1000 A.M. until 500 P.M. Monday through Friday on Saturday the library is open from 900 until noon.
15. Having worked overtime all week, Josephine looked forward to a weekend break so she made some hotel reservations, packed her suitcase, and raced to the train station.

16. Dorothea Dix 1802–1887 worked to improve the treatment of the mentally ill through her efforts, many states established hospitals for the insane.
17. When Hank Aaron slammed his 715th home run April 8, 1974, he broke Babe Ruth's record Aaron's record, by the way, was subsequently broken by a player in Japan.
18. I hear that Japanese subways are so crowded you won't believe this that official "pushers" help jam passengers into the cars although it sounds bizarre, their system is extremely efficient!
19. There are three basic shapes of triangles equilateral, which has three equal sides isosceles, with two equal sides and right-angle.
20. Juan spends all of his money on art supplies paints, brushes, canvas, and crayons except for essentials food, for instance.

The Hyphen

The *hyphen* is used to link the parts of some compound words. It also links the parts of a word begun on one line and finished on the next. Be sure to consult a dictionary if you are uncertain about how to hyphenate any particular word.

1. Use a hyphen when a word is divided at the end of a line.

Place the hyphen only between syllables. Do not hyphenate a word if doing so would leave just one letter on either line. If a word already contains a hyphen *(self-control)*, divide it only at the hyphen. Do not hyphenate proper nouns or adjectives or abbreviations.

> Rome is a large, bustling, and cos-
> mopolitan city.

> Reporters swarmed about the President-
> elect.

Compound nouns are discussed on page 364.

2. Use a hyphen to link the parts of compound nouns that begin with the prefixes *ex-*, *self-*, and *great-* or that end with the suffix *-elect.*

ex-wife   president-elect   all-star

Proper nouns are explained on pages 363–364, proper adjectives on page 438.

3. Use a hyphen to link all prefixes with proper nouns and adjectives.

pre-Columbian   pro-American   anti-American

4. Use a hyphen to link the parts of compound nouns that include a prepositional phrase.

father-in-law   jack-in-the-box

Note: Many compound nouns are not hyphenated. Some are two separate words *(tennis court)*; others are one word *(baseball)*. Check a dictionary if you are unsure about any given word.

5. Use a hyphen to link the parts of a compound adjective when it precedes a noun.

muscle-building routine | up-and-down relationship
well-known author | high-paying job

Note: Do not use a hyphen when the adjective follows the noun *(The essay was well written)* or if the first modifier ends in *-ly (easily understood motive).*

6. Use a hyphen to link parts of a fraction used as an adjective.

one-half acre | two-thirds majority

7. Use a hyphen to link the parts of a compound number between twenty-one and ninety-nine.

sixty-three cents | forty-seven days

The Apostrophe

The *apostrophe* is used to show the omission of letters or numbers, to form the plural of letters and numbers, and to form possessive nouns.

1. Use an apostrophe to show that letters have been omitted from a contraction.

can't [*cannot*] | don't [*do not*]

2. Use an apostrophe to show that the first two numbers have been omitted from a year.

the gold rush of '49 | the hurricane of '22

3. Use an apostrophe to form the plurals of letters, numbers, and words.

"We have some *8*'s, but we're out of *10*'s," the salesperson informed us.

Mena pronounces her name as if it had two *e*'s.

Note: An apostrophe is not necessary when making centuries and decades plural *(1900s, the '30s).*

For more complete information on possessive forms of nouns, see pages 374–375.

4. Add an apostrophe and an *s* to make a singular noun possessive or to make possessive most plural nouns not ending in *s*.

Maggie'**s** whiskers | children'**s** laughter

5. If a plural noun ends in *s*, show possession by adding only an apostrophe.

chickens' feed | the candidates' speeches

Note: The possessive forms of personal pronouns do not have apostrophes. Be careful, especially in the case of *its*, not to confuse the possessive forms with contractions.

its [possessive]	it's [contraction]
their [possessive]	they're [contraction]
your [possessive]	you're [contraction]

6. To show possession in hyphenated words and in words showing joint possessions, add an apostrophe and *s* only to the last word.

    brother-in-law'**s** company

    Doyle Dane Bernbach'**s** offices

    Deborah and Bob'**s** apartment

Note: When two or more people each possess something separately, make each of their names possessive.

men's and women's shoes

Julio's and Maurice's dreams

If the second word is a possessive pronoun, then the first word is also possessive.

Kendra's and my idea

7. When words of time, date, and money are used as possessives, they require an apostrophe.

    ten minutes' worth of work

    twenty-five cents' worth; one cent's worth

Exercise 10

Write out the following sentences and use hyphens and apostrophes where necessary. Circle the marks you insert.

Examples

a. Ive eaten so much deep fried chicken I feel like a two ton truck.

a. I'ye eaten so much deep-fried chicken I feel like a two-ton truck.

b. My daughter in laws house has a twenty one foot wall of windows in its living room.

b. My daughter-in-law's house has a twenty-one-foot wall of windows in its living room.

1. Barb and Julios collection of twenty three post Impressionist paintings hangs in a well lit and carefully guarded room.
2. Im sure that Hectors twenty three year old cat couldnt possibly scale that forty foot wall, arent you?
3. "If youre going to speak professionally, you must eliminate all the *I means* and *you knows* from your speech," Mindys self taught elocution teacher advised.
4. Manuels father signed a long term lease on a well run, carefully designed apartment, which was also well located.

5. Each one of the windows in Hectors and my second story apartment overlooked a rose filled garden, which was at least forty six feet long.
6. His son in laws recently opened restaurant was terrible: its five course dinner consisted of sour tasting soup, day old bread, overcooked meat and half cooked potatoes, dressing soaked salad, his great grandmothers stale cookies, and foul smelling cheese!
7. When she was in her twenties, my friends name was spelled *Judee* (with two *es*); in her thirties it was *Judy;* and by the '80s shed settled on the mature sounding *Judith.*
8. At the games excitement filled climax, a two thirds majority of the pro Dodger fans rushed toward the All Star teams dugout.
9. Carries mother in law gave her a mother of pearl necklace from the '30s, an obviously well read book, and her ex husbands gold filled watch.
10. Tims twin engined plane flew low over the palm lined shore; within twenty minutes time wed landed, set up our foldaway table and chairs, and unpacked our well stocked picnic baskets.

Quotation Marks

Quotation marks usually occur in pairs. They enclose a word or group of words and separate them from the rest of the sentence.

1. Use quotation marks to enclose a speaker's exact words.

   Raoul reminded her, "Don't forget your tickets."

   "When I earn my first million," Janet dreamed, "that's when I'll travel around the world."

In the preceding example the words *Janet dreamed* interrupt the direct quotation. Notice that the second part of the quotation does not begin with a capital letter. Use a capital letter to begin each quotation and each new sentence within a quotation.

Note: Remember to use quotation marks to enclose only a speaker's exact words. Do not use quotation marks in an indirect quotation.

Sheryl advised that we not underestimate Leo. [indirect quotation]
"Don't underestimate Leo," Sheryl advised. [direct quotation]

2. Use quotation marks to enclose the titles of short stories, essays, short poems, songs, single television programs, magazine articles, and parts of a book.

   "Causes of the Russian Revolution" was a complicated chapter in the Russian history book.

   Have you seen "A Plague on Our Children," a show about toxic chemicals, which was shown on PBS's *Nova?*

3. Use quotation marks to enclose nicknames and slang expressions.

"Lizard" LaRue is a devious character.

What does "You dig" mean?

Sometimes, other marks of punctuation appear within quotation marks. Commas, for example, often separate a direct quotation from the rest of the sentence. The following rules explain how to place other marks of punctuation when they are used with quotation marks.

4. Always place commas and periods inside closing quotation marks.

"Jefferson grew broccoli at Monticello," Denise told us.

We left after Gloria sang "I Will Survive."

5. Place colons and semicolons outside closing quotation marks.

Toni Cade Bambara wrote "Raymond's Run"; she didn't, on the other hand, write "Bryon's Run."

Here's why that street is called "The Serpentine": it's very winding!

6. Place question marks and exclamation points inside closing quotation marks if just the quotation is a question or an exclamation. Place the marks outside the closing quotation marks if the whole sentence is a question or an exclamation.

Connie asked, "Is that a chicken?"
Was Rocky nicknamed "The Italian Stallion"?
Connie shouted, "What a catch!"
How Alicia loves the song "Call Me"!

In general, two end marks should never appear together. When you are considering using a comma and another mark of punctuation together, drop the comma and use the other mark.

An asterisk (*) indicates a sentence with a feature that is not a part of Edited Standard English.

*"When does the shop open?", we wondered.
"When does the shop open?" we wondered.

*Manuel shouted, "Watch out!".
Manuel shouted, "Watch out!"

Exercise 11

Write out the following sentences and use quotation marks as necessary. Circle the quotation marks you insert.

Examples

a. Please call, Jackie said, if you'll be late.

a. "Please call," Jackie said, "if you'll be late."

b. Our spirits fell when we read the sign: Closed for the winter.

b. Our spirits fell when we read the sign: “Closed for the winter.”

1. Before checking in Chapter 7, Household Hints, Lorraine asked her friend, Do you know if club soda will remove berry stains?
2. Juan wrote three episodes for the television series: Caught in the Middle, Out on a Limb, and Long Walk on a Short Pier.
3. Did you know that these two songs have each been recorded in over 1,000 different versions: Yesterday and Tie a Yellow Ribbon Round the Old Oak Tree?
4. Paulo Lucky Santos and Paul Mr. Money Moran have opened a disco called Winners; they're sure it will be successful.
5. Remember when every other word Mickey said was a slang expression such as groovy, far out, pad, hip, or bummer? Well, now he's changed his act and sounds like an Oxford professor!
6. What an amazing discovery! June exclaimed. Would you ever have suspected that a clam was capable of all that?
7. Having prepared for your debut for all these months, Charlene moaned, you can't give up now. What's the matter? she asked. Have you panicked?
8. Who said, A nod is as good as a wink to a blind horse?
9. Ms. Androtti asked whether we'd read any of the following articles: Alternatives to the Automobile, Let's Cycle, or An Invigorating Hike.
10. How can I pretend that I know how to ski, Don asked, when I've never even seen snow?

Single Quotation Marks

Use single quotation marks to enclose a direct quotation or title that occurs inside another quotation.

> Charles reminisced, “I remember hearing Ezio Pinza sing ‘Some Enchanted Evening.’”
>
> “Who,” asked Pete, “was nicknamed ‘The Phantom’?”

Notice that in the preceding example the direct quotation is a question; however, the nickname *(‘The Phantom’)* within the quotation is not a question. Therefore, the question mark is placed *outside* the closing single quotation mark but *inside* the closing mark of the direct quotation. (The period in the first example is placed inside the closing quotation marks because periods always go inside the closing mark of a quotation.)

Writing Dialogue

When you write dialogue, you quote the words said by two or more people who are having a conversation. You enclose the exact words of the speakers in quotation marks. The speakers are often identified by phrases such as *Alex argued, Kim sobbed, Elaine laughed.* These "words of saying" are not enclosed in quotation marks and are separated from the quoted material by commas or other marks of punctuation.

> Liana said triumphantly, "We've won!"
>
> "Where are we going?" John asked.
>
> "Those lilies close at night," Helen said, "and open again in the morning."

1. When you write dialogue, begin a new paragraph whenever the speaker changes.

> "Videotape is the wave of the future," declared Clarissa. "There's no doubt about it! Not only is it a popular medium for today's artists, but it has practical applications as well."
>
> "You're right," Angelo agreed. "Video has been a boon to us on the swimming team—even when we don't like what we see! When we see ourselves on tape, however, we see immediately where our shortcomings are: a kick that's uneven or too much time lost at the turn."
>
> "I work with emotionally disturbed children," mused Carmen, "and, now that you mention it, videotaping the teachers at work would really be helpful. It would give us a chance to study our interaction with the children and see where we might improve or change our approach."
>
> "Well, I guess we have our work cut out for us," Clarissa said. "If we all become masters of the video camera, we'll be on the road to success!"

2. Sometimes, one speaker's words run for more than one paragraph. When this happens, use quotation marks at the beginning of the quotation, at the beginning of each subsequent paragraph, and at the end of the whole quotation.

> "I read a spell-binding mystery yesterday," Agnes said. "It gripped me on the first page, and I couldn't put the book down until I had finished.
>
> "The plot is simple, almost classic. Five people are sitting in a room watching home movies. When the lights come on, one of the people is dead. Who did it? How was it done?
>
> "Of course, no one has entered or left the room during the movies; thus, one of the other four people in the room has done it. I, of course, thought of poison—but that was wrong.
>
> "Well, the detective arrives, the questioning begins. As the story unfolds, you learn that everyone has a motive. The plot thickens. The mystery isn't solved until the last page, and it had me fooled. Whew! I'm exhausted from the suspense!"

Underlining *(Italics)*

Underlining has several uses, but is used most frequently to indicate that a specific word or group of words is a title or name. While printers use special type *(italics)* for titles *(Huckleberry Finn)*, writers use underlining (<u>Huckleberry Finn</u>).

1. Underline the titles of all the following:

Books, plays, and long poems	Pride and Prejudice Romeo and Juliet Paradise Lost
Newspapers, magazines, and pamphlets	The New York Times Today's Teen How to Can and Preserve Fruit
Films, radio and television series	Star Wars All Things Considered Masterpiece Theatre
Paintings, sculpture, and ballets	The Card Player Black Majesty Giselle

2. Underline the names of ships, aircraft, and spacecraft.

   Queen Elizabeth II   Mariner

3. Underline words, letters, and numbers referred to as such and foreign words.

   How many r's are there in the word occur?
   The numbers 7 and 9 are frequently hard to read in your records.
   Please define the Latin term carpe diem.

Exercise 12

Write out each of the following sentences and insert underlining wherever it is required. Circle the words you underline.

Example

a. When is the drama club holding tryouts for roles in Don't Go Near the Water?

a. When is the drama club holding tryouts for roles in Don't Go Near the Water?

1. Last month's Science Fiction Facts contained an interesting interview with the author of Stranger in a Strange Land.
2. This article on advertising in the Daily Recorder used the phrase caveat emptor; what do you suppose that means?
3. Mr. Sanchez asked me to revise the essay and eliminate all the so's at the beginning of sentences.
4. According to Everyman's Almanac of Trivia, the first aircraft to successfully cross the Atlantic was called the Lame Duck.
5. Picasso's cubism is very evident in the painting The Card Player.

6. The youth symphony played a selection from Carmen and all of Berlioz' Symphonie Fantastique.
7. Here's the error in your algebra problem, Raoul; you wrote a 6 rather than a 5.
8. Janet interviewed one of the aeronautical engineers who worked on Skylab's landing gear.
9. I read Newsweek and the Tribune at the airport and watched the movie Star Wars during the flight.
10. Alexander Calder created the large sculpture Three Arches in 1963.

Mastery Test A

Write out the following paragraphs and add any necessary punctuation. Since more than one mark of punctuation could be used correctly in some instances, be ready to explain the marks of punctuation you choose. Circle the punctuation marks you insert.

Every era spawns its own distinctive decorative style and the style of the 1970s and 80s seems to be *high-tech* Deriving its name from the two terms high-style and technology, *high-tech* takes commercial and industrial furniture gym lockers factory lamps restaurant stoves and moves them from the factory to the home.

Does it seem strange Well it's really a very practical solution to many problems Industrial furniture and fixtures often have two clear cut advantages theyre inexpensive and durable that is built to withstand wear and tear.

Of course every commercial object cant be converted to an article for the home. What for instance would the average apartment dweller do with a factory boiler On the other hand chemical glassware beakers and flasks and graduated cylinders make wonderful vases often obtainable directly from the manufacturer these well made attractive glass containers are a find.

High-tech offers never ending options for the imaginative person. For example school gym lockers which can be brightly painted make convenient sturdy at home closets plumbing pipes they can also be painted can be used to build sleeping or storage lofts. Need an extra rug Call Ace Truckers Inc for a furniture pad the type that movers use to protect furniture in transit. Heres another suggestion an empty banana crate tossed onto the sidewalk by a market might just be the storage bin or planter youve been seeking Let your imagination run wild and keep your eyes open!

Mastery Test B

Write out the following dialogue and add all necessary marks of punctuation. Remember to check the placement of quotation marks with other marks of punctuation. Circle the marks you insert.

Much of the life of a Navaho family Professor Moriarty explained centers around the hogan the traditional Navaho dwelling. One type of hogan the professor continued is called the cribbed roof A six sided building this hogan has six foot high walls made of logs and mud The door of the hogan always faces east and the rising sun.

Excuse me Professor Lucy interrupted. What is the roof like

Professor Moriarty replied The roof too is made of logs and mud as a matter of fact theres traditionally an opening in the roof to allow smoke to escape.

The professor continued During formal gatherings inside the hogan people sit in this a traditional arrangement at the western side sits the husband facing the door. According to tradition the husband a warrior would be able to see any approaching enemies. The other men sit on the south side of the hogan women and children sit on the right.

Hogans were usually set far apart so each family's sheep would have sufficient grazing land around the house. Since the land was arid many acres were needed to supply enough land for the sheep thus the hogans were often isolated and really were the center of each family's life the professor concluded.

23 Capitalization

Capitalization in Edited Standard English

By mastering the capitalization rules of Edited Standard English, you can make your writing clear and assure that your use of capitals is consistent. Capital letters indicate the start of new sentences, distinguish proper nouns and adjectives, and indicate titles. Other capitals are used, where tradition dictates, in certain abbreviations (such as C for *centigrade* or *Celsius*) or in the salutation of a letter. Although the use of capitals may vary a bit with style, the rules and examples that follow should guide you in your use of capitals.

Capitals That Set Off Groups of Words

1. Capitalize the first word of a sentence.

A capital immediately signals a new sentence and separates it from the sentence that precedes it.

> **B**ecause next Monday is a national holiday, all the banks will be closed.
> **I** have a check but can't deposit it. **A**ll the banks are closed today.

2. Capitalize the first word of a direct quotation.

If a direct quotation is interrupted, capitalize only the first word of the quotation. Do not capitalize the word that begins the second part of the quotation.

> "**W**e've just bought a new home," Anna announced.
>
> "**W**e've bought a house," Anna explained, "**w**hich is not far from town." She added, "**I**t's very convenient."

3. Capitalize the first word of a complete line of poetry.

(Although the use of capitals in poetry might vary according to a poet's style, the first word of a line is usually capitalized.)

> **I**f music be the food of love, play on;
> **G**ive me excess of it, that, surfeiting,
> **T**he appetite may sicken, and so die.
>
> —*William Shakespeare*

4. Capitalize the first word, the last word, and all other important words in the title of any work of art.

This rule applies to the titles of books, chapters, stories, magazines, poems, plays, movies, newspapers, musical works, works of art, historical documents, and so on. Do not capitalize prepositions and conjunctions that have fewer than five letters when they appear within a title. However, do capitalize *a, an,* or *the* (as well as all prepositions and conjunctions) when they are the first word of a title.

Isak Dinesen's ***O**ut of **A**frica* tells about her life in Kenya.

William Faulkner, author of the American novels ***I**ntruder in the **D**ust* and ***A**s **I** **L**ay **D**ying,* also helped write the screenplay for the film ***T**he **B**ig **S**leep.*

The record album ***M**usic of the **C**ivil **W**ar* contains two excerpts from **L**incoln's **G**ettysburg **A**ddress and the "**B**attle **H**ymn of the **R**epublic."

I located the poem "**I**s **W**isdom a **L**ot of **L**anguage?" in a collection of Sandburg's poetry called ***H**oney and **S**alt.*

Exercise 1

Write out the following sentences, using capital letters where necessary. Underline the words you capitalize.

Examples

a. "last night," Joanna said, "we went to the movies to see *the african queen* and *guess who's coming to dinner.*"

a. "Last night," Joanna said, "we went to the movies to see The African Queen *and* Guess Who's Coming to Dinner."

b. although Fats Waller recorded and popularized "it's a sin to tell a lie," he didn't write the song. i'm not sure who did.

b. Although Fats Waller recorded and popularized "It's a Sin to Tell a Lie," he didn't write the song. I'm not sure who did.

1. according to an article in *playbill* magazine, some plays have had some strange titles. have you ever heard of *the devil in the cheese* or *a worm in the horseradish?*

2. frank Sinatra's album, *in the wee small hours of the morning*, is now popular with a whole new group of listeners. three generations of fans have admired "old Blue Eyes!"
3. "have you ever read *the wind in the willows?* Lucy asked. she added, "it's a classic."
4. the *chronicle* used to be the only paper in town, but now there are also the *daily gazette* and the *times.* at least there's more than one paper to read.
5. these words by Benjamin Franklin offer good advice: "dost thou love life? then do not squander time, for that is the stuff life is made of."
6. "we went to the opening of Paulo's show," Muhammad exclaimed. "it was wonderful. my favorite painting was entitled, 'reflections inside a golden eye.' "
7. while researching for her sociology report, "feline fans—common personality traits among cat admirers," Helga read the books *cat people* and *working cats.* both books were filled with quotes from cat owners.
8. didn't Jack say that he had seen *the empire strikes back* four times? after seeing *star wars*, Jack declared, "if there are a million sequels to this picture, I'll see each of them at least four or five times."
9. "if you're planning to diet," Kim said, "read *shape up, thin from within*, and *get slim.* each book offers intelligent plans for diet and exercise."
10. "next week's film festival," the announcer said, "boasts some of the worst films ever made! two of the films that will be shown are *the attack of the killer tomatoes* and *plan nine from outer space.*"

Capitals That Set Off Proper Nouns and Adjectives

The following rules, organized into logical groups, apply to the capitalization of proper nouns and adjectives.

1. Capitalize the names of specific people.

While visiting New York, **B**ernie **C**ohen met **M**eryl **S**treep and **M**elba **M**oore.
Last weekend **A**lice and **M**axine stayed at the **C**oopers' house.

Note: Sometimes, capitals occur within a surname, such as **M**c**C**luskey and **O'H**enry. However, the spelling of these surnames varies.

2. Capitalize a title preceding a person's name or a title replacing a person's name, as in direct address.

One of the most active senators on the committee is **S**enator James.
Do you expect, **G**overnor, to run for another term?

Note: When the words *president* and *vice president* do not precede a person's name they may be capitalized only when they refer to the highest officials of the government.

The **P**resident [of the United States] is inaugurated in January.
Vice **P**resident Ford later became **P**resident Ford.
Juan's goal is to be president of the company within five years.

3. Capitalize the abbreviation for a person's name or title.

Capt. **W**m. Jordon will see you now, **P**rof. Clarke.
Harry Brown, **S**r., and **D**r. Bertha Shapp own that building.

4. Capitalize words that show family relationships when they precede a person's name or when they replace a person's name.

My sister went to Mexico with **A**unt Irene.
I wonder, **F**ather, when you'll be ready to leave.
I'm looking forward to meeting my long-lost cousin.

5. Capitalize *Miss, Mrs., Ms.,* and *Mr.*

Miss Ella Brown will head the special task force.
In American history **M**rs. Eleanor Roosevelt is one of the most admired women.

6. Capitalize the names of specific places and proper adjectives formed from the names of specific places.

Fifth **S**treet in **P**lainfield becomes **N**orth **A**venue in **W**estfield, but it's the same street.

The **C**aribbean islands of **A**ruba, **B**onaire, and **C**uracao are known as the "**ABC I**slands."

Five counties in southern **N**ew **J**ersey want to secede from the state. The new state would be called **S**outh **N**ew **J**ersey.

According to this map, **K**ahalui **B**ay is north of **H**aleakola **N**ational **P**ark.

Note: Capitalize the names of compass directions only if they refer to a specific region or are part of an address.

Don't visit the **S**outhwest in August!
If the museum is located at 75 **E**ast Huron, it is not on the northwest side of the city.

Exercise 2

Write out each of the following sentences and use capital letters where necessary. Underline the words you capitalize.

Examples

a. My aunt lives in cape may, a town at the southern tip of new jersey.

a. My aunt lives in Cape May, a town at the southern tip of New Jersey.

b. Jake's cousin, dr. wm. march, was elected president of the kiwanis club in jefferson, wisconsin.

b. Jake's cousin, Dr. Wm. March, was elected president of the Kiwanis Club in Jefferson, Wisconsin.

1. When asked if she could name all fifty state capitals, aunt marcella missed two—augusta, maine, and sacramento, california.
2. When did you move south to atlanta, reverend ames? I thought you lived in south carolina.
3. If don's cousin sherwin goes north to seattle this summer, chris and jenny will live in his house in los angeles.
4. Did you know, mother, that dr. yates, ms. aleta, mrs. knowles, and sen. coles met while traveling in south america? They visited venezuela, peru, and colombia.
5. When he visited washington, d.c., paulo morales, jr., who is the president of our student council, met the president and vice president of the United States at a restaurant in georgetown.
6. aunt ruth, uncle henry, and their daughter allison (my favorite cousin) took a mediterranean cruise, stopping in france, italy, sardinia, and tunisia.
7. Many old western trails began in texas and led north to the great plains, the rocky mountains, and california; for example, the shawnee trail ran between texas and kansas city, and the california trail led from texas to san francisco.
8. For his birthday my friend alonzo received a pair of fabulous cowboy boots made by the bootmaker tony lama, jr., whose company is located on tony lama street in el paso, texas.
9. Eleanor's cousin tommy lives on pudding street in bedford hills, a small town in westchester county just north of white plains and new york city.
10. Last summer jaimie's aunt, who is a professor at ohio state, taught a course in florence, italy, and then traveled with her sister, dr. celia ling, to rome and milan, and then across the english channel to london.

7. Capitalize the names of buildings, institutions, monuments, businesses, and organizations.

The **A**merican **M**edical **A**ssociation has an office in the **S**peidel **B**uilding.

In 1912 Juliette Low founded the **G**irl **S**couts of **A**merica.

Is **M**idwestern **M**utual the insurance company that gave away plastic replicas of the **L**incoln **M**emorial last year?

8. Capitalize the names of nationalities, religions, races, and languages. Also capitalize the proper adjectives formed from these nouns.

Jennie Lee has a **F**rench poodle and a **S**iamese cat.

Because he lived in North Africa, Alan speaks both **F**rench and **A**rabic and is a respected scholar in the **M**oslem faith.

This basket was made by a member of the **H**opi nation.

9. Capitalize the abbreviations A.D., B.C., A.M., and P.M.

> Tomorrow's sunrise is at 5:14 **A.M.**
> Who won the Battle of Hastings, fought in **A.D.** 1066?

Note: Do not capitalize the abbreviations *am* and *fm* (pertaining to radio) or abbreviations for measurements such as *kg*, *cm*, *oz.*, *sec.*, and *min.*

10. Capitalize the names of planets, stars, and other heavenly bodies.

> Sailors used the **N**orth **S**tar—**P**olaris—to guide them.
> Which planet shines red in the sky—**M**ars or **V**enus?

Note: The words *sun*, *moon*, and *earth* are not usually capitalized. Never capitalize them when they follow the word *the*.

> The term *heliocentric* refers to the belief of early scientists that the earth, not the sun, was the center of our solar system.

Exercise 3

Write out the following sentences, using capital letters where necessary. Underline the words you capitalize.

Examples

a. The american museum of natural history is across the street from the new york historical society.

a. The American Museum of Natural History is across the street from the New York Historical Society.

b. Which planet is larger, neptune or saturn?

b. Which planet is larger, Neptune or Saturn?

1. The african country of zaire—formerly the belgian congo—has rich deposits of copper and cobalt.
2. Did you know that New York's temple emanuel is the largest jewish synagogue in the world?
3. A fine example of japanese carpentry is the golden hall, a buddhist temple built in a.d. 679.
4. Don't forget that the league of women voters will sponsor a panel discussion on Tuesday night at 7:30 p.m. at the city center motor inn.
5. Last Saturday we ate at casa patron, a wonderful spanish restaurant around the corner from the minskoff theater.
6. The chinese have been practicing acupuncture since 3000 b.c.; recently american doctors have accepted acupuncture as a treatment for certain ailments.
7. Every year many artists and writers apply for grants from organizations such as the national endowment for the arts, the national endowment for the humanities, and the ford foundation.

8. The exhibition at asia house includes japanese screens, chinese porcelain, chinese ivory, and korean silks.
9. French, mexican, spanish, italian, and canadian diplomats met at the white house to discuss trade agreements; the meetings, which ran from 9:00 a.m. until 9:00 p.m., were broadcast over fm radio.
10. Professors and administrators from boston university, emerson college, harvard university, simmons college, and amherst attended a meeting of the massachusetts association for continuing education last week at the powell building.

Review Exercise A

Write out the following sentences, using capital letters where necessary. Underline the words you capitalize.

Examples

a. Combining their resources, the astronomers club and the science fiction society have produced an amusing play called *rocket magic: a historical spin through space.*

a. Combining their resources, the Astronomers Club and the Science Fiction Society have produced an amusing play called Rocket Magic: A Historical Spin Through Space.

b. While visiting london, marta's brother paul saw a viking ship on display at the british museum.

b. While visiting London, Marta's brother Paul saw a Viking ship on display at the British Museum.

1. "did you know," asked alice, "that dr. dotti, who's a psychiatrist in italy, is married to audrey hepburn?"
2. While researching a report entitled "unusual names of ordinary people," pablo found these two humorous examples: minnie magazine, an editor at *time* magazine in new york; and u. s. bond, an employee of the harvard trust company in cambridge, massachusetts.
3. "Some dentists," said marco, "have names well suited to their profession." he explained, "there's dr. gargle in florida, dr. pull in minnesota, and dr. pulls at st. mark's clinic in new york."
4. According to *the cowboy catalogue*, winston churchill, general custer, "calamity" jane, and the duke of windsor had one thing in common: they all wore hats made by a famed hatmaker named stetson.
5. In the 1850s john b. stetson, originally from new jersey, traveled west to missouri and designed the hat that became a symbol for the american west.

6. Manuela explained, "high-heeled boots were brought west from asia by genghis khan. unlike others who had to walk, genghis khan's hordes rode horses and could comfortably wear high-heeled boots!"

7. In the 1940s a bootmaker in san antonio, texas, began making pairs of boots to honor each of america's states. (the first pair, of course, honored texas!) today these boots, which have toured museums from the atlantic to the pacific, are owned by acme boots, inc.

8. When china's vice-premier teng toured the united states the new york *post* reported that he donned a cowboy hat and enjoyed a rodeo in the southwest.

9. The roman pliny the elder (a.d. 23–79) wrote a book called, in latin, *historia naturalis*, which listed herbal remedies for ailments.

10. I think, father, that the word *mesmerize* comes from an austrian doctor named franz mesmer, who was the first modern physician to use hypnosis.

11. I heard that jane's father, paul langly, sr., does stunts in hollywood movies. next month he is going to europe to film a german movie about mountain climbing in the alps.

12. Kim wong, who is becky parson's sister-in-law, is the president of the chinese cooking gallery on pell street. well-known in the east, wong will tour the midwest and southwest and then continue west to washington and oregon.

13. You'll be surprised to hear, mother, that dr. raina perez, who is chief of cardiology at mercy hospital, writes mysteries in her spare time. writing under the pen name alice bones, the doctor is working on a new book, *murder under our noses*.

14. The lecturer, prof. geo. rourke, said, "wild animals that lived in north africa around 3,000 b.c. are depicted on a rocky plateau located in the sahara desert in algeria."

15. My aunt's family are all involved in the literary world: karen, who used to be a broker on wall street, writes a column called "financial advice" for the portsmouth *gazette;* uncle will's play, *mayhem from eight until twelve*, is playing at the morton theater in phoenix; and my cousin beth's poetry appears monthly in antioch college's literary magazine.

16. Beginning at 4:00 p.m., the barkoff theater on north wedgewood drive in ketchum, idaho, will show movies honored by the directors association of america. the films include *on the waterfront*, *strangers on a train*, and *and then there were none.*

17. Nikki read, "on saturday alberto durance, jr., will conduct the minneapolis symphony orchestra at carter hall. there will be guest performances by the russian violinist mitzi volkov, the spanish pianist kara garcia, and the dutch cellist hans groot."

18. "dr. lynn fargo, rev. thom. marth, ms. helga tropez, and prof. adam mendoza all teach at yuma community college," jan said. "the school is in colter, a small town just east of sante fe."

19. "if you don't like the current policies of the internal revenue service, mrs. bulgar, you can write to your representative in washington," mayor jones explained. "or," he added, "you can write to the president himself."

20. When elana heard the lead soprano singing on yesterday's 10:00 a.m. opera broadcast over station 99.3 fm, she could think only of these lines from samuel coleridge's poem "on a volunteer singer":

    swans sing before they die—'twere no bad thing
    should certain persons die before they sing.

11. Capitalize words referring to the Deity, Holy families, and Holy books of all religions. Capitalize personal pronouns when they refer to deities.

The evangelist urged, "Believe in the **L**ord and **H**is power."

The prayer begins, "Blessed art **T**hou O **L**ord our **G**od."

Our philosophy class compared sections of the **T**almud with portions of the **O**ld **T**estament.

Note: Do not capitalize the word *god* when it refers to a god of ancient mythology; capitalize the names of specific ancient gods.

The ancients attributed natural phenomena to their gods; for example, stormy seas might mean that **N**eptune, the god of the sea, was angry.

12. Capitalize the names of months, days of the week, holidays, and special events; capitalize historical events and periods.

Isn't **E**arth **D**ay in **A**pril?

The **S**enior **P**rom is on **F**riday, **J**une 3.

As a result of the **S**panish-**A**merican **W**ar, the U.S. annexed Puerto Rico.

Unfortunately, I stated on my essay exam that Wordsworth was a **R**enaissance rather than a **R**omantic poet.

Note: The names of seasons are not usually capitalized.

That restaurant closes in winter.

13. Capitalize the names of school subjects that are formed from proper nouns or that name a specific course.

Since you plan to major in art, you must take **F**undamentals of **D**rawing, a basic art course, before **D**esign 204.

I believe that **L**iterature III focuses on the American short story; it's an interesting literature course.

Note: Capitalize most nouns followed by a number or letter.

Isn't **R**oom 422 in use on Tuesday afternoon?
Mrs. Ortega found **P**lan C met all of her insurance needs.

14. Capitalize the names of political parties, the names of government agencies, departments, and bureaus or their abbreviations.

When is the **D**emocratic convention?

If you want information on national parks, you should write to the **D**epartment of the **I**nterior. The **ICC** (**I**nterstate **C**ommerce **C**ommission) has a helpful booklet on moving; why don't you send for a copy?

15. Capitalize the names of specific ships, trains, planes, and spacecraft.

Don's boat is called ***S**easpray*.

Who was the commander of the starship ***E**nterprise*?

Agatha Christie wrote a mystery about the ***O**rient-**E**xpress*, the luxurious European train that traveled between Calais and Istanbul.

16. Capitalize brand names of specific products.

Daisy detergent is the least expensive cleanser in this market.
Jell-**O** is one brand of gelatin dessert.

17. Capitalize the first word and each noun in the salutation of a letter. Capitalize the first word in the closing.

My dear **D**r. **K**ramer, **D**ear **M**rs. **W**aller: **V**ery truly yours,

18. Capitalize the pronoun *I* and the interjection *O*.

I don't know where **I** put my eyeglasses!
Where, oh where, should **I** go, **O** Father?

19. Capitalize the first word of each topic of an outline.

I. **H**ollywood idols
   A. **S**tars of silent films
   B. **S**tars of "talkies"

Exercise 4

Write out each of the following sentences and use capital letters where needed. Underline the words you capitalize.

Examples

a. Marissa's course, yoga for beginners, meets on tuesday evenings, february through may, at 6 o'clock in room 750.

a. Marissa's course, Yoga for Beginners, meets on Tuesday evenings, February through May, at 6 o'clock in Room 750.

b. My dog, i think, prefers bonz-o dog chow to bark bites.

b. My dog, I think, prefers Bonz-O Dog Chow to Bark Bites.

1. You cannot, i understand, take modern art 12 without first having taken introduction to art 1.
2. Sometimes a Presidential candidate splits from the democrats or republicans to run on a third-party ticket; for example, Teddy Roosevelt formed the bullmoose party.
3. At the auction i attended last tuesday, lot 49 included a huge poster of the luxury liner *normandie.*
4. Yes, easter is always on a sunday, but it is not always the same date; it is, however, usually in april.
5. Next sunday, may 12, is mother's day; we're giving our mother a midnight cruise around the island on the ferryboat *glistening maiden* and a bottle of chanel perfume.
6. Jenny wrote, "dear aunt lynn, i'm writing—with my new jackson bros. pen—to let you know that i am coming on thursday, july 28, and will stay until saturday, august 15. i have reserved room 803 at the martin hotel, so i'll see you then. Oh, i can't wait! fondest regards, jenny."
7. Julio outlined his paper on the occult:
   I. unexplained events from may until august
      A. crying in room 412
      B. sinking of the *flying cloud* in the harbor
      C. hail on labor day
8. Religious thought 12 covers these holy books: old testament, new testament, koran, and tibetan book of the dead.
9. The mayor's department of consumer affairs (suite 3100) rates the following brands of typewriters as comparable buys: addison, adler, and march bros.
10. You'll have a long weekend for washington's birthday (february), memorial day (may), independence day (july), labor day (september), thanksgiving (november), and christmas (december).

Review Exercise B

Write out the following sentences and use capital letters where necessary. Underline the words you capitalize.

1. in 1926 gertrude ederle swam the english channel in record-breaking time and won america's heart; crowds lined new york's broadway to see her, and even the president honored her.
2. oh, myrtle, on this dreary tuesday morning, let's remember shelley's lines from "ode to the west wind":

   the trumpet of a prophecy, o wind,
   if winter comes, can spring be far behind?
3. in 1912 a professor at yale university, dr. bingham, discovered the ruins of the incan city of machu picchu in peru's andes mountains.

4. the ranch house was developed by the american architect frank lloyd wright. although there are few examples of wright's work in the east, many of his buildings exist in the west and midwest; my aunt lives in a wright house in oak park, illinois.
5. "the nebraska historical society has photographs documenting the settlement of omaha," ritchie said. "i know," he added, "that j. younger, jr., who teaches at the university of nebraska, found a photo of witkin's drug store where his great-grandfather worked."
6. on october 4, 1957, the russians launched *sputnik 1* into space and thus began the space race, which culminated in the american landing of *apollo 11* on the moon in july 1969.
7. a hallmark, i think, of the civil rights movement in the south was martin luther king's bus boycott in montgomery, alabama, in 1955.
8. josé's uncle raoul has worked for *the new york times*, the san francisco *chronicle*, and the st. louis *post dispatch;* now he lives in swarthmore, a town just west of philadelphia, and teaches fundamentals of journalism at swarthmore college on monday, wednesday, and friday at 10:00 a.m. in memorial hall, room 212.
9. do you suppose, dr. lang, that i should do research with doctors at caldwell medical school? if i begin in september and work through june, i will be able to get a job at massachusetts general hospital next summer.
10. "after the civil war, the u.s. war department bought negatives from the photographer matthew brady," duane explained. "these pictures document the war and american life, both in the north and in the south."
11. "i saw a photograph," janet remarked, "that showed the statue of abraham lincoln being placed in the lincoln memorial in 1920." she continued, "amazing! the statue of the president was still in pieces."
12. a skilled and versatile scientist, benjamin banneker was appointed by president washington to survey the site of the capital in washington, d.c.
13. my cousin elaine used to ride the baltimore and ohio railroad between plainfield, new jersey, and philadelphia. since that train no longer runs, elaine now takes the amtrak at newark and arrives at philadelphia's 30th street station.
14. our science professor, prof. geo. colombo, explained that the brightest star, polaris, is part of the constellation ursa minor; polaris, also known as the north star, shines in the handle of the little dipper.
15. every summer my parents, my sister anne, my cousin billy, my aunt jo, uncle ike, and i vacationed in the berkshire mountains in western massachusetts. traveling north, we'd drive through great barrington, then east on rte. 23 to our cabin on lake garfield, where we'd stay until labor day.

16. i think, mother, that juan found most of the information he needed for his report, "economics on trial," in mayor caan's study at 23 west pruitt drive. the mayor's books included *a short economic history of the united states, the federal reserve system and how it works,* and *guide to good investments in bad times.*

17. the republican party's candidate hoped to win votes from registered democrats who were unhappy with their party's candidate. although the gallup poll showed the republicans in the lead, the answer would come on election day, november 5, when voters from florida to oregon cast their votes.

18. the painting at the chicago institute of fine arts depicts the trinity of hindu gods: brahma, the creator; vishnu, the preserver; and shiva, the destroyer. the painting appears on the cover of the show's catalogue, *religious art of india,* published by karma press, duluth, minnesota.

19. in ms. hanson's fifth-grade class at clarkson elementary school, pedro rodriguez memorized the gettysburg address, the declaration of independence, and the preamble to the constitution. now, twenty years later, he performs with the eatontown vaudeville troupe, reciting passages from shakespeare in record-breaking time. in fact, pedro's reading from *much ado about nothing* qualified him for listing in the *guinness book of world records!*

20. dolores and i bought records—irish folk songs and french chamber music—during the christmas sale at holiday record shop on jones road; all labels, including columbia, elektra, rso, casablanca, and rca, are on sale through new year's day and, perhaps, the first week in january.

Mastery Test A

Each of the words or groups of words that follow contains capital letters. Some of the capitals are used correctly; others are not. Write out each of the groups of words, using correct capitalization. If a group of words is correct as written, write *correct.* Underline the words whose capitalization you correct.

Examples

a. the President of priceright markets

a. the president of Priceright Markets

b. a Spring dance at the High School

b. a spring dance at the high school

1. waikiki Beach in hawaii
2. the Southern coast of japan
3. a Professor of Irish Art
4. Techniques of Drawing 121
5. a Holiday supper at the Church on Nicholas avenue

6. rabbi pearlman at temple Beth Sholom
7. mayor barnes, rev. clark, and Dr. k. Unizo spoke at greenwood school.
8. orange county south of Los Angeles, California
9. a river that is a tributary of the Danube river
10. is april the cruelest month of Spring?
11. Vice president johnson became president.
12. Sitting bull, a chief of the sioux
13. The lord is my shepherd, i shall not want.
14. the North entrance of the Museum, on East Lansing drive
15. two Siamese cats and a Persian rug
16. The five Lakes are huron, ontario, michigan, erie, and superior.
17. a narrow street off Richmond street
18. the lenni-lenape, a tribe that lived in new jersey
19. a Doctor (Dr. lorne Grey, m.d.), a nurse (ms. L. Hutton, r.n.), and the dean of cornell medical school
20. Professor j. ling, an expert on chinese history, teaches introduction to chinese history.

Mastery Test B

Write out the following paragraphs and use capital letters where necessary. Underline the words you capitalize.

Ask any record company executives—whether from columbia records or a & am, inc.—to list important pop recording artists of the decade, and no doubt they will mention josé feliciano. Now a recognized star both in the united states and abroad, josé endured many hardships on his way to fame. After moving from puerto rico to new york, he had to fight to stake his claim; in addition, he had to overcome the problems of being blind.

José's father, who had been a farmer, left the caribbean to try his luck in manhattan. it was hard for five-year-old josé. He had no friends and had to learn english; so he spent much of his time indoors, by himself, listening to elvis presley and ray charles on the radio.

Inspired to become a musical star, José learned to play the concertina and the guitar. At first he played at school, and his performances at charles evans hughes high school on west 18th street won him fans.

His first job was in detroit, michigan. Then he returned to the east to perform in greenwich village. Encouraged by his wife, hilda perez, he kept working away. Then in 1968 his song "light my fire" secured his career.

With that hit, José began playing all over the country, from the atlantic to the pacific, from canada to mexico. Fans on both sides of the mississippi rushed to his concerts. Today, having won the music industry's grammy award, José continues to work hard. As usual, his next concert, june 24, will be before a sell-out crowd.

24 Spelling

Learning to Spell

As early as 1768 Ben Franklin had experimented with a phonetic system to simplify spelling. However, responding to Franklin's system one woman wrote that she could "si meni inkanveniiniensis, as uel as difikyltis." Although numerous scholars since Franklin have also suggested simplified spelling systems, those systems have created as many difficulties as they tried to solve. Because of its irregularities, American spelling is difficult, but by mastering the basic spelling rules, proofreading carefully, and working on individual errors, you can reduce your spelling problems.

1. Proofread carefully.

Proofreading for spelling errors requires that you focus attention carefully on one word at a time. This is often easier if you begin at the bottom of the page and cover every word with a ruler except the one you are looking at.

2. Check the dictionary.

When you are not sure about a word's spelling, look the word up in a good dictionary. If the word does not appear as you have spelled it, try alternate spellings until you locate the correct one. Use the dictionary to check the pronunciation of words you misspell frequently since students often misspell words because they pronounce them incorrectly.

3. Keep a personal record of spelling errors.

Recording your own spelling errors in a notebook will help you understand why you misspell specific words. In the first column of your personal record write the correct spelling of the word and underline the letter or letters you are misspelling. In a second column break the word into syllables and show the accent and pronunciation. Finally, in the third column, add any explanation or note that will help you avoid misspelling that word. The following entries show how a student spelling record might look.

formerly	for′·mer·ly	Means "in the past"—don't confuse with *formally.*
hospitable	hos′·pit·able	Pronounce the *able* ending clearly.

Remember to keep your spelling record up-to-date and review the list before you proofread writing assignments.

Glossary of Troublesome Words

The common words in the following list present special problems because they are often confused. These troublesome words either look or sound alike and often confuse students who do not understand their meanings. Work on those words that cause problems for you and learn the distinctions between them.

1. **accept**	Although Kim is blind, she **accepts** my help only if the school halls are very crowded. *Accept*, a verb, means "to receive with consent."
2. **except**	Dan packed everything **except** his toothpaste and toothbrush. *Except*, a preposition, means "excluding."
3. **advice**	If you had followed the manufacturer's **advice,** this problem wouldn't have occurred. *Advice* is always a noun.
4. **advise**	At the lumberyard Ms. Wilson **advised** Ramona about the best wood for her project. *Advise*, a verb, means "to suggest" or "to recommend a course of action."
5. **affect**	The lobbyist was unable to **affect** the Wisconsin Senator's ideas on farm prices. The verb *affect* means "to influence" or "to change."
6. **effect**	Your doctor should inform you if this prescription has any side-**effects.** The noun *effect* is the result of an action. The verb *effect* means "to accomplish."
7. **aisle**	During the wedding a white carpet was placed over the center **aisle** of the church. An *aisle* is a passageway.

8. **isle** — What British poet wrote a poem about the **Isle** of Innisfree?
An *isle* is a small island.

9. **all ready** — The NASA engineers hoped to have the space shuttle **all ready** for an early 1987 launch.
All ready means "all in readiness" or "all prepared."

10. **already** — Although he appreciated the gift, Mr. Romero had **already** read the novel *Emma* by Jane Austen.
Already means "previously."

11. **all right** — When she toured the structure, the city building inspector found the construction work was not **all right.**
All right is the only acceptable way to write this phrase.

12. **all together** — Once my grandfather had the fallen limbs **all together**, he broke them into small kindling for the fireplace.
All together means "gathered in one place."

13. **altogether** — The report provided **altogether** too little information on the new industry's plans to control pollution.
Altogether means "wholly" or "entirely."

14. **altar** — Throughout December the **altar** was adorned with large red poinsettias.
An *altar* is a table used for religious ceremonies.

15. **alter** — It is too late now to **alter** these plans.
The verb *alter* means "to change."

16. **angel** — The tiny crystal **angel** hanging at the top of the tree was a gift from a friend in Ireland.
An *angel* is a supernatural being.

17. **angle** — Anna had to turn the bookcase on an **angle** to move it through the door of the apartment.
An *angle* is a corner or the meeting of two lines.

18. **ascent** — The women began their **ascent** of the mountain before dawn.
The noun *ascent* refers to a rise or a climb.

19. **assent** — Without proper research and documentation the senator will never give her **assent** to this project.
Assent means "consent."

20. **capital** — While state government is located in a city called the **capital**, county government is located in a town or city called the county seat.
The noun *capital* refers to a city or to money used to set up a business; the adjective *capital* means "important" or "excellent."

21. **capitol** — The murals in the state **capitol** were painted by WPA artists during the thirties.
The *capitol* is the building in which a legislature meets.

Exercise 1

Write out the following sentences and insert the correct word from the choices in parentheses at the end of each sentence. Use the sentences in the previous section to aid you. Underline each word you choose.

Example

a. Although it was half superstition, alchemy did ______ the development of modern chemistry. (affect, effect)

a. Although it was half superstition, alchemy did affect the development of modern chemistry.

1. To be ______ at most junior colleges, applicants must submit a transcript of their high school grades. (accepted, excepted)
2. Because she had ______ completed an advanced chemistry course in high school, she did not have to take the freshman science course at the university. (all ready, already)
3. Modern methods of mining gold have not drastically ______ the old prospectors' method of washing material in a sieve. (altared, altered)
4. The huge rock placements at Stonehenge resemble gigantic ______, but actually Stonehenge is an astronomical clock. (altars, alters)
5. If Agatha Christie's publications were placed ______ in one list, that list would include over one hundred titles. (all together, altogether)
6. As she escorted patrons to their seats, the usher's flashlight spread a glow across the theater's center ______. (aisle, isle)
7. Dr. Theodore Lawless' medical research had an important ______ on the treatment of leprosy. (effect, affect)
8. I followed my grandfather's ______ about letting the bread rise overnight, and it turned out perfectly. (advise, advice)
9. The ______ of Queen Elizabeth I to the British throne inaugurated the period of English history known as the Elizabethan era. (assent, ascent)
10. We admired the sharp ______ and small gables of the old Victorian house. (angels, angles)

11. Of all the relatives she describes in her autobiography, Pauli Murray's grandfather _______ her the most. (affected, effected)

12. In many states the _______ is also the largest city. (capitol, capital)

13. The student council promises that the gym will be _______ for the Homecoming Dance by noon on Saturday. (already, all ready)

14. Small businesses sometimes fail because their owners do not accurately estimate the _______ needed to support the business during the first six months. (capital, capitol)

15. _______ for a four-hour break in the middle of the day, Mrs. Ortiz, who drives a city bus, works from six in the morning until eight in the evening. (Accept, Except)

22. **complement**	The students' excellent performance was **complemented** by the attractive sets the Art Club built for the musical. The verb *complement* means "to make complete"; the noun *complement* refers to something that completes or makes perfect.
23. **compliment**	The senior citizens received many **compliments** on their restoration work at the historic Reed house. The noun *compliment* is a pleasing or flattering remark; the verb *compliment* means "to express something flattering."
24. **council**	The student **council** includes representatives from every class and organization. A *council* is a group that meets together for some purpose.
25. **counsel**	Several of last year's graduates **counseled** the seniors to submit their college applications in the fall. *Counsel*, a verb, means "to advise."
26. **councilor**	All sixteen **councilors** were present at last week's city council meeting. A *councilor* is a member of a council.
27. **counselor**	Before she became the assistant dean, Marge Hagemann was the admissions **counselor.** A *counselor* is one who advises.
28. **des′·ert**	One of the three botanic domes in Milwaukee houses a display of **desert** vegetation. A *desert* is an arid, sandy region.
29. **de·sert′**	At dusk when the mosquitoes come out, the family **deserted** the backyard for the com-

forts of the screened porch.
Desert, a verb, means "to abandon."

30. **dessert** — That watermelon you have raised will make a wonderful **dessert** in another month.
Dessert, a noun, is the last course in a meal.

31. **dyeing** — Jim is **dyeing** the wool for his next weaving according to directions he found in an early settlers' journal.
Dyeing changes the color of a material.

32. **dying** — The **dying** embers of the campfire sent up a small glow in the darkness.
Dying is the process of losing life.

33. **formally** — The President and his cabinet **formally** greeted Margaret Thatcher, the British Prime Minister.
Formally means "properly" or "with decorum."

34. **formerly** — This building was remodeled and turned into a restaurant; **formerly** it was a neighborhood fire station.
Formerly means "in the past."

35. **hear** — You can usually **hear** the birds starting to sing about an hour before dawn.
To *hear* is to perceive sound.

36. **here** — **Here** is some information about ethnic groups you may want to include in your report.
Here means "in this location."

37. **its** — **Its** fur matted and dripping, the puppy raced toward another mud puddle.
Its is the possessive form of *it.*

38. **it's** — **It's** still possible to see the exhibit of Gordon Parks' photography at the art center.
It's is a contraction of *it is* or *it has.*

39. **knew** — Even when she was still a teenager, those who heard Marian Anderson singing **knew** she would become an outstanding vocalist.
Knew is the past tense of the verb *know.*

40. **new** — Be sure to save the care instructions for your **new** smoke alarm.
The adjective *new* means "recent in origin."

41. **later** — Without carefully investigating the property, he invested in it; only **later** did he learn the land was undeveloped.

Later means "after a period of time" or "more late."

42. **latter** — Both Anne and Charlotte Brontë wrote novels; the **latter's** most famous work is *Jane Eyre*. *Latter* refers to the second of two.

Exercise 2

Write out each of the following sentences on a sheet of paper, inserting the correct word from the choices given in parentheses at the end of each sentence. Then underline the word you choose. Refer to the sentences in the previous section for extra help.

Example

a. To reduce the rush hour congestion downtown, the city ______ voted to make Washington Boulevard a one-way street. (counsel, council)

a. To reduce the rush hour congestion downtown, the city council voted to make Washington Boulevard a one-way street.

1. The legal ______ advised their client not to file the civil suit until they contacted more witnesses. (councilors, counselors)
2. Modern irrigation techniques made it possible to raise crops in the ______ climate. (desert, dessert)
3. The quote from Ruby Berkley Goodwin's autobiography ______ the rest of your ideas about the book. (complemented, complimented)
4. As a member of the National Youth Administration, Mary McLeod Bethune ______ President Roosevelt about youth-related issues. (counciled, counseled)
5. The senator was ______ on her years of volunteer work with the Red Cross. (complemented, complimented)
6. In 1929 it took travelers approximately twelve hours to cross this desolate stretch of ______. (desert, dessert)
7. Although they met for two days in January, members of the state economic ______ did not agree on a course of action until much ______. (council, counsel), (latter, later)
8. These tomato plants are ______ because the soil in the garden is too sandy. (dyeing, dying)
9. He could have fixed broccoli or green beans, but he ______ the family preferred the ______. (new, knew) (later, latter)
10. Although he has already completed his studies, José will be ______ graduated from the university in January. (formally, formerly)
11. Because her research in cell structure is so ______ and innovative, the students were anxious to ______ her lecture. (knew, new) (hear, here)

12. Although she was ______ a cook at a private clinic in Berlin, ______ in America Mrs. Lance learned to manage an asparagus farm. (formerly, formally) (hear, here)

13. We ______ that ______ the old, yellowed sheets would give them a fresh look. (new, knew) (dyeing, dying)

14. The poem contained several excellent images, but ______ meter was flawed. (its, it's)

15. The court martial revealed that the two sentries had not ______ their posts. (desserted, deserted)

43. **loose** Doctors recommend wearing several layers of **loose** clothing during severe cold weather.
Loose means "not tightly secured."

44. **lose** Everyone in New Jersey admires Rep. Fenwick; I can't believe she will **lose** the election.
The verb *lose* means "to experience a loss."

45. **miner** Until legislation improved working conditions, many **miners** contracted black lung disease.
A *miner* works in a mine.

46. **minor** In the sixties many people thought energy conservation was a **minor** problem; today everyone knows it is a major issue.
The noun *minor* refers to a person under legal age; the adjective *minor* means "less important."

47. **moral** Some people believe the government should divorce itself from **moral** issues.
The adjective *moral* means "good or right"; the noun *moral* means "a lesson in conduct."

48. **morale** The team's **morale** reached a peak just before the district tournament.
Morale is a noun, meaning "state of mind."

49. **passed** Raoul **passed** the freeway exit he wanted.
Passed is a form of the verb *to pass.*

50. **past** In the **past** valuable natural resources were sometimes squandered.
Past means "ended," "beyond," or "bygone."

51. **personal** Sheila moved her **personal** belongings herself; the moving company transported her office furniture.
Personal, an adjective, means "private" or "related to the individual."

52. **personnel** The company established a profit-sharing plan in which all **personnel** could participate.
Personnel, a noun, refers to the employees of a business.

53. **plain** By June his grandmother had transformed the **plain** yard into a colorful garden.
The adjective *plain* means "clear," "simple" or "unadorned."
The noun *plain* refers to a flat area of land.

54. **plane** She used the **plane** to shave tiny slivers of wood from the edge of the warped door.
The noun *plane* may refer to a tool, a flat surface, or an airplane.

55. **principal** Our **principal** spends one hour every day talking with students in the cafeteria.
The noun *principal* refers to the head of a school.
The adjective *principal* means "primary" or "most important."

56. **principle** Ms. Watanabe, our debate coach, is dedicated to the **principles** of thorough research and frequent practice.
A *principle* is a basic truth, standard, or rule of behavior.

57. **quiet** The doctor recommended **quiet** bed rest and fluids to cure his cold.
Quiet means "silent" or "still."

58. **quite** Winning second place in poetry and a first in short stories, Jim was **quite** pleased with his performance in the literary festival.
Quite means "to a great extent or degree."

59. **shone** The day she bought it, Maria waxed that old used car until its surface **shone.**
Shone is the past tense of the verb *shine.*

60. **shown** Kim has certainly **shown** me that her recent handicap will not prevent her from finishing college.
Shown is the past tense of the verb *show.*

Exercise 3

For each of the following words write a separate sentence in which you use each word correctly. Put your sentences on a sheet of paper and underline the word as you use it. Check the explanations in the previous section to ensure that you have spelled and used the word correctly.

Example

a. principal

a. Before he devoted his time completely to writing, Charles Waddell Chestnut was a school principal.

1. quite
2. principle
3. shown
4. minor
5. loose
6. morale
7. plain
8. personnel
9. moral
10. past

61. **stationary** — The walls in the resource center are not **stationary**; they can be arranged to handle large groups.
Stationary means "fixed, unmoving."

62. **stationery** — Rosa designed the letterhead for the **stationery** used by her company.
Stationery is used for writing letters.

63. **straight** — After the Homecoming parade the high school band will go **straight** to the football field.
Straight means "without delay" or "not crooked."

64. **strait** — The **Strait** of Dover separates France and England.
A *strait* is a narrow passage between two bodies of water.

65. **their** — The teens were pleased to learn that **their** volunteer efforts allowed the day care center to continue its work.
Their is the possessive of *they*.

66. **there** — **There** are several pages missing from the paperback you gave me.
In the preceding sentence, *there* is used as a function word to indicate that the subject follows the verb. *There* is also used as an adverb meaning "at that place."

67. **they're** — **They're** planning to attend Kwanza, the seven-day Afro-American celebration held after Christmas.
They're is a contraction of *they are*.

68. **threw** — Unfortunately he **threw** his bibliography cards away before he finished his research paper.
Threw is a form of the verb *to throw*.

69. **through** — **Through** the efforts of many noted men and women, the NAACP came into being in 1909. *Through* means "by means of" or "in one side and out the other."

70. **to** — Jacob Lawrence produced an entire sequence of paintings after his trip **to** Nigeria in 1964. *To* is a preposition.

71. **too** — Many health problems are the result of **too** much cholesterol in the diet. The adverb *too* means "in addition" or "more than enough."

72. **two** — For several years Dean Dixon was the musical director for **two** orchestras: one in Frankfurt, Germany, and one in Sydney, Australia. *Two* is a number.

73. **waist** — Fitting the pattern correctly will require accurate **waist** and hip measurements. The *waist* is the middle part of the body.

74. **waste** — When he cooks, my dad plans family meals carefully to avoid **waste.** The noun *waste* means "unused material." The verb *waste* means "to squander."

75. **weather** — Although they enjoy the mild **weather** of Georgia, the Ortegas miss their friends in Green Bay. *Weather* refers to the condition of the earth's atmosphere.

76. **whether** — **Whether** she gets the position or not, Ms. Quinn knows the job interview was a good experience. *Whether* indicates doubt or an alternative.

77. **who's** — **Who's** running the neighborhood clean-up campaign in Congress Park? *Who's* is a contraction of *who is* or *who has*.

78. **whose** — The factory provided bonuses for employees **whose** attendance records were outstanding. *Whose* is the possessive form of *who*.

79. **your** — Ali, **your** photographs are the best ones in this year's student exhibit. *Your* is the possessive form of *you*.

80. **you're** — Is it true that **you're** entitled to deduct the cost of uniforms and union dues on an income tax return? *You're* is a contraction of *you are*.

Exercise 4

On a separate sheet of paper, write out each of the following sentences and insert the correct word from the choices in parentheses at the end of each sentence. Underline the word you choose. If you need extra help, refer to the sentences in the previous section.

Example

a. Elena plans ______ spend six weeks on a ranch. (to, two, too)

a. Elena plans to spend six weeks on a ranch.

1. Margaret Thatcher, ______ known as the "iron lady" in Britain, was elected Prime Minister in 1979. (who's, whose)
2. ______ concerned about ______ energy so they always turn down the thermostat in the morning when they leave. (Their, There, They're) (waisting, wasting)
3. The park district will not open the pond for skating until the ______ turns much colder. (weather, whether)
4. The analysts still are not certain ______ a poor voter turnout will hurt ______ candidate. (weather, whether) (there, their, they're)
5. Did ______ aunt really receive an invitation to the President's inauguration? (your, you're)
6. ______ her novels and short stories, Zora Neale Hurston acquainted readers with the rich folklore tradition of Afro-American culture. (Threw, Through)
7. In this state it is illegal to dump ______ into rivers or streams. (waste, waist)
8. ______ was a narrow ______ between the two lakes, but it was interrupted by a beaver dam. (Their, They're, There) (strait, straight)
9. If ______ not certain about the spelling of a word, check a good dictionary. (your, you're)
10. Business letters and job applications should be typed on plain, standard-size ______. (stationary, stationery)
11. After the success of his ______ volumes of poetry, Claude McKay received a scholarship and traveled ______ the United States. (to, two, too) (to, too, two)
12. Dave ______ a load of clothes in the washer and added the detergent he had measured into a small cup. (through, threw)
13. Early nurses of Appalachia, ______ work often carried them into rugged mountain areas, often traveled on horseback. (who's, whose)
14. Looking ______ the want ads in ______ local newspaper, the Smith family located several good used car possibilities. (through, threw) (there, they're, their)
15. In this state ______ required to have car insurance even if ______ car is an older model. (you're, your) (you're, your)

Review Exercise A

The following letter contains many of the troublesome words discussed in the previous sections. Rewrite the letter, inserting the correct word from the choices given in parentheses. Underline the words you choose.

101 N. Boulevard
Naperville, IL 60540
March 15, 1984

L & M Manufacturing, Inc.
1225 N. Washington St.
Naperville, IL 60540

Dear Ms. Ramirez:

My aunt, (who's, whose) been an employee of (your, you're) company for the (passed, past) six years, (adviced, advised) me that as (personal, personnel) director (your, you're) now (accepting, excepting) applications for summer employment. I am interested in a part-time summer job in your (new, knew) business office.

I am seventeen years old, 5'10" tall, weigh 160 pounds, and my health is (quite, quiet) good. I am currently a junior at Central High School and have (already, all ready) completed (to, too, two) courses in typing and a course in computer programming. The (later, latter) course was offered (through, threw) the junior college. I have (complimented, complemented) these courses with a course that provided a basic knowledge of office practices and electives in math and English.

(Formerly, Formally) my family lived in Yorkville; we moved (hear, here) this fall. At Yorkville I was a member of the tennis team and also participated in speech activities. I was elected to the student (council, counsel) as a sophomore and (later, latter) served as the treasurer of that group. I have been involved in these programs at Central High School, (to, too, two). I plan (to, too, two) attend college but am not sure (weather, whether) I will major in accounting or computer programming.

From June until September of 1981, I worked as a clerk in the Acme Hardware Store. My employer, Mr. Alvarez, often (complimented, complemented) a change I made in the filing of sales slips that (affected, effected) an improvement in organization. Mr. Alvarez has said he would be happy to send you a (personal, personnel) recommendation.

I would be pleased to meet you for an interview at your convenience. I have enclosed my home phone number and can be reached (their, there). (Accept, Except) for one-week family vacation during early June, I would be able to work the entire summer. I will look forward to (here, hear)ing from you in the near future.

Sincerely yours,

Jon Kuskie

Jon Kuskie

Spelling Rules

Learning the following basic spelling rules will help you spell hundreds of words correctly. Even though some words are exceptions, mastering the rules will help you avoid many unnecessary errors in spelling.

1. In words containing an *ei* or *ie* combination that sounds like the long *e* in *feet*, use *ie* except after *c*.

   ie sounded as long *e:* bel*ie*ve, n*ie*ce, sh*ie*ld
   ei after *c:* conc*ei*ve, c*ei*ling, dec*ei*tful

   Exceptions: *ei*ther, n*ei*ther, l*ei*sure, prot*ei*n, sh*ei*k, s*ei*ze, financ*ie*r, spec*ie*s

2. In many words containing an *ei* or *ie* combination not sounded as long *e* (especially words with a long *a* sound as in *weigh*), use *ei.*

   ei sounded as long *a:* fr*ei*ght, r*ei*gn, v*ei*n
   ei not sounded as long *e:* forf*ei*t, th*ei*r, counterf*ei*t

   Exceptions: fr*ie*nd, handkerch*ie*f, sc*ie*nce, p*ie*r, and words with a schwa (ə) sound: consc*ie*nce, defic*ie*nt, profic*ie*nt, quot*ie*nt

3. Words containing a syllable pronounced like the word *seed*, are spelled with one of the following forms.

1	2	3
supersede	exceed	accede
	proceed	concede
	succeed	intercede
		precede
		recede
		secede

The only word in the English language spelled with the *-sede* form is *supersede.* Three very common words use the *-ceed* form: *exceed, proceed, succeed.* All other words with a *seed* sound have the *-cede* form.

Exercise 5

Write out each of the following sentences, adding the correct *ei* or *ie* combination or *seed* sound that is missing in each blank. Underline the word you complete in each sentence.

Example

a. Working in a law firm during the summer improved Manuel's profic ______ ncy in shorthand and typing.

a. Working in a law firm during the summer improved Manuel's proficiency in shorthand and typing.

1. Because of her bel ______ f in service for her constituents, Millicent Fenwick is often called "the consc ______ nce of Congress."
2. Tonight's news report warned local businesses to beware of counterf ______ t twenty dollar bills.

3. The insuffic ______ ncy of operating funds super ______ ed all other problems at the school board meeting.
4. My fr ______ nd, I think you've had more than a small p ______ ce of that limburger cheese.
5. Benjamin Banneker's many ach ______ vements as an astronomer far ex ______ ed those of other men with years of formal education.
6. The new legal br ______ f super ______ ed the one prepared six months earlier.
7. The dental hyg ______ nist pro ______ ed to clean his patient's teeth.
8. Bes ______ ged with calls from the media, the famous film star finally con ______ ed to an interview.
9. Muhammad Ali, who rec ______ved an Olympic gold medal early in his career, also won the world heavyw ______ ght championship twice.
10. Suc ______ ing to the throne after her father's death, Queen Elizabeth had r ______ gned since 1952.

Prefixes are discussed on pages 265–266.

4. When a prefix is added to a root word, the spelling of the root word does not change.

ir + responsible	The *irresponsible* driver did not slow down even though the roads were icy.
un + certain	Tina is still *uncertain* about her career plans.
in + expensive	The young couple believed the remodeling would be *inexpensive* if they did the work themselves.

Exercise 6

From the following list choose the prefix and root combination that correctly completes each of the following sentences, using a dictionary to define unfamiliar words. Write out each of the sentences on a sheet of paper, inserting the correctly spelled word. Underline your inserts.

Example

dis + regarding in + correctly
dis + similar un + reliable

a. ______ the instructions, the applicant filled out the entire form ______

a. Disregarding the instructions, the applicant filled out the entire form incorrectly.

PREFIX + ROOT LIST

dis + orderly	im + proved	over + rated
dis + satisfied	in + accurate	over + rule
il + legible	in + equality	re + mover
im + mature	mis + understood	re + organize
im + partial	non + violence	un + realistic
im + plausible		

1. Sojourner Truth devoted her life to speaking out against ______ .
2. The lawyers questioned the woman to be sure she would be an ______ member of the jury.
3. The ______ customer wrote that the varnish ______ did not perform as expected.
4. Commenting that the film was highly ______ , the critic said the plot was ______ and ______ .
5. Because the chemist's experimental records were ______ , valuable research time was lost.
6. Ms. Igrek, our new accountant, immediately suggested a way to ______ our bookkeeping system that ______ efficiency.
7. The secretary ______ the message because of the receptionist's ______ handwriting.
8. The Supreme Court can ______ the decision of a lower court.
9. Martin Luther King, Jr., never wavered in his devotion to ______ as a means of reform.
10. The seniors felt the ______ freshmen at the play were rude and ______ .

Suffixes are discussed on pages 266–267.

5. When a root word ends in an *e*, drop the *e* before adding a suffix beginning with a vowel.

survive + al	The infant's *survival* depended on an immediate blood transfusion.
regulate + ion	The contest *regulations* stated that entries had to be submitted by midnight on March 3.

Exceptions: *serviceable* (service + able), *changeable* (change + able), *advantageous* (advantage + ous). In words such as these, the final *e* is retained to create the soft *c* or *g* sound. Other words keep the final *e* for clarity: *acreage, dyeing, singeing.*

Do not drop the final *e* from the root word when the suffix begins with a consonant.

care + ful	*Careful* proofreading will help you avoid errors in your writing.
safe + ty	For *safety* the machine operators were required to wear goggles.

Exceptions: *argument* (argue + ment), *judgment* (judge + ment), *ninth* (nine + th), *truly* (true + ly), *introduction* (introduce + tion), *reduction* (reduce + tion).

Exercise 7

On a separate sheet of paper, write a sentence using the word formed by each of the following roots and suffixes. Underline the correctly spelled word in each sentence.

Example

a. please + ant

a. Watching the blizzard from my window was a pleasant experience, since I knew school would be canceled.

1. advise + or
2. bare + ly
3. ridicule + ous
4. peace + able
5. outrage + ous
6. waste + ful
7. disintegrate + ion
8. price + less
9. confuse + ion
10. argue + ment

6. When a root word ends in a *y* preceded by a consonant, change the *y* to *i* before any suffix not beginning with *i*.

hasty + ly	It is never wise to make a major purchase *hastily*.
hurry + ed	She *hurried* through the crowd of commuters in the subway station.
boy + hood	At fourteen, still in his *boyhood*, Charles Waddell Chestnut helped support his family by teaching school.

Exceptions: *drily* (dry + ly), *gaily* (gay + ly).

When a suffix begins with *i*, do not drop the *y*.

try + ing	The historical society is *trying* to save the old church from demolition.
study + ing	*Studying* all night is no way to prepare for semester exams.

Exercise 8

Write out the following sentences, in each blank inserting the correctly spelled combination of the word and suffix given in parentheses. Underline each word you form.

Example

a. Mom's comments as master of ceremonies were even _______ than we expected. (funny + er)

a. Mom's comments as master of ceremonies were even funnier than we expected.

1. The day could not have been more _______ ; we visited the art museum, had a nice lunch, and saw an excellent film. (satisfy + ing)
2. _______ _______ the rim off the worn tire, Liz created an inner tube for the children. (Ready + ly), (pry + ing)
3. _______ discouragement and other obstacles, Althea Gibson _______ had the satisfaction of standing in the winner's circle at Wimbledon. (overcome + ing) (final + ly)

4. The form asked all applicants who ______ for the position to list their previous experience. (qualify + ed)
5. The length and ______ of the official greetings created ______ in the hot crowd standing in the summer sun. (wordy + ness), (uneasy + ness)
6. Alice Walker's *Revolutionary Petunias and Other Poems* presents incidents ______ her own ancestors. (involve + ing)
7. W. E. B. Du Bois did publish some poetry although it lacks the stature of his ______ and ______ writings. (historic + al), (sociologic + al)
8. We had to postpone my aunt's ______ birthday party because she was still ______ with the last details of a special assignment for the state police. (fifty + eth), (occupy + ed)
9. Typical of most ______ poetry, Phillis Wheatley's works contain numerous mythological references. (neoclassic + al)
10. ______ in her refutation of the plaintiff's facts, the elderly lawyer ______ ______ the defendant's case. (Mercy + less), (easy + ly), (justify + ed)

7. Double the final consonant before a suffix beginning with a vowel when both of the following conditions are met:
   a. The root word has one syllable, or the accent is on the last syllable.
   b. The word ends in a single consonant preceded by a single vowel.

plan + ing	*Planning* each truck's route is part of her job as a dispatcher. [one-syllable root]
con·fer′ + ed	The principals and superintendent *conferred* about the rise in vandalism at several schools. [accent on the last syllable]

If both of these conditions are not met, the final consonant is not doubled before a suffix.

look + ing	*Looking* back at what she had written, she found several errors. [single consonant preceded by two vowels]
ben′·e·fit + ed	The neighbor's garage sale *benefited* the family who lost their home in the tornado. [accent is on the first syllable]

Exceptions: The accent on words such as *con·fer′*, *de·fer′*, *pre·fer′*, *re·fer′* sometimes shifts from the last syllable when a suffix is added.

Exercise 9

On a separate sheet of paper, write the correctly spelled word formed from each root and suffix combination. Then use that word in an interesting sentence, underlining the correctly spelled word. A dictionary will help you find the accent in words of more than one syllable.

Example

a. de·fer + ed

a. Langston Hughes' poem questions the consequences of a dream deferred.

1. in·suf·fer + able
2. soak + ing
3. re·fer + al
4. de·vel·op + ment
5. con·trol + ed
6. for·got + en
7. hap·pen + ing
8. be·gin + er
9. de·fer + ence
10. re·mit + ance

Mastery Exercise A

The following paragraph contains twenty-five words formed from prefix, suffix, and root combinations. On a separate sheet of paper, rewrite the paragraph and insert the correctly spelled words for the combinations given in parentheses. Underline the words you form.

Jesse Owens' (participate + ion) in the 1936 Olympics was marked by an (extra + ordinary) (illustrate + ion) of good sportsmanship. Owens, who had (early + er) broken three world track records in American (compete + tion) almost failed to qualify for the broad jump. (Race + ing) six inches past the takeoff mark in his first jump, Owens heard the referee (cry + ing) "Foul" as he landed. Shaken by the crowd's (hostile + ty) but filled with fresh (determine + ation), Jesse (concentrate + ed) on not (over + step + ing) the line. Although he did not foul, his second jump fell short of the (qualify + ing) mark. His legs (tremble + ing) with (nervous + ness), Owens thought it (im + possible) to succeed on the third jump. In a (surprise + ing) move, the German (athlete + ic) star Luz Long walked over and (re + assure + ed) the American. Long's words were (un + important), but his (demonstrate + ion) of good will cheered Owens. (Show + ing) his true talent, Owens made a (success + ful) final jump and went on to win the gold medal in that event. (Set + ing) a new Olympic record in the broad jump and (win + ing) three other gold medals, Owens never forgot the gesture of (encourage + ment) that made his success possible.

PART

8 Speaking/Listening

25 Developing Speaking/Listening Skills

Making Critical Decisions

You are confronted daily with a vast number of choices. Some choices you make (such as whether or not to sleep an extra fifteen minutes) affect only your daily routine, while other choices (your decision to marry, for instance) may change your life's direction. Making choices may be based on nothing more than a flip of the coin, a momentary whim, or a superstitious belief. On the other hand, the choices you make may be decided by rational means.

You use rational means to make a decision when you test opinions and assumptions logically and examine the consequences of actions before you act.

When you take a critical, objective approach to decision making, when you refuse to rely on prejudice, bias, and superstition, you are actually involved in the activity of debate. The debate may be no more than a tossing around of ideas in your own head, or it may be a face-to-face confrontation with someone else about the "truth" in a given situation. In either case your ability to argue successfully for a certain point of view will often determine the outcome of a decision.

In this chapter you will learn how to debate—how to prove a statement, how logically to attack and defend an idea, and how to verbalize your thoughts quickly and clearly. Learning to debate for the sake of debate makes little sense. The value of learning to debate is that it can prepare you to make critical, objective choices, an essential skill of survival in today's world.

Debating will also sharpen important skills of critical thinking. You will learn to analyze arguments as you prepare for your own debates and listen to others. You will also learn to evaluate the soundness of reasons given to support an idea. These are skills that you will need throughout your life, living in a society dependent on the spoken word.

Choosing Debatable Propositions

In debate terminology a course of action that is supported by one side (the affirmative) and rejected by the other side (the negative) is called a *proposition*. It is judgment expressed in words about what should be done or should be believed.

Debate propositions can be labeled as one of three types.

1. *Propositions of Fact*

When debaters argue whether something is or is not true, or will or will not happen, they are arguing a *proposition of fact*.

Lawyers debate propositions of fact whenever they try to prove the guilt or innocence of a defendant. "Resolved: That Ron Kallas is guilty of fraud" is an example of a proposition of fact. The prosecutor (the affirmative side) will have to prove that Ron Kallas is guilty of fraud, while the defense attorney (the negative side) has the burden of proving Ron's innocence. The distinguishing characteristic of a proposition of fact is that a definite answer exists. The jury will find Ron guilty or innocent, and one lawyer wins the case while the other loses. If you argue that candidate *A* will win the Presidency in November's election, eventually people will know whether you are right or wrong.

2. *Propositions of Value*

If you try to prove that your opinion or value judgment about an issue is right, then you are arguing a *proposition of value*.

The affirmative side arguing a proposition of value contends that something is good, right, proper, desirable, or beneficial. When debating a proposition of value, you cannot absolutely prove that your position is correct or true as you can a proposition of fact. You can, however, try to prove your position beyond a reasonable doubt. An example of a proposition of value is "Resolved: That American cars are better built than foreign cars." You could argue this statement all night in a "bull session" and still not come up with a definite answer.

3. *Propositions of Policy*

When a debater suggests that a certain rule, course of action, law, or policy should be pursued, that debater is arguing a *proposition of policy*.

The debate in a proposition of policy centers around whether or not changes should be made in the way people do things, and this type of proposition characterizes all legislative debates. It also characterizes much of the debate that takes place in organizations, clubs, and businesses. Typical proposition-of-policy statements are "Resolved: That the United States government should provide a free medical care system for all United States citizens"; "Resolved: That Anderson High School should establish an open lunch policy for all students"; and "Resolved: That the Hinkley Electronics Company should build three new stores." All propositions-of-policy statements suggest a change from what currently exists.

Wording the Debate Proposition

In most discussions speakers do not present their propositions in a formal manner, with the word *resolved* preceding the topic. The closest most people come to formalizing their request may be a statement such as, "I think that the government should pass legislation requiring the wearing of seat belts."

For formal debate, however, the basis for argument must be clearly defined and must be worded in a way that ensures a clash between two opposing sides. If the proposition is vaguely and improperly worded, then the debate will be unorganized and ineffective. To make the debate profitable, you should consider certain guidelines in choosing your proposition and in phrasing it.

1. The proposition should be controversial.

When you choose a topic, be certain that the topic is two-sided and that a difference of opinion exists about what should be believed or acted upon. If there is no conflict, then there is no need to debate. Thus, a proposition that states, "Resolved: That American democracy rests on the people's right to vote" is neither very debatable nor very interesting. However, a proposition that states, "Resolved: That the Electoral College should be abolished" is debatable because it is controversial.

2. The proposition should involve only one main idea.

Confusion will reign if there is more than one debatable topic in a proposition. A proposition that reads, "Resolved: That the senior class sponsor a paper drive on December 26 and use the money toward the senior gift to the school" is too much. The debaters involved not only will clash over whether a paper drive is the best way to earn money, but they will also have to debate the date for the drive and the eventual use of the money. Each main idea demands a separate proposition and a separate debate.

3. The proposition should be worded affirmatively.

The proposition should always be worded so that the affirmative side supports the new idea stated in the proposition and so the negative side rejects it. In other words the affirmative should always be put in a position of suggesting a change in the present situation, while the negative must defend what presently exists. A proposition that states, "Resolved: That compulsory education should be eliminated in the United States" fulfills this requirement because the affirmative is in a position of suggesting a change (supporting the proposition), while the negative must reject that change.

4. The proposition should be phrased in a single, neutral sentence that begins with the word *Resolved.*

Because a proposition should not give the edge to one side or the other, it should be written in the clearest possible language, and it should be free of bias. To state in a proposition, "Resolved: That the murderous, unethical, repressive act of capital punishment should be abolished" is unfair to the negative debaters. Let the arguments evolve from a fairly worded statement that reads, "Resolved: That capital punishment should be abolished."

Also, be certain that the proposition is worded as a declarative sentence rather than a question and that you precede the statement with the word *Resolved*. Notice that a colon follows *Resolved* and that the first word of the following sentence is capitalized.

Activity 1

Identify each of the following propositions as a proposition of fact, value, or policy.

1. Resolved: That English is a better subject than math.
2. Resolved: That the U.S. will enter into a recession later on this year.
3. Resolved: That the federal government should nationalize all public utilities.
4. Resolved: That Supreme Court Justices should be elected to office.
5. Resolved: That swimming is the best form of physical exercise.
6. Resolved: That the National League will adopt the designated hitter rule.
7. Resolved: That women should compete with men in all interscholastic athletic competition.
8. Resolved: That women are equal to men.
9. Resolved: That a woman will be elected President in the next election.
10. Resolved: That all smoking in public places should be prohibited by law.

Activity 2

Working alone or in a group, create five propositions of fact, five propositions of value, and five propositions of policy. Share your ideas with your classmates.

Activity 3

The following statements break the guidelines for wording propositions. First decide why each statement is not a proposition. Then rewrite the statement so that it becomes a proposition, following the guidelines discussed in the preceding section.

1. Should high schools drop courses in driver education?
2. The American custom of tipping
3. Resolved: That mandatory retirement ages should not be abolished.
4. Cheating is wrong.
5. Resolved: That women should not be drafted in time of war.
6. The irrational, insane, practice of spanking children should be outlawed.
7. Students who flunk courses

Activity 4

Clip out three different editorials from any newspaper or magazine. Then using the topics discussed in each editorial, phrase three different propositions of policy.

Activity 5

Brainstorming is discussed on pages 29–30.

The following is a list of subject headings. Either individually or as a group, brainstorm to discover controversial topics that fall under each of the headings and that would interest your classmates. After you have discovered the potential controversies, phrase each controversy into a proposition of policy.

Business	Medicine	Public people
Politics	Justice/Law	Teenagers
Life styles	Environment	Parents
Music	Education	Marriage
Sports	Television/Films	Taxes
Science	Books	Foreign policy

Affirmative and Negative Obligations

Once you choose a debatable proposition, the next step is to decide which side of the proposition you want to take. For the sake of the research you will do, limit yourself to propositions of policy. Neither propositions of fact nor of value lend themselves adequately to a research approach, since a proposition of fact is too easily settled and a proposition of value relies too much on personal opinion.

Before making your final decision about either supporting the proposition (debating affirmatively) or opposing it (debating negatively), you need to understand some of the obligations both sides must fulfill.

First of all, the affirmative side has the obligation known as *burden of proof.* Since a proposition of policy suggests that a change should take place in the status quo (present system), the affirmative must prove that there is a need for that change. By proving beyond a reasonable doubt that certain problems exist in the status quo, the affirmative is accepting its burden of proof. In fact, the affirmative has to prove that the problems are significantly harmful and that the only answer is to accept or adopt the proposition.

As the affirmative hammers away with the harm done by the present situation, the negative must be able to defend itself by fulfilling its obligation known as *burden of rejoinder.* Basically, the negative must meet head-on each of the affirmative's attacks, and it must show that the status quo is innocent of all of the affirmative's claims. In a proposition that states, "Resolved: That America's prison system should be significantly changed," the affirmative might attack the present system by saying that prisons do not really rehabilitate criminals. Because the affirmative has the burden of proving a need to adopt the proposition, it must be able to prove that claim. The negative, then, must defend itself by clashing directly with the affirmative's attacks. The key to understanding burden of proof and burden of rejoinder is realizing that both affirmative and negative speakers are under the obligation of proving any statements they make.

Activity 6

Divide up into small groups and then choose three propositions of policy you have already drafted or that you draft for this activity. Put each proposition on a separate sheet of paper and draw a line down the middle. In the left-hand column write the heading *Affirmative Attacks* and in the right-hand column write *Negative Responses.* As a group think of as many affirmative arguments as possible that show problems with the status quo and prove that the proposition should be adopted. Write these arguments under the *Affirmative Attacks* heading. Then think of negative responses to those arguments and put them in the right-hand column.

Activity 7

Have an informal class discussion about one of the following propositions or about one of your own choosing. After the argument is over, list on the board all of the affirmative attacks that related to problems with the status quo and all of the negative statements that were made in the defense of those attacks. Can any of these arguments stand alone without further proof?

Resolved: That training for American Olympic athletes should be funded by the Federal government.
Resolved: That female soldiers should be assigned to combat units.
Resolved: That all corporal punishment in schools should be abolished.

Developing the Proposition

Debate is actually a two-step process. First you make a statement about what you think is true in a given situation. Then you must prove that statement.

A good debater spends little time talking; instead, the majority of time is spent in preparation for those few minutes when the arguments and evidence are finally presented to an audience for its critical judgment. To prepare valid arguments backed by solid evidence and reasoning means that there should be some organizational pattern to your research. One approach is to consider research as having six different components.

1. Read for background knowledge of the topic area.

Researching a proposition means that you first must gain some background about the subject matter. Reading is one of the best ways to do this. Newspaper and magazine articles, chapters in a book, pamphlets, and encyclopedia entries can all help to broaden your perspective on the topic by suggesting ideas for you to explore as you prepare your opinion and its defense.

2. Uncover the issues in the debate.

If you have thoroughly explored the printed sources about your topic, you should then be prepared to articulate the issues in the debate. The *issues* are the main points about which the affirmative and negative disagree. They are the topics that must be analyzed by both sides and that will determine who wins the debate. They are the pivotal concerns in a debate because once the issues are uncovered, the actual arguments used to prove that a proposition should either be adopted or rejected can be developed from those issues.

The essential issues in a debate should be phrased as questions to which the affirmative must answer *yes* and the negative must answer *no*. The following diagram illustrates how issues are uncovered about the proposition, "Resolved: That private firms be allowed to deliver first-class mail."

Resolved: That Private Firms Be Allowed To Deliver First-Class Mail.

AFFIRMATIVE ARGUMENTS	NEGATIVE ARGUMENTS
First Issue: Is the present system of delivering mail inefficient?	
Yes	*No*
a. The service is deteriorating. b. The cost of mail delivery continually rises. c. The Postal Service seems always to be operating on deficits.	a. The Postal Service is becoming more mechanized. b. The cost of everything is rising due to inflation and not inefficiency. c. The Postal Service operates on a deficit only because of a clumsy rate-making structure.
Second Issue: Is the Postal Service's monopoly of mail service harmful?	
Yes	*No*
a. Because there's no competition, there's no incentive to improve. b. Because there's no improvement, there have actually been cutbacks in deliveries and changes from doorstep to curbside delivery.	a. Rural areas would be harmed because private firms would serve only profitable urban areas. b. A monopoly actually provides for an equality of service, which cannot be duplicated by private firms.
Third Issue: Would private firms create more jobs?	
Yes	*No*
Competition and reduced rates would mean expanded service and more jobs.	There is no guarantee that more jobs would be created. In fact, jobs would be cut because there would be no union protection.
Fourth Issue: Would the proposed system of having private firms deliver first-class mail be more efficient?	
Yes	*No*
a. Competition would cause companies to deliver mail more efficiently.	a. The present system is already doing a good job of mail delivery, and there is no need to change.

b. Competition would cut the cost of mail delivery.

b. The cost for transportation, employees, and maintenance would be the same for private firms as it is for the government.

Three general questions apply to almost all propositions of policy. These questions are called *stock issues*, and they can guide your thinking as you look for the specific issues dealing with your proposition.

Is there a need for a change?

Will the proposed change be practical, and will it solve any of the problems found in the status quo?

Will the proposed change produce advantages over the status quo?

You can also discover your proposition's issues by answering questions like the following ones.

With what problems does the topic seem to be concerned?

What are the causes of these problems?

How harmful are these problems?

What are the effects of these problems?

Is the present method of solving these problems working at all? If not, why not?

Is there a way of improving the present system without drastically changing it?

Will the adoption of the proposition really solve the problems uncovered?

Will the adoption of the proposition be practical, inexpensive, and beneficial?

Will the adoption of the proposition do more harm than good?

The important consideration about issues is not how you go about uncovering them, only that you do. Your research will be meaningless and your debating ineffective if you are uncertain about the major controversies involved in your topic.

Activity 8

Beginning with this activity, you will begin researching a proposition of policy that you will eventually debate for the class. First, divide yourselves into groups of four. Each group of four should then choose an interesting proposition of policy. You also need to choose a partner from your group so that two of you will be debating the affirmative side while the other two will debate the negative side. After a proposition of policy is chosen, partners are paired, and sides of the topic are decided, you are ready to begin your research. In your library each group member should read at least three general articles about the topic. Once the articles are read, each individual should develop a list (three to five) of issue questions that pertain specifically to the proposition, and then you should share your list with the other three in your group. As a group put all of your lists of issues together and pick the major three to five issues upon which the proposition rests. When you are in agreement about the issues, you are ready to proceed to the next step of research.

3. Select the contentions you will use.

Since you and your opponents have now settled on three to five issues with which to focus the debate, you are ready to develop your contentions.

Contentions are the arguments used to support your side of an issue.

Contentions, written as declarative sentences, are opinions that need to be proved to show that your side of the debate is right. In the diagram on pages 622–623, notice that both the affirmative and negative sides have made statements in response to each issue raised. These statements are the contentions that will actually be used during the debate.

Several contentions are usually necessary to establish your side of an issue, and it *always* takes evidence and reasoning to establish a contention.

Activity 9

Working with your partner, list the contentions you will need to prove to support the three to five issues you have already selected. These contentions should reflect your side of the debate and should be worded in simple, declarative sentences.

4. Find evidence to support your contentions.

Finding specific evidence to prove your contentions is by far one of the most demanding tasks you will face in preparing for your debate. Most debaters have little trouble deciding on the contentions or conclusions they want to develop. However, adequately supporting those conclusions with valid evidence is another story. In fact, you may find that some of your contentions are unwarranted and must be replaced with other arguments that can be proved.

For more help with using the library, see the chapter "Library Resources."

The library is your most important research tool. Libraries maintain bibliographies, indexes, vertical files, and reference books in which you can find the specific information you may need to support your claims. The following list contains some of the most common library reference works that deal with topics of current interest.

Readers' Guide to Periodical Literature
New York Times Index (Describes all news items; usually is on microfilm)
Public Affairs Information Service
Vertical File Service (Catalogues subjects of current interest/pamphlets)
World Almanac
Information Please Almanac
Congressional Record Indexes
United States Government Publications; Monthly Catalog

Education Index
Catholic Periodicals Index
Statistical Abstract of the United States
Index to Legal Periodicals
Biography Index
Editorial Research Reports (Thorough analyses of important current topics)
Yearbook of World Affairs
Britannica Book of the Year
Brookings Institute Publications
Black's Law Dictionary
Encyclopaedia Britannica
Collier's Encyclopedia

The *Readers' Guide to Periodical Literature* can help you to take a sweeping survey of the library to find specific magazine articles relating to your topic. Again there are certain publications, such as those in the following list, that tend to deal more with current topics and that can benefit you greatly when you are familiar with what they contain. Along with the magazines there are also noted newspapers that can provide you with the evidence you need.

Time
Newsweek
U.S. News and World Report
Fortune
Business Week
The Nation
Atlantic Monthly
Saturday Review
Harper's
Wall Street Journal
The New Republic
Foreign Affairs Monthly
Congressional Quarterly
The New York Times
Christian Science Monitor

Although the library will be your primary source for finding information, it is by no means the only avenue you can take. Interviewing knowledgeable people and corresponding with private and governmental agencies can also be useful to you as you research your topic.

Activity 10

Choose one of the references listed on pages 624 and 625 or any other helpful reference that is in your school library. Then prepare a short report about the kinds of information contained in that reference and about how to use the reference.

Activity 11

Dividing up the workload between you and your teammate, do a thorough search of the library sources that provide information about your proposition. List each source and its date so that you can return to it later to find specific information that supports your contentions. Do not, however, neglect sources giving information in support of your opponent's view. Finding out what others say against your position can help you to strengthen that position when you debate.

5. Test the evidence you would like to use.

The evidence you look for will be of two types: *empirical evidence* and *opinion evidence.*

Whenever you find controlled scientific studies resulting in factual data or whenever you read about controlled observations of events, you are involved with empirical evidence. For example, studies showing that certain agents cause cancer can be accepted as proof if the studies follow proper scientific rules of experimentation, such as variables that are controlled and repeated experiments that generate the same results.

A more common type of empirical evidence is the observation evidence that is based on controlled observation of events. Carefully developed examples and statistics that make generalizations are the types of observational evidence. Opinion polls are good examples of this type of evidence since they seek to draw conclusions about the way people think about issues. As long as the poll can prove validity (the pollsters actually observe what they claim to be measuring) and reliability (the same results would be gathered if the polls were repeated or if they had been gathered by another pollster at the same time), it can be accepted as evidence.

Even though empirical evidence is probably the strongest support you can gather for a contention, it is not always available. Instead, you may find yourself using opinion evidence. In using *opinion evidence* you rely on expert testimony to prove your point. If you quote an expert's opinion in an area in which he or she is qualified and competent, you are then using the weight of that person's authority to support your claim. In addition, if you quote a publication, such as a newspaper or magazine, that is noted for reliable, fair reporting, you are relying on that publication's reputation for supplying expert testimony. For example, a chemist may make a statement about the dangers of chemical warfare, and you may want to use that quotation as evidence. You are free to use the chemist's expert testimony or any empirical evidence you find as long as the evidence passes the tests described in the following statements.

a. The evidence must be clearly written so that it can be understood by you and by your potential audience.

b. The evidence must directly prove the contention, or it should not be used.

c. The evidence must be consistent with other known evidence. (One study showing that cigarette smoking does not cause cancer is not credible since all other studies indicate otherwise.)

d. The source for the evidence must be free from bias and must be objective and responsible. (A geologist who works for an oil company may not be free from bias when reporting facts about oil recovery.)

e. The evidence must be the most recent available. (Outdated evidence proves nothing more than times have changed.)

f. The evidence must be abundant. (The more pieces of evidence you have to prove the same idea, the stronger your argument will be.)

6. Record and file your evidence.

The final step in your research is to record and file your evidence so that you know what you have at a glance and so that it is easily retrievable. By using either 4″ × 6″ or 5″ × 8″ index cards, you can record one item of evidence per card, in a format that readily identifies it. Each note card should include a proposition heading that indicates whether your side is negative or affirmative, a subject matter heading, a citation heading (author's name, title of article and magazine or book, place and date of publication, and page number), and an exact quotation of the evidence you want to use. A typical evidence card might look like the following one.

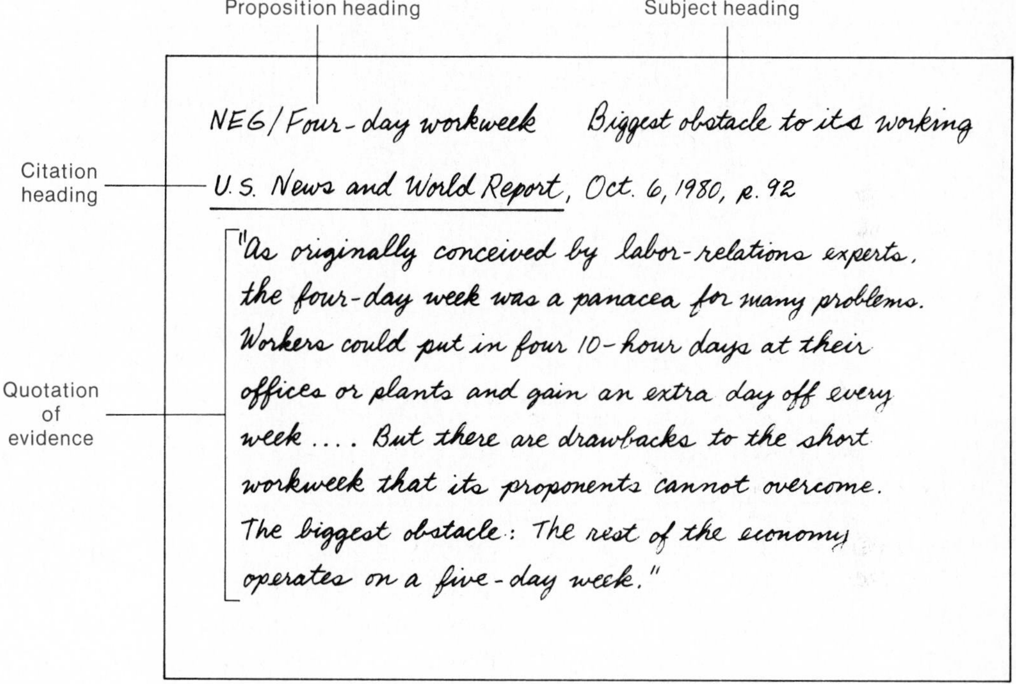

Proposition heading
Subject heading
NEG/Four-day workweek
Biggest obstacle to its working
Citation heading
U.S. News and World Report, Oct. 6, 1980, p. 92
Quotation of evidence
"As originally conceived by labor-relations experts, the four-day week was a panacea for many problems. Workers could put in four 10-hour days at their offices or plants and gain an extra day off every week .... But there are drawbacks to the short workweek that its proponents cannot overcome. The biggest obstacle: The rest of the economy operates on a five-day week."

Activity 12

Bring into class a recent newspaper or magazine editorial in which the writer uses evidence to support his or her position. Then prepare a brief presentation in which you read the editorial to the class, discuss the writer's main contention, and analyze the evidence he or she uses. Does the evidence pass the tests described on page 626?

Activity 13

Bring to class three examples of empirical evidence and three examples of opinion evidence. Again, apply the tests of evidence to your examples to see if they pass your examination.

Activity 14

Dividing up the workload between you and your teammate, begin recording evidence that supports the contentions you have developed. Record each piece of evidence on a note card. Include the proper headings.

Activity 15

Choose one of your contentions and prepare a three-minute speech in which you present to the class your proposition, the issue from which you developed your contention, the contention itself, and the carefully chosen evidence that proves it. After you prove your one claim to your class, let the class discuss and test the evidence you used.

Choosing a Competitive Debate Format

Most debate formats establish a pattern through the use of two sets of speeches—constructive speeches and rebuttal speeches.

In *constructive speeches* both affirmative and negative speakers build a series of arguments known as a *case.* Part of building the case during constructive arguments is done by attacking your opponents' case. Therefore, there must also be a series of speeches that give you time to repair any of the damage your opponents inflict upon your case during the constructive speeches. This time is known as the *rebuttal period.* Not only do you have a chance during rebuttals to rebuild your case, but you also have a chance to summarize the constructive arguments that have not been damaged. The rebuttals, then, become your final parting shot at proving your side of the proposition.

Refuting Your Opponents' Arguments

During a debate you will be confronted with many arguments presented by your opponents. Since debate, however, rests on the premise of two sides clashing or arguing about the truth in a given matter, you will have to take each one of your opponents' arguments, analyze it quickly, and present valid objections against it. This process is known as *refutation,* and it is not an easy skill to use unless you familiarize yourself with the ways to attack an argument and with the means to organize the attack.

Refutation involves three general strategies that can be used individually or together to refute an argument or to analyze any idea.

1. Attack the evidence used by your opponents.

Any evidence used should be analyzed carefully because it may provide a weak spot in your opponents' argument. When you listen to an argument, ask yourself the following questions to see if you can refute the argument by attacking your opponents' use of evidence.

a. Was there evidence used to support an argument?

b. Does the evidence directly relate to the argument it is to support?

c. Does the argument need more evidence to support it than was used?

d. Is the evidence too general to really prove anything?

e. Is the evidence outdated?

f. Is the evidence clearly written?

g. Is the evidence consistent with other reliable evidence?

h. Does the evidence have a bias? Is it from an unqualified source?

Fallacies in logical reasoning are discussed on pages 162–167.

2. Attack the reasoning used by your opponents.

Evidence alone is not enough unless conclusions can be drawn from that evidence. The process of drawing conclusions from the facts is known as *reasoning*, and it, too, must be analyzed in a debate. Not all conclusions reached are valid, and you may be able to poke some holes in your opponents' arguments by attacking their reasoning.

a. Do your opponents use hasty generalization when they jump to a conclusion without enough proof to support that conclusion? Example: "I've met three corrupted politicians in my life. That just goes to show that all politicians are crooks!"

b. Do your opponents commit the fallacy of non sequitur when they draw a conclusion from facts that do not provide adequate, logical grounds for that conclusion? Example: "Jones is a good father. Therefore, he will make a good senator."

c. Do your opponents try to oversimplify a really complex topic by arguing in terms too simple to take all issues into account? Example: "Slavery was the cause of the Civil War."

d. Do your opponents try to compare two situations that are not enough alike in all essential regards to make the comparison work? Example: "Nationalized health care works in Great Britain so it will also work in the United States."

e. Do your opponents try to say that one thing caused another thing to happen when there may really be no relationship between the two or not a strong enough one to make a difference? Example: "The heavy amount of rain we had this summer must have been caused by that volcanic explosion out in Washington."

f. Do your opponents beg the question by assuming that something is true that requires proof, but yet they do not prove it? Example: "Because the use of chemical weapons in warfare is normally wrong, it should be prohibited. Because the use of chemical weapons in warfare should be prohibited, it is normally wrong."

3. Defend your own case.

You have probably heard the sports-related cliché that a good offense is the best defense. This bit of wisdom holds true for debaters too. One way to refute your opponents' case is to establish and defend your own. When you deal with an opponents' argument against your case, do not forget about the following refutation strategies:

a. Use evidence that contradicts your opponents' evidence.
b. Point out arguments that your opponents have dropped as the debate progresses.
c. Minimize the significance of their arguments while maximizing the significance of your own.
d. Point out inconsistencies in what your opponents have said.
e. Dismiss their irrelevant arguments that have nothing to do with the real issues at hand.
f. Point out emotional appeals that your opponents are using.

Once you have decided what strategies to use against an opponents' argument, you next have to organize your refutation. Unless you let your listeners know what you are trying to do, your refutation will be ineffective. Therefore, organize your refutation around the following four steps.

1. State your opponents' argument that you want to refute.
2. Tell your listeners the objections you have against that argument.
3. Support with evidence or explain your objections.
4. Explain how your objections weaken your opponents' case while strengthening yours.

Activity 16
Bring to class a newspaper or magazine article about a controversial topic and isolate one argument that is used in the piece. Then refute the argument by organizing your refutation around the four steps listed above.

Activity 17
Each of the following statements can be attacked in some way. Identify what is wrong with the statement and what attack could be used against it.

1. He comes from a wealthy suburb; therefore, he must be rich.
2. Because of the lack of morality among its people, the Roman Empire fell.
3. Compulsory wage and price controls should be rejected in this country because the Communists favor them.
4. They are all good speakers so they should make an excellent debate team.
5. Harry started using Ultra Light toothpaste, and then he had lots of dates. That just goes to show that Ultra Light will make a person more attractive.
6. Scott says that the school dress code should be revised. But what does he know? He can't even keep his shoelaces tied!

7. Either we keep a strong military structure, or we will have WW III.
8. Clothing made by Tucker is the longest wearing clothing you can buy. How do you know? Because it is made by them, and they are a brand name.
9. The time has come to throw this do-nothing, corruption-riddled administration out of office.
10. Prison conditions are appalling, which is why they do not work.

Activity 18

As a culminating activity for the work you have done in preparing to debate, have each group of four students present a debate to the class.

Listening to Debates

Even though you have prepared yourself for the debate, your success depends on one more skill—the ability to listen and take notes. You cannot refute an argument that you have not heard accurately nor remembered completely. Most debates last about an hour. Without a note-taking system, it is almost impossible to remember everything that is said by both teams during that time.

As you listen to debates, or even to informal arguments, you should train yourself to listen for the speaker's proposition (or main idea) and for the argument set forth to support his or her position. Listening to a debate in order to follow the main ideas is similar to taking notes on the main ideas of a book that you are reading. You will find that speakers emphasize their main ideas, often by stating them first or with the words, "I believe that. . . ." In listening, transition words such as *first, second, finally,* and *in conclusion* help you to identify the supporting arguments. You will probably find it helpful to jot down notes as you listen in order to outline the main ideas of the argument.

If you are listening as an audience member to a speech or debate, you are expected to make a critical choice about which side most effectively presented its case. To do so, you need to have some criteria by which you can judge the speech or debate. Use the following six criteria in evaluating the arguments of a single speaker or of a debate team:

1. *Analysis.* How well did the speaker (or team) grasp the proposition and the opposing viewpoint?
2. *Reasoning.* How valid were the conclusions presented, based on the evidence? How strongly did the evidence support the conclusions?
3. *Evidence.* How believable was the evidence presented? Were the sources of the evidence cited?
4. *Organization.* How well organized was the argument? How easy was it to follow?

5. *Refutation.* How well did the speaker (or team) attack and refute the opposing viewpoint?
6. *Delivery.* How well did the speaker (or team) present the argument? Was the delivery clear, direct, and forceful?

Activity 19

Listen to a speech on television by an elected official or a candidate for office. Perhaps you can find some recorded debates to listen to. Choose one speech, and evaluate the speech according to the six criteria listed in the preceding section. Be prepared to state the speaker's main idea and the main supporting arguments.

Activity 20

Develop a rating sheet in which you use the six criteria found on pages 631–632. As your class debates, rate the speakers individually against the six criteria and then rate the teams against the criteria. Include on the sheet a place for comments about the team and complete a sheet for each debate you hear in class. Share your evaluations with the debaters.

PART 9 Testing

26 Preparing for Tests

Tests of Vocabulary, Reading and English Comprehension

Regardless of your future plans—a job, the military, a specialized training course—you will probably be asked to take standardized tests as a measurement of your interests and abilities. Such tests can be divided into two general categories: *achievement tests* and *general aptitude tests*.

Achievement tests measure specific skills and knowledge that you have been taught in school.

General aptitude tests measure more general skills of learning, such as the ability to comprehend, to think clearly, to organize ideas, and to express yourself with logic and conviction.

The purpose of aptitude tests is to assess the likelihood of your succeeding in more advanced study. These tests may also be used to predict your probable success in learning a particular skill such as small appliance repair or aircraft maintenance.

When applying for college, you may be asked to take one or more of the following tests: the tests of the American College Testing Program (ACT); the test of the College Entrance Examination Board; the Scholastic Aptitude Test (SAT); and the English Composition Test, known as the "English Achievement Test." Even when colleges do not make the tests an entrance requirement, they may ask that you take one or more of them to determine the course you should take.

The armed services and many employers require applicants to take tests in such areas as vocabulary, reading, and grammar and usage to determine the applicants' strengths and weaknesses.

Preparing for Tests

The most important preparation for standardized tests is to apply yourself in your high school courses. You cannot prepare for these tests in late-night sessions a week before the event—in fact, such cramming might do you more harm than good.

The following specific suggestions will help you as you prepare for and take standardized tests.

1. Try to remain calm during the test. These tests were designed so that the average student will answer about half of the questions correctly, so do not become upset when you cannot answer every question.
2. Have a positive attitude. The purpose of the tests is to help you make choices about college and a career, not to penalize or frustrate you. Try to think about the tests as a learning experience.
3. Listen carefully to the instructions for the test. Some instructions may be read aloud to you, some you may be asked to read silently. Follow the instructions exactly.
4. Work the sample questions that often are included as a part of the instructions, even if they seem very simple. This activity will help you to "warm up" for the main event.
5. Read the entire question before marking an answer. Read all the choices before picking one. Many questions ask for the "best" choice, so compare the alternatives before making the decision.
6. Work rapidly but carefully. Answer questions you find easy first, skipping questions that give you difficulty. Then when you have worked to the end of the section, spend the time you have left on the difficult questions. Unless you are told otherwise, all test questions have equal value.
7. The answers are usually coded with letters, as is the answer sheet. Be certain you are marking your choice in the correct space for the item and answer you intend. Check at least every fifth item to be sure you are in the right place.
8. If you change your mind about an answer, be certain you erase your first choice thoroughly. The answer sheet is "read" by a very sensitive electronic scanner that will read both your answers unless the first is well erased. If the machine reads two marks, it will count the answer as wrong.
9. Plan your time. Be aware of the length of the test and the amount of time you have to work. Try to be certain you are about halfway through the test when half the time is up. (Do not spend too much time watching the clock, however.)
10. If you finish before time is called, go back and check the answers you have marked.

In the next several sections of this chapter, you will find practice questions for standardized tests. By becoming familiar with the question formats for various kinds of tests, you increase your chances of performing well. Answers to the sample questions are found on page 651.

Tests of Vocabulary

Vocabulary tests usually examine a student's understanding of the sophisticated words found in formal writing—both fiction and informational nonfiction—rather than the common words used in conversation or informal writing. Familiarity with this vocabulary is thought to be an indication of the student's current reading ability and language experience; it is all viewed as a good predictor of the individual's ability to learn and use new words in advanced study.

Four common formats are used to test vocabulary: *vocabulary in context*, *synonyms*, *antonyms*, and *verbal analogies*.

Vocabulary in Context

Vocabulary-in-context questions often are presented as incomplete sentences that students complete by selecting the best response from four or five possible answers, or options. Sometimes, students are asked to choose a synonym for a word in the incomplete phrase. In other questions the incomplete sentence includes a descriptive phrase, and the student completes the statement by selecting the word defined by that phrase. A third possibility is the reverse of the previous one—that is, the student selects the option that best defines a term in the incomplete sentence. The following exercise is an example of vocabulary-in-context questions.

Answers to sample questions are marked with a dagger (†). All other answers are on page 651.

Example

A. Someone who is loquacious is:

a reticent
†b talkative
c fervent
d polite

Exercise 1

Read the beginning of each of the following sentences and the choices that follow it. Choose the answer that best completes the sentence.

1. A gregarious person is:

a deviant
b childish
c introverted
d sociable

2. An erudite article is one which is:

a sarcastic
b scholarly
c controversial
d simplistic

3. To work adroitly is to work:
a willingly
b carelessly
c diligently
d cleverly

4. A nebulous statement is one which is:
a succinct
b intelligible
c vague
d abusive

5. Things which are analogous are:
a similar
b opposite
c transposed
d convoluted

Synonyms

Two or more words or phrases that share essentially the same meaning are called *synonyms*. Sometimes, several words may have closely related meanings, although there are few instances in which two words are completely identical in meaning, tone, or "feel." Therefore, the "correct" answers in synonym test items are usually more accurately described as "best" answers. Careful reading will help choose the response that is better than the others.

Answers to sample questions are marked with a dagger (†). All other answers are on page 651.

Example

A. abate
a release
b increase
c shrink
†d subside

Exercise 2

For each of the following questions, choose the synonym (word most similar in meaning) to the underlined word.

1. meretricious
a sincere
b worthwhile
c gaudy
d genuine

2. germane
a relevant
b Teutonic
c developing
d insignificant

3. quell
   a quibble
   b foment
   c immerse
   d quiet

4. aversion
   a prevention
   b ability
   c greed
   d antipathy

5. leery
   a suggestive
   b distrustful
   c rash
   d lascivious

Antonyms

Words that have almost opposite meanings are called *antonyms.* Since there are very few true antonyms in English, you must look for the best answer. Remember that the negative form of a word, in many cases, is not always the best antonym. For example, something that is "*not* sour" (negative form) is not necessarily "sweet" (antonym of *sour*). By the same token, something can be "not sweet" without being "sour."

Answers to sample questions are marked with a dagger (†). Answers for all exercises are on page 651.

Example

A. acute
   †a mild
   b chronic
   c habitual
   d occasional

In the preceding example, two of the options—*chronic* and *habitual*—are synonyms, but they are not both antonyms for *acute.*

Exercise 3

For each of the following questions, choose the antonym word (most nearly opposite in meaning) to the underlined word.

1. ambiguous
   a obscure
   b explicit
   c ardent
   d pretentious

2. taciturn
   a surly
   b quiet
   c anxious
   d talkative

3. inane
   a wise
   b silly
   c necessary
   d lively

4. esoteric
   a private
   b trivial
   c certain
   d well-known

5. crass
   a obtuse
   b helpful
   c discriminating
   d gentle

Verbal Analogies

Synonym and antonym vocabulary items require an understanding of the relationships between a pair of words. In analogies, the test taker must match two pairs of terms to demonstrate understanding of the relationships among those terms. Usually you will be given one pair of words or phrases. You must identify the relationship between those two terms and then find another pair of words with the same relationship. Sometimes, you will also be given the first word of the second pair, and will have to choose only the fourth term. The following is one example of a verbal analogy test item.

Answers to sample questions are marked with a dagger (†). Answers to all exercises are on page 651.

Example

A. Pride is to lion as gaggle is to—
   a bear
   b eagle
   †c goose
   d hawk

In this case *pride* is the term used for a group of lions. *Gaggle* is a parallel term applied to geese.

Sometimes, only colons are used to suggest the relationship between the terms, as shown in the following example.

Example

B. QUARRY: STONE::
   a rock: mineral
   †b mine: ore
   c soil: field
   d oil: drill

Exercise 4

In the following items, choose the pair of words whose relationship is most similar to that of the first pair.

1. LIGHT: FEATHER::
   a hard: nails
   b lead: heavy
   c molasses: slow
   d grass: green
2. BEAR: DEN::
   a bird: cage
   b tent: camper
   c beaver: water
   d fox: lair
3. LETHARGIC: ENERGETIC::
   a eager: lazy
   b mollify: soften
   c apathetic: enthusiastic
   d capricious: vigorous
4. PLEASURE: PAIN::
   a madness: sanity
   b happiness: sorrow
   c gentleness: amiability
   d intolerance: patience
5. WORDS: SCRIPT::
   a ink: pen
   b computer: digits
   c notes: score
   d letters: sounds

Reading Comprehension

Reading comprehension tests are used to assess a student's ability to read with accuracy and comprehension. On these tests, you will usually be asked to read a passage of some length—several hundred words, perhaps—and then to answer questions about what you have read. If the subject matter is unfamiliar, do not worry about that. The examiners are not interested in your previous knowledge of the subject. Rather, these tests are designed to measure how well you can derive information from the passage itself and how well you draw appropriate inferences from the facts given to you.

Some questions are about specific information found in the passage—literal or factual data. Other questions may ask you to define a term in the context in which it is being used. More often, however, the questions will require you to draw conclusions, synthesize a number of details, or evaluate the author's purpose, point of view, and so forth.

Turning your regular reading assignments into practice tests is a good way to prepare for tests of this sort. Read a few paragraphs in your social studies or literature textbook and then do the following:

1. Briefly state the main idea or focus of the paragraph.
2. Restate each important idea presented in the passage in your own words.
3. Look for words that can have more than one meaning and define each word in terms of its use in this paragraph.
4. Identify statements that are expressions of the author's opinion. Are they well founded and based on facts presented in the passage?
5. Identify value judgments, expressions of bias or prejudice, exaggerations, and understatements.
6. Try to identify the author's purpose or reasons for writing this particular passage. What is its tone? Is it descriptive, persuasive, argumentative?
7. What inferences can be drawn from what is stated?

English Mechanics and Usage

Tests of English mechanics and usage assess your understanding and use of the most basic skills of English composition. You may also be asked to write a short essay or writing sample, but more frequently, you will be given a multiple-choice test including sections on spelling, grammar, and usage. The test may also include exercises that evaluate your sensitivity to language and your ability to organize thoughts into a logical whole.

Spelling

Spelling test items usually assess your understanding of basic spelling rules or ask you to identify misspellings of frequently used words. The most common format is to present several words, one of which is misspelled. (Sometimes, one option is "no error.") Another format tests understanding of *homophones*—words spelled differently but sounding the same—such as *peace* and *piece* or *two* and *too.*

Exercise 5

For each of the following questions, choose the one word that is misspelled. If no word is misspelled, mark *N* for "no error."

1. a cemetery
   b chastise
   c analyze
   d acommodate
   N
2. a current
   b medicine
   c possability
   d pejorative
   N

3. a category
   b innoculate
   c nickel
   d guidance
   N
4. a illicit
   b mischievous
   c height
   d fallacy
   N
5. a irresistable
   b knowledgeable
   c irrelevant
   d millionaire
   N
6. a thorough
   b quizzes
   c rarity
   d seighe
   N
7. a personal
   b preceed
   c perfectible
   d prevalent
   N
8. a absence
   b simultaneous
   c sophmore
   d burglar
   N
9. a democracy
   b efficient
   c optimist
   d conquerer
   N
10. a wierd
    b succumb
    c sympathize
    d vacuum
    N

Error Recognition

Error recognition test items ask students to identify errors in short written passages. Sometimes, you may be asked to indicate the nature of the error.

Other formats require only that you indicate the *presence* of an error. The following are examples of both these types.

TYPE 1

Mark your answer sheet:
a -if the sentence contains an error in diction (choice of words)
b -if the sentence is verbose or redundant (wordy)
c -if the sentence contains a cliché or mixed metaphor
d -if the sentence contains an error in grammar
e -if the sentence is correct as it stands.

EXAMPLE

A. The young man was fit as a fiddle. (c)

TYPE 2

Mark the letter of the line containing an error in spelling, punctuation, capitalization, grammar, or usage. If there is no error, mark N for "no error."

EXAMPLE

B. †a the canadian flag has
b a red maple leaf on a
c ground of white

Answers for sample questions are marked with a dagger (†). Answers for other questions are on page 651.

Exercise 6

TYPE 1

Mark your answer sheet:

a. if the sentence contains an error in diction (choice of words)

b. if the sentence is verbose or redundant (wordy)

c. if the sentence contains a cliché or mixed metaphor

d. if the sentence contains an error in grammar

e. if the sentence is correct as it stands

1. After such a grueling game neither the player nor the coach are going to celebrate the victory.
2. Tourists taking extended journeys to the Far East that last a long time may become tired and exhausted.
3. The incumbent's campaign rested on the hope that most people would think a bird in the bush was safer than changing horses in midstream.
4. Each complaint to the discotheque manager was followed by a temporary deduction in noise level.
5. Some of the eggs purchased from the farmer early last week is rotten.
6. The president asked his advisor, who he knew had attended the scientific conference, to give him a complete report on DNA research.

7. Scientists predict that solar studies of the sun will become an important object of scientific study in the future.
8. While hurrying out of the building, the lights went on before the burglar escaped unnoticed.
9. The juror claimed his decision was not effected by his previous knowledge of the case.
10. Fond memories were stirred as she looked through the photo album thinking that a picture is truly worth a thousand words.

Exercise 7

TYPE 2

Mark the letter of the line containing an error in spelling, punctuation, capitalization, grammar, word choice, or usage. If there is no error, mark N for "no error."

1. a Less than half of the present
   b 152 member states were original
   c members of the United Nations.
   N
2. a Each of the women attending the
   b state conference were asked to
   c participate in the international assembly.
   N
3. a Due to the declining birth rate,
   b the amount of children attending elementary
   c school is decreasing each year.
   N
4. a After the fire it was discovered
   b that the flames had originated
   c in an electrical outlet in the school liberary.
   N
5. a Although she is as strong as, if not
   b stronger, than most of her teammates
   c she is not the best player.
   N
6. a Convertible automobiles lacking a roll bar,
   b having been found unsafe, are
   c hardly never seen on the roads today.
   N
7. a Assignments for the combined history and
   b government course have been
   c seperated to make grading easier.
   N

8. a John could of helped her
   b take care of the building if
   c he had asked for work.
   N

9. a An easy way to publicize the lecture
   b is to distribute announcements for it among
   c the students attending tonight's concert.
   N

10. a To help prevent shoplifting, many
    b storeowners post warnings that state that
    c shoplifters will be persecuted.
    N

Organizing Paragraphs

Exercises involving scrambled paragraphs indirectly assess your ability to organize thoughts and present them logically. The test format usually consists of a passage with sentences in random order, which you must organize into a paragraph.

After reading the sentences, try to order the paragraph in your mind. Look for clues, such as transitional words or phrases within the sentences. Notice pronouns that refer to something in another (and therefore earlier) sentence. If necessary, jot down the order of the sentences on scrap paper. Then answer the specific questions you are asked.

Example

P Myths, on the other hand, are born, not made.
Q A fable is a story, made to order, intended for instruction.
R They owe their details to the imaginative efforts of generations of storytellers.
S A distinction must be made between myths and fables.

1. Which sentence did you put first?
   a Sentence P
   b Sentence Q
   c Sentence R
   d Sentence S
2. Which sentence did you put after S?
   a Sentence P
   b Sentence Q
   c Sentence R
   d None of the above. Sentence S is last

The correct order of these sentences is S, Q, P, R. S is a topic sentence and makes sense only as the first sentence. As a final sentence it would be silly unless it included *therefore* or *thus* or *in summary, then,* or some such phrase.

Sentence P needs to come after Q because of the phrase *on the other hand*. The *they* in Sentence R refers to myths, not fables, so the order is established.

Exercise 8

Each group of sentences in this section is actually a paragraph presented in scrambled order. Each sentence in the group has a place in the paragraph; no sentence is to be left out. You are to read each group of sentences and decide the best order in which to put the sentences so as to form a well-organized paragraph.

P An important step in taking a good photograph is to previsualize the result.

Q One then thinks of possible improvements and makes necessary changes.

R Essentially this means that while looking through the viewfinder the photographer visualizes or imagines how the shot will look when printed.

S Thus by making all adjustments to lighting and composition before the shutter is released, the final photograph comes close to what was wanted and expected.

T For professional photographers good photographs do not just happen; they are made.

Which sentence did you put first?

1. a Sentence P
   b Sentence Q
   c Sentence R
   d Sentence S
   e Sentence T
2. Which sentence did you put after Sentence P?
   a Sentence Q
   b Sentence R
   c Sentence S
   d Sentence T
   e None of the above. Sentence P is last.
3. Which sentence did you put after Sentence Q?
   a Sentence P
   b Sentence R
   c Sentence S
   d Sentence T
   e None of the above. Sentence Q is last.
4. Which sentence did you put after sentence R?
   a Sentence P
   b Sentence Q
   c Sentence S
   d Sentence T
   e None of the above. Sentence R is last.

5. Which sentence did you put after Sentence T?
   a Sentence P
   b Sentence Q
   c Sentence R
   d Sentence S
   e None of the above. Sentence T is last.

Writing Samples

Since the best test of whether a student can write effectively is to have the student write something and evaluate that product, some tests of English composition skills ask students to prepare a writing sample. Because writing samples cannot be scanned by a machine or graded with complete objectivity, they are far more difficult to evaluate than multiple-choice test items.

There are two common methods used to evaluate writing samples. One approach is *holistic scoring*. Using this system, the trained reader/scorer reads your essay or paragraph quite rapidly and gives it a rating—perhaps on a scale of 1 (low) to 5 (high). The rating is based on an *overall* impression of the piece (hence the term *holistic*) rather than on any quantitative or even qualitative evaluation of specific elements. Spelling, punctuation, grammar, usage, organization, tone, even handwriting probably "count" to some degree, but they are not assessed or tallied separately. When writing samples are scored holistically, at least two readers will rate each sample independently. When the readers disagree, a third reader is often called on to make a final assessment.

A second method of scoring requires reading the writing sample several times and rating elements such as ideas, organization, wording, flavor, mechanics, and presentation (penmanship, neatness, spacing, etc.) separately. Each element may be rated 3 (excellent), 2 (average), or 1 (poor), and the ratings averaged to come up with a total score. If you have not had experience in writing short descriptive or persuasive pieces, you might want to practice writing "on demand" in preparation for this kind of test. The following is a short list of topics similar to those you might be asked to address in a writing sample.

1. Explain how to make a food/object.
2. Describe a favorite place you have visited.
3. Discuss improvements you would make to a high school.
4. Describe someone you like well.
5. Discuss your views on war.
6. A Job I Would Like to Have
7. Music I Enjoy
8. The World in A.D. 2000
9. An Autobiography
10. If I Were President

Taking Essay Examinations

An *essay examination* requires that you demonstrate your knowledge of a topic by writing about it.

Essay questions may be included as part of an examination in almost any school subject. The steps involved in writing essay answers are similar to those found in other types of exposition: work with a limited topic, development of a thesis statement, and support of the thesis with specific details. Sometimes, students are allowed to use their textbook and notes as sources of supporting detail such as examples, reasons, facts and figures, and so on. Often, however, students are expected to rely on memory for these supporting details.

The best way to prepare for an essay examination is to develop good study habits. The SQ3R (Survey, Question, Read, Recite, Review) method is one way to prepare for essay examinations. This method involves the following steps.

1. Survey the material, noting the title, reading the introduction and summary, looking at illustrations, paying special attention to subject headings, marginal notes, and vocabulary words in **boldface** and *italicized* print.
2. Using chapter titles, topic headings, or hints from your teacher, formulate a list of questions that should be answered as you complete the reading assignment.
3. Read to find the answers to your questions.
4. Recite answers to the questions you have asked yourself and record your answers as reading notes.
5. Immediately after reading, review your list of questions and answers, trying to answer the questions without looking at your notes. After one week, review again.

Exercise 9

Select a section or chapter from one of your textbooks to read and study using the SQ3R method. On a sheet of paper, write down the questions you ask yourself in the *question* step and the notes you develop to answer those questions in the *recite* step.

Writing Essay Answers

The following suggestions will help you improve your performance on Essay Examinations.

1. Look over the test carefully before you begin.

Read the instructions to find out if you must answer every question or if you have a choice of topics. Then read the topics and decide which will be the easiest to discuss and which might offer you the most problems.

2. Schedule your time.

If you must write on three topics in an hour, allow fifteen minutes for each topic, ten minutes for note-taking, and five minutes for review. If one question carries more weight than the others, adjust your schedule to allow more time for that topic.

3. Analyze each essay topic carefully.

Most essay test items contain "clue words" that suggest how the essay should be written. Verbs such as *discuss, describe, compare, contrast, define, refute* suggest how a topic should be treated or developed. Notice the other development clues provided by the words in the following essay examination topics.

> Explain *three services* that a life insurance agent should provide for a buyer.
>
> What *characteristics* of romanticism can be found in Wordsworth's poetry?
>
> Explain the *major functions* of the United States Supreme Court.

Notice that sometimes a topic will specify a number of items that should be discussed:

> Describe *three* major causes of water accidents.

Questions may also consist of several parts:

> According to the definition of propaganda provided in this chapter, what modern occupations could be classified as propagandistic? Discuss each occupation's relationship to the spread of propaganda. To answer this question students must discuss two things: (1) occupations that spread propaganda, and (2) how each occupation spreads propaganda.

4. Quickly gather information before writing your answer.

Jot down facts from reading and class discussions as rapidly as you can; if you have forgotten an important idea, go on to the next question and come back to your list later. The systems for gathering information (brainstorming, the Pentad, or the *who? what? why? when? where? how?* questions) are often helpful.

5. Briefly outline your answer and begin writing.

Remember that your essay should possess the qualities of an abbreviated expository essay. The essay question itself already tells you how the topic should be limited. Often the question can be restated as the thesis or main idea in your essay answer. Reread your list of notes, cross out irrelevant information, and number the remaining information in the order it should logically be presented.

Keep your time limitation in mind; if you must develop three points in your answer, divide your time equally among the three. Write concisely, stating the most important information first.

6. Save a few minutes of your scheduled time to reread your answer, making necessary changes and proofreading.

Your ideas will make a more favorable impression if they are stated clearly and correctly. Be especially careful to spell words and names given in the essay question correctly.

Exercise 10

On a sheet of paper, list the clue words in each of the following sample essay examination questions. Then indicate how many parts there are to each question and what they are.

1. Discuss the five approaches to the study of religion in terms of the contribution each makes to human understanding.
   —from *Sociology: The Study of Human Relationships*
2. Discuss the importance of the labor force to production, service, and distribution systems. What would happen to these systems if labor was not available?
   —from *Sociology: The Study of Human Relationships*
3. Compare the view of nature developed in "A Sunrise on the Veld" with the view developed in O'Flaherty's "The Wild Goat's Kid." Contrast the ways in which these views emerge.
   —from *Adventures in English Literature*
4. What are the advantages and disadvantages of each kind of life insurance below for a 20-year-old person?
   a. 5-year term insurance
   b. endowment insurance
   c. limited-payment life insurance

   —from *The Consumer in America*

A Sample Essay Question and Answer

The essay examination answer in this section was written in response to the following question.

QUESTION

In what ways do government services aid consumers and businesses? Illustrate your answer to this question by discussing the roles of three federal agencies or commissions.

ANSWER

Government services aid both consumers and businesses by shaping the direction in which the economy develops and by protecting the consumer's health and safety. For example, the FDA (Food and Drug Administration) carefully tests new drugs before they are made available to consumers to ensure that the drugs are effective and do not have harmful side effects. The FDA also sets up guidelines for food so that shoppers can purchase safe, carefully prepared, wholesome items in their local stores. The information about nutritional value that now appears on the packages of prepared foods is the result of FDA legislation.

Another government group, the FTC (Federal Trade Commission), oversees advertising and sales practices. The FTC protects the consumer from illegal price fixing by companies and dishonest advertising. In some cases, the commission has filed suits against companies and forced them to change deceptive magazine or television advertisements. The commission also investigates thousands of consumer complaints that are brought to their attention every year.

A third agency, the EPA (Environmental Protection Agency), protects consumers by setting standards for the pesticides that are used in American agriculture. The agency also sets standards for air, water, and noise pollution to ensure that businesses do not damage the environment in the process of manufacturing their goods.

While the FDA, FTC, and EPA were developed primarily to protect consumers, they also direct the economy by setting up guidelines that force American businesses to compete honestly and fairly, according to set regulations, for the consumer's dollar.

KEY

Exercise		1	2	3	4	5	6	7	8
Item	1.	d	c	b	a	d	d	a	e (or a)
	2.	b	a	d	d	c	b	b	b
	3.	d	d	a	c	b	c	b	c
	4.	c	d	d	b	N	a	c	b
	5.	a	b	c	c	a	d	b	a (or e)
	6.					d	d	c	
	7.					b	b	c	
	8.					c	d	a	
	9.					d	a	N	
	10.					a	c (or b)	c	

Glossary of Terms

Achievement test A test that measures specific skills and knowledge taught in school

Active voice The form of the verb when the subject performs the action

Acronym A word formed from the initials of a group of words

Ad hominem The fallacy of attacking a person instead of an issue; the Latin words mean, "against the man"

Adjective A word used to modify a noun or pronoun

Adverb A word used to modify a verb, an adjective, or another adverb

Affix A word element, such as a prefix or suffix, added to a root to change its meaning

Analogy A comparison in which two things are shown to have at least one quality in common

Antagonist A character against whom the protagonist struggles to resolve the conflict

Apostrophe Punctuation mark used to show the omission of letters or numbers, to form the plurals of letters or numbers, and to form possessive nouns

Appositive A word or phrase that renames or explains a nearby noun or pronoun

A priori The fallacy of offering a conclusion without any evidence to support it; the Latin words mean, "from the first"

Bandwagon appeal An appeal to the emotional need to be like everyone else

Begging the question The fallacy of arguing that a conclusion is true without offering any evidence or reasons

Bias The coloring of events or descriptions from a particular point of view

Black English A major American dialect spoken by many black people in the United States

Brainstorming Stimulating creative thinking by letting one's mind wander freely over a subject

Card catalogue A file of cards listing books and other reference materials

Card-stacking Withholding information in order to persuade

Central theme The main idea developed in a piece of writing

Clause A group of words containing a subject and a predicate that functions as part of a sentence

Cliché An overused expression

Climax Turning point

"Clincher" sentence A sentence that provides a strong ending for a paragraph

Coherent paragraph A paragraph in which the links between sentences are made clear to the reader

Collective noun A noun that names a collection, or group, of persons or things

Colon Punctuation mark that calls attention to the word, phrase, or list that follows it

Comma Punctuation mark used to separate words, phrases, or clauses within a sentence

Commentary The writer's statements, reflections, and observations about the central theme

Comparison Identifying ways in which items are similar and ways in which they differ

Complement A word or group of words that completes the meaning of the verb and the subject

Compound Having two or more parts

Compound sentence A sentence containing two or more independent clauses and no subordinate clauses

Compound-complex sentence A sentence composed of two or more independent clauses and one or more subordinate clauses

Complex sentence A sentence composed of one independent clause and one or more subordinate clauses

Conjugate To show a verb's different forms according to voice, mood, tense, number, and person

Conjunction A word that connects words or groups of words

Connotation Feelings associated with a word

Critical writing Writing that analyzes, evaluates, and comments on selected elements of another's work

Dangling modifier A modifier that has no word or words for it to modify

Dash Punctation mark used to call attention to a word or group of words that precedes it
Declarative sentence A sentence that states a fact
Deductive reasoning Reasoning that begins with a general statement, adds a related statement, and ends with a conclusion drawn from the two statements
Denotation The explicit meaning of a word
Dewey decimal system A method of dividing nonfiction works into ten categories
Diction Choice of words
Direct object A word or group of words that receives the action of the verb
Edited Standard English The written form of Standard English
Either–or fallacy The fallacy of arguing that only two alternatives are possible in a given situation
Euphemism A word or phrase substituted to make something offensive sound more agreeable
Exclamation point Punctuation mark used to end imperative sentences
Exclamatory sentence A sentence that expresses strong feeling
Expository writing Writing whose purpose is to explain
Facts Information that can be verified
Factual statement A statement that can be proved or disproved by measurement, experiment, or research
Fallacy An error in logical thinking
False analogy A farfetched comparison
Final bibliography A list of all the sources actually used in writing a research paper
First-person narrator A character who refers to himself or herself as *I*, narrates the story, and plays a part in it
***5WHow?* questions** A method of organizing writing by asking *Who? What? When? Where? Why?* and *How?*
Flat character One that is static and does not grow or change during a story
Footnotes The sources of information or of direct quotations used in a research paper
Foreshadowing The technique of hinting about events to come
Formal outline An outline showing the relationship of major and minor ideas in a research paper with Roman numerals, capital letters, and Arabic numerals
General aptitude test A test that measures general skills—the abilities to comprehend, to think clearly, to organize ideas, and to express oneself with logic and conviction
Gerund A form of the verb used as a noun
Glittering generality A loaded word or phrase with strong positive connotations
Gobbledygook Jargon used to confuse and exclude others
Hasty generalization The fallacy of basing a conclusion on inadequate sampling
Hyphen Punctuation mark used to link the parts of compound words or to divide a word at the end of a line
Imagery The use of language to appeal to the senses
Imaginative writing Stories, novels, plays, and poetry
Imperative sentence A sentence that gives a command or makes a request
Independent clause A clause that can stand on its own as a sentence
Indirect object A word that tells *for whom* or *to whom* the action of the verb is done
Indo-European A parent language spoken in central Europe about 4000 B.C.
Inductive reasoning Reasoning that begins with a series of specific details and ends with a conclusion based on those details
Infinitive A form of the verb preceded by the word *to* and used as a noun, adjective, or adverb
Interjection A word that expresses strong feeling
Interrogative sentence Asks a question
Intransitive verb An action verb that does not take a direct object
Ipse dixit The fallacy of citing an unreliable authority; the Latin words mean, "He said it"
Library of Congress system A method of classifying books, more comprehensive than the Dewey decimal system
Linguist A scholar of language
Linking verb A verb that joins the subject of a sentence to a noun or adjective that identifies or describes it
Loaded words Words with strong connotations
Logic Clear and orderly thinking
Metaphor An implied comparison between two unlike items, stated without the use of linking words
Meter A formal rhythmic pattern of sound in poetry
Middle English The language developed from Old English, spoken from about A.D. 1066 to 1450
Modern English The English language developed from Middle English, spoken from about A.D. 1450 to the present
Mood The speaker's attitude toward his or her statement
Narrative The relating of incidents or experiences in chronological order
Nonrestrictive clause A clause that does not add essential information to the sentence
Non sequitur The fallacy of drawing a conclusion that does not necessarily follow from the evidence; the Latin words mean, "It does not follow"
Noun The name of a person, place, thing, or idea
Objective complement A complement that follows a direct object and describes or renames it
Old English A language developed from Anglo-Saxon, spoken from about A.D. 450 to 1066
Omniscient narrator A narrator who is not a character in the story but knows everything that happens, and can describe what all the characters think and feel
Only-cause fallacy The fallacy of naming a single cause for a complex situation
Opinion Belief, view, judgment, or appraisal based on an interpretation of facts
Outline A listing of the main points of a piece of writing

Parallel structure Similar wording or arrangement of words in a sentence or series of sentences

Paraphrase Rewording

Parentheses Punctuation marks that enclose elements within a sentence

Participle A form of the verb used as an adjective

Passive voice The form of the verb when the subject receives the action

Pentad A method of organizing writing by asking five questions (about *action*, *actors*, *scene*, *method*, and *purpose)*

Period An end mark following a sentence or an abbreviation

Personal journal A record of the writer's experiences, thoughts, and observations

Personification A metaphor attributing human characteristics to nonhuman subjects

Persuasive writing Writing whose purpose is to change the opinions or actions of the reader

Phrase A group of words, without a subject and its verb, that functions as a single part of speech

Plot A story-line or plan of action that centers on a conflict and is brought to a conclusion

Population The group or class of things that is being studied in inductive reasoning

Post hoc, ergo propter hoc A fallacy that occurs when one event is said to be the cause of a second event because both occurred in sequence; the Latin words mean, "After this, therefore because of this"

Predicate The part of the sentence that says something about the subject

Predicate adjective An adjective that follows a linking verb and modifies the subject of the sentence

Predicate nominative A noun or pronoun that follows a linking verb and renames the subject

Prefix A syllable that is put before a root word

Preposition A word that shows the relationship of a noun or pronoun to another word in the sentence

Prepositional phrase A preposition, its object, and any modifiers of the object

Primary sources Firsthand documents

Process analysis Writing in which the author's purpose is to explain how something works

Pronoun A word that takes the place of a noun or another pronoun

Proofreading Correcting a manuscript before submitting it to another reader

Propaganda Persuasive materials put out by a group to further its purposes

Proposition The statement of the writer's position in persuasive writing

Protagonist A character who must solve a problem or resolve some conflict

Question mark Punctuation mark used to end interrogative sentences

Quotation marks Punctuation marks enclosing a word or group of words to separate them from the rest of the sentence

Readers' Guide An index to widely read magazines that is published twenty-one times a year

Reference books Books used to locate information

Regional dialect A variation of a language shared by people in a particular region

Research paper An extended, formal composition presenting information gathered from a number of sources

Restrictive clause An adjective clause that is essential to the meaning of the sentence

Résumé A summary of personal data, background, and experience in outline form

Retained object An object that continues to function as a complement in the passive construction

Review A critical evaluation

Revision The process of making changes to improve a piece of writing

Rhyme A pattern of repeating sounds at the ends of words

Root word A word from which others have been derived

Round character One that is dynamic, capable of growth and change

Run-on sentence Two closely related sentences joined only by a comma or by no punctuation

Sampling In inductive reasoning, the number of specific cases of the population that are examined as evidence

Secondary sources Documents written about some aspect of the primary sources

Semicolon Punctuation mark used to separate independent clauses not joined by a coordinating conjunction, items in a series when one or more of the items contain commas, and independent clauses when commas appear within the clauses

Sentence A group of words that expresses a complete thought

Simile A comparison between two unlike items using words such as *like*, *as*, *than*, *seems*, and *appears*

Simple sentence A sentence containing one independent clause and no subordinate clauses

Slang An informal language of words and phrases that carry a special meaning for members of a group

Slug A topic heading on a note card

Standard English The form of English most accepted in business, industry, and commerce

Stanzas Patterns of repeating lines in poetry

Stereotype A hasty generalization about groups of people

Subject The part of the sentence about which something is said

Subjunctive mood The mood used to express wishes, possibilities, statements contrary to fact, and indirect commands

Subordinate clause A clause that cannot stand on its own as a sentence

Suffix A syllable added to the end of a root word

Syllogism The three-statement argument in deductive

reasoning (major premise, minor premise, and conclusion)

Symbol A concrete object or place that suggests complex ideas and associations

Thesaurus A dictionary of synonyms

Thesis The point the writer intends to make

Tone The attitude of the writer toward his or her readers

Transitions Words or phrases that help link sentences

Transitive verb An action verb that takes a direct object

TRI pattern A method of paragraph development using *T*opic, *R*estriction, *I*llustration

Truism A statement that is true but is too obvious to mention

Turning point In a plot, an unexpected discovery, a crucial decision, or a resolution of the conflict

Unity The quality of wholeness

Verb A word that describes an action or a state of being

Verbals Participles, gerunds, and infinitives formed from verbs but not functioning as verbs

Vertical file A filing cabinet for storing reference materials that cannot be put on shelves

Working bibliography A list of all the possible sources for a research paper

Index of Authors and Titles

Index

A

B

C

D

E

F

Q

R

S

U

V

W

Y

Z

Skills Index

C 4
D 5
E 6
F 7
G 8
H 9
I 0
J 1